TAWAIFNAMA

Saba Dewan is a documentary film-maker. Her documentaries have focused on issues of gender, sexuality and culture. This is her first book, and has emerged from her trilogy of films on stigmatised women performers: *Delhi–Mumbai–Delhi* (2006) about the lives of bar dancers; *Naach* (The Dance, 2008) on women dancers in rural fairs and *The Other Song* (2009) about the art and lifestyle of the tawaifs or courtesans. The research and writing of the book was supported by a fellowship from the New India Foundation. Saba lives in Gurgaon.

Praise for *Tawaifnama*

'As a historical text, *Tawaifnama* is a feat. Dewan bridges generations of private memories with public archives to compile a thorough and tender account of tawaif life. Most significantly, she approaches a 20th century culture with the nuance of 21st century gender politics.' – *Mint*

'This is easily one of the most ambitious new non-fiction books to come out of the subcontinent.' – *Open*

'*Tawaifnama* combines history, biography, gender studies, politics, culture and music, and walks the reader through a forgotten landscape of Banaras.' – *The Hindu*

'Dewan combines the wealth of academic scholarship available on the subject with highly original research and gives us a work of immense depth and sensitivity.' – *Wire.in*

'A comprehensive, well-sighted, and necessary book, *Tawaifnama* is not just sensitive handling of the topic, but also a demand for a more positive acknowledgment of things past, and things as they are.' – *The Telegraph*

'Many books and academic papers have been written on the life of courtesans, but where Dewan scores is her effortless weaving oral history, myths and legends with historical facts and data.' – *Outlook*

'In *Tawaifnama* Saba Dewan tells a gripping multigenerational story of a culturally erased community.' – *Scroll.in*

'... a *tour de force* of cultural history, sociology and biography.' – *Asian Review of Books*

'Well-researched and intricately written, *Tawaifnama* presents a nuanced account of the tawaif community's history when few such writings exist in the public realm.' – *Himal Southasian*

'Saba Dewan's pathbreaking book *Tawaifnama*, celebrates the invisible history of tawaifs, courtesans, female singers of classical traditions, musicians, artistes, lyricists and entertainers who enriched Indian culture.' – *The Tribune*

'Dewan's writing is as intimate as it is seductive. Weaving in history from chronicles and gazetteers, Dewan never loses the dream-like quality—the magic of folktale underpinned with history.' – *The Week*

'Saba Dewan's *Tawaifnama* is not merely a book tracing a family of tawaifs, it is understanding the sexuality associated with these women in the given society and the times that they lived in.' – *The New Indian Express*

cntxt

TAWAIFNAMA

SABA DEWAN

cntxt

First published by Context, an imprint of Westland Publications Private Limited, in 2019

Published by Context, an imprint of Westland Books, a division of Nasadiya Technologies Private Limited, in 2022

No. 269/2B, First Floor, 'Irai Arul', Vimalraj Street, Nethaji Nagar, Allappakkam Main Road, Maduravoyal, Chennai 600095

ISBN: 9789395073592

10 9 8 7 6 5 4 3 2 1

Typeset by SÜRYA, New Delhi
Printed at Replika Press Pvt. Ltd.

In memory of my father,
Dewan Berindranath 'Zafar Payami'

Contents

INTRODUCTION

Ibtida

YOUR EYES SHINE WITH EXCITEMENT as I walk into the room. Without a word, you thrust into my hands a yellowing black-and-white photograph. You had found it last night while searching for some documents in the old, dented tin trunk you jokingly refer to as your jaidad, your inheritance. It belonged to your mother and is still full of her things; clothes you hadn't the heart to give away after her death, random pieces of jewellery including the green- and gold-flecked glass bangles she wore during her last days, old photographs like this one.

Three rows of unsmiling women stare fearlessly into the camera. The six oldest are seated on chairs. Behind them stand the younger women, and in the front row, the little girls sit on the floor. You identify a pretty eight- or nine-year-old wearing a faintly supercilious expression as your elder sister Asghari. The timid-looking girl clutching her tightly, you guess, is your cousin Rani. Then you point out your mother, a plump, dark, simply dressed woman to whom you bear a startling resemblance, and her two cousins, Phoolmani and Pyaari, both quite young and resplendent in silk saris and heavy jewellery. Of the dour-looking matriarchs in the middle row, you are able to identify only your nani and your chhutki nani, your maternal grandmother and 'younger' grandmother, her sister. The baby perched on her lap is your cousin Rajjo, you speculate.

It is an unusual family portrait, one in which there is no space for the men and boys of the household. I point this out, but you don't find the omission strange. 'This is how it always was in our families,' you say with finality. I now know you well enough to recognise that.

I clearly remember the first time I met you. It was a warm summer afternoon of May 2004, and I was interviewing Shanney Khan Sahib, a well-respected sarangi player, at his family home in Chahmama in

Banaras. At some point, you dropped by. Middle-aged, dusky and pleasantly plump, you momentarily reminded me of a primary-school Hindi teacher that I was a bit in awe of as a child. Perhaps it was the crackling starchiness of your pastel cotton sari or the lace-trimmed handkerchief you held delicately in the palm of your hand or the lavender perfume of the talcum powder that had mixed with perspiration and formed faint white ridges in the crevices of your neck and shoulders. It was with some surprise that I realised you were a musician, when Shanney Khan Sahib introduced you as his shagirda, his student.

I had been visiting Banaras since 2002 to research and film a documentary on tawaifs, the courtesans and entertainers who had, until almost the mid-twentieth century, played a significant role in the cultural and social life of northern India. Enjoying sacred status in religious texts and scriptures as one of the holiest Hindu places of pilgrimage, Banaras has also for long been a major hub for literature and music. Tawaifs congregated here in large numbers, making the city a premier centre of the arts associated with them, including their distinctive musical style, the bol banao thumri and its associative genres such as hori, chaiti, kajari and dadra. Kathak dance too was linked closely with the tawaifs.

Highly skilled professional singers and dancers, tawaifs were expected to play multiple roles in pre-colonial society, including those of being companions and lovers to men from the local elite. Besides long and arduous training in music and dance, in order to be successful, tawaifs had to be educated in a range of other skills, such as a grounding in literature and politics as well as knowledge of the intricacies of social etiquette and of erotic stimulation. Bharatendu Harishchandra, nineteenth-century scion of an aristocratic merchant family of Banaras, writer, poet, journalist and playwright, often called 'the father of modern Hindi', confessed that he visited tawaifs regularly to acquire and cultivate a knowledge of the arts.

Feted as artists and sought after as lovers, elite tawaifs enjoyed access to high prestige and considerable wealth. Yet, their non-marital sexuality and the stigma attached to women who were in the public gaze, accessible to all, placed them on the margins of 'respectable' society; neither totally contained within pre-colonial patriarchy nor entirely outside it. It was this liminal space that I was interested in exploring.

This space was to be recast from the late nineteenth century, when the cultural and social position of the tawaif was not only marginalised but also branded as deviant and obscene. I wanted to understand and analyse the processes by which this change took place. In particular, my attention was focused on the colonial discourse and the Indian nationalist response, and the construction of the tawaif within both. I was also interested in how tawaifs had negotiated the onslaughts by colonialism and nationalism upon their way of life and art practice, the strategies that they had adopted to survive the hostility, and the extent to which they had been successful.

My canvas was vast and progress slow. Research into the history of music and musicians in India is necessarily based upon the retrieving and reading of fragments of oral memories and material traces. The histories of tawaif artists, not surprisingly, are even more fragmentary, since this is a community that has always stood on the margins of patriarchy and, therefore, necessarily its historiography. The process of retrieval is further complicated by the fact that the history of the tawaif and her arts over the last century and a half is also a history of erasure and silencing.

I got ample proof of this in my journeys through the social and cultural life of Banaras. In the twenty-first century, the city continues to see itself as a centre of Hindustani music, validated no doubt by the regularity of concerts organised here in both formal and informal settings, as also the presence of a large number of well-known, mostly male musicians, patrons, music schools and local music societies.

Where did the tawaif live in the city's memory, I wondered, as I tried to trace her in mehfils or musical gatherings hosted by wealthy merchant families in the opulent music halls of their homes. I asked the people that thronged concerts organised by religious bodies on the ghats of the river Ganga, and everywhere received one answer: the tawaif was dead. She sang no more those beguiling melodies that made men forget their way back home. Almost everyone insisted that they had no idea about the current whereabouts of tawaif families.

I met with several accompanist male musicians in Banaras, tabla and sarangi players like Shanney Khan Sahib, who had begun their careers performing with tawaif singers, I was told. Initially, none admitted to any past link with courtesans. In my early days in Banaras, I had in fact been cautioned to never directly enquire of the male musicians if they had ever accompanied tawaifs since it is considered very impolite to do so.

Over time, however, several tabla and sarangi players, including Shanney Khan Sahib, opened up about having been accompanists to the great gayikas, women singers, like Siddheshwari Devi and Rasoolan Bai. The euphemism came in handy, as the influx of non-tawaif, middle-class women musicians and dancers into performance spaces through the twentieth century has bestowed respectability and social acceptability to the identity of the female professional performer. A general term for any female singer, 'gayika' is reassuringly free of the anxiety-provoking sexuality that seems to charge the word tawaif, which, laden with moralistic, value-loaded connotations, is now synonymous with a 'fallen and dangerous' woman—bluntly put, a prostitute.

I also spoke with soloist musicians, male and female, music collectors and descendants of patron families. Many seemed happy to share the nostalgia associated with the lives of celebrated gayikas in the past, especially those who had managed to find a space for their music in post-Independence India. With the exception of a notable few, however, most of my respondents, even while extolling the richness of the women's art practice and their service to music, attempted simultaneously to distance them in subtle ways from their tawaif backgrounds. Their struggles as individual women musicians were duly commended, but the details of their backgrounds and the cultural contexts in which they first started performing were kept hazy and vague.

Clearly, in the cultural dispensation of modern India, the tawaif's art practice has been wrought acceptable only after being separated from the sexuality and lifestyle of its practitioner. As opposed to the gayika, the figure of the tawaif in twentieth-century archival and oral accounts is that of a woman outlaw, stigmatised both by the state and by society.

That afternoon at Shanney Khan Sahib's home, as you gracefully passed around cups of tea, I noticed your glittering nose pin and, for no logical reason, momentarily wondered whether you came from a tawaif background. Your prim persona, however, did little to raise my hopes.

We all made polite conversation about the exceptionally hot summer of that year and of the music culture in Banaras. You graciously invited me to visit your home the next time I was in the city. Significantly, it was located in Nariyal Bazaar, an area that was once populated mainly by tawaifs.

Over the past two years, I had spent several fruitless days roaming the lanes of Nariyal Bazaar and other adjoining courtesan neighbourhoods of old Banaras, like Chowk, Dal Mandi and Raja Darwaza, trying to trace the few tawaif families that I heard still lived in apartments located above the crowded bazaars. My attempts at asking busy shopkeepers about the whereabouts of these families were met either with smirking and innuendo or an impatient hand waving me away—talk to us if you want to buy something, otherwise don't waste our time. Even when I was able to make contact with some tawaif families living in the area, through the efforts of musicians like Shanney Khan Sahib, my first obstacle was introducing the subject of my research.

In deference to the morality of the cultural elite, the tawaif community itself more usually employs the colloquial term 'ganey wali', singing women, for themselves, instead of the Sanskritised 'gayika'; the euphemism, with its emphasis on singing, coming in handy to survive a hostile environment. I used it too, but that did little to diffuse the anxiety that rose up as I explained the scope of my project to the former tawaifs. Almost all of them had moved away from any direct connection with their past lives, and their families were now engaged in other professional spheres. Understandably, the last thing they wanted was to have a filmmaker turn up at their doorstep, raking up a past best forgotten. Sometimes, other family members raised objections even if the older women showed an interest in the project. Our meetings would usually end soon after.

So it was with some trepidation that I climbed up the steep flight of stairs to your home in Nariyal Bazaar. I was still not sure whether you did, in fact, come from a tawaif background. And even if you did, there was no saying whether you would want to share that aspect of your life with me.

The first part of my apprehensions was laid to rest when you ushered me politely into the visitors' room of your three-storey house. Located on the first floor, above a sari store, the medium-sized room opened on to a balcony that overlooked the street below. The other walls were covered with full-sized mirrors that must have once sparkled in the bright lights of the chandelier that still hung from the ceiling. Time had been ruthless in its passage through the room. The mirrors were covered with a patina of grime and dust, and the chandelier had lost most of its arms. More than half the room was slightly raised as a platform, lined on three sides with mattresses covered with threadbare, once-white sheets, and sagging bolsters were strewn on them.

There was little doubt that this room must once have been a tawaif's kotha, or salon. Visitors would have sat on the mattresses, facing the performer as she sang and danced on the lower part of the floor, watching her steps in the twinkling mirrors around. It was obvious too that the room had long since lost its original use. The battered television placed high up on a partially open almirah stacked with clothes, the children's toys scattered on the floor and a sewing machine standing in one corner imparted a humdrum domesticity to its faded grandeur.

You were a courteous and generous host, plying me with snacks and lassi. In the setting of your own home, you looked indefinably different. Although you were dressed in a similar pastel sari as the last time I saw you, there was a laidback confidence in your manner and an easy smile that travelled from your eyes to reach your lips. Your glass bangles seemed to clink more mischievously and your voice sounded more lilting.

A bit disoriented by this subtle transformation, I somewhat anxiously spoke of my interest in researching the lives and art practices of ganey walis. You were attentive but noncommittal. You talked in general terms about your love for music and hinted at the opposition you as a woman vocalist, a gayika, had to face from the family and, to some extent, society. At my request, you sang a bit, a hori, '*Aaj Braj mein hori khelat hain*; Today Holi is being played in Braj'. You had a strong, full-throated voice, but it was evident that you had been out of practice for some time.

From somewhere in the house came the relentless rattle of a sewing machine. Your younger daughter, Meenu, a 'BA pass', contributed to the household income by taking up sewing jobs for the sari shop below. You did the same on the machine in the room. Besides this piece-rate work, you also tried to earn by giving sporadic music tuitions, mainly to foreign tourists passing through Banaras.

We continued meeting whenever I visited Banaras, which was often. Over time, I moved beyond the formal visitors' room to the family rooms on the second and third floors. This was where you lived with your daughter, daughter-in-law, son and grandson, and sundry relatives either passing through or staying on semi-permanently. In Banaras for work, medical treatment, further education or to escape poverty at home, the guests were all expected to make themselves useful and, with a few incorrigible exceptions, most did: the men and boys ran errands, the women and girls helped in the cooking and other housework. You were the undisputed captain of the ship. From the minor to the most major, you made all the decisions regarding the running of your large household.

My visits had a well-worn pattern. You were often reading the newspaper when I dropped by. With your glasses perched low on the bridge of your nose, you commenced perusal of the paper every day with news from the gold market. After sighing about the inexorable ascent in the price of your favourite metal, you then turned to the main page and caught up on the rough and tumble of the world beyond. Next, you proceeded to the local pages and sighed a bit more about the chronicles of crime, political intrigue and civic disrepair plaguing your city. And then on to the sports columns, where you checked on the fortunes of Indian cricket. That accounted for, you would settle down to savour your favourite sections: the lifestyle and cultural pages. You giggled at the jokes, seriously considered the beauty tips and commented on concert reviews.

On my arrival, you would call out for tea. It would always come paired with snacks that Salma, your daughter-in-law, had prepared in anticipation of my visit. You took food seriously, and Salma was a good cook. Feeding and eating out of the way, I would spend some time chatting with Meenu and Salma and playing with baby Haaris, your much-adored grandson.

If I reached early enough in the morning, I would also get to briefly meet your son, Nanhe, on his way to work at a jeweller's shop in Chowk. Your only son and eldest child, Nanhe is mentally challenged and has difficulties with his speech and hearing. You have had him examined by various doctors in Banaras and Delhi but to little avail. I was surprised to learn that he did a regular job. You explained that it was your idea; you wanted Nanhe to be as independent as possible. The jeweller was a family acquaintance and had obliged by giving Nanhe a job that he could do: help open the shop for the day, dust it, serve tea and paan to customers, and run small errands. The salary wasn't much but it gave Nanhe a tremendous sense of self-confidence to be, as he described himself earnestly, 'a working man'.

I would usually end up staying much longer than planned; our meandering conversations winding their way through the day. In a rare displacement of the professional and one-sided researcher–subject relationship that I had thus far experienced on my earlier projects, I found myself talking to you about my life in Delhi, my family, my interests and concerns, and my progress and difficulties on the work front. You always listened patiently, with concern and empathy, without passing judgement. You gave an opinion only when it was sought, and it would invariably be an astute and measured one. I began to see in you a trusted friend.

Over time, you too felt comfortable enough to dispense with the fig leaf of gayika or ganey wali, and began referring to yourself as a tawaif. There was an unmistakable ring of pride in how you used the term—naturally, without fuss, strikingly different from the embarrassed half-tones in which I had occasionally heard you use it in front of outsiders to the community.

You belonged to a well-known tawaif family in Bhabua, Bihar, you told me. There were several women in your family, including your aunts and cousins, who had begun their careers as tawaifs in Bhabua but later made their way to Banaras and set up kothas in rented houses in the city's courtesan quarters.

The house in which you lived had, in fact, originally been taken on rent more than half a century ago by your elder sister, Asghari, when she moved to Banaras to begin her career as a tawaif. You inherited the tenancy of the house once you made the shift to the city, and she in turn moved back to Bhabua, like other women in the family had when they retired from the 'line', the shorthand used by your community for its line of work.

Almost all of them had, through their earning years in Banaras, invested in houses in Bhabua as insurance against old age and homelessness. You too had done the same, although unusually, you chose to stay on in Banaras after retirement. You allowed your twin sister to live rent-free in your house in Bhabua along with her husband and children, on the understanding that they would make space for you if you ever decided to move back. You visited 'home' regularly to attend to illnesses, births, marriages, deaths and the feast days that marked the family calendar, and maintained close links with your large network of relatives living there.

In Banaras, I often found myself accompanying you on visits to your wide circle of friends, extended family members and former accompanist musicians. With the exception of a few families of male musicians who still try and maintain a tenuous link with their traditional vocation, almost all the others had long shifted from their now-stigmatised tawaif past to 'respectable' professions as small-time traders, shopkeepers, petty contractors, tailors, tourist guides, fixers, taxi drivers and home-based piece-rate workers. Carrying memories of a rich tradition of music, dance and a way of life, once so intrinsically bound with the elite cultures of Banaras, they are now part of the largely invisible working population, the sinews of this chaotic, seemingly anarchic city.

The only connection that some of these families have with performance arts is through dance bars. During the early years of my fieldwork in Banaras, I had occasionally heard rumours that, with the exception of well-off elite tawaif households, which have withdrawn into 'respectable' seclusion, many others send their girls to work in the dance bars of Mumbai and other cities and towns of western and southern India. It was very difficult to confirm the truth of this gossip. The former tawaifs I met usually dismissed my question, saying that they did not personally know any family where girls had become bar dancers. Everyone in their acquaintance, they would insist, had long since withdrawn from the line.

Over time, I discovered that the reality was more complex. My growing friendship with you and my extended stays in Banaras and Bhabua revealed that the norm today in several tawaif households is to marry off most daughters, barring one or two who are sent off to dance bars to contribute to the family income. This is in contrast with the earlier practice, where every daughter considered suitable was trained as a tawaif, with the exception of those either deemed unattractive or without any aptitude for music and dance. Mostly employed on short-term contracts, bar dancers, though pilloried as immoral and obscene by society, are an indispensable feature of the popular culture of a rapidly transforming India.

You emphasised that, even though there were a few bar dancers among the tawaif households you knew, your family had chosen the more difficult but izzatdar, honourable, path of not living off the earnings of daughters any more, preferring instead to 'settle' them in marriages. Your family had bid goodbye to the profession with its head held high and learnt to make do with the earnings of the sons, you proudly said. Your elder daughter was married and the younger one, Meenu, was waiting in line for a good match.

You were single-minded in grooming your daughters for matrimony. Over the years, Meenu had gathered several diplomas in beauty treatment, glass painting and embroidery, besides her BA degree. She spent considerable time embroidering sundry wall-tapestries of cooing doves, dancing peacocks and bouquets of roses, which all formed part of her ever-expanding dowry. Neither of your girls was taught any music. You said that this was because of their lack of interest.

One morning, however, when you sang for me—*Lagat karejwa ma chot, Phul gendwa na mar*; My heart is wounded, Do not throw flowers at me—a thumri made immortal by Rasoolan Bai, the great tawaif singer from Banaras, much to my surprise, Meenu correctly identified it as being set to raga Bhairavi. You asked Meenu how she knew about the raga. And Meenu said, 'Amma, I have heard you sing ever since I was born. Even if you haven't bothered to explain all this to me, I am neither deaf nor stupid!' But Meenu maintained that she was not interested in music and firmly ended the conversation there.

Visibly proud of your daughter's self-gained musical knowledge, you remarked, 'Who teaches baby fish to swim? They learn of their own accord since they live in water. As children, we too learnt simply by hearing all the music played and sung in the house. I began learning music formally only when I was almost twelve years old. By then, I had already picked up the rudiments by just hearing the others sing.' You then changed track and added, 'But there is no future in music now for our girls even if they want to pursue it. People stopped listening to our songs years ago.'

You often shrugged at your marginalisation in Banaras: '*Sab* time-time *ka khel hai*. It is all a play of time/fate.' In the early years of our acquaintance, I would frequently ask why you hadn't shifted back to Bhabua like your sister and aunts. You paid a high price for living on in Banaras: besides the material costs of monthly rent and living expenses, the scorn that the city had heaped upon you, the space that it had denied to your music practice and to your identity as a musician.

Your response would always be: 'Banaras gave me my music, my profession, all the colours of my life. I tasted great success here as a tawaif, I experienced love, I became a mother in this city, and I also suffered my share of heartbreak and sorrow here. Banaras has made me the woman I am.'

Through you and your friends and relatives, I got to know a Banaras beyond the celebrated pilgrimage circuit of imposing ghats, Brahmin priests and majestic temples propitiating the great deities of the Hindu pantheon. Your Banaras and that of your extended circle is one of modest neighbourhood mosques calling out to the faithful, small shrines dedicated to local Sufi saints, crossroads memorials daubed with vermilion in veneration of unknown Bir Babas (warrior elders and protectors of a locality, respected across religious and caste divisions), and hole-in-the-wall altars lit with single-lamp offerings to Mais or Mothers, turbulent, autonomous goddesses that have thus far refused to be domesticated by brahminical Hinduism.

We often went out for evening walks on the ghats. You always carried some kneaded flour dough to feed the fish. I remember laughing the first time I saw you solemnly sprinkle little bits of dough in the muddy waters. Unthinkingly, I teased you about the improbability of fish surviving in its polluted, toxic depths. You, a practising Muslim, had looked hurt and murmured about the miraculous powers of Ganga-ji to cleanse 'herself'.

At other times, we would go shopping in the serpentine bazaars of the old city. Your pleasure came not so much from buying something new but simply wandering past the shops, admiring the window displays. When you did buy something, it was usually quite inexpensive. I would pay.

It took me a while to realise that somewhere along the way, you had placed me in the role of a minor patron. It began innocuously. Some medicines needed to be bought or Salma had run out of ghee. Could I spare some cash? You would square up later. You did square up—with time, attention, courtesies, concern and friendship. Money was never spoken of directly between us but, for you, the rules were simple. You were a retired tawaif with no patrons or a regular source of livelihood. I was a researcher interested in understanding your life. You extended yourself to me. In return, I was expected to make myself useful through small monetary contributions, little presents.

It was a relationship that you understood well. And you gave it your best. You sat by my bedside night and day, nursing me through a heatstroke during a particularly warm summer in Banaras. Slowly and imperceptibly, over the span of my visits to Banaras, you took charge of my eating arrangements, insisting I join you if I was at your place during mealtimes, otherwise sending across tiffin carriers of home-cooked food to my hotel room.

You have been an extremely generous and enthusiastic participant in my research into your life, family history and tradition; encouraging your relatives and family friends to share their memories with me, excavating memorabilia related to your musical past—letters, song books and photographs, like the family portrait that you have found for me now. Staring at it again, a memory of another family portrait, much closer home, comes to me in a flash.

One long summer afternoon in her home, Bua-ji, my father's widowed elder sister, had taken out her embossed, leather-jacket album of old family photographs to entertain a restless and bored schoolgirl. She showed me photos of my father's journey from childhood to becoming a young man, photographs of my uncles and their male cousins, and of my rather stern-looking grandfather and his older brother. And then Bua-ji came to the centrepiece of her album: the family portrait. Three rows of unsmiling men and boys staring straight into the camera. All looking quite stuffy, to my little-girl eyes, in their formal sherwanis and suits and with their heads covered in a bewildering variety of headwear: safas or turbans, topis and Western-style hats.

Innocently, I asked, 'But where are you and the other buas and dadi-ji in this photo?' She hesitated, perhaps trying to frame a reply that an eight-year-old could understand. And then said, 'In our families, women did not go about getting photographed, and certainly never with the men.' As compensation, she had found for me precisely five photographs of the elusive, invisible women of the house. Of these, one was a faded photograph of my grandmother, taken in her late middle age. Another was a similar one of my grandaunt. The remaining three inadequately chronicled my three buas' lives in the ancestral haveli, the family mansion in Kapurthala, Punjab. One, of my youngest aunt, her father's pet, as a young three- or four-year-old wearing a frock and holding a long stick menacingly in her chubby little hands. Another, of the three sisters as teenagers in kurtas with baggy shalwars, their heads decorously covered with dupattas and their eyes partly shut against the sun's glare, smiling shyly into the camera. This photograph was taken around the time my aunt had got engaged. The eldest daughter of the house, she had been allowed to study only till class eight. At fifteen, she was married off to a young but upcoming lawyer. The last photograph had my three aunts, my grandmother and grandaunt seated around the new bride of the family, my eldest uncle's wife. I didn't recognise her because her face was almost entirely covered by a heavily embroidered veil.

Over the years, I would look at those photographs again. I would ask my aunts endless questions about their lives as girls in Kapurthala. Amused by my curiosity, they would talk of the happy times spent in dyeing and crinkling dupattas and then putting them out to dry. The long, sometimes tedious hours of elaborate embroidery that they were made to do. The afternoons spent in gossiping and laughing with neighbourhood girls. They had to be careful though. Girls in their kind of families neither spoke nor laughed loudly. They would remember the never-ending preparations for family weddings that consumed so much of their time and energy.

'To tell you the truth, child, we always had so much to do that we never knew how our time went by!' my aunts would exclaim.

As I grew older, I began to realise that the lives led by my grandmother and aunts had followed a predetermined script for women who lived in havelis. Hidden behind the veil, these lives were dictated by the strict rules of seclusion enforced upon daughters, sisters and wives of upper-caste families to ensure the purity of patriarchal lineage. Confined to the world of the inner courtyard, they had limited access to their husbands whose domain as men lay outside the confines of the zenana, the women's quarters.

This was not considered unusual; husbands and wives occupied very different spaces, literally as well as at a more subliminal, emotional and intellectual plane, in upper-caste households. Deprived of opportunities for formal learning and of contact with the outside world, most upper-caste women could share only in a limited manner in their husbands' lives. Neither were they expected to. Since marital alliances were meant to bring together suitable families in a contract of mutual advantage, rather than two individuals, the relationship between the married couple was largely dictated by conventions of duty and responsibility. Emotional, physical and sexual compatibility often came up short in such an arrangement.

It was not considered socially reprehensible for men from such backgrounds to seek companionship instead, with a variety of women performers and entertainers belonging to castes and communities that stood outside the veil of upper-caste 'respectability'. I would occasionally overhear my aunts make coded references to the 'women kept in the outhouse' by some granduncle or the other in the past; women that my female relatives were not allowed to meet or even come face-to-face with for fear of the 'polluting' influence their 'promiscuity' would have on the chastity of my aunts, grandmother and grandaunt.

Tied to each other through intertwined and yet conflicting histories, you and I would spend long hours piecing together for each other our family chronicles. I told you about my maternal grandmother, Sita, one of the first girls in her community to graduate from college; her quest for freedom beyond her destiny as a purdah-observing daughter became a source of inspiration for the women in my family. Enrolled in one of the earliest schools for women in northern India, the Kanya Gurukul in Dehradun, Sita was to chart her own course in life not only as a thrifty homemaker and loving mother to five children but also as a freedom fighter and a trade unionist.

The entry of 'respectable' women like Sita into public space coincided with the branding of the tawaif and her arts as 'immoral' and 'obscene' by the very same nationalist reformers whose espousal of the right to education for purdah-bound girls had made it possible for my grandmother to step out of the haveli. Simultaneously, they projected the tawaif's presence in public spaces as a threat to the moral and physical well-being of Indian society. The anti-nautch movement of the late nineteenth and early twentieth century attacked the tradition of holding nautches (or nach, dance and music performances by tawaifs) by the upper classes on festive occasions. This was matched by demands in various north Indian cities, including Banaras, for changes in municipality laws that restricted the tawaifs' place of residence to certain specified areas of the city. In effect, public space was being sanitised for 'respectable' women like my grandmother to step out without being mistaken for tawaifs.

You, in turn, told me stories about the lives of your aunts, grandmothers, great-grandaunt and great-great-grandmother. Ranging from itinerant entertainers to elite courtesans, the lives of these self-made women from humble origins held a mirror to me of the everyday struggles that tawaifs had waged to not only survive but also to practise their arts in an increasingly hostile environment: your great-great-grandmother

Dharmman, early nineteenth-century tawaif-turned-warrior in the cause of the Rebellion of 1857; your great-grandaunt, Sadabahar, tawaif musician whose magical voice attracted mystical beings; your mother, Teema, forced to prostitute herself for her family's survival; Bindo, your aunt, who dreamt of becoming the greatest gramophone singer ever; your aunt Phoolmani and her tryst with theatre; Pyaari, your younger aunt, who made her name on the radio; your beautiful and tempestuous sister, Asghari, and her aborted bid for eminence; and you, a tawaif in an era that officially signed the death certificate of your tradition.

Over the years that we have known each other, these stories multiplied, as I spoke with women and men from your family and extended social circle, and with male musicians and patron families that I met in Banaras and on my journeys to Jaunpur, Bhabua and Arrah. Together, these narratives formed a rich tapestry that represents the social history of tawaifs from Banaras and its cultural hinterland of eastern Uttar Pradesh, or UP, and western Bihar, from the early nineteenth century to the present.

You were always by my side when I needed you as an interlocutor, guide and friend. You wished to remain unnamed in this book to spare your married daughters and sons-in-law any embarrassment. And it was you who suggested that I change the names of all the individuals from tawaif backgrounds and those related to them who feature in its pages. You said it would not only liberate me to tell their stories without fear of causing social awkwardness for my protagonists but also free them to share their stories without inhibition. I have followed your advice. Names have been changed and identities have been blurred, but my endeavour has been to be faithful to the narrating of the tales as they were told to me.

CHAPTER 1

Dharmman Bibi and Kunwar Singh

A SMALL, RAGGED RED FLAG flutters tentatively atop an abandoned temple. From my rear-seat window, I can see the thirsty plains of southwest Bihar stretch out in the shimmer of a noon-day dream as our car climbs the bumpy road that threads its way up the Kaimur hills, poor cousins of the mighty Vindhyas. Sitting in front, Jawed, your seventeen-year-old, bright-eyed nephew turns around and announces excitedly, 'Mao-wadis, Maoists, have hideouts in these hills!' Next to him, Ramesh, the taxi driver who has brought us here from Banaras, shifts nervously in his seat. Unperturbed, you smile fondly at your nephew and say with barely concealed pride, 'My Jawed reads the papers daily. He loves to watch the news on television.'

Jawed, I am aware, is also a cricket fiend. As far as his classmates were concerned, he was practically Sachin Tendulkar and his teachers had predicted that the boy would one day bat on a state-level pitch and bring glory to their dilapidated Bhabua high school. But Jawed is no longer in school. His father, Naeem, your twin sister Ghafuran's husband, is an overworked, poor tailor. With ten mouths to feed, spending money to keep a grown-up boy in school so that he could play cricket seemed to him an inexcusable indulgence. Even after passing class twelve, in all likelihood, Jawed would end up as his father's assistant; he might as well begin right away. Jawed now spends his time stitching women's blouses. Whenever he can, he plays cricket on the sly, away from his father's disapproving eyes. In this packed working day, it seems Jawed also finds time to contemplate the prospects of an uprising. 'Mao-wadis rob the rich and give to the poor. Mark my words, they will not sit quiet until there is a revolution here.'

Something in Jawed's fervent tone makes you narrow your eyes. 'I hope, son, you are not mixing around with people who can get you in trouble? Your father will skin you alive. You know that, don't you?' you say in your 'aunty' voice.

Jawed falls silent, a picture of injured innocence, his eyes no longer sparkling. You seem to notice this, because your tone shifts to conciliatory complicity. 'This is a family trait. We have always played our part in any just cause.'

Jawed turns his back to both of us.

'In the times before the ghadar [the revolt of 1857], there lived in Arrah a tawaif named Dharmman Bibi.' You lower your voice to a conspiratorial whisper when saying the word 'tawaif', as you always do when outsiders are present. You needn't have worried about Ramesh, though. It's doubtful if he can hear you from his front seat above the din of the Anoop Jalota bhajans he has been playing on the car stereo throughout the drive.

'Dharmman Bibi is our first illustrious purkhin, ancestress. I heard her story from my mother, who had heard it from her mother. Tall and lithe, Dharmman Bibi was as strong as any man living within a 50-km radius of Arrah. She had hair as long and black as the night of lovers' separation, a face as radiant as the dawn of their reunion, and full, high breasts, a narrow waist and bountiful hips so exquisitely proportioned that even an angel would be led astray. Adept at handling the sword with the same sure touch with which she caressed a lover, Dharmman Bibi could ride a horse bare-backed. She could, and frequently did, challenge wrestlers throughout the district of Shahabad to a good bout.'

Shahabad no longer exists on the map of Bihar. Carved into smaller districts—including present-day Kaimur, Rohtas and Bhojpur—in the decades following Independence, it now lives on only as a memory of times gone by when it was an in-between land; a corridor between the northern Gangetic plains and Bengal and other regions in the east. Its history was shaped by its geography: the territory had long been camping ground for sundry passing armies, invaders and rebels. During the rule of the British East India Company, the rocky ranges of the Kaimur hills marked the southwestern boundaries of Shahabad, and the alluvial plains of the river Ganga surrounding Arrah defined the northern and northeastern limits. Sasaram, Buxar and Dumraon were the main towns apart from Arrah, which was the district headquarters.

'Blessed with a powerful voice, Dharmman Bibi was famous all over Arrah and beyond for her mastery of music and dance; it was said that she could sing for a full day and night, her notes becoming stronger with each passing hour. The only break that she would take was to offer namaz five times daily, regardless of whether she performed at a princely court or in her home.'

You pause and spit out of the window the remains of your paan, no doubt adding to the many red splotches on the exteriors of the taxi. Even as I worry about Ramesh's reaction, he follows suit and contributes his own share of betel stains to the car paint. Ignoring my censorious look, you open the old and dented aluminium paandaan that travels everywhere you go. It has small compartments for paan, betel leaves, which are always covered with a moist red cloth, choona or lime paste, kaththa or catechu, sliced supari or areca nut, chhoti elaichi or green cardamoms, and roasted tobacco. With practised precision, you take out a fresh betel leaf, daub it with choona and kaththa, and place upon this palette of green, white and maroon a few bits of supari, two cardamoms and a pinch of tobacco.

We have been in Bhabua, the main town of Kaimur district, for the past two days. You are here to spend time with your terminally ill aunt. I have come along to get to know your hometown and family better. Today, perhaps wishing to give me a break from the gloom of impending death enveloping your aunt's home, you are taking me sightseeing to the Mundesvari temple in the Kaimur hills. Widely regarded as one of the oldest temples in Bihar, it is the most important landmark in the district, and is about 15 km from Bhabua. Jawed has attempted to impress upon me the significance of the temple by sharing that two reigning stars of Bhojpuri cinema, Manoj Tiwari and Ravi Kisan, make it a point to come and seek the blessings of Goddess Mundesvari before the release of any film. Always one to add drama, he also mumbled about 'wild beings' that stalk the hills surrounding the temple.

While we have yet to chance upon the wild, it has been a bone-breaking journey, and I can feel the remains of breakfast heave uneasily in my stomach as the taxi lurches over potholes. These, for some inexplicable reason, have been filled with large stones without being covered with tarmac—perhaps to test the faith and fortitude of pilgrims visiting Mundesvari.

With a freshly made paan tucked inside your mouth, you are now ready to launch into the tale of your first-known purkhin. 'With her multiple talents, Dharmman Bibi was naturally the envy of all the others tawaifs in Arrah. What set her above the rest was, of course, her status as the mistress of Babu Kunwar Singh of Jagdishpur, one of the most distinguished zamindars of the district.'

Dharmman Bibi had been all of eighteen when she first caught the eye of Kunwar Singh, then nearly fifty-five years of age. She had come to perform at the annual Shivratri fair at Jagdishpur, organised by its zamindar. Such fairs were a regular feature across Shahabad. Rich and poor, peasants and traders, jugglers and entertainers of different types would gather here in large numbers to transact business and to seek and provide distraction from the worries of everyday life. Tawaifs were a special attraction and earned a great deal from their nightly performances of music and dance.

And so it was that, in the flickering light of burning mashals, or fire torches, the beautiful and vivacious Dharmman Bibi was dancing for a large gathering of notables of the district when Babu Kunwar Singh was ushered into the mehfil. Their eyes met and Dharmman Bibi bowed low to offer her salaam. Acutely aware of his pre-eminence in this congregation of local elites, Dharmman Bibi danced all night as if he were the only person present.

Kunwar Singh had known many women before, yet he was spellbound by this tall, well-built girl. Dawn came, the mehfil ended but not the passion that babu sahib felt for Dharmman. Making her his mistress, he remained steadfast in his ardour for as long as he lived.

Heedful that babu sahib placed her above all others, Dharmman reciprocated his feelings with unfaltering love, trust and fierce loyalty. Neither age nor status or religion came in the way of the great bond they shared. He would visit her as frequently as he could at the imposing, beautifully furnished house that he had bought for her in Arrah. Or she would come and stay with him for long periods at his estate of Jagdishpur, about 35 km from Arrah.

Covered with vast tracts of fertile rice-growing lands irrigated by the river Ganga, Babu Kunwar Singh's estate was amongst the largest landholdings in district Shahabad. His status, however, accrued as much from his illustrious pedigree as from the vast landholdings. Belonging to the high-ranked clan of Parmara Rajputs, better known in the area as Ujjainiya Rajputs, his family traced its history to the descendants of the legendary king Vikramaditya of Ujjain as well as Raja Bhoj, ruler of Malwa around the tenth century. Many zamindars of Shahabad belonged to this clan, while others belonged to the Chauhan and Sakarwar Rajput clans.

Rajput clans claiming Kshatriya descent had risen to prominence in the sixth century as soldiers and rulers in northern, western and central India. From the twelfth century on, as many of their principalities were successively invaded and conquered by Turkish, Afghan and Mughal armies, several Rajput warlords and their clans began retreating eastwards. In search of new lands to dominate, they arrived in the eastern Gangetic plains, including the lands that would later become part of Shahabad district. The region, once ruled by the Mauryas, Guptas, Harshavardhana of Kannauj, the Shailas of central India and the Palas of Bengal, was then controlled by the indigenous tribes—the Cheros and the Kharwars. Through a series of petty clashes and strategic marital alliances with indigenous chieftains, the Rajputs emerged as the dominant group of warrior-landholders in the Shahabad region.

The Turkish-Afghan rulers of Delhi arrived soon after. Over countless battles, Shahabad got passed around—from the Khilji sultans to the Sharqi rulers of Jaunpur, then into the hands of the Lodis and subsequently to Sher Shah Suri. By the mid-sixteenth century, the territories of Bengal and Bihar, including Shahabad, were conquered by Akbar's armies and became part of the vast Mughal empire.

Regardless of the change of rulers at the provincial level, Rajput warlords continued to form the local landed aristocracy in Shahabad, enjoying power and prestige as hereditary landholders, clan chieftains and notables. They kept extending their control over cultivable lands in the area by vanquishing indigenous tribes and reducing cultivators from less privileged castes to abject dependence. Under the Mughals, they began to act as revenue collectors for the empire. In exchange, the more notable amongst them were bestowed with the title of raja, or king, by the emperors. Given their control over clan militia, these Rajput rajas were also made responsible for the maintenance of law and order in their dominions.

Wielding authority from their mud-and-brick forts, the zamindars effectively controlled as quasi-proprietors the land under their sway. Some of this land was cultivated directly by hired and bonded labour, while the remainder was tilled by cultivators who normally possessed an inalienable and hereditary right of occupancy over their family plots. They could usually not be ejected from the land as long as they continued to pay a share of their produce to the zamindars. In many instances, they also paid tax for grazing their cattle in the village commons and for gathering forest products.

In 1764, Shahabad passed into the hands of the East India Company, after its victory in the Battle of Buxar over the combined forces of the nawab of Bengal, Mir Qasim, the nawab of Awadh, Shuja-ud-Daulah and the Mughal emperor Shah Alam II. It became one of the six districts that comprised the Bihar province, or rather the Patna division of the Bengal presidency, under the Company's direct jurisdiction.

The Company's most significant gain from its victory in the Battle of Buxar was exclusive control over land revenue from Bengal, Bihar and parts of Orissa. The revenue would be used to finance its unending wars, and for the needs of its other two presidencies in Bombay and Madras and of its treasury in far-off Canton.

With these future requirements in mind, the Company nearly doubled its demand for revenue in Bengal and Bihar between 1765–66 and 1793, when the Permanent Settlement came into effect. This revenue settlement bestowed upon erstwhile zamindars ownership of their landholdings as private property, with the power of sale and transfer, while fixing forever the amount they would pay the Company, based on an assessment of their estate.

In the initial decades of this settlement, many landholders found it difficult to meet the inflexible high rates of revenue demanded by the Company that made no allowance for times of drought, flood or other natural disasters. As a result, several among them fell into arrears. Failure to raise and pay the assessed sum on time could, and did, result in the forfeiture of the estate by the colonial government, and its auction to bidders who included Indian officials in the Company's government, as well as merchants and bankers. To avoid seizure of their estates, zamindars used every means to extract the maximum rents from the tenant cultivators.

In Shahabad, a great majority of such estates were controlled and managed by the old landed aristocracy of Rajput landlords, like Kunwar Singh's family. Pathans amongst the Muslims and Bhumihar Brahmins amongst the Hindus were the other communities in Shahabad that were landed and had estates under the Permanent Settlement system.

❁

An ear-piercing noise drowns Anoop Jalota's plastic notes. With a start I realise that our taxi has come to a halt. An impatient tractor trolley, its horn on full throttle, threatens to push us off the narrow ribbon road. Ramesh has to grudgingly make way. Squeezed into the tractor trolley, half of Kaimur district sails past: bleating goats, wailing babies, shrieking children, silent women with veiled faces and scowling men carrying an assortment of ancient rifles and air guns. Old habits die hard. At the sight of babu sahibs, as Rajput men are addressed in these parts, you hastily move the paan discreetly to the centre of your mouth and cover your head deferentially with the end of your sari.

A huge annual fair held at the Mundesvari temple in celebration of sawan, the rainy season, is just a few days away. You tell me that the trolley-load is on their way up to offer the goats to the goddess. In the old days, the animals were slaughtered within the precincts of the temple, but now, they are only symbolically offered to the Devi, then taken back to the village and let loose. You have no idea when the practice changed or why.

Ramesh is furious. He sticks his head out of the window to let his feelings be known. You immediately stop him. 'Brother, hold your peace. We will reach the temple in good time. These people have always enjoyed right of way in the area. Besides, they don't take kindly to being ticked off by strangers.'

We drive on behind the tractor. As the car bumps and swerves over potholes, you grip tightly the tiffin box in your lap. It contains lentil-stuffed puris, spicy potatoes, curried pumpkin and gulgulas, which are sweet dumplings made of flour, jaggery and milk kneaded together. Our picnic lunch comes from the leftovers of the elaborate repast cooked in your sister's home yesterday on the occasion of the monsoon festival, Kajli Teej, or simply Teej.

With no personal experience of its celebration, I had thus far associated the festival only with Hindu married women. Yesterday, as you spoke of past Teej celebrations in your family home in Bhabua, I realised I was wrong on both counts. In the era gone by, neither was Teej an exclusively Hindu festival nor was it celebrated only by married women. Amidst the cooking and feasting, you reminisced about the times when Teej was a much-awaited festival for tawaifs, both Hindu and Muslim, in western Bihar and eastern Uttar Pradesh. It was amongst the many shared festivals that women, non-tawaifs and tawaifs, across communities and castes, celebrated together.

The older women in your family recalled the bygone days when Bhabua had resounded to songs celebrating the rains, sung in unison by tawaifs: 'Jhulas would be tied to the neem tree in the clearing of the tawaifs' neighbourhood. The tree has long since been chopped down. Large groups of tawaifs would sit down and begin singing, and the rest would take turns to swing on the jhulas in pairs. Our accompanist musicians would come and join in the celebrations and play tabla and sarangi as we sang kajari, jhula, sawan—all songs of the rainy season. We applied henna on each other's hands as we sang. The younger women danced. The bangle-seller arrived and we all bought new glass bangles. Green, gold, blue, silver, red, yellow, they shimmered so prettily on our wrists. Hindu tawaifs would perform puja in their homes and their daughters-in-law observed a fast. Muslim tawaifs too offered niyaz that day to the dear departed. It's all gone now. There are no tawaifs left, no swings and no songs.' The old women sighed in unison.

Most Muslim families, whether tawaif or non-tawaif, no longer celebrate Teej since it is seen as un-Islamic. Your family, loyal to the old ways, has continued with the feasting even though the songs have long since fallen silent and the swings have disappeared. Hindu tawaif families, no doubt mimicking the ways of their more socially respectable, upper-caste neighbours, have begun imbuing the fun festival with far greater religiosity than was observed earlier. The emphasis is now on the fast observed by the married women in the family and recitation in the evening of the katha, or religious lore, rather than on the singing and dancing that used to be the central feature of the celebrations.

'It's not just the festivals that have got divided. All aspects of shared cultures, norms, beliefs have got divided.' You give the example of vermilion powder that was used by daughters-in-law in tawaif households in the region, whether Hindu or Muslim, to colour their hair-parting as a sign of their married status. I have noticed that Salma, your daughter-in-law, still puts vermilion in her parting and a bindi of the same on her forehead, in the fashion of Hindu married women. You say that vermilion in the hair differentiated daughters-in-law from daughters in the erstwhile tawaif families.

With the solidifying of religious identities, however, most married women in Muslim families from tawaif backgrounds, including your own elder daughter, have stopped doing this. Your son-in-law considers it too 'Hindu' to be appropriate for a good Muslim wife. You are pained by the hardening of boundaries. Muslims, you conclude sarcastically, are keen to become 'proper' Muslims, and Hindu tawaif families have begun aping the ways of upper-caste Hindus.

Gazing out of the window, you sigh at the landscape fleeting past. Withered, worn out and wasted, these hills have long since been stripped of the sal, bamboo, mahua, kendu, koraiya jungles that feature in the early nineteenth-century accounts I came across about the Kaimur plateau, written by Dr Francis Buchanan, a Scotsman sent by the Company to tour and report on areas directly under the Bengal presidency.

In 1813, on his way to the estate of Sahebzadah Singh, the raja of Jagdishpur and Kunwar Singh's father, Buchanan had to negotiate dense, widespread forests that abounded in wildlife, including tigers, cheetahs, hyenas, deer, nilgai and monkeys of several varieties. Getting lost more than once in the verdant woodlands, he was attacked by bands of langurs he had tried to scare away from his path.

Exhausted and irritable, Buchanan finally reached Jagdishpur only to find a small, unprepossessing town of about a thousand mud-walled houses. Its only noteworthy building, he noted, was the 'abundantly' large but in 'no way ornamental' brick-and-mud ancestral fort of Sahebzadah Singh.

The old zamindar probably found it galling to have his estate and its affairs put under the scrutiny of a white stranger. Unable to refuse Buchanan's proposed visit, Sahebzadah Singh expressed his displeasure by not meeting him personally. Excusing himself on grounds of being indisposed because of a hunting accident, he had Kunwar Singh, the eldest of his four sons, receive Buchanan and show him around the estate.

If he perceived the slight, the guest was too seasoned a traveller to lose sleep over it. A man of many parts, Buchanan was a physician by training whose wanderlust had brought him to India. He served in the Bengal Medical Service from 1794 to 1815 and made significant contributions as a geographer, zoologist and botanist. From 1807 to 1814, under the instructions of the government of Bengal, he made a comprehensive survey of the areas within the jurisdiction of the Company, including Shahabad, and reported copiously on an exhaustive range of subjects that included topography, history, antiquities, the condition of the inhabitants, religion, fisheries, forests, mines, quarries, agriculture, fine and common arts, and commerce.

Confronted with the staggering diversity of India, the Company had, since the late eighteenth century, deputed a host of colonial administrators, missionaries and travellers to carry out surveys and enquires about the natives in territories under colonial rule—their faiths, laws, property relations, social, economic and cultural conditions and beliefs, customs and styles of living. The voluminous surveys by these self-styled ethnographers would form the basis on which the colonial rulers classified their subject populations.

The representations in these surveys, annals, gazetteers and travelogues were usually unencumbered by the complexity of reality. They reduced all natives to essentialist stereotypes to fit the self-serving premise of colonialism: that Indians were unsuited to govern themselves. The colonised masses were thus most usually represented as trapped in moribund social and cultural beliefs, divided into mutually antagonistic and exclusive groupings of Hindus and Muslims, and further fragmented by an all-pervasive, never-changing, hierarchical caste system. Caste became the dominant paradigm for the classification and quantification of entire populations. Each caste, it was claimed, had certain characteristics, a compilation of which became a reductionist ready-reckoner for the colonial administrator, who could thus claim to 'know' the natives he governed.

The knowledge thus gathered was further tempered by the interests and prejudices of the local elite whom Buchanan and his ilk of surveyors consulted in the course of their investigations. Represented primarily by Brahmin ritual-and-text specialists, upper-caste landowners and native officials like village headmen, these informants were chosen for their 'natural' status as community leaders, and for their perceived expertise on religion, native society, law, land relations and cultural practices. Buchanan's accounts of caste were thus ordered on the basis of the hierarchy valorised by his native elite informants, and had no space for self-representation by communities classified as 'lowly', 'vile' and 'abominable' by them.

In his travels through Bengal and Bihar, Buchanan was surprised to find that many groups and tribes had little idea of brahminical ideals such as dowry, child marriage, prohibition of divorce and remarriage of widows, and dietary regulations, with many consuming liquor and meat during festivals that had no place in the brahminical calendar. Yet, he was dismissive of the understanding that these vast masses of artisans, tradesmen and peasant groups had about their own social position. Even more confusing for early British surveyors was the presence in Bengal and Bihar of large numbers of groups with syncretic customs and beliefs and no fixed identity of themselves as neatly Hindu or Muslim. This did not deter colonial writers from attempting to construct over a period of time, imagined, homogenised and mutually exclusive communities of Muslims and Hindus, the latter neatly organised on the principles of brahminical caste ranking.

Well looked after and escorted everywhere by Kunwar Singh, whom he described as 'very obliging', Buchanan spent several days surveying the estate of Jagdishpur. His first impressions of Sahebzadah Singh's lifestyle were favourable. 'His domestics amount to 350 and 100 persons are fed daily from his kitchens,' wrote Buchanan of the raja's large retinue. 'He keeps 1 elephant, 10 horses, 8 carriages drawn by oxen and a large establishment of hawks and dogs.' While commenting on the relatively low standard of living of other landlords in Shahabad, Buchanan marked out Sahebzadah Singh along with his kinsman, Jai Prakash Singh, the raja of Dumraon, and Ali Hussein, the estate holder of Koyatur, as the few zamindars who 'live in the style becoming gentlemen'.

Raja Sahebzadah Singh was, however, something of a maverick. He had inherited the estate from his uncle Bhup Narain Singh, who had died without a male heir. A few years later, Sahebzadah Singh had found himself embroiled in a protracted legal battle with a branch of his own family that contested his succession. This, many said, was the reason for his lifelong antipathy to the ashraf or respectable people in his estate, many of whom had supported the claims of his rival. Feeling betrayed and isolated, he reposed trust in his mostly Kurmi and Dusadh employees and agents, who, on account of their low-caste status, were disparaged by Buchanan as 'the dregs of impurity'.

Sahebzadah Singh seems to have most enjoyed spending time on hunts in the deep forests that covered his estate. In the bargain, Buchanan alleged, he paid little attention to his landholdings. If indeed Sahebzadah Singh was careless about his duties as a landholder, he was following the norm rather than being an exception. Virtually free of any accountability, except for paying the predetermined revenue on time to the colonial government, many landholders delegated their responsibilities to a series of intermediaries in exchange for a share in the takings from the land. Buchanan, for instance, reports the presence of revenue contractors, or thikadars, who had purchased leases from the zamindars to collect rent on their behalf from the cultivator tenants. Many thikadars, in turn, subcontracted the work to another set of intermediaries, the kut kinehdars. The natural outcome of this parasitic system of landlords and intermediaries was rapacious exaction from tenant cultivators to ensure a sufficient share for all involved, together with a lack of responsibility and accountability towards the attendant obligations of land improvement.

Buchanan complains that Sahebzadah Singh was neither interested in overseeing the regular repairs of water reservoirs, nor in clearing forested lands and extending cultivation. Yet, even Buchanan had to concede that Sahebzadah Singh was extremely popular with his tenant cultivators. One possible reason for this could have been that when the rice crop in his estate had failed successively in the previous years, the raja, much to Buchanan's disapproval, had not shown any inclination to use 'legal process or violence' to extract the maximum possible rent from his tenants. This was a serious lapse as far as the colonial government was concerned. While a landlord like the raja of Dumraon earned praise for his ability to 'exact what is due to him with some rigour', estate owners like Babu Sahebzadah Singh ran the risk of having their lands seized if they were perceived as being lax in their chief duty of ensuring timely payment of revenue to the Company's coffers. To avoid seizure of their estates when the takings from tenant cultivators fell short, the zamindars had no option but to turn to moneylenders.

Sahebzadah Singh was caught in an acute financial crisis. Already in debt because of the long-drawn-out family lawsuit, he was forced to borrow more money to pay the land revenue due from his estate. From Buchanan, we know that the raja of Jagdishpur owed moneylenders almost Rs 300,000, on which he paid nearly Rs 60,000 annually as interest. Laying the blame for his pecuniary distress on Sahebzadah Singh's choice of employing low-caste and hence unsuitable people, besides his maintenance of an excessively large retinue of dependents, Buchanan sternly concludes that the raja and his family seem to be 'on the eve of ruin'.

If major zamindars like Sahebzadah Singh faced financial distress, there can be little doubt that the condition of tenant cultivators and landless labourers would have been very dire indeed. The Permanent Settlement, by bestowing upon zamindars complete proprietorial rights over land, had stripped the cultivators of the protection that pre-colonial customs had provided against unfettered exactions by landholders and eviction from holdings. As the district collector of Champaran was to point out in 1855, 'The cultivator, though nominally protected by regulations of all sorts, has practically no rights in the soil. His rent is continually raised; he is oppressed and worried until he is actually forced out of his holding.'

Shahabad was thus not an easy place to live and survive in, in the early nineteenth century. From Buchanan we know that, in proportion to the total population of the district, the number of beggars was very high. Epidemics, especially of fevers, and consequent deaths in large numbers seem to have been a feature of daily life. Malnutrition must have been quite high since Buchanan mentions that the poor, especially in the Kaimur hills area, lived off dried mahua flowers and 'the kernels of the mango sakuya and kend fruits'.

Out-migration from the district was rampant amongst all communities, and Buchanan writes about not only the lower castes but also 'high-born' men belonging to poorer families with small landholdings amongst the Rajputs, Bhumihars and Kayasths being forced to move out of the district to seek their fortunes in distant lands. Shahabad had the highest number of men enlisted in the army as compared to any other district in Bihar province.

Amongst the few communities that seemed to have thrived in the harshness of Shahabad were the tawaifs. A pervasive musical culture seems to have flourished here, given the many categories of tawaifs and women entertainers that find mention in Buchanan's accounts of 'prostitutes', or the different 'sets of girls who dance and sing accompanied by musical instruments, the performers on which are men'.

Colonial writers like Buchanan routinely described women who practised a vast spectrum of female sexualities that existed outside marriage as 'prostitutes'. This representation was informed as much by

Victorian morality as by Hindu and Muslim laws newly fashioned under the Company rule to administer justice to the natives according to their separate religious canons. The process of this law-making was based on the search for, and translation of, brahminical scriptures in Sanskrit and Quranic injunctions, seen by colonial rulers as a 'historically fixed' and 'authentic' body of laws and codes representing the customs and beliefs of all Hindus and Muslims respectively. Interpreted by Brahmin priests and maulavis, these laws represented the worldview of the traditional elites and glossed over the traditions and practices of a wide range of less privileged castes and communities, which, lacking textual sources, might have sought their legitimacy in customary laws.

Patriarchal norms of rigid control over female sexuality and emphasis on marriage as indispensable for all women got codified as law under Company rule. These became the default setting by which all native women would be judged; even custom-based female sexual activity that fell outside marriage would be punished as 'incontinence', 'unchastity' and 'prostitution'. Under this legal framework, communities of women performers, including the highly accomplished temple dancers in peninsular India and privileged courtesans of the north, who had traditionally entered relationships of concubinage with men of the local elite, now got grouped with the more humble brothel-based prostitutes.

Colonial writers and commentators became enthusiastic votaries of this reformulated, codified, brahminical patriarchy. Thus, even while providing a surprisingly nuanced account of the varied social and economic status of women entertainers and performers in Bihar and the cultural skills associated with them, Buchanan chooses to essentialise them under the overarching category of 'prostitutes'.

We get a detailed and vivid description of different classes of 'prostitutes' from Buchanan's account of his travels through the neighbouring district of Behar in the previous year of 1811–12. About the 'dancing girls' in Patna, whom he refers to as 'bais', he writes that they 'are considered by the natives as very accomplished'. He suggests that the term 'bai' was considered derogatory and used for 'upstart sets, who are also sometimes called Natin'.

According to Buchanan, distinct from the more plebeian bais or Natins, there existed a category of 'prostitutes' whose predecessors had 'obtained a certain rank from former princes. Some of them, if not all, were allowed small endowments in land, which in the southeast part of the district a few still retain. These ennobled ladies of easy virtue and enticing manner were by imperial authority reduced to four classes—Domni, Hurkini, Kangchani and Ramjani: the last are Hindus; the first three are Muhammedans.'

Buchanan then painstakingly enumerates the rates charged by different categories of women singers and dancers in Patna and Gaya. We are told, for instance, that in Patna, on 'ordinary occasions', the 'good sets are usually paid 15 rupees for a night's performance. The lowest sets are allowed 5 rupees.' He singles out for special mention Mehtab, a Hindu singer and dancer who lived in Patna. Buchanan describes her as a 'dancing girl in the highest request. Like the others she usually goes to Calcutta during the Durga puja; and when she first appeared, being about 15 years of age she was paid 1000 rupees for the three nights' performance.'

About Shahabad, he notes that the 'prostitutes are mostly Muhammedans, only in the western parts of the district there are some of the Gandharvinis ...' While stating that the girls who sing and dance, both Muslims and Hindus, 'possess no celebrity', Buchanan concedes that 'no women have a fairer character than those of this district'.

Buchanan enumerates various types of male musicians he encountered in Shahabad, like the Dhari-Mirasis, who 'perform at marriages'. Amongst the oldest communities of musicians in north India, Dhari men from the late seventeenth century onwards find regular mention as sarangi players and teachers to courtesans. They performed at weddings as accompanists to tawaifs whose singing and dancing was an indispensable feature of landholding Rajput and Bhumihar marriage celebrations. Closely associated with tawaifs as their tabla and sarangi players as well as teachers, Mirasis performed occupational roles so similar to the Dharis that the two often got clubbed together.

In his accounts of nineteenth-century Shahabad, Buchanan mentions the Kathaks, who he describes as Brahmins belonging to 'a sacred order'. Kathaks as a community of male performers have a shared history with the evolution of kathak, the dance form that, by the eighteenth century, became identified with tawaifs. In the role of their dance teachers and also as tabla players, Kathaks shared a close relationship with courtesan performers. Some Kathaks in pockets of eastern India seem to have continued with their ancient role of katha vachaks, or storytellers of Hindu epics and mythology, especially episodes from the life of Krishna, through the use of mime, drama and dance.

Buchanan also notes the prevalence in Shahabad of the Kalawants whom he describes as 'ballad singers' and 'converted Brahmans of the Kathak kind'. Also enumerated are the Bhaats or bards, both Hindu and Muslim, and the bajawalas or 'common musicians' who 'are all shoemakers or sweepers' and 'perform on the fife and drum'.

His accounts further include 'the Baazigars who sing, play legerdemain tricks and show feats of activity and are of the Nat tribe'. A widely dispersed, semi-nomadic community, the Nats have traditionally included in their fold a broad spectrum of entertainers, including acrobats and conjurers in rural areas, and groups of urban tawaifs referred to as Natins in Mughal and later accounts, including Buchanan's.

Patronage to tawaifs and their large retinues of accompanist musicians, family members and servants came from the Rajput and Bhumihar zamindars of the region. They patronised courtesans and entertainers, just as they made endowments for the construction of temples and mosques, financed feasts for the poor on festive or ritual occasions, gave gifts to religious functionaries, and indulged in pomp and ceremony.

Babu Kunwar Singh, who inherited the estate of Jagdishpur from his father in 1826 at the age of forty-four, inherited too the heavy burden of debts that had given Sahebzadah Singh so much grief. This does not seem to have dampened his spirit of charity, though. The Arrah Zillah School was established in 1846 on land he donated, along with a cash endowment of Rs 101.

Catholic in his philanthropy, Kunwar Singh not only got a Shiva temple and a tank built at Jagdishpur but also made a generous grant for the maintenance of a Muslim shrine in Patna city. Far from being seen as extravagances unsuitable for a debt-ridden landholder, Kunwar Sigh's munificence marked him as one of the more generous zamindars of Shahabad.

Kunwar Singh's interests were as wide-ranging as the recipients of his largesse. From the gazetteer of Shahabad, we get to know that 'spirited and adventurous by nature, Kunwar Singh was inclined to strenuous outdoor life'. He was 'a patron of men well versed in martial sports, such as riding, shooting, archery etc. He invited such experts to Jagdishpur and retained them for long periods to train his men in those arts.' There is mention too of his tawaif concubines, including Dharmman Bibi. In deference to her religious beliefs, Kunwar Singh, a devout Hindu, made 'endowments for the construction of a mosque in the heart of the town of Arrah'.

Kunwar Singh's patronage of Dharmman excited much envy amongst other tawaifs in Arrah, many of whom had been vying for his attention. The fortunes of a tawaif rested on finding—on the basis of her talent, beauty, sharp wits and luck—a wealthy and generous zamindar patron who would maintain her and her family, by providing them material security. If a tawaif faltered and tied her affections instead with a lover of meagre means, then she charted her own course and that of her family towards hunger, homelessness and the swelling ranks of the poor in Shahabad.

Before Dharmman Bibi met Kunwar Singh, she had been involved briefly with a young Rajput, Dalip Singh. They had met at a wrestling bout that he was participating in and that Dharmman Bibi had gone to see. His tall, powerful frame rippling with sinewy muscles had towered above all the other wrestlers. One by one, Dalip Singh had made them all taste mud. When there was no one left, he had arrogantly turned towards the gathering and dared anyone amongst them to a final bout. Unable to resist a challenge, Dharmman Bibi had stepped out of the crowd and announced that she would take him on. Dalip Singh laughed. Then he refused to take up her offer. He was not going to wrestle with a mere woman, he said. But when Dharmman Bibi, her eyes flashing, taunted him for being scared of losing to her, he had no option but to reluctantly agree.

Hitching her sari up between her legs and securely tucking in the end of the pallu that covered her head so that it would not slip off, Dharmman Bibi entered the wrestling arena. From the very first clasp of the other's shoulders, it was obvious to both the wrestlers that this would be no ordinary bout. An electric charge seemed to run through them when they touched each other. With rising passion, they wrestled long and hard. Dalip Singh's chiselled features, aquiline nose and brown eyes made Dharmman Bibi melt like wax each time he put his arms around her. Likewise, he felt dizzy with desire whenever she tried to pull him down. Although she did bring him very close to the mat several times, Dalip Singh was perhaps the only man Dharmman Bibi could not conclusively defeat in the wrestling arena. Eventually, the bout ended with neither competitor conceding defeat. It was obvious to both that they were a perfect match for each other.

Night after night, they would stay awake in each other's arms consumed by an inexhaustible passion. As part of her education to become a tawaif, Dharmman Bibi had been taught all the wiles to make any man fall in love with her. As importantly, she had been repeatedly cautioned never to fall in love with a patron; it was an emotion, she had been warned, that confused the mind, blurred judgement and weakened the tawaif's capacity to extract the maximum from her lover while the going was good. Thus far in her career, Dharmman had wisely adhered to each rule that had been laid down for her. But this time, her heart betrayed her head; she fell madly in love with Dalip Singh. It was said that she would fall ill if separated from him for any length of time. He too had eyes only for his Dharmman. But both knew that their love was doomed. Dalip Singh, though a Rajput, was too poor to afford a courtesan mistress.

His family had once controlled sizeable landholdings around Arrah. Over the generations, due to successive fragmentation of land, Dalip Singh and his six brothers were forced to cultivate their small, uneconomical holdings themselves, in disregard of brahminical injunctions against upper-caste landholders tilling the soil with their own hands. The colonial government's demands for high rates of land revenue further threatened their precarious elite status. Desperate to keep up appearances of a lifestyle considered appropriate to their Rajput pride, Dalip Singh's brothers decided to migrate and seek employment as soldiers in the Company's army.

Dalip Singh, the youngest of the brothers, was the last to leave home. Dharmman Bibi prayed for a miracle that would make him stay back in Shahabad, but this was not to be. Delayed rains, withered crops and a cruel drought forced him to harden his heart, bid her farewell and set off to join the Company's army.

Dharmman was heartbroken. However, her aunt Zahooran, who had brought her up like a mother and was her only family, was most relieved. In the community, it was said that the fortunes of a tawaif were like quicksand. One false step and the descent from riches to rags was sudden and inexorable. Having passed on the family legacy of music, dance and material assets to Dharmman and groomed her to become a popular tawaif, Zahooran had been scathing in her reprimands when her niece got involved with the unsuitable Dalip Singh. With him out of the way, she hoped that Dharmman would make a wise choice. Her prayers were answered when no less a personage than Babu Kunwar Singh offered to maintain her as his mistress.

Dharmman herself was far from ready to accept Kunwar Singh's proposal. She refused to take on as lover a man old enough to be her grandfather. She did not care if he was amongst the most illustrious of the babu sahibs of Shahabad. Daily, she and Zahooran would have bitter arguments on the issue. The mini-army of servants and accompanist musicians in the house would quiver as the shouting and ranting smashed through the walls and hurled out into the street. One or the other, aunt or niece, would have to give in—but who would it be? Each woman was as strong-willed as the other. Then, an unexpected tragedy decided for Dharmman her course in life.

CHAPTER 2

The Arrival of Umrao

'KIDNAPPERS HAVE STRUCK AGAIN!' JAWED's declaration brims with the drama of a Hindi film. He has sighted a torn, dirty white shirt hanging limply from a neem tree some distance away. It's a ransom sign, he explains with solemn authority, and also a warning to the victim's family of the sure death awaiting their loved one if they don't pay up. As we draw closer, Jawed squints and stares some more, and claims to spot bloodstains on the shirt. I strain my eyes but discern no such marks.

Looking irritated, you refuse to be the indulgent aunt this time. 'Such fanciful stories you think up, boy! If you spent half as much time thinking of your work, you would reach places.'

I am not sure that thinking more about the petticoats and blouses he stitches in his father's tiny shop in small-town Bhabua will necessarily reach young Jawed anywhere, but I hold my tongue. Not that your rebuke dampens Jawed's excitement. 'Badki amma, this is no fanciful story. Rich people are often kidnapped for ransom by criminal gangs with hideouts in the Kaimur hills. They then tie some clothing worn by the victim to a tree as a signal to the relatives to pay up. I would suggest we drive away as fast as we can. Danger lurks close by.'

Our driver Ramesh, attention diverted from his non-stop bhajans, looks panic-stricken and pushes down hard on the accelerator. As we lurch forwards on the bumpy road, you snort in exasperation and tell Ramesh to calm down and drive carefully.

Looking straight at your nephew, you say sternly, 'Son, I know all there is to know about abduction and ransom. I personally know people who have been abducted. I have also run into those who live by kidnapping. But kidnappings don't happen in our parts where almost everyone is too poor to pay up. And not all shirts flapping on trees are ransom notes.'

Turning to me, you add in lowered tones that abduction is a mini-industry in Bihar. Controlled by the rich and powerful with political connections, kidnapper gangs have attracted even educated, unemployed young men to crime. Lowering your voice further to a furtive whisper, you tell me that in the past you had performed a few times at wedding parties organised by former zamindars who, you got to know later, headed such gangs. Everyone in the area knew about their involvement in the abduction business but, because of their political influence, not even the police had the guts to bring them to book.

His ears straining to catch your whispers, Jawed looks visibly impressed by your knowledge of the abduction industry. Wishing perhaps to register his considered views on the subject, he adds in earnest tones, 'Of late there has been a spurt in these kidnappings even in our district. Some people say it is the Maoists who are doing it, but I don't believe it. Maoists don't stoop to such petty deeds.'

'Son, stop wasting your time thinking about criminal gangs and Maoists. Focus on your own life and stop poking your nose into the affairs of others.' The advice you give Jawed is your life's dictum. You have told me often that, as a tawaif, you saw and heard much that was out of the ordinary, but following your mother's teachings, always kept your own counsel. 'I am but a poor tawaif. I have never interfered in anyone's business. And I don't like anyone interfering in mine,' you frequently say.

Tucking a fresh paan inside your mouth, you now pick up the threads of the story that Jawed had interrupted. 'Dharmman Bibi's aunt, Zahooran, was an extremely popular tawaif in Shahabad as a young woman. Though well into middle age by the time Dharmman caught Babu Kunwar Singh's fancy, Zahooran had not still retired and had a few select wealthy and influential lovers at her beck and call.'

Known for her clear-sighted choice of patrons, it was said that Zahooran could count the feathers on the wings of a bird in flight. But she was destined to make one fatal error of judgement. Much to Dharmman's surprise, she began entertaining on a regular basis a rakishly handsome new arrival in town, Khanazad Khan, about whose background no one knew anything.

Suave, charming and always expensively dressed, Khanazad Khan from Patna specialised in preying upon affluent tawaifs living on their own. They were usually among the wealthiest women in any town. Their homes were open to all manner of visitors, which made access relatively easy and the police too were less likely to zealously pursue a case involving tawaifs than one which involved an upper-class, 'respectable' victim.

Posing as a rich travelling trader, Khanazad Khan would gain the confidence of a courtesan, with an extravagant show of wealth, solicitous concern and courtesy. Once trust was won, he would poison her drink or food and decamp with all her jewellery and cash. After several successful strikes on courtesans across Bihar, and before that in the North-West Provinces, Khanazad Khan reached Arrah. Always thorough with his research, he zeroed in on Zahooran, one of the best-off tawaifs of the town, living with just a niece in the largest house in Arrah's tawaif quarters.

Over the next few months, he lavished Zahooran with thoughtful gifts, fulsome but sincere-sounding compliments and exhilarating love-making. When he was sure of her complete capitulation, he struck one evening when Dharmman was away attending the wedding of a relative. In the course of a night-long session of music and dance, Khanazad Khan laced Zahooran's drink with a special slow-working poison.

Once all the servants in the house and accompanist musicians had retired for the night, he made love one final time to the dying Zahooran. When she was dead, he tenderly laid her body on the bed and offered pious prayers for the departed. He then proceeded to stealthily and meticulously remove all the valuables and cash from the house. By first light of dawn, he had disappeared forever from Arrah, carried by his loyal steed across forests and rivers into oblivion.

Dharmman was now left alone in the world. Inconsolable in her grief over the loss of the aunt she had loved as a mother, she was wracked with regret about the bitter quarrels that had marred her last days with Zahooran. Dharmman knew that her aunt had only wanted the best for her. She blamed herself for Zahooran's death—had she not caused her aunt so much heartache, perhaps she would not have lost the good judgement she was so admired for. Her friends and well-wishers tried to console Dharmman, but her soul shrouded in anguish, she was beyond being comforted.

Babu Kunwar Singh prevailed upon the colonial police to launch a massive manhunt for Khanazad Khan across Shahabad and beyond. His own band of armed militia searched in vain every forest, hill range, field and home in and around Arrah. He was constantly by Dharmman's side through this difficult period.

Over time, Dharmman began finding solace in his presence. Kunwar Singh's kindness and concern in the lonely months following her aunt's murder were reassuring and yet gently unobtrusive. Without fussing, he tried to give her relief through thoughtful gestures. His efforts to trace her aunt's murderer further endeared him to Dharmman. Here was a man she instinctively felt she could trust. In the absence of a family, he would provide her the loyal, steadfast companionship she desperately sought. As a tawaif on her own, accepting babu sahib's proposal would be the right choice for her, and one her aunt would have approved of. Accordingly, Dharmman shifted into the new house Kunwar Singh bought for her, away from the memories crowding her old home. There, installed in great comfort, she entered into a life-long relationship with the old Rajput.

A young girl in school uniform, about thirteen or fourteen years of age, gaily pedals past us on a cycle. She is followed by ten or fifteen girls, talking, giggling and tinkling their cycle bells. Instinctively, you and I exchange smiles with them. Jawed informs us that under a government scheme in Bihar, cycles are presented to all girls who clear class nine. I am pleasantly surprised. You rue your fate for having been born forty-five years too early.

Jawed then goes beyond the headlines. A large number of families in Bhabua have sold off their daughters' cycles for much-needed cash, he says. In many other homes, the cycles have been appropriated by the men in the family. Allowing girls to gad about freely on cycles, people said, was inviting catastrophe. Who could predict when the girls would get the wrong ideas, have love affairs and elope? I watch the last of the girls disappear from sight around the bend of the hilly tract and silently wish her luck. Always an optimist, you point out that many more girls go to school today than they used to in earlier times.

In 1812–1813, Francis Buchanan, commenting on the state of formal education in Shahabad, wrote, 'in general ladies of the highest rank understand only the common form of the vulgar dialect'. With the exception of 'ten or twelve Hindu ladies [who] have acquired the dangerous art of reading and writing letters', formal education in Hindi, and definitely in Persian, seems to have been absent amongst upper-caste women.

Buchanan's grim report on the educational status of women in Shahabad makes no mention of tawaifs. Tawaifs, prostitutes and female entertainers, as a rule, were never included in accounts that related to women in any colonial survey, gazette or travelogue. Had Buchanan investigated and reported on the tawaifs' skills in reading, writing and numbers, his representation of native women's lack of access to formal learning might have revealed some patches of light in the overall bleakness.

And bleak it certainly was. Even leaving margin for the sensational that so often characterised colonial representations of purdah-observing upper-caste Indian women's lives, there was no denying that their destinies were inexorably tied to marriage and the reproduction of patriarchal lineages. Child marriage was the norm amongst the Rajputs, Bhumihars and other privileged castes in Shahabad. A girl was sent to her husband's home as soon as she reached puberty. In general, access to learning was considered neither necessary nor desirable, and most times her only education was in the skills associated with being an ideal wife and mother.

Kunwar Singh was married to the daughter of Raja Fatah Narain Singh, a wealthy zamindar of Deo in Gaya district. We have little information about this woman whose name even remains unknown. We are told that, from her, Kunwar Singh had a son, Dalbhajan Singh, who died young. If she had any daughters, they find no mention in biographical accounts of Kunwar Singh.

Whether Kunwar Singh's wife ever received any formal education can only be speculated upon, but we can be fairly certain that she would have been married when she was a mere child. Hidden behind the veil, she would have spent the better part of her life within the women's quarters of the large mud-and-brick fort of her husband's family. Occupying a world very different from that of her husband, her primary duties and responsibilities would have entailed producing a male heir for his family, looking after the comforts and needs of Kunwar Singh, their children and his relatives, and observing appropriate religious rituals and fasts for his well-being.

I wonder if she resented her husband's many lovers, felt jealousy and pain in sharing him with his tawaif concubines such as Dharmman Bibi. You, clear-eyed through experience, reply that she would probably have had little choice but to accept it as normal. Maintaining tawaif mistresses is what zamindars were expected to do. Moreover, how else would men like Kunwar Singh pass their time? Part of a long and parasitical chain of revenue collectors, zamindars like him had plenty of leisure to indulge in a wide range of interests, ranging from hunting to martial arts to music and dance.

The Rajput aristocracy in Shahabad had long been part of the vast Mughal political, administrative and social edifice. They shared the aesthetics of the Indo-Islamic cultural synthesis that had flowered under Mughal rule and, following its disintegration, found localised expression in regional power centres. Dharmman Bibi's extensive and exacting education in the arts, letters and etiquette would no doubt have been tailored to fit the cultural norms and preferences of her zamindar patrons.

Kunwar Singh, therefore, might have enjoyed listening to Dharmman Bibi sing the thumri, which was prevalent in the eighteenth and nineteenth centuries in provincial centres like Banaras and Gaya. Less classicised than its aristocratic cousin, the bandish thumri of Lucknow, this thumri of the east was characterised by its folk form and metre. According to scholars, it was this folk-based thumri that would provide the foundation for the bol banao thumri style that emerged in Banaras and surrounding areas around the late nineteenth century.

You add that Dharmman Bibi would most certainly have sung for Babu Kunwar Singh the dadra and hori, forms closely linked with the thumri. Her repertoire would have included folk songs of the region, like the languorous chaiti that heralds the onset of the summer heat and the longing-imbued kajari, which celebrates the dark clouds of the monsoon rains. Traditionally sung by the local women, these folk songs, as part of the repertoire of tawaif musicians, evolved into classicised versions of the originals and came to be regarded as associative subgenres of thumri. She would also have been trained in kathak, performed to the accompaniment of the thumri.

It is possible that Kunwar Singh, who as a Rajput landholder would have received some Persian education, might have also had a taste for the ghazal, which Dharmman Bibi would have been trained to perform. She would no doubt have enthralled her patron with the sensuous kaherwa, set to eight beats and accompanied by song types of the same name. A folk song and dance of the region, kaherwa involves dexterous movements of the waist and abdominal muscles and was closely associated with tawaif performers. Her repertoire must have included too the dadra dance, set to six beats and which accompanied the usually playful and flirtatious dadra songs so closely associated with the thumri and with tawaif performers.

You now narrate what you confess is amongst your favourite stories about Dharmman Bibi: 'Kunwar Singh had once organised at his fort in Jagdishpur a mehfil, as he was wont to do, in honour of a visiting gora sahib, a white official.'

On account of his lineage and eminent position, Kunwar Singh was well known and respected in the colonial circles of Bihar. A generous host, he would entertain often and lavishly, inviting colonial officials to sumptuous feasts and spectacular nautches. The celebrations would be remembered for months on end in British and Indian circles for their splendid extravagance.

'On this occasion too he had arranged for some of the finest tawaifs in Arrah to come and entertain his guest with music and dance,' you say. 'Dharmman Bibi was staying at Jagdishpur at that point. She was not scheduled to perform in the evening's mehfil because Babu Kunwar Singh did not wish to have his publicly acknowledged mistress dance in his home in front of strangers, including a gora sahib. In our parts, although there was no formal rule against it, it was considered bad form to do so.'

Everything seemed to be going well. One well-known tawaif after the other sang, danced and cast a spell on everyone invited to the mehfil—everyone except the gora sahib, who looked out of sorts and bored. Concerned, Kunwar Singh enquired if something was amiss. The official replied that he had heard much about Dharmman Bibi and had hoped to see her perform that evening. He was a bit disappointed that she was not part of the mehfil. Kunwar Singh was now in a fix. He did not wish to ask Dharmman to sing and dance for the Englishman's entertainment, and yet how could he refuse a guest?

Rajputs prided themselves on their hospitality, for treating their guests like gods. Moreover, this guest was a representative of the colonial government. Kunwar Singh needed to keep officers like him happy. There was no way he could allow the Englishman to leave his home disappointed. So, he sent word to Dharmman Bibi to get ready and join the other tawaifs in the mehfil.

Dharmman, though surprised, realised that her babu sahib must be under some pressure. Without fuss, she quickly changed into a peshvaz, the elite tawaif's ceremonial dress for performance, comprising a long-sleeved, close-fitting bodice that flared out into a full skirt reaching almost to the ankles, traditionally made out of cloth woven with threads of gold or silver metal and silk. Its weight and emblematic importance would be often likened by tawaifs, semi-jokingly, to the metal-plated body armour worn by the elite soldiers of the Mughal army. To don a heavy peshvaz and dance in it with the swiftness of an eagle and grace of a deer, as if it were made of gossamer, needed arduous training and practice.

That evening, Dharmman wore a beautiful, green, yellow and gold peshvaz, paired with green silk pyjamas. As she lined her large eyes with kohl, her two personal maids dressed her thick, lustrous hair in a long plait, adorning it with freshly made gajra of sweet-scented flowers. Next, they applied delicate patterns of red alta on Dharmman's feet, as she selected the ornaments that would complement her costume. Much of her jewellery had been gifted by Kunwar Singh; the rest she had either received from former lovers or bought out of her own earnings.

Her hair, forehead, ears, nose, neck, waist, forearms, wrists, fingers, ankles and toes glittering with precious stones inset in gold, Dharmman now covered her head and draped her shoulders in a long, golden-yellow, semi-diaphanous scarf woven from the finest silk. She made a dazzling entry into the ceremonial audience hall where the mehfil was underway, and offered her salaams to the English guest, who looked delighted by her appearance.

Dharmman Bibi began her performance with dance as was the norm. Every time she completed a circle, the visitor would offer her money, insisting that she herself take it from him. He would then try and grab her hand. Dharmman seethed silently. This firangi, foreigner, was behaving as if she, the leading tawaif of Shahabad, was a humble nachaniya, a low-placed dancer, or worse, a poor prostitute selling sex to English soldiers.

In her early days as a tawaif, when she visited cities like Banaras and Calcutta to perform for the local elite, Dharmman had noticed the crowds of women, young and old, with faces pinched and stomachs hungry, that arrived there daily from villages in search of work. Mainly artisan women pauperised by the arrival of cheap British imports into the Indian market, or wives and daughters of peasant families facing destitution because of the high rates of revenue extracted from them by the colonial state, many of them drifted into selling sex in fast-expanding cities like Calcutta.

Several women were recruited into chaklas, or brothels, set up at the behest of colonial authorities in the Lal Bazaar area of cantonments, designated for regimental prostitutes. Engaged by the military establishment to provide sexual services exclusively to European soldiers, these women were registered by the Cantonment magistrate and issued licences to live and work there. Even their fee was fixed by the military authorities. Besides brothels, the Lal Bazaar also housed the lock hospital, a venereal disease 'hospital', where prostitutes who were considered diseased would be forcibly sent for treatment and detained until 'cured'.

Outraged at being treated no better than the unfortunate denizens of the Lal Bazaars, Dharmman suppressed her urge to plant a slap across the face of the boorish visitor. Several English officers kept courtesans as mistresses, and many more were routinely invited to nautches such as this one. All of them were aware of the decorum to be observed with elite courtesans. Was this offensiveness a deliberate attempt to humiliate Dharmman's patron?

Under normal circumstances, Dharmman would have stopped performing in protest against the insulting behaviour of the firangi. This mehfil, though, was not routine. Heavily in debt, Kunwar Singh desperately needed to keep English officials on his side. Even though the total annual income of his large estate was about Rs 300,000, out of which he paid an annual revenue of Rs 148,000, the burden of debts that he had inherited from his father had over the years grown to an astronomical sum of Rs 1,300,000. He had made applications for a remission of his dues to the state revenue board. The only card he had in hand was the friendship and goodwill he enjoyed with the colonial officers in Shahabad. They could help put pressure on the state revenue board to bail him out of a situation where he stood in danger of losing his estate and his title.

Dharmman Bibi saw the helpless rage in Babu Kunwar Singh's eyes, his clenched fists. She knew of his difficult financial position. She realised too that the status she enjoyed as an eminent tawaif was linked directly to the patronage she received from babu sahib. Besides, she had come to respect and even love Kunwar Singh for the kindness, generosity and consideration he extended not only towards her but to all those who served him. His actions inspired loyalty, and Dharmman was not one to betray a benevolent patron. Swallowing her pride, she ignored the leering white guest's clumsy advances and continued her dance with a smile on her lips. She had been trained to perform in the most adverse circumstances, and today she put those long years of learning to good use.

As Dharmman Bibi danced, she became increasingly aware of the hungry look in the Englishman's eyes. She knew exactly what the foreign visitor would expect when he retired to bed that night under babu sahib's roof. She did not fancy the thought, and worried too that the request would put her patron in an intolerable situation. A refusal would result in alienating the firangi. And yet she knew that it would be impossible for babu sahib to agree to let his guest sleep with his mistress. It would compromise completely the old Rajput's sense of honour, his masculinity.

So, swirling faster and faster as the dance piece drew to an end, Dharmman Bibi thought of a way out. It was quite a simple plan actually. For the rest of the evening, she kept pouring wine in the gora sahib's glass and encouraging him to drink up quickly. Soon enough, she had him completely drunk. When the evening drew to a close, a stumbling sahib had to be helped to his room by Babu Kunwar Singh's staff.

Meanwhile, Dharmman Bibi retired quickly to her quarters and changed out of the peshvaz and jewellery that she had been wearing that evening. Giving these to her personal maid who resembled her in height and build, Dharmman requested her to go in her stead to the gora sahib that night. The maid covered her face with Dharmman's scarf and slipped into the Englishman's room.

The officer took his leave the next morning. Pleased with his hazy recollections of the previous night's encounter, he never once realised that he had been fooled. Kunwar Singh bade goodbye to his guest with a sense of relief. His mistress's quick thinking had saved what could have been a truly humiliating situation for him. He felt a new respect for her intelligence, resourcefulness and, most importantly, her loyalty towards him and his honour. Standing on the terrace, as she watched the Englishman depart, Dharmman Bibi felt only a cold, hard rage well up in the pit of her belly and reach her heart. She would neither forget nor forgive the firangi's insulting behaviour.

'A whore pretending to feel insulted is like a pot complaining about being put on the fire!' Ramesh comments sarcastically, looking pleased with his turn of phrase. Engrossed in the telling and listening of Dharmman's encounter with the English officer, neither you nor I had noticed that, somewhere along the way, our taxi driver had switched off his selection of dreary bhajans to eavesdrop. The story seems to have outraged his sensibilities.

As I grope for an appropriate response, your voice, razor-sharp, cuts through the pregnant pause. 'Brother, you are being paid to drive, not to give your opinion on matters about which you obviously have little knowledge and even less understanding. Don't barge into conversations that have nothing to do with you. You will be better off concentrating on your driving, which so obviously needs attention.'

As if on cue, the taxi splutters in agreement and an abashed Ramesh, muttering under his breath, changes gear. The sharpness of your rebuke is accentuated by the quiet, measured tones in which it is delivered. Usually mild-mannered, your gentleness, I am aware, cloaks sharp steel. To float like a butterfly, to sting like a bee—as apt for a champion boxer as for a true-blue tawaif—the lines run in a loop in my mind.

With seeming calm, you make yourself another paan. I notice the almost imperceptible tremor in your hands. And with a tug recognise the vulnerability masked by the cultivated hauteur of your gaze. Jawed seems lost in thought. Perhaps mulling the possibility of running into kidnappers or Maoists; perhaps not. And Ramesh sulks in the driver's seat. I feel almost glad when he switches on his stereo and Anoop Jalota's sickly sweet singing drowns the congealed silence in the car.

Pulling a wry face, you put a finger in each ear. This makes me laugh. You smile back. Tension ebbs and normalcy is restored when, uncaring now about Ramesh, you pick up again the threads of Dharmman's tale.

There was just one sorrow that cast a shadow over Dharmman's happy life with Kunwar Singh. Dharmman desperately wanted a child, preferably a daughter, from her Rajput lover. In the tawaif community, the birth of a daughter was an occasion for celebration and thanksgiving. Daughters inherited the music and dance, property and other assets of their mothers. As bearers of their families' musical tradition, they were vested too with the responsibility of earning for their household, of decision-making and of running the affairs of the kotha and home.

Dharmman dreamt of a daughter who would have the broad forehead of her father, his steadfast manner and gracious bearing. She would inherit from her mother her physical beauty, musical skills, charm, intelligence and ingenuity. She would be the abiding symbol of the great love Kunwar Singh shared with Dharmman. She would, moreover, be Dharmman's security in old age when Kunwar Singh, given the years that separated them, would not be by her side.

Dharmman made pilgrimages, visited countless shrines and kept endless fasts. Yet her womb remained empty. Years went by. Kunwar Singh entered old age and Dharmman's youth reached its apex; like the noonday sun, it would now begin its journey into the fading light of middle age. And though it was said that a bull and a Rajput man never grew old, Dharmman's hopes of conceiving a child from Kunwar Singh began to fade too. She decided to adopt a girl child whom she could groom to succeed her as a tawaif. In return, the girl, she hoped, would take care of her in her old age and illness. This was the norm in the tawaif community.

Customarily, tawaifs (both Hindus and Muslims) in the north, along with devadasis and other female singer and dancer communities in peninsular India, were the only section of Indian women that enjoyed the freedom to adopt children. Hindu married women could only adopt a son on behalf of their husbands, while non-tawaif Muslim women could not adopt at all.

Adoption of girl children amongst childless tawaifs was most common, but it was not considered unusual for tawaifs with biological daughters of their own to adopt as well. More daughters in the family meant more earning members and prosperity for the kotha.

Adoptions usually happened within the family and extended social circle: daughters of brothers, married sisters and cousins, and sometimes even of close women friends. Adoption by purchase was also common in those times. Montgomery Martin in his survey of eastern India in 1838 (based in large part on compilations of Buchanan's earlier accounts), writes that tawaifs, both Muslims and Hindus, 'adopt girls of any caste, whom they procure by purchase'.

It would appear reasonable to presume that those tawaifs who could buy girl children for adoption would have been women of some means. Martin confirms this assumption by noting that 'several of the prostitute families are rich, and a few in Behar have trifling endowments in land'.

The majority however, he concludes, 'are rather poor. They are not however as in Europe neglected when they become old, their adopted daughters supporting the aged.'

Martin was not the only British observer struck by the bonds of love, concern and mutual care that seemed to exist in most instances between foster mothers and their purchased and adopted daughters. In 1827, Arthur Steele in his survey of the *Laws and Customs of the Hindoo Castes within the Dekhun Provinces Subject to the Presidency of Bombay* had noted that girl children purchased by dancing girls and 'taught the usual accomplishments of the profession, sometimes rise to become the head of the establishment. They cannot leave the purchaser without the consent of the latter and the parties generally live harmoniously together. Sometimes the mistress and slave exchange the appellations of mother and daughter, the latter supporting the former ...'

Tawaifs were not the only ones who purchased children. In early nineteenth-century colonial Bengal and Bihar, the sale and purchase of children and adults, both male and female, was recognised with caveats and restrictions by Hindu and Muslim law. Parents were allowed to sell their children, and husbands enjoyed the right to put up their wives for sale; the transaction being duly registered on a deed of sale. Gosains and sanyasis, priests and ascetics, purchased boy children whom they initiated into their sects and groomed to become their spiritual successors. Both Buchanan and Martin in their accounts of Shahabad and Behar mention slaves, called Kamkar or Kamia and Molnazadah, who formed part of many upper-caste and elite Hindu and Muslim households and performed menial housework and agricultural labour. Girls and women were often purchased to be made into concubines and performers attached to aristocratic households. Europeans living in India purchased slaves too, to work in their houses and even to provide sexual services.

Besides the deed of sale, elaborate contracts that laid out the terms and conditions of servitude would be drawn up during the time of sale and signed by both the buyer and the bought. These contracts were recognised by law courts and used frequently by purchasers of disobedient or runaway slaves to justify punishment or demand restitution, as the case might be.

Slavery pre-dated colonial rule in South Asia. It took many forms and existed in varied contexts but arose primarily out of either enslavement in war or impoverishment. Under colonial rule, the high and inflexible demand for land revenue by the Company, aggravated by a cruel cycle of devastating famines and the resultant penury and hunger, contributed manifold to the existing trade in children and adults. Starvation often forced the rural poor to sell their offspring and sometimes even themselves in order to survive.

Zahooran had been adopted too; purchased on an impulse in the late eighteenth century by Dharmman's grandmother, Batoolan, while on a visit to Calcutta during Durga Puja to perform in mehfils that the rich organised as part of the festivities. One morning, she had seen five little girls and two boys, all aged between two and six, brought in for sale by a dealer at the home of the tawaif she was staying with.

Severely emaciated, the bedraggled group sat huddled together on the stone floor. They had been brought into Calcutta, Batoolan was told, from the drought- and famine-struck villages of Dhaka district. With evident relish, masked by a show of sympathy, the dealer, a well-fed and loquacious mountain of a man, conjured up for Batoolan and her hostess the spectre of hundreds upon hundreds of starving and dehydrated adults and children lying in exhausted stupor on the banks of the river Brahmaputra. Every time a passenger boat or trading vessel sailed past, they would feebly flail their arms to supplicate for something to eat in exchange for their own and their children's freedom.

The entire trade in human beings in this blighted region was controlled by hard-headed, stone-hearted Portuguese, said the dealer, distancing himself primly from the unsavoury business of profiting from misery. Slave traders preferred buying children over adults and girls over boys. Girl children were easier to control, made fewer demands and were prized for their reproductive and sexual capacities. From Dhaka, the shipments of children would make their way to varied destinations, including Ceylon. The exigencies of a long journey, suffocation and starvation would take their toll, and nearly half the freight perished on the way. Some such vessels negotiated the treacherous marshes of the Sundarbans to reach Calcutta, where the cargo would be sold to yet another chain of middlemen.

With loud protestations of faith and good intent, the dealer presented himself as a god-fearing saviour, sullying his hands in this murky business only so that he could help these unfortunate young ones find food, shelter and care in good homes. Tawaifs, he knew, brought up the children they bought as their own, the dealer added with such obvious obsequious insincerity that both Dharmman's grandmother and her friend burst out laughing. Advising him to save his sales talk for more gullible customers like the pompous rajas and nawabs who employed such children in dozens to wash dirty dishes and clean their mansions, Batoolan's hostess, a worldly-wise woman with kindly eyes, pointed at two little girls with fair faces and chiselled features she wished to buy for herself.

Batoolan already had a daughter of her own and had never entertained any thoughts of adopting another by purchase. The story of penury, starvation and death told by the wily dealer had shaken her, though. She knew it could well be a lie cobbled together for profit by the man fawning on them right now. But the huge, empty eyes of the children he was selling told her that, whatever the truth of their background, it was an intensely unhappy one. Batoolan wished she could have provided shelter to each of them in her home, but practical financial considerations dictated that at most she could afford to take in one of the children.

She decided to make as her own the darkest-complexioned, most shrunken and ordinary-looking little girl of the lot, four or five years of age, whom she knew no tawaif would choose. The child would probably end up being bought to work as a menial in an aristocratic zenana or a European trader's home: both spaces vying for the dubious distinction of being the harshest hell-holes of female slavery. On the other hand, in her home, Batoolan felt confident, the little girl would bloom again with health and vitality.

Not all courtesan establishments were nurturing spaces, Batoolan was well aware. While many tawaifs did share a loving, fostering relationship with their adopted daughters, there were those who treated the purchased girls as property to be used at will for financial gain. They felt no compunction in using the purchase contract to file police complaints against girls who eloped with patron lovers. Similarly, there were umpteen cases of girls who, either fed up with their controlling, exploitative, manipulative tawaif owner-mothers, or wishing to set up independent dance troupes of their own, or desiring to settle down with their lovers, filed appeals to magistrates alleging mistreatment and pleading for emancipation.

Confident in her capacity to love another's child like her own, Batoolan brought the little girl back with her to Arrah. Following the norms set out for adoption in the courtesan community, she invited all the tawaifs of the town along with their accompanist musicians to her house for a feast. There, with the entire community as witness, the local maulavi ceremonially placed the little girl in Batoolan's lap. Prayers were recited, the child was named Zahooran and her formal adoption as a daughter by Batoolan was deemed complete. In the years to come, so intense was the love shared between Batoolan and her two daughters, Ameeran and Zahooran, that few in the family and almost no one outside would remember which girl was adopted and which one related by blood. Both girls received similar education and training in music and dance, both were launched as tawaifs in great style by Batoolan.

Tragedy struck unexpectedly when Ameeran died young while giving birth to Dharmman, and a year later, Batoolan fell prey to the fevers that periodically raged through Shahabad. Customarily, courtesans inherited the property and other assets of their mothers or aunts. In addition, they earned and invested in property and assets, which they held exclusively. The head of the household vested with decision-making powers was always the senior-most matriarch, or nayika, of the family. Zahooran inherited Batoolan's properties as also the attendant responsibilities of being the decision-maker of the family. She brought up Dharmman like a daughter and prepared her to be a worthy inheritor of the tawaif legacy.

After fruitless years of trying to conceive, when Dharmman finally decided to adopt, she could not find a child within her own social circle. She had no brothers or sisters who might have been happy to give her their child. And there was no one amongst her cousins, friends and acquaintances willing to give away a daughter in adoption.

Over time, Dharmman's desire to become a mother became known in the bazaar. Almost every other day, she would be visited by young tawaifs offering themselves up for adoption. But Dharmman wanted a child, the younger the better, with no memory of a past that might come in the way of completely accepting her as mother. Sick and tired of these unsuitable claimants to her maternal affections, Dharmman had almost given up hope when a retired tawaif from Monghyr came to meet her.

The woman had fallen on hard times and resorted to trading in children. She had brought with her a little girl about two years old, whom she offered to sell to Dharmman, complete with a deed of sale drawn up by the qazi of Monghyr. This, she claimed, was all that Dharmman needed for her adoption to be recognised as legal by the Company.

One look at the child and Dharmman knew she had found her daughter. Neither dark nor fair, the little girl's complexion was that of burnished copper, much like Dharmman's own. She had a wide forehead, doe eyes that were shut just then in angelic sleep, a fine nose and lips that seemed to have been lovingly etched by the Creator himself. Dharmman took the baby in her lap and was enveloped by a feeling of deep peace and contentment. This was her daughter, her beautiful Umrao.

The first person that Dharmman informed of her transaction was Babu Kunwar Singh. Much to her shock and dismay, babu sahib was furious with Dharmman for buying a child from an unknown woman without first consulting him. He had cautioned her nearly a year ago when she had first broached the idea of purchasing a child.

Colonial attitudes towards adoption by purchase by tawaifs were increasingly unsympathetic, even hostile. Bracketed in colonial law along with prostitutes, they were being projected as predators preying upon domestic 'felicity' and marriage. In a representation to the government, J. Eliot, a magistrate of the suburbs of Calcutta in the early decades of the nineteenth century, referred to the miseries to which the poorer classes were exposed 'from the wives, children and the female relations of their families being seduced away from them for the purposes of prostitution'.

Accordingly, in 1819, seduction, adultery and elopement for purposes of prostitution were made punishable offences. Buttressing the control of husbands over their wives and of fathers over their daughters, the colonial government passed Regulation 7 that year. This empowered a magistrate to punish any person who enticed a married woman away from her husband or an unmarried woman under the age of fifteen from her parents for the purposes of 'rendering her into a prostitute or concubine'.

The colonial state's hypocrisy is evident from the fact that, regardless of Regulation 7 of 1819, the recruitment of women, many of them runaways from abusive marriages and impoverished homes, to service the sexual needs of European soldiers continued as before in Lal Bazaar regimental brothels. Moreover, whereas the enticement of an unmarried girl was punishable so long as she was under the age of fifteen, no such exception was made for married women. Under the law, therefore, the husband had a lifelong right over his wife.

The concept of 'family' was also being narrowed to a patriarchal one, in which legitimate members shared ties of blood and women were subservient to the will of the male head of the household. The boundaries of this idealised domestic sphere were jealously guarded by the law. Domestic arrangements like those of the tawaifs, on the other hand, where blood relations and purchased members often lived together in close ties of kinship, were increasingly denied the privilege of being recognised as a family.

During the same period, there was a rising chorus about the 'reprehensible' trafficking of female slaves linked with prostitution. Colonial authorities—while choosing to ignore the use of slaves in agriculture out of self-serving concern for the impact any such intervention might have on revenue generation, and displaying remarkable concern for the rights of 'respectable' men, elite Indians and Europeans over the slaves in their households—felt no hesitation in responding with moral outrage to the sale and purchase of children by prostitutes and dancing girls.

Faced with large-scale dislocation of the rural poor, the colonial state, while refusing to recognise the terrible toll their revenue policies were taking on the countryside, attributed the growing numbers of women and girl children being sold and purchased to the demands of prostitution. W.H. Sleeman, Commissioner for Thuggee and Dacoity, for instance, claimed in 1839 to have 'discovered' yet another form of thuggee, for which he coined the term 'megpunnairm', which is the killing of poor parents and the stealing of their children for sale to prostitutes.

Similar narratives—of abduction, of parents being 'duped' with false promises into parting with their children and girls being forced into prostitution—became a staple of colonial lore to gloss over the inconvenient truth of voluntary sale of their wards by the poor struggling to survive Company rule. Amidst such sensational focus on 'immorality' and 'crime', claims made by tawaifs and prostitutes over their purchased wards in colonial law courts were being increasingly struck down.

Kunal M. Parker, in his paper 'A Corporation of Superior Prostitutes: Anglo-Indian Legal Conceptions of Temple Dancing Girls 1800–1914', quotes the case of Chutroo, a tawaif from Banaras, who in 1822 sued Jussa, a girl she had raised from infancy, for defaulting on the contract drawn at the time of purchase entitling the foster mother to a part of her adopted daughter's monthly earnings in lieu of the money that she would spend on the latter's upbringing, education and training to become a courtesan. The Sudder Diwanny Adawlut of Bengal, however, refused to enforce the claim. Striking down the contract, the judge ruled against Chutroo on the grounds that Jussa was not a legal slave. The expenditure that Chutroo had spent on raising the girl had been sufficiently compensated by Jussa's earnings thus far, and the girl was free of any obligations towards her foster mother, the ruling said.

While delivering the verdict the judge observed, '... it is a well-known fact that in Banaras many children are annually stolen from their families and sold to persons who profess singing and dancing; besides, it is equally notorious that those persons obtain much of their livelihood by the practise of prostitution. It is incumbent on the judicial authorities to obtain, without the fullest proof of free will, from countenancing the servitude of any individual entitled to freedom ...'

Similarly, in other cases involving suits brought by tawaifs for the restitution of runaway girls, the courts increasingly ruled against the claimants with much show of concern for the defendant's autonomy. Such solicitousness for the freedom of the individual was, however, singularly missing in cases involving irate husbands demanding the return of wives who had left them. In almost all such cases, regardless of the woman's plea for freedom from a marriage she did not wish to be in for various reasons, the judge ruled in favour of the husband. In one such case in 1851, while deciding that Latchmee, who had left her husband, be restored to him, the judge opined that 'A wife's virtue is safe only in her husband's keeping; there is her proper place ... What may be the influence he may exercise over her, the Court has nothing to do with ... I will not ask what may be her own wishes in the matter: even should she tell me she has no desire to go, I should be obliged to say that she must return to her husband.'

Given the targeting of tawaifs and prostitutes as responsible for the continuing trade in human beings, Kunwar Singh reasoned with Dharmman that the purchase of a child for adoption, regardless of the good intent behind the act, could get her—and by association, him—on the wrong side of the law. He reminded her of Gulab, a tawaif with whom Dharmman had a passing acquaintance. In 1841, she had been arrested for trying to sell five girls to tawaifs in the bazaar of her town of Sirajgunj. Her pleas that the girls had been voluntarily sold to her by their poverty-stricken parents in the hope that they might find better life in tawaif homes had fallen on deaf ears, and Gulab had been imprisoned.

But Dharmman was beyond all reason. Several other tawaifs in the bazaar had purchased little girls for adoption without much fuss or trouble from the police. And what about the zenanas of Rajput havelis that luxuriated on the sweat of slave labour? Why, babu sahib himself had inherited his father's slaves, bonded to his family for generations to come. Would any English officer dare to demand an inspection of his zenana or a headcount of the slaves that toiled in it and out in the fields? Why didn't babu sahib free those bonded to him in servitude before demanding that Dharmman abandon the child she would bring up with love as a daughter? Dharmman raged long and hard. She had fallen in love with her Umrao at first sight, and would not be parted from her under any circumstance. Even the threat of being forsaken by Kunwar Singh could not change her mind.

In the face of her headstrong fury, Kunwar Singh fell silent. He wanted Dharmman to be happy, but worried about a run-in with the law. Slavery had been legally abolished in India in 1843. While it had made little real difference to the use of bonded labour either in agriculture or in aristocratic homes, with trade in human beings carrying on as before under the guise of either marriage or repayment of debt, the law hung like a sword over adoption by purchase by tawaifs. However, Babu Kunwar Singh knew that once Dharmman's mind was made up, only the force of destiny could change it. Hoping for the best, he patted a sullen Dharmman gently on the head and gave her his blessing.

CHAPTER 3

Ghadar

Ah chhod re firangiya hamar deswa!
Lutput kaile tuhun, majwa udaile
Kailas des par julum jor.
Sahar gaon luti, phunki, dihiat firangiya
Suni suni Kunwar ke hridaya me laga lagiya
Ab chhod re firangiya hamar deswa!

(Oh British! Now quit our country!
You loot us and enjoy a life of luxury
And oppress our countrymen.
You have looted and destroyed our cities and villages
Listening to all this Kunwar's heart rages with fire
Oh British! Now quit our country!)

WE HAVE REACHED THE CLEARING in the forest where vehicular traffic comes to a halt. Nearby, a steep flight of steps cut into the hill leads to the Mundesvari temple at the top. The area is crowded with pilgrims on account of the forthcoming sawan fair. Little makeshift shops have come up to cater to the visitors. Selling inexpensive trinkets, posters of Hindu gods and goddesses, simple snacks like puffed rice and some rather stale-looking mithai, the shops reflect not just the simple tastes but also the limited purchasing power of their potential customers in this poverty-stricken area. We settle for soda lemonade that, at Rs 15 a glass, is among the more expensive items being sold here. As we sip our drinks, you resume the story of Dharmman Bibi.

'Happy in her newfound motherhood, Dharmman would spend her days taking care of Umrao, bathing, feeding and playing with her for hours at length and singing lullabies at night while patting her to sleep.

Kunwar Singh had come around to accepting Umrao's presence and would watch indulgently while his mistress fussed over her child. All seemed to be going well and nearly a year had passed when, one day, a posse of policeman knocked on Dharmman's door.'

The old tawaif from Monghyr had been arrested on the charge of selling girl children for the purpose of prostitution. In her confession, she named several tawaifs to whom she had sold children, including Dharmman. The police had come to verify if her statement was true.

Luckily for Dharmman, Kunwar Singh was present in the house at the time. Taking charge of the situation, he asserted that the old tawaif was lying. Dharmman had indeed adopted a child but not by purchase. The child belonged to her cousin, who had parted with Umrao out of love and goodwill for the childless Dharmman, and not for pecuniary gain. Confronted with one of the biggest and most influential zamindars of Shahabad, the attitude of the police changed from the usual belligerence to deferential amenability. It didn't take long for Kunwar Singh to prevail upon them to leave without questioning Dharmman.

Throughout the ordeal, a frightened Dharmman sat in the innermost room of her house clutching little Umrao to her breast. Babu sahib's warnings, she now realised, had not been unfounded. The police had been turned away today. But what if they returned tomorrow with proof that the old tawaif's claims were indeed true? How could she bear to part with her Umrao? And what would happen to the child? With panic in her heart and tears streaming down her face, Dharmman prayed desperately for deliverance from such an eventuality.

'And then the ghadar broke out,' you say, referring to the great uprising of 1857 against the rule of the British East India Company. On 10 May 1857, sepoys of the Company's army stationed in the town of Meerut revolted against their officers and marched overnight to Delhi, 67 km away. Next morning, they had proclaimed the old and frail Bahadur Shah 'Zafar', last Mughal occupant of the Red Fort, emperor of Hindustan.

The news sped across the summer of northern India, sparking hope and rebellion. Overthrow of the exploitative and despised colonial rule seemed an imminent possibility, fuelling the dreams of diverse sections of society—peasants and zamindars, town-dwellers, royalty and common soldiers. In the following months, several mutinies and civilian rebellions flared up across present-day Uttar Pradesh, Bihar and northern Madhya Pradesh.

'When news of the revolt reached Arrah's tawaif quarters, Dharmman's first reaction was of happy relief,' you say, sipping the lemonade. 'The police and the administration would now be too busy quelling the flames of an uprising to have time to investigate the veracity of an old tawaif's confession. Her Umrao would remain with her. In silent thanksgiving, that evening she fed the poor and made generous donations to the mosque and temple in the neighbourhood.'

Destiny had other plans for Dharmman, though. All of a sudden, just a day later, Umrao came down with high fever. Convinced that the ill-will of the English had cast a malicious shadow over her daughter, Dharmman bought charms, burnt dried red chillies and uttered a thousand prayers to rid Umrao of the firangis' evil eye. Not willing to take a chance, she also summoned the most venerable hakim of Arrah to treat her daughter.

In the end, nothing worked. The fever burnt Umrao's frail little body for many days before devouring her. Dharmman was overcome with grief. In the madness that followed, she tore at her clothes, pulled open her hair and beat her head against the walls. For days on end, the house echoed with her terrible howling. Cursing the British, she wished upon them death for casting their malevolent gaze upon her little flower, her Umrao. Then rage would give way to tears, and Dharmman would cry out for her little one to wake up from the dead.

Finally, the tears ran out, her voice died down, but not the pain. In a daze, Dharmman restlessly shuffled from one room to another, uncaring of the waves of nausea that rose from the pit of her stomach and reached her throat. And then she began to retch, the vomit pouring out of her mouth in torrents of grief.

Babu Kunwar Singh, fearing that Dharmman too was falling prey to the fever that had killed Umrao, hastily called for the learned hakim. After reading her pulse and peering into her eyes, the hakim's diagnosis was simple. Dharmman was pregnant.

Tossed between the grief of losing a child and the joy of becoming a mother again, Dharmman found her bearings finally in the conviction that Allah had returned Umrao to her. Reshaped this time out of her own flesh and nourished by Dharmman's own blood, Umrao would belong to her and her alone. No power in the world would be able to snatch her daughter away again.

Prayers rose to Dharmman's lips. His will was truly mysterious. He took away and He restored. As a mere mortal, she could only bow her head in gratitude at His munificence. The knowledge of being in His keeping, enveloped her in a deep feeling of serenity.

'And then, one day, an old faqir reached her doorstep,' you continue softly. 'After giving him alms, Dharmman waited for the blessings she hoped would rise to his lips. But the faqir had a warning to share with her instead. She must take utmost care through the pregnancy, he cautioned, because her womb had conceived under the shadow of a sword. There was grave danger ahead to her own being and also to the life she carried within her.

'Dharmman Bibi was hard put to comprehend this forecast—what possible danger could she and her yet unborn child face when they lived in the protection of Babu Kunwar Singh and, above all, in Allah's safekeeping? It was only when babu sahib informed her that he had decided to join the ghadar and lead the rebel sipahis in the war against the firangis that Dharmman Bibi realised the truth of the old faqir's words.'

History records Kunwar Singh as one of the heroes of the revolt of 1857. The zamindar had good reasons to feel bitter against the rule of the Company. In its single-minded exaction of land revenue, it had stripped several defaulting zamindars in Shahabad of their estates, displaying scant respect for their status and prestige as notables of the area.

Neck-deep in debt, Kunwar Singh had applied to the colonial Board of Revenue for remission of dues. Several British officers, including William Tayler, the commissioner of Patna, who shared a personal friendship with Kunwar Singh, had strongly supported the Jagdishpur zamindar's case. However, after extended parleys, the Board had decided to turn down his application. On the eve of the uprising in 1857, Kunwar Singh found himself on the brink of bankruptcy, and faced with the humiliating prospect of his estate being confiscated by the colonial authorities and put up for auction.

Meanwhile, in Patna, on 3 July 1857, a local bookseller Pir Ali, along with other associates, raised the banner of popular rebellion in Bihar. With flags flying and drums beating, they paraded the streets of the city. Dr Lyell, the deputy opium agent of the Patna Opium Agency, was among the first to be killed. This was seen as an attack on a major source of colonial revenue, since Gangetic Bihar, together with the Banaras-Ghazipur region, was the main area of opium production in the Company's territories. The Company enjoyed monopoly over the lucrative trade in opium, which they forced the peasantry to grow. The opium was then smuggled and illegally sold in China by the Company, where it was banned.

The Patna uprising spurred soldiers belonging to three regiments stationed at the cantonment of Danapur (or Dinapore in colonial records) on the outskirts of Patna to rebel against their officers on 25 July. They marched into neighbouring Shahabad, where, heading to Jagdishpur, they requested Babu Kunwar Singh to lead them in the war against the British. Many of these soldiers belonged to the Rajput community in Shahabad that had, in the decades following the battle of Buxar in 1764, contributed sizeable numbers of fighting men to the colonial army.

As soldiers, they shared their comrades' grievances about racial discrimination in promotion opportunities, low pay and insensitivity to their religious beliefs displayed by colonial authorities, which had fuelled the uprising in the army. As Rajput cultivators, they resented bitterly the unjust colonial demands for high rates of land revenue and the resultant poverty, indebtedness and fear of dispossession, which threatened the gentry status they had traditionally enjoyed. And, as loyal clan members, they shared the sense of outrage against colonial rule for stripping their traditional leaders, the zamindars, of their customary power and prestige derived through the control of large landholdings.

Amongst the soldiers who now begged Kunwar Singh to become their leader was Dalip Singh, the man Dharmman Bibi had loved passionately in her youth. Once she became Babu Kunwar Singh's mistress, Dharmman had given up all thoughts of Dalip Singh, although he would go over to her house to offer greetings whenever he came to Shahabad on leave. On his part, Dalip Singh was mindful of the boundaries that now separated him from Dharmman. He respected Babu Kunwar Singh both for his position as a community elder and for the reputation that he had earned as a fair-minded leader. Dalip Singh thus felt no conflict between the love he still felt for Dharmman and the pledge of loyalty that he was prepared to take to follow Babu Kunwar Singh to the very end in the war against the British.

After some deliberation, Kunwar Singh decided to cast in his lot with the forces of ghadar sweeping across Shahabad. Totally against the idea, Dharmman Bibi was furious with him for taking a decision that could jeopardise their world. She nursed a deep anger against the British following her run-in with the Company official who had treated her like a prostitute. The anger had turned into hatred when Umrao had fallen prey to fever after the colonial police visited their house. And yet, she doubted the wisdom of challenging the might of the East India Company.

She pointed out to Kunwar Singh the lack of parity between the thousands of trained sipahis that the colonial rulers had at their disposal and the few hundred renegades that he would be leading into war. What chance did he have of winning? Everything he had now could be lost, including, god forbid, his own life. The old zamindar, for once, was deaf to Dharmman Bibi's reasoning and pleading. He had drawn his sword. It was too late now to go back on his word.

Realising the futility of her attempts, Dharmman decided that there was only one course of action open to her. She would not stand in his way, she told Kunwar Singh, but only if he allowed her to join him in the war against the firangis. It was his turn now to reason and plead with her. She was pregnant with their child, he reminded her. How could she put a defenceless life in such enormous danger? But Dharmman Bibi too was unmoved by all reasoning. Like him, once she committed to something, it was impossible to change her mind.

Babu Kunwar Singh had attracted a large number of followers, including his brothers Amar Singh and Ritnarain Singh, and his nephews Nishan Singh, Jai Krishna Singh, Thakur Dayal Singh and Bisheswar Singh. Several other Rajput landholders and many more proprietor cultivators swore allegiance to Kunwar Singh's cause. Beyond Shahabad, Raja Arjun Singh of Singhbhum as well as Arjun Singh's brother sought to help Kunwar Singh by sending their forces to join him.

Support for the rebellion seems to have extended beyond the lines of caste loyalty. At the age of seventy-eight, Kunwar Singh found himself leading a popular uprising of Hindus and Muslims, sepoys, artisans, peasantry and landholders cutting across religious, clan and caste divides in Shahabad. They brought with them varied reasons for joining the uprising.

British officers in Bihar, like William Tayler, had warned the government nearly two years before the revolt broke out that 'the people of the districts were in a very restless and disaffected state'—the primary reason for this rising 'tension and disquiet' being the perceived attack by the government on 'Indian customs and religion'. Inspired in varying degrees by colonial expediency, evangelicalism and racial prejudice, the attempts by the British to bring in changes in the social, cultural and educational fabric of Indian society—such as the promotion of Christian missionary activity and Western education, the abolition of sati and the sanction given to widow remarriage—had generated widespread fears about the imminent destruction of the traditional social system and forcible conversions to Christianity.

These grievances sharpened the edge of agrarian distress in the countryside. Large sections of the rural population had been dispossessed of their land through mortgage and sale to rapacious moneylenders in their attempts to pay the high rates that British revenue policies demanded. The revolt thus saw attacks on the much-hated local moneylenders, and looting and burning of their credit books.

In urban areas, the de-industrialisation that was to acquire an acute form in the late nineteenth century had already by the 1830s begun affecting the artisan communities. Those employed in cloth-weaving were the worst hit, as the volume of foreign cloth imported into India reached significant proportions. Ruined weavers from the districts of Bihar had either become landless agricultural labour, or migrated to cities like Calcutta and Bombay to work as mill-hands and coolies. Large numbers of women from the community had been forced to join the rank and file of sex workers in cities.

The immediate focus of the rebels in Shahabad in those tumultuous days of July 1857 was the small European community stationed in the district headquarters. Buchanan, when he had visited Arrah in 1812–13, had found it singularly unimpressive: 'A close built town' with about 2,775 houses, 'in general mean', and with a population of around 22,000 people. The exclusively white European section of Arrah, on its northwest outskirts, was the 'most handsome part of the town', built around 'an open lawn, in which are placed the court houses, the accommodation of the judge of circuit, and the houses of the judge and surgeon of the station'. Beyond these buildings 'is the office of the collector, and his assistants' houses, and some belonging to Europeans, who are not in the Company's service. None of these buildings are at all ornamental. The jail is a very sorry work.' This is where the Indians arrested for sundry crimes were kept in appalling conditions.

On 27 July 1857, according to the records of the Imperial Gazetteer, 'a body of rebels consisting of about 2,000 rebel sepoys from Dinapore and four times as many armed villagers under Kuar Singh [Kunwar Singh] marched on to Arrah'. On reaching the town they 'released all the prisoners in jail and plundered the treasury amounting to 84,000/- rupees'. The next target of attack was a newly constructed building that housed land records and the civil courts. Every last shred of these land deeds and records was destroyed by the rebels.

The colonial presence in Arrah was not taken unawares by the uprising. Rumours of an imminent attack by the local population and native soldiers had been circulating for some time in the local bazaars. As a precaution, all the European women and children in the town had already been sent away, and there remained in Arrah just 'about a dozen Englishmen and three or four Christians of other races'.

Richard Vicars Boyle, a British engineer posted here to supervise work on the East Indian Railway, had in anticipation of an armed attack 'fortified and provisioned' two adjoining houses located in the European quarter. As the rebels approached Arrah, all the European residents took refuge in these two houses. A siege soon ensued, with fifty sepoys loyal to the Company defending the house against 'artillery and musketry fire from the rebels' led by Kunwar Singh with Dharmman Bibi by his side.

Two days later, on 29 July, 400 men commanded by Major Dunbar were sent from Dinapore to relieve Arrah. But this force was ambushed by the rebels about a mile from the siege, defeated and driven back. On 30 July, Major Vincent Eyre, who was going up the Ganga river with his troops, the 5th Fusiliers, reached Buxar and heard about the siege at Arrah. Changing course, he immediately began marching towards the town. On 3 August, Major Eyre and his men reached Arrah and successfully ended the eight-day-old siege. Babu Kunwar Singh and Dharmman Bibi were forced to retreat to Jagdishpur but were pursued by Major Eyre. The colonial forces took over Kunwar Singh's ancestral seat, which they looted and set on fire.

Your narration of the 1857 Uprising includes events that find no mention in historical records. 'Defeated but not disheartened, Babu Kunwar Singh and Dharmman Bibi, along with a handful of surviving soldiers, including

Dalip Singh, sought a safe hideout where they could regain their strength, replenish their numbers and take on the enemy once again. Stealthily riding through the nights and hiding in the daytime, they journeyed across the district and took shelter at the temple of Mundesvari Devi located in the thick jungles of the Kaimur hills.'

We begin a slow climb up the steps to the temple. You know the place well and steer me past the various guides-cum-priests who swoop upon unsuspecting visitors. We pause only to buy, at your insistence, flowers, incense and vermilion to offer to the goddess. A practising Muslim, you bow at every Hindu, Sikh and Christian shrine that comes your way. Once, when I commented about this, your reply reflected characteristic pragmatism. 'Why take chances? I think it's safest to have all the gods on my side.'

The temple stands on a table-top summit. It is octagonal and much smaller than I had imagined. Inside, the small idol of Goddess Mundesvari is depicted with ten hands bearing weapons, corresponding to the familiar representation of the goddess as Mahishasuramardini, the destroyer of the buffalo-demon Mahisha. In one critical detail, though, the icon stands out as tantalisingly different. Generally, Mahishasuramardini is represented in the act of killing the demon in the shape of a buffalo. At the Mundesvari temple, however, the goddess is shown riding a buffalo.

Some recent scholars are of the opinion that the goddess installed in the Mundesvari temple might well have been a deity worshipped originally by the aboriginal population described in Vedic and post-Vedic texts as asura and daitya. In the long-drawn-out struggles between the forces of invading Brahmanism and the indigenous population of the Kaimur area, the goddess seems to have been usurped and made part of the Hindu pantheon.

> *Bhado mas andheria badariya gagan here ji,*
> *Tahl rate challe, Kunwar Singh lare laraiya ji*
>
> (In the month of Bhadon, when dark clouds covered the sky,
> Through the night, Kunwar Singh fought the battle)

Sitting in the shade of one of the few trees that dot the by-now blazing table-top, you sing for me a rather unusual sohar, a ritual song sung by women to celebrate the birth of a child. This particular sohar, you inform me, is still very popular in the areas around Arrah as an abiding memory of the tumultuous ghadar of 1857.

'Dharmman Bibi was now in the final month of her pregnancy,' you resume your story. 'On a rain-drenched, moonless night of Bhadon, just as Dharmman Bibi went into labour, news came of an imminent attack by British troops who had tracked babu sahib to the Kaimur region and were massed at the foot of the hill. Hurriedly placing Dharmman Bibi at the feet of the goddess, Babu Kunwar Singh rushed off to repel the enemy.'

Alone in the temple, Dharmman Bibi prayed hard to Mundesvari to watch over her as a mother would and protect her child's safe passage into this world. Outside, the fighting continued for many hours. As Kunwar Singh put scores of men to death in the jungle, Dharmman Bibi gave birth to twin girls in the safe sanctuary of the Devi. Every time the enemy troops tried to enter the temple, fierce lightning would surround the building in a protective shield, forcing them to retreat. By dawn, the enemy forces were beaten back, but the battle had taken its toll: babu sahib was badly wounded and unconscious, and almost all his men were dead. The only surviving soldier was Dalip Singh. Bathed in blood, he now stood guard over the unconscious Kunwar Singh, oblivious to his own injuries.

Dharmman Bibi knew that she could not afford the luxury of post-partum rest. Decisive action had to be taken and fast. The enemy would take some time to regroup and mount another assault. Before that, she had to remove her new-born twins to safety and get medical help for Kunwar Singh.

Leaving him in Dalip Singh's watchful protection, Dharmman took off on her horse with a child strapped to each breast. She rode 8 km to Chainpur, where her distant cousins—twin sisters Bullan and Kallan—lived and worked as tawaifs. She planned to leave her new-borns with them and return with a local vaidya or hakim to save the life of her babu sahib.

Bullan and Kallan gave their word to Dharmman that they would protect her twins from all harm. At no cost would the girls' identity ever be made known to anyone, nor the secret of Kunwar Singh and Dharmman's whereabouts. They also arranged for a trusted hakim to accompany Dharmman to tend to Kunwar Singh's injuries. Kissing her little girls goodbye, Dharmman named them Sadabahar and Gulshan, and rode away, uncertain whether she would ever see them again.

Nothing is known about Dharmman Bibi after her departure from Chainpur. She has disappeared into the mists of time, leaving behind the glow of unmistakable pride that I now see in your eyes. The memory of the valiant Dalip Singh too has been erased by the passage of history. As for Kunwar Singh, saved from probable death by the hakim brought by Dharmman Bibi, he reached Lucknow in December 1857. In March 1858, he occupied Azamgarh but was soon forced to leave the area and retreat to his home in Bihar with Brigadier Douglas in thick pursuit.

On 23 April 1858, while nearing Jagdishpur, Kunwar Singh was successful in defeating the forces led by Captain Le Grand. In the battle, he was, however, seriously wounded in the arm. Popular legend has it that, undaunted, Kunwar Singh severed the injured limb and flung it into the Ganga flowing close by, as an offering to the holy river. Three days later, on 26 April 1858, he died in his ancestral village, Jagdishpur.

After Kunwar Singh's death, the rebels in Shahabad gathered under the leadership of his younger brother Amar Singh and continued to fight the colonial troops; police posts were taken, prisoners released and several British-owned indigo factories and plantations in Shahabad burnt down. For some months in 1858, Amar Singh was successful in occupying the greater portion of the district and establishing a parallel government. However, by December 1858, the revolt was finally crushed, and Amar Singh was forced to leave the district and seek refuge in the Nepal Terai.

To honour Babu Kunwar Singh's memory and his contribution to India's freedom movement, the Republic of India issued a commemorative stamp on 23 April 1966, and Veer Kunwar Singh University was established in Arrah in 1976. Dharmman Bibi's role in the uprising of 1857 remains unrecognised beyond a passing mention in some biographical notes about Kunwar Singh, of her 'joining him in the war against the British'.

Relegated to a footnote in the official history of the great revolt, Dharmman suffers a fate less known than that of another tawaif-turned-warrior, Azeezan. A camp follower of Nana Sahib's troops in Kanpur, and lover of Shamsuddin Khan, soldier-spy of the rebels, Azeezan's spirited role in the city's uprising has evoked wildly varied responses. British accounts tend to vilify her as a bloodthirsty supervisor of the massacre of English women and children by rebel troops in Kanpur; Indian narratives of the revolt, on the other hand, bestow upon her a heroic revolutionary status.

The afternoon sun has begun waning to a golden sheen. I wonder aloud about the possible reasons that made Dharmman Bibi and Azeezan join cause with the rebels in 1857. It is not difficult to comprehend their anger against a regime that had little respect for the tawaifs' way of life and their art practice, and which attacked the rights they had customarily enjoyed, like adoption by purchase. Tawaifs would have sympathised too with the grievances felt by other sections of the population, particularly landholders like Kunwar Singh who were traditionally their patrons. The spectre of forfeiture of landholdings and status that haunted the zamindar would undoubtedly have engendered resentment amongst tawaifs who were materially dependent upon the generosity of their wealthy and powerful lovers. Could these fears for the future have spurred women like Dharmman Bibi to join the rebels?

You understand the choice made by Dharmman Bibi a bit differently. '*Unhoney namak ka haq poora kiya.*' She was true to her salt, you say to me. The lives of the zamindar Babu Kunwar Singh and his tawaif concubine Dharmman Bibi were intricately entwined with threads of reciprocal duties, responsibilities and obligations. As a patron, he had provided her with not only material wealth and emotional security but also love and respect. In return, Dharmman's complete loyalty to babu sahib in his hour of need was the cornerstone of her principles as a true tawaif. Besides, she loved and respected him in reciprocation of his feelings for her. Adding an edge was the humiliation she had experienced at the hands of the firangi officer and her suffering as a mother following Umrao's death.

With a sad smile, you conclude your story of love, loyalty, courage and vengeance: 'It is said that on moonless nights Dharmman Bibi can be seen around this temple riding a horse, sword in hand, eyes blazing a terrible fire, seeking retribution from the firangis who had destroyed forever the world that had been hers.'

CHAPTER 4

Sadabahar, the Child

IN THE HUMID, DARK STILLNESS, she tosses restlessly between sleep and wakefulness. You sit at the foot of her bed and silently keep watch. The room smells faintly of mildew, soiled bedsheets and the open gutter running outside. It's been raining since morning and a hesitant breeze fleetingly dispels the gloom and the odour. Ravaged by cancer, Pyaari khala is dying. She is your mother's cousin and your favourite aunt, and it is to be with her through these last, difficult days that you have come to Bhabua, your home town.

I first met Pyaari khala two or three years ago at your house in Banaras. She walked in without warning, interrupting an interview I was filming with you. Fair-complexioned, tall and well built, she had looked remarkably robust for someone in her late seventies or early eighties.

She wore a crumpled and slightly faded printed cotton sari that stopped, in the manner favoured by women in rural eastern UP and Bihar, a few inches above her ankles. The sari pallu covering her head had slipped to reveal wisps of thinning white hair bundled into a little ponytail that masqueraded as a bun. Amidst your cries of welcome and her greetings, Pyaari khala's eyes kept darting inquisitively to us, the film crew.

Without much ado, she demanded to know what we were doing there. And even before I could begin explaining, she wrinkled her nose and stared nervously in the direction of the rather large microphone held up on a boomrod by the sound recordist. 'Aah, I understand now! You people have been sent by the health department to spray mosquito repellent!' she announced with confident finality in Bhojpuri. Bewildered, we gaped back at her.

Beaming at us toothlessly, she then pointed at the camera and added, 'And that is to give proof that you have been actually doing your job and not gadding about like the other scoundrels in your department.'

Gathering my wits, I tried to explain, 'Umm, we are film people shooting here ...'

Arching an eyebrow coquettishly, the old lady shot back in impeccable Urdu, 'But you should have said as much at the very beginning! I am so very sorry I mistook you for a bunch of mosquito killers.' Her electric metamorphosis from a Bhojpuri-speaking rustic to a sophisticated, Urdu-speaking woman of the world was so sudden that it was some moments before we realised the joke had been on us all along.

That morning, Pyaari khala performed, sang and had us in splits with her jokes. Her humour was mostly self-deprecatory and never unkind. When you told us that, once upon a time, she had been a well-known tawaif in the Dal Mandi area of Banaras, Pyaari khala retorted with feigned hurt, 'What do you mean "once upon a time"? I retired just a couple of years ago!' And she then burst into Hafiz Jallundhari's Urdu nazm celebrating eternal youth: *Abhi to main jawan hoon*; I am still young ... She sang with perfect control in an unusually low-pitched, pleasing voice, not once hitting a false note even though, as she confided later, she had stopped performing formally at least forty years ago.

Pyaari khala was a frequent guest at your home. I remember her vividly, leaning against the bolsters in the visitors' room, one leg resting upon the other, a cigarette in hand. She smoked like a man, holding the cigarette between her thumb and index finger.

She was fun to be with, and had a ready supply of Urdu verses for every occasion. These ranged from the fairly plebeian *Bhoolne wale se koi keh de zara, Iss tarah yaad aane se kya fayada*; Someone should remind he who has forgotten, The futility of creeping thus into my memories—when talking about a now-dead patron lover—to Jigar Moradabadi's *Yeh ishq nahin aasaan bas itna samajh leeje, Ik aag ka dariya hai aur doob ke jana hai*; Understand, love does not come easy, It's a raging river of fire one has to dive into and swim across—when commenting on your struggles to gain recognition as a concert singer.

Pyaari khala's repertoire of songs was equally wide-ranging and impressive. She could seamlessly shift gears from an Urdu ghazal to a Bhojpuri dadra, with a bhajan and a thumri thrown in for good measure.

She was also a great cook. While your culinary skills don't extend beyond tea and eggs, Pyaari khala's gastronomic range was as varied as her songs. During her visits, on popular request, she would oblige us all with qorma, biryani, meat and vegetable salan and litti and chokha, turning meal-times into sublime occasions.

When I complimented her on her cooking skills, she would reply with eyes twinkling that a tawaif had to know all the arts of seduction. In her experience, the route to a lover's heart (and pocket, she would add, laughing) was indeed through his stomach.

Easygoing and affectionate, Pyaari khala had something to say to everyone in the house, including the children. I was struck by her friendship with your son, Nanhe. Most other visitors to your home either uncomfortably ignore him or speak to him in a false, patronising manner. Pyaari khala treated Nanhe with the warm regard of an equal, sharing private jokes with him, showing genuine interest in his life. She was the only visitor he showed enthusiasm in meeting.

She was also the only member of your family who complimented Salma generously about her cooking and housekeeping skills. Most others, including you, seem oblivious to your daughter-in-law's daily efforts to keep house and lay out meals that meet your exacting standards.

Not surprisingly, Pyaari khala was everyone's favourite aunt. Without any children of her own and 'free of cares', as she liked to describe herself, she spent her time visiting relatives, helping out whenever needed. The day I first met her, she had come from Bhabua to accompany you to the wedding of a grandniece for whom you had played matchmaker. You enjoy the role and take a great deal of satisfaction in having found appropriate brides and bridegrooms for most of the boys and girls in the family.

During my last meeting with her at Banaras, Pyaari khala had said, pulling a face, 'Everyone parrots just one word now—Marriage! Marriage!! Marriage!!! All the girls in our family are either married or in the process of being married.' Pointing to you, she had added, 'Her elder daughter is married too. The younger, upstairs, is engaged with only the wedding date to be finalised.'

Meenu's engagement had taken place a few months before. Her fiancé, Arshad, you had gently boasted, belongs to an affluent and respected tawaif family in Bahraich, which had once entertained only the nobility. The family moved away from the tradition well before most other households, including yours, had. Arshad, an educated, hard-working boy, running the family's electronics shop along with his father, is by all parameters a good catch. To celebrate your daughter's success in the marriage market, you had spent so lavishly on the engagement that several guests, you told me with great pride, had likened it to a 'mini' wedding.

You are normally careful with money, almost parsimonious—making do with less rather than more. I was shocked to learn that you had withdrawn substantially from your bank deposits to finance the engagement. With some hesitation, I questioned the wisdom of such extravagance. Your earnings through music tuitions and piece-rate stitching work are sporadic. Your only regular source of income is the modest rent that comes from the agricultural lands you own in Bhabua and the monthly interest from your bank savings.

You waved away my objections. Your izzat, honour, was at stake here. The reputation that you had earned over the years as a tawaif, for your music, your honourable ways and your perceived affluence had to be maintained at all costs.

'Even if at times,' you had said, 'my children and I have been forced to make do with roti-chutney, I have never allowed the world outside to see my poverty. You don't understand. This world is very cruel. The very people who lower their eyes while speaking to me would sit on my head if they knew my true financial position. Let them think I have treasures buried away somewhere. At the very least, this ensures respect for me and my girls.'

Pyaari khala, who was visiting, had interjected in an approving tone, 'People look at her in wonder and awe that she got her elder daughter married after having retired from the line. They naturally assume that she must be very well off.'

Looking pleased but trying to sound humble, you said, 'I could get her married only because of the support of family members like you, khala. I am preparing now for the younger one's wedding, although only Allah knows how I will gather the means to do it properly. I will need everyone's help to fulfil my responsibility well.' I wondered then whether you were hinting that Pyaari khala must extend financial support for Meenu's forthcoming wedding. You had gently pressed upon me a similar commitment earlier.

You have told me that, of all the women in your family, Pyaari khala is the best off. Her house in Bhabua, where she moved after retiring as a tawaif in Banaras, is the largest and best-constructed of all your relatives' homes in the town. An impressive three-storey building, two of its floors are rented out to various tenants, while Pyaari khala lives alone on the ground floor. Not only are her needs met quite adequately from the rent, she also owns agricultural land that she lets out to share-croppers. Besides, she has fabled amounts of gold jewellery. 'A tawaif without gold is no tawaif,' is a saying I often hear from you and others in your family. 'A good tawaif ensures that, no matter what, she has gold put away for good times and bad.'

Then, about three months ago, Pyaari khala was diagnosed with cancer. It had by then spread to large parts of her body. Bedridden, she needed to spend extended periods at a hospital in Banaras. You were a loving and dutiful niece, visiting her almost daily.

After surgery and painful chemotherapy sessions, the hospital had discharged Pyaari khala. In the last stage of cancer, she was prescribed only palliatives; the hospital had ruled out any further medical intervention as unnecessary and useless. She was shifted back to Bhabua. You and other relatives in Banaras visit her often, but for daily care she has had to depend on the affection and sense of duty of family members who live in Bhabua.

In the past week, Pyaari khala has taken a turn for the worse. The end seems imminent, and most of her family from Bhabua and outside have gathered to be with her in these last days. This afternoon, though, only you and I are at her bedside, the others taking a much-needed siesta after staying awake all night because of a rapid deterioration in her condition. By mid-morning, she had stabilised, so the others left to bathe, eat and sleep, while you stayed on, unwilling to leave her side.

Rim jhim khola ho kiwadiya, hum bideswa jaibena
Jo toohara jaa bideswa jaibena
Hamre baba ghar pahoonchaye da
Ham peeharwa jaibena

Pitter patter [falls the rain], open the door, I have to leave for foreign lands
If you must leave for foreign lands
Drop me off first at my father's house
I want to go to my natal home.

You sing softly into the hush enveloping Pyaari khala's room. I haven't heard you sing this sweet, lilting Bhojpuri song before.

'This is a dialogue between a man and a woman. It is raining and the woman is refusing to let her husband leave for a faraway land,' you explain in whispers. 'My mother told me that this kajari used to be sung by her grandaunt, Sadabahar.'

Reminded of the conversation on our trip to Mundesvari temple, I ask, 'Wasn't Sadabahar one of Dharmman Bibi's twins whom she entrusted to her cousins Bullan and Kallan in 1857?'

You nod, and patiently continue the tale.

Bullan and Kallan became twin mothers to Dharmman Bibi's daughters, Sadabahar and Gulshan. They told everyone in Chainpur that the girls belonged to their sister who had been married into a distant village and was no more. Times were such that, if the truth came out that they were the rebel Dharmman's daughters, there was no saying what terrible fate would have befallen the baby girls and their adoptive mothers.

British reprisals following the quelling of the rebellion in December 1858 had involved large-scale destruction of native property and life in places that had been centres of the revolt, including Shahabad. Hundreds of people suspected of being rebels or sympathisers were barricaded in their villages and shot or sabred 'like rats'. Thereafter, the villages were burnt down and stored grain was destroyed. Countless men were summarily tried, then were tied to cannons and blown to death. For the victorious British soldiers, mass public hangings of 'natives' rounded up on the way became grisly amusement.

To escape colonial terror, there were large-scale migrations to foreign lands. In the decades following 1857, Shahabad saw the emigration of sizeable numbers of its population to Mauritius and British colonies like Demerara, Trinidad, Jamaica and Grenada.

Rim jhim khola ho kiwadiyaa, hum bideswa jaibena ...

Kunwar Singh's family fort at Jagdishpur was burnt down. His zamindari estate was confiscated, with one Ernest Mylne obtaining the settlement of a large part of it. The moveable assets of Kunwar Singh's younger brother Amar Singh, valued at about Rs 30,000, were seized, and Messrs Burn and Company of Calcutta were given the contract for clearing the forests surrounding Jagdishpur.

Other Rajput zamindars deemed guilty of participation in the revolt were not spared either: 869 estates in Shahabad were confiscated and auctioned, entire Rajput clans suspected of participating in the revolt were forcibly disarmed and their forts systematically destroyed.

'In our eastern parts, Rajputs have been the main patrons of tawaifs and their music,' you say. 'So, tawaifs naturally faced very difficult times in the aftermath of the ghadar. Many of them were forced to sell their homes and kothas and migrate to other areas in search of livelihood.'

Many tawaifs moved either to Banaras, which had remained unaffected by the revolt, or to Calcutta, where money and patrons now resided, since it was the capital of the British empire in India. There were others who, lacking the means to relocate, had little choice but to join the ranks of glorified prostitutes, forced to service the sexual needs of British soldiers camping now in large numbers in Shahabad.

Then there were those tawaifs, especially from Arrah and around, who had participated in some manner in the ghadar. Free of the restrictions imposed by the veil, even those tawaifs who did not ride into battle as Dharmman Bibi had, acted as spies and couriers for their rebel patrons. Their homes had served as convenient meeting places for the insurgents. The colonial government confiscated their houses and, in many instances, lands and other property gifted to them by their Rajput patrons. Heavy penalties and fines were imposed. Several tawaifs in and around Arrah were raped and killed by British soldiers.

'Those were dreadful times,' you whisper animatedly. 'Even old women were not spared. My mother had heard from her elders that a distant aunt of Dharmman Bibi was repeatedly questioned about her niece's whereabouts. When she could provide no satisfactory answer, the old woman's face was blackened and she was paraded on a donkey in the bazaars of Arrah. No one dared come to her rescue. Shahabad seemed to be in the grip of a calamity.'

The rebellion brought an end to the East India Company's rule in India. By the Government of India Act 1858, the Company's ruling powers over India were transferred to the British Crown. Once the reprisals in the immediate aftermath of the revolt had satisfied the colonial thirst for revenge, it was decided that the prime object of the restored British government should be the 'tranquillisation of the public mind'. 'Caution and conciliation' were to mark the government's attitude towards the social and religious beliefs of the 'natives'.

It was widely agreed in British circles that the attempts made by the East India Company to 'interfere' with indigenous traditions of the Hindus and Muslims had contributed significantly to the stirring of popular discontent. The abolition of sati, the passing of the Widow Remarriage Act and the supporting of evangelical activity, it was felt, had alienated large sections of the Indian population. In the decades following the revolt, therefore, the government did not initiate any major legislation that would challenge the fundamental structure or functioning of the patriarchal family and the position of women within it.

The dawn of Crown rule in India saw the bifurcation of law into 'personal' and 'public' domains. All matters pertaining to property, marriage, separation, inheritance and adoption were placed under the category of 'personal' laws—Hindu, Muslim, Christian etc.—to be governed by religion-based rulings outside the purview of state intervention. Patriarchal controls over women's economic and sexual mobility thus continued with some modifications in the garb of 'personal' laws. This was a politically expedient move to reassure and win over the more traditional and conservative elements in an alienated subject population.

'Public' laws, on the other hand, exemplified most notably in the Indian Penal Code of 1860, dealt with criminal law and were upheld as an intrinsic component of the 'civilising mission' of European imperialism. Their formulation and implementation were used to project the colonial state as an impartial and firm law-giving despotism.

Women outside the domain of the patriarchal family, including tawaifs, found themselves in the grip of both 'public' and 'personal' laws; their sexuality was criminalised by public laws, while their customs and norms were eroded by the imposition of personal laws. With far-reaching implications, these developments increasingly undermined tawaifs' customary rights to property, succession and inheritance by placing these under male-dominated personal laws.

In addition to the already-existing offences of adultery and enticement, the Indian Penal Code made the procuring, sale, hire and purchase of minors under the age of sixteen for the purpose of prostitution a criminal offence under its sections 372 and 373. Prostitutes and 'dancing girls' were forbidden from adopting children, since this was presumed to be for the purpose of inducting them into prostitution. The right of adopted daughters to inherit the property of their tawaif foster mothers also became legally invalid. Colonial law-making, thus, contributed substantially to the dissolution of the autonomy and privileged position as independent women of substance that courtesans had customarily enjoyed.

In the coming years, the Indian Penal Code of 1860 and the Contagious Diseases Act sought to further increase state surveillance and control of the tawaifs' extra-marital sexuality. When it became known, for instance, that more European soldiers had died in 1857 due to venereal diseases than in actual combat, the colonial government was quick to apportion blame to the Indian prostitutes, a category in which they included the tawaifs. Although it was European soldiers and sailors who had introduced syphilis to India in the sixteenth and seventeenth centuries, the nineteenth-century British authorities, in keeping with precepts of colonial medicine that attributed the disease to Indian climate, sanitation and social mores, viewed Indian prostitutes as part of a disease-bearing environment.

Accordingly, the Cantonment Acts of 1864 were passed, which instituted compulsory medical examination of all practising prostitutes, including the tawaifs in cantonments, not just those in regimental brothels. Medical authorities had to carry out regular check-ups on prostitutes, and the police could enforce punitive measures if the women refused. If a woman was declared to be infected, she would be confined in a 'Lock Hospital' until deemed 'cured'. Tawaifs now had to deal with the pathologisation of their sexuality as 'diseased'.

The Contagious Diseases Act of 1868 (CDA) widened the ambit of the Cantonment Acts beyond the cantonment to the cities. While aiming to control venereal diseases through enforced medical checks on prostitutes, the Act also specified where prostitution could be practised, and provided for the compulsory registration of women involved in commercial sexual activity.

Similar laws had been passed in England as well, around the same time. The Contagious Disease Act in India, however, was far more coercive than the English CDA. Whereas there were limits on the amount of time a woman could be detained by the police in hospitals in England, Indian prostitutes could be forced to stay inside for indefinite periods. They were also to be compulsorily registered, whereas in England, after 1883, the system became voluntary.

The soldiers for whose 'protection' these laws had primarily been enacted in India were never brought under the scope of the CDA. The possibility of banning commercial sexual activity was rarely discussed; it was felt that, as men of the lower classes, soldiers lacked the moral resources for continence. Preventing them from having sex with prostitutes, it was argued, would lead to offences such as criminal assaults, rape and unnatural crime against 'respectable' women.

In the midst of this changing world, Bullan and Kallan remained steadfast to the promise they had made to their cousin. Unaware that it would have no legal validity in the years to come, they formally adopted Sadabahar and Gulshan in a simple ceremony. Most tawaifs in Chainpur accepted the adoption as an act of love by Bullan and Kallan for their dead sister. The ones who suspected the truth of the girls' parentage kept quiet out of loyalty to the sisters and respect for Dharmman's sacrifice in the revolt.

Others outside the community were too busy trying to survive the harsh times to pay attention to the adoption of two little orphan girls by a pair of tawaifs. The great famine of 1860, which claimed a huge number of lives in Bengal and Bihar, held Shahabad in its grip through most of the following decade. Food was scarce and expensive. Starvation, disease and death stalked the district. The area around Chainpur in the arid Kaimur plateau region was denuded of its population. Those amongst the poor that survived, swelled the ranks of the kangla, or beggar squads, formed by the colonial government to work on roads in return for a daily pittance.

Bullan and Kallan had seen good times as tawaifs in their prime. With advancing age and no source of regular income, the difficult times hit them hard. They had little choice but to mortgage their house, agricultural lands and jewellery bit by bit, not only to feed and clothe young Sadabahar and Gulshan but also to finance their education and grooming. Bullan and Kallan hoped that one day the twins would bring back wealth and fame to the family as successful courtesans.

By the time the girls grew out of babyhood, however, it became obvious to the mothers that only one of them, Sadabahar, would become a tawaif. Little Gulshan demonstrated little aptitude for music or dance, and was happiest playing with the pots and pans in their kitchen. While Sadabahar showed an avid interest in the music that at all times played in the tawaifs' quarters of Chainpur, Gulshan was preoccupied with learning domestic skills. Both girls had inherited their mother's good looks. However, while Sadabahar's shokh, or vivacious temperament, enhanced her beauty even in childhood, Gulshan's homely demeanour made her look plain-faced and drab. The sisters, therefore, decided to focus their attention and their scarce resources on grooming Sadabahar.

You speak of Sadabahar's prodigious musical talent even as a child. She had heard her mothers and other tawaifs perform in their kothas, at community celebrations, festivals and in their own homes, music that ranged from raga-based thumri, dadra and ghazal to lilting folk melodies. She had memorised these compositions without any conscious effort, and begun singing these songs at an age when most children recited nursery rhymes. Her foster mothers and other women in the community were thus her first teachers.

In the tradition of Hindustani art music, however, while women could learn and become performing musicians, they could not formally assume the status of teachers. That prerogative belonged to men. A tawaif had to learn from a reputed male ustad in order to be recognised as a trained, professional singer. Accordingly, Bhure Khan, the venerable old man of sarangi in Chainpur, was appointed to teach Sadabahar music.

Bhure Khan Sahib had taught and accompanied on the sarangi nearly all the tawaifs in and around Chainpur, including Bullan and Kallan. He belonged to a well-established Dhari clan of Arrah that traced its roots to Delhi. No one was sure when Bhure Khan Sahib had come to Chainpur, since he seemed to have been there forever.

Dharis (also spelt Dhadis) are amongst the oldest communities of musicians in north India and are identified closely with the sarangi. Originally wandering folk musicians from Rajasthan and Punjab, they specialised in singing war songs to the accompaniment of the dhadh, a small dhol or drum to which they owed their name, and the kingra, perhaps an earlier version of the sarangi. At some point, they converted to Islam and many of them began migrating and settling in urban centres.

Dharis were a recognised community of musicians in Mughal courts. Abu'l Fazl's *Ain-i-Akbari* names five Dharis, all men, as principal musicians in Akbar's court. It also makes mention of Dhari women who sang 'Dhurpad and Sohla songs'. From the late seventeenth century, as sarangi players, male musicians from the Dhari community were to become closely associated with courtesans in the role of accompanists and teachers.

In 1872, British missionary M.A. Sherring, writing about the Dhari community in the Banaras region, describes them as 'a class of Mahomedan players. Both men and women perform on musical instruments, or sing, or dance, wherever they can obtain employment.' Subsequent references, mainly colonial, make no mention of women in the Dhari community as musicians or dancers.

In conversations with me on the subject, senior musicians of Banaras like Shanney Khan Sahib and tabla maestro Kishan Maharaj, seemed to hold the opinion that Dhari women sang in public along with the men when they were still wandering folk musicians. However, as sections of the Dharis began settling in urban centres, and the men joined art music practice as sarangi-accompanists and teachers to tawaifs, the role of the women folk singers became increasingly marginalised. Since the community was fairly widespread, the process and pace of urbanisation and entry by men into art music practice would have varied from region to region.

Late nineteenth-century colonial commentators are disparaging of the strong links that Dhari men shared with tawaif performers. Given that tawaifs were increasingly coming under hostile scrutiny from colonial quarters, it is hardly surprising that the communities linked with them, like the Dharis, were stigmatised by association. W. Crooke, a civil services official and ethnographer of the period, describes the Dhari as 'a musician and singer' who because of his 'habit of going about with women of bad character has rather an unsavoury reputation'.

Your account of old Bhure Khan Sahib is far removed from such tawdry descriptions. In your family history, he is remembered as a tall, painfully thin man with a glorious mane of white hair and a flowing beard. He cut an imposing figure, practising his sarangi even as he walked slowly from one tawaif household to another to give lessons to young, aspiring courtesans. It was said that Bhure Khan spent all his waking hours in dialogue with his sarangi, stopping only for the few hours he slept at night when it would lie by his side like a faithful lover.

The thick ridges of his cuticles and the deep grooves that marked the nails of his gnarled and calloused hands were proof of the discipline and perseverance of his long riyaz, music practice. His single-minded concentration, it was said, was so intense that several times he had failed to notice snakes and scorpions that crawled over him as he played the sarangi. Daily riyaz, intensive and correctly done, he would tell all his students, held the key to becoming a true musician.

The term riyaz, from Arabic, connotes abstinence, devotion, discipline and hard labour. At a mundane level, regular riyaz is necessary for a flawless performance before an audience. True riyaz, however, Bhure Khan would tell his students, is a never-ending quest, beyond the goals of worldly success, towards unattainable perfection. Only Allah, the old musician would say, is perfection personified. We mere mortals can only aspire with all humility to strive towards near-perfection, not perfection itself. Riyaz for him was worship, an act of dedication and devotion.

When Sadabahar was about six or seven, Bhure Khan Sahib was summoned by Bullan and Kallan to commence her formal education in music. The occasion was marked by the customary ceremony. Bhure Khan Sahib, along with other musician members of his family, all men, assembled at Bullan and Kallan's house for a feast. Special saffron-flavoured sweet rice and other delicacies were prepared for the occasion.

Bhure Khan Sahib read the fatiha, prayers that form the opening chapter of the Quran. Bullan and Kallan presented him with a new set of clothes, some sweets and a token sum of money. Bhure Khan in turn gave Sadabahar a handful of black gram and jaggery to eat. He then sang the sargam, the seven notes of the musical scale, and made her repeat it after him. The sweet zarda was then distributed to everyone present. In this manner, the ustad and his shagirda entered into a relationship of teaching and learning based on reciprocal duties and responsibilities.

Sadabahar would now have to be dedicated to serving her ustad's smallest needs. Through sincere devotion to music, and service, respect and loyalty to her ustad, she would hope to inspire love in her teacher, so he would share with her knowledge beyond the call of duty. As Bhure Khan himself was fond of saying, 'Any ustad will teach as his duty all his students. It is only with the special few who win his heart that he will share the more subtle depths of his music.'

Bhure Khan's male disciples were boys from his own family—his sons, nephews and, over the decades, grandsons and even great-grandsons. They all lived with him in the same house and had the advantage of imbibing his music all the time, not just within the confines of formal lessons. It was understood too that, since they came from the same lineage, and would contribute to the fortunes and musical reputation of the family, the old ustad would teach them with greater care and generosity. This was not an assumption that any of them could take for granted, however.

Bhure Khan Sahib was an exacting but fair-minded teacher. He had taught enough students by now to gauge quite early on the aptitude, interest and dedication of each. His musical legacy was precious to him and he would not thoughtlessly bestow it upon those unworthy of nurturing and presenting it in its right form. He shared its riches in varying measure with students who met his rigorous standards, irrespective of whether they were his own blood, or outsiders—the daughters of tawaifs whom he taught in their houses. So far, in all his years of teaching, he had not found a student to whom he would be happy to leave all the music he had learnt from his father.

One look at Sadabahar's serious and determined little face, and Bhure Khan knew that finally Allah had blessed him with the student he had been seeking. From the very first day of their lessons together, she did not disappoint him. Eager to learn, she would memorise even difficult passages quickly and correctly. It was obvious that the child had been blessed with a sharp brain and a keen pair of ears.

He had a rule that all his students should wake at the crack of dawn when the muezzin at the local mosque called out to the faithful for the fajr namaz, and do riyaz on their own for two hours. He knew, of course, that few followed his rule, though they all swore to him that they did. Their voice quality during lessons later in the day betrayed their lies. In the first few months, Bhure Khan Sahib hadn't expected little Sadabahar to wake up so early. He was amazed, therefore, to note the growing strength and suppleness of her voice, the evidence of her being diligent about the daily riyaz.

Bullan and Kallan confirmed this. The child was out of her bed on her own as soon as the call for prayer rang out in the stillness of the newborn day. After a quick wash and prayers, she would sit cross-legged and straight-backed as the ustad had instructed her to, and begin the series of exercises he had taught her, to expand her chest cavity, regulate her breath and strengthen her vocal cords. She would then practise the particular music piece being taught to her.

Two hours later, Bullan and Kallan would give her a tall tumbler of freshly boiled milk mixed with a paste of ground almonds, raisins and two roughly crushed peppercorns fried in a tablespoon of homemade ghee. A nourishing diet, they believed, would give her body the strength that intensive riyaz requires. For the next few hours, Sadabahar was a regular child, running around the house, chasing butterflies, playing with her sister and enjoying her mothers' embrace.

Her ustad would arrive mid-morning. Even as a young child, her head was always covered in deference to her teacher. She personally carried in the tray of refreshments and served him, even though for her own needs Sadabahar had her two foster mothers and her sister Gulshan at her beck and call. Despite the poverty in which she had been brought up, Sadabahar was treated like a princess. Exempt from doing all housework, her day was spent in preparing to become a tawaif.

Bhure Khan Sahib trained her in raga-based music, with organised patterns of melody and rhythm. He would either sing or, more usually, play a phrase of a given song on his sarangi, and she would repeat it, memorising by rote every word, every note and each embellishment.

Over the years, he would teach her the musical repertoire associated with tawaifs in eastern United Provinces and Bihar—thumri, tappa, dadra and ghazal, along with raga-based versions of hori, chaiti and kajari. In the first years, however, he focused on the khayal. This was a necessary prerequisite to providing Sadabahar with a sound foundation in the intricacies of raga structures.

The taan technique of khayal enriched her rendition of bandish thumri, which was the centrepiece of the music education she received from Bhure Khan. Originally a song accompaniment to dance, bandish thumri had come into its own by the mid-nineteenth century as an independent music genre associated closely with tawaifs. Since it had flowered under the patronage of the nawabs of Lucknow in the late eighteenth to early nineteenth century, musicians across northern India, including Bhure Khan Sahib, generally referred to the bandish thumri as the Lucknow ang, or Lucknow style, of thumri-singing.

As its name connotes, the bandish, or composition, was (and continues to be) of the greatest significance in the musical rendition of bandish thumri. The poetry of its compositions mainly focuses upon narratives of Krishna's dalliance with the gopis, milkmaids. A few deal with other themes, notably that of biraha, or a woman's longing for an absent lover. The texts are usually narrative and, in the nineteenth century, provided the framework for storytelling in a dance performance. Usually set in medium to fast tempo (teental), bandish thumri is (generally but not always) performed in light classical ragas like Ghara, Kafi, Pilu, Zilla, Mand, Manj Khamaj, Des, Tilang and Jhinjhoti, and in Sadabahar's time used to be sung to the accompaniment of tabla and sarangi.

Sadabahar learnt to lay stress on the text of the bandish, to bring out its meaning musically by repeating the composition of the thumri over and over again in quickening tempo. She learnt the technique of bol baant, or word division: improvising passages with a phrase from the thumri text. This she did either through bol taan—taans using words from the text—or varying different stanzas of the thumri to create rhythmic and melodic patterns that were then interpreted through dance.

There was no time frame set for mastering a particular musical composition or bandish. It depended entirely on how quickly young Sadabahar learnt a piece. At times, she would master an entire bandish in just a few days, and at others, they kept practising a particular phrase in the bandish for weeks to get it just right.

Bhure Khan Sahib was a patient and gentle teacher, not easily given to anger—unless he perceived a lack of concentration and application by his student. Then his temper would rise like a heavy hail cloud that would let loose a shower of searing chastisements. Sadabahar weathered these occasional storms with her head bowed respectfully, in silence.

'Once, when she was about ten or eleven, despite repeated attempts, she couldn't sing a particular phrase as the ustad wanted her to.' This is one of your favourite stories from Sadabahar's childhood. 'He motioned to her to stop; then in a deceptively soft voice commanded her to spit in the palm of her hand. How would spitting in her palm help her sing the line right, Sadabahar silently wondered? Anyhow, after some hesitation, she did as she was told.

'His voice now rising like a whiplash, the old ustad ordered her—*Ab thook ko chato!* Now lick the spit! Sadabahar froze in mortification. Her eyes stung with tears but she said nothing. In the adjoining room, Bullan and Kallan's hearts reached out to their child, yet they knew better than to intervene. They had never raised a hand against Sadabahar, but they understood that harsh words and punishment from her ustad were part of her education to become a great singer.'

❁

Pyaari khala's room is now full of shadows. Afternoon has made way for dusk and the return of other family members. Sitting around the bed now are Phoolmani and Sakeena, her two surviving sisters, one older, the other younger—Pyaari is the third of four. Also in the room are Pyaari's nieces: your cousins and sisters.

Sakeena sits next to me. Married off by the family, she lives in Bhabua. A short, thick-set, quiet woman, she is usually dominated by her more assertive sisters and nieces. Today she is accompanied by her two chronically unemployed sons, the incongruously named Nawab and Wazir.

Keeping her distance even in this relatively small room is the dour-looking Phoolmani, the second amongst the four sisters. Their oldest sister Bindo being long dead, Phoolmani has assumed the role of the family elder. She has travelled all the way from Mumbai, where she lives with her younger daughter Seema. Phoolmani was a tawaif and a theatre actress in her younger years but, according to you, she always remained aloof from the rest of the family; a choice you attribute to the 'smallness' of her heart.

Seated beside Pyaari is her favourite niece and Phoolmani's elder daughter, Rajjo. Settled in Banaras, she is among your closest friends. In her youth, Rajjo had begun her career as a moderately successful tawaif but moved on to become a highly popular qawwali singer in Banaras. Bearing a strong resemblance to Pyaari, with her full-throated laughter, amiable disposition and sparkling eyes, Rajjo is usually the life of any family gathering. Today, she sits quietly, gently stroking the head of her much-loved aunt.

Seated side by side as always are Rani, your cousin, and Asghari, your much older sister. They are next-door neighbours in Bhabua and close friends. Rani, the late Bindo's only child, sits with her eyes shut, counting her rosary and mumbling prayers. Asghari drums her fingers on her knees and looks distinctly edgy.

Both had once been tawaifs—Rani a spectacularly unsuccessful one who opted to retire early; Asghari the toast of Banaras in her prime and still, in her mid-seventies, exceptionally good-looking. Rani now spends most of her time in prayer or visiting Sufi shrines in and around Bhabua. Asghari, who I notice has appropriated the only comfortable chair in the room, apparently keeps busy with more worldly concerns. After moving to Bhabua, she spends her time, according to you, battling with family members and neighbours, usually over trivial issues.

Perched precariously on a small stool next to Asghari is the tall and statuesque Seema, Phoolmani's younger daughter. Although you hardly ever talk about her, I have heard from your aunts and cousins that, had Seema not opted out of the line early to become the mistress of a jeweller in Mumbai, she could have posed a serious challenge to your status as the most popular tawaif singer of your time.

Hovering around and serving tea to everyone is Ghafuran, your twin and Jawed's mother. For reasons I have never quite been able to comprehend, the family chose to marry her off, though she is good-looking and has spoken of her love for music. The youngest and financially least well-off in this assembly of matriarchs, Ghafuran is timid and eager to please. She is always the most hard-worked in family gatherings, delegated the responsibility of running the kitchen and managing household tasks.

Ghafuran is assisted by the family's many daughters-in-law who remain invisible presences in family gatherings like these. Along with their children and the young daughters of the family, they occupy the back rooms and kitchen. Cooking, hushing babies back to sleep and chatting, they pass time waiting for Pyaari khala to breathe her last.

The men in the family are conspicuous by their absence. Most of them, no doubt, are still away at their jobs or small businesses, and will join the younger women in the rooms at the back of the house once they return. Had it not been raining, the younger boys would have loitered outside, waiting to run errands if there was need. Today, while some of them crowd in the back rooms, the others have disappeared.

Men and boys in your family are rarely seen and even more rarely heard. Decision-making and delegating duties is the prerogative of the senior tawaif matriarchs. This is gradually changing though. In a significant departure from tradition, Pyaari khala has chosen to bequeath her property to her sister Sakeena's sons, Nawab and Wazir. According to them, this is in recognition of the care they have taken of their ill aunt. The status of being her heirs has earned them the right to join the older women in keeping vigil over Pyaari khala as she approaches death.

Presiding over all these descendants of Dharmman Bibi is you. Though younger than the others, and not the financially best-off, you inspire the respect and deference due to a choudharayin, the senior-most matriarch of the tawaif community. I have noticed that it is you the family turns to for important decisions. It is you whom Ghafuran consults about dinner arrangements for everyone gathered. Nawab and Wazir too confer with you about Pyaari khala's fast-deteriorating condition.

With electricity playing truant as usual, one of the daughters-in-law has silently come in and placed a lit kerosene lantern in the room. Its orange flame valiantly battles the gloom as dusk dissolves into the night and the rain outside gathers momentum.

All of a sudden, Pyaari khala wakes up from her narcotic-induced stupor and peering around, demands in a surprisingly strong voice, 'What are all of you sitting and whispering to each other? I am still alive, sisters. Will someone bother to speak to me?' Pyaari khala is clearly in one of her few and far between painless moments.

You reply gently, 'Khala, you were sleeping and we didn't want to disturb you. Do you feel like eating something?'

Pyaari refuses food but orders you and Seema to sing for her instead: 'Come on girls, the rains are here. And we are all together after a long time. Let's have a kajari, like in the old days.'

You begin to weep. Impatiently, your elder sister Asghari orders you to shut up. 'Khala is feeling better for once, and you waste time shedding tears! Stop howling this very instant and sing her the kajari she wishes to hear.'

Pyaari khala hoots with laughter. 'That must be my Asghari. Bless her honeyed tongue! She sheds flowers when she speaks.'

Rajjo begins giggling and Ghafuran conjures up a dholak from somewhere.

By now, the room is bathed in an orange glow. Seema and you move in closer and decide upon a song. In your performer's voice, you announce, 'We will sing our family's favourite kajari. Everyone here has to join in.'

Rajjo takes charge of the dholak and plays on it a few trial beats. After a couple of false starts, you and Seema begin the song I heard you sing sotto voce earlier in the afternoon.

Rim jhim khola ho kiwadiyaa, hum bideswa jaibena ...

As the song comes to an end, Pyaari khala turns to me and explains that this kajari belongs exclusively to your family. Like a treasured heirloom, the song has been passed down from one generation of tawaifs to another in abiding memory of Sadabahar, the greatest singer ever in the family's history. And again, you take up the telling of her story.

✿

So rapid was young Sadabahar's progress that, after a few years of teaching her, Bhure Khan Sahib declared her ready to receive a rare privilege. In a ceremony held at his home, where all the male musicians from the Dhari community in Chainpur were invited, Sadabahar presented Bhure Khan Sahib with sweets, betel leaves and areca nuts, a sherwani and money in nazrana. In turn, the ustad tied the ganda, or black thread, on Sadabahar's wrist and gave her black gram and jaggery to eat. From being a pupil, she thus graduated to becoming his disciple—the black thread formally tying her name to the music of her ustad and his family. Henceforth, with the musicians' community as her witness, she could formally claim her ustad's musical legacy as her own.

Bhure Khan Sahib taught several students but granted the privilege of giving his name formally as their mentor only to a worthy few. This was a usual feature of the ustad–shagirda or guru–shishya relationship in Hindustani music. With her ustad's permission, Sadabahar sang in front of his community members, her first time in public. Her formal initiation as one of his chosen disciples was now complete.

Over the coming years, every morning without fail, tanpura in hand, Sadabahar sat in front of Bhure Khan Sahib. At noon, once her music lesson was over, she was given a nourishing meal of fresh vegetables, dal and some meat cooked in ghee to replenish her strength. Then she would sleep; prescribed diet and judicious rest being as important in the training to become a musician as daily riyaz, dedication to one's ustad and discipline.

'By late afternoon, Pannu Guru would come in to teach her dance,' says Rajjo with a smile, taking over the story from you. 'With his huge girth, bald and shining pate, twinkling eyes and nimble feet, Pannu Guru looked like a happy, dancing Ganesh. Even as a little child, Sadabahar marvelled at the grace and agility of her guru-ji's kathak, despite his tree-trunk legs and a mountainous belly in which, he would tell her impishly, there lived a perennially hungry mouse. Pannu Guru made lessons feel like playtime, with his jokes and stories. He rarely lost his temper, but inspired such affection for himself and interest in dance that even his most difficult students were brought in line.'

Pannu Guru belonged to a small community of Kathaks in Chainpur whose main source of livelihood was teaching kathak dance and music to the tawaifs. If the Kathaks had migrated here from elsewhere, their older origins are not known. Associated closely with the history of the rise and development of kathak, the dance form, Kathaks as a community have their antecedents in professional male performers in the Agra-Mathura, Braj region of Krishna worship. They would relate Hindu epics and mythology through storytelling, mime and dance, and from this evolved kathak as a formal dance form. Brahmins by caste, in the eighteenth and nineteenth century, some of them migrated to Lucknow. The patronage provided to them by the nawabs there was instrumental in moulding kathak into a sophisticated and mature dance genre performed by tawaifs in the courts.

W. Crooke, writing in 1892, describes the Kathaks as a 'caste of story-tellers, singers and musicians ... equal to Brahmans, and all castes, including Rajputs, salute them and beg a blessing'. And yet Crooke sanctimoniously declares, 'While they hold a fairly respectable position, their business degrades them to some extent.' This 'business' is being teachers and accompanists to 'ordinary dancing girls, who are often prostitutes'. He also notes that, besides worshipping all the gods venerated by Hindus, Kathaks especially revere Saraswati, the goddess of speech and learning, whom they regard as their 'clan' deity. They also 'worship Ghazi Miyan, (a revered Sufi saint whose shrine is in Bahraich), and offer him sweet cakes in the months of Kuar and Chait'.

Pannu Guru's best friend in Chainpur was the old Bhure Khan, and the two could often be seen together, walking the streets of the town. This sight generated much mirth among the tawaifs who had affectionately nicknamed the pair Alif and Sifar, the long, angular and dour first alphabet of the Urdu script accompanied by the round, cheerful zero. Together, the teachers scored a perfect ten from their students, the tawaifs' daughters who had to learn music and dance to become performers. Only a handful, however, gained mastery in both.

Sadabahar never gave Pannu Guru any reason to fault her for lack of either dedication or effort. The girl put her heart into learning and executing all the steps guru-ji taught her. But it was obvious to both Pannu Guru and Bhure Khan Sahib that, while Sadabahar would flower into a remarkable singer, her dancing would never scale the heights of her musical notes. Still, it was proficient enough to complement her singing even in the most culturally sophisticated mehfil. In the late nineteenth century, in a formal performance, a tawaif would enact through facial expressions, hand gestures and dance movements each line of bandish thumri, ghazal or other song type she sang. This performance in its entirety was called mujra.

'Music and dance were just one part of the intensive education Sadabahar received,' Pyaari khala chips in, her pain momentarily forgotten. 'Mastery of the letters too was considered an important aspect of a tawaif's learning process. Deep in the evening, when shadows lengthened to the sound of bells round the necks of cows returning home, Sadabahar would sit bathed in lantern light in the company of books and the maulavi sahib from the nearby mosque. Guided by him, she would read and write Urdu, and learn Farsi, Persian. She could not hope to sing ghazals with the right understanding and feeling without gaining proficiency in these languages. Our family is Bhojpuri-speaking, so maulavi sahib took care to correct and polish Sadabahar's pronunciation and fluency in Urdu. Her mothers had taught her the Devanagari script since early childhood, and by the time she was eleven or twelve, Sadabahar could read Hindi effortlessly.'

Bullan and Kallan paid the greatest possible attention to teaching Sadabahar the etiquette of formal zamindar mehfils and the elaborate social courtesies associated with the kotha: the deep lowering of the neck and shoulders, accompanied by the salute of the adaab, the making and folding of paan and presenting it gracefully to guests, the witty repartee and amusing conversation during interludes in the performance. Sadabahar had to adopt these as a natural part of her being.

'Through her childhood and youth, her mothers constantly monitored her use of language, mannerisms and body posture, and quickly reprimanded and corrected her when anything was out of line,' you add, as Pyaari khala's voice falters. 'As she stepped into adolescence, Sadabahar learnt by watching the other tawaifs in the community the skills that could never be taught in formal lessons.'

Now Asghari breaks in. With no patience for your coy allusions, she spells out what Sadabahar learnt through observation—the tawaif's use of sexuality in subtle and overt ways to attract male patrons. 'Why did men come to our kothas? They came seeking distraction from wearisome worldly affairs. With us, they wanted the pleasure of being treated like lovers. Their wives were too busy in the affairs of running the house to play these games with them. We would entice and attract them through our music, dance, conversation about poetry and politics, our gestures, flirtation and adaa, even through the lowering and raising of our eyes. It was part of our duty to learn the art of rijhana—to attract and captivate a patron completely.'

CHAPTER 5

Sadabahar, the Tawaif

THERE IS AN APOLOGETIC COUGH at Pyaari khala's door. Shambhu Lala stands there, looking a bit lost as usual. He owns the largest cloth shop in Bhabua, and has been visiting your aunt in the evenings ever since she moved back from Banaras about forty years ago. A self-effacing, quiet man in his eighties, Shambhu Lala is neither tall nor short, neither dark nor fair, neither fat nor thin. Dressed in a simple cotton dhoti and a crumpled kurta, his singularly ordinary appearance is offset by the deep love in his eyes for the old and ill woman lying on the bed in the room.

They first met when she came to his shop to buy a sari. Recently retired, Pyaari was at that time in her forties. He was around the same age, a widower with married children and no experience of any woman other than his long-dead wife. Entranced by her fair face and twinkling, bold eyes, Shambhu Lala made a mistake in calculating the bill for the first time in his life. Pyaari laughed—a full-throated, good-natured laugh—and Shambhu Lala fell hopelessly in love.

He found himself dropping in at her house every other evening on some pretext or other. Soon the excuses were dispensed with, and he became a regular presence in Pyaari's home. She would talk with him, and make him laugh with her jokes and stories. Sometimes she would sing. Even without accompanists, her voice and the way she looked into his eyes while singing made the ageing cloth-seller's breath catch. They would make love. Occasionally, she let him spend the night with her.

In a matter-of-fact tone, Pyaari khala has described Shambhu Lala to me as her ashiq, lover, a term that over the years has come to encompass romantic lover, patron, friend, companion, confidante and, now, simply a deeply worried, heartbroken old man. He stands shyly at the door while you call out to Ghafuran to get a glass of water for him. In his kurta pocket, Shambhu Lala carries a quarter bottle of whisky and, in his hand, a quarter kilogram of lamb liver which Ghafuran will cook for him.

He will spend the next couple of hours or more at Pyaari khala's bedside, silently finishing his whisky and nibbling at the spicy fried liver. Periodically, he will ask her if, like in the old times, she wants a drink. She might, depending upon the level of pain flooding her frail frame, either indulge him by taking a sip or two from his glass or wave his offer away irritably.

Occasionally, she might demand he light a cigarette. Shambhu Lala doesn't smoke but has, from the earliest days of their acquaintance, always carried a packet for Pyaari. Torn between anxiety for her cancer-eaten lungs and desperation to make her happy, he will first pretend to have no cigarettes to give her. She will then tell him to get the hell out of her house. He will reason, she will rage, cajole and beg.

Beaten, finally, Shambhu Lala will guiltily take out a cigarette and light it for her. Smoking and coughing, she will quickly push back the cigarette into his fingers when warning footsteps approach the room. Much of this is play-acting, since Pyaari knows that no one will enter her room while he is there without discreetly knocking first.

Before leaving, he will, not daily but fairly regularly, slip a few notes under her pillow. She likes this. She values money, of course. Who doesn't? But Pyaari values much more the fact that even on her deathbed she has an ashiq willing to pay for her company. It makes her feel in business yet; she is the tawaif who, even after formally retiring, never ran out of admirers.

I have heard all this from you and from Pyaari khala, who addresses her old lover as 'lala'. He calls her 'bai'. In deference to his relationship with your aunt, you and your sisters and cousins address Shambhu Lala as mausa, or maternal uncle.

Flashing at him a coquettish smile, you now exclaim in a tone of mock hurt, 'I can see, mausa, that old age is fogging your memory! Or have you stopped caring for your niece? I have been here several days now and you have not once dropped by at my house to exchange two words.'

Shambhu Lala stammers something about being preoccupied with the shop. To this, you reply, laughing, 'Mausa, spare me the explanations. *Ghayal ki gati ghayal janey*; only the wounded knows the pain of another's wound. Why should you care if I am heartbroken by your neglect?'

I am amazed at your transformation. The prim matron I know has in the blink of an eye taken on the avatar of a playful femme fatale. Pyaari khala cackles with delight. 'Lala! I am leaving you in capable hands. This girl will make the fool of you I never could!'

Shambhu Lala manages a bashful smile and you, satisfied with having dispelled the gloom, revert to the sturdy, no-nonsense manner I know. Briskly straightening Pyaari khala's bedclothes and smoothing back her hair, you signal your aunts and cousins to follow you out of the room. It is time now for Pyaari khala to entertain her ashiq.

That evening, battling mosquitoes that swarm the terrace of Pyaari khala's house, as we wait for Shambhu Lala to take his leave, you remember your aunt's winning ways. 'In her days as a tawaif, no one could hold a candle to khala. My mother would often say that of all the women in the family, it was Pyaari who had inherited the spirit of Sadabahar. Like her, Pyaari's beauty, musical talent and charm, even as a child, convinced her family and teachers that she had a great future as a tawaif.'

It was just as well, however, that Pyaari khala, otherwise true to Sadabahar in most respects, had not inherited her grandaunt's eyes. Eyes, the wise say, are gateways to the soul. Wide-set, thickly lashed and large, Sadabahar's eyes were a startling mix of blue, grey, green and silver. Unfathomable mysteries seemed to lurk in their depths. Some said she had the eyes of a magician. Others claimed that only mad mystics were born with eyes like hers. She was destined to wander unknown lands, they said, lands out of bounds for ordinary mortals.

Sadabahar's powerful but exceedingly sweet voice too had a haunting quality. Passers-by were rooted to the spot by her singing. They were not the only ones spellbound by the girl's music. One evening, Bullan and Kallan discovered the smell of burning incense in the room where Sadabahar had been practising alone. The sisters hadn't burnt any, so who had? On another occasion, they found the room bathed in jasmine perfume.

Bhure Khan Sahib confirmed their worst fears. Sadabahar's music was other-worldly, he warned. That, along with the mystical destiny foretold by her blue-grey-green-silver eyes, held the dangerous possibility of spirits and djinns, known to be attracted by music, seeking out

Sadabahar when she practised alone. What if one of them fell in love with the beautiful girl? It was known to happen. And if it did, she would be lost to the real world; spirits and djinns were known to be possessive lovers. The only way to prevent such a terrible eventuality was never to leave her on her own, certainly not when she was singing.

'Such talk naturally frightened Bullan and Kallan.' Warming up to the story, you speak in dramatic tones. 'They resolved to keep Sadabahar safe in their warm embrace, and prove the soothsayers wrong. But who can change the course of destiny?'

On the rare occasion they had to leave Sadabahar alone, Bullan and Kallan came back to find her singing and chattering away to thin air. Sadabahar would look perplexed when questioned. Why were her mothers asking who she was talking to when the old man in the yellow robes and long white beard stood right opposite them? Her answer caused Bullan and Kallan to go pale. Was it possible that Harshu Brahm, the ghost presiding over Chainpur, had begun visiting their daughter?

Local folklore has it that, hundreds of years ago, Harshu Baba was a Kannaujiya Brahmin and family priest of Raja Salivahana in Chainpur. Instigated by his queen to falsely believe that Harshu Baba was conspiring against him, Raja Salivahana had the priest's house pulled down and burnt. To avenge this humiliation, Harshu Baba fasted unto death at the gates of the king's palace. When his body was taken to Banaras for cremation, much to everyone's shock, Harshu Baba appeared standing on the steps of the burning ghats. He informed the mourners that he had turned into a brahm, or Brahmin ghost, and would take revenge on the king for his unjust treatment. True to his word, Harshu Brahm destroyed Raja Salivahana and his family, sparing only a princess who had been kind to him. Since then, he has been propitiated at the temple built in his name in Chainpur.

Removed from the romance of mythology, it is more probable that Salivahana, in fact, suffered defeat and death at the hands of Sher Shah Suri, the Pathan ruler from Sasaram who rose to briefly become emperor of Hindustan. Annexing Salivahana's territories to his empire, Sher Shah Suri left behind several impressive monuments in Chainpur that survive to this date, including the remains of a fort and the mausoleum of Bakhtiyar Khan, his close associate. Even through the colonial era, the area was largely dominated by Pathan landholders.

On our way back from Mundesvari temple yesterday, you took me to Chainpur, about 15 km from Bhabua, to visit the shrine of Harshu

Brahm, which stands on a hillock rising above the town. Raja Salivahana is believed to have ruled during the sixteenth century, but the temple seems to be of more recent vintage.

A sacrificial fire burns at all times in the main structure, which is surrounded by a courtyard bordered by a rectangular, covered gallery. Seated in one of the alcoves of the gallery was a troubled-looking young man who seemed to be in great physical pain. In another alcove, a woman was in paroxysms of convulsions, her hair flying.

Surrounding the woman was a group of exorcists attached to the temple which, you whispered, is a playground for spirits. Even the most incurable cases of possession are freed here of the evil ghouls that have taken over their bodies. Beaten into submission by resident exorcists, the restless spirits are then consigned forever to the flames of the sacrificial fire that blazes day and night inside the temple.

Little wonder then that Bullan and Kallan, fearing that Harshu Brahm himself had begun visiting Sadabahar, forbade her from ever going anywhere near the temple. Crowded with ghosts and bloodthirsty apparitions, it was no place for young girls, they tried to scare her. But Sadabahar, born on a moonless, rain-drenched night under the protective gaze of Goddess Mundesvari, had the fearlessness of her mother combined with the curiosity of a seeker.

One evening, as darkness began falling, the temple priest found Sadabahar, then barely ten or eleven, sitting alone in the deserted courtyard, singing of the pain of separation in the rainy season:

Rim jhim khola ho kiwadiya, hum bideswa jaibena …

Recognising her as Bullan and Kallan's daughter, the priest had enquired gently, 'Child, why do you sit here and sing alone?'

Sadabahar answered, 'Baba, we are not alone. Look at all these people gathered around. They look so sad that I thought of cheering them with a kajari.'

It's begun raining again and we are back in Pyaari's room. She is awake and groaning in pain. Shambhu Lala has long since left. It is uncomfortably warm inside the house and several people are fanning Pyaari khala with newspapers to keep her cool. Even in normal times, electricity graces

Bhabua for just about a couple of hours a day; now, the rains have ensured that there is almost continuous power breakdown.

You look worried and angry. Pyaari khala has to be made comfortable through her terrible ordeal. You asked Sakeena khala's sons, Nawab and Wazir, two days ago to arrange for a portable generator. They haven't managed to organise one so far, and I see you purse your lips in exasperation.

I quietly offer once more to contribute money towards buying a generator if hiring one is proving difficult. You impatiently signal me to keep silent. This is your family and they must take responsibility for Pyaari khala's care. As the sole beneficiaries of Pyaari's will, Nawab and Wazir should be arranging and paying for all her material needs. Personally, I feel it is not the most appropriate time to make the brothers accountable, at the expense of your aunt's comfort, but keep my own counsel. We have discussed this before and I know your views.

I wish it would stop raining so I can step out. I want to briefly escape the heat and the helplessness of the sick-room. You are focused on the tasks at hand, and busy calling a doctor. He comes, despite the late hour, to deliver the painkiller that temporarily relieves Pyaari of her anguish. There is nothing more that can be done.

In the silence that descends, I go over what you told me of the life and times of Sadabahar earlier in the evening. The story of Bullan and Kallan's young daughter whose music enchanted even the resident spirits of Harshu Brahm's temple spread far and wide. Soon enough, Bullan and Kallan's former patron, the zamindar-raja of Bhagwanpur, heard the strange tale and expressed a keen desire to hear Sadabahar sing. Once he did, the raja was so impressed that he decided to finance Sadabahar's further education in music and dance. When she grew a bit older, he declared, she would sing in his court on all major occasions and celebrations.

The Bhagwanpur raja belonged to the Sakarwar Rajput clan that traces its descent to King Puru, or Porus, the ruler of Takshila who bravely fought the invading armies of Alexander in 323 BCE. Raja Salivahana, the accursed ruler of Chainpur, also belonged to this clan. The descendants of his daughter were known locally as 'raj kuar', literally 'royal princes'. Many of them were zamindars in the area around Chainpur and Bhabua. Possibly the largest of these landholdings was Bhagwanpur, south of Bhabua, founded by Bhagwan Singh, a forefather of Sadabahar's patron.

During the revolt of 1857, while several Muslim landholders of Chainpur had thrown in their lot with the rebels fighting under the leadership of Babu Kunwar Singh, many Rajput zamindars of the area, including the Bhagwanpur family, had remained loyal to the British. Once the revolt was crushed, they were all richly rewarded for their loyalty, and some of them, such as the landholder of Bhagwanpur, were allowed to use the title of raja.

The critical role played by loyalist princes and landholders across northern India in containing the revolt had led to realisation in British circles of their potential as valuable allies. Lord Canning, who was governor-general during 1857, described them as 'breakwaters in the storm'. The aim of the government, therefore, increasingly became to 'enlist on our side those natives who have, from their birth or their position, a natural influence in the country'. Consequently, efforts were made to conciliate this class to become 'useful instruments' of the empire and help 'restore order and tranquillity'.

In Bengal and Bihar, the policy of auctioning the landholdings of zamindars who were in arrears was largely abandoned; in fact, increasingly, the government was expected to rescue encumbered landholders from the weight of their debts. Over time, in any case, as more forests were felled and land brought under the plough, the fixed revenue under the Permanent Settlement became progressively less of a burden for landholders. Zamindars were additionally invested with magisterial authority, and thus given a recognised place in the local administration. These powers, alongside the freedom they enjoyed to extort as much rent as they liked from their tenants, gave landholders almost complete control over the peasantry.

With landholdings and titles becoming secure, even minor zamindars indulged in the paraphernalia associated with royalty. Artists, notably singers and dancers, found patronage in the courts of these petty potentates. A large number of local male musicians and tawaifs performed regularly in the court of the raja of Bhagwanpur. Once Sadabahar reached puberty, the raja cemented his patronage of her music education by proposing that she be made the mistress of his much younger half-brother Kunwar Chandrabhan Singh.

By norm, a girl chosen by her family to become a tawaif would be presented to a suitably eligible aristocratic patron once she reached puberty. This coming-of-age rite was called 'sar dhakna', literally 'covering the head', among tawaif communities in Bihar and eastern United Provinces. I remember that you shrugged with distaste when I innocently asked whether sar dhakna was akin to the better-known nath utarana, the 'removing of the nose-ring' ceremony that marked the sexual initiation of a virgin tawaif into the profession. You told me that, although the ceremonies were similar, families like yours never used the term nath utarana. Only lower-placed tawaifs and prostitutes would use such a crude expression, you said.

Celebrated like a wedding, the sar dhakna ceremony marked the first sexual encounter of the debutante courtesan. The opportunity to 'deflower' a virgin tawaif was highly coveted among Rajput patrons of the area, and regarded as a marker of virility. It was not unusual for them to compete to be chosen for the privilege. The selected lover patron not only paid for all the expenses incurred at the ceremony—clothes and jewellery for the girl and a feast for the tawaif community—but also presented gifts and money to the courtesan's family.

Sadabahar's sar dhakna ceremony, financed by the old raja himself, was a grand occasion that would be remembered for years to come. The occasion also marked her first public appearance as a professional musician. Bullan and Kallan invited the entire community of tawaifs and male musicians of the area, as well as prominent members of the Rajput aristocracy, for musical mehfils spanning several nights in their home. As the undisputed star of these soirees, Sadabahar impressed everyone present with her resonant voice, her command over each musical note and her vivacious beauty. Dazzling in the heavy Banarasi silks and glittering gold jewellery gifted by Kunwar Chandrabhan Singh, she wore a large gold ring in her nose that he would ceremoniously remove during their first night together. Thereafter, Sadabahar would wear a nose-stud as all tawaifs did after their initiation.

After the sar dhakna ceremony, she entered service as Kunwar Chandrabhan Singh's mistress, and was entitled to a handsome monthly maintenance. There were no fixed rules about the duration of the relationship between a debutante tawaif and her first lover patron. In many cases, patrons were interested only in buying the privilege of spending the first night with a virgin tawaif, after which the girl was free to enter into sexual relationships with other men. This was the pattern most prevalent amongst the lower-placed tawaif families in the community. In the upper echelons of the community, to which Bullan and Kallan belonged, more usually, the debutante tawaif became the mistress of her first lover patron, as Sadabahar did. This was referred to as naukri karna, entering service, or even pabandi mein rehna, living within boundaries.

The tawaif was obliged to remain sexually faithful to her lover patron as long as he wished to continue the relationship and could afford to maintain her. But she was usually free to perform as a musician in mehfils in her own kotha or in the homes of the local elite. Occasionally, the tawaif stopped performing for others altogether if her lover patron wished it and could afford to exercise exclusive rights over her.

After 'entering service', sometimes a tawaif would shift to a house arranged by her lover patron, while still maintaining close links with her family. She would transfer her earnings to them. Generally, though, tawaifs continued to live in their natal home—as Sadabahar did, with Bullan and Kallan managing her life and career. She would sing at the raja's court whenever required, including all important occasions, but would also perform at other places she was invited to. By norm, it was understood that if Sadabahar had any children from Chandrabhan Singh, they would belong to her family with no rights either to their father's name or his property, unless, as did happen in emotionally intimate relationships between tawaifs and patrons, he specifically made arrangements for them.

Monitoring Sadabahar's every action to ensure it was pleasing to her lover patron, Bullan and Kallan continually stressed upon her the imperative of following the professional code of the tawaif. On no account, they warned her, should she fall in love with Chandrabhan Singh. The alliance with a lover patron was binding from the tawaif's side, they emphasised, only as long as he was financially in a position to provide for her and her extended family and dependents in the kotha.

Moreover, there was always the real danger of a lover patron turning fickle, a motif familiar in thumri and ghazal poetry. As long as he was completely devoted to the tawaif, her professional code demanded that she play the role of a woman in love adeptly so as to extract as much from him as possible. Her financial security, and that of her family, depended upon this.

Intrigued, I had asked you and Asghari—who had joined us on the terrace—if either of you had ever broken the tawaif's professional code and fallen in love with a lover patron. While you had chosen to remain silent, Asghari flashed a heart-wrenching smile and exclaimed, *'Ghoda agar ghas se yari karega to khayega kya?'* If a horse falls in love with the grass, what will it eat?

Among the sixty-four necessary courtesan skills that the sixth-century *Kamasutra* enumerates, is the art of pretence, the feigning of love. In Mirza Hadi Ruswa's early twentieth-century Urdu novel, *Umrao Jan Ada* (tr. by Khushwant Singh and M.A. Husaini), about a tawaif of Lucknow in the mid-nineteenth century, the protagonist Umrao describes the game of love that courtesans were so adept at playing: 'I am but a courtesan in whose profession love is a current coin. Whenever we want to ensnare anyone we pretend to fall in love with him. No one knows how to love more than we do; to heave deep sighs; to burst into tears at the slightest pretext; to go without food for days on end; to sit dangling our legs on the parapets of wells to jump into them; to threaten to take arsenic. All these are parts of our game of love.'

Sadabahar, who had been taught the intricacies of this game from childhood, never got around to playing it with Chandrabhan Singh. Her relationship with him was cordial but nominal. Apart from the social obligation of maintaining at the very least a well-known tawaif mistress or two, the kunwar's interest in women was negligible. For his sexual needs, he much preferred natuwas, the boy dancers so popular in the area. There was always a troupe of these boys with pretty faces and slender waists stationed in his quarters. This suited Sadabahar just fine. Free from the duties of sexually entertaining a lover patron, she focused all her time and energy in perfecting her music.

Bullan and Kallan were far from satisfied by this arrangement, though. Had they known of Chandrabhan Singh's sexual preference earlier, they might have found ways of politely side-stepping the Bhagwanpur zamindar's offer. Undoubtedly, the honour of becoming the kunwar's official mistress had brought prestige to Sadabahar and her family, and her handsome allowance had substantially improved the household's financial health. But this did not compensate the loss of an additional income—expensive presents, jewellery and land—that Sadabahar could have earned had Chandrabhan Singh been a besotted lover and not just a rubber-stamp patron more interested in boys.

It could be argued that the ageing tawaifs were being greedy, but they saw it as being pragmatic. It was the extras that a young tawaif could cajole, bargain and extract from an enraptured admirer that turned her from being merely well-off into a wealthy woman of substance.

Meanwhile, Babu Rudra Bahadur Singh, cousin of Chandrabhan Singh, had begun displaying a keen interest in Sadabahar. He was often present at the mehfils in which Sadabahar, as part of her duty, performed exclusively for the pleasure of the kunwar and his close friends, and was effusive in his praise.

Living off a generous inheritance, Rudra Bahadur spent much of his time and wealth in maintaining and indulging tawaif mistresses. They were his hobby, passion and main activity. He was, in Bullan and Kallan's estimation, an imminently suitable patron lover for their daughter. But they knew that he would never agree to enter into a sexual liaison with Sadabahar while she remained his cousin's mistress. In the Rajput code of conduct, this would have been considered an unpardonable impropriety and a breach of honour. They would have to find a way to free Sadabahar somehow, and quickly, before another tawaif caught Rudra Bahadur's fancy.

Bullan and Kallan knew that Sadabahar could walk out of her relationship with Chandrabhan Singh only at the peril of death. Powerful Rajput zamindars did not take kindly to being rejected by mistresses. In the end, as destiny would have it, they had to do nothing. Out on a hunt in the Kaimur hills, Chandrabhan Singh was fatally wounded in an encounter with a tiger. By the time he was brought back to the family house in Bhagwanpur, he was dead. After the mandatory period of mourning, Sadabahar was free to enter into a relationship with Babu Rudra Bahadur Singh as his new mistress.

In her journey through life, Sadabahar would have many lovers but none in her estimation as experienced and generous as Rudra Bahadur Singh. Guided gently by him, Sadabahar discovered the joy of giving and receiving sexual pleasure. Love-making, he would say, was an art that only those who had patience, passion and love for life could master.

To Bullan and Kallan's relief, Sadabahar's mystical preoccupations too seemed to wane. Some said this was bound to happen now that she had entered the worldly life of a tawaif and a sexual relationship with a man; djinns and spirits of the outer world didn't like sharing with mere mortals the affections of a woman. Others warned that it was a passing phase. The pull of the mystical world would most likely return once the young girl's initial fascination with her new life ebbed.

❁

Looking out of the only window in Pyaari khala's room, I notice an orange light wade through the inky darkness. Shambhu Lala is hurrying towards his lover's house, carrying a lantern in one hand and a large can in the other. He is followed by two younger men, who carry a portable generator between them. Lala seems to have decided he will not allow his bai to suffer through yet another night of power breakdown.

Without any explanation or fuss, he gets the two young men—his grandsons, I later get to know—to install the generator. The diesel in the can is poured into the generator and its lever yanked. Pyaari's ceiling fan whirls into motion and the bulbs in her room light up.

Even old, retired lovers have their uses, Phoolmani mutters under her breath. You smile gratefully at Shambhu Lala, as do Rajjo and Rani, and express warm thanks. Asghari, half-seriously, flirts with lala, asking him to arrange a free generator for her house as well. Clearly uncomfortable with all this attention, Shambhu Lala keeps wiping his flushed face with his gamchha, the cotton multipurpose scarf worn by many men in UP and Bihar.

His grandsons seem to be familiar with the relatives of their grandfather's mistress. Ghafuran insists they have tea and, before they can refuse, hurries inside. She returns with steaming cups for everyone, and we celebrate the installation of the generator with tea and piping-hot gulgulas, a favourite snack of the monsoon season.

Asghari, Rajjo and you are charming and vivacious hostesses, Rani exudes serene benedictions and even the usually grim Phoolmani and Seema manage an occasional smile in Shambhu Lala and his grandsons' direction. The only one who sits unsmiling and silent is Sakeena. Nawab and Wazir have in the meanwhile quietly slipped out of the room.

Once Shambhu Lala and his grandsons taken their leave, the mood instantly transforms from the jovial to accusatory. Old Phoolmani, looking directly at Sakeena, opens the offensive by remarking that it's just as well Pyaari maintained a lover rather than being totally dependent on unreliable family members.

Seema berates Sakeena for not exerting enough pressure on Nawab and Wazir to be more responsible. 'Khala has placed her trust in them. Do they think we will allow them to gobble up her inheritance once she is gone when they seem to be doing so little for her while she is living? Had they been my sons I would have made sure they fulfilled their duties,' she declares forcefully.

I know that you share your relatives' low opinion of Nawab and Wazir. Yet, perhaps out of consideration for your sleeping aunt, you refuse to be drawn into the tirade against Sakeena. Instead, you attempt to use Sadabahar's memory to broker peace amongst her squabbling descendants. 'Since everyone is here, this is a great opportunity to record our family history,' you say to me. 'My aunts can share with you stories about Sadabahar that even I do not know.'

When neither the combative Phoolmani nor the timid Sakeena show any enthusiasm, you resolutely launch into the story yourself. 'Sadabahar's life as a popular tawaif in Shahabad shimmered with the light and colour of mehfils. No musical gathering, including those organised by the biggest Rajput zamindars and rajas of the region, was deemed a success unless Sadabahar had performed in it. Her earnings were considerable, making her family the best-off among tawaifs in Chainpur. Bit by bit, Bullan and Kallan were able to free the house and agricultural lands that they had mortgaged to take care of Sadabahar and Gulshan.'

Sadabahar was the only tawaif in Chainpur, you say with obvious pride, who had her own horse-drawn carriage. She loved going out on rides with its hood drawn back, revelling in the looks of admiration and envy that came her way.

I am reminded of a similar anecdote about the acclaimed tawaif-diva Gauhar Jan of Calcutta in the late nineteenth–early twentieth century, who enjoyed taking evening rides through the city in her carriage drawn by four white horses. A particularly favoured route, it seems, went through the white quarters of Calcutta, in flagrant violation of the law that denied access to Indians. Gauhar is supposed to have thought nothing of paying a hefty fine whenever the desire to ride through the white area overtook her.

The tawaif here is a figure charged with sexuality, and proclaiming with flamboyant confidence not only pride in her identity as a *public* woman but also her power to access and use at will the public space, a privilege reserved for men from the feudal aristocracy and Europeans. This reversal of socially sanctioned gender rules is reflected in your telling of Sadabahar's story as well.

At her home in Chainpur, Sadabahar was looked after much like senior earning male members are in patriarchal households. A mini-army of relatives and retainers lived in Bullan and Kallan's house, dependent entirely upon her generosity for their survival. In return, they were obliged to make themselves useful. If Sadabahar wanted a hot meal on her return home after a late-night performance, then someone would be woken up to cook whatever she desired. If she complained of aching limbs, someone would give her a massage, all night long if necessary.

Yet Sadabahar did not allow the luxurious living, or the heady exhilaration of having lovelorn admirers, expensive gifts and lavish praise, diminish her commitment to music. In all seasons, every day, mid-morning, her old ustad Bhure Khan would troop in for lessons as he had always done. Until, one day, he did not come.

It was such an unusual occurrence that a worried Sadabahar sent someone to his house to enquire about his well-being. One of those merciless fevers that regularly swept through Shahabad district had taken a grip of her old teacher. Worse, there was no one to look after him. Over the decades, his family tree had branched off in different directions, and the men and their immediate families had migrated to various zamindaris in search of patronage as musicians. Bhure Khan Sahib, his old body feeble with high fever, lay alone, surrounded by flies and the spectre of imminent death.

As soon as she heard this, Sadabahar set off to bring her ustad to her own home. Here, she tended to him like a daughter. The best hakim in the entire district was summoned to take charge of his medical needs. Heedless of her own sleep or hunger, Sadabahar sat by Bhure Khan Sahib's side constantly, mopping his brow, feeding him and cleaning without hesitation his soiled clothes and bedsheets.

One morning, the ustad seemed to be feeling much better. Some colour had returned to his lips and his eyes too shone again. Motioning to Sadabahar, he asked in a surprisingly strong voice, 'How long has it been since you last did riyaz?' Her eyes welling up, Sadabahar said nothing. 'This just won't do, girl!' her teacher exclaimed crossly. 'Go and get your tanpura and settle down to some singing.' Sadabahar said a silent prayer to Allah for sending her teacher back to her. She ran and brought her beautifully carved tanpura into his room and, settling down on the floor, began strumming it gently.

On his instructions that morning, she sang *Babul mora naihar chhuto hi jaye*; Father, my maternal home slips away. Said to have been written by the last nawab of Awadh, Wajid Ali Shah, when he was exiled by the British from Lucknow to faraway Calcutta, the thumri set to raga Bhairavi was very different from the fast-tempo, bol-baant style of bandish thumris that were generally the staple of Sadabahar's repertoire. Slower in tempo and deeply reflective in tone, the song had reached Bhure Khan Sahib fairly recently through a relative based in Banaras. Profoundly impressed, he had been teaching it to Sadabahar just before he took ill.

At one level, the thumri is the cry of a young bride forced to leave the sanctuary of familiar faces after marriage; at another, it is also a song of the exile from a beloved homeland. At a third level, it is a meditation on death: of the journey made by the soul away from mortal life. Her eyes shut, Sadabahar sang with passion and precision, bringing out the multiple meanings embedded in the deceptively simple lines of the song. *Char kahar mili doliya utthaye, apno begana chhuto jaye*; Four bearers together carry my palanquin, Loved ones and those estranged, both slip away.

This would be her finest performance ever. There was silence in the room when Sadabahar concluded the thumri. She opened her eyes to find herself alone. In the course of her song, her teacher had taken his leave from the mortal world.

Sadabahar had loved her old teacher, mentor and guide like a father. He, in turn, generously shared with her his greatest treasure: music that could neither be bought nor stolen. She knew that this was a debt she could not hope to repay; the best she could do was to fulfil her duties and obligations as a disciple, a shagirda. There is a saying amongst the Dharis that a tawaif is the best son a sarangiya, sarangi player, can hope for in his old age. Sadabahar was proof of its truth. Just as she had looked after her teacher when he was alive, she left nothing wanting in his funeral and after-rites.

By now, Sadabahar was counted amongst the leading tawaifs not just of Chainpur but across the borders of district Shahabad, in major zamindaris like Bettiah and Darbhanga, which were also prominent centres of music, particularly of the ancient genre of dhrupad. She was regularly invited to perform in both these places. She may, you tell me, even have lived for a few years in Bettiah and learnt from the descendants of Pandit Shivdayal Mishra, who is said to have established dhrupad singing here. Since dhrupad was out of bounds for women, Sadabahar must have been taught informally, without being taken on as a disciple. Although she is not known to have ever publicly performed dhrupad or dhamar, you point out that the influence of her training in these musical genres was reflected in her rendition of thumri and hori. Some of those compositions came down the generations to you and others in the family.

Sadabahar also learnt music from Ustad Nabbu Khan, a khayal singer from a Khurja-based Kalawant family that had originally belonged to Delhi. She had been visiting some relatives in Calcutta when she met him at the home of a wealthy middle-aged tawaif, Sayeeda Bai, who was originally from Chainpur. The hugely talented Nabbu Khan was languishing in Calcutta for want of patrons. Sayeeda Bai, taking pity on his impoverished state, had taken him on as a lover-cum-teacher and provided him shelter, food and some pocket money.

However, she was now tiring of his constant complaints, his extended bouts of self-pity and his greed. He wanted her to buy him a house, so that his family back in Khurja could join him in Calcutta. Every time they were alone, Nabbu Khan would plead with Sayeeda to agree, assuming that she would finance his family's upkeep as she did his.

Sayeeda Bai had no patience for emotionally manipulative lovers. As a tawaif who had made a fortune out of playing with the hearts of wealthy patrons, she knew the game of love better than a down-and-out Kalawant. Thus, when Sadabahar met him, Nabbu Khan, though an amusing enough companion, a satisfactory lover and a great singer, was on his way to being thrown out of Sayeeda Bai's bed and her kotha.

Sadabahar was impressed by Nabbu Khan's mastery over khayal and his impeccable Kalawant family lineage, which could be traced back to Miyan Tansen himself. An association with him would greatly add to the lustre of her accomplishments as a tawaif. And so, she took him under her protection and brought him to Chainpur.

A small town in the rural backwaters of Bihar was not exactly the destination that Ustad Nabbu Khan had in mind when he had left Khurja at the age of thirty-five to seek his fortunes in Calcutta. But the ustad was a practical soul and, realising he had little choice, made himself comfortable in a spacious room overlooking a private terrace in Bullan and Kallan's sprawling home. For the next three or four years, in return for food, shelter and a far-from-modest allowance, he would add to Sadabahar's repertoire with the highly respected musical style associated with his family.

Practitioners of dhrupad and khayal, Kalawants enjoyed a pre-eminent position in the hierarchy of art music practitioners in the nineteenth century. About them, the Protestant missionary and colonial ethnographer Matthew Atmore Sherring writes, 'These are Mahomedan performers, but are much higher in rank than the Dharis; are regarded, indeed, as persons of reputation and respectability.'

Since Mughal times, Kalawants had enjoyed high prestige as favoured imperial musicians because of their mastery of dhrupad, the genre of music patronised by the court. They were also closely associated with the rise in popularity of khayal, which evolved as a more ornate and lively alternative to dhrupad, and found favour as court music during the reign of the Mughal ruler Muhammad Shah 'Rangila' in the mid-eighteenth century.

As members of established families of hereditary musicians who could trace their descent from well-known ancestors, the Kalawants' elite status was derived as much from the purity of their lineage as from the artistry of their music specialisation. Marrying exclusively within the group, the music tradition of a Kalawant family was passed down exclusively to direct patrilineal male descendants. While male students from outside the community were also taught, the corpus of old and rare musical repertoire, such as the achhop or hidden, secret ragas, was held within the family.

With the erosion of Mughal authority through the eighteenth and nineteenth centuries and its complete erasure with the revolt of 1857, Kalawant families had been forced to migrate from Delhi, which had thus far been their main centre of patronage, to various principalities of northern, central and western India. There was fierce competition among them to win patronage on the merit of the distinctive musical styles associated with different families. Reluctant to share their repertoire with outsiders, from the late nineteenth century, Kalawant families developed into unique musical institutions, the gharana.

Derived from the term ghar, or house, each gharana was distinguished by an impressive lineage of hereditary musicians, a select circle of disciples and a particular musical style that they represented. A premium was placed on teaching and practising in exactitude the distinguishing style of the founding fathers of the gharana, which was generally named after the hometown of the founders, or the place where it flourished. The late nineteenth century, for instance, saw the emergence of the Gwalior, Agra,

Khurja, Hapur, Secunderabad, Atrauli and Jaipur gharanas of khayal singing, of which the Gwalior gharana is considered the oldest.

Until well into the early twentieth century, gharanas did not formally recognise women disciples, either from within the Kalawant families or outside, as inheritors of their music tradition. Life stories of tawaifs and gharanedar musicians, however, reflect that individual Kalawants often did take on courtesan students, either impressed by their musical talent or attracted to the handsome fees offered. This was an informal arrangement and for relatively short periods of time as compared to the long-drawn-out education imparted to formally recognised male disciples.

Established tawaifs were often financially better placed than male musicians. Their musical repertoire, considered more accessible than the khayal practised by male ustads, enjoyed greater popularity with a broader spectrum of patrons. Besides, male musicians always complained, the physical charms of a woman musician gave her an unfair advantage. Whatever the reason, there are countless stories of wealthy tawaifs providing food, shelter and monetary remuneration to hard-up ustads in return for coveted gharana-based music learning. There are instances too of tawaifs helping gharanedar musicians find generous patrons.

Nabbu Khan could not become Sadabahar's lover as he had hoped. She had been mildly attracted to him as a man, but after a couple of unsatisfactory attempts at physical intimacy, it became obvious to her that Nabbu Khan would be best utilised as a teacher. In this department, he did not fail her. There was much—rare ragas, perfection in layakari and diverse new compositions—that Sadabahar learnt from him.

On her part, she was a generous and grateful student. Not only did she look after Ustad Nabbu Khan's material comforts during his stay in Chainpur but also made it a point to introduce him with lavish praise to all her powerful and wealthy patrons. Eventually, she put to use the high esteem in which she herself was held in Darbhanga to find a place for him there as a court musician.

Pyaari khala has woken up now. A bit disoriented by the unexpected return of electricity and the loud whirr of the generator outside, she looks around silently, eyes wide open. Then, with some effort, she asks Rajjo, who is sitting closest, about the source of the whirring sound. On being informed about Shambhu Lala's gift, her face creases into a delighted smile, 'That old miser! How his heart must have fluttered shelling out money for a generator! I know him so well. He gets even potato peels cooked in his home, he is that stingy. But for the sake of his bai's comfort he spends thousands on a generator!'

Her disparaging words are burnished with affection for her lala. Deeply disappointed about sleeping through his second visit, Pyaari khala reprimands her sisters and nieces for not waking her. She relents only when everyone solemnly assures her that lala and his grandsons were well cared for while they were here.

Unlike her sister and nieces, Pyaari does not seem to be troubled by the fact that Shambhu Lala has fulfilled a need that ought to have been Nawab and Wazir's responsibility. Turning to Sakeena, she says with obvious relief, 'Thank god for lala's generosity! My poor boys have been spared the bother of raising money for a generator. You tell them now to relax. I know how worried they have been on that count.'

While Sakeena musters a weak smile, Phoolmani snorts in disgust, 'Pyaari, you remain a fool! Those rascals you call boys are making merry with your money while doing nothing for you in return, and yet your heart still beats for them! When will you grow up?'

'Too late now, appi, for me to grow up. Allah Miyan is beckoning me back already,' Pyaari says wryly. Then adds earnestly, 'You are truly mistaken about Nawab and Wazir. They are good boys and have always loved me like their own mother. For my sake, I beg you to stop saying such terrible things about them.'

Phoolmani opens her mouth as if to make another retort but decides otherwise under Rajjo's disapproving stare. Having silenced her mother, Rajjo gently strokes Pyaari's hair. 'No one will say anything against Nawab and Wazir, khala.'

Patting Rajjo's cheek Pyaari calls her a 'good, sweet girl'. Her attention now turns to the cool breeze of the ceiling fan and the brightness of the well-lit room. With childlike delight, she savours her new comforts. Tiredness, however, soon overtakes her excitement. After one last loving look at the moving electric fan, Pyaari khala sinks back on to her pillow and drifts into sleep. The wet sound of the rain that's begun to beat down outside mingles with the constant whirring of the generator.

CHAPTER 6

Gulshan

GHAFURAN SLOWLY MAKES HER WAY up the straight and narrow stairs that lead from the ground floor of your house, where she lives, to the two rooms on the terrace that you use during your frequent visits to Bhabua. She holds a glass of warm, sweetened milk that you always drink at bedtime.

Sharp-featured, tall and slender, Ghafuran bears little physical similarity to you with your short and stout frame. Crumpled to your primly neat, she wears a worn-out sari that she seems to have carelessly thrown on. As she draws closer, I notice the heaviness of her walk, the dark circles under her eyes and the deep lines of exhaustion on her face. Ghafuran is your twin, but, as another long day draws to a close, she looks five to ten years older than you.

'Come on, sister, drink this milk quickly before it turns cold,' she says lightly. Sprawled out on the bed, dressed in a flowery kaftan, your eyes shut, you heave a contented sigh and gesture to her to leave the glass of milk on the adjoining table. Ghafuran's daughter Naseem is massaging your scalp and hair with warm coconut oil, while Shameem, her youngest, is busy kneading copious amounts of cold cream onto your face.

Ghafuran and I exchange an amused look. Pointing at you, Ghafuran says with an indulgent laugh, 'Someone should learn from her how to behave like a queen.' Though you get very little time off, you take leisure seriously. 'Just as it is important to work hard, it is as important to learn how to relax,' you often say, particularly to me. You frequently chide me for carrying my work around at all times.

Placing the glass of milk on the table, Ghafuran asks me politely, as she does every night, 'Are you sure you don't want milk? I can make tea if you like.' I assure her that I need nothing. Just as she turns around to leave, I suggest that she too get her head massaged.

Ghafuran smiles wryly, 'Who will clear the mess downstairs if I let down my hair and relax?' And before I can reply, she leaves the room quietly.

With your eyes closed, you mutter, 'There is no point asking her to relax. Her work and worries never get over.' Then, opening your eyes, you briskly order Naseem and Shameem to run downstairs and help their mother clean up for the night.

From the ground floor, I can hear the faint rattle of the sewing machine. Naeem is still at work in the front room that doubles as his tailoring shop during the day and a bedroom for him and Ghafuran at night. After clearing the dinner dishes, Ghafuran will join him, sewing on hooks and buttons way after all of us are asleep.

With eight children to bring up, life has been difficult for the couple. You are their only security. They live rent-free in the house that you built when your career was at its zenith. Although you did not shift here as originally planned, the house came in handy when Ghafuran and Naeem were forced to move out of his family home. Your twin describes you as her 'brother', a protective anchor for her and her family.

Ghafuran's children address you as badki amma, or older mother. You have subsidised their education, sent them the clothes your children had outgrown, financed the marriages of the two older daughters and promised help with the weddings of the two younger girls. Ghafuran's four sons have all at some point or other lived for long periods in your Banaras house. Monty, her third-born, shares your home now and works as a shop assistant at a sari store in Nariyal Bazaar, a job that you have arranged through your vast network of acquaintances and well-wishers.

Ghafuran, in turn, has shunted over the years between her home in Bhabua and yours in Banaras to look after your house and children as their chhutki amma, or younger mother. You have needed her presence during your long absences from home as a tawaif, and even now, well into your retirement, it is Ghafuran who comes and takes charge in the event of celebrations or emergencies. When your older daughter Shama got married, Ghafuran stayed for several months to look after the domestic arrangements before and after the wedding. Similarly, when your grandson Haaris was born, it was Ghafuran again who took charge of Salma and the baby. During Meenu's engagement, she was the one to maintain household order. You are, she chuckled once, clueless about such matters.

'She can work hard like an ox, go out into the world and earn for the family, but my poor sister knows little about how to run a house,' Ghafuran has told me more than once. She takes obvious pride in your 'manly' qualities. She is your house-bound 'feminine' twin.

You say this is how your relationship has been since childhood when, left largely to your own resources by an overstretched mother, you and Ghafuran learnt to look after each other. Tied by bonds of love, loyalty and interdependence, as both of you grew older, one a tawaif and the other a wife, you have always shared your responsibilities and duties.

I remember the pride with which you made Naseem sing for me the other night. Never taught music, Naseem knows either patriotic songs she has learnt in school or film songs she hears on television. Without needing much coaxing, she sang *Aye watan, aye watan, humko teri kasam, teri rahon mein jaan tak luta jayenge*; O' beloved country we pledge, For you, we will sacrifice our lives. The song, dedicated to the revolutionary martyr Bhagat Singh, is from the 1960s film *Shaheed*.

The girl has a good voice and is naturally tuneful. She is also very pretty. There was a time when Naseem would have been trained by the family to become a tawaif. In the present, though, you had brought the house down when well-wishers of Ghafuran and Naeem suggested that Naseem, like some other girls from tawaif families in Bhabua, be sent to Mumbai to become a bar dancer.

I was with you in Banaras when Ghafuran tentatively broached the subject. She sounded open to the idea. But you were furious. Had she taken complete leave of her senses, you thundered at your twin. Were she and Naeem so greedy for a few extra currency notes that they were willing to throw mud over all the sacrifices that the family had made to gain community respect? They were welcome to send Naseem to Mumbai, you said, your lips drawn in a thin line, but only after severing all ties with you and your family. This dire warning ended any further talk of making Naseem a bar dancer. She stayed on in her Bhabua home, helping her mother with housework and waiting for the marriage that you would in due course arrange for her.

The incident made me aware of the iron that lies covered in the velvet of your outer being. I saw it again when you heard of Shameem's romantic involvement with a boy the family considered unsuitable. You have always described Shameem as Ghafuran's 'wild' daughter. The boy she fell passionately in love with was from your neighbourhood in Bhabua. His mother had been a tawaif once, though you believe she conducted herself little better than a nachaniya. This went against Shameem's boyfriend, but it was the fact that he did no work and lived off the earnings of his sister, who was a bar dancer in Mumbai, that truly negated his prospects.

I was in Delhi at the time but heard from you over the phone about the daily unfolding developments. Reaching Bhabua as soon as you heard of Shameem's love affair, you first vented your wrath on Ghafuran and Naeem for being careless parents, granting their daughters the freedom to roam around as they pleased in the neighbourhood. Your own girls were never allowed to leave home unescorted. Under your orders, Shameem was brought to Banaras. I was aghast to learn that you kept her under lock and key in your house to ensure that she did not elope. Next, you met with the boy's mother. And though you were uncharacteristically cagey about sharing with me the details of your conversation, it resulted in the boy being packed off for good to Mumbai to 'look after' his sister there.

Shameem was heartbroken. Released from her prison and allowed to return to Bhabua, she spent several months talking to her boyfriend on the phone and perhaps plotting her escape. When, after repeated entreaties, he failed to give her the commitment she sought, Shameem, all of sixteen years, was forced to confront her life's first major disappointment. After brooding and sulking for a long time, she was finally reconciled to reality. And much to your relief, she even made peace with you, where earlier she had refused to speak with you directly.

Shameem's goalposts too have shifted. Academically the brightest of the siblings, she now nurses ambitions of a college degree, a job in the big city and an independent life. Her hopes rest on you. Her parents, especially her father, were desperate to get her married once her love affair became public knowledge. But you supported Shameem and helped her reach the final year of school. Partly, I suspect, you were working your way back into your niece's heart. But more importantly, you truly believe in the life-transforming possibilities of education. Your daughter Meenu is a graduate, thanks to your consistent pressure. Trained to shrewdly evaluate the potential of daughters, you have bolder dreams for Shameem. You want her to become an officer sitting behind an impressive desk in a grand office, rewriting the history of your family. To this end, you finance her computer classes in Bhabua and encourage her efforts to learn spoken English from self-help guides.

Ghafuran has often held you up to me as an example of a true tawaif—honourable, strong-willed, wise and fierce when the need arises to protect the family. She rarely talks about herself. 'I am just a housewife,' she says whenever I ask about her life. Aptly, the only story that this quiet, diffident woman has told me is that of Sadabahar's twin, Gulshan, who remains a shadowy figure in your family's chronicles. Neither you nor your tawaif sister, cousins and aunts have ever seemed interested in remembering or recounting her history, although I have asked several times.

From childhood, Ghafuran tells me, Gulshan had no interest in the tawaif's way of life. Forever compared to her winsome twin, she grew up into a shy, nervous and hesitant girl. Unlike Sadabahar, who passionately loved not only the seven notes that make music but also the bright lights of the mehfil, the bold-eyed appraisal of male admirers, the excitement of travelling to strange, new lands, the shimmer of silk and the glitter of gold, Gulshan found sustenance in the security of home, the warmth and familiarity of known, loved faces. Bullan and Kallan, therefore, secured for Gulshan the domesticity they thought would suit her best. Around the same time that Sadabahar made her debut as a courtesan, Gulshan was married off to the son of a tawaif family in Chainpur.

'But Gulshan had pain written in her destiny,' Ghafuran says with a sigh. 'For nearly five years after her marriage, she remained childless. Her pregnancies would either end in miscarriage or in stillbirth if they reached full term. She was routinely humiliated by her husband and his family for carrying a cursed womb. When finally, she did give birth, it was to a son. Worse, the boy was born blind. Bitterly disappointed, her husband and his family threatened to throw Gulshan out if she did not produce a daughter soon.'

To everyone's relief, Gulshan's next child was a girl. There were celebrations not just in her husband's family but also in her natal home. Happy that her sister would finally be accepted in her husband's house, Sadabahar fed the poor, lit lamps filled with ghee and made offerings of thanksgiving at all the mosques and temples in Chainpur.

This joy proved short-lived. Gulshan's baby girl died within six months of birth. Several failed pregnancies later, Gulshan gave birth to yet another boy. Discarded as useless by her husband and his family, she was finally thrown out of their house. Along with her two sons, Gulshan returned to her foster mothers' home. Her two little boys, Bullah Miyan and Sa'dullah Miyan became the responsibility of her twin Sadabahar, who promised to look after them as she would her own children.

Gulshan's life makes for chilling listening. It is a familiar story in India, except for one critical difference: it is the mothers of daughters who are humiliated and abused in patriarchal families that worship sons but think little of killing baby girls in the womb.

In the tawaif community, on the other hand, the birth of a daughter was an occasion for celebration and thanksgiving. As future breadwinners, girls were coveted and loved, while boys were treated as unwelcome burdens, a drain on the family's resources. With little role to play in the economy of a tawaif household, boys were the forgotten children of the family. Deprived of the attention and indulgence that daughters marked out to become tawaifs received, boys usually grew up without schooling or any other work-related training. Very few, if any, men from the tawaif community learnt music, and even those who did were never considered good enough to become accompanists, a role reserved for professional musicians from hereditary castes.

Some men in tawaif families played supportive roles as escorts or errand-doers for the earning women; a minuscule few, in the absence of older retired tawaifs in the family, even took on the task of managing the careers of their sisters, daughters and nieces. Most simply did nothing. Receiving 'pocket money' for their personal expenses from their mothers, sisters, daughters, even adult men were treated as children. This relationship of dependence is reflected most vividly in the term 'baap–bhai', or father–brother, used within the community as a synonym for a parasitic life.

'You one-eyed donkey, when will you learn to serve tea less clumsily,' Rajjo's harsh tones slice through the mellow glow in Pyaari khala's room as old, cataract-ridden Mamu Farid shuffles in with a tray laden with teacups. Son of a long-dead cousin, he is an integral though largely invisible part of Rajjo's house in Banaras. Phoolmani laughs out loud, joined by the other tawaif matriarchs in the room, including you. Mamu Farid keeps serving tea and biscuits with a shamed, miserable smile.

He is the family's sad clown. It is a role he has played ever since he was a little boy brought up on the charity of his tawaif sisters in Bhabua. When Rajjo shifted to Banaras to set up kotha there, Mamu Farid was sent along as male escort and attendant. It's been over fifty years that he has been general handyman and errand-runner in her home. In return, Rajjo has provided him with food and shelter. When in a generous mood, she even gives him some money to buy the afeem, opium, he licks on the sly, and usually turns a blind eye to his petty pilfering when his craving is greater than the cash in his pocket.

The scorching manner in which Rajjo shouts at Mamu Farid is a shock to me; she's amiable enough otherwise. She often calls him a thief, a lazy lout, a liar. Mamu Farid never protests, although occasionally, Ghafuran, braving derisive comments from her relatives, speaks out in his defence. Her empathy for Mamu Farid is, perhaps, fuelled by protectiveness of her own husband Naeem's dignity. As the wife of a tawaif's son, she understands only too well the mix of contempt and pity with which men in courtesan households were treated for being born 'boys'.

Dismissed as unreliable and too weak to take responsibility or to negotiate the world outside, Naeem too was treated by his mother and sisters as a liability. His daily humiliation at their hands made Ghafuran's blood boil with helpless rage. Luckily for her, she had you for support, and was able to muster the courage to convince Naeem to leave his family home.

It had not been easy. Brought up with little confidence in his own worth or abilities, Naeem was panic-struck at the thought of leaving the daily little tyrannies of his mother's household for the unknown terrors outside. His limited tailoring skills, acquired through his own initiative as a boy, were completely untried and rusty. Without his mother to support them, how would he and his family survive, he fretted.

Little wonder then that, when he finally agreed to leave his family house and seek sanctuary in yours, he sought and found in you an authority figure to take the place left vacant by his mother. As an earning man and the husband of Ghafuran whom you love dearly, Naeem is spared the taunts and ridicule that are the lot of Mamu Farid. But only just. His meekness and status of being a ghar jamai, a man living in his in-laws' home, his poverty and intermittent dependence on your support to provide for his children, make Naeem the recipient of a curious dismissive deference from you and your extended family.

Addressed by all except the older women as 'dulhe bhai', or bridegroom brother, Naeem has little say in the decisions, major or minor, made by you for his family. 'You don't need to bother your head with all this', or 'Leave it, dulhe bhai, you won't understand this', is your routine response on the few occasions when Naeem does try and intervene in a family matter. His desire to marry off Shameem after her aborted affair counted for little in the face of your decision that she must continue her schooling. He was able to prevail upon Jawed to join him in work after he finished his matriculation only because you chose to turn a deaf ear to the boy's appeals and seconded Naeem's decision.

A wispy presence in the house, Naeem's life centres in the daytime on his sewing machine and by early evening on his bottle of country liquor. During times when the family didn't have the security of their next meal, you stepped in not only as bread-giver but also as provider of Naeem's daily drink. You reason that his drinking has never come in the way of his attempts to earn for his family. Quietly sipping his glass of hooch, Naeem, red-eyed and flush-faced, pedals away on his sewing machine till late into the night.

Men, you say seriously, almost compassionately, remain childlike and emotionally frail even as adults. They need something to get through the harshness of life. In the old days, addiction to alcohol and drugs was commonplace among men in your community, you tell me. At times indulgently, most times grudgingly, their mothers, sisters and daughters supported their addiction in the belief that this was what men did.

Women, on the other hand, you maintain, are made of sterner stuff. Many tawaifs smoked or chewed tobacco. Some, in the company of lovers also took to drinking and even occasionally smoking marijuana. Most did not become slaves to their indulgence—with vast families to support, they simply could not afford to. Moreover, it was believed that, while moderate consumption of alcohol might benefit music practice, alcoholism was ruinous for a tawaif singer. Many, like you, abjured alcohol completely.

Some feminist scholars have focused upon the reversal of socially sanctioned gender rules in their exploration of tawaif lifestyle in the kotha. While the affirmation that the tawaif received from her family has been extolled, there has been silence about the discrimination borne not only by male members of tawaif households but also by daughters who were groomed for marriage.

You and others have said that the decision to become a tawaif or be married was one that a girl was allowed to make for herself once she reached puberty. Most girls, including you, had voluntarily chosen to become tawaifs. On the other hand, I remember Ghafuran's silence when I asked if she had chosen marriage as her destiny. Evading my eye, she looked deep into her tailor's box, as if searching for an answer amongst the hooks, buttons and zippers.

Finally, after a very long pause, she murmured, 'I can't remember. It was so long ago.'

To my next question, about whether she regretted being married, all that Ghafuran was willing to say was, 'This is destiny. I was destined to be a wife and so I was married. We mere mortals should not question Allah's will.'

My conversations with a large cross-section of people, including former tawaifs, other members of courtesan families and accompanist musicians, seem to suggest that, while theoretically, the choice was left to the girl, the weeding-out process took place in childhood itself. A family could decide not to invest the considerable resources needed to educate and groom a daughter to become a tawaif if it became obvious from early on that she did not possess the requisite talents. Admittedly, it was not a choice tawaif families were happy to make, given that their survival depended on the earnings of daughters. Former tawaifs and male accompanist musicians like Shanney Khan told me stories of families who tried desperately to train their musically challenged daughter in music and dance, only to be advised by teachers and other well-wishers to not waste resources on a girl who had limited prospects as a performer and would be better off being trained in the domestic chores of a purdanasheen grihasthan, a purdah-observing housewife.

Whether there were instances of families forcing a daughter eager to be married to become a tawaif is not recorded in courtesan narratives. Everyone across the community categorically stated that the few girls who did choose to become wives were married off by their families. The tawaif's way of life, it was stressed, needed a certain temperament, or tabiyat, which included a love and talent for music and dance, but equally, assertiveness, fearlessness and independence of mind and spirit.

A girl could be forced to learn music and dance, but the tabiyat, I was told, could never be forcibly instilled. A timid girl, always seeking protection, simply could not make it as a tawaif. She was better off married.

The polarity between a tawaif's way of life and that of a purdanasheen grihasthan was a valorised ideal in the kotha. It was also a zealously enforced norm. The physical layout of a tawaif home was defined on the basis of purdah. While the first floor or front rooms, as the case might be, were reserved by norm for the kotha or salon—where male outsiders, including accompanist musicians, visitors and patrons, were received by the tawaif—the secluded upper storeys or back rooms, including the kitchen, was the domain of the purdah-observing daughters and daughters-in-law in the family. In these domestic quarters of a tawaif household, accessible only to relatives, the family carried on with its everyday life.

References to the observance of purdah in tawaifs' quarters can be found as early as in the eighteenth-century novel *Nashtar*, the love story of a young man of noble birth, Hasan Shah, and a tawaif, Khanum Jan, who belonged to a travelling troupe of performers. When the troupe is visited by a courtesan Mewa Jan and her foster daughter, who has been brought up in purdah to be married off, a portion of the tawaifs' tents are accordingly secluded from male outsiders to become suitable accommodation for the purdah-bound girl.

In the early twentieth-century account of the lifestyle and culture associated with Lucknow, *Qadeem Lucknow ki Aakhri Bahaar* (The Last Spring of old Lucknow), author Mirza Jafar Hussain writes about the zenanakhana, women's quarters, located in the back portion of the palatial home of the leading tawaif sisters, Nanuha and Bichhua Jan in the Chowk area of the city. The front portion housed the reception hall and visitors' rooms, while the zenanakhana was the family residence in which lived the brothers, their wives and children in seclusion. Similarly, there are mentions of purdah-based living arrangements within kothas in *Yeh Kothewaliyan* (These Women of the Kothas), a journalistic account by Amritlal Nagar of the declining fortunes of tawaifs in Lucknow in the late 1950s. While talking about the daughters-in-law in courtesan families, one of the tawaifs interviewed by the author says, 'We all live in one house. But the house is partitioned into two. Our section is the bazaar (open to all) while their section is the actual home, closed to outsiders.'

Daughters marked out for domesticity and marriage in tawaif households were rarely, if ever, allowed to venture into the outer rooms or interact with the visitors who were received there. A premium was placed on the virginity of prospective brides in tawaif homes, just as in male-centred families.

Over the years of our acquaintance, Ghafuran, initially guardedly but later more openly, has described to me the austere, cloistered life that Teema, your mother, compelled her to lead. She was kept away not only from music and dance but also the vivacious conversation, coquettish airs and charming manners that you and Asghari were encouraged to learn from the older tawaifs. Girls destined to be wives should not behave like tawaifs, Teema would say. Ghafuran would be better off taking lessons in cooking, cleaning, docility and obedience.

Forced to make do with cast-me-downs so that she might get used to the want that was part of a married woman's life, Ghafuran remembers longing for the pretty clothes, glittering bangles and twinkling earrings worn by Asghari, already a tawaif by the time she was growing up. With childlike vehemence, Ghafuran asserts that Teema loved her as much as she loved Asghari and you. And yet Teema refused to indulge her for fear of making her too 'soft' to adjust to the harshness of life as a daughter-in-law in another household.

Life in Naeem's home had indeed been difficult. As the wife of a dependent, non-earning son, Ghafuran's status was, if possible, even lower than Naeem's. While he at the least received pocket money from his mother, Ghafuran, like the other daughters-in-law of the family, had no income at all.

Expected to provide unpaid domestic and reproductive labour—cooking, cleaning, sewing and producing children for the benefit of their husband's family—married women like Ghafuran enjoyed no rights either in their mother's property or that of their mother-in-law. Their only hope lay in giving birth to daughters who, if they were groomed by their husband's family to become tawaifs, might take better care of their mothers. With the changing times, Ghafuran's hopes today rest on her sons. Meanwhile, she looks upon you as her protector from homelessness and want—and occasionally, even from Naeem.

I noticed one morning the bruises that spread blue-black on the paleness of Ghafuran's neck and shoulder, which she kept covering with her sari while feeding us breakfast. She said a heavy bag hanging on a nail above her bed had fallen on her while she was sleeping. Your eyes narrowed but you said nothing. Much later, after dinner, I happened to pass by Ghafuran's room on the ground floor and overheard you talking to Naeem, 'Dulhe bhai, it is time you controlled your drinking. You have a daughter-in-law in the house now. How will she respect her mother-in-law if she sees her with bruises all over her body?' A bit embarrassed about overhearing a conversation not meant for me, I hurried off upstairs.

Next morning, when Ghafuran came up with freshly washed and ironed clothes, you muttered without preamble, to no one in particular, 'Men will be men.' Then shaking your head dismissively, you added, 'Even those men who are powerless and meek lambs otherwise, even with their own children, vent their masculinity on their wives.'

Ghafuran leapt to her husband's defence. 'He is a good man. Sometimes, the combination of frustration and alcohol gets the better of him, but you know as well as I how much he regrets it later.' She then quickly left the room to begin cooking lunch.

Following her retreating figure with admiring eyes, you said to me, 'My sister is a gem. She will not hear a word against her husband even when he is in the wrong. A lesser woman would have fought back, even threatened to leave, but not my Ghafuran!'

Marriage has been a fervently guarded institution in the community. While tawaif daughters could and did exercise relative freedom in their choice of patrons and lovers, marriage was a one-way street. Fidelity in married women was highly valued, and so, once a girl was married, she couldn't walk out of the arrangement and become a tawaif, or she would be ostracised by the entire community. A woman's natal or marital family too were forbidden from making her join the profession once she was married; the defaulting family would be punished with a heavy fine and excommunicated.

Customary rules were relatively less harsh about remarriage for women who were either abandoned by husbands or widowed. And yet, remarriage was frowned upon among the upper echelons of the tawaif community, especially if the woman had children from her first marriage.

For the brave women who dared to run away from unsatisfactory marriages, remarriage came at a high cost. Customary laws ordained that the second husband's family financially compensate the previous one for the loss of a productive daughter-in-law. Besides, there was the social stigma faced by the woman's natal family, especially in the higher ranks of the community. The fear of losing face made families like yours force their daughters to continue in bad marriages and waste little time in snapping links with them if they failed to meet their expectations.

Though times are changing, and I do hear about divorces in the community, the shame attached to a woman separated from her husband is still high. You have told me that, in the initial years of marriage, before her children were born, Ghafuran had pleaded with you to be allowed a way out of the grinding poverty and daily humiliation she faced as Naeem's wife. You, on the advice of family elders like Pyaari khala and Phoolmani, had offered support on the firm condition that Ghafuran would continue in her marriage to Naeem. Else, she would have to fend for herself.

Nearly a century ago, Gulshan would have had fewer choices still. The option of becoming a tawaif was barred. She could have been remarried within the community. But who would marry a woman well past her youth and with two sons in tow? Even if her family had been able to find a suitable second husband for Gulshan, would she have been willing to face a possible repeat of the same misery?

On the other hand, she would have known the claustrophobic, dependent and back-breaking existence awaiting her as an abandoned wife in the home of her mothers and sister. Treated for most of her adult life as no better than a womb attached to a pair of hands, Gulshan would now be expected to spend endless hours in the kitchen cooking for Sadabahar's many visitors and admirers. She would wash and clean and keep the house worthy of her sister's status as the leading tawaif of Shahabad. And she would live out her remaining years clothed in hand-me-downs, fed on leftovers and bathed in rancid pity.

Her foster mothers and sister might have, in their own way, cared for the unfortunate Gulshan; perhaps they even loved her. And yet, she wouldn't have expected them to give her, a wife castaway by her husband for giving birth to sons, more than was considered appropriate in the community. Their position as members of a leading tawaif family in Shahabad was dependent on living within the boundaries sanctified by the community.

For days after her return to her natal home, Gulshan withdrew into the windowless, cell-like room next to the kitchen that had been allotted to her. She hardly ate or slept or talked. Bullan, Kallan and Sadabahar let her be. It was natural they thought that Gulshan should be mourning the end of her days as a wife. Once her grief ebbed, they felt sure, the always-docile Gulshan would submit to her new life in her old home.

Little did they realise that, sitting in her dark, airless cell, Gulshan was dreaming of realms far beyond the hemmed-in horizons sanctioned for women like her. Miraculously, the years of deprivation, neglect and abuse had kindled in Gulshan a desperate desire to reclaim her lost life. To live, finally free of the duties and responsibilities of a purdah-bound woman.

One moonless night, when everyone had gone to sleep, she rose from the floor and wrapped herself in a black shawl. Then she tiptoed into Bullan and Kallan's room, where her sons Bullah and Sa'dullah slept next to their grandmothers. Embracing them in a gaze full of love and longing, Gulshan turned away and silently made her way out of the sprawling house. Resisting the desire to look back, she stepped into the inky darkness outside and left behind her the night.

CHAPTER 7

Nachney Ganey Wala Samaj

As I SCRAMBLE PAST AN open garbage dump in the centre of the vegetable market in Bhabua, it occurs to me that I will have a difficult time describing your hometown. The term that comes to mind is nondescript. Bhabua looks no different from the countless grimy, thoughtlessly put-together settlements that dot northern India. The much-awaited monsoons have made it even shabbier, and decidedly more uncomfortable to negotiate. My chappals squelch in the muddy rivulet that in dry weather serves as a potholed, filth-littered thoroughfare. The drains have flowed over and generously contribute their offal to the flooded streets. If indeed there are authorities of the state responsible for the upkeep of this bedraggled town, their presence is marked only on the numerous signboards of badly constructed buildings housing sundry arms of district governance.

In colonial records, Bhabua sounds like a blighted place, frequently visited by floods, famine and epidemics of fevers, the plague, influenza, smallpox and cholera. Then, and in the decades following Independence, the town was the headquarters of a subdivision, also named Bhabua, in Shahabad. In 1972, it became part of the newly created Rohtas district, but deprivation and disease still stalked the town. On the rare occasion that Bhabua found mention in contemporary newspapers, it was usually on account of an epidemic threat or a citizens' protest over the absence of sanitation, electricity and drinking water.

The town's prospects seemingly brightened in 1991, when Kaimur district was carved out of Rohtas, and Bhabua got promoted to district headquarters. But to my outsider's eyes, the elevation in status seems to have brought little change to the state of decrepitude, neglect and lack of basic civic amenities that has been its lot through the past century and more.

I am in for a surprise though when I share my thoughts with you, a Bhabua girl. 'But Bhabua was such a great centre of music and dance! People came from far to hear the singing of tawaifs in this town. It was known as Lahura Banaras, Little Banaras, since the singers and dancers from Bhabua were as accomplished as those in that city, and many eventually made a name for themselves there. I have heard from my mother and aunts about the beautiful evenings in Bhabua when the town echoed with music wafting out of the many kothas here.

'In those days, the tawaifs in the town were khandani, belonging to lineage-based old courtesan families. They had principles. No tawaif would ever agree to enter into a relationship with a patron already involved with someone else in the community.

'I was born in Bhabua and spent several years of my childhood here. All the tawaifs, Hindu and Muslim, lived side by side. While playing, we would run in and out of all the houses in the neighbourhood as if they were our own. To tell you the truth, although I have made Banaras my permanent address, I still think of Bhabua as my watan, homeland. There is much more warmth here, people genuinely care for each other.'

You pause a tad uncertainly at this point. Perhaps the twin images of the uncaring Nawab and Wazir rise in your mind's eye.

'Of course there are people everywhere who are small-hearted and selfish,' you add a footnote. 'But look at the way Pyaari khala is being cared for by the entire neighbourhood. And you must have noticed the respect with which I am greeted even today by others, the non-tawaif families of this town, especially those who have lived here for generations. My identity is not hidden from them. But they have seen the true culture of tawaifs and, therefore, don't look down on us.'

Our narratives of Bhabua seem to run parallel to each other without crossing paths. While I notice only the civic disrepair, you talk of its people. And yet, as you step gingerly around the many garbage heaps, I hear you softly curse the sarkar, government, that has abandoned the people of Bhabua to their fate. So you do see the flooding, the filth and flies. But for you, Bhabua is home, invested with history, memory and the daily experience of living with others; beautiful in ways that as an outsider I cannot see.

We have reached your modest, two-storey house located at the centre of the former tawaifs' quarters of Bhabua. It looks no different from the other, slightly poorer localities of the town. Time and changed circumstances have taken their toll. Even the once-imposing houses of wealthier tawaifs look badly in need of a coat of paint. Many former tawaifs have moved away and either sold off their properties or rented them out. As a result, you inform me, the neighbourhood has several 'outsider' families.

You point out the motor-repair, tailoring and weaving workshops, a private English-medium 'convent' school, computer training and internet centres, and even an institute teaching spoken English. Bhabua, as I see it through your eyes, is no longer the early twentieth-century municipal town that could boast of only one public building: a sub-jail large enough to accommodate fourteen prisoners. The total population of Bhabua in 1901 amounted to a modest 5,660 men, women and children. And it is to this town that Sadabahar and her family fled after the terrifying turn of events in Chainpur. A rather strange story, it was one of the earliest you narrated to me.

'Once, the raja sahib of Bhagwanpur was presiding over a full court, with the prince and courtiers in attendance. Perhaps it was a function to celebrate the prince's wedding. Sadabahar was singing and everyone was spellbound. Unnoticed, a cobra slithered onto the prince's lap. As the song came to a close, people saw the snake and panicked. The cobra's head was huge and it had the mark of a crescent moon on its forehead.'

Trained to mime words with action, you made graceful movements of your hands to outline the approximate size of the cobra's skull and drew an arc above your eyes to mark out the crescent moon. 'Naturally, everyone present got up to kill the snake but Sadabahar requested that its life be spared. At this, the courtiers drew their swords at Sadabahar and said, "Your singing has drawn this snake here. Your singing must make it go back. Else you will be beheaded." She agreed and resumed singing. As if mesmerised, the cobra lay absolutely still in the prince's lap while Sadabahar sang.

'Suddenly, hearing the sound of the azan, Sadabahar stopped and, folding her hands, addressed the cobra, "Maharaj, it is time for my prayers. I have to take your leave now." The cobra then slid off the prince's lap and, without harming anyone, made its way out of the court. Pleased with Sadabahar, the raja rewarded her with the title of Koeli, nightingale. As a mark of his appreciation, he also gifted her with fifty-two bighas of land.'

But Sadabahar and her mothers were not destined to claim the land as their own. Family lore has it that it was guarded by seven djinns, who resided in seven pots of gold buried under the land. When the family slept, the djinns would enter their dreams and say, 'Please take over the land and gold from us.' Their condition was that either the first-born male child or an ox be sacrificed in return.

Much as the family wanted the land and the riches, how could they agree to such a condition? It would have meant sacrificing Bullah, Gulshan's first-born. Sadabahar, childless herself, loved her nephew deeply. Since the boy had been born blind, she had always felt great protectiveness towards him. They could not sacrifice an ox either. That would amount to slaughtering a cow, and cause offence to the religious sentiments of Hindu neighbours, patrons and acquaintances.

Deciding to get rid of the djinn-infested land, Sadabahar gave it away for free to a local teli, oil presser and seller. Dismissing her story about the djinns and their demands as foolish fancy, he began tilling the land without first making the sacrifice that she had warned him about. Soon, his entire family perished. Only one child survived, and he was sickly and of unsound mind.

Sadabahar's woes were not over, though. Every night, a snake would come and coil itself on blind Bullah's chest. The door to his room was secured with seven locks and yet the snake would sneak in. It was the same cobra that had appeared on the prince's lap when Sadabahar was performing. In love with Sadabahar's voice, it had followed her home. Every night she had to sing while it swayed on poor Bullah's chest. At dawn, it would leave without harming the boy.

Desperate to be rid of this unwanted admirer, Sadabahar appealed to the presiding deity of Chainpur, Harshu Brahm. The Brahmin ghost advised Sadabahar to lure the snake to his temple with her singing. So, one night, when the cobra appeared, Sadabahar sang an exceptionally sweet basant, a song of spring, which you say belongs exclusively to your family.

Ayo basant mana le suhagan, apne piya ko mein paoon,
Pehla basant nabi ji key dwarey,
Phoolon ney mangal gaya, pariyon ney dhol bajaya.

Spring is here, celebrate O lovely one and claim the love of your life!
Let the first spring of love be celebrated at the doorsteps of
the Prophet
To auspicious songs sung by flowers and to the beat of drums played
by fairies.

As she sang, Sadabahar walked backwards, one step at a time, towards Harshu Brahm's temple, which was a considerable distance away. Enthralled, the cobra followed her all the way. At the temple, Harshu Brahm chanted magic incantations to create a snare made of seven spells and trapped the snake.

The ghost then told Sadabahar that he could not commit the sin of either killing a cobra or imprisoning it forever. He advised her to leave Chainpur and go away to a place where the snake would not be able to find her and her family. And so it was that Sadabahar, along with her elderly mothers and young nephews, fled her home in Chainpur and settled down in Bhabua.

I haven't quite known what to make of this story of the family's flight from Chainpur. Was there some reason so unspeakable that it had to be cloaked in allegories of serpent admirers and magic spells? The family's choice of refuge, however, made perfect sense. Bullan and Kallan owned a small house in Bhabua and some agricultural land in its immediate vicinity, gifted to them by a Rajput patron from a neighbouring village. The house would provide shelter, and the land would bring in grain and some income to sustain the family till Sadabahar established her presence in the thriving tawaif community of the town.

Bhabua had long elicited comment in colonial records on account of its inordinately large proportion of 'prostitutes' to the total population. They were described as belonging to the Gandharva and Nat communities. Their prevalence in Bhabua and its surrounds seems to have been so widespread, in fact, that they were said to be found in 'almost every big village' besides the exclusive settlements of Nats in various places in the subdivision.

Traditionally, courtesans from the Gandharva community were the elite among tawaifs in Bhabua, as in Banaras. Their high ranking accrued in large measure, I was told, to their patronage by the local aristocracy and their raga-based music practice. They invested time, effort and money to learn music and dance from the best possible teachers.

Even today, although most Gandharva families I met during my travels have long snapped their links with music and dance, they continue to be the wealthiest in the community, with their children well placed in different professional spheres. Asghari had introduced me to her best friend, Kameshwari Bai, an erstwhile tawaif belonging to a prominent old Gandharva family in Bhabua, when she dropped by one day to share gossip, paan and a cup of tea. While one of her sons is a public works contractor, the other works for a pharmaceutical company. Her three daughters are educated and married into notable Gandharva families.

Kameshwari Bai described the Gandharvas as originally being celestial musicians and dancers in the court of the Vedic god, Indra. Then, one day, Indra's favourite dancer broke the rule that forbade any alliance with mere mortals, by falling in love with a prince and eloping with him. Furious at this transgression, Indra punished the entire Gandharva community by banishing them from the heavens forever and condemning them to life as mortals on earth. Here too the Gandharvas continued to practise music and dance, ever wandering new lands in search of patrons.

This story tracing their origins to celestial musicians and dancers feeds into the claims made by Gandharva tawaifs to high caste and elite status within the courtesan community. I subsequently heard several versions of this legend from other members of the Gandharva community, both in Bhabua and in Banaras.

The most recurrent one traced the origins of the Gandharva tawaifs to Urvashi, the apsara, or celestial courtesan, who fell in love with the mortal prince Puruvasa and lived with him on earth for several years. She eventually left Puruvasa when he was forced to break his promise that he would never allow her to see him naked. The story finds reference in the Puranas and the Mahabharata.

In the version that I heard from members of the Gandharva community, since Urvashi had consorted with a mortal man and become pregnant by him, she was not allowed back into the heavens and was cursed instead to become a swan and inhabit the waters below. She was subsequently reunited with Puruvasa who, recognising the beautiful swan as his lost Urvashi, begged the gods for mercy. Taking pity on the lovers, the gods transformed Urvashi into a woman, and then she and Puruvasa lived happily together. Their progeny, in the contemporary telling of the myth, were the ancestors of the Gandharva tawaifs—a community living predominantly in the areas of eastern UP and Bihar.

References to the Gandharva can be found in medieval accounts, where they are classified as musicians who knew both Desi and Marga ragas, new and old ragas respectively. In colonial accounts from the nineteenth century, the term finds mention in the context of the hereditary, family-based practice of music and dance by women of the Gandharb or Gandharva community. While describing the different classes of 'dancing girls' in early nineteenth-century Shahabad, Buchanan wrote: 'Gandharvinis hold a still higher rank; and admit none to their embraces but Hindus of pure birth and consequences. No one disputes the purity of their birth, nor scruples to drink water from their hand.'

Buchanan's observations were corroborated by almost everyone I spoke with in Bhabua and Banaras. Positioning themselves historically as 'highborn' within the brahminical caste system, Gandharva tawaifs, I was told, took on as lovers only 'high-caste' Hindu men. Although they did accept invitations to perform for Muslim rulers and aristocracy, rarely did a Gandharva tawaif openly enter into a sexual relationship with a Muslim patron. A century ago, the community would have excommunicated such a tawaif. In more recent history, the rules had become a bit more relaxed but to take on a Muslim lover, however highborn, would still earn social censure.

Almost everyone I spoke with, including Gandharva and non-Gandharva tawaifs, and male musicians, seemed very willing to share narratives about the community. On the other hand, my attempts to learn about the social history of tawaifs from the Nat community, who find mention in colonial records about Bhabua, ran into choppy waters from the start. My questions were usually met with silence, evasion, partial truths—the extent of which I realised only as I began piecing together the puzzle of the Nat tawaifs of Bhabua.

Since your family traces its history in the town to roughly the late nineteenth century, I asked you about the Nat tawaifs referred to in the census records of 1901. Instead of answering me directly, you chose to talk about Bhabua's Gandharva and Muslim tawaifs.

When I asked about the caste of the Muslim tawaifs, including that of your own family, Asghari, who was also present, replied that artistes had no zaat or sectarian identity. 'Singers and musicians keep getting divided into different biradari, brotherhoods or clans. Some claim to be of one biradari, others to some other. Beyond these superficial differences, we are all really one, united by our love and practise of music and dance.'

Asghari looked pleased at her espousal of these lofty ideals. You too nodded sanctimoniously. And I felt more than a bit bewildered. After all, Asghari had been happy enough to talk about the Gandharvas and their special social status, then why this negation of differences now? Not quite knowing how to proceed, I dropped my questions for the time being. A couple of days later, the opportunity presented itself again.

We had just finished lunch at Pyaari khala's house. While the others drifted off to their afternoon siestas, you settled down to read the day's newspaper to your aunt, whose fast-failing eyesight is a constant source of sorrow for her.

Pyaari khala, like you, has always been a newspaper enthusiast. Neither cancer nor fading vision stop her from buying the local Hindi daily, which she then demands that someone read aloud to her. On that afternoon, you were doing the honours. You read about impending local body elections and of contesting politicians' promises to voters. Pyaari and you chuckled over the political arithmetic of caste and community loyalties. Who would the Dalits vote for and who inspired the Muslims' trust? Which path would the 'forwards' take and in which direction were the 'backwards' and the 'other backwards' headed? This was the blood, sweat, sinews of Indian democracy at work.

Ultimately, the delicious quiet of an overcast, cool afternoon prevailed over the excitement of political speculation. Your reading became fainter, segueing into gentle snores. Pyaari khala and I smiled at each other. She holds tight to every hour of wakefulness granted to her before eternal sleep carries her away.

Our conversation then wandered into territory that I had not travelled with you and your relatives. Pyaari khala conjured for me times when your ancestresses, with origins in landless communities, carried their poverty and their folk songs from one place to another on horseback. 'My father told me that, in those days, our family was very poor and wandered long distances, from Banaras to Patna and beyond, in a dera, mobile encampment, on horses. This is perhaps why they were also called ghudcharis, or women atop horses,' Pyaari said.

'In those early days, our family had no permanent address. They stopped wherever there were celebrations in well-off homes, and the women danced and sang at the festivities. Too poor to afford musical training from ustads, they sang simple folk songs that had been passed down the generations in our family. Sometimes, the entire dera stayed on at a place for longer periods if one or more of the girls in the group caught the fancy of rich patrons. At other times, the dera moved on, leaving behind a senior member to safeguard the girls.'

At some point, the family's wanderings led it to Shahabad, an area abounding in patrons. The family decided to settle down in Arrah, and over subsequent generations, girls in the family began to learn the intricacies of music and dance and all the other skills required to become successful tawaifs. Dharmman Bibi's talents as a singer and dancer helped her find a well-placed and committed patron in Babu Kunwar Singh. Sadabahar made an even bigger name for herself as a musician. From then on, the family, Pyaari khala said, began to be considered a prominent tawaif household in the district.

'Our family had relatives in various towns of Shahabad. Tawaifs, it used to be said, had wings on their feet. They had to be prepared to move from a known home to strange lands if the circumstances demanded it. Wherever they went, tawaifs would invariably find kinfolk to help them settle down. We belong to the Baisi biradari, the Baisi clan, as do several other Muslim tawaif families in Bhabua. Baisi are small in number compared to other tawaif biradaris. You won't find too many of us outside these parts, except for a few in Banaras, and they too are originally from here or from places around Allahabad.'

Before I could ask Pyaari khala more about the Baisi and their possible connection with the Nat, you woke up and hastily moved the conversation to other topics. I began increasingly to get the feeling that you were uncomfortable with my interest in the family's social origins. I decided to wait until you felt ready to discuss the subject.

Meanwhile, you and your relatives spoke about Muslim Nat tawaifs in Bhabua and Banaras who belong to the Magahiya biradari. They had, I was told, originally been a nomadic community that moved from village to village performing acrobatic tricks like rope-walking. On the side, they would also provide sexual services to the wealthy and powerful. Over the generations, the Magahiya Nat had settled in places like Bhabua and Banaras, learnt some music and dance, and upgraded their skills and status to become lower-placed entertainers and sex providers in the tawaif community.

Older women like Pyaari said that, earlier, Magahiya women were not really counted as 'proper' tawaifs either in Bhabua or Banaras because of their 'loose' ways. Over time, they had begun to adopt the practices of the khandani tawaifs, including the crucial taboo on indulging in indiscriminate sex work.

Through you, I met some Magahiya families in Bhabua and Banaras. They initially refused to identify as Nat, and instead talked about their origins as courtesans, singers and dancers in ancient Magadha, the seat of powerful dynasties like the Mauryas and the Guptas. The term Magahiya is derived from Magadha, they said. With its collapse as an epicentre of imperial power, the Magahiyas were forced to wander in family deras in search of patronage. The women would perform acrobatic tricks, sing and dance to earn a livelihood. At some point, as a group, they converted to Islam.

Over the generations, different Magahiya families, I was told, settled down in places in Bihar and UP that had a tawaif tradition, and began to practise singing and dancing. Interestingly, while the Magahiya families I interviewed took some time to admit their own links with the Nat, they were quick to ascribe that identity to yet another group of women performers who are better known in Bhabua and Banaras simply as Basukawalis or those from Basuka.

Basuka village near Banaras is mostly inhabited by Muslim Nat tattoo-makers. In fact, you and others use the term Basukawali interchangeably with godnewali, or tattoo-maker. A small number of families originally from Basuka, I was told, have been living in Bhabua for the past three to four generations, but much larger numbers are to be found in Banaras.

In the narratives of erstwhile tawaifs from Bhabua and Banaras, the Basukawalis are described as being latecomers to the line. This and their alleged lack of musical skills and practice—and therefore complete dependence on sex work—were the reasons they were placed on the lowest rung of the tawaif hierarchy. Dismissed as 'mere' prostitutes, the families from Basuka, I was told, now send their daughters to work as bar dancers in Mumbai and other towns in western and southern India.

All the Basukawali families that I spoke with in Bhabua and Banaras admitted to their Nat identity—the only group associated with the tawaif tradition in these places that did so without hesitation. They described their hereditary profession as that of wandering tattoo-makers but vehemently contested any association with prostitution. One elderly woman I interviewed in Bhabua said that families in Basuka used to primarily practise tattoo-making, but since they were Nat, music and dance 'flowed in their veins'. So, over time, they gave up the low-paid tattoo work, settled in places like Bhabua and Banaras and took to gana-bajana, singing and music-making. Most Basukawalis were very reluctant to admit any connection with bar dancing, saying that while some girls might have been put in the line by their parents, most daughters were now being married off 'respectably'.

Accidental, spontaneous conversations sometimes reveal truths that are otherwise difficult to admit. One day, Asghari, Phoolmani, Pyaari and you were talking about the great tawaif singers of the past. Vidyadhari, Siddheshwari and Rasoolan Bai were invoked. Then Pyaari said, 'Did you know that Rasoolan Bai belonged to our biradari? Baisi might be few in number but we have had many important singers. She was not from Bhabua. Her family originally belonged to a place called Kachhwa Mandwa that falls between Banaras and Allahabad.'

Your aunts and sister nodded proudly, and Phoolmani recalled that, at one point, Ghafuran's marriage had been fixed with Rasoolan Bai's nephew. Negotiations fell through at the last moment causing considerable embarrassment to the family.

In a flash, I was reminded of a long-ago conversation in a tranquil house, in a predominantly Muslim locality in Okhla, Delhi. Surrounded by stacks of files stuffed with old newspaper cuttings, official letters and spiritual discourses, an eighty-year-old man with a long flowing beard coloured red with henna, and deep-set eyes, sat opposite me, recreating a lost world.

A magician with words, Malik Dilbar Hussain, or baba as I have called him since childhood, conjured up an era when his mother, the imperious, wealthy and powerful Mumtaz, was choudharayin of the tawaif community in Delhi. He chronicled the dazzling careers of his six beautiful and accomplished aunts, Mumtaz's younger sisters, who had dominated the cultural firmament through the early decades of the twentieth century as celebrated singers, dancers and actors in theatre and cinema.

Malik Dilbar Hussain has been part of my extended family ever since, as a young man, he had declared himself a murid, or disciple, of my father's cousin, a communist-turned-Sufi and a self-styled healer. Baba was a constant presence in my uncle's house, which was open at all times of the day to his myriad friends and followers. When not attending to my uncle's needs, he looked after his mother's many properties in Delhi and also ran a small second-hand car sale business of his own. At some point, he had chosen to attach the suffix 'Tawaifzada', or son of a tawaif, to his name in public recognition of his mother, Mumtaz Choudharayin.

I had been too young to understand the significance of either his new name or his courage in publicly reclaiming the tradition into which he was born. But I do vividly remember the many musical evenings that took place in my uncle's house, with baba as main organiser and master of ceremonies. These were usually qawwali sessions with male musicians singing Sufi poetry late into the night. The mehfils were public events overflowing with the regulars in my uncle's vast social circle along with neighbours, local shopkeepers and even complete strangers who were lured by the music into that large hall.

One evening, baba presented a group of performers whose appearance caused some initial excitement in the assembled mehfil as they trooped in and settled down: three women along with male accompanist musicians on the tabla, sarangi and harmonium. These were singers from baba's own community. In deference to the spiritual preoccupations of the host, my uncle, heads decorously covered with sari ends, they sang songs written by mystic poets like Amir Khusrau, Bulleh Shah and Shah Hussain.

Their shimmering saris, glittering jewellery, powdered faces, painted lips and kohled eyes held me enthralled. They provided such a happy contrast, in my eight- or nine-year-old eyes, to the drab appearance of the male qawwals I had seen more frequently in these mehfils that I broke from my routine of falling asleep halfway through the music session. I was awake when the police arrived to bring the joyous music to an end.

Some neighbours had apparently taken offence that ganey walis were performing in their respectable locality and lodged a complaint. The policemen were polite, even apologetic, and left soon after ascertaining that no 'immorality' was taking place. My uncle insisted that the musicians continue performing. But the mood had irrevocably changed from festive to gloomy, and the mehfil faltered and dipped for a bit and then disintegrated.

A few years later, my uncle migrated to Italy. And my parents' contact with baba dwindled to occasional meetings when my uncle visited India. After my uncle died, baba disappeared altogether from our family-scape. We learnt that he had moved to Bombay to live with his businessmen-sons.

The shift proved temporary, though. Baba returned to Delhi, feeling unwanted and unappreciated. He and his wife, Bitto, went back to living in the small house he had bought in Okhla just before they left for Bombay. His main preoccupation now was the promotion of his ideas on spiritualism and Sufi thought through pamphlets he printed and the impromptu lectures he delivered to bored and sniggering neighbours in the market, at the local mosque and in the lane outside his house. When I began visiting him for my initial research, we made a deal. For every question he answered about tawaifs, I would have to hear one thought of his on spiritual matters.

'We are Nat!' Baba said with no hesitation when I asked him about his family's background. 'I have heard my elders say that our forefathers originally belonged to Chittor and were warriors in the Rajput army. When Akbar attacked Chittor, our forefathers refused to accept Mughal suzerainty and chose instead to go to war against the mighty enemy. Defeated and dispersed, we were forced to wander new lands as fugitives. We moved from Chittor to areas of present-day Rajasthan, Haryana, Punjab, Uttar Pradesh, Bihar and Madhya Pradesh. To escape the eagle eye of the Mughal forces, some of us began to call ourselves Nat.

'Some groups among the Nat converted to Islam while others remained Hindu. Landless, and with no other source of livelihood, we began to teach our daughters music and dance. These girls did not get married but instead earned for their families by performing for the powerful and wealthy. The Nat got the best ustads and gurus to teach their daughters. Our girls became tawaifs to the Mughals, to Hindu rajas and to the nawabs and zamindars. Other Nat clans became acrobats, tattoo-makers and cattle-dealers.

'Nat are divided into twelve clans. My family belongs to the Madaar clan. The Madaar were supposed to have possessed magical powers with which they could tame wild animals like tigers, lions and bears, and make them perform tricks. My mother's aunt extended those powers to captivate men and bring them under her control. In her times, she was the leading tawaif of Patiala, enjoying the patronage of the maharaja himself. So pleased was he with her that he gifted her part of the estate of Kilaat that now falls in modern-day Haryana. My mother, Mumtaz, who succeeded her, also possessed these powers. She could prevail over any man.

'Nat, along with the Kanchan and Gandharva, produced the finest tawaifs. Why, even Rasoolan Bai was a Nat, although she was not from the Madaar clan. Her clan was different. One of our girls married her nephew.'

Sitting in Bhabua with your family, the jigsaw puzzle fell into place for me. If Rasoolan Bai belonging to the Baisi clan was a Nat, then so must your family be. A bit dizzy with this epiphany, I wasn't quite sure about how to proceed, and stumbled in another direction on a blind guess. 'Do you know of Malik Dilbar Hussain, the son of Mumtaz Choudharayin in Delhi?'

Phoolmani pulled a face and said, 'Know of him? Of course we knew him and Mumtaz Choudharayin rather well. With their fancy family and high connections, they lorded over tawaifs not just in Delhi but even in faraway centres like Bombay, Banaras and Lucknow. Will you believe it, that Dilbar broke our Ghafuran's marriage negotiations with Rasoolan's nephew by pushing his niece on the boy! Obviously, we were no match for his rich and well-connected family. Rasoolan chose to bring the high and mighty Mumtaz's granddaughter into her home as a daughter-in-law. The word of a true tawaif, it is said, is akin to a line drawn in stone. But the great Rasoolan not only went back on her promise, she did so with people belonging to her own biradari, with us.'

'That's not true, appi!' Pyaari protested vehemently. 'Rasoolan aapa did not break her promise to our family. She tried till the end to convince her stuck-up nephew to marry Ghafuran. But what could she do in the face of his threats to commit suicide if he wasn't married to Dilbar's niece?'

While the two sisters argued afresh about a long-dead marriage proposal, my thoughts went over my research on references to Nats through history. In Sanskrit, the word 'nata' means a dancer, and the Nat were traditionally associated with various kinds of performances that included acrobatics, jugglery, rope-walking, magic tricks, singing and dancing. The *Arthashastra*, an ancient treatise on statecraft dating to the Mauryan era (fourth to second centuries BCE), describes the Nati as an actress, while enumerating different categories of courtesans, entertainers and prostitutes, such as Ganika, Pratiganika, Rupajiva, Vesya, Dasi, Pumschali and Rupadasi. The *Kamasutra*, dated variously between last centuries BCE and early centuries CE, enumerates the Nati among actresses, entertainers and prostitutes found in society.

The medieval-period *Ain-i-Akbari* makes mention of male Natuwas who trained slave girls in music and dance. The word 'Natin' finds regular mention in later Mughal accounts as courtesan and entertainer. Nawab Dargah Quli Khan's *Muraqqa'-i-Dehli* (1739) enumerates Natin, along with Kanchani, Domini, Hurkiya and others, among tawaif performers.

Buchanan in his account of travels in early nineteenth-century Patna writes of women singers and dancers referred to as 'Bais ... who are also called Natin'. His accounts of district Shahabad include reference to 'the Baazigars who sing, play legerdemain tricks and show feats of activity and are of the Nat tribe'. Buchanan also makes mention of the Nat who wandered through Shahabad to tattoo women. 'In the favourable season they make distant excursions.'

The Nat, a widely dispersed landless and semi-nomadic social group, seems to have been composed of subgroups or clans with diverse skills and lifestyles—the range extending from nomadic and poor entertainers, acrobats, tattoo-makers, cattle dealers and artisans in rural areas to groups of urban, musically accomplished tawaifs, singers and dancers. In the twentieth century, several Nat clans, I was told by Malik Dilbar Hussain, had formed the aristocracy among tawaifs in northern India, along with communities like the Kanchan and the Gandharva. Why then was I confronted with such silence in families like yours about their connection with the Nat?

One possible reason could be that the Nat occupy the lower rungs of the caste ladder. Nat families connected with the tawaif tradition have had to, therefore, negotiate not only the stigma of sexual deviancy but also that of being 'low caste'. The conversion to Islam might have been in part motivated by an attempt to escape their caste status by embracing a religion that professes equality among all believers. In the South Asian context, however, the practice of Islam has incorporated to a great extent the observance of the caste system and the prejudices associated with it. One of the ways in which Nat tawaif families like yours seem to have negotiated this 'low' status is by obscuring their caste origins and foregrounding, as the situation required, either the Muslim or the more difficult-to-place clan identity.

The reluctance to be identified as Nat could also be linked to the legacy of stigma that the community still suffers as a direct result of the Criminal Tribes Act (CTA) of 1871. The Act authorised the colonial government to declare by notification any tribe or group of persons 'addicted to the systematic commission of non-bailable offences' as a 'criminal tribe'. Thus, a person was deemed criminal under the law merely on the basis of belonging to a particular community.

Under the Act, several landless, nomadic communities were notified as 'habitually criminal' and their members registered by the government. Restrictions were imposed on their movements, with adult male members of such groups being required to report weekly to the local police, failing which they could be arrested without a warrant. The Act also gave the government vast powers to forcibly settle, remove from a particular place, detain and transfer members of a notified 'criminal tribe', and even to separate children from their parents. The Nat were among the communities marked as criminal tribes because of their perceived marginal or illegal behaviours.

This form of criminal ethnography had been first used in the earlier part of the nineteenth century to identify and stigmatise entire groups as 'thugs'. Later historians and commentators questioned the factual basis and the methods used of such a classification. The anti-thuggee campaign led to the formation of an archive of police ethnography which, in turn, was used subsequently to identify and designate increasing numbers of people as members of 'criminal' tribes and castes. The colonial state used an elaborate apparatus of surveillance to study and classify behavioural patterns, habits, physical features, social and cultural practices and the 'modus operandi' of suspect groups and communities to detect and identify their 'inherent criminality'.

Along with the Nat community, nineteenth-century colonial records classified other landless, nomadic and semi-nomadic groups, such as the Bedia, Sansi, Kanjar and the Habura, as criminal and describe them as 'gypsies', 'vagrants', 'dissolute' and 'disorderly'. Historically, these communities led an itinerant and subsistence lifestyle, moving in family groups from one village and town to another, providing entertainment, goods and services to settled populations.

Colonial rule marginalised the traditional occupations of such nomadic groups to a great extent. The network of roads and railways established in the 1850s, which connected many outlying villages to each other and to cities and towns, drastically cut down the scale of their operations. The services of nomadic traders, artisans and entertainers were now restricted to areas where wheel traffic could not yet reach. Further, under newly imposed forest laws, the British government did not allow tribal communities to graze their cattle in the forests or to collect the bamboo and leaves that were needed for making simple items like mats and baskets for their own use and for sale. The nineteenth century also witnessed repeated and severe famines, which further put at peril their subsistence economy. Driven by the threat of starvation, even death, some members of these communities appear to have taken recourse to petty crime. Jail records of the famine periods in Bengal, for instance, show a higher incidence of criminal activity by them.

Several nomadic communities participated in the revolt of 1857 in protest against colonial rule. There were also nomadic and tribal groups, especially in the hills and forests, that had a long history of resistance against the state. The imposition of the CTA came in handy as a tool of repression and control for the British over these rebellious communities. It invoked the Act to kill and imprison thousands of men.

Ideologically too the nomadic and subsistence lifestyle of several notified communities did not conform to colonial notions of civilised living: of settled agriculture and waged labour. These ideas had their roots in nineteenth-century Europe's anxieties about nomadic lifestyles as a threat to the territorial sovereignty of the nation-state, to private property and to social stability. The notion of criminal tribes also drew from Victorian ideas of heritability of criminal behaviour. The working-class slums in England, for instance, were seen as breeding grounds for 'dangerous classes' and 'habitual offenders'.

These ideas were transposed to the colonial understanding of the Indian caste system by linking profession, upbringing and background. The eminent jurist James Fitzjames Stephen, for instance, while introducing the CTA in 1871 noted: '... people from time immemorial have been pursuing the caste system defined job-positions: weaving, carpentry and such were hereditary jobs. So there must have been hereditary criminals also who pursued their forefathers' profession'.

When I first read about the Nat being notified as a 'criminal tribe', my thoughts immediately turned to the mystifying story of Sadabahar and her kin fleeing Chainpur to escape the snake that threatened Bullah's life. Could the actual cause of the family's flight—around the late nineteenth century—be linked to their Nat identity? Could the threat to Bullah's life have been from the heightened vulnerability to arrest and imprisonment of male members in Nat families?

Tempting though the narrative was, further investigations pointed to the relative immunity and security that established Nat tawaif families like yours enjoyed from the CTA. Practising music and dance or even sex work as tawaifs and prostitutes evoked moral condemnation from the colonial state and a newly emerging Indian middle class, but were not considered criminal activities per se under the law. Nat families like yours with old links to tawaif communities were, therefore, relatively safe from police harassment. Still, Sadabahar's decision to shift to Bhabua might have been dictated to some extent by the desire to be part of the town's established and large tawaif community, which perhaps afforded greater security due to numbers.

The relative immunity from CTA-related police harassment seems to have attracted to the tawaif fold other clans from the wider Nat, Bedia and Kanjar groups that had traditionally practised lifestyles and occupations now defined as criminal. Where men had played a significant role in the family's economy, now women came increasingly to the forefront of earning for the family, since they would not face harassment under the CTA. In such contexts, the work associated with women in the social group's traditional occupations became their chief means of livelihood.

In the case of the Bedia, for instance, it has been argued that, once the group was notified as 'criminal', family-based prostitution by women (which had thus far been one of the several occupations practised by the community) became increasingly the main means of livelihood. Certain clans among the Bedia also seem to have joined tawaif communities. Similar considerations might also account for Nat clans like the tattoo-makers of Basuka joining the lowest ranks of urban tawaif communities.

Across northern India, tawaif communities seem to have been a refuge historically for women belonging to resourceless castes and communities.

That this process was not confined only to the period after the imposition of the CTA is confirmed by oral evidence of tawaif groups being joined by new entrants throughout the eighteenth and nineteenth centuries. Your own family's history of poor, rural Nat singers and dancers transforming over the period of a few generations through accumulation of cultural skills and well-placed patronage to high-end courtesans points towards the hope of betterment of opportunities that the tawaif community offered to socially and economically disadvantaged groups.

William Crooke, in his 1896 ethnographic account *The Tribes and Castes of North Western Provinces and Oudh*, while writing about tawaifs describes them as 'plural of taifa, a troop of dancing girls'. He enumerates the varied 'castes and tribes' that constituted the tawaif community in the census of 1891: Gandharva, Kanchan, Kashmira, Ramjani, Rasdhari, Patar, Naik, Hurkiya, Baksariye, Brijwasi, Magahiya, Kabutari, Chhata, Janghariya, Naurangi, Domini etc. While the Gandharva, Ramjani, Naik, Patar, Kashmira, Brijwasi and Rasdhari are identified as Hindus, the others had returned themselves in the 1891 census as Muslims. Interestingly, the Natin, which had found repeated mention in Mughal and early nineteenth-century colonial ethnographic accounts, is not mentioned as a category by Crooke although several subgroups in the tawaif community enumerated by him (including Kashmira, Kabutari, Baksariye, Brijwasi and Magahiya) are identified either in his own accounts, or in earlier colonial writings such as Sherring's, as clans belonging to the wider Nat community.

It would be impossible to hazard a guess about the antiquity of the links of these various groups to the tawaif tradition. Some, like the Ramjani, Kanchan, Gandharva, Hurkiya and Domni, are mentioned in Mughal records and in the writings of European travellers of the time, like Bernier, Manucci and Pelsaert.

The Gandharva, Ramjani and Kanchan continued to be closely linked with the tawaif tradition in the twentieth century. Like the origin stories of the Gandharvas, the multiple meanings and narratives embedded in the term 'Ramjani' throw light on the social background of various other tawaif groups.

Ramjani tawaifs have played an important role in the courtesan tradition of eastern UP and Bihar. They find repeated mention in accounts of eighteenth- and nineteenth-century colonial observers. The well-known Orientalist Henry Thomas Colebrooke, who during the 1780s lived in

Tirhut and Purnea in Bihar, writes about them, '... the Ramjenis (Hindu dancing women) have been all day dancing and singing before the idol'.

British observers of the eighteenth century, like Colebrook and James Forbes, suggested that the north Indian Ramjanis, much like the devadasis of the south, were attached formally as dancing girls to temples. There are references, no doubt, to temple-based women singers and dancers in northern India during the Mauryan and Gupta periods. With the onset of Muslim rule, however, the practice seems to have ebbed in the north, as patronage of music, musicians and dancers shifted to the imperial courts. With this, the patronage or ritual sanctions provided by religious institutions declined. But tawaifs continued to be invited on festive occasions to perform at temples in their secular role as singers and dancers.

The number of Ramjani tawaifs seems to have been so considerable that they make their presence felt in the Anglo-Indian vocabulary as well. The *Hobson-Jobson*, a dictionary of Anglo-Indian terms, traces one of the meanings of the term 'Rum-Johnny' used by British soldiers and sailors to mean 'a prostitute' to Ramjani or 'a dancing girl'. Buchanan too mentions Ramjani, Domni, Hurkini and Kangchani as courtesans.

In 1876, Sherring, in his *Hindu Tribes and Castes as Represented in Benaras*, describes the Ramjani or Ramjana as '... a tribe of professional musicians ... The caste is devoted to prostitution. The female children born in the caste are brought up to immorality and vice.' He concludes by noting that Ramjanis differ from other castes in Banaras because of their practice of 'admitting women from various castes into the order'.

Yeh Kothewaliyan in the mid-twentieth century too mentions the important place occupied by the Ramjani in the tawaif tradition of Banaras. Based upon tawaif and non-tawaif narratives, Amritlal Nagar's book describes them as 'women of other communities who through difficult circumstances have become tawaifs ... Some great singers have been Ramjanis.' In another instance, he writes, 'Ramjani are those who tawaifs buy and then give ... a thorough education in music to become courtesans.'

Almost half a century later, during my own journeys through the tawaif tradition of Banaras, I encountered varying meanings attached to the term 'Ramjani'. Most non-tawaif music enthusiasts invariably enumerated it as a 'caste' of Hindu courtesans who, along with Gandharva and Muslim singers and dancers, had contributed significantly to the arts of the city. Some others described them as a 'caste' of women from 'good' families who, falling upon 'bad' times, became tawaifs.

On the other hand, almost all respondents belonging to former tawaif families or accompanist musicians, including you, insisted that Ramjani was not a 'caste'. Shanney Khan, for instance, used the literal translation of the term Ramjani or Ramjana as someone 'born of Rama, belonging to Rama' to explain it as a euphemism used by a certain section of tawaifs to 'hide the illegitimacy of their children born out of wedlock'. This explanation begged the question why only a certain section felt the need to adopt such a euphemism, when tawaif offspring were all born outside of socially sanctioned marriage.

'Ramjani is no caste! They are Bedia and their kin, the Kanjar and Nat. These people extend all the way to Agra, Bharatpur. They were originally prostitutes. Those among them that set up kothas and began singing and dancing began calling themselves Ramjanis. We did not maintain *beti–roti ka rishta*, relations of either marriage or inter-dining, with the Ramjanis,' Saraswati Bai and Susheela Bai, elderly Gandharva sisters, your neighbours in Banaras, said to me.

I received a similar explanation from a cross-section of people across Banaras's tawaif community. No one appeared to know when the term came into being and gained currency. To my question about why tawaifs from these communities would have chosen to call themselves Ramjani, you shrugged, 'To hide their low social status, of course. These were communities like the Bedia that had traditionally moved and lived in the beehad, ravines, unlike our clans of khandani tawaifs who moved in deras and put down base in populated areas. Where could they have learnt music and dance in forests? So, their daughters became prostitutes.'

According to you, although the great majority of Bedia lived by prostitution, some of them, at an unknown point of time, began to learn music and dance and set up kothas. They developed intimate relations with wealthy, upper-caste men. 'It is possible,' you said, 'that these tawaifs invented the term for themselves to advance their status, brighten their prospects.'

How would taking on a euphemism have helped to improve the Ramjanis' social status since everyone in the tawaif community would have known the truth about their origins? 'Yes, but outsiders didn't know,' you said. 'We don't go about broadcasting each other's stories to outsiders. In the community, everyone knows and observes their boundaries.'

Over time, and through extensive conversations, I came to understand that the term Ramjani connoted Hindu groups like the Bedia and Kanjar within the tawaif community. Those who belong to Hindu Nat clans are also called Ramjani.

I met Meena, an acquaintance you said belonged to a Ramjani family. But Meena insisted that she came from the Kashmira biradari. She dismissed the term Ramjani as a 'fig leaf' used by Bedia and Kanjar tawaifs to hide from 'outsiders' their 'low caste'.

'In a manner of speaking, we are all Ramjani. And yet, since Ramjani is not a biradari or a zaat, it can as easily be said that none of us belongs to it,' Lakshmi, a former tawaif, said to me with a mischievous glint in her eyes. Quite forthright about her Ramjani identity, she explained to me that, in the community, where everyone is aware of each other's biradari, no one uses the term for themselves or for others. It was a euphemism that non-Gandharva Hindu tawaifs in Banaras and other places in eastern UP and Bihar had adopted while dealing with 'outsiders' because it provided a 'convenient' shared identity to several kindred clans and groups.

Lakshmi said that she came from the 'ancient' tawaif biradari called Patar. They find mention in the *Kamasutra* and other ancient Sanskrit texts, according to her. At this point, you interrupted her and said that the term 'paturiya' or prostitute comes from Patar. Lakshmi did not look at all happy but chose to ignore the interjection. Instead, she said, 'The Muslim tawaifs of this area too come from different clans and groups. Most of them are Nat. In the community, we know that, of course. But just like most non-Gandharva Hindu tawaifs in this region call themselves Ramjani to outsiders, the Muslim tawaifs, if you ask them, simply say they are Muslim. It is more convenient.' Lakshmi settled the score, casting a dark look in your direction.

I tried to investigate whether Ramjani might also have been a euphemism for children of women from 'respectable' families, forced by circumstances to become tawaifs. But no one I spoke with in the community, including women and men in their eighties and nineties, knew of such courtesans. They pointed out that an 'outsider' could not hope to gain recognition as a courtesan unless she was formally adopted as a foster daughter by a practising tawaif. This usually occurred when girl children were formally adopted by childless tawaifs.

In the extremely rare case of an adult woman from 'outside' wishing to join the line, she too would need to convince a respected tawaif to adopt her as a daughter if she wanted recognition and sanction from the community. This ceremony was dauntingly expensive, with the foster daughter making gifts in cash and jewellery to her adopted mother and her family.

I was often given the example of the legendary Gauhar Jan, the first well-known musician in India to record for the gramophone in 1902. She came from a non-tawaif background, being of mixed Armenian-Jewish-Anglo-Indian descent. Though she achieved success and popularity that few women musicians in her time could dream of, Gauhar hankered for formal recognition as a courtesan. At the height of her musical career in the early twentieth century, she convinced the choudharayins of Lucknow, the sisters Nanuha and Bichhua Jan, to adopt her as a daughter in exchange for extravagant gifts and huge amounts of money.

Not everyone wishing to become a tawaif had Gauhar's resources. Therefore, while there might have been women who had taken to dancing and singing in their adult life, tawaifs would not recognise them as part of the community. Naturally, these women would not be able to use the term Ramjani to describe themselves, because the tawaifs who identified with the term would never allow it.

The use of euphemisms like Ramjani point to the anxieties experienced by members of the tawaif community about public identification with groups like the Bedia, Kanjar and Nat that were considered low caste. These groups faced stigmatisation even within the tawaif community because of their historical dependence upon family-based prostitution.

Internalising the sexual morality of patriarchal society, tawaifs have traditionally accorded to themselves a status superior to women in prostitution not only on account of their skills in music and dance and their wealth but also their self-professed abstinence from indiscriminate sex work. As highly paid artistes, lovers and companions to the male elite, they could afford to be selective about their sexual relationships. Nat, Bedia and Kanjar clans that had entered the community earlier than the others had, over a period of time, carved out a higher status. They positioned themselves as khandani—old lineage-based tawaif families, with little in common with the poorer clans that lived by prostitution. With the colonial and nationalist discourse branding tawaifs as 'prostitutes', there was an added edge to the community's insistence on distinguishing themselves from women living by sex work.

These anxieties would no doubt have been exacerbated by the imposition of the CTA. For the Nat, Bedia and Kanjar clans that had entered the tawaif tradition well before the imposition of CTA, while their identity as khandani, and in many instances wealthy, tawaifs enjoying the patronage of the local elite would no doubt have protected them from harassment under the law, they would still have wanted to avoid any public association with communities notified as 'criminal'.

This does not mean that caste identities do not carry an internal significance for tawaif groups with origins in the Nat, Bedia and Kanjar communities. They have traditionally shared customs, lifestyles and histories of origin, and many within these groups inter-marry.

Malik Dilbar Hussain described Bedia, Kanjar and Sansi as kin communities of the Nat, with shared origins as fugitive former soldiers in Rajput armies. 'To escape the eagle eye of the Mughal forces, some of us began to call ourselves Nat. Others went into the forests and ravines, and became Bedia. Then there were those who began calling themselves Sansi or Sansiya and Kanjar. We are like different fingers of the same hand.'

This sense of community works at two levels. As erstwhile nomadic and semi-nomadic groups, the Nat, Bedia and Kanjar share a socio-cultural identity that is internally significant for members of these communities. As members of a wider tawaif community, they share with other groups such as the Gandharva a common art practice, norms of lifestyle and sexuality, traditions and life-cycle rituals particular to the courtesan tradition, and a common history of persecution by the state from the nineteenth century onwards.

Their identities as Nat, Bedia and Kanjar are, however, slippery. While these are terms used most often by 'outsiders' to define and categorise them, among themselves, members more frequently use markers such as locality and clan to identify each other. Thus it is common to identify a group by their place of origin—Basukawali or Chaandeywali or even Bhabuawali, for instance. These location-based identities carry internal meanings and personal history for community members.

Lakshmi, while differentiating between those Ramjani tawaifs with older claims to the tradition and those who are relative 'newcomers', said, 'There is a lot of difference between us from the poorab, east, and those from Agra-Bharatpur. We are khandani, while they did dhandha, prostitution, till very recently.'

Those identified as Agra-Bharatpurwali are most usually the Bedia, who originally come from this region. However, Bedia is not necessarily synonymous with Agra-Bharatpurwali because, in this group, I have also met Nat women. In such a case, it is their identity of belonging to Agra–Bharatpur that casts them in tawaif narratives as linked to prostitution.

By far the most important unit of identification among tawaifs belonging to the erstwhile nomadic and semi-nomadic communities is that of clan. Non-Gandharva tawaif groups, whether Hindu or Muslim, foreground their clan identity, which might cut across caste identities. Therefore, while members of a clan might identify as Nat in one place, in another area, the clan could be seen as Bedia.

You told me about the 'saat taat' or seven mats—the seven clans that constituted the community of Muslim tawaifs in Bhabua. These were the Magahiya, Nigaadi, Baisi, Chaubisi, Pacheesi, Godnewali and Sahban. 'In our nachney ganey wala samaj, Sahban are considered the highest, while Godnewali are the lowest. This is in our Bhabua. In other places, it would be different. Baisi, for instance, are mainly found in Bhabua and a few other places. We are very small in number and spread out, whereas the Magahiya are found across this region,' you said.

Similarly, the various 'Ramjani' clans had their own version of the taat system of community composition. Various taats of tawaif groups in a given place then formed town- or city-specific community of courtesans. The tawaif community of Bhabua, for instance, included all the Gandharva and Muslim tawaifs of the town, and had its own panchayat or council for the laying down of rules for conduct, and for the redress of grievances and disputes. The choudharayin of this panchayat was by norm a senior courtesan from the Gandharva group.

I first came across the term deraydar in my readings on early twentieth-century Lucknow. Deraydar courtesans are often described as the elite in the tawaif community. Their origins are traced to eighteenth-century tawaifs' deras, mobile encampments, that were an extended part of the military expeditions of the early nawabs of Lucknow.

However, Crooke makes no mention of deraydars in his detailed, late-nineteenth-century descriptions of various castes, communities and classes of tawaifs in the region. There is no mention of the term either in the Urdu novel *Umrao Jan Ada*, published in the early years of the twentieth century. This absence is significant since not only does the novel revolve around a group of tawaifs that would fit the description of being deraydar but also has been hailed for its realistic and nuanced portrayal of the culture and social life of the community in mid-nineteenth-century Lucknow.

Deraydar tawaifs find mention in Mirza Jafar Hussain's *Qadeem Lucknow ki Aakhri Bahaar*, a detailed account in Urdu of the social and cultural life of nineteenth- to early twentieth-century Lucknow. He describes the different classes of tawaifs and prostitutes in the city, including the khangi, prostitutes from among purdah-bound women, and kasbi, brothel-based prostitutes.

Hussain then describes the different categories of bazaar-based women performers, which included the randi, lower-placed women singers and dancers who also provided sexual services. Several among them, he says, were highly accomplished and patronised by the elite. He distinguishes this category from deraydar tawaifs about whom he writes, 'Their music and dance skills, cultural refinement, impeccable mannerisms, sophisticated behaviour and integrity endowed deraydar tawaifs with superior status among all the women of the bazaar.'

Amritlal Nagar too interviewed several women in Lucknow in 1959 who describe themselves as deraydars, 'the highest category among tawaifs'. Deraydars, they say, are both Muslims and Hindus and divided into several groups and clans. They describe deraydars 'as self-respecting and honourable women like those of respectable families. This was so since deraydar tawaifs were taught from childhood to live with decency and dignity.'

The eminent twentieth-century Urdu writer Qurratulain Hyder, who has written several insightful stories about tawaifs, describes deraydars as 'the most eminent class of tawaifs'. Hyder writes that the deraydars 'had their own caste rules'. Interestingly, the term does not appear in the 1790 novel *Nashtar*—translated into English by Hyder, and according to her, the first novel written in Urdu—the story of a group of eighteenth-century tawaifs who moved from one place to another in deras.

'Nonsense! Deraydars were no special class of eminent tawaifs.' Malik Dilbar Hussain exclaimed with some exasperation. 'The term deraydar,' he explained, 'comes from the word dera. It refers to all those tawaif families that had originally moved in deras from one place to another. Gandharva, Nat, Ramjani, Kanchan and other biradaris, whose daughters had practised family-based gana-bajana, moving earlier from one place to another, were called deraydars. These women were from hereditary tawaif families, which had their own rules, their unique way of life. They were different from prostitutes like khangi and kasbi, or women from other communities who might have practised some music and dance or were kept as rakhails, mistresses. All these other categories of women and their families were not included within the deraydar.'

In my subsequent travels through Banaras and Bihar, I received similar explanations from others. You, your aunts, cousins and sister explained that the deraydar community included tawaif families of varied types, elite and humble, some highly skilled in music and others less accomplished, rich and poor. It had well-defined boundaries, excluding from its fold all those perceived as 'outsiders'.

Thus, prostitutes, who in many instances lived and worked in brothels located in the tawaif quarters of a town, were not part of the community of deraydars. Similarly, women singers, dancers and performers, like the mirasins and gonaharins, with origins in social groups outside the constellation of communities and clans traditionally associated with the practice of tawaif lifestyle, sexuality and art were not part of the group. Nor were women musicians like Gauhar Jan, born outside the tawaif community.

Why then the attempts in places like Lucknow, from the early twentieth century onwards, to use the term to suggest a category of 'superior' tawaifs? A possible answer could lie in the tawaifs' anxiety about being cast as women in prostitution. Under increasing attack from colonial and nationalist quarters for their non-marital and therefore 'prostitute' sexuality, the khandani tawaifs might have attempted to ascribe to the term deraydar a meaning that would not only distance them in public perception from prostitution but also from the lower-placed and new entrants to the line, who were seen to be indiscriminate about doing sex work.

In actual usage among tawaifs, the term deraydar, in its broadest sense, simply connotes the community of hereditary tawaif families like yours. It is also commonly used to refer to sons, brothers and uncles in courtesan families, especially male relatives who played a significant role as managers in the careers of their tawaif daughters and sisters, or exerted influence in the community as leaders and spokesmen, or were musicians in their own right, usually tabla and sarangi players; in short, the few men of substance in the tawaif community.

The community also uses 'deraydar' to connote a more subliminal meaning: of a way of life, ethics, integrity and morals associated with 'true' tawaif families. This meaning was especially embodied in its usage to refer to retired tawaif heads of family, or leaders of the community, as also respected men occupying similar positions. These people personified in some manner the valorised ideal of the tawaif's way of life. This ideal is reflected, for example, in the discipline and control these deraydar elders exerted over the family or larger group. Deraydar guardians were renowned for their uncompromising insistence upon the etiquette and decorum expected from their own girls and from visitors within their premises, as well as for maintaining the sanctity of music and dance practice associated with the tradition.

Many people from the community narrated incidents that illustrated the deraydar elders' commitment to professional ethics. As managers of a tawaif's career, once they gave their commitment to a mujra assignment, no inclement weather, bad roads, illness or family problems would hinder a deraydar elder from reaching the group of performers to the promised venue on time. I also heard stories about the 'hawk's eye' that deraydar elders would keep on the visitors allowed to enter their kotha, sternly 'removing the grain from the chaff', weeding out anyone perceived as rowdy or poor.

Most of all, being a true deraydar meant observing and enforcing rules and norms that governed the lifestyles, sexualities and choices available to the women and men living in the family kotha. You proudly told me, 'My mother was a true deraydar. If someone began acting too boisterous during my mujra, one look from her was all it took to throw water on his excitement! Elders like her ensured that kothas maintained their sanctity and did not degenerate into brothels. They were strict and maintained discipline like the true deraydars that they were.'

CHAPTER 8

Sadabahar in Banaras

IT'S AROUND 5.30 IN THE evening, and the mainly pedestrian traffic on Kachori Gali, flanking the Vishwanath temple, has slowed to a crawl. Dedicated to Shiva, Lord of the Universe, the temple enjoys pre-eminent status in Banaras. Pilgrims jostle in serpentine files to gain entry to it in time for the evening arti. Touts promising cheap deals on everything, from beating the queue to silk saris and hotel accommodation, add to the squeeze in the narrow lane. As do the mainly American and European tourists clicking photographs of 'exotic' Banaras to show back home. Cycle- and two-wheeler-borne residents yell and beep their way through the chaos, while shopkeepers and hawkers swoop down on unsuspecting visitors to cajole them into buying incense sticks, flower garlands, water bottles, film rolls and more.

I am back in Banaras for a few days to catch up on appointments thrown into disarray by my longer-than-anticipated stay in Bhabua. You are still with Pyaari khala. Making my way through the milling crowds, I edge past the large posse of armed policemen posted 24x7 in the lane—a constant reminder of the threat posed by right-wing Hindu groups to the Gyanvapi mosque adjacent to the Vishwanath temple.

Textual and mythological references to the Vishwanath shrine date back to early medieval times. Historical evidence shows that the temple certainly existed in the twelfth century and was destroyed in 1194 by Muhammad Ghori. It was rebuilt around the fourteenth century by Rajput dynasties ruling the area only to be razed to the ground again in subsequent conquests of the city by the armies of the Delhi Sultanate.

A reconstruction of the Vishwanath temple was once again undertaken in 1585 during the reign of the Mughal emperor Akbar by his minister, Raja Todarmal. Besides this temple, Akbar's reign also saw the building of various other Hindu shrines and schools of Sanskrit learning in Banaras. But the Vishwanath temple was demolished once again in 1669, this time on the orders of the Mughal emperor Aurangzeb, who had the Gyanvapi mosque constructed on the site.

The temple was rebuilt in its present form, adjacent to the mosque, by the Maratha queen Ahilyabai Holkar around 1765. Over the two centuries that followed, the Vishwanath temple and Gyanvapi mosque coexisted in relative peace, attracting the devout of their respective faiths to prayer and worship.

This calm came under siege in the late twentieth century, when various groups affiliated to the Hindu nationalist Rashtriya Swayamsevak Sangh (RSS), including the Vishva Hindu Parishad (VHP) and the Bharatiya Janata Party (BJP), began selectively raking up and distorting history for political gain. Advocating the politics of Hindutva, an exclusivist ideology that equates being Indian with being Hindu, the VHP and the BJP sought political mobilisation of Hindus on the ownership of three religious sites: the Vishwanath temple–Gyanvapi mosque in Banaras, the mythical birthplace of the Lord Rama in Ayodhya and that of Lord Krishna in Mathura. All three sites have shared space with mosques since the medieval period.

In 1992, Hindutva protesters demolished the sixteenth-century Babri mosque in Ayodhya, which they claimed stood on the birth place of Ram. Emboldened by their success, the VHP and the BJP have been whipping up sectarian passions against the Gyanvapi mosque in Banaras and Mathura's Shahi idgah, calling for them to be similarly 'liberated'.

The security forces stationed in Kachori Gali are now as much a part of its landscape as the numerous little shops selling aloo kachori, from which the lane derives its name. This is cheap, filling food, mostly bought by the droves of poorer, rural pilgrims and mourners who pass this lane daily on their way to the Vishwanath temple and numerous other shrines in its vicinity, or to the ghats for a ritual dip in the Ganga, or to cremate their dead on the burning pyres of Manikarnika.

The real earnings of this narrow, winding lane, however, come from the crores that ride on the glorious Banarasi silks brought in an evening rush of Muslim weavers and middlemen to Hindu wholesale merchants waiting for them in their unprepossessing cubbyhole offices on the first floors of shops lining one end of Kachori Gali. From here, the silk makes its way to tens of thousands of retail stores in Banaras and elsewhere.

Silk, thick, rich and lustrous ties together the destinies of the Muslims and Hindus of Banaras. It defines the economy of this city. And plays an integral role in its religious rituals. Woven by Muslim artisans, stoles of traditional Banarasi silk and brocade are part of the offering made by wealthy Hindu devotees to the presiding deity at the Vishwanath temple.

At the end of Kachori Gali, I reach Chowk, the epicentre of four thoroughfares that cut across old Banaras. Chowk is also a major wholesale market for Banarasi saris. From here, the road towards my left goes to the market centre of Godolia, and from there to the Muslim weavers' locality of Madanpura and then onward to Banaras Hindu University, or BHU. To my right, the same road, intersected by Chowk, winds through the Hindu-majority sections of the old city, Thatheri Bazaar, Neechi Bagh and further on to the open space of Maidagin. The third road, facing me, runs through the Muslim neighbourhoods of Dal Mandi to Nai Sarak, and the fourth which I have just traversed, Kachori Gali, connects Chowk to the Vishwanath temple and the Ganga river-front.

Rickshaws, cars, two-wheelers, fruit stalls, hawkers, shoppers and labourers throng the busy crossroads of Chowk. In the middle of it all, the mazar of Baba Zahid Shareef, a local Sufi saint, stands serene. This tiny and unassuming shrine, no more than a raised concrete platform surrounded by wrought-iron lattice on three sides, has just enough room for a handful of devotees to pray at a time around the saint's grave.

I have accompanied you here several times. The shrine is located close to your house in Nariyal Bazaar, which adjoins Chowk. As much a part of your Banarasi identity as your ritual of feeding fish at the ghats, you come here almost daily to seek Baba's blessings. As do, I have noticed, large numbers of Hindus, men and women, from localities surrounding Chowk. The marble plaque in the shrine with its list of donors stands testimony to the love that Baba receives from the neighbourhood cutting across religious divides.

In the late nineteenth–early twentieth century, the Chowk and its adjoining mohallas, Dal Mandi, Nariyal Bazaar, Raja Darwaza and Chhatte Tale, were famous as the tawaif quarters of Banaras. Tawaifs occupied—quite literally—the centre of the city. The buildings here had shops on the ground floor, while their upper storeys customarily housed tawaifs' kothas. The daily mehfils in these salons were renowned for their high quality of music, dance, conversation and sophisticated seduction.

Crossing Chowk, I enter Dal Mandi. Early twentieth-century police records of Dal Mandi list Muslim and Hindu Gandharva tawaifs, Dhari-Mirasi Muslim male musicians, Hakims or Muslim practitioners of Unani medicine, Baqr Kasab or Muslim butchers, and Beniya or Hindu traders and shopkeepers as the main residents of the neighbourhood. Many wealthy tawaifs owned extensive property here.

With its large Muslim population, Dal Mandi was, through the nineteenth and early twentieth century, also a literary centre for Urdu, attracting writers, poets and dramatists. Agha Hash'r Kashmiri, often referred to as the father of Urdu drama, lived here for some time. Renowned poets like Mir Anis and Mirza Ghalib stayed in Dal Mandi during their visits to Banaras, and participated in mushairas, poetry-reading sessions, organised by lovers of Urdu poetry, many of them tawaifs.

Dal Mandi in its present avatar is a somewhat shabby, predominantly Muslim locality and a thriving market for cheap readymade clothes, electronics goods and music and film CDs. Tawaifs have long since shut down their elegant salons, here as elsewhere. Those who lived and worked out of rented kothas have moved out of the area, while those who own property have stayed on to lead vastly transformed lives.

'You goat-headed fiend, what have you done with the rest of the money? Used it to give your unknown fathers a halfway decent funeral, have you?' I hear Chanda well before I reach her doorstep on the first floor of one of the few well-maintained buildings located in Dal Mandi's main street. A former tawaif and a BHU graduate in music, Chanda is as famous in Dal Mandi for her English as for her colourful Bhojpuri expletives. Older than you by several years, she owns an entire katra, or cul de sac, of buildings in Dal Mandi. As one of the best-educated residents and wealthiest property owners in the area, she is also a local leader here.

Chanda is also almost always drunk—not enough to dull her razor-sharp business acumen and ferocious intelligence, but enough to keep her eyes bloodshot and her temper on a short fuse through the day. Responding to my timid, polite knock with a snarl to 'Stop knocking the place down and come in', on seeing me, Chanda tries to compensate with a smile that doesn't quite reach her eyes.

As always, she lies sprawled on her bed in the front room that serves as her boudoir and office. From here, Chanda controls not only her flourishing property business but also the lives of her five sons, daughters-in-law, many grandchildren, innumerable poor relatives and servants who scurry around in her rambling home spread over three floors.

Exceptionally tall and big-built, Chanda looks more like a retired wrestler than a tawaif. A retired wrestler of seventy-odd years, with short-cropped hair hennaed a dull orange and small, sharp eyes that miss nothing. Dressed as usual in a worn-out housecoat thrown over a petticoat and blouse, she takes a swig from the hip flask she carries the way other women carry their purse. All the cash that she will need through the day as a businesswoman is stuffed in a large wallet tucked in the one-size-too-small blouse that only partially covers her generous breasts.

Chanda's room is enveloped in silence once the hapless employee makes a hurried departure. Seemingly oblivious to my presence, she spends some time making entries in her diary. That done, she turns to make a call, and her petticoat rides up to reveal a thick, hairy leg. Scratching absent-mindedly at her exposed calf, she doesn't bother to cover up. You have told me, your tone part censorious and part awestruck, about Chanda's supreme indifference to modesty, 'She can pee standing anywhere like a man, she can change her clothes in front of anyone. Chanda has no sense of shame at all.'

You like Chanda. She is rich, successful and influential. She owns properties and shops across Dal Mandi, Chowk and your own locality of Nariyal Bazaar. Politicians of different hues fawn over her. They cannot hope to function in the area without first currying favour with Chanda.

Chanda, you say, uses her influence to help others. I have seen the queue of supplicants thronging her house in the mornings. From procuring a job to securing a bed in a government hospital, from admission in schools and colleges to approvals of bank loans, from redressal of civic woes to resolution of disputes—life in urban India is a daily struggle. And it is Chanda that the people of this area turn to for small miracles.

You like her even more because she comes from an old and illustrious tawaif family, among the very best in Banaras. Chanda's mother, Tara, was at one time a leading tawaif in Banaras. Tara's mother, Gulab Jan, and aunt, Mannan Jan, find mention in early twentieth-century police records as among the most 'notable and respectable' persons of Dal Mandi. Mannan Jan went on to become the choudharayin of the tawaif community in Banaras, and is still remembered for her fair-mindedness and sagacity.

I find the names of the women—Chanda, Tara, Gulab—beautiful in their non-denominational simplicity. The family has Kanchan antecedents, unusual among tawaifs of eastern UP and Bihar. Kanchan tawaifs, so prominent in the northern parts of undivided India's Punjab and Delhi, are very rarely to be found in the east. Originally from Punjab, the women in Chanda's family migrated to this area several generations ago as camp followers of conquering Mughal armies.

The family, however, has a unique identity that sets it apart from Muslim Kanchan tawaifs elsewhere. While the daughters in Chanda's family have always identified as Muslims, the sons have customarily been brought up to be Hindus. When I once asked Chanda the reason for this, she mumbled about a mannat or promise that one of her ancestresses had made to 'Ganga-ji' in exchange for returning alive her son who had been swept away by a strong current while bathing in the river. Desperate with grief, she had prayed to the Ganga for his life to be spared and promised that, in return, all the sons in the family would henceforth be dedicated to the river and would follow the Hindu faith.

The family has kept its word. While Chanda is a practising Muslim, her five sons have been brought up as Hindus. You once joked that almost every day of the year is celebrated or observed as festival, feast day, fasting day or a day of mourning in Chanda's house—Holi, Ramzan, the two Eids, Teej, Shivratri, Barawafat, Navratras, Dussehra, Diwali, Shab-e-Barat and the ritual forty days of mourning for Moharram.

Times are changing, though. Chanda has never mentioned it, but you told me that, of her five sons, three have been attempting to reconfigure the heterogeneity of their family's religious identity. While her eldest son has voiced his reluctance to bring up his daughters as Muslims, Chanda's youngest two sons have embraced Islam. These developments have left Chanda disconsolate and resulted in bitter quarrels between her and her sons. You remain hopeful that she will be able to prevail upon her boys to maintain the family's unique plural character.

Your intimate knowledge of Chanda's family comes from old ties. Your great-grandaunt Sadabahar was a good friend of Chanda's great-grandaunt Shehzadi, a friendship that has endured over generations. The doors of Chanda's home are always open to you and your relatives. Chanda is among your most trustworthy confidantes in Banaras; you describe her as a deep well from which no secret ever comes out. Yet you hesitate to call her your friend.

That's the way Chanda is, you say. She has dependents, followers and, as a tawaif, she had lovers—but never any friends. Alcohol is her only friend. According to you, she has never had the time or inclination to invest in the emotional give and take needed to forge a friendship. No one really knows what Chanda thinks or feels. She is supremely self-sufficient, you say, people and their opinion of her have never mattered to Chanda. She has no interest in other peoples' affairs, except those that they bring to her to solve.

Chanda has been courteous to me in her own rough and ready manner the few times that I have accompanied you to her house. Beyond greetings and perfunctory offers of tea, however, she has made amply clear her lack of interest in entertaining my queries either about her own life or about her community's social history. Though her indifference has not helped my research, over time, I have come to respect Chanda and the boundaries that she has clearly drawn.

I have come today to meet her mother, Tara, who everyone estimates to be a bit over a century old. This is going to be my first meeting with her. Despite her age, Tara prefers to live for the greater part of the year in Dewa Sharif in Barabanki district, famous for its dargah, shrine of the Sufi saint Waris Ali Shah. Looked after by a relative, Tara stays close to the shrine in a small house that Chanda has bought for her, and spends almost all her time praying at the dargah. Extreme summer and winter provide Chanda the excuse to drag her mother back to the comfort of Banaras. But not for long. As soon as she can, Tara returns to the spiritual sanctuary of Dewa Sharif.

Chanda has arranged my appointment with Tara. And, in some time, she has a young daughter-in-law escort me to Tara's room.

I am not sure what I had expected Chanda's mother to look like. But I am surprised when I step inside and see the small, sprightly old woman seated on the bed, plaiting her damp, wispy strands of white hair. Tara looks like a cheerful little sparrow that has just had a bath. Her voice is crystal clear and lively, 'So you are the filmmaker Chanda mentioned! Come in, child, and sit down here in front of me.'

Tara's blind eyes are opaque, but her wizened, animated face mirrors her excitement at receiving a guest. 'Who has the time to visit an old bone like me,' she hoots with laughter. 'And so I wondered, who is this miss who wishes to interview me? And why? I am just an old ruin waiting for redemption at the hands of my Maker.'

Tara's jolly sociability makes for a striking contrast with her daughter's taciturn aloofness. Neither does Chanda look anything like the petite old woman beaming at me. Tara's face, with its high cheekbones and a pert button-nose, is still strikingly beautiful. The only gene that Tara has conclusively passed on to Chanda is her dark complexion. Yet, while Chanda's duskiness is dull, Tara's radiates vitality.

Unlike her daughter, Tara enjoys talking. She tells me that when Gandhi-ji and Nehru-ji came to Banaras, as a young girl then, she had attended their meetings in Town Hall. She was almost middle-aged when India gained Independence. Breaking into her memories, I ask if, as a child, she had known Sadabahar.

'Sadabahar? The one from Bhabua? She was a friend of Shehzadi nani, my grandaunt who had brought up my mother, Gulab Jan, as her own along with her own daughter, Mannan Jan. Sadabahar khala would often stay with Shehzadi nani when she came to Banaras for a mujra. She was a frequent visitor to the city, and loved my mother and Mannan khala whom she had seen grow up in front of her eyes,' Tara says.

'My mother said that Sadabahar khala specially came to Banaras when I was born. She died a few years later, but I have heard so much about her from my mother that it always felt as if I knew her well. Sadabahar khala was very popular with the wealthiest merchant-banker families, who were among the biggest patrons of music in Banaras. They invited her to come all the way from Bhabua to perform at their mehfils. Such was the charisma of her singing!'

Tara talks about a bullion merchant in Banaras who fell in love with Sadabahar at first sight. He had a reputation for flitting from kotha to kotha and throwing money at any tawaif who caught his fancy. During one of Sadabahar's longish stays in Banaras, so besotted was he by her that he stopped visiting other kothas and spent every evening in her company.

One day, much to Sadabahar's surprise, the merchant's wife paid her a visit. Their young son was dying of a serious ailment, she said. Even the best hakims and vaidyas of the city had given up on the child.

Well-wishers had advised that the boy be shown to doctors of English medicine. But the merchant had become blind to his duty towards his family; instead of sitting by his son's bedside, he spent all his time with Sadabahar. He had neither the money nor the inclination to take the child to Calcutta, where the best doctors were available. Over the years, his fascination with tawaifs had made him neglect his business, resulting in huge losses. Now he was showering all his remaining wealth on Sadabahar, including the jewellery that belonged to his wife. His family could only watch helplessly as the child drew closer to death.

Sadabahar was very distressed at hearing this. The merchant had never mentioned his son's illness to her, or the financial difficulties he was facing. As a tawaif, she had been taught the guiles to make a lover shower her with riches while the going was good. Wealth was a tawaif's only surety in old age, she knew well. Yet, Sadabahar was not greedy or selfish. Unlike other tawaifs, who might have thought nothing of bringing an infatuated lover to ruination, she never wished for more than what her admirers gave of their own accord. Remorseful that she had inadvertently contributed to the suffering of her lover's wife and son, Sadabahar immediately returned to her all the jewellery that the merchant had gifted her, and solemnly promised to sever all links with him.

When this story spread in the bazaar, most tawaifs made fun of Sadabahar. Some called her a fool, while others tried to find some hidden motive in her sympathy for the wife. But Tara's grandaunt Shehzadi knew that Sadabahar had been propelled only by the integrity of her own character.

'Nani understood khala well because both of them were childhood friends since Chainpur,' Tara says. 'Before shifting to Banaras, our family too belonged to that town. As girls, nani and khala had played together, learnt from the same teachers and had become tawaifs around the same time.'

Shehzadi's mother Bhagirathi had decided to bring her beautiful and talented daughter to Banaras once she reached puberty. Besides its pre-eminence as a place of pilgrimage, nineteenth-century Banaras was the largest city of northern India, second only to the colonial capital Calcutta. Cultural hub of the Bhojpuri-speaking region, it was also a centre of intense commercial activity. Its breathtaking river-fronts, magnificent temples, luxurious havelis, bazaars laden with goods and crowded with pilgrims and visitors from across the country and outside, all spoke of its economic prosperity.

The city commanded a rich agricultural hinterland that filled its grain marts with rice, barley, maize and other foodstuff. Besides, Banaras had for long been a centre for the production and trade of textiles, including silk, that were exported to distant lands: 'From the looms of Benares went forth the most delicate silks that adorned the balls of St. James' and of the Petit trianon,' wrote Thomas Babington Macaulay in 1867 (in an essay included in his *Critical Historical, and Miscellaneous Essays and Poems, Volume* 2).

Strategically located, the city had also risen to become an important commercial centre of trade between eastern and northern, central and even southern India. Thus, Bishop Heber, the Anglican Bishop of Calcutta, in his travels through Banaras in 1824 (accounts of which are collected in *Bishop Heber in Northern India: Selections from Heber's Journal*), would comment, 'Benares is, in fact, a very industrious and wealthy, as well as a very holy city. It is a great mart where the shawls of the north, the diamonds of the south, and the muslins of Dacca and the eastern provinces centre and it has very considerably silk, cotton, and fine woollen manufactories of its own.'

Nineteenth-century Banaras was presided over by the Bhumihar king, the merchant-banker aristocracy and the Gosains or mendicant trader-soldiers who controlled the vast resources of the rich temples under their charge. This triumvirate provided generous patronage for literature, art and music to flourish in the city. A centre of diverse genres of Hindustani music—dhrupad, khayal, tappa and thumri—Banaras thronged with musicians ranging from dhrupadiyas (dhrupad vocalists), kalawants and binkars (instrumentalists who played upon the Rudra vina, sitar and sarod) to tawaifs and their accompanists, Dharis, Kathaks, Kinnars and Bhaats.

Dhari Muslims in Banaras traced their descent to the eighteenth-century musician, Shori Miyan, who is known as the founder of the musical form tappa. Originally from Punjab, Shori Miyan migrated to Lucknow, after which a branch of his family is believed to have shifted to Banaras. Mostly sarangi players, Dhari musicians in the city were known not only for their mastery of thumri and dadra associated so closely with courtesan singers but also of tappa, a genre that they helped establish in the musical life of the city.

They were joined in performance at the tawaifs' kothas by Hindu accompanist musicians, the Kathaks and Kinnars. Kathak musicians in the city were associated closely with the tabla and traced their origins to Lucknow. Among them, Ram Sahai, who learnt the percussion instrument from Maudu Khan in the court of Nawab Wajid Ali Shah, is revered in Banarasi music history for giving shape to the distinct Banarasi baj, or style of tabla playing. As music teachers to tawaifs, Kathaks popularised the dance-based bandish thumri that had reached its maturity in the nawabi court of Lucknow. They are also credited for bringing to Banaras the kathak dance, which they taught to the tawaifs. Kinnar male musicians, on the other hand, claimed ancient Purana-based origins and were associated primarily with the sarangi, although a few did play the tabla.

Tawaifs ruled the destinies of these communities of male accompanist musicians. Among the wealthiest women in Banaras, they hailed from different places across northern India. While some came from distant Lucknow, Delhi and beyond, many like Shehzadi, had migrated from towns and villages in the Bhojpuri-speaking belt.

Contemporary accounts reveal that the kotha-based community in Banaras was broadly stratified based on the class of patrons that the tawaifs entertained as also their musical and other cultural talents. The categories were fluid and narratives reflect how a poor tawaif could, through her beauty, talent and luck in getting a rich patron, make her way up the ladder of success.

At the highest rung were the famed elite tawaifs of the city. They embodied the aesthetic and erotic refinement of Banaras. A great majority of them came from Gandharva and Muslim Nat communities. They entertained an exclusive category of aristocratic patrons and were among the wealthiest women in the city. The financial security provided by wealthy patrons enabled these tawaifs to invest in the best available music and dance teachers, expensive clothes and jewellery, and a luxurious ambience in the kotha—all essential to ensuring their success and popularity as performers. The kotha's prestige attracted to it well-known male musicians, poets and other members of the literati, thus marking it as a musical and cultural institution.

Elite tawaifs were invited to sing at the court, at family celebrations in the homes of merchant-bankers and in prominent temples and the ghats of the Ganga during important religious functions. In his early twentieth-century travelogue, E.B. Havell says of the courtesans of Banaras that 'they sang free in the akhada of Sadhu Kinnaram, in the Vagishwari temple on the occasion of Saraswati Puja, in front of the Shitala temple in the month of Chaitra, near Panchganga Ghat in the month of Kartik, in the akhada of Naga Baba near Gai Ghat'.

Tara now tells me a story that I have also heard from you and your family. 'At the height of her glory, Sadabahar khala received blessings that all musician families in and around Banaras craved,' Tara narrates. 'Once a year, all musicians, big and small, men and women, would gather at Baba Kinnaram's akhada in the city. They would all take turns to perform free at the saint's shrine and seek his blessings.'

Baba Kinnaram was a much-venerated Shaivite ascetic and is credited with establishing the headquarters of the Aghori sect of wandering mendicants or sadhus in the eighteenth century at Ramgarh near Banaras. A deeply secretive cult, the Aghori ascetics are devotees of Bhairava, the fierce manifestation of Shiva associated with annihilation.

Challenging conventional distinctions between the notions of purity and pollution as illusionary, Aghori sadhus seek to realise the self's identity with the absolute through various practices, including rituals that challenge social taboos like drinking alcohol, smoking marijuana, ritualistically eating human flesh, using a human skull as a begging bowl, meditating at cremation grounds and having sex as part of worship. These intense practices, it is popularly believed, bestow Aghori sadhus with magical powers.

Many contemporary musicians and tawaifs, both Hindu and Muslim, in Banaras have talked to me about the boons that performers received from Baba Kinnaram at the musical gatherings in the akhada. Tawaifs, in particular, performed in large numbers on these occasions. Colonial ethnographic accounts of the late nineteenth century mention that Baba Kinnaram's akhada 'is frequented by dancing girls in hope of success in their profession'.

'Sadabahar khala too had gone to perform hazari there one year,' Tara tells me. 'When her turn came to sing, such was the magic of her voice that all the people present were enthralled and even the birds stopped chirping and the cows in the akhada stopped grazing.

'Naturally, Baba Kinnaram was very pleased and, speaking through a medium, said, "Sadabahar, you whose name means eternal spring, ask for any boon you wish." Sadabahar khala, her head bowed in reverence, replied, "Baba, I wish for a voice for my family." Granting her wish, Baba Kinnaram declared, "Rest assured, Sadabahar! Your future generations will be blessed with a voice so exquisite that even celestial musicians will feel jealous."

'And so it was,' Tara concludes the tale. 'Many of the women in Sadabahar's family sing so beautifully that, when they perform in a mehfil, even seasoned musicians cannot hold their own before their voice. They are a family blessed by Baba himself.'

Chanda's daughter-in-law staggers in carrying a tray laden with pakodis, laddus and tea. Directed by Tara, she proceeds to pile up a plate for me despite my protestations that it's too much.

'Nonsense! It's nothing! We have a saying in our community—never refuse an invitation to khana, food, and gana, singing,' Tara urges me on like she would a child. 'And while you eat, I will recite for you a poem that I used to sing in my mehfils.' She takes off with effortless ease:

Taoqi, Maena, Umda, Gunna
Uttam, Jagmag, Tara, Munna
Chandrakala, Gulbadan, Janaki
Faijan, Bibba, Manaki
Chanchal, Chandar, Champa, Sundar
Heera, Maanik, Panna, Mundar
Zohra aur Mushtari, Kundan
Sadabahar, Bulaakan, Gulshan
Pancham aur Amila, Ganno
Naazo aur Allahdei, Banno ...

This recitation of names, Tara tells me, is part of a Hindi poem, *Veshya Strotra*—Invocation to the Prostitute—written by Babu Bacchu Singh 'Bhakta' Vaishnav, a scion of Banarasi merchant aristocracy and regular visitor to her grandaunt Shehzadi's kotha. A signed copy of the poem he presented to Shehzadi had been a prized family heirloom but is now lost.

I was subsequently able to hunt down a copy of *Veshya Strotra* in the archives of BHU's Bharat Kala Bhavan museum. Wildly popular in the late nineteenth century, it had a foreword written by Bharatendu Harishchandra and ran into a third edition in 1896. Part laudatory, mostly satirical, this ode to the prominent courtesans of Banaras begins by invoking 108 of them by name. The name Sadabahar finds mention in the invocation. And though there is no conclusive evidence to prove it, I am tempted to believe that this is a reference to your great-grandaunt who had performed so often in Banaras.

The rest of the poem is divided into four-line verses, or chaupayi, describing the musical, literary, conversational, amorous and other skills as also the temperament and physical attributes of many of the 108 tawaifs invoked in the opening section. One of these chaupayis is dedicated to Shehzadi. Described as 'Pathan's Shehzadi', because of her long-term romantic relationship with a Pathan moneylender in the city, Tara's grandaunt is extolled thus:

> Her innocent face is winsome, she keeps her ways simple,
> This beautiful daughter of a Kanchan, bestows grace upon her lovers when she sits in their laps,
> The aesthetes agree that she has much to teach as an instructor in matters of the heart,
> Imbued with a rare delicacy amongst flighty tawaifs is Shehzadi ...

'Shehzadi nani,' Tara says, 'was legendary for the gentle courtesy she extended towards all. Prince or pauper, nani was polite and well-mannered with everyone, unlike those who simpered at the rich and snarled at the poor. She was a great singer and dancer but was admired too for her fluency in Urdu, Hindi, Maithil, Bangla and Farsi, besides Bhojpuri, of course. In later life, she also learnt some English from a Christian lady teacher.

'Her kotha in Dal Mandi, very close to where we live now, was luxuriously appointed with furniture made of the finest Burma teak, cut-glass chandeliers, silk and satin curtains and gilded mirrors. Her hospitality was legendary. Besides her daily mehfils, nani would also frequently host musical events called jalsa to celebrate weddings and the birth of a girl child in the family, or in honour of a visiting courtesan or male musician from outside Banaras.'

Tara tells me that Shehzadi would often organise a jalsa when her best friend Sadabahar visited. Tawaifs from Banaras were invited along with select patrons and male musicians. The high point of these gatherings was the music, with all the assembled musicians taking turns to perform. Bhaiyya-ji Ganpat Rao, the greatest harmonium player of the time, credited with popularising the instrument in Hindustani music, was a familiar face at her gatherings, as also Ustad Mojuddin Khan, the well-known thumri exponent.

A meeting at one such jalsa forged a lasting friendship between Sadabahar and the premier Gandharva courtesan of Banaras, Husna Bai, who was nominated choudharayin in Banaras in the early twentieth century. A well-respected musician, Husna Bai was renowned for her deep knowledge of literary texts in Sanskrit, Persian, Urdu and Hindi. She had regular correspondence on literary matters with the tallest literary figure of nineteenth-century Banaras, Bharatendu Harishchandra, who was also a patron of the arts.

Her handwriting, both in Urdu and Hindi was, I have been told by old Banarasis who have seen her letters, 'as well formed as that of a man', a compliment in those times when men were better educated than women. She was also a regular and highly respected participant—and the only woman—in the city's many literary and philosophical gatherings, where men from the local intelligentsia met informally to discuss and debate literature, spirituality, philosophy and religious texts.

Husna elicits fulsome praise from Bacchu Singh 'Bhakta' Vaishnav:

> Mistress of letters, Husna has the mightiest and most worthy at her beck and call,
> The wealthy camp outside her house and vie with each other to bestow upon her countless riches …

'As a girl, I accompanied my mother to Husna Bai's house in Raja Darwaza,' Tara says. 'It was the most majestic mansion in the entire locality. Two dazzlingly liveried sentries were always posted at her door to prevent riff-raff from entering. Visitors to her kotha were entertained only by prior appointment. Past the entrance, a huge elephant made of solid silver greeted guests in the reception hall. Persian carpets richly embroidered in silk were strewn all over the gleaming marble floors. I was used to the magnificence of Shehzadi nani's house but Husna Bai's palace was in a league of its own. My mother would tell me that Husna Bai always insisted upon having Sadabahar khala stay with her for at least a few days whenever she visited Banaras.'

> This restless heart is captive to the memory of her alluring eyes,
> Sighing with yearning, this lover of beauty finds no peace,
> His body burns with desire, his mind is turbulent,
> Smitten by the arrow of Myna's music he wanders the streets injured …

Sadabahar's keenest rival in Banaras was Myna Bai. Her deep, sonorous and exquisitely trained voice, it was said, could be heard on the riverfronts of Banaras when she performed for the maharaja of Banaras at his fort in Ramnagar on the opposite bank of the Ganga. Recognised as one of the greatest musicians produced by the city, Myna was extolled not only for her mastery over thumri and its sub-genres, dadra, hori, chaiti and kajari, but equally for her dazzling rendition of khayal and tappa. A great favourite of Maharaja Prabhu Narayan Singh of Banaras and his son Ishwari Narayan Singh, she was invited to perform at all court celebrations. Tara tells me that Myna was addicted to marijuana and smoked her chillum all the time, especially before the start of a mehfil.

Myna belonged to a Gandharva family that had produced an illustrious line of singers and dancers. She had inherited her kotha from her aunt Rati Bai, a well-known vocalist of her time. And now Myna Bai had introduced with much fanfare the next generation of musicians from her family, Rajeshwari and Shyama Bai, her beautiful and gifted daughters. However, such was the charm of Myna Bai that her large number of patrons still far outstripped Rajeshwari and Shyama's impressive array of admirers.

'Myna Bai's allure was eternal,' says Tara, who in her childhood had seen the diva. 'It was not as if she was exceptionally beautiful. My Shehzadi nani was by far lovelier. Her own daughter Rajeshwari radiated youthful beauty. And yet, she paled before her mother.'

Legend has it that one of her admirers was so besotted by Myna Bai and her singing that he would turn up at every mehfil where she performed, irrespective of whether he was invited or not. Braving royal censure and even possible imprisonment, he once gate-crashed an exclusive mehfil organised by the maharaja of Banaras, just to prove his love for Myna.

During her visits, Sadabahar must certainly have also met the emerging star of thumri, young Vidyadhari Bai, of whom the *Veshya Strotra* says:

> Her rising breasts are as beautiful as the sharpness of her intellect,
> Her words carefully chosen and accompanied by a radiant smile, cast a spell on the listener,
> Let aside the praise of connoisseurs even in the eyes of this humble poet,
> Vidyadhari is the embodiment of a lovely fairy ...

Vidyadhari was originally from Jasuri, a village close to Banaras, and belonged to the same distinguished family as Myna Bai. Her education to become a tawaif had been long and intensive. Besides learning music from Ramsumer Mishra and Dargahi Mishra in Banaras, she had also been a student of Nasir Khan and Bashir Khan in Darbhanga, and was famed for her musical rendition of Jaideva's epic poem *Geeta Govinda*. Vidyadhari was also known for her culinary talents and her skill at playing cards.

Widely travelled, Vidyadhari had performed in princely mehfils from Kashmir and Punjab to Kutch and Dhaka. In recognition of her musical genius, she was appointed court musician at a relatively young age by the maharaja of Banaras. She was also one of the earliest, most acclaimed exponents of the slow-paced and deeply reflective style of thumri rendition that was still developing in Banaras at that time.

Based on the region's folk songs, brought in by migrant tawaifs and male musicians from their original homes in the villages and towns in present-day eastern UP and Bihar, this new style was marked by a deceleration of tempo and emphasis upon bol banao, or elaboration of the multiple meanings embedded in a text. Instead of the classical teental, the newly evolving bol banao thumri used folk-derived metres like sitarkhani and deepchandi. It was associated closely with elite tawaif singers of Banaras, who performed it along with the still-dominant bandish thumri, which focused on speed and rhythm and was complemented by the accompanying kathak dance.

Almost all the women performers in Tara's narrative and mentioned in the *Veshya Strotra* belonged to the elite sections of the city's courtesan community. Placed below this group were tawaifs from the lower-ranked Nat, Bedia and Kanjar clans. Though many of them were skilled musicians, they did not have the resources to be as discriminating about their choice of patrons. They would be looked down upon by the elite tawaifs for standing on their balconies in the evening to attract the attention of passers-by in the bazaar below.

Though they did sing thumri, and also tappa, their repertoire in the main consisted of popular ghazals, dadras and folk music and, down the decades, even songs performed in Parsi theatre and films. It is the repertoire of these tawaifs in the early twentieth century that finds disparaging mention in literary Hindi writing of the period for being 'vulgar' but hugely popular with the 'common' people in the bazaar.

Still lower in the hierarchy, one finds mention of female performers like gonaharins, who were not counted as tawaifs at all. Besides performing mainly for purdah-bound women at family celebrations, they danced in religious and cultural processions on public thoroughfares and streets, considered taboo by the elite courtesans.

Brothel-based prostitutes formed a separate category altogether. Primarily engaged in sex work, some among them also had rudimentary music and dance skills. Their ranks were filled by women from the Bedia and Kanjar communities, and from Nat clans like the Magahiyas. A large number of women and girls sold off by their destitute peasant or artisanal families, or fleeing from the hunger and want of an impoverished countryside, or escaping ill-treatment in their marital or natal homes, also made their way into the by-lanes of Dal Mandi inhabited exclusively by sex workers, or to the Lal Bazaar brothels of the cantonment area.

'Are there any sex workers still in Dal Mandi?' I ask Tara.

'The prostitutes were driven out of here first, around the early 1970s. A bit later, tawaifs were forced to shut down their kothas. Dal Mandi today is a respectable locality of honourable, decent people,' Tara says sardonically.

When I eventually take my leave, and walk down the narrow, busy streets of Dal Mandi, I notice that there are very few women around. The few I see are mostly shoppers draped respectably in an array of veils—matronly housewives covered in the indigenous burqa, school- and college-going girls wearing headscarves, mostly in black or white but also in stripes that seem to be the latest fashion trend in hijabs.

I spot young women swishing past in shiny new imported abayas, brought no doubt by their husbands or other male relatives from Saudi Arabia and other Gulf countries, where thousands of men from this city and around have headed to over the years in search of jobs. Braving appalling living conditions and exploitative terms of employment, they work there as construction labour on opulent high-rises, chauffeur luxurious cars, and cook and serve in high-end restaurants. They consider themselves lucky for getting salaries that—though abysmal by local standards—are much higher than what they could hope for back home.

Their absence from the streets of Dal Mandi is marked as much by the flowing georgette abayas of their womenfolk as by the shiny new exteriors of their refurbished houses. Many of the old kotha buildings in the area have gone through such hideous alterations that their original structures can barely be discerned. Yet others have been demolished altogether to make way for shops, workshops and godowns, where the men that remain in Dal Mandi ply their trade as shopkeepers, craftsmen, electricians and tailors. The din of their working days drowns out memories of an earlier time when these streets dozed through the day and woke up refreshed in the evening to the singing and laughter of the bare-faced, bold-eyed women who held sway here.

CHAPTER 9

Bhang, Paan, Mela, Masti

'Do you have a booking here, madam?' asks the imposingly whiskered and liveried guard on duty at the padlocked gates of the Nadesar Palace hotel. His question is well founded. With my crumpled shalwar-kurta, dusty sandals and hair tousled from the auto-rickshaw ride, I hardly look a likely guest at the most expensive hotel in Banaras.

Hurriedly trying to flatten my wayward curls, I admit that I am not a prospective lodger but wish to have a look at the property. 'I am sorry, madam, but that will not be possible. Only guests are welcome on the premises,' is the smooth reply.

Normally, I might have smiled at the sentry's assumed superiority and taken it as part of his job brief, but today for some reason I find it galling. Maybe it's because I am irritated with myself for coming here on an impulse without first arranging a research visit with the management. Or it is the alacrity with which the sentry unlocks the gate for the black limousine that imperiously glides past me into the tree-lined driveway of the hotel. Maybe it's just the sun and the sticky perspiration I feel trickling down my back. But I feel stubborn. I had decided to see Nadesar Palace today. And I will see it. Without thinking too much, I find myself doing something I haven't done since I was a rookie documentary filmmaker using all means to expose murky realities. I lie; or rather, I stretch the truth.

'I would like to speak with your manager, please'—remembering in the nick of time the name that I read on the hotel website before coming here, I repeat it hoping fervently it's still the same man. 'He is expecting me. Please tell him that the filmmaker whose office had contacted him is here.' I sound more confident than I feel.

As always, the 'filmmaker' bit works. The assistant manager is soon on the line sounding puzzled. No, neither the manager nor he has been contacted by anyone from my office. What did I say my name was? I soon find myself walking down the shady driveway flanked by immaculately kept lawns, mango orchards, and flower and vegetable gardens, to the colonial-style, white-painted Nadesar Palace hotel that nestles among 2.5 acres of greenery.

Located beyond the labyrinthine lanes and chaos of old Banaras, next to the cantonment area, the recorded history of the building dates to the late eighteenth century when it served as residence to a Mr Davis, the then British magistrate in Banaras. It changed hands a century later, passing from the British to the maharaja of Banaras, Ishwari Narain Singh, who ruled from 1835 to 1889, and after his death to his successors. Now owned by the Taj group, it is positioned as an exclusive boutique hotel for those with deep pockets and deeper aspirations to 'live like Maharajas'.

'I am sorry you were stopped at the gates. The hotel and its grounds are out of bounds to non-guests. Even guests from our Gateway Hotel next door are not allowed entry here. So, tell me, how I may help you?' asks the young, polite assistant manager who has hurried across the front lawns of the hotel to meet me.

My own introduction and stated purpose of my visit hover between fact and fiction. I am a filmmaker based in Delhi, which is true. I am here to research the history and present status of Nadesar Palace on behalf of an award-winning French director who is planning to make a travel film and is interested in finding out if the hotel is worthy of inclusion in his documentary—some parts true, most parts fiction.

'What is the name of his company, ma'am?' the young assistant manager wants to know. I hadn't thought of that. For a moment, my mind goes blank, but then inspiration strikes.

'Arc de Triomphe Productions,' I reply with a serene smile. 'They are based in Paris. And last year won the best travel documentary award at Cannes.' This was becoming fun.

Looking suitably impressed, the young man timidly asks his final question, 'And what is the name of the filmmaker, ma'am?'

I juggle between the new wave masters—Truffaut, Godard, Rohmer, Chabrol—but then decide on paying homage to cinema vérité instead. 'Jean Rouch. He is a very important filmmaker from France,' I reply with stout conviction, hoping that my young host is not a world cinema aficionado.

'Would you like a tour of the hotel, ma'am?' His enthusiastic reply tells me he is not. Any twinge of conscience that I feel at lying so blatantly to this innocent young man I put to rest at the altar of research. Beyond wishing to see the interiors of Nadesar Palace, I come here with no sinister agenda.

Guiding me towards the main veranda of the building that serves as foyer, the assistant manager tells me, 'This is a heritage site. We have made renovations without changing the main structure. The hotel still houses many valuable paintings from the maharaja's collection as also select pieces of furniture. Our aim is to provide our guests a sense of old-world tranquillity and the experience of being treated like royalty.'

As if on cue, a small brass band materialises out of nowhere, led by a photographer and a posse of Brahmin priests carrying between them a welcome thali of kumkum, a lit diya, bells, conch-shell and garlands. No doubt mistaking me for an arriving guest, they scurry forth to give me the customary 'royal welcome'. I recall the ecstatic reviews by former guests, mainly Americans, cited on the hotel's website, about the 'ancient Hindu' ceremonial reception they had received, complete with the mandatory photograph taken on arrival.

Looking a bit sheepish, the assistant manager discreetly signals them to back off before ushering me inside the foyer that opens into a luxuriously appointed dining hall. 'We have only ten suites and rooms in the hotel,' he informs me. 'The rooms are named after dignitaries, Queen Elizabeth, Lord Mountbatten, Pandit Jawaharlal Nehru and others, who have stayed here in the past.'

Nadesar Palace was used by the rulers of Banaras as their city residence. While their ancestral home, Ramnagar fort, lay across the river Ganga, they used the Nadesar Palace to host visiting dignitaries and to entertain guests on ceremonial occasions.

'The elite of the city assembled at 8 p.m. at Nadesar Palace at the invitation of the maharaja. The commissioner, collector and other British notables were also present. Everyone was very pleased with the plays that were staged as part of the evening's entertainment and with the performance of nach.' That is the Hindi newspaper *Bharat Jiwan* describing a spectacular evening of entertainment organised by the maharaja in 1887 to celebrate Queen Victoria's golden jubilee as monarch of the British empire. Earlier in the day, the Brahmins of the city had conducted elaborate religious rituals at Dashashwamedh and Manikarnika ghats to pray for the queen's long life and reign. On both occasions, the city's ruling elite—the Bhumihar king, merchant aristocracy, Gosains, Brahmin scholars and ritual specialists—had been present in full force along with the British residents to reiterate their loyalty to the queen.

The fortunes of the city's elite had long depended on aligning their destiny with the ruling dispensation of the day. Their ascent to political, economic, social and cultural dominance had coincided with the disintegration of the Mughal empire in the early eighteenth century. They had then been swift in promising allegiance to the nawab of Awadh, who during this period was vested with political power over Banaras.

It was around this time that Mansaram, a small but ambitious Bhumihar landowner, entered the employment of the nazim, or representative of the nawab of Awadh in the Banaras region, Mir Rustam Ali. Besides being a great patron of music and musicians, Mir Rustam Ali is also credited with building Mir ghat, and with introducing the Burhwa Mangal boat festival in Banaras.

Through intrigue, bribery and diplomacy, in 1734, Mansaram was able to wrest control of Mir Rustam Ali's position by promising Nawab Safdar Jung of Awadh Rs 4 lakh more in revenue than had been given by the former nazim. Balwant Singh, son and successor of Mansaram, further consolidated his family's control on Banaras. During the Battle of Buxar in 1764, he chose to secretly extend support to the British even though he was in the employ of the nawab of Awadh, who, along with the nawab of Bengal and the Mughal emperor, Shah Alam II, was fighting against the colonial troops. After the defeat of the Indian rulers at Buxar, the British rewarded Balwant Singh by recognising his claim to possession of the Banaras region in exchange for a massive tribute of Rs 8 lakh.

Balwant Singh's successor Chait Singh fell out with the British when he was unable to meet their demand for an arbitrarily raised tribute. As punishment, the British deposed him and installed Chait Singh's relative Mahip Narayan as king in 1781. From this period onwards, the Bhumihar rulers of Banaras were relieved bit by bit of all administrative, revenue and judicial authority over their territories, which was now controlled directly by the British. Still, the dynasty, with active encouragement from its colonial overlords, continued to play a significant role in the cultural and religious life of Banaras, imbuing it with a distinctly Hindu identity.

The maharajas of Banaras played an integral part in celebrations of festivals like the Burhwa Mangal and the Ram Lila of Ramnagar, both of which were organised under their aegis. They were also great patrons of Sanskrit learning and literature, and provided patronage to Brajbhasha poetry, both devotional and erotic. Painting flourished in the Banaras court. During the long reign of Ishwari Narayan Singh, painters like Dullu Lall and Kamlapati from Patna moved to Banaras and found employment at the court, also training other artists. The maharaja commissioned numerous group portraits, a series of paintings of the famous courtesans of the city as well as works to commemorate important occasions. Musicians too, men and women, vocalists and instrumentalists, congregated here from other courts.

On the economic front, British support to the Bhumihar rulers of Banaras led to a phase of relative peace and security that benefited both agriculture and trade. There was widespread construction of river embankments and irrigation tanks. Markets came up along the Ganga and trade routes became more secure, spurring overland long-distance commerce, much of which was controlled and facilitated by the Gosains.

A religious sect of armed ascetics, Gosains engaged in trade, banking and soldiering. In the eighteenth century, they were the largest owners of property in Banaras, controlling many of the large temples and monasteries. Venerated by the ordinary people, the Gosains' monopoly over long-distance trade was bolstered by their religious status and their military prowess.

After the breakdown of the Mughal empire, Gosains enjoyed a reputation through the eighteenth and early nineteenth centuries as mercenary soldiers who served competing political powers, including the nawabs of Awadh, the Marathas and the East India Company, often changing allegiance to the winning side. In payment, they amassed landholdings across northern and central India, thus further consolidating their control over trade routes.

The establishment of colonial suzerainty over large parts of the country in the nineteenth century led to the waning of the Gosains' soldiering activities. But they continued to be a formidable presence in Banaras, presiding over many of its rich temples and monasteries, and wielding influence in the commercial, religious and cultural activities and institutions of the city.

The Gosains led a lavish lifestyle and were generous patrons of music and musicians. Almost all the major temples in Banaras they controlled had a tradition of inviting musicians, including tawaifs, to sing and dance at the special celebrations of sringar, literally meaning decoration or beautifying of the presiding deity. Held annually, but sometimes more than once a year, sringar involved decking up the deity for darshan by the devotees, special cleaning and illumination of the temple, cooking of special offerings to the deity, and performances by courtesans and male musicians. Tawaifs were also invited to perform in temples on festive occasions, such as the nine-day celebrations of Navratras, Saraswati Puja and during the festivities that preceded and followed Holi.

Forming the backbone of Banaras's economy were the third group of the city's elite—the wealthy merchant-banker families who had made their fortunes from the city's vibrant commerce. Their banking operations had been boosted phenomenally with the downfall of the Mughal empire and with it the collapse of the provincial treasuries in the eighteenth century. In the absence of imperial security, hundis or bankers' credit bills became the only means of transferring money across the subcontinent. The merchant-bankers also extended loans to other traders, as also to landowners and rulers in return for security in the form of land revenue.

By the late eighteenth century, the city's merchant-bankers were quick to extend support to colonial expansion into the countryside, earning for themselves the privilege of being recognised as British subjects, which further assured their economic pre-eminence in Banaras. The consolidation of colonial rule and consequent establishment of a network of imperial treasuries across British India, along with the introduction of the uniform silver rupee in 1835, meant that the hundis of merchant-bankers were no longer needed. The losses they sustained as a result were somewhat compensated for by changes in the landowning pattern following the Permanent Settlement. By the mid-nineteenth century, 40 per cent of the land in the Banaras region had slipped out of the hands of traditional landowner families to become the property of civil servants and merchant-bankers.

'My nani-ji converted this mehfil ghar, music room, into a temple a few years after my grandfather passed away,' says Krishna Kumar Rastogi, or Rastogi-ji as he is generally known. The hall occupies an entire wing on the first floor of his family haveli. Courteously ushering me inside, he leads the way through the gloomy darkness. While his voice matches his actual age of around sixty years, Rastogi-ji's laboriously slow movements and his stooping and shuffling gait make him seem a quarter-century older.

Outside, Thatheri Bazaar is enveloped in the drowsy stupor of a monsoon afternoon. Deriving its name from the many shops of copper and brass utensils located here, Thatheri Bazaar is the main thoroughfare of Chaukhamba, in the past the poshest address in Banaras. The still-imposing exteriors of the once-grand havelis that line Chaukhamba's alleys, stand testimony to the wealth and power of their owners, the city's merchant aristocracy.

From deep within Rastogi-ji's family haveli, one of the oldest in Chaukhamba, I hear faint sounds of a familiar music track. Someone is awake this sleepy afternoon, watching family dramas on television. However, silence reigns in the first-floor hall, in which I am just about able to make out the shadowy outline of Rastogi-ji pulling hard at the worn-out knobs of tall Venetian windows with wooden shutters.

Finally, one of the windows reluctantly creaks open to let in sunlight, revealing the mildewed and ruined grandeur of a once stately and luxuriously appointed music room. Its Italian marble flooring is chipped and stained with neglect. The elegant fountain in the centre of the hall, which must have invigorated warm summer nights with the cool splashing of running water, is broken and dried out. The peeling, thick walls look badly in need of a whitewash, and the Belgian cut-glass lamp-holders and chandeliers are cracked with time and stained with thick coatings of dust. Most of the paintings that decorate the niches and the fluting columns holding up the ceiling have faded beyond recognition, or have been superimposed by relatively new and crudely executed religious motifs—perhaps deemed more appropriate for a temple than the voluptuous nayikas and virile heroes that had earlier peopled the mehfil ghar.

The only portion of the hall that looks well maintained is the temple, built to one end. It is partitioned off from the decrepit and disused mehfil ghar by ornately carved wooden doors. Past the doors is the gold-plated inner sanctum, a space restricted to members of the immediate family.

The presiding deity of the temple, Rastogi-ji tells me, is Laddoo Gopal, Krishna in his avatar as a baby clutching a ball of butter in his palm. In Shiva's city Banaras, a majority of merchant-banker families, including Rastogi-ji's, have traditionally been followers of the Krishna worship–centred Vallabha Sampradaya or Pushti Marga. Founded by the sixteenth-century theologian and philosopher Vallabhacharya and his son Vitthala, Vallabha Sampradaya with its rejection of monasticism and emphasis on devotion to Krishna by householders to attain salvation, continues to be popular with mercantile communities across northern and western India.

The responsibility of serving the family gods rests squarely on Rastogi-ji, since his children, two daughters and a son, are completely absorbed, he often comments with great pride and no rancour, with their college classes, computer-training, and accounting and brokerage courses. His highly competent wife Radha is similarly busy taking care of the house and running a children's day-care centre and kindergarten.

Rastogi-ji spends several hours every morning and evening offering worship in the family temple. The remainder of his day is dictated by the Hindu almanac, which he consults religiously to keep track of the date of every fast, every penance or special worship ordained. His deep religiosity, though, does not come in the way of his wistful longing as a musician and music-lover for the lost glory of the music room. Originally built by his great-grandfather, Babu Jagannath, it was furnished luxuriously over subsequent years by Rastogi-ji's grandfather, Babu Purshottam Lall. Both of them, he says, would invite musicians, women and men, to perform in mehfils here.

Originally traders from Gujarat, Rastogi-ji's forefathers migrated to the east in the early eighteenth century, and made their initial fortunes as bankers and revenue collectors in Ballia, which today falls in eastern UP. Over the decades they extended their control over landholdings in Bihar and Bengal. Once their banking operations dried out, Rastogi-ji's forefathers moved into trading in silk cocoons, rice and mango-based products. Shifting base to Banaras in the late eighteenth century, they settled down to the life of business magnates and absentee landholders in a set of sprawling twin havelis located in Chaukhamba, melding into the affluent business community of the area.

Rastogi-ji's ancestors took pride in amassing great fortunes but leading an austere lifestyle dictated by piety and religious rituals. The family was renowned in the city for both prudence and parsimoniousness. Though careful to avoid extravagant display of wealth either on the upkeep of the haveli or on daily living expenses, the family spent generously on a battery of Brahmin ritual specialists who trooped in daily to perform elaborate religious ceremonies. Large sums of money were also donated to Pushti Marga temples. This choice of lifestyle was not unique to Rastogi-ji's family. It was an ideal subscribed to by the larger merchant community in the city. A reputation for frugality, it was felt, added to one's creditworthiness in the market.

Not all merchant families of the time followed this model, of course. There were also those who lived the life of merchant princes in sumptuously furnished palaces and spent freely on fine food, clothing and concubines. Connoisseurs of music, dance and literature, they were munificent patrons of the arts: a lifestyle most flamboyantly exemplified by Bharatendu Harishchandra, whose profligacy was as prodigious as his literary and cultural contribution to the intellectual life of the city. Born into one of the premier merchant-banker families of Banaras, Harishchandra used his vast inheritance to finance his literary and cultural activities and support his extended circle of friends. Equally, the family money was spent on maintaining a large harem, patronising tawaifs, hosting extravagant parties and grandiose entertainments.

Attracted to the power and glamour surrounding such extravagance yet fearful of the threat that it could pose to mercantile credit, Rastogi-ji's great grandfather, Babu Jagannath, a hard-headed merchant-banker but also a music lover, tried to walk the fine balance between parsimony and piety on the one hand and pleasure-seeking on the other. In a significant departure from the frugality expected of him, he had this music hall constructed. Yet, he did not spend excessively on its furnishings and fittings, and contented himself with hosting only the occasional soiree to celebrate a special occasion.

He was succeeded by his son, Babu Purshottam Lall in the late nineteenth century, who inherited his father's business acumen but not his vast fortunes. Bitter property feuds and litigation had resulted not only in huge losses to the family business but also a decimation of its share of landholdings in Bihar and Bengal.

Babu Purshottam Lall moved away from the family business of trading in silk cocoons to dealing in gold and silver. His shrewd business sense soon propelled the family back among the ranks of the wealthy of Banaras. A great lover of music, his indomitable will was tempered by an almost childlike fascination with extravagant ostentation.

As his fortunes soared, so did Babu Purshottam Lall's enthusiasm for staking a claim as a cultural leader among the merchant elite of Banaras. He had the modestly appointed mehfil ghar renovated and refurnished with the finest fittings and furniture imported from Europe. Here, he organised music gatherings often and without reason other than to celebrate the opulent lifestyle of the city's merchant princes.

'Very often, my grandfather's music mehfils lasted ten days or more,' Krishna Kumar Rastogi says. 'The best tawaif singers of Banaras, including Husna Bai, Myna Bai, Shiv Kunwar Bai, Shehzadi and Badi Moti Bai, were invited to perform for a select audience of powerful and wealthy merchants. The tawaifs held my grandfather in very high esteem. Many of them were also his tenants, since our family owned considerable property in Dal Mandi, Nariyal Bazaar and Raja Darwaza.'

The tawaifs, their accompanist musicians and the audience virtually camped in Babu Purshottam Lall's haveli through the period of the festivities. Going home at daybreak after performing through the night, tawaifs would return a few hours later in time for the Bhairavi ki mehfil, a music soiree unique to Banaras and its cultural hinterland, dedicated to songs in Bhairavi, a raga loved by all for its sweetness and poignancy. Though a morning raga, by convention, Bhairavi can be performed at any time of the day. It is also the raga most performed to bring a mehfil to a close.

Freshly bathed, with flowers in their still-damp hair and paan sweetening their breath and staining their lips a becoming red, the tawaifs would sing mostly thumri and dadra, and appropriate seasonal songs like hori, chaiti and kajari in Bhairavi. From the spiritually imbued *Babul mora naihar chhuto jaye*; Father, my maternal home slips away, to the romantic *Baju band khul khul jaye*; My arm-band keeps getting undone, the tawaifs cast a magic spell with their music.

With the ascent of the noon-day sun, the Bhairavi mehfil would draw to a close, and a battery of the finest Brahmin cooks would lay out a banquet of Banarasi delicacies cooked in pure desi ghee. Seated in orderly rows inside the mehfil ghar, the guests would feast upon malai ki poori, malai ki gilori, malai ka samosa, chewra matar, dal ki kachori, kalonji of various vegetables, magdal, dal bati and other delicacies served on pure silver thalis placed upon beautifully embellished chaukis, low wooden stools.

Repast over, the guests returned home for an afternoon siesta. They reassembled around five o'clock to be refreshed by fine quality bhang, paan and music performances by tawaifs and their attendant musicians. Very often, bhands, male performers who sang and danced and played the role of jesters, were also invited to enliven these mehfils with their humour and the banter they exchanged with the assembled audience, but especially with the tawaifs present.

Skilled in the art of sophisticated conversation and clever repartee, the tawaifs matched the bhands rejoinder for rejoinder, couplet for couplet, in a competitive exchange of wits. They simultaneously engaged in flirtatious dialogue with the guests, their performance of pretty preening and pouting, of intimate whispers and seductive glances, laughter and cultivated wordplay as dazzling in its virtuosity as their music and dance.

Many of these assemblies were khadi mehfil, or standing mehfils, in which the tawaifs would stand and perform for guests who were reclining comfortably on mattresses with cushions. The courtesans sang and at the same time danced, while their accompanist musicians too stood and played, with the tablas or sarangi tied to their waists.

By the late nineteenth century, baithaki ki mehfil, where tawaifs and their accompanists sat and performed, was also gaining popularity. The emphasis in baithaki ki mehfil was on expressive singing and bhav batana—the exposition of the multiple meaning of the lyrics through vocal virtuosity, facial expressions and hand gestures.

Dinner would be served around 8–8.30 in the evening and then the music would resume. At this late hour, when the audience mostly consisted of serious lovers of music, the emphasis shifted from the flirtatious and light to intellectually engaging forms like khayal but also tappa, tarana and thumri, in ragas of the night, like Yaman, Kedar, Kamod, Hansadhwani, Darbari, Shahana, Desh and Durga.

As night moved towards dawn, individual performances made way for group songs called gajra, or garland of flowers. Groups of tawaifs, their arms linked, stood and sang together. Still further into the night, the quest for musical perfection took the shape of dangal, or singing competitions, between tawaif performers, resulting in dazzling performances, charged emotions, dizzying triumphs and crushing defeats.

Rastogi-ji is happiest when describing these mehfils from a past before he was even born. Self-effacing music lover, obsessive collector and meticulous archivist, Rastogi-ji has spent the greater part of his life in sangeet seva, service to music. At my insistence, he speaks with characteristic shy earnestness, about his journey through the world of raga and tala.

He was barely six or seven when he was introduced to the khayal singing of the Gwalior gharana as part of the grooming considered necessary to inherit the cultural capital of his merchant family. Simultaneously, the young Krishna Kumar Rastogi had begun collecting. While other boys his age played hockey and cricket, or as they grew older, squandered their fathers' fortunes on the good life, serious-minded Krishna first collected coins, moving on next to stamps and then to music records.

His business family, happy that Krishna's hobby reflected the merchant ideals of thrift and hoarding, encouraged his collections. Their feelings about his other passion were less than ecstatic, though. No one in the family had foreseen that the young man would fall so deeply in love with the khayal, that his ambition of becoming a full-time musician would clash with their expectations that he fulfil the traditional role of merchant, music connoisseur and patron.

Krishna Kumar Rastogi's father drew the line. It was all very well to learn music, but no son of his would be allowed to bring disrepute to the family name by becoming a mere gavaiyya, professional singer. Merchant families like theirs provided benevolent patronage to musicians. They did not sully their name and squander their fortunes by entering the somewhat unsavoury and decidedly erratic business of music-making.

Rastogi-ji was heartbroken. But, brought up to be an obedient son, he bid farewell to his dream and joined the family business that, after the death of his grandfather, had been going steadily downhill. There was one promise he made to himself, though. He would continue serving the cause of music, if not as a musician, then as a collector, archivist and patron.

And to this day he has kept his pledge. Rastogi-ji has spent most of his time and, I suspect, almost all his inheritance, saving rare recordings from being sold to private collectors by contemporary Banarasi families oblivious to the worth of music, and salvaging and restoring old photographs of musicians from discarded trash. Making good use of the high esteem that he is held in by most business families in the city, he feels no embarrassment in going door to door collecting funds to organise a concert, or to felicitate a forgotten musician.

The family business died at the hands of Rastogi-ji's preoccupation with music. He remained unmoved, content to trade profit for sangeet seva. The twin havelis owned by his family, including the one in which he lives with his wife and children, have been partitioned and let out to tenants. The rents, along with the income from his wife's pre-nursery school and crèche, are the family's financial mainstay.

Rastogi-ji's only claim to his merchant lineage is a small electronics shop that he runs from a room of the haveli on the ground floor. The shop, with its meagre and dust-laden inventory of ancient transistor radios, obsolete two-in-one radio-cum-cassette players and vintage television sets, sees few actual shoppers. But it opens out into the bazaar and serves as a space where Rastogi-ji and his music-lover friends can spend hours listening to rare recordings and animatedly discussing the strengths and weaknesses of various musicians and their performance styles.

This is where Rastogi-ji ushers me after his guided tour of the mehfil ghar's peeling grandeur. As I settle down, my host orders a kulhad of lassi for me from the adjacent milk shop. While we wait for it, he pulls out a faded print of a nineteenth-century painting of the river festival unique to Banaras. Epitomising the fabled Banarasi masti, joyfulness and abandonment, Burhwa Mangal was an extraordinary gathering of people. It followed the spring festival of Holi and marked the first Tuesday of the month of Chaitra in the Hindu calendar that straddles March and April. Hosted by the city's merchant aristocracy, the fair had as its chief patron the maharaja of Banaras. Princes and zamindars from other places too especially visited Banaras to participate in the celebrations.

'Burhwa Mangal used to be a four- to five-day celebration of the Ganga and its ghats, of music and dance. Everyone in the city eagerly awaited and enjoyed it,' says Rastogi-ji, lightly tracing with a finger the fading contours of the painting. 'Hundreds of barges and boats beautifully decorated and lit, covered the river along its eighty ghats, creating a parallel city. The best-known tawaif singers of the city performed on boats owned by the maharaja of Banaras and the merchant aristocracy. Other boats resounded with the singing of more humble tawaifs and gonaharins.

'The entire city, Hindu and Muslim, upper caste and lower caste, rich and poor, kept awake through this period, with those who couldn't afford boats standing on the ghats to enjoy the tawaifs' music. The barges were decorated in pink. Tawaifs too wore pink peshvaz, with matching pink minakari jewellery. Even the guests assembled wore pink turbans. Pink rose petals were strewn on the barges as the tawaifs sang chaiti. The atmosphere was truly magical.'

Burhwa Mangal was one among the many melas that reflected Banaras's composite culture, and its love of fun and masti cutting across communities and classes. Banaras boasted no less than forty fairs in the period of a year. While some, like the Burhwa Mangal, were organised and funded by the city elite, the others had more popular patronage. Many of these fairs, such as Lolark Chhat, Durga-ji Mela, Sorahiya Mela and Shankudhara Mela, also saw much music and dance by tawaifs, gonaharins and male musicians.

By the late nineteenth century, however, the legendary love of Banarsis for melas had begun to come under hostile attack by morality drives launched by newly emerging groups of English-educated, Hindu elites and middle-class reformers. Espousing the cause of Hindu nationalism, based upon the imagining and mobilising of a collective Hindu identity, these groups were making their presence felt through the rallying cry: *Chahu jisko nij kalyan, toh sab mili Bharat santan, Japau nirantar ek zaban, Hindi, Hindu, Hindusthan*; Those who desire personal salvation should together, as children of India, chant in one voice, Hindi, Hindu, Hindu nation.

Hindu nationalism based its ideal in a mythical 'golden age' when Hindus had built a great and glorious world-conquering civilisation. Locating its 'downfall' in 'foreign' rule, first by the Muslims and subsequently by the British, Hindu nationalist discourse projected Islam and Muslims as 'enemies' of the Hindus, far more dangerous than even the British. Described as 'foreign conquerors', Muslim rulers were seen to have plundered India, destroyed and pillaged Hindu temples, forcibly converted Hindus to Islam and dealt a body-blow to Hindu religion and civilisation.

The Hindu nationalists were by no means a homogeneous group, and were divided often into mutually antagonistic reformist and revivalist camps. Notwithstanding their differences, however, they were joined in common cause on the fundamental issue of promoting 'Hindu interests' in the colonial polity.

Among the earliest issues they took up, polarising Banaras and the rest of northern India on the basis of religious identity, was the demand that Hindi and the Devanagari script in which it was written, posited as the language and script of the Hindus, be declared the official language—as opposed to Urdu, disparaged as Muslim and foreign. Cow protection, with an emphasis on protecting cows from beef-eating Muslims, was another deeply divisive issue. Barring the entry of Muslims into Hindu temples was also a frequent demand, and one that the colonial administration seems to have granted on some occasions. 'We are intensely happy to note that Mr Porter, the very able magistrate of our city Kashi, has issued an order banning the entry of Muslims in Shri Vishwanath and Shri Annapurna temples. The endeavours of Babu Kali Prasad Khatri towards demanding this order are indeed commendable. We are hopeful that soon other famous temples in the city too will put up similar signboards banning Muslim entry so that our religion is not further destroyed by them,' wrote the *Bharat Jiwan* on 16 June 1884.

Attempts were also made to tame the often plural, overlapping identities of people into a singular homogenised religious identity. Public sermons by Hindu publicists and newspaper editorials expended much time and effort in rebuking those who indulged in syncretic practices. 'There are Brahmins in Kashi who think nothing of visiting Ghazi Miyan's shrine in Bahraich in the company of Muslim daflis [players of a tambourine-like instrument] and gonaharins. Worse, these esteemed Brahmins also carry back the prasad from the shrine and distribute it to all and sundry! When will such foolish, dark practices be destroyed?' bemoaned the *Bharat Jiwan* on 9 June 1884.

By the late nineteenth century, Hindu nationalists were also launching morality drives aimed at 'cleansing' 'corrupt' practices among Hindus, which had crept in, it was argued, as a result of Muslim rule. Influenced by the 'degenerate' lifestyle and beliefs of the Muslims, Hindu society too, it was claimed, had become ensnared in ignorance, immorality and vice. The preoccupation with pleasure had drained Hindu masculinity, making it a submissive slave, first of the Muslims and now the British.

Ironically, colonial morality became the parameter by which the Hindu nationalists differentiated the moral from the immoral. After the war of 1857, colonial authorities had assiduously constructed Indian society as backward and effete, steeped in barbaric customs and decadent pleasures, symbolised by debauched nawabs and princes and their merry-making with the 'prostitute' tawaifs. Internalising the Victorian moral code, Hindu nationalists of all hues were obsessed with the identification and cleansing of immorality and obscenity from the Hindu domestic realm and public spaces.

Little wonder then that they frowned upon the mixing of religion with public merry-making that made fairs so enticing. Condemning the collective pleasure-seeking aspect of such events as a sign of moral and religious degeneration in Hindu society, they made their voices of condemnation heard through contemporary newspapers of the city, which began carrying regular articles complaining about the rowdyism and violence, vulgarity and immorality rampant in fairs, attributing these to the presence at these gatherings of the multitudes of 'uneducated', 'boorish' and 'low-born' labouring poor. Music and dance and the presence of tawaifs, prostitutes and gonaharins, all described increasingly now as obscene and immoral, too came under attack.

The participation by 'respectable' and educated members of 'high-born' castes and classes in such excess was considered especially reprehensible. As privileged and influential opinion-makers in the community, it was argued, they would do better to lead by example and help cleanse and regenerate Hindu society by rejecting vulgar public entertainments.

The most significant casualty of Hindu nationalist morality was the legendary Burhwa Mangal, undoubtedly the premier fair of the city. By late nineteenth–early twentieth century, adverse reports about the festival began appearing in local newspapers. While the leading role played in it by the maharaja and the city's merchant elite ensured that the festival itself was still not questioned, the large participation of the 'disorderly' lower classes and their allegedly antisocial, immoral behaviour came in for increasing censure. On 23 March 1903, the *Bharat Jiwan* wrote, 'Last Friday night, violence broke out between rowdy elements on Dashashwamedh ghat during Burhwa Mangal celebrations. It is a matter of shame that certain sections of the illiterate, ignorant and criminal population in the city always mar public events such as Burhwa Mangal with their uncouth behaviour.'

Patronage of tawaifs and prostitutes, consumption of alcohol and indulgence in other 'bad habits' too came in for shrill condemnation on the grounds that these sapped the vigour and vitality of the Hindu nation. Even Bharatendu Harishchandra, a leading light of Hindu nationalism, was not spared. Respected highly for his literary writings and contribution to the making of modern Hindi, his philanthropy and enthusiastic participation in religious celebrations and traditional festivities of Banaras, Harishchandra also periodically came under attack for the perceived hedonism and licentiousness of his lifestyle. In the late nineteenth century, the Aggarwal community, of which his family was a prominent part, publicly reprimanded him for his close association with tawaifs.

The tawaif was posited in the Hindu nationalist discourse as the embodiment of the 'other'. A series of popular cartoons circulated widely by Hindu publicists to promote the cause of Hindi as opposed to Urdu, for example, depicted 'Begum Urdu' as a tawaif, the embodiment of the alien, untrustworthy, decadent, morally corrupt Muslim 'other' in contrast to 'Mother Devanagari', the upper-caste, respectable, honest and homespun mother of every true Hindu son.

Upper-caste Hindu women were significant subjects of the Hindu nationalist discourse. The cultural expression and practices associated with purdah-bound women, such as wedding songs with sexual allusions, their intermixing in the domestic realm with lower-class and lower-caste working women, such as servants and goods vendors, seen now as a bad influence, their bathing on ghats and visiting fairs elicited much criticism from the Hindu nationalists on grounds of immorality and obscenity.

The period was also marked by heated debates between reformist and revivalist Hindu nationalists on the social and educational status of upper-caste women and the need for their movement out of purdah. The 'new woman', constructed by this conflicting set of worldviews, would enjoy the benefits of education but also cherish the 'innate values' of Indian womanhood—modesty, chastity, purity. Bharatendu Harishchandra himself was to advise readers of the magazine *Bala Bodhini* (Wise Woman), which he published to promote women's education, that 'Like Sita, Anusuya, Sati and Arundhati, women all over the world should adopt the qualities of decorum, modesty and learning.'

With a few notable exceptions, debates on tawaifs and prostitution were rarely articulated in the context of women's reforms. Instead, they were placed in the sphere of public morality, law and order, sanitation and urban space management. In the Hindu nationalist discourse, the tawaif was categorised with the 'other' that included Muslims, lower-castes and lower-class goondas, or bad characters. Her presence in public spaces was projected as a threat to the moral and physical health and well-being of Hindu society. This was matched with demands in various north Indian cities, including Banaras, for changes in municipality by-laws so as to restrict the tawaifs' quarters to specified areas of the city.

The anti-nautch movement in the early twentieth century attacked the tradition of holding 'nautches' and the open presence of tawaifs on public occasions. Under the onslaught of this movement, tawaifs' participation in temple celebrations came in increasingly for sharp criticism from the votaries of reform. 'Last Tuesday took place the annual sringar of Sri Batuk Bhairon and Sri Kali ji. Prostitutes were gathered there all night. Instead of this, had some bhajan group been called, would it have been a sin?' questioned the *Bharat Jiwan* on 30 July 1917.

These morality drives were strengthened by the participation of various caste associations, which had emerged in the 1880s to jostle for social recognition, jobs and political representation in the colonial political economy. In the face of the far-reaching changes that colonialism wrought in Indian society through improved means of communication and the spread of English education and print media, upper-caste groupings attempted to reinforce their traditional status through periodic calls for moral rejuvenation and cleansing. Meanwhile, various associations of upwardly mobile intermediate castes adopted upper-caste Hindu norms as a strategy to claim higher social status commensurate with their improving economic position and aspirations. Increasing controls on women's sexuality and the emphasis on curbing immorality, obscenity and vice, and adoption of brahminical religious symbols and rituals were part of these attempts at upward social mobility.

As Rastogi-ji and I sit exchanging notes on the tawaif history of Banaras, I notice him discreetly look at his watch. It is time for me to take my leave. Thanking him for his hospitality, I step out into the still-scorching late-afternoon sun. Walking down Thatheri Bazaar, past shops selling papads, pickles and other condiments, I reach Bharatendu Harishchandra's sprawling ancestral haveli, which remains a major landmark here. A portion of the haveli is occupied by his descendants, the rest fragmented into a cluster of shops and offices.

Further on, I walk past a row of deceptively nondescript confectionery shops that sell the most expensive sweets in all of Banaras. Prepared from almonds, pistachios and cashew nuts, these sweets, I am told by connoisseurs like Rastogi-ji, are exclusive to the city. In days of yore, such extravagant delicacies were part of the regular menu in households of merchant-bankers like Babu Purshottam Lall. Today, they are a Banarasi status symbol bought on special family occasions or as temple offerings.

Here, I run into Chanda's eldest son, Jaipal. We have met a few times before. Jaipal is a skilled electrician and runs a thriving shop in Dal Mandi, specialising in sound equipment for hire at wedding venues and cultural programmes. Clad as usual in matching dark shades of shirt and trousers, Jaipal is as big-made and stout as Chanda. He has inherited too her lack of social graces. Apart from acknowledging my greeting with a slight nod, he shows little enthusiasm in seeing me.

Falling in step with Jaipal, I politely ask about the well-being of his mother and grandmother. Mopping his brow wearily, he replies that they are well. Silence brews as we walk past the line-up of modest shops in Thatheri Bazaar, selling temple finery, metal idols, hand-embroidered silk and brocade apparel for the gods, brass bells of all sizes, lamps to light the sacred flame, and other objects used in Hindu religious rituals and prayers. All of a sudden, without preamble, Jaipal mutters that his mother is in a bad mood because of him.

'And why is that so?' I ask, partly guessing the answer. You have told me that Jaipal, once the favourite son, now has a rather strained relationship with Chanda because of his decision to bring up his three daughters as Hindus like him.

'Tell me, didi, what have I done wrong?' Jaipal asks. 'What is the crime if my children follow the religion of their father? Children inherit all that belongs to their parents—their wealth and property and also their financial losses. It is only right that they inherit their parents' religion. That is how family ties are strengthened. How can any family survive if the father follows one faith and his children another?' Jaipal uses the logic of patriarchal inheritance and religious dogma to counter the heterodoxy of his own tawaif family.

I try and defend Chanda as best as I can. 'Jaipal, as a complete outsider, perhaps it is not my place to say this, but Chanda-ji is only trying to safeguard the family's old traditions.'

My support for his mother elicits an agitated response from Jaipal: 'Didi, what tradition are you talking about? The tawaif tradition is long dead. And alongside are dead all the old customs associated with it. Good riddance! How much shame and ridicule we have had to suffer because of our mother's background, only I and my brothers know. If now we are being accepted as equals by respectable people in the city, it is only because we have chosen to lead honourable, decent lives. Is that a crime? Why should we be condemned to carrying on our backs forever the corpse of tawaif culture?

'My mother is furious with me. Unlike my two other brothers, who have insisted upon becoming Muslim, I never offered resistance to being brought up as Hindu. What sin have I committed if I want my daughters to be brought up as Hindus like me? By god's grace, I have done well for myself. Can I not hope one day to marry my daughters into educated, respectable families? But which good boy from the outside will agree to take the hand of a girl, no matter how generous her dowry, who belongs to a strange family, where the father is Hindu and daughter a Muslim? Will my mother feel happier if my girls are condemned to marry only within tawaif families that abound in half-literate, good-for-nothing boys?

'My mother is also angry with my two younger brothers. But, tell me, how are they wrong to be following the religion of their mother, grandmother and great-grandmother? From childhood, they have always thought of themselves as Muslim, even though my family insisted they were Hindu. Is it a crime that they want to bring up their sons as Muslims? If the boys are brought up, as our mother wants, to be Hindus, how will they explain to their teachers and friends in school why their father and grandmother are Muslims? Our mother loves the past so much that she gives no thought to the future.'

Jaipal's words flow in a torrent, as if a dam has been breached. Hearing him speak, my thoughts go to Tara, his centenarian grandmother. When I had broached the subject of her grandsons' decision to break with family custom, her reply had been as sad as it was compassionate: 'Chanda's boys are just trying to fit in with the times. These are the times of boundaries and walls. People's vision has become narrow and their hearts have shrunk. They have divided god. They have destroyed each other's mosques and temples in the name of religion. Our boys have had their share of suffering for being born in a tawaif home. They don't want further ridicule for their family's belief in the oneness of god. And so they are trying to make their peace with the times by dividing their mother's faith into neat little parcels labelled Hindu and Muslim.'

CHAPTER 10

Mamu Shafiq

I RETURN FROM BANARAS to Pyaari khala's home on an overcast and humid day that presses heavily upon the muddy lanes, grimy mohallas and bedraggled bazaars of Bhabua, rendering the town a dull grey. Inside, the house is plunged in depressing darkness.

The undercurrent of tension that I had earlier felt between Pyaari khala's sisters and nieces is now in full flow. Faces drawn with anxiety, lack of sleep and resentment, the family's matriarchs have called a meeting in a room on the first floor. Phoolmani, Rajjo, Seema, Rani, Asghari, Ghafuran and you are present, as are Sakeena and her sons, Nawab and Wazir, who sit huddled together in a corner looking nervous. Pyaari's decision to bequeath all her assets to the two of them has generated much bitterness. The family that was united in loving and being loved by Pyaari is now, with her impending death, divided over her property.

Customarily, certain communities of women singers and dancers, particularly from peninsular India, privileged courtesan daughters over sons in the share of their mother's inheritance. Most other courtesan communities, however, including Nat clans in Bihar and Banaras like yours, held that tawaif daughters, both biological and adopted, sons and even nieces brought up and regarded as daughters, and if surviving, the mother or aunts (if they had brought up the deceased tawaif as a daughter) enjoyed equal rights to property.

The self-earned moveable and immoveable assets owned by a childless tawaif were divided after her death equally between her mother, if alive, her courtesan sisters and her brothers. If she had adopted daughters, they would inherit her property if she bequeathed it solely to them; otherwise, they would get an equal share with the other claimants. Married sisters and other relatives, like nephews and uncles, would not have a share in the inheritance unless specifically indicated by the tawaif during her lifetime or in her will.

The general consensus in this case seems to be that Pyaari khala ought to have followed the norm and divided her property equally between her sisters and nieces, there being no brothers in the family. Phoolmani, Rajjo, Seema, Rani, Asghari and even you feel hurt and let down. Each one of you lays claim to having been more generous and loving in caring for Pyaari than the married Sakeena, who you all feel has always been too preoccupied with her family to spare the time for a sister.

Rani and Asghari, being Bhabua-based, assert their closeness to Pyaari, their ready presence in times of need. Phoolmani grimly reminds everyone that Pyaari would come and stay several months in a year with her and her younger daughter, Seema, in their house in Mumbai. Rajjo has claims of her own: not only is she Pyaari's favourite niece, but she would come and stay with her aunt whenever she needed help with running the house. Her sons have always been at Pyaari's beck and call, coming all the way from Banaras to Bhabua to run her errands, do maintenance-related chores, unlike Sakeena's boys who never showed up when there was work to be done.

You are more modest in your claims but remind everyone that Pyaari has spent long periods of time in your home in Banaras. When she was hospitalised, you went daily to sit by her bedside. Your house became camping ground for the many relatives from outside Banaras who came pouring in upon hearing about Pyaari khala's cancer surgery.

Pyaari's sagacity in choosing Nawab and Wazir over the other boys in the family is also debated indignantly. By their inability to hold on to any job have they not proven themselves utterly incapable of shouldering family responsibilities? If Pyaari's wealth is to go to sons, there are others in the family who do regular work and are more deserving candidates.

Sakeena khala does not utter a word. Nawab and Wazir are grilled by Phoolmani and Rajjo about their laxity in meeting Pyaari's needs. Why had they not shifted her, given her critical condition, to the greater comfort of their home? Even if she had stayed on in her own house, could not the brothers have moved in here with their families to look after her better? Was it not true that Ghafuran often brought food for Pyaari from her own kitchen since Nawab and Wazir's wives wouldn't remember to cook her meals on time? Could they deny that Pyaari khala had to depend on her other relatives for her daily care?

The inquisition goes on for several hours. Nawab and Wazir come out of it rather badly, their shifty eyes and nervous demeanour doing little to help. Although in their fifties, they look like a pair of overwhelmed schoolboys. They have few answers to any of the angry questions hurled at them by their aunt and cousins.

In their defence, they claim to be spending on Pyaari khala's ongoing care from their own pockets. The size of her agricultural holdings, they insist, was not as vast as the family imagines. Pyaari had long ago sold off most of the land that she owned. Her fabled gold jewellery, they say, does not amount to more than a couple of bangles and a few rings.

I wonder if the brothers are speaking the truth. Is it possible that her relatives carry an inflated impression of Pyaari's wealth? An impression that she may have encouraged in order to gain respect in the family and outside, much as you do? The family does not seem to harbour any such doubts. Visibly angry, Phoolmani points out that Nawab and Wazir have no jobs. How did they then have the money they claim to be spending on Pyaari? Everyone present at the meeting seems to believe that the brothers have eaten up Pyaari's property and gold, and are now making lame excuses.

You are the only one who tries to put behind your personal disappointment and hurt, and take a more objective view of Pyaari's decision. Later at night, when we return to your house, you tell me about Pyaari khala's special relationship with Sakeena and her children. 'Sakeena khala has two sons and three daughters. From the time that the first child was born, Pyaari khala has always looked after the entire family.'

I am surprised to hear this. 'Didn't Sakeena's husband contribute anything?'

You explain, 'Sakeena khala, as you must have noticed, is not nice-looking. This is why she was married off. But the man chosen for her was very handsome. This was my mother's fault, since she fixed the marriage. She should have found a more appropriate match for Sakeena. In those times, however, such things were not given much importance. Pyaari khala too supported my mother's choice. Poor plain-faced Sakeena khala was never accepted by her good-looking husband. Therefore, all her children were born in our family home in Bhabua. He would visit Sakeena intermittently, make her pregnant and disappear. Then he married another woman and severed all connection with Sakeena khala.' There is quiet compassion in your voice.

Although the third among her siblings, Pyaari khala, you say, has always taken on responsibilities that ought to have been discharged by her elder tawaif sisters, Bindo and Phoolmani. Feeling remorseful about the decision that ruined Sakeena's life, she took it upon herself to take care of her and her children. She loves all her nieces and nephews equally but has always felt a greater protectiveness for Sakeena's children. She arranged the marriage of each of Sakeena's girls as if they were her own daughters.

You say that Pyaari's decision to bequeath all her property to Nawab and Wazir comes out of her sense of responsibility for that household, more so since, unlike the other boys in the family, these two have never found work that they could stick to. Perhaps she wishes to ensure some security for them even if all else fails.

'But why didn't she keep aside something for her sisters and nieces?' I ask. 'Surely all of you too could have done with some help.'

You reply, 'When daughters were breadwinners of the family, they had an equal share in the inheritance. But times are changing. We are marrying off our daughters and expect our sons instead to earn for the family. Surely then it is they who must now inherit whatever we have.' You are implacable in your expectations of Nawab and Wazir, though. 'Pyaari khala has chosen them above all others to be her heirs. They cannot hope to enjoy her property without taking care of her in return. The family will not let them off so easily.'

'Once Pyaari khala is gone, the family, I suppose, might consider going to the courts to challenge her decision,' I suggest tactlessly. 'I am not sure her desire to bequeath all her property to Nawab and Wazir to the exclusion of the others in the family will stand the scrutiny of law.'

Your irritation obvious, you snap back, 'The family will do no such thing! Pyaari khala's wishes, however misplaced, have to be respected while she is living and more so once she is dead and unable to defend her decisions. She has the right to bequeath her hard-earned property to anyone she chooses. Moreover, in our community, we do not drag family matters into courtrooms. We resolve our domestic disputes by ourselves. The community spits on the faces of tawaif families that wash their dirty linen in public courts.'

And so it is that you come to tell me about Mamu Shafiq, Bullan and Kallan's only surviving sibling, their younger brother. He had used this fact to live in style at their expense in Chainpur while keeping busy with fanciful get-rich-quick schemes. Unheeding of his sisters' repeated advice to work hard and practise patience, Shafiq chased chimeras and constantly cajoled his sisters into giving him money.

Mindful of their duty to provide for their brother, Bullan and Kallan grudgingly financed Shafiq's many ventures in the hope that one would succeed at last. Thus far, Shafiq's most daring enterprise had involved sweet-talking people in and around Chainpur into buying from him a charm he claimed could turn copper to gold. Soon enough, the so-called alchemist's charm had been exposed for the hoax that it was. And irate buyers thronged his sisters' house demanding reimbursement of their money. When confronted, Shafiq pleaded innocence. He had sold in good faith a charm made from a formula that had been taught to him by a wandering magician. How was he to know that the magician had played a prank on him?

Wishing to believe in their brother's innocence, Bullan and Kallan had accepted Shafiq's story. Their patience ran out, though, when they heard rumours that he had graduated from petty fraudulent activities to a decidedly criminal enterprise. In partnership with a down-at-heel tawaif, Bibia, whom he had met near Arrah at a highway sarai, or inn, Shafiq had hatched a new scheme.

A runaway from an overbearing dance-troupe owner in Agra, Bibia desperately wanted to reach Calcutta, the city of endless possibilities. Her resourcefulness and the gold she had managed to bring away had only got her to the outskirts of Arrah. Down to her last cowrie, she agreed to Shafiq's proposal.

Bibia would charm rich travellers staying in highway sarais into spending the night with her. Then, she would mix a drug with sedating properties that Shafiq procured into their food or drink. As soon as the victim was unconscious, Shafiq would enter the room, tie up and gag the sedated traveller, and the two of them would decamp with all the valuables.

Over several months, night after night, the duo preyed upon unsuspecting travellers across sarais in Bihar. And though rumours abounded about their possible involvement, Shafiq and Bibia managed to evade the police. They ultimately fell out, and Bibia resumed her journey to Calcutta, while Shafiq went into hiding in Banaras for more than a year to let the trail cool. Bullan and Kallan snapped all links with their brother and refused to let him into their house when, worn-out and gaunt, he returned one day begging for food and shelter.

Then, the revolt of 1857 blazed across northern India. Shahabad was taken over by the rebels. Shafiq, by then living in Arrah, found a new vocation as a spy for the beleaguered colonial troops, passing on to them information about rebel plans and movements that he gathered as bazaar gossip. This brought in much-needed money in the form of baksheesh, tips. More importantly, it provided Shafiq an opportunity to cultivate valuable contacts in the district's colonial circles. Once the revolt had been crushed, the collaborators, mighty and petty, were rewarded for their support by way of titles, landholdings and contracts for forest clearing and road construction.

Shafiq thrived for a while as a minor sub-contractor in Arrah, involved with the laying of railway tracks. However, after some years, he tired of the hard work that the job entailed, and drifted into gambling, hoping to multiply his fortunes quickly. Soon enough, he not only lost the savings he had made as a sub-contractor but also found himself neck-deep in debts he had incurred from Badri Prashad, a moneylender in Arrah, to finance his gambling.

Desperately in need of money, Shafiq came up with a plan. Over the years, he had kept himself informed of the goings-on in his sisters' lives. He knew about the adoption of Dharmman's daughters by Bullan and Kallan, and had keenly followed Sadabahar's rise in popularity as a tawaif and the consequent soaring of the family's fortunes. He was aware of their hurried migration to Bhabua, and that their house and landholdings in and around Chainpur had gradually been taken over either by the families of patrons who had originally gifted these to Sadabahar, Bullan or Kallan, or by other claimants and even usurpers. Appalled at his sisters' thoughtless decision, Shafiq had even visited Chainpur to stake his claim on their properties, only to be beaten back by the new holders.

Frustrated and furious, Shafiq cast his eyes towards Bhabua, where Sadabahar was now the pre-eminent tawaif, and had managed to add to Bullan and Kallan's old landholdings. The sisters had invested a major part of her earnings into renovating and enlarging their small house, a gift from their old patron, to make it a mansion worthy of Sadabahar's status. They had also bought agricultural land to augment their existing holdings.

Shafiq was determined to wrest for himself a chunk of the properties that Sadabahar had built for the family. He knew his sisters were unlikely to agree amicably to his demands, and so resolved to use blackmail, failing which he would go to the courts to press his claims. Shafiq knew enough about the law to feel fairly confident of his eventual victory in any court battle with his sisters. However, since litigation would entail heavy expenses, he convinced the moneylender Badri Prashad to finance the case with the promise of a major share in the properties they would win.

It was around 1890 when Shafiq presented himself at his sisters' home in Bhabua. Shocked to see their prodigal brother after so many years, Bullan and Kallan welcomed him with as much enthusiasm as they could muster. But they realised soon enough that Shafiq had little interest in re-entering the family fold. He came straight to the point: he wanted his share of their properties in Bhabua, including in the house and agricultural lands that he claimed belonged to their mother. Furthermore, laying similar claim on the house and landholdings in Chainpur, he demanded compensation for his share in these properties that had been lost to the family upon its flight from the town. Besides, as their only surviving sibling, he wanted his sisters to draw up a will and name him as the sole successor to all that they owned.

Shafiq gave his sisters an ultimatum. He knew as well as they did, he said, that their story about Sadabahar and Gulshan being the daughters of their deceased sister was a lie. Shafiq just had to report the truth of Sadabahar and Gulshan's real parentage to the police, and Bullan and Kallan would be arrested for illegal adoption. To avoid such an eventuality, they would do well to accede to his demands.

The sisters heard him out and then calmly told him to go to hell. Their properties had accumulated in the past years from Sadabahar's earnings. And it was Sadabahar, their daughter and the only breadwinner of their kotha, who would inherit everything they owned. Shafiq was welcome to go to the police and file his case in the law courts. And then Bullan and Kallan had their brother thrown out.

Later, when they discussed Shafiq's demands with close friends and old patrons, Bullan and Kallan were shocked to learn that he had not made empty threats. The law courts would most certainly declare their adoption of Sadabahar and Gulshan illegal. Sadabahar would not be recognised as their legal heir. In cases where adopted daughters found their inheritance rights contested, the courts had almost always ruled against their claim. Under the Indian Penal Code of 1860, adoption of children by prostitutes and 'dancing girls' was illegal, since this was presumed to be for the purpose of inducting them into prostitution, thus 'perpetuating immorality'. Moreover, colonial law could indeed benefit Shafiq if he was able to prove in the courts that the properties under dispute had originally belonged to their mother.

Customary laws of the tawaif community pertaining to property and inheritance laid out that all those who lived in the kotha and helped in some manner to perpetuate the name of the family were entitled to the moveable and immoveable property, including kotha premises, landholdings and, in the modern times, even bank accounts belonging to the deceased tawaif. Her jewellery would most often pass to the women, with sons enjoying no claim on it.

The most worthy daughter or niece would inherit too her mother's or aunt's place as head of the establishment, vested with the duties and responsibilities of managing its affairs. Married daughters got jewellery and whatever else the family wished to present to them at the time of marriage. Beyond this, they had no further claims on their mothers' properties. Unworthy and renegade daughters and sons got nothing. Under customary law, therefore, Shafiq had long forfeited any claim to his sisters' properties.

Kotha premises could not be partitioned or sold off as a whole or in part by any member without the consent of all the others who collectively owned and lived in it. Individual members were free to dispose of in any manner they wished their share in assets like jewellery, landholdings and money in the bank.

Through the late nineteenth century, however, the colonial judiciary refused to recognise the inheritance-related customs of tawaifs, since it rejected in the first place their claims of being a community. These assertions were, instead, disparaged by the courts as being akin to a band of thieves or a group of card sharpers claiming corporate distinctiveness based on tradition. The customs and norms of tawaif communities were similarly dismissed by the learned judges as self-serving rules formulated by 'prostitutes' to profit from encouraging 'vice' and 'immorality'.

Tawaifs and other communities of women singers and dancers from peninsular India were placed within the ambit of personal laws, Hindu or Muslim, depending on their perceived religious affiliation. These laws, based upon patriarchal religious injunctions privileged the right of sons over daughters to a greater share of inherited property. Cases that reached colonial courts involving property disputes between tawaifs and their male relatives, therefore, mostly went in favour of the men.

Shaken by these revelations but unwilling to give in to Shafiq's false claims and arm-twisting, Bullan and Kallan refused to reach an out-of-court settlement with their brother as advised by well-wishers. Sadabahar followed her mothers' wishes, although Babu Rudra Bahadur Singh, her patron lover at one point in time and now a close friend, repeatedly cautioned her against litigation. There was no saying, he warned, what details of their private lives might get flung around in public courts.

Shafiq went ahead and filed a case for his share of the properties in Chainpur and Bhabua. He alleged that his sisters, Bullan and Kallan had, upon moving to Bhabua sold off, without either informing him or giving him his due share, the house and agricultural properties in Chainpur, which he claimed had been accumulated by their mother from her earnings. He further charged that his sisters usurped his share in the properties in Bhabua that again, he claimed, had belonged originally to their mother. He charged them with illegally passing on his share of properties in both places on to Sadabahar and Gulshan, who he described as 'slaves' bought in infancy by Bullan and Kallan and illegally adopted to be brought up to become 'prostitutes'.

Bullan and Kallan countered Shafiq's claims by contending that their mother, Shabaratin, had been a tawaif of modest means, living on rent in the house of another courtesan in Chainpur. She had neither house nor agricultural lands or any other property in her name. The family fortunes brightened only after the two sisters began their professional life as tawaifs. Their mother, in keeping with the norms of the community, had managed her daughters' professional matters and enjoyed complete control over the earnings they brought into the family. She had invested a part of these earnings into building the house in Chainpur, where the family shifted from its earlier rented accommodations. The landholdings too had either been gifted to Bullan and Kallan by patrons or bought from their earnings by their mother. They, therefore, had every right to dispose of the property in any manner they chose without either informing Shafiq or giving him a share.

Contesting the allegations about a clandestine sale of their Chainpur properties, Bullan and Kallan narrated the story of their hurried flight to Bhabua. Shafiq, they asserted, had no right to any part of their property in Bhabua. The house and agricultural lands here had never belonged to their mother but had been gifted to them by a patron during their days as highly popular tawaifs in Shahabad. Though he was long dead, his sons would be able to corroborate the veracity of their claims.

Shafiq, they said, was just a usurper trying to lay false claims on property that did not belong to him. On the contrary, he owed them gratitude for the long years they had provided him food and shelter besides money to invest in all his failed ventures. They pointed out his criminal past and the unsavoury reputation he enjoyed in all of Chainpur on account of his crooked dealings.

As for Sadabahar and Gulshan, the sisters asserted that they had not bought the twins but had adopted them from a relative in keeping with the norms of their community. They had witnesses from Chainpur, from the community and outside, who were present at the adoption ceremony of the girls and could back the validity of Bullan and Kallan's claim.

Sadabahar was not a usurper but a rightful co-sharer of the properties they had built but subsequently lost in mortgage, the sisters said. It was Sadabahar who, as a daughter, had not only redeemed their assets in Chainpur and Bhabua out of her earnings as a tawaif but also considerably added to them. And as their adopted daughter, she enjoyed customary right to inherit their share of the properties after their death.

From the start, when the lower courts ruled against Bullan and Kallan, it became obvious that they were fighting a losing battle. But, convinced that truth was on their side, the sisters kept seeking redressal in higher courts of appeal. The case dragged on for years and finally reached the Privy Council in London. After some deliberation, this final court too opined in Shafiq's favour.

Shafiq enjoyed the advantage of his gender in approaching a judicial system that favoured the rights of men over women. He also used to his benefit his familiarity with the workings of the colonial police, courts and revenue department. He produced in the courts authentic-looking forged property documents, and managed to successfully bribe local officials and buy off other witnesses to give testimonies in his favour. And he bandied about intimate details of his sisters' relationships with patrons that served not so much to bolster legal arguments in his favour but cast a slur on Bullan and Kallan's reputation in the colonial courtroom, where any sexual alliance outside marriage was defined as 'prostitution' and 'immoral'.

Bullan and Kallan, on the other hand, were drawn into combat on an unfamiliar terrain, with unfamiliar rules. With no previous experience of colonial law courts and their demand of affidavits and stamp papers, they sought to prove their case instead on the basis of norms, customary usage and oral testimonies. More than anything, they were caught unawares by the low esteem in which they, once the most venerable tawaifs of Chainpur, were held by colonial judges and lawyers who, much to their horror, referred to them repeatedly as 'prostitutes'.

Waving aside Bullan and Kallan's assertions, the judges gave credence to the legality of Shafiq's skilfully forged land deeds and false witnesses. Concluding that the properties in Chainpur and Bhabua had belonged to their mother, Shabaratin, judgement after judgement declared Shafiq a co-sharer in the inheritance. The judges ruled that, under Muslim law, Shafiq was entitled to double the share of the property as compared to his sisters.

The counsels for Bullan and Kallan had argued that Muslim law was not applicable since the parties belonged to Nat clans that were originally Hindu and had retained several Hindu customs even after conversion. That the parties in question did not have allegiance either with Muslim or Hindu law was evident from the fact that they did not follow the rules of any of these legal systems related to issues like inheritance but instead practised the tawaif community's customs in matters of property and succession. The rulings pertaining to their case should, therefore, take into consideration the tawaif community's customary norms of equal shares in the property for sisters and brothers.

This argument was rejected by the judges who held that customs among the dancing girls, which aimed at the continuance of prostitution as a family business, were contrary to the law, immoral and not enforceable. They further ruled that, regardless of whether Bullan and Kallan had sold off the properties in Chainpur or had abandoned them, as they claimed, Shafiq was entitled to his share in these. This would be due along with his share in the properties in Bhabua.

The courts further held the adoption of Sadabahar and Gulshan by the 'prostitutes' Bullan and Kallan as illegal since it contravened the provisions of Section 373, Indian Penal Code, and was, in any event, 'immoral'. No criminal charges were made against the sisters since the adoption had taken place before the promulgation of the IPC. Moreover, the honourable intentions of the two 'prostitutes' in adopting the girls was noted in the fact that one of them, Gulshan, had been married off and made into a 'respectable' woman.

In the context of Sadabahar, the courts declared that, since her adoption by Bullan and Kallan was illegal, her status in their house was that of a mere nochi—a girl customarily brought into a tawaif establishment and taught singing and dancing, after which her earnings belonged to the tawaif, in a mistress-employee relationship. Bullan and Kallan had trained Sadabahar in the art of singing and dancing. This training could only be with a view to making her a prostitute—that, as a matter of fact, she was now, announced the judges.

According to the courts, a nochi might through the earnings she brought into the establishment contribute to the augmentation of her mistresses' properties. This gave her no claim as a co-sharer to those properties, nor did she enjoy any natural right to inherit the properties. Bullan and Kallan could, under the Muslim law, bequeath by a written will not more than one-third of their share of the property to Sadabahar if they so wished.

The case was closely followed by leaders of tawaif communities across Bihar and other parts of northern India. Its outcome they knew would impact all future litigation involving members of their communities. The colonial courts had put under the label of 'dancing girls' various communities of women singers and dancers, including devadasis, tawaifs and other women across the country who performed in different settings and contexts, both religious and secular. Any case pertaining to 'dancing girls' served as precedent for another.

The court rulings in two previous cases—of which the first involved women singers and dancers from the Naikan community of Bombay, *Mathura Naikan v. Esu Naikan* (1880), and the second concerned tawaifs from the Kanchan community in the Punjab, *Ghasiti v. Umrao Jan* (1893), had been extensively cited in the judgements given in Shafiq's case against Bullan and Kallan. The rulings in the earlier cases had underlined that colonial courts did not recognise the norms and customs practised by communities of 'dancing girls'. The rulings on these cases had been made according to 'Mahomedan' law, since the court adjudged the concerned parties to be 'Muslim', regardless of the fact that those involved had refused to be categorised as either Muslim or Hindu.

In the decades to come, cases involving 'dancing girls' that reached colonial courts would be settled in accordance with the Hindu or Muslim personal law, according to the perceived religious identity of the concerned parties. This contributed substantially to the erosion of the autonomy and privileged position as independent women of substance that courtesans had customarily enjoyed. In the long run, the imposition of personal laws also facilitated the consolidation of homogenised Hindu and Muslim identities governed by patriarchal religious injunctions not just among tawaifs but also among other communities that had until well into the nineteenth century traditionally followed more syncretic practices and customs.

Realising that justice would not be forthcoming from hostile law courts, and recognising the threat that judicial intervention posed to the distinctive corporate identity and lifestyle of the courtesans, the community elders of Bhabua convened a meeting of great significance a few months after the Privy Council judgement on Bullan and Kallan's case. All the tawaifs of Bhabua attended, from the youngest to the oldest, from the poorest to the wealthiest.

After prolonged discussion, the gathering decided that, henceforth, any disputes in the family and community—whether over inheritance, adoption, sale and purchase of properties or any other domestic matter, and even personal rivalries between courtesans over patrons or accompanist musicians—would be brought and resolved exclusively in the community council, panchayat, and never taken to the courts. Any tawaif family found violating this injunction would be ostracised by the community and readmitted to the fold only after it withdrew its case from the courts.

Perhaps following the example laid out by tawaif elders in Bhabua, or maybe arriving at the decision independently, over the coming years, other courtesan communities across northern India placed a similar prohibition on accessing public courts to settle internal disputes. The efficacy of the ban in northern India is manifest in the notably few cases involving personal disputes between tawaifs or in their families that are available in the archives. On the other hand, there is a plethora of similar litigation by devadasis and other communities of women singers and dancers from peninsular India, where no such internal embargo seems to have been enforced.

You inform me that even in your times as a tawaif in late twentieth-century Banaras, the injunction against approaching courts to resolve internal disputes was followed in the community. All such cases were generally settled by the panchayat. I am sceptical. Would men accept the ban on going to court on issues related to inheritance when clearly they had much to gain by appealing to the law?

You point to men's everyday dependency on their mothers, sisters, aunts and nieces for their needs. Barely literate, men in your community rarely had the financial backing to take on their better-placed and more educated women relatives. Moreover, the fear of social ostracism was very real. Cut off from the community, they would have no one to turn to for support in times of crises. No mourners would share their grief in a death, no merry-makers would add to their joy in celebrations. Most men would, therefore, accept their share in inheritance as sanctioned by customary norms. In the absence of steady work and a regular income, this inheritance depleted fast, and very soon the men were back to being dependent on the tawaif women in the family.

With the passage of time and the disappearance of tawaifs from the urban landscape of northern India, the community councils have lost their relevance. However, tawaif families continue to be reluctant about taking personal matters to court. Internal conflicts are more often than not resolved informally by community elders and negotiators in a manner similar to the times when the panchayat settled them formally.

'We keep to ourselves,' you say. 'We follow our own rules for property distribution, succession and inheritance. With changing times, we too have had to amend our rules, but we do so on our terms. We don't tell outsiders to our community how to conduct their affairs and don't take kindly to being advised about ours.'

In the tawaif community as a whole, the practice of adopting girl children from outside the family, whether by purchase or otherwise, seems to have died out by the early twentieth century. Families like yours that I have met in Bhabua and Banaras have no personal experience or recall of any such adoption taking place in the past two or three generations. Despite the state's non-recognition of it, the practice of adopting girls from the immediate family seems to have continued among tawaifs across northern India.

While the community was busy trying to protect its norms and customs from a fast-changing and hostile world, Sadabahar and her family had to deal with the more immediate problem of surviving the huge losses, both material and emotional, that the successive adverse court rulings had inflicted on them. The family had exhausted much of its savings in paying the lawyers' fees and other related expenses over the long years that the case had taken to reach the Privy Council. Now, faced with losing their hard-earned assets to the dissolute Shafiq and, worse, of suffering defeat at his unworthy hands, Bullan and Kallan were engulfed in despair.

Sadabahar had been more prepared for the final bitter outcome, from the very first adverse ruling. Left to her, the case would never have been sent for appeal. Still, the final verdict left her stunned. With a stroke of the pen, she had been divested of properties she had redeemed and built upon with her earnings. The landholdings and jewellery in her name were but a small fraction of the savings she had invested in properties held by Bullan and Kallan—most of which was now in Shafiq's hands. Much of her mothers' depleted properties, including their share of the Bhabua house and agricultural lands, would have to go in repaying the loans that they had taken from various moneylenders to fight the prolonged and expensive court case. Even the agricultural lands in Sadabahar's name and her jewellery would have to be sold to pay Shafiq his fraudulent share in the properties lost in Chainpur. Sadabahar's family, once among the wealthiest in Shahabad, now found itself on the brink of destitution.

CHAPTER 11

Bullah and Sa'dullah

YOUR HOUSE IN BHABUA IS redolent with the fragrance of festive cooking. Jawed and the other boys are stringing up brightly coloured plastic decorations on the doorways, while little children run around, squealing with excitement.

You are at the centre of all this activity, supervising the preparations for the thanksgiving prayer your family offers annually at the shrine of a local Sufi saint on a Thursday of sawan, the rainy season. Pyaari khala has insisted that the tradition, unbroken since Sadabahar's time, is observed with full ritual this year since everyone in the family is together in Bhabua after so long.

Quite unexpectedly, she appears to be making a marginal recovery. Over the past couple of days, though pain still convulses her frail body, Pyaari khala spends more time awake, chatting and laughing with the family gathered around. I mention this, hoping it will dispel some of the sadness in your eyes. You continue to look troubled. 'The flame burns brightest just before it goes out,' is all you say.

You are doing your best to ensure that the thanksgiving ritual is observed as elaborately as Pyaari khala wishes. Under your watchful eyes, Ghafuran, her daughter-in-law and daughters are cooking the ritual offering. Wheat flour, ghee and melted gur, jaggery, are kneaded together into a dough that is rolled out, cooked and stacked into a massive pile of rotis. These are then crumbled into a coarse, sweet powder, or malida, which is stored in a thaal, a huge brass platter, covered with a green silk napkin. The platter belonged to your mother, Teema, and is used exclusively for this offering to the resident Sufi saint of Bhabua, popularly called Baba Court Shaheed.

With all due respect to the saint, I find his name a bit strange. And, last evening, I had unthinkingly indicated as much to the old and rather deaf maulavi sahib, who guides your family through religious observances, when he came by to see Pyaari khala. Maulavi sahib has spent a lifetime teaching basic Urdu and readings from the Quran to the children of Muslim tawaifs in Bhabua. In return, he is assured, besides the token monetary fee, an easy welcome and something to eat in the homes of your neighbourhood. As a young girl, you too had been his student and I noticed the endearing mix of deference, familiarity and affection with which you welcomed him.

His slight frame, fair, pointed little face, white beard, kindly eyes and serene smile reminded me of the pictures of genial pixies in my childhood storybooks. This made me a little careless, perhaps, in framing my question. Taking my cue from you and the others present, I shouted out loudly, 'Maulavi sahib, was Baba Court Shaheed the saint's real name?'

Maulavi sahib roared back louder still, 'What a stupid question! Think for yourself. Can anyone, let alone such a venerable saint, be named *Court*? Baba's name was Hazrat Syed Usman Daata Rehmatullah Alai. You had better write it down lest you forget. Very few people are aware of his real name. He became god's own by erasing his identity.

'In British times, there used to be a police station and court near his dargah in Bhabua. The simple people of this area began calling him Baba Court Shaheed after the court. In 1947, the government relocated the court to another building, but Baba continues to be known by the name.

'Huzoor belonged to the family of Gharib Nawaz, Shahenshah-e-Hind Rehmatullah Alai,' said maulavi sahib, referring to Khwaja Moinuddin Chishti, the most prominent Sufi saint of the Chishti silsila, or order, in South Asia. 'Preaching and practising the gospel of universal love and the brotherhood of man, Khwaja Moinuddin Chishti Rehmatullah Alai believed that the highest form of devotion meant helping the poor, the distressed and the downtrodden. Accordingly, he is popularly called Gharib Nawaz, or benefactor of the poor. Now that you know the history of our Huzoor in Bhabua don't go about asking silly questions.'

A bit disconcerted at being ticked off loud enough for your entire neighbourhood to hear, I posed another question, 'Did Baba Court Shaheed originally belong to Bhabua?'

Maulavi sahib thundered, 'This question is even more stupid than the previous one! Where did Hazrat Khwaja Moinuddin Chishti Shahenshah-e-Hind Rehmatullah Alai come from? He came from Sanjar, which falls in Iran. This is why he is also called Sanjari. Baba Court Shaheed was from the same family. How could he then be from Bhabua?'

Maulavi sahib glared at me, looking so much like an exasperated pixie that I felt a terrifying urge to laugh. You were, I noticed, giggling softly with your face averted. Wishing that you had warned me about your old teacher's rather severe manner of imparting knowledge, I tried to cover my laugh with a cough.

Oblivious to our mirth, maulavi sahib was in full flow, bellowing away about Baba Court Shaheed's mystical powers, 'I once saw a girl climbing up the steps to his dargah. She was crying, and clutched in her hand was a bottle that she slowly raised to her lips. Before she could drink from it, however, she staggered and fell as if someone had slapped her. The bottle slipped out of her hands and shattered on the steps.

'I asked Huzoor, "Khwaja Hazrat, what is happening to this girl?" All at once I knew the answer. The girl had been trying to drink poison, and Huzoor had stopped her from taking her own life. I hurried down to the girl and asked, "Child, have you made a mistake?" The girl replied, "Yes, baba, I have made a terrible mistake. I have become pregnant before marriage." I told her, "You have been forgiven by Huzoor. Now run along."'

The earlier severity had left maulavi sahib's voice. There he sat, his face creased in a toothless smile of happy remembrance; a gentle pixie dipping a glucose biscuit in his cup of tea. In the confines of Pyaari khala's humid, dark room, he had given me a glimpse of a world where the sanctity of life is valued over narrow sexual morality and compassion overrides punishment.

He peered at you and inquired about preparations for the family thanksgiving the next day. Then, turning to me, he shouted genially, 'This ceremony is performed exclusively by their family in the whole of Bhabua. It's a special privilege that Huzoor bestowed upon their great-grandaunt, Sadabahar.'

Pyaari khala now seemed to have decided that maulavi sahib could not be allowed to do all the talking for the evening. This was her grandaunt's story, which by right she must tell. Cutting him short, she launched into the tale.

'After Sadabahar had been cheated by mamu Shafiq of her properties, she began seeking solace in Baba Court Shaheed's dargah, spending long hours there every day, singing his praises. Baba was very pleased with our grandaunt. Of all the houses in Bhabua, therefore, he chose to grace only our home with his presence, and of all the tawaifs, he selected Sadabahar to be his medium. *Un par sawari aati thi*; she would be possessed by him.

'When Baba manifested himself through her, other tawaifs of the neighbourhood, whether Hindu or Muslim, gathered around and sang. Musicians were called in to accompany them. One day, a tabla player said, "She is just pretending to be possessed." This made Baba Court Shaheed very angry and worms began crawling out of the tabla player's nose and mouth! Realising his mistake, the man begged forgiveness and the worms miraculously disappeared!

'Sadabahar had implored Baba Court Shaheed to always guide and protect her family's musical destiny. In return, she took a vow that the tawaifs of her family would present a thaal full of malida to Baba every year without fail during sawan. And so, over the generations, we have kept her promise. We carry the thaal to the dargah and sing all the way. I remember clearly, when I was young, the older women in our family would make me sing on that day at the shrine. Baba loves music.

'Although everyone is involved in the preparations for the thanksgiving—the daughters-in-law and daughters help in the cooking, the sons carry the thaal on our behalf—the offering to Baba and all other rituals at the dargah are performed, as Sadabahar had ordained, only by the tawaifs in our family. Since I live here permanently, I have been doing it on behalf of my side of the family, while Asghari represents her mother, my cousin Teema's branch of the household.

'But times have changed. With all our daughters being married off, who will do it after we, the old tawaifs, are gone? I don't know. I hope Baba will accept the offering from our sons and daughters-in-law once we are dead. Otherwise, this thanksgiving ceremony will end in our family, and we might lose Baba's continuing blessings and benevolence.'

Pyaari khala's concern is shared by you and the other family members. In South Asia, Sufi mystics are venerated as saints and viewed as intermediaries between mere mortals and god. Believers share an intensely personal relationship with Sufi mystics. Undeterred by harsh criticism from religious orthodoxy, which considers veneration of saints un-Islamic, devotees turn to Sufi mystics for guidance, redress, problem-solving, spiritual fulfilment and salvation.

The discourse of divine love, or ishq-i-haqiqi, is central to the personal and individualised relationship between devotees and Sufi saints, man and god. Distinct from the love between mortals, which is seen as transient and isolating, divine love leads the self towards eventual union with divinity or the 'ultimate truth', al-Haq.

Sufi saints in South Asia have a special following among musician communities. This is due, in large measure, to the fact that music plays an important role as an instrument of devotion in Sufism, especially of the Chishti silsila. Moreover, with their catholic outlook, humanism and stress upon a strong personal element in devotion, Sufi saints attract to their shrines pilgrims cutting across divides of religion, class, caste, gender and sexual morality.

Baba Court Shaheed is the patron saint of all the courtesan families of Bhabua, whether Muslim or Hindu. He is equally revered by the town's non-tawaif residents. For your family, the exclusive privilege of offering thanksgiving at the shrine not only provides a sense of security about being in Baba's safekeeping but has also contributed to its special spiritual status in the tawaif community in Bhabua.

Pyaari khala is in no state to go to the dargah this year. Phoolmani, being the eldest, takes her place, while Asghari leads your side of the family. You, Rani, Rajjo and Seema complete the depleted group of six tawaifs left in your family to offer the thanksgiving prayers at the shrine located atop a mound. The dargah had once marked the outer boundaries of Bhabua but now is very much within town limits. Adjacent to it is a Shiva temple. A shared water tap stands between the two shrines. I am told that Baba Court Shaheed and Shiv-ji get along fabulously. Recognising this friendship, their devotees offer salutations to both, even if specifically visiting one of them.

The mound is swarming with people on this Thursday evening. It is one of the few green, open spaces in Bhabua, and the weather is perfect: cool, breezy and cloudy, a classic monsoon evening of the sort traditionally celebrated by the songs of the season, kajari, sawan and jhoola, that your family has sung for generations. While many visitors seem to be out enjoying a break from the heat and humidity—there are multiple groups of men and boys flying kites—others have more spiritual pursuits in mind. Thursday evenings are regarded as a particularly favourable time to visit Sufi shrines.

Your family's combined offering of the two thaals, each full of malida, a ghee-filled lamp and flower garlands, are carried up ceremoniously by Jawed and Nawab. Flanking them are Phoolmani and Asghari and behind them follow the rest of the family, all dressed in their best.

As your family climbs up the mound, you begin singing a hamd, a devotional song very different from your repertoire of romantic and erotic compositions. Made famous originally by the well-known qawwal from Hyderabad, Aziz Ahmed Warsi, the song is a particular favourite of yours:

Kab tak, merey Maula? Kab tak, merey Maula?
Mein harf-e tamanna hun
Badi der sey chup hun
Kab tak, merey Maula?

For how long, my Master? For how long?
I am but a syllable of desire
Waiting in silence for my turn
For how long, my Master? For how long?

Just outside the shrine, the lamps are lit and Phoolmani and Asghari take the thaals from the men and ceremonially present them to Baba Court Shaheed. The family then offers thanksgiving prayers. The flower garlands and lamps are removed from the thaals by the dargah attendants and placed on Baba's grave. A small portion of the malida too is placed as an offering, while the rest, after being symbolically presented to the saint, is returned to Phoolmani and Asghari.

The thaals are brought home, covered and kept away. The festivities have just begun. Very early the next morning, Ghafuran and the other women in the family begin feverishly cooking a huge feast of mutton pulao, chicken qorma and sweet saffron-flavoured rice.

'Today we will offer food to our purkhin, ustads and other buzurg (family elders), pir and auliya (venerable saints) who have steered the family's journey in music and dance,' you say. 'Since we are a musician family, the first name to be invoked in thanksgiving is naturally that of Miyan Tansen, from whom our singing originated. Then everyone else's names will follow.'

Around mid-morning, Asghari, as the eldest tawaif from your side of the family, takes out the thaal and ceremoniously 'breaks' the mound of malida into smaller portions. Phoolmani will do the same with the other thaal. Meanwhile, Ghafuran announces that food is ready. Laughing gently, she says to you, 'Sister, now invite your ustads to eat the qorma and pulao!'

You take out small portions of the feast in little saucers. Old maulavi sahib, who has been hovering around all morning, is summoned to do nazr-o-niyaz, dedicate the food in the name of the family to ancestresses, musicians and saints—a long line-up of names, starting from Miyan Tansen and including Batoolan, Ameeran, Zahooran, Dharmman, Bullan and Kallan, Sadabahar, your mother Teema and Rani's mother Bindo. Once the prayers are offered, the food, along with the malida, is distributed among family and neighbours.

By late afternoon, there is a lull in the feasting and festivities, leading to a much-needed siesta. We are back in Pyaari khala's house. It's begun raining again and, except for her, you and I, everyone else is resting. The excitement of the past two days seems to have energised Pyaari khala. Despite your repeated requests that she rest, khala is in full flow, recounting family history.

'My father would tell us that they saw very difficult times through their childhood and adolescence in Bhabua,' Pyaari khala recalls. 'After losing the court case, Sadabahar tried to rebuild the family's lost fortunes anew. For some time, it seemed that her efforts would bear fruit, but her heart was clearly elsewhere. She had begun to lose interest in the bright lights of mehfils, the admiration of male admirers and the accolades that came her way after a performance. All she seemed to want was to spend her days in prayer and meditation at the dargah of Baba Court Shaheed.'

Slowly, the invitations to mehfils began to dry out. Sadabahar was past caring. She stopped performing even in her own kotha. With no earnings coming in, the family lived for some time off the money that Sadabahar had earned in the immediate aftermath of the court case. Bullan and Kallan had already spent a portion of these savings in buying a smaller house in Bhabua after losing their own to Shafiq. Sensing that Sadabahar was increasingly lost to the real world, her foster mothers had also invested some of her money in buying two cows to ensure regular supply of milk for the family, and a horse with a tonga-carriage, which Sa'dullah Miyan began driving when he was a mere child.

Through those years, the district of Shahabad seemed to be under some terrible curse. Floods would follow droughts, and epidemics turned vast tracts into graveyards. The horse too died of starvation. Bent with age, Bullan and Kallan, along with the able-bodied and young Sa'dullah, were forced to join the kangla squads and work on roads in return for a daily pittance.

The elder son of the family, Bullah Miyan, born blind, could not join them. Every day, he would set out to graze the family's cows in pasturelands surrounding Bhabua. There was little grass to be found, and the starving cows would desperately munch even on stones in the hope of finding nourishment. In search of fodder, Bullah would have to take the animals further and further out of town. The jingle of the bells tied around their necks would keep him informed about the cows' whereabouts, while his faithful walking stick guided him through unfamiliar trails.

The animals were the family's only resource. The sisters sold a portion of their fast-decreasing supply of daily milk to augment the earnings from the beggar squad. The rest of the milk supplemented the family's frugal diet of sattu, made of parched and pounded barley, or marua, a local millet.

In Bullah's day-long wanderings, his most loved companion was an old sarangi left behind by one of Sadabahar's former accompanists. On this, Bullah had taught himself a few simple tunes. Playing on it while his cows grazed, the blind Bullah was a familiar figure in and around Bhabua. Hearing his sarangi's wail, there was always someone to guide him back if Bullah wandered off in the wrong direction, or to help him find the cows if they strayed too far.

One day, as Bullah sat under a tree cluster playing the sarangi, he became aware of approaching footsteps. He called out greetings but received no answer. Now he could hear angry murmurs. Long used to making his ears do the work of eyes, Bullah estimated a crowd of nearly fifty people closing in on him.

He called out a greeting again. This time, a harsh male voice asked him who owned the cows he was grazing. Unaware of the danger looming in front, Bullah replied that the cows belonged to his family. Another stranger's voice demanded to know his family's religious identity. As soon as he said that they were Muslim, blows and kicks descended upon him, accompanied by abuses that made Bullah's blood turn cold. His last thought before he lost consciousness after a lathi blow to his head was: 'Who are these men and what do they want?'

❁

The group that attacked Bullah comprised men of various castes from villages neighbouring Bhabua. Mobilised by the gaurakshini, or the cow-protection movement, mobs like these had become a common feature in district Shahabad in the last two decades of the nineteenth century.

The movement had originated in Punjab around 1882 under the aegis of the Arya Samaj, which sought to use the cow as a symbol of Hindu religion and mobilise Hindus for its protection. It soon found support from leaders, sadhus and supporters of Sanatan Dharma Sabhas and other Hindu groups who spoke of the cow both as a nurturing mother goddess and mother of the Hindu nation. The protection of her life-giving and sacred body was stressed as the paramount duty of all Hindus. Propagated through pamphlets, leaflets and chain letters, the cow-protection movement spread rapidly across northern and central India, and became especially strong in the Bhojpuri-speaking districts of Azamgarh and Shahabad.

Initially, the movement stressed upon caring for ailing, old and abandoned cows. Soon, the focus shifted almost entirely to the danger posed to the cow by beef-eating non-Hindus, portrayed in gaurakshini discourse primarily as Muslims. They were, it was argued, not only the enemies of the cow mother—and, by extension, of the Hindu religion—but also all Hindus.

In the Bhojpuri-speaking region, the cow-protection movement received active support from middle-class lawyers, clerks, officials and teachers as also local traders, moneylenders and Brahmin priests. Rajput and Bhumihar landholders—whose dominant status was being eroded due to the successive subdivision of landholdings, the closing of avenues of alternative employment, like army service, and the rising assertion of the tenantry—were at the forefront of the movement.

Taking the lead in the cause of protecting Hindu religion through protecting the cow became a means to assert their traditional role as upper-caste 'protectors' and 'warriors'. They also encouraged poorer members of their communities to align with the cause. In addition, their tenants and servants, who belonged to a range of intermediate castes—like the cow-herding and cultivating tenant communities of Ahirs, Kurmis and Koeris—and were aspiring for a higher status in the caste hierarchy, also joined in the movement.

By the 1890s, there was an outbreak of sectarian strife and bloodshed in eastern parts of the United Provinces and west Bihar, as gaurakshini mobs began attacking Muslims accused of either transporting cattle for slaughter or of killing cows. Gaurakshini sabhas, or cow-protection societies, that had come up in various towns and villages of the Bhojpuri belt began demanding iqrarnamas, or bonds, from Muslims that they would not slaughter cattle. These demands were backed up by threats of social and economic boycott and plunder of Muslim-owned properties. In this atmosphere of intimidation, suspicion and escalating tension, violence would break out at the smallest pretext, and peak during Eid al-Adha, when Hindu mobs targeted Muslim localities and villages alleged to have sacrificed cows during the festival.

Meanwhile, in the same region, the revivalist Faraizis and Wahabis, especially the latter, had been mobilising Muslims to follow practices of a 'purer' Islam. In reaction to the cow-protection movement's propaganda, certain sections among Muslims—many of whom had earlier avoided beef-eating or sacrificing cows on Eid al-Adha out of respect for their Hindu neighbours—now claimed it as their right as 'true' believers.

In many instances, the British authorities played an instigating role by revoking the ban upon the killing of cows for food that had been imposed in pre-colonial times by Muslim rulers in deference to the sensibilities of their Hindu subjects. In 1863, for example, the Azamgarh District Magistrate, Henry Lushington, declared that Muslims were free to kill cows behind closed doors. Under pressure from local Hindu inhabitants, this order was subsequently revoked. However, in 1888, the North-Western Provinces High Court decreed that a cow was not a sacred object, and its slaughter for food was not illegal. These contradictory positions by colonial officials on the issue of cow slaughter contributed to further escalation of hostilities between Hindus and Muslims.

In many areas, like Patna and around, Muslim butchers were employed by colonial authorities to provide beef for the Europeans troops stationed in cantonments like Dinapore. Interestingly, while gaurakshini supporters mounted attacks on these Muslim butchers, they remained conspicuously silent about the consumption of beef by the British in India.

In 1893, Eid al-Adha was marked by vicious riots in Azamgarh and Shahabad. The number of Muslims in Shahabad was the lowest in all of Bihar, amounting to about 7 per cent of the district's total population. The *Bengal District Gazetteer for Shahabad, 1906* describes the riots in village Koath in the Sasaram subdivision, where the Muslim population was higher than the district average, in the following words: '… a large concourse of Hindus assembled from the neighbouring villages and made a raid on the Muhammadan butchers of Koath, who were charged with having caught and slaughtered a Brahmani bull. In revenge for this outrage, the Muhammadans attacked the Hindu quarters, in the course of which guns were used, and several persons were severely injured. Additional police force was accordingly quartered for one year in Koath and forty-six other villages.'

An uneasy calm prevailed for some years after this, fractured periodically by 'minor' incidents, like the assault on Bullah. Through all this turbulence, the tawaifs' locality in Bhabua remained an island of genuine peace, where Hindu and Muslim families continued to live side-by-side in neighbourly amity. Reviled and attacked alike by the Arya Samaj and the Wahabis, the tawaifs had little sympathy for, or interest in, the proselytising and propaganda of these reformist and revivalist religious movements.

You are justifiably proud of the fact that Bhabua, and in particular the tawaifs' quarters, has no history of communal violence. You attribute this not only to the tawaifs' own good sense but also to the benign influence of Baba Court Shaheed, beloved of all in Bhabua. Baba, you assert, has never discriminated among his devotees, sharing with them in equal measure his love and grace.

A Hindu shopkeeper of Bhabua witnessed Bullah being attacked and ran back to the town for help. Bullan, Kallan and Sa'dullah were away at work, but their tawaif neighbours, Hindu and Muslim, along with their sons and other menfolk ran to his rescue. They arrived too late. The mob had left. Bullah lay unconscious in a pool of blood. His sarangi had miraculously escaped damage. His cows were gone, robbed by the mob in the name of protection.

A loud and incessant knocking rudely breaks into Pyaari khala's narrative. Manohar, who drove me back to Bhabua from Banaras two days ago, stands at the door. Quivering with self-righteous indignation, he announces that he will immediately return to Banaras. He will not stay a moment longer, he declares, in the vicinity of 'Muslim prostitutes'. It isn't clear which part of this identity is more abhorrent to him.

Ever since I returned to Bhabua, I had noticed that he refused the water, tea and food that you tried to serve him. He refused too to sleep in your house, despite your warm offer to set up a bed for him in one of the rooms. Without any explanation for his churlishness, Manohar had insisted on buying his food and tea from the market and sleeping in the cramped discomfort of his taxi.

Today, he has decided to break his silence, raging that he won't have his purity compromised by drinking your water, eating your food, ferrying you in his car. Hearing his loud rant, a small crowd of curious passers-by have gathered outside the house for an afternoon's free entertainment. Addressing them and us, Manohar declares that he is a high-born Brahmin from Banaras who would rather starve than take orders from 'lowly Muslim whores'.

Telling him to get lost, I settle his dues and shut the door on his malevolence. My hands are shaking. You and Pyaari khala have been silent through the entire episode. I dare not look into your eyes. I hold myself responsible for imposing the man upon you and your family.

Taking a deep breath, I attempt an awkward apology but you gently cut me short, 'Do not take to heart the venom that man spewed. You are not responsible for what he says. He is not the first man to abuse us and, sadly, he will not be the last. Believe me, khala and I have heard worse. And not only have we survived, we have given back in good measure. So, don't worry for us. Just spit away his memory. He deserves no better.'

From her bed, Pyaari khala intones gravely, 'I hope he gets diarrhoea on his way back to Banaras. May he find no water to wash himself. And may his car break down, so he is left stranded in a place without water and with shit smeared on his bottom!' Mimicking the rumblings of an upset stomach, she hoots with laughter.

You giggle. I am a bit taken aback. Does your laughter mask the humiliation inflicted by the driver's ugly words, I wonder. I have no way of knowing, and not wishing to cause further hurt, I let it go. And join you and your aunt in laughing the memory away.

A bit later, Nawab's wife brings in the evening tea. Asghari, Rani, Phoolmani, Seema and Rajjo arrive to spend the evening with Pyaari khala. Once the cups are cleared, all of you join in to tell me of the trials and tribulations faced by Sadabahar's family in Bhabua.

❁

'I am your whore, my beloved, Throwing shame away I dance for you.' Sadabahar sang as she whirled in ecstatic frenzy at the shrine of Baba Court Shaheed. Unknowing, she was repeating the lines of another Sufi mystic and poet separated from her by distance, time and language—Bulleh Shah.

Sadabahar now lived almost permanently at the dargah. Occasionally, her foster mothers would drag her home for a bath and change of clothes. But even they were reconciled to losing her to the world beyond. Twice a day, they would visit the dargah and feed Sadabahar, comb her hair and bemoan their ruined fate.

With the theft of Bullah's cows, the family had no assets save its own capacity for labour. Thanking Baba Court Shaheed for saving Bullah's life, his grandmothers and brother continued foraging for work and sustenance with greater urgency.

Bullah spent a long time at home, recovering from the assault. Once he was better, the family was shamefacedly forced to send him out to work. Stumbling from door to door, playing his sarangi, Bullah Miyan, brought up like a prince by his aunt, was now reduced to begging.

'Sadabahar remained enveloped in her mystical preoccupations, oblivious to the family's suffering,' Pyaari says. 'The prophecy foretold by her blue-grey-green-silver eyes had finally come to pass. Destined to wander unknown lands, she had indeed moved away from the mortal world into realms open only to mystics, magicians and the mad. Captive to her enchantment, her eyes had become blind, her ears deaf and her heart had hardened to the wretched poverty that had hold of her home.'

The family's spectacular fall in fortunes was not unusual in the community. As self-made women, the tawaifs' material well-being hinged upon finding wealthy and generous patrons willing to provide regular financial support to their kotha. Cautionary tales abound about tawaifs, who for the sake of love or spirituality or any other reason abdicated their responsibilities as breadwinners, and were reduced to penury or low-paid prostitution. Plentiful too are stories about the rise to fame and riches of its responsible, ambitious and hard-working daughters.

Sadabahar's family urgently needed a daughter to steer it out of the economic straits it found itself in. Given Sadabahar's preoccupation with mystical matters and advancing age, there was little hope that she would ever become a mother. It was imperative, therefore, that Bullah and Sa'dullah be married off as soon as possible. But who would agree to give their girls in marriage to paupers?

Finding wives for sons was not easy in the tawaif community. The Gandharvas and socially higher-placed clans among the Nats, like the Baisi, set aside for marriage those daughters considered neither musically gifted nor physically attractive, nor with the aptitude to become tawaifs. By norm, these communities and clans married within their respective groups; the prestige and respect they enjoyed in the wider tawaif community were linked to the exchange of girls within these boundaries.

Needless to say, the numbers of marriageable girls in these groups were far fewer than those chosen to become tawaifs. Families with boys, therefore, had to spend considerable money and energy in persuading relatives of girls who observed purdah to agree to their marriage proposals. Socially and financially well-placed families naturally stood the best chance of being accepted. In poorer tawaif households, it was not unusual to find men long past marriageable age still waiting for a wife.

By norm, the bride's side was expected to spend only a nominal amount on the wedding, which included gifts to their daughter, the groom and his family. The major share of wedding expenses was borne by the boy's household. This comprised gifts for the girl and her family—the haisiyat, or status, of the bridegroom's side being judged by how expensive these were. The boy's family was also expected to organise a wedding feast, walima for the entire community once the bride was brought home. This too played an important role in determining the status of the boy's family and added to its prestige in the community.

Lower-placed tawaif families, like the Bedia and Kanjar, and Nat clans like the Magahiya, involved in the low-end practise of music and dance as also sex work, could not afford to keep any of their daughters from earning. Regardless of looks, musical talent or aptitude, almost all their girls were recruited into the profession. Since these families did not have daughters to offer in marriage to other tawaif households, they could not hope to get wives for their sons either. They had to buy wives from outside their social groups by paying a bride price. Prospective wives for sons of these clans were provided by communities like the Gohriya. Once regarded as 'low caste' by tawaifs, Gohriya men specialised in curing animal hides, which they then used to make the faces of tablas and dholaks.

The Gohriya families I spoke with in Bhabua, however, asserted that they were a biradari from among the 'Khan sahibs', the Dhari Mirasi

Muslim accompanist musicians. Over the past few generations, many Gohriya have entered the field of tabla-playing, which might account for their contemporary claims to musician status.

The Gohriya traditionally prohibited their women from practising either music and dance or prostitution. Instead, their daughters were sold for a bride price as wives to tawaif clans like the Magahiya. These tawaif groups would also buy wives from other castes and marginalised communities willing to sell their girls to the highest bidder.

Belonging to the higher-placed Baisi clan, Sadabahar's family considered buying wives below their social status. Ideally, they would have wanted wives from the Baisi or other similarly higher-ranked Nat clans, like the Sahban or the Nigaadi. The problem was that not one among the many families with marriageable daughters that Bullan and Kallan approached was willing to even consider their proposal.

Not only were Bullah Miyan and Sa'dullah Miyan penniless orphans without the security provided by an earning tawaif relative, but the older boy was also blind. Bullan and Kallan were advised by well-meaning clan members and friends to consider buying wives for their two grandsons. But this too proved futile. Down to their last savings, Bullan and Kallan had to beat an embarrassed and hasty retreat every time marriage negotiations reached the all-important discussion of bride price. Everyone wanted to fleece tawaifs, they would fume on their way back home. Twenty-one silver coins for each girl besides new clothes for their extended families and a wedding feast replete with mutton pulao—did these low-borns think that tawaifs held keys to Kuber's treasure? They would lament the greed of daughter-sellers.

Meanwhile, the number of rejections kept growing, as did the age of Bullah and Sa'dullah. Finally, Biggan, a tawaif in Bhabua, taking pity on the family, broached with Bullan and Kallan the possibility of negotiating a deal with Ramzani, the 'leper', for his two eldest daughters.

Ramzani, a Gohriya by birth, could often be heard wailing about his fate, about being the most unfortunate person in town. On account of the stigma of leprosy, he and his family were treated as pariahs and forced to live outside the boundaries of Bhabua.

His earlier profession of covering tabla and dholak with hide had long since come to an end. No one would touch anything he made. His wife, unable to bear the stigma and poverty, had abandoned him and their children to their fate. Apart from a ramshackle hut, one partially broken charpoy and a few old and dented utensils, the family now owned nothing.

Shakuran and Saleeman were the oldest of Ramzani's six children; there were also three much younger boys and a little girl. The family survived on the earnings brought in by the hardy, industrious older daughters. Daily, the sisters walked several miles to the forests in the Kaimur hills and, braving attacks from wild beasts and predatory men, collected firewood, which they would then sell in Bhabua.

Clothed in rags, hair matted with dirt, the younger children would accompany their father to the dargah of Baba Court Shaheed and beg from all those who came there. Maintaining their distance from the wretched-looking family and averting their eyes from Ramzani's oozing wounds, the devotees would toss food or coins at his children and hurry away.

Bullan and Kallan would see the ragged group during their daily trips to the shrine in search of Sadabahar. Barely managing to keep their hearth fires lit, they would nonetheless carry leftover sattu gruel for Ramzani's hungry brood.

The idea of marrying into his stigma had sounded preposterous to the sisters when Biggan first broached it. For days, they wept and ranted. They kept reminding each other (since no one else seemed to remember) that they had once been among the foremost tawaifs in Chainpur, and their daughter Sadabahar was the most illustrious singer Shahabad had known. Would fate be so cruel as to force them to bring in as daughters-in-law the girls of a Gohriya leper? Once their outrage had exhausted itself, Bullan and Kallan came to a difficult but pragmatic decision.

No one ever visited Ramzani, and so he was astonished to see two old and bent women hobbling their way to his hut one evening. His amazement turned to shock when Bullan and Kallan, while refusing to enter his home or his offer of water, expressed interest in Shakuran and Saleeman as prospective daughters-in-law. But they wanted to inspect the girls thoroughly to make sure that they were not infected with their father's dreaded disease.

A silent prayer rose from Ramzani's heart. He had all but given up hope of ever being able to marry off his daughters. He was deterred neither by Bullah's blindness nor Bullan and Kallan's impoverished circumstances. Being the wife of a blind son from a poor tawaif family was, he believed, a huge advancement from being the unmarried daughter of a starving Gohriya leper.

Shakuran and Saleeman were summoned and presented to the sharp-eyed Bullan and Kallan. Dark, stocky and short, the girls were unremarkable to look at, which did not overly worry the sisters. They assessed the girls' respective ages as no more than fifteen and sixteen summers each; a bit past marriageable age but with long years still ahead to produce several healthy children. Their wide hips and flat bellies met with satisfied approval; these girls were made to be mothers. Then followed a hawk-eyed inspection of limbs, torso and back for any wounds, scratches or marks bearing disease. Reassured with the girls' unblemished skins, Bullan and Kallan now turned towards Ramzani to conduct the business of give and take, the bargaining and the cajoling that would conclusively seal their new relationship.

Ramzani was so desperate that he would have agreed to give his daughters away for free. More for keeping up appearances than any real expectation, he murmured about the difficulties his family would face without the labour and earnings provided by his two eldest daughters. Bullan and Kallan had come prepared for this. Having scraped together the last of their savings, they were ready to offer Ramzani two silver coins and new sets of clothes for him and his children in exchange for the girls.

The deal was struck in no time. The next day, Bullan and Kallan, along with a handful of clan members, accompanied Bullah and Sa'dullah to the local mosque. Ramzani was waiting for them with Shakuran and Saleeman. Wearing new saris presented by their prospective grandmothers-in-law and with hair neatly oiled and combed into plaits, eyes lined with kohl and feet coloured red with alta, the girls looked transformed from the wild-maned, scruffy creatures Bullan and Kallan had inspected the previous evening.

For the first time in very long, the old tawaifs felt hope spread like warm ghee in the arid recesses of their hearts. Their last-ditch investment in their grandsons' futures and that of the family would not be in vain. Some intensive training in the ways expected of daughters-in-law in tawaif households, and the girls would be ready to take on the responsibilities of silently and obediently cooking, cleaning and bearing children, especially girl children who would earn back for the family its lost fortunes and prestige. With these happy thoughts, Bullan and Kallan watched the local maulavi entwine the destinies of Bullah with Shakuran and Sa'dullah with Saleeman in simple nikah ceremonies celebrated with small pieces of gur and sweetened water, which was all that Ramzani could afford to feed his guests.

Late into the evening, just as Pyaari finishes the story of Bullah and Sa'dullah's wedding, Reyaz, a local taxi owner and driver, presents himself at her door. News travels fast in Bhabua. Having heard of the showdown with Manohar, with easy confidence, Reyaz announces his decision to provide me with a taxi whenever I need it through the remainder of my stay in the town.

'You can verify my background with the khalas here,' he announces, settling down comfortably at the foot of Pyaari's bed. 'My family and I live in this neighbourhood. Everyone in Bhabua knows me. Just ask for Reyaz or Randhir Singh, and people will give you my entire life history.'

Seeing my mystified expression, he chuckles. Then winking at you and Pyaari khala, he explains, 'My mother, Buddhan, is Muslim. She is an old friend of this family. In her times, she too was counted as a good singer. She gave me the name Reyaz. My father, Babu Rajbir Singh, is, as you might have realised from his name, Hindu. He named me Randhir Singh when I was born. So I have two names. Muslims call me Reyaz and Hindus, Randhir. You can choose, aapa, to call me by whichever name you like.' Reyaz has a forthright charm that makes me smile.

You courteously add the details that Reyaz/Randhir Singh had modestly held back. Babu Rajbir Singh, you say deferentially, is one of the most prominent Rajput landholders of the area and an important public works contractor. Besides, he owns several properties in Bhabua. He has set up Reyaz's business by buying for him the three taxis he runs. Reyaz's older brother Aijaz, or Ajay Singh, is an influential politician of the district.

In a region where tawaifs were an accepted presence in the everyday life of upper-caste men, their children bore no stigma of illegitimacy. Times might have changed, and tawaifs rendered extinct, but their progeny living in Bhabua and around continue to enjoy a relative measure of social acceptability. In a continuation of past practice, though not given legal recognition or share in the ancestral property of their mothers' upper-caste lovers, several tawaif offspring like Reyaz enjoy relatively secure connections with their fathers. This is more usual in the case of long-term relationships between tawaifs and their lovers. Children from such unions continue to be assured of quasi-formal but unquestioned recognition of their father's name. In several cases, the fathers also provide their offspring from tawaifs with some measure of financial security.

You have often described your three children as your Rajput patron lover Maheshwar Singh's most precious gift to you in a relationship spanning nearly twenty years till his death. In deference to their father's religious identity, your children, though brought up as Muslims, like Reyaz/Randhir, carry two sets of names. Your eldest Shama is also Shyama, while your younger daughter Meenu is Mehrunissa as well. Your son, nicknamed Nanhe, is Nadeem alias Narendra.

'Reyaz and Aijaz are good boys,' murmurs Pyaari khala from her bed. 'Even though Aijaz has become a big man, he continues to look after the interests of his own people. Just recently, when the local chemist did not have the medicines I needed, Aijaz and Reyaz had them brought from Banaras the same day. I can never bless these boys enough.'

Reyaz presses Pyaari khala's feet in happy response. With a theatrical flourish he announces that, since I have come all the way from Delhi, he will personally drive me wherever I wish to go. 'I have heard, aapa, that you make films. I love films. This way, I can get to hear all about my favourite actors and actresses.'

'I make documentary films, Reyaz. I know little about the lives of Bombay stars,' I hasten to clarify.

'Documentary films? Like what they show on Discovery? Those are good too. Good for knowledge,' Reyaz reassures me kindly. Then after a momentary pause, he adds, 'You might consider making a film about my life? Reyaz/Randhir Singh's story, as told by him.' Without waiting for my response, he takes his leave as breezily as he had arrived, 'I will call you tomorrow morning to find out your plans for the day. Till then, Khuda Hafiz!'

CHAPTER 12

Teema

ASGHARI TAKES A LONG, LOVING look at herself in the mirror. Closer in years to Pyaari than to you and Ghafuran, your older sister stoutly dismisses all questions related to age. As far as Asghari is concerned, she is still the prettiest, most talented and, yes, the youngest of all her tawaif relatives, even into her mid-seventies.

Her opening remarks when we meet are invariably along the lines of, 'I stepped out this morning to get some fresh air when two young men, strangers to our neighbourhood, wouldn't stop staring at me. Tiring of them, I told them to get lost. They apologised for staring but said they had never seen a woman as beautiful as me in their lives. Fancy that!'

She had told me a similar story the first time I met her in Banaras. You sat through it in silence and later, when we were alone, said in a sour tone that Asghari had not left the house at all that morning. This was her opening conversation with everyone. You were right. And though I know that you find her vanity irritating in the extreme, I am usually rather captivated by Asghari's unabashed self-adoration.

Petite and fair-skinned, Asghari is beautiful by north Indian parameters. Her hair is still plentiful and long; her eyes are thickly lashed. She has a perfectly proportioned nose above bow-shaped lips. Unlike you and others of your generation in the family, Asghari spends considerable time on her make-up. Her face is always powdered, her eyes kohled and her lips and nails painted. The pink saris she favours, the glittering plastic pins and bands decorating her hair, and her high-pitched little girl's voice create around her an aura of exaggerated femininity. This impression disappears as soon as she loses her temper, which is often. The torrents of abusive expletives that pour forth from her painted lips would wilt the sturdiest soul.

'You sister-fucking pimp! Has your whore daughter stopped earning that you need to cheat an honest woman of her hard-earned savings?' Asghari rants at the old tea-stall owner who has come in to collect his cups and has calculated, by mistake or design, a rupee extra on the total bill.

We are visiting Asghari's home in Bhabua and being treated to the special lal chai, or red lemon tea, for which the hapless shopkeeper is justifiably famous. You arch your eyebrows in smug satisfaction at Asghari being exposed to me in what you describe as her 'true colours'. Rani, your cousin and Asghari's faithful shadow, merely tugs harder at her rosary and shuts her eyes.

The elderly tea-stall owner, Asghari's neighbour for several decades, feebly attempts a rebuke, 'Bai, hold your tongue. Even streetwalkers speak better than you.'

Her eyes flashing, Asghari jumps up and, taking her slipper in her hand, thunders back, 'You vermin-eaten, impotent bastard! You dare to open your filthy mouth in front of me. Get the hell out of here before I stuff your shrivelled little dick in your mouth!'

Leaving the cups behind in panic, the tea-stall owner scampers out of Asghari's house.

Rani tells me that he will return once Asghari's thunder has calmed. Then, with a coquettish wink, she will make him a peace offering of paan and without fuss pay her bill. Grumbling under his breath about her 'loose tongue', the tea-seller will grudgingly accept the paan and money and pretend to scowl as he leaves, with Asghari blowing air kisses at him.

Asghari's charm is as formidable as her fury. She can hold one captive with scintillating stories of her life as a popular singer and dancer. Age has slowed neither her memory nor her steps and if requested repeatedly and flatteringly enough, she will dance with greater agility and grace than performers half her age.

That said, Asghari is enchanting only as long as she is the centre of attention. If the conversation veers towards anything else, a petulant tone enters her voice, her lips develop a sulky droop and her eyes glaze over with boredom. The sole exception is the talk of Teema, the mother of you three sisters, the one person apart from herself whom Asghari seems to have loved deeply.

✽

You have often talked to me about Teema. I can sense your deep love for her, your protectiveness of her memory. From you, I have heard about Teema's much-awaited birth. She arrived just when Bullan and Kallan had decided to throw out her mother, Shakuran, if her next baby too was a boy.

Named Rafeeqan but called Teema by all, blind Bullah's daughter was vested with responsibility from the moment she was born. Desperate for her to transform the family's destiny, Teema was the sun that her entire household—her great-grandmothers, parents, uncle and aunt, and her two older brothers, Yahiya and Yaqub—revolved around.

Bullan and Kallan devoted all their waking hours to telling her stories about illustrious tawaifs like Dharmman and Sadabahar who had brought glory to their family. At an age when children believed in fairies and witches, little Teema was taught about the magic of music and dance. Her father, Bullah Miyan, would play on his sarangi and teach her the seven notes of music-making while she was still a lisping toddler. Sa'dullah Miyan, her uncle, would go out daily to work on road construction and in peoples' fields to ensure that Teema never went hungry to bed. Her mother and aunt, Shakuran and Saleeman, swallowing their shame as purdah-observing wives, would go to the homes of wealthier tawaifs and help with housework in exchange for cast-off clothes, a glass of milk or a bowl of yoghurt or ghee for their little Teema. Clothed in hand-me-downs and fed on charity, Teema's infancy was spent being pampered and doted upon by her family.

The only person oblivious to her existence was her grandaunt Sadabahar. Baba Court Shaheed now resided for longer and longer periods in her emaciated form. A medium for his pronouncements, the once-celebrated singer had lost her own voice. She had lost too memory of her links with her family and the world around. She was usually to be found speaking feverishly on behalf of her saint or lying semi-conscious in the dargah. She had stopped eating, taking only a few sips of the water that Bullan and Kallan pressed upon her dry lips. Realising that their daughter's days with them were numbered, they helplessly watched her slip away, till one day they arrived at the dargah to find a crowd of devotees gathered. Sadabahar lay sprawled out at the foot of Baba's grave, her soul at peace and with the Maker.

Bullan and Kallan were the only ones who mourned Sadabahar's loss. Bullah Miyan was too engrossed in making a singer out of Teema, while her uncle and brothers were preoccupied with earning a livelihood for the family. Teema's mother, Shakuran, made pregnant almost every year by Bullah, was grieving yet another miscarriage. And her aunt Saleeman, after giving birth in quick succession to five boys, each one of whom had died in his infancy (much to the family's relief), was busy nursing a new pregnancy in the hope that she would have a girl.

Worn out with old age and the long struggle to keep the family afloat, Bullan and Kallan too passed on not long after Sadabahar. Teema was by then nearly eight years old. The last prayer on their lips was for her, that she inherit Sadabahar's prodigious musical talent and her spectacular success as a performer.

Teema was, however, no Sadabahar in the making. Her voice lacked the magic evident in her grandaunt even as a child. Teema's less-than-satisfactory progress in music learning as she grew older, dashed the dreams of even the most optimistic family members. Bullah and Sa'dullah borrowed money from wealthier tawaifs to engage a dance teacher for her in the desperate hope that she might prove to be a better dancer than she was a singer. In a few months, the kathak guru, Ramji Maharaj, a man known for his honesty and integrity, advised Bullah and Sa'dullah to stop wasting their scant resources on a lost cause. The girl simply could not dance.

To make matters worse, Teema had inherited her mother and aunt's thickset, short frame. Her family would bemoan her sallow complexion and bulbous nose, her too thin lips and irregular teeth. There was no hope that she could become a popular tawaif like some others whose good looks compensated for mediocre singing and dancing. Had the family been wealthier, they would have probably pushed Teema into purdah for training in the skills expected of married women. This choice the family was in no position to make.

Bullah wished he had not been born blind, had been younger and better placed financially so that he could have kicked Shakuran out and got himself a new wife. Cursing his luck for being tied to a liability, he issued her a grim warning that he would keep making her pregnant till she gave him another daughter.

Saleeman, meanwhile, had at long last given birth to a daughter. Named Bindo by Sa'dullah, the child was the family's only hope. She was still too young, though. Moreover, investment in her future career as tawaif would involve considerable expense, for which Bullah and

Sa'dullah had banked upon Teema's success as a performer. Teema had to be made to earn, and fast, to ensure the family's survival.

Bullah extended her hours of learning. She had been his redemption for being born a boy and blind; his only hope of gaining some respect and status lay in Teema's future success as a tawaif. Every false note from the child curdled this hope to sour bitterness, which Bullah marked in angry, rough welts with his sarangi bow on her little arms. She would cry out in pain but, with Bullan and Kallan dead, who would come to her rescue?

Her uncle Sa'dullah had his own grievances. None of the fathers, uncles, brothers or sons in other tawaif homes in Bhabua lifted a finger to earn a living. Sa'dullah envied the ease, comfort and pocket money they enjoyed in the protection of their tawaif daughter, niece, sister or mother. Teema's arrival had promised liberation from the gruelling labour he had been forced to do since childhood. Teema's quivering, unsure notes shattered his dreams.

Sa'dullah now resented every morsel the girl ate from his earnings. In hopeless rage, he would join Bullah in raining blows upon the child when her singing and dancing fell below the desired expectations, which was often. The two sons of the family, Yahiya and Yaqub, now in their adolescence, would also vent their fury upon the hapless Teema for the years of neglect they had suffered while she had been indulged.

Shakuran and Saleeman would initially just watch and shed tears. Trained by the exacting Bullan and Kallan into timid obedience, they had long shed the feisty spirit with which as girls they would walk deep into forests in search of firewood. Unable though to watch Teema being abused daily, they began to throw themselves upon the girl and receive the blows meant for her on their own backs. Often, hearing their cries, tawaif neighbours were forced to rush in and pull Bullah, Sa'dullah, Yahiya and Yaqub away.

You begin to cry whenever you tell me about Teema's life. I have noticed that your account of her story is punctuated by silences and gaps. From episodes of Teema's childhood, you go straight to the point when she became a mother, without filling me in on what came in between.

Hoping that Asghari might say more, I ask about her mother. In the darkening shadows of her airless room, she makes no immediate comment but gets up instead to open the solitary window to let in the last light of the setting sun and a post-shower breeze.

Asghari lives alone in her double-storeyed house. While the upper floor, I have been told, lies empty, she occupies the two rooms downstairs. The outer room has a crumbling mud chulha used for cooking. On a shelf next to the chulha lie scattered bottles of basic spices like turmeric, red chillies and cumin, a few old and soot-blackened aluminium pots, chipped plates, two steel glasses and a weed basket used to store onions and potatoes.

Opposite the kitchen space is a hand-pump screened by a torn sari stretched over a rope. This serves as the bathing area. Facing it is a corner crammed with suitcases, a couple of broken chairs and a pile of dirty, discarded clothes. The small and cramped inner room in which we sit has a solitary bed, an almirah and a mirror on top of a dressing table which, in stark contrast to the want engulfing the house, is crammed with cosmetics—lipsticks of various shades, gleaming bottles, and jars full of cream, powder and face colour.

Except for the now-open window and the main door, which is kept shut for safety and privacy, the house has no openings. The breeze from outside has died down, and it's uncomfortably warm. I murmur that there must be a power cut in the neighbourhood, which is why the electric fan is off. You cast a quick look at your elder sister but say nothing. In mocking tones, Asghari informs me that her power connection has been cut by the electricity department since she couldn't afford to pay for it. I begin to understand her fury—if not her abusive outburst—over the inflated tea bill. I also notice for the first time the candle stubs littered around the house.

After delicately wiping the sweat off her face, Asghari tells me, in her characteristically blunt manner, the parts of Teema's life that you have found so difficult to speak about. Teema was only eleven years old when she was raped by Babu Prabhuddhanarayan Singh, a Rajput landholder with a penchant for very young virgins. She had begun menstruating early; too early according to the old women in the neighbourhood, wise about such matters, but not early enough for her father and uncle who had been anxiously awaiting her puberty.

Teema had whimpered with fright when she first saw menstrual blood on her thighs, convinced that she was going to die. Neither her mother nor her aunt explained what was happening to her. The one silver lining was that, for the first time, Teema got a break from the music lessons she loathed.

She hated the wailing of the sarangi. She dreaded the long, exhausting hours spent with her father, the tedium of repeating the same song over and over again, his shouting and his beatings. Prohibited now from activities like music learning because of her 'impure' menstruating state, Teema was free, while the bleeding lasted, to play with her little cousin, Bindo, sit in her mother's lap and enjoy her childhood.

Then the bleeding stopped, and after a long ritual bath, Teema was forced to go back to the dreaded music lessons. Meanwhile, ignoring the advice of tawaif neighbours to delay Teema's sexual initiation until her body had matured a bit more, her uncle Sa'dullah was busy negotiating the best deal for Teema's virginity.

He would have done this earlier had it not been for a strict rule in the community prohibiting sexual activity in pre-pubescent girls. Free now to set his plans in motion, Sa'dullah struck gold with Babu Prabhuddhanarayan Singh. The old Rajput would pay an astronomical figure of a hundred rupees and rice enough to feed Teema's family for an entire month in exchange for spending one night with the child.

Back home, Shakuran and Saleeman reasoned and pleaded with their husbands, but to no avail. Bullah and Sa'dullah were adamant. If the good-for-nothing girl could not bring fame and respect to the house through music and dance, she would at least have to bring in earnings and food with her youth and body.

Dispensing with the rituals and fanfare of the sar dhakna ceremony, which would eat into the much-needed money, Sa'dullah ordered Teema to get ready quickly and come with him one evening. Teema was not sure where her chhote abba, younger father, was taking her, but her mother and aunt's tears made her anxious. As frightened of her uncle as she was of her father, Teema said or did nothing that would enrage him and invite his blows.

Timidly, she wore the new red sari thrown at her by Sa'dullah and asked her mother to darken her eyes with surma as her uncle had directed. At this, Shakuran wept some more, and fearing her chhote abba's impatience, Teema applied the surma herself, her unpractised hands smearing it all around her eyes in the process. She then quietly followed her uncle to the outhouse of babu sahib's stately haveli in a neighbouring village.

As Asghari grimly narrates the terrible events that marked her mother's entry into the line, you begin crying quietly with your head averted. Rani is sighing into her rosary. I have no desire to cause distress, especially to you, and I interrupt Asghari to fetch a glass of water for you to drink. Hugging you tight, I apologise for enquiring about the details of your mother's life. I had no idea about the darkness your silence had concealed. You hug me back and then, wiping your tears and clearing your throat, take over the story from your sister.

'Years later, in an attempt to make me change my mind about joining the line, amma had told me about her initiation. She couldn't recall the details of that horrifying evening. All she could remember were fragments. An old woman, perhaps a servant, had taken her inside while our granduncle Sa'dullah remained standing in the courtyard. Amma recalled a vast room with a huge bed on the edge of which she saw herself, a child of eleven, sitting and waiting in fear. Even after the passage of so many years, she remembered the stuffed animals with glassy eyes that had frightened her so much. An old, very thin man then sat with her on the bed. His white, dry skin looked as if it was paper. He asked her to sit on his lap. Her teeth began chattering loudly, and her limbs became paralysed with terror. He laughed and pulled her to him. After that, her memory ran blank, except for the searing pain.'

Sa'dullah had waited patiently outside while Prabhuddhanarayan Singh assaulted his niece in the outhouse. Around midnight, babu sahib emerged, smoothing his kurta. Without a word, he thrust a wad of notes into Sa'dullah Miyan's grasping hands and walked away to the respectability of his ancestral haveli. After some time, Teema too came out. She could barely walk and had to be half-carried by the same old woman who had taken her inside. Her torn sari was thrown carelessly over her plump child's body, her surma had spread in black streaks across her face, her hair was dishevelled and eyes dazed.

That night, while Shakuran and Saleeman shed tears over Teema's wounds, Sa'dullah counted again and yet again the notes he got from Prabhuddanarayan Singh. This was to be the first of the many, many times that Teema would be raped, and the money in Sa'dullah's hands the first of his earnings as her pimp. Next day, mutton pulao was cooked after years in the family kitchen. Dharmman's family was back in business.

By the time she was in her mid-teens, Teema had been forced to have sex with more men than her father and uncle could keep count. The only community rule that they followed was to send Teema only to men of the 'upper' castes in the area—Rajputs and Bhumihars, Brahmins and Baniyas. Aligning their destinies with their elite patrons, tawaifs had adopted the prejudices and exclusion practised in the brahminical caste system. Traditionally, tawaifs, especially those from khandani clans, did not perform music and dance for, or enter into romantic and sexual alliances with, the 'lower' castes.

Bullah and Sa'dullah's flagrant prostitution of Teema evoked contempt and even censure in the Baisi and other tawaif clans. The tawaif panchayat in Bhabua had been forthright in its condemnation, stopping short only of excommunicating the family.

The brothers were past caring. Teema's sex work liberated them from the need to labour, from chronic hunger and want. They now pinned their hopes on little Bindo to reverse the decline in their family's status in the community. The child showed promise of great musical talent. Unlike Teema, she was sure to make a mark as a singer and dancer, and in so doing, restore the family to its earlier eminent position.

What Teema's feelings were about her daily prostitution we do not know. You and Asghari describe her as gentle, forbearing and forgiving. I imagine a young girl who had a strong sense of duty towards the family, which was ingrained in her from infancy. As the eldest daughter, she had been told repeatedly not just by her relatives but also others in the community that her family was her responsibility. It is possible that Teema might have seen her lack of the aptitude and skills necessary to meet these expectations as a personal failing.

With sadness, you say that Teema felt no rancour against the father and uncle who had violated her childhood for their greed. Her one ambition was to someday find a rich and devoted lover who would take care not only of her but also of her family. Given her less-than-pretty looks, this was a lofty expectation but not outside the possible. Despite the stones that life had hurled at her from childhood, Teema never lost hope for the future. And for a change, destiny responded to her generously.

The unexpected sound of footsteps breaks into Teema's story. You momentarily fall silent and look towards the door. A young woman of around twenty stands at the entrance.

'Khala, I have locked up the room upstairs. Here are the keys,' she says, extending her hand to Asghari. Behind her, I see the back of a man quietly open the main door of the house and slip outside. The girl is dressed in jeans and a man's shirt. She hesitates at the doorway on seeing us. It is obvious she didn't expect Asghari to have company.

Clearing her throat, Asghari says in a bright voice, 'Oh! Have you finished studying for the day? It's getting late. Your mother must be waiting. You had better run home fast.'

I am unable to fathom the look that passes between Asghari and the girl who, after greeting Rani and you, walks away. Asghari tells me that she is the daughter of an old friend in the neighbourhood. Preparing for her college exams, she finds it difficult to study with a tutor in her own small, noisy and crowded home. 'So I allow her to study in the room upstairs,' Asghari says earnestly, in a self-congratulatory tone. 'If I can be of some help to the daughter of an old friend and in the process earn merit by serving the cause of education, then why should I grudge the use of the extra room in my house?'

I am pleasantly surprised; Asghari is not exactly famous for being helpful. Later, I would get to know from you that the girl, though indeed the daughter of her old friend, a retired tawaif who lives in the same neighbourhood and enrolled in the second year of her college degree, does not come to study in Asghari's house. She uses the upstairs room for sex work and gives a part of the money she earns to your sister as rent for using her room.

A couple of other girls in the locality too use Asghari's room for the same purpose. The entire neighbourhood, including the girls' families and the local police, know of the arrangement. It works well for everyone. Confining this motley group of sex workers and their male customers to Asghari's house allows the wider neighbourhood to stake its claim to respectability. The girls' families, which include purdah-observing daughters-in-law with young children, are spared the harassment and humiliation of periodic police raids. As keeper of the only brothel in the locality, Asghari scrupulously pays up the money due from each girl to the police on a weekly basis. In return, Asghari, asset-less and poverty-ridden in old age, earns a small but much-needed income.

Asghari's brothel-keeping embarrasses, even shames, you and your family, and is a source of considerable friction between the two of you. You are unforgiving of what you see as your sister's betrayal of

Dharmman and Sadabahar's legacy. As a proud deraydar tawaif, you have tried to measure up to the propriety and decorum associated with the tradition. Post-retirement, you have invested the better part of your life in seeking respectability, conforming with immense pride to the iron-cast rules of middle-class morality.

You have ensured that not just your own but even Asghari and Ghafuran's daughters are either married or waiting for marriage. You have frequently boasted about the considerable money you spent on your nieces' weddings. Being relatively better off than your sisters, it was your duty, which you never shirked.

I have never dared to ask you to consider your choices had you been as ravaged by poverty as Asghari. Respectability does not come cheap. The course of your mother's life is testimony to the narrow divide that separates the 'honour' associated in your community with a deraydar tawaif from the 'indignity' linked in courtesan narratives to the prostitute.

Sitting in Asghari's decrepit home, however, I am innocent of the tug-and-pull over respectability that pits you against your sister. Once the girl leaves, Asghari hastily resumes the telling of Teema's story, while you sulk in the shadows lengthening across the room.

Around her seventeenth year, Teema found a man who noticed the intelligence in her twinkling eyes, the warmth in her engaging smile and the soothing calm of her countenance. Daya Singh, a middle-aged Rajput, recognised in Teema a rare beauty. His vast experience of women told him that here was a woman who had much to offer beyond pretty smiles, sweet talk and lilting songs. Possessing a loving heart and a steadfast mind, she was a woman that he would, after a long day's work, like to return home to.

Moreover, Teema knew how to make a man happy in bed. Pushed too early into sexual activity, she had a complicated relationship with sex. Until she met Daya Singh, Teema had not enjoyed sex. And yet, over the years, dismissed as a failure in the many other talents associated with tawaifs, she had mastered the skills of giving pleasure to the countless lovers foisted upon her on a nightly basis. After spending just one night with her, Daya Singh offered to keep Teema as a permanent mistress, provided she stopped entertaining other men.

The usual arrangement in such situations was that the woman would leave her family home and shift into a house bought or rented by her lover. This was referred to as baith jana, literally 'sitting down', wherein a tawaif retired from her career as singer and dancer, and entered into an exclusive, monogamous (from her side) relationship with one patron. He was obliged not only to provide for her needs but also to financially compensate her family for the loss of income from her singing and dancing. Such relationships could last lifelong and even translate into shared children and marriage, or they could end quickly if either of the partners decided to move on.

Daya Singh was by all parameters a good catch. He belonged to a well-off Rajput family from Chand, a village not far from Bhabua. The family had once controlled substantial landholdings. Over the generations, successive fragmentation of land had forced the sons of the family to move into complementary economic activities to finance the lifestyle expected of Rajput landholders.

Daya Singh and his four brothers were among the wealthiest and most powerful government contractors in the region, making huge profits from the natural resources of forests and mines that district Shahabad was so rich in. In the aftermath of the revolt of 1857, the dense jungles that had provided cover to rebels like Babu Kunwar Singh had been extensively cleared for the laying of road and rail networks to ensure more rapid movement of colonial troops in the event of any future uprising. During the decades to come and, especially in the early twentieth century, under government sanction, contractors like Daya Singh and his brothers had become rich by felling and selling bamboo and sal wood from the Kaimur hills. They also controlled the quarrying of high-quality sandstone, which was found in abundance in the area. On excellent terms with local colonial officials, who regularly awarded them lucrative forest and mining contracts, Daya Singh and his brothers had extended their business beyond Shahabad to the adjoining forest district of Palamu.

Sa'dullah and Bullah were initially reluctant to accept Daya Singh's proposal. It would mean letting go of the regular daily income brought in by the girl. More importantly, their control over Teema would weaken once she was under his protection.

On the other hand, Daya Singh had promised a more-than-handsome down payment for removing Teema from her family, as also continued gifts and a monthly 'salary' to her father and uncle for as long as she remained his mistress. Besides, Sa'dullah and Bullah understood only too well that Teema's earnings from prostitution would not outlast her youth.

There was also Teema to consider. Thus far meekly obeying their bidding, she was now showing signs of quiet assertiveness. Daya Singh, she realised, was the generous lover she had been waiting for. The rare respect he had shown her on their first night together had won over the girl's heart. Instead of heaving himself on her as soon as they were alone, Daya Singh had sat next to her on the bed, asked her name, her age, about her family, and waited till she pulled him towards herself.

Tall and well built, Daya Singh evoked in Teema an erotic desire she had never felt before. In a break from her past timidity, therefore, she made it clear to Bullah and Sa'dullah that she wished to accept Daya Singh's offer to become his mistress.

Her father and uncle realised that they were now faced with a situation dreaded by tawaif families. Teema had grown not only in years but also experience and confidence. It was not unusual for earning tawaifs to branch out on their own, rebelling against controlling relatives, leaving them destitute. Bullah and Sa'dullah's best option would be to go along with Teema's wishes, rather than risk losing both the girl and the largesse that Daya Singh promised. Their decision would also satisfactorily settle the recurring nuisance that came in the form of Daya Singh's younger brother, Veer Bahadur Singh.

There is an imperious knock on the main door. You get up and open it to a middle-aged man dressed in a white khadi kurta-pyjama. Head covered with a crocheted, white prayer cap, shoulders draped in a green kaffiyeh and his beard neatly clipped, he is the very picture of piety. As Asghari hurries out to welcome him, I am surprised to learn from Rani that the visitor is Reyaz's elder brother, Aijaz/Ajay Singh, local politician and self-proclaimed champion of Muslims in district Kaimur.

Aijaz bears no resemblance to his friendly and chatty brother. Reyaz is fair, short and plump, while Aijaz is dark and tall and painfully thin. Reyaz is charming, Aijaz is quite clearly not. His lips, set in a thin line, do not seem to have smiled in a long time. His eyes, piercing and forbiddingly cold, speak of intelligence and severity.

Out on his weekly rounds as the politician of your neighbourhood, he has dropped in at Asghari's home to enquire about her well-being. Preferring to stand at the doorway rather than come inside, his very first word is directed not at Asghari, who is beaming at him, but at Ghafuran's young daughter, Shameem, who tries to squeeze past into the house. 'Dupatta!' he says in reproving tones that mirror the look of distaste on his face.

Shameem's non-comprehension is met with an impatient gesture from Aijaz that makes his meaning crystal clear. Hurriedly, Shameem disciplines her flyaway scarf to cover her head and shoulders modestly. Then, muttering a quick salaam, she flees inside Asghari's home.

On cue, all three of you, including the usually pugnacious Asghari, meekly drape your heads with sari ends to conform to Aijaz's expectations of good Muslim women. Pretending that he hasn't noticed, Aijaz's eyes momentarily halt at me who stands bareheaded. And then he averts his gaze even as you make stumbling introductions. The five minutes that he spends standing at Asghari's door crawl by under the burden of enforced sombreness.

Aijaz enquires about her electricity-related woes but seems disinterested in hearing the details. Cutting Asghari short just as she begins complaining of the faulty electricity meter and its inflated readings, Aijaz says that he will see what can be done. Then, pausing, he adds a quiet, grim warning: 'Khala, do keep an eye on the comings and goings in your house. I have been hearing all kinds of stories.' Before Asghari can respond, however, he bids all present a strict 'Allah Hafiz' and moves on to the next house. On his way, he warns the boys loitering in the lane that he wishes to see them present every Friday for prayers at the local mosque.

Asghari is the first to remove the sari end from her head. With mock disdain, she snorts, 'Allah save us from the pious!' I notice though the pallor on her face and the nervousness in her eyes. You and Rani titter uneasily in response. Behaving like a bunch of abashed schoolgirls, each of you tries to cover up her discomfort at the encounter by exchanging good-humoured anecdotes about Aijaz's religious zeal.

Asghari says that his mother, Buddhan, is forced by him to wrap herself in a chador every time she steps out of the house. A chain-smoker, she is also forbidden from smoking in public. Amidst much laughter, Asghari recounts Buddhan's attempts to smoke covertly at a wedding.

'There we sat, all the women of the neighbourhood, waiting for the nikah to be solemnised. I smelt a cigarette burning but could see no woman smoking. Then what do I notice? Curls of smoke swirling out from under old Buddhan's chador in which she sat all huddled up. Pretending that I hadn't noticed, I whispered to her to take the chador off now that we were all only women sitting together inside the bride's house. Coughing, poor Buddhan croaked that she was fine. In some time, people noticed that the oldie's chador was on fire! Water was hastily brought in and the chador doused. And poor old Buddhan, drenched like a rat, was pulled out from deep within its folds. And guess what? In her utter shock upon discovering that she was on fire, she had forgotten to throw away the cigarette. There she stood wet and shivering with a half-smoked damp cigarette in hand!'

Turning to me, Rani adds, 'You see, Aijaz, even as a little boy, never liked his mother to be out in public. From childhood, he would spend as much time at his father's family house as at his mother's in Bhabua and was known more by his other name, Ajay Singh. He was very close to his half-brothers, Maheep and Kuldeep, and wanted to be just like them in all respects. And although he was by nature always serious-minded and quiet, while his half-brothers were boisterous brats of the first order, I remember how he would insist that Buddhan buy him the exact same shirts, shorts and trousers that Maheep and Kuldeep wore.

'Naturally, he would feel embarrassed when he overheard people in his father's village discuss Buddhan. You know how men talk about women like us. He felt it lowered him in the eyes of his father's family. And so, even when he was barely ten or twelve years old, he forbade his mother from ever performing in public.'

You add further details. Ajay Singh was aware from an early age that, though he suffered no stigma in Bhabua on account of his mother being a tawaif, he would never be considered equal in status and privileges to Maheep and Kuldeep, the 'legitimate' sons of Babu Rajbir Singh. He spent most of his time cementing ties with his half-brothers by making himself useful to them. He would cover up for them when they got into brawls with other boys and lie on their behalf when they got into trouble. His loyalty endeared him to his father who, even when furious with his other two sons for their rowdy ways, would forgive them on Ajay Singh's request.

As they grew older, Ajay Singh would arrange alcohol for Maheep and Kuldeep to party behind their father's back, procure girls from his neighbourhood for sexual encounters and bribe local policemen if they found themselves on the wrong side of the law. Ajay also took care to be an obedient and loyal son to his father. For years, while Maheep and Kuldeep enjoyed their youth, Ajay worked hard at managing Rajbir Singh's property business in and around Bhabua. Little wonder then that his father rewarded Ajay by setting him up as an independent property dealer. Maheep and Kuldeep too helped. Among the biggest public works contractors in west Bihar, they provided Ajay useful contacts, opening several doors for him. Property dealer and owner of petrol and diesel stations, Ajay Singh did well for himself.

Along the way, his father decided that the family could do with an in-house politician to safeguard and promote its many business ventures. Aijaz/Ajay Singh, with his cool head, razor-sharp intelligence and shrewdness, was the obvious choice. With Rajbir Singh's blessings, and Maheep and Kuldeep's backing, Aijaz—foregrounding his identity as Ajay Singh—graduated from local businessman to full-time politician.

Aijaz had hoped to garner political support of the Muslim population in the area through his mother, and through the influence of his father and powerful half-brothers of the numerically more sizeable Rajput community in these parts. In the initial years, though, his calculations had proved utterly wrong. Far from getting elected to the municipal board as he had hoped, he suffered a humiliating defeat in his electoral debut as an independent candidate.

Upon introspection, he concluded that his attempts to project for himself a syncretic distinctiveness as the son of a Muslim mother and Rajput father had proved counterproductive in a polity divided deeply along the fault-lines of caste, religion and community. In the eyes of the people he wished to lead, the identity of Ajay Singh/Aijaz connoted merely a half-breed, neither fully Muslim, not even close to being a Rajput.

Proud of his ability to learn from mistakes, Aijaz bid farewell to Ajay Singh. Next, he joined the Rashtriya Janata Dal, which has a strong presence among the state's minorities, and re-launched himself in the political arena in the avatar of a true-blue 'Muslim' leader.

CHAPTER 13

Veer Bahadur Singh

'GOOD MORNING, AAPA,' COMES THE cheery salutation. As promised, Reyaz/Randhir Singh has been presenting himself on the dot whenever I have needed his car.

With his humorous quips and expert driving skills, Reyaz makes journeys along district Kaimur's appalling roads almost fun. He is also immensely resourceful. From finding me internet access to locating former tawaif families now living in remote interiors of the district, to fixing my temperamental mobile phone, Reyaz is driver, guide and general handyman all in one. And unlike Aijaz, his elder brother, Reyaz carries no weight of pious self-righteousness.

My destination today is Chand, the village to which Daya Singh and his family belonged. I have been informed that that none of his immediate descendants live there any longer, having dispersed to Patna, Ranchi and even Calcutta many years ago. All the same, I am keen to visit the village that is so closely tied to your family's history.

You are not happy with my plan. As my protective hostess in Bhabua, you feel obliged to accompany me wherever I wish to go. You know the village well. In the past, you regularly performed in Rajput villages in the area, including Chand, which you have told me was your favourite performance venue because people here understood music and appreciated musicians. And yet, as a former tawaif, you are reluctant to revisit a space that has known you only in the persona you now wish to leave behind.

I have tried to convince you that I can take care of myself but you remain hesitant. Kaimur is not welcoming of strangers, you say. Unfamiliar female visitors here run indescribable risks. This area is a law unto itself, you keep repeating.

You yield only when Reyaz gives his solemn promise that he will under no circumstances leave my side while we are in Chand. And, despite my protestations, Jawed has enlisted himself as an additional escort.

Just as we are about to take our leave, Asghari arrives and, upon hearing my plans, announces that she will accompany me to Chand. You look alarmed. Clearly, you have no faith in your elder sister's abilities to be my chaperone. Cutting her short, you declare that you have decided to go along after all. Realising that my proposed trip might inadvertently trigger a family squabble, I almost shelve my plans. Just then, Pyaari khala, asserting her position as senior matriarch, overrules you. 'Asghari might be headstrong and foul-mouthed. But she is no one's fool. And she is fierce. Your friend will be safer with her in Chand than with any of us.'

You have little choice but to give in and, with reiterated instructions to Reyaz and Jawed never to let me out of sight, you bid us all a reluctant goodbye. Asghari settles herself comfortably next to me on the back seat and Jawed sits in front with Reyaz.

On the way, Asghari tells me about Veer Bahadur Singh, who had been so instrumental in Bullah and Sa'dullah's decision to accept Daya Singh's proposal. It adds to all that I have already learnt of Veer Bahadur from his distant relatives who still live on in these parts, and from the families of his political associates and work acquaintances in Arrah.

Daya Singh's youngest and most favourite brother, Veer Bahadur Singh, was the first person in and around Chand to study beyond high school. An academically inclined young man, he was sent by his eldest brother to study at the prestigious Calcutta University. And though sending him to Calcutta had not come cheap, it was a source of immense pride for Daya Singh. He had dreams of Veer Bahadur someday becoming a lawyer, bringing to the family not only prestige in the Rajput community of the area but also much-needed in-house legal services to fight the many land- and business-related cases that Daya Singh and his brothers had in the courts at all times.

A small-built, painfully thin and shy boy, Veer Bahadur Singh was initially overwhelmed by the urbane sophistication of the students at the university. Feeling like a rustic bumpkin, he tried to hide his discomfort under a veneer of scholarly reserve. He made few friends during the first year in Calcutta, preferring instead to spend all his time diligently attending classes and studying in the library.

By his second year, however, Veer Bahadur's aloofness crumbled under the pervasive influence of the anti-colonial Swadeshi movement. Begun as a boycott of British goods to protest against the partition of Bengal in 1905, the scope of the movement had quickly widened to include rejection of colonial education and administrative institutions. The setting up of indigenous industries, schools and colleges, and attempts at rural improvement through village-level samitis, or volunteer organisations, came to be associated closely with the Swadeshi movement that spread from Bengal to other parts of the country, like Maharashtra, Punjab and Madras, rising soon to the call for Swaraj, self-rule.

The politics of the Swadeshi movement came to be closely identified with attempts to combine nationalism with Hindu symbolism. People were encouraged to take vows to follow Swadeshi in temples. Boycott of British goods was often sought to be enforced through traditional caste sanctions, and the curriculum taught in national schools and colleges often had a strong Hindu content. *Vande Mataram*, the poem celebrating the motherland in the form of the Hindu goddess Durga, became the rallying cry of the movement. Leaders like Lokmanya Tilak used Hindu festivals like Ganesh Chaturthi to spread the message of Swaraj in Maharashtra, while Lala Lajpat Rai in Punjab had strong sympathies and links with the Arya Samaj and was, in his own words, 'wedded to the idea of Hindu nationality'.

Moved by the eloquence of these leaders, Veer Bahadur began attending nationalist meetings and made friends with like-minded students. He became a volunteer in the many strikes organised to protest colonial rule and would march the streets singing *Vande Mataram*, his heart swelling with love for Bharat Mata, Mother India.

At a personal level, too, he set about changing his lifestyle. Never particularly devout before he joined university, Veer Bahadur Singh became increasingly ardent about his Hindu identity. He began reading religious scriptures, particularly the Bhagavad Gita, and became a devotee of Goddess Kali, whom he saw as a form of Mother India. Life stories of Hindu rulers like Shivaji and Maharana Pratap became his source of inspiration: they had fought for the liberation of the motherland against the 'foreign' Mughal rulers, and Veer Bahadur Singh wished passionately to follow their example and free Mother India from the yoke of colonial tyranny.

Meanwhile, many of his Bengali friends were becoming members of secret societies that advocated revolutionary terrorism to rid India of the much-hated British rule. This struggle took the form of planning the assassinations of oppressive European officials, dacoities to raise funds for arms and individual acts of self-sacrifice that cast a spell upon the minds of educated young men like Veer Bahadur Singh.

The heroism of the revolutionaries appealed to Veer Bahadur Singh's Rajput masculinity. Brought up to take pride in the mythology of Rajput valour as personified by Babu Kunwar Singh and Babu Amar Singh in India's first war of independence, Veer Bahadur began to dream of himself as a warrior waging spectacular battles for his motherland. There was one hurdle, though. And it came in the form of Veer Bahadur's elder brother, Daya Singh.

Notwithstanding his zeal for annihilating the colonial enemy, Veer Bahadur was pragmatic enough to recognise the importance of the material security his brother provided. Daya Singh had placed him before all others in the family, incurring considerable expense on his college education in Calcutta. But his brother would not tolerate any act that might jeopardise the cordial and beneficial relationship that the family enjoyed with the colonial authorities.

Daya Singh was formidable when provoked, and settled scores in the time-tested manner of landholding Rajputs in Shahabad. The large number of court cases against him and his brothers included several of criminal assault, and even murder, of business rivals and land claimants. In his more melodramatic moments, Veer Bahadur Singh felt sure that before he could get around to assassinating a British official, his brother would kill him if he became aware of his plans. Even if he escaped such fatal consequences, Veer Bahadur knew for certain that any direct involvement in revolutionary activities would certainly cast him on his own. Daya Singh would waste little time in cutting him loose from the family's purse-strings.

Veer Bahadur's financial concerns seemed to him disagreeably petty when compared to the lofty ideal of love for the motherland. However, try as he might, these anxieties kept his revolutionary nationalist fervour confined to participation in relatively safe activities like public meetings and marches, and beating a hasty retreat when the police cracked down. In the security of his hostel room, Veer Bahadur would spend long hours praying to Kali, reading up on the need for righteous action as propounded in the Bhagavad Gita, and in intensive physical exercise to turn his frail frame into the sinewy and strong body of a revolutionary hero.

We arrive in Chand. Almost the size of a mini-town, Chand continues to be overwhelmingly Rajput. From the moving car, I notice the tall houses in the village, the dish antennae dotting its skyline and the tractors with trolleys parked along its semi-metalled lanes, all reflecting a prosperity not shared by the wider district.

Our entry into Chand evokes excited comments from Asghari. She was loved by everyone here, she declares. At weddings and other festivities, the Rajput villagers would insist that, of all the tawaifs invited, they wanted Asghari, and Asghari alone, to perform for them.

Reyaz nods agreement. 'My mother has told me about the mehfils here and about Asghari khala's popularity. No other singer or dancer would want to perform at a mehfil to which khala was invited since she was always sure to get the maximum applause and inam, prize money or tips.'

Preening with pleasure, Asghari is in a mood to be generous. As we walk along the semi-paved muddy lanes of the village, she says to Reyaz, 'Your mother, Buddhan, was quite popular too. And since she was under the protection of Babu Rajbir Singh, she commanded a lot of respect in all Rajput villages, including Chand. Although, of course, once she had all of you, her career took back seat.'

'Arrey, Asghari, what brings you here after so many years?' exclaims an elderly man sporting a spectacularly luxuriant moustache, as sparkling white as the dhoti-kurta he wears. He has stepped out of a house just ahead of us. On his shoulder hangs, incongruously, a vintage .22 air gun. Eyes twinkling, he boldly appraises Asghari's pink prettiness and passes judgement, 'Why, bai-ji, you have become an old woman now!'

Asghari, who had simpered at the old Rajput's initial greeting, stiffens at his mention of age. In a tone dripping with icy politeness, she states, 'Brother, I am afraid I have not recognised you.'

Laughing incredulously, the old man replies, 'I am heartbroken, Asghari! With advancing age, not only has your memory got blunted but, worse, you now call me brother! Don't you remember me? I am Ramavatar Singh.'

Asghari, clearly enjoying herself, now exclaims, 'The only Babu Ramavatar Singh that I knew in Chand was a strapping, handsome young man, not some derelict wreck. Little wonder I couldn't recognise you!' Asghari smiles charmingly at her old admirer and falls in step with him, while Jawed, Reyaz and I obediently follow behind.

The narrow lane is lined with large, cemented houses, ringed by spacious courtyards with buffaloes, cows and goats. By the standards of rural Kaimur, where ramshackle mud-and-thatch homes contain empty pots, hunger and want, we are in the midst of plenty here. Squeezing past a huge tractor-trolley that arrogantly blocks the entire width of the lane, I remark on the complete absence of women. In the other villages that I visited in the district, they have been a visible presence, hard at work outside their homes and in the fields. Even the task of drawing water from the well nearby is being done by young men.

'Rajput women stay in purdah. If they do have to step outside their homes, they do so only under the cover of a thick veil,' Reyaz whispers to me. Just then two young girls walk past us with books in their hands. Evidently, with changing times, some women in this Rajput village are emerging from confinement. The knowledgeable Jawed informs me that a handful of girls from Chand are enrolled in the women's college in Bhabua and travel there daily to attend classes.

Deep in discussion about gender and education, we have failed to notice that Ramavatar Singh has taken a break from flirting with Asghari and is staring at Reyaz and me with avid curiosity. Reyaz steps forward and politely touches Babu Ramavatar's feet.

'You are Ajay's brother, aren't you, son?' asks the old Rajput.

Folding his hands humbly, Reyaz nods. 'With your blessings, uncle, I run a taxi business of my own in Bhabua,' he politely asserts an independent identity. Grunting acknowledgement, the old man states that Babu Rajbir Singh has been fair to all his sons, never discriminating between Maheep and Kuldeep and Ajay and his brothers.

Next, it is my turn to be introduced by Asghari. I try my best to address Ramavatar's inquisitiveness, without going into unnecessary details about the exact nature of work that has brought me here. Just then, without warning, heavy showers come pelting down. We take shelter under the awnings of a nearby house. Drying his head and face with his gamchha, Ramavatar continues to quiz me about my purpose in visiting Bhabua and, in particular, his village.

He has heard about Daya Singh's family, although he does not know them personally. He looks flummoxed, however, when I mention Veer Bahadur Singh. It is obvious that Ramavatar has never heard the name before. Loath to admit his ignorance of this notable-sounding son of his village, he grills me instead for details about his life.

Veer Bahadur Singh returned to Chand with a law degree in hand and love for Mother India in his heart. He dutifully took over the many civil and criminal cases filed by and against the family in the dusty courtrooms of Arrah. Not a particularly successful lawyer, he found the atmosphere and people in the district courts dull and depressing. Everyone, the lawyers and their clients, seemed to him singularly self-serving, interested only in either litigating against each other or currying favour with colonial officers for petty, personal gain.

He hated their hypocrisy. While most of his lawyer-colleagues paid pious lip service to the ideals of Swadeshi and Swaraj to his face, he knew they made fun of him behind his back and mocked his attempts to enthuse them to rise above the cause of the self to a nobler ideal of service to Bharat Mata. At such times, he desperately missed his comrades in Calcutta and their idealism. Feeling isolated, Veer Bahadur tried to spend as little time in the courts as was possible.

At home in Chand, he felt equally disengaged and disconsolate. Much against his wishes, the family had brought home the bride to whom he had been married as a child. As a student, Veer Bahadur had secretly idolised the educated refinement and high-mindedness of the young Bengali women he had seen participate in Swadeshi activities in Calcutta. The modesty of their dress, chasteness of behaviour and seriousness of speech had made a deep impression on him.

In comparison, his child-like, high-spirited and talkative wife, Rukmini, who seemed interested only in clothes, jewellery and cooking, appeared to him intolerably crude, frivolous and ignorant. As much as possible, Veer Bahadur would contrive excuses to avoid visits to the room allotted to them.

Equally, he found it difficult to renew ties with the men in the family. He had spent his childhood being pampered by them, but now he felt he had little in common with his brothers and cousins. He found them aggressive, rude and raucous, inspiring fear not only among outsiders but also within the household, especially among the women and children. Governed by the logic of profit, vendetta and false prestige, their conversations held little interest for Veer Bahadur. When not plotting ways to win new contracts, eliminate rivals and settle scores, they would, to Veer Bahadur's intense displeasure, waste time and money on tawaifs, alcohol and gambling.

At times, when his life seemed intolerable, he would make up his mind to return to Calcutta and join the revolutionaries. Just when he began packing, though, Veer Bahadur would be assailed by doubts. How would he survive without family support? He would also remember the vivid descriptions of police torture he had heard about, and a cold terror would seize his heart. He would then hurriedly postpone his plan to become a revolutionary to a more opportune time.

Glossing over his own fears and failings, Veer Bahadur felt resentful towards his family. Surely if his brothers had been more understanding, he would by now be laying down his life in a blaze of glory for the country, instead of rotting in mundane oblivion in the backyards of Shahabad. He blamed his eldest brother the most. If only Daya Singh was less obsessed with money and family prestige, he would not have stood in the way of Veer Bahadur's dream.

Ironically, the one person who had some understanding and sympathy for Veer Bahadur and his idealism was his eldest brother. Daya Singh was shrewd and ruthless when it came to promoting the family's interests but, unlike the other men in the household, he was a soft-spoken person of few words. Fair-minded and considerate, he inspired respect and loyalty within his family, and among clan members and his retinue of dependents. He felt sorry for his well-read and high-minded brother who was surrounded by a bunch of boors.

Daya Singh had received only basic schooling. Veer Bahadur's university education was a source of immense pride to him, and he enthusiastically paid the bills for all the books the young man ordered by mail. He would reverentially enter the small library Veer Bahadur had built for himself in the family house, and take delight in the sight of his young brother reading studiously. He never joined the other brothers in berating Veer Bahadur for his lack of success as a lawyer. If anything, he proudly justified it as an example of the young man's inability to indulge in the falsehoods and sophistry necessary to win court cases.

He was amused and intrigued by the long hours Veer Bahadur spent in prayer and reading from the scriptures. In their family, religion had always been the domain of women; men, preoccupied with worldly affairs, participated in rituals perfunctorily. Daya Singh would tease Veer Bahadur affectionately about being a sadhu, a faqir. And though he never said this, he saw the young man's preoccupation with god and books as redemption for his and the family's absorption in the material world.

That said, Daya Singh was no votary of the nationalism sweeping across the country. He had been deeply anxious when he heard of Veer Bahadur's participation in Swadeshi activities in Calcutta. When it became obvious that the young man would not allow his patriotism to come in the way of duty towards the family, Daya Singh became generous in his acceptance of his brother's love for the country. He saw it as yet another example of Veer Bahadur's upright nature. Moreover, in the wake of the Swadeshi movement, even in Shahabad, nationalists were being looked upon with admiration and regard. If Veer Bahadur's love for the motherland could bestow nationalist respectability to the family's blood-stained reputation, Daya Singh saw little reason to restrain his brother from singing *Vande Mataram* loudly from the terrace of the house every morning.

Daya Singh would not have been happy about Veer Bahadur's revolutionary ambition, of course, had he known of it. However, consumed by his sense of victimhood, Veer Bahadur said nothing of it to his family, turning for friendship instead towards the small but vocal group of Arya Samaj preachers and educationists he struck up acquaintance with in Arrah.

'How is Ajay doing nowadays? Ever since he became a leader of the Miyan-log, he has stopped coming to our village.' Ramavatar Singh's question is directed at Reyaz. The torrential rain has slowed to a mild drizzle and Asghari's old friend is preparing to take his leave.

Ignoring the jibe, Reyaz mumbles about Aijaz being busy with his many commitments. Ramavatar Singh laughs and, slapping Reyaz on the back, steps into the lane. Then he pauses, as if struck by a thought. Turning back, he invites us to his home.

Asghari looks surprised and takes her time responding to this unexpected invitation. I am more receptive. I don't know Ramavatar's reasons for extending hospitality. Perhaps he wishes to relive his youth by spending more time with Asghari. It's as likely that his curiosity about me and my research has led to this invitation. Whatever his motives, this is an opportunity to visit a Rajput home in Chand and, before Asghari can say anything, I accept enthusiastically.

Located not far from where we waited for the rain to stop, Ramavatar's home looks smaller and humbler than the other houses we passed. It stands in a sea of wet mud that, in drier weather, must serve as a courtyard. Trying not to slip, we gingerly make our way across to the pistachio-green cemented front room, behind which stands the mud-walled and thatch-roofed main house.

From the suffocating humidity that greets us as we step in, it seems that the room gets few visitors. Its unplastered inner walls, unlevelled mud floor and thatched roof hint at a drying up of funds after the initial flurry of cemented construction. Sacks of stored grain, piled up almost to the roof, occupy much of the room, the remaining space being strewn with cans of pesticide, coils of thick rope and other odds and ends of an agricultural life. Clearly, whatever the original intentions behind its construction, the room is now used as storage space.

And it is here that Ramavatar ushers us to, instead of the main house behind—the tawaif background of my companions and my status as an unknown female outsider no doubt playing some part in this choice. Ramavatar might exchange flirtatious banter with Asghari and acknowledge Reyaz as the son, albeit an illegitimate one, of a caste member, but there is no forgetting the social hierarchy that separates him from them. And, clearly, Asghari, Reyaz and Jawed are equally mindful of this equation.

Gone is the mischievous playfulness in Asghari's eyes, the erotic femininity of her gait and the easy confidence of her bearing. Instead, as she stands next to me in that room, face almost half-covered with her sari, eyes deferentially downcast, posture drawn in, Asghari suddenly looks old and vulnerable. Reyaz and Jawed hover awkwardly in the doorway. Ignoring them, Babu Ramavatar pulls out a stringed cot from behind the sacks of grain and makes himself comfortable. With an imperious wave of the hand, he gestures to Asghari and me to seat ourselves on the moorhas, or rush-mat stools, that he has dug out from among the heaps of coiled ropes.

Over the next couple of hours, Ramavatar holds court to a group of elderly men from the village who have trooped in for a close-up view of their yesteryears' object of desire and the city woman she has brought with her. While I wilt under this collective male scrutiny, Asghari seems to fare rather well. With the arrival of old admirers, the sassy siren I am familiar with is back.

Her sari pallu slips ever so often from her head. Her eyes sparkle with animation and her uninhibited laughter resounds in the dank and musty storeroom. But she has not forgotten her responsibilities as my escort. Almost imperceptibly, Asghari positions herself between me and the men surrounding us, shielding me from further enquiry and inspection. Every question directed at me has to go past her. She answers on my behalf and, when unsure, repeats the question to me as though we are alone in the room. My questions to Ramavatar and his friends are similarly negotiated through Asghari.

Like Babu Ramavatar, most of the men gathered don't appear to have heard of Veer Bahadur Singh, although many of them know of Daya Singh's family. And yet, perhaps impressed by the sketchy hagiographic details proffered by the few who do recognise his name, everyone present seems to feel compelled to claim a connection with the reflected glory of this 'most famous' son of Chand.

Since 1878, Shahabad had been an important centre of Arya Samaj activities, which included the setting up of schools and orphanages. Over the decades, with its trenchant critique of the caste system and philanthropic activities, the Arya Samaj was successful in attracting to its fold a considerable following among lower-placed communities like the Kurmis, Ahirs and Musahars. Arya Samaj preachers and publicists were also at the vanguard of promoting the politics of Hindu nationalism. Following the end of the Swadeshi movement in 1908, along with supporters of groups like the Hindu Sabha, founded by the maharaja of Darbhanga, they had been working to rekindle the gaurakshini movement in Bihar.

Veer Bahadur found in the Arya Samajis of Shahabad his soulmates. Though a devoted follower of the tenets of Sanatan Dharma, Veer Bahadur admired his Arya Samaji friends' love of Hinduism and Hindus. Encouraged by them, he became actively involved in organising and addressing meetings for the promotion of cow protection among his lawyer colleagues as also the Rajput clans in his area. Unlike in the past, when he had been either mocked or ignored for his earnest lectures on nationalism, this time he found a receptive audience to his appeals to save Gau Mata, since he was advocating an issue his listeners were familiar with and sympathetic to. A failure as a revolutionary, as a nationalist, as a lawyer and as a family man, Veer Bahadur finally found success and respect as a champion of the Hindu cause.

The Arya Samaj's social reform agenda, especially its emphasis on character-building and its strident opposition to drinking and patronising tawaifs and prostitutes too left a deep impression on him. Having led an abstemious and disciplined life himself, under the influence of his new friends, Veer Bahadur became a passionate votary of the moral regeneration of Hindu society as a political imperative. So far, he had despised his male relatives' fondness for alcohol and tawaifs as a weakness of character. Now, he began to locate this pleasure-seeking in a wider historical context—the long and unremitting rule over the Hindus by 'degenerate' and 'depraved' Muslim princes and nawabs.

In the golden age of the Vedas, his friends said, the Aryans had adhered to an ideal and virtuous way of life and had thus ruled the world. Hindu men must once again adopt the moral conduct of their ancestors and thus purify the mind and body to regain the masculine vigour needed to free the motherland from the shackles of foreign rule.

This revelation charged Veer Bahadur with an enthusiasm he had not felt since his days as a student in Calcutta. Decisive action had to be taken to cleanse Hindu society and return it to its ancient, pristine glory. Buoyed by his success as a speaker for the Gaurakshini movement, Veer Bahadur Singh was confident that his arguments against vice would be accepted just as enthusiastically.

Arya Samaj preachers readily joined him in launching an earnest crusade for the moral renaissance of Shahabad. They had long argued that the consumption of alcohol and marijuana—and worse, keeping the company of lowly, degenerate women like tawaifs and prostitutes—led to impoverishment of the home, tension in the family, diminishing of health and clouding of judgement.

In his speeches, Veer Bahadur often quoted the nineteenth-century social reformer from Bengal, Keshub Chandra Sen, who said of the prostitute: 'In her breast is a vast ocean of poison. Around her comely waist dwell the furies of hell. Her hands are brandishing unseen daggers ever ready to strike unwary or wilful victims that fall in her way. Her blandishments are India's ruin. Alas! Her smile is India's death!'

In a land that worshipped women as pure, nurturing and self-sacrificing mothers, these wanton, greedy and grasping women, Veer Bahadur would declare passionately, were a blot on Indian womanhood. Prostitutes and tawaifs were man-eating non-mothers, the grotesque antithesis of exalted motherhood represented by Bharat Mata and Gau Mata.

The tawaif's music and dance too came under attack for being obscene and immoral. Equating her songs to the filth that littered public streets, Veer Bahadur would argue that, just as dirty and unhygienic surroundings endangered public health, so also the obscenity imbued in the tawaif's art practice corrupted the minds and morals of all those who heard and saw her performance. The need of the hour was to ensure cleanliness in physical surroundings and cultural expression.

Around the same time, in 1915–16, newspapers in Bihar too began reflecting a growing preoccupation with obscenity and the need to cleanse public and private life of it. The Bihar press fulminated about a range of cultural practices it termed obscene, ranging from the patronage of tawaifs and their 'lascivious' song and dance to the 'vulgar' songs sung in public celebrations of festivals such as Holi.

Editorials denounced the evil practice of organising nach during weddings and other celebrations. Keeping their mainly middle-class readership in mind, newspapers also stressed on the need for thrift and the huge drain on income that consumption of alcohol and patronage of tawaifs posed.

Social reform had been slow in coming to Bihar. While educated public opinion in cities across northern India, inspired by the anti-nautch movement, had begun a boycott of nach at public and family celebrations by the early twentieth century, Bihar was not overly impacted by this morality drive. The educated middle classes, the backbone of the anti-nautch movement in cities like Banaras, had but a tenuous presence in Bihar. Even by the second decade of the twentieth century, districts like Shahabad remained predominantly agrarian. Towns were few, industry nascent and the presence of an educated middle class confined to limited pockets.

The dominant, landholding Rajput and Bhumihar castes in Shahabad were still strongly attached to their old ways. Patronising tawaifs was traditionally linked to their status and prestige; no wedding or other public and family celebration was deemed complete without mujra performances by more than one tawaif. So, they heard with good-humoured indulgence the earnest speeches of Veer Bahadur and his associates, nodded polite agreement and then proceeded to ignore their advice and exhortations.

Disappointed but not disheartened, Veer Bahadur decided to take his war on immorality into what he described as the 'heart of darkness'. Henceforth, he would concentrate on cleansing the tawaif and prostitute quarters of vice and obscenity.

As in cities across northern India, tawaifs in Shahabad district too lived mainly in the centre of towns like Arrah, Sasaram and Bhabua. They would have to be forced to move out, he decided, if Shahabad was to be purified and its menfolk morally regenerated. And so began a campaign of petitions and memorandums to the colonial authorities to remove tawaifs and prostitutes from town centres, backed with picketing in these areas to pressure the women to shift out.

Bhabua, the town closest to his village, became the focus of Veer Bahadur's zeal. The men from Chand lavished considerable money and time on the tawaifs of the town. Gathering around him a motley group of followers comprising young students, a couple of school teachers and a few shopkeepers, Veer Bahadur began regularly picketing the tawaifs' quarters in Bhabua.

Holding a handkerchief to his nose as a precaution against moral contamination, Veer Bahadur would lead his followers to raise slogans against tawaifs and prostitutes, demanding that they leave Bhabua, and try to stop visitors from entering their homes. Occasionally, his followers roughed up the men and boys from tawaif families. They heckled individual tawaifs who crossed their path and jeered at the male musicians who came into the locality to teach and accompany the women in performance.

Bitter fights erupted almost daily between the tawaifs and Veer Bahadur's moral brigade. The police were often called in. Since many of the protestors, including Veer Bahadur, belonged to well-connected upper-caste families, the law enforcers did little but watch.

Under siege, tawaifs in Bhabua appealed to their wealthy and powerful patrons for help. They obliged by sending their strongmen armed with lathis to protect their mistresses and their homes. In many instances, wealthy tawaifs hired their own local wrestlers and lathaits, lathi-wielders, for personal security. Rajput patrons and well-wishers of the tawaifs also tried to reason with, threaten and subdue the enthusiasm of Veer Bahadur's young followers, many of whom were relatives.

Ramavatar begins to laugh when he hears my description of Veer Bahadur Singh's picketing of the tawaifs' quarters in Bhabua. Apprehensive that I might have caused offence, I fall silent. But he does not in the least seem affronted. Addressing Asghari, he says, 'Just as well, bai-ji, that neither you nor I were around back then, or we would have been deprived of each other's company!'

Asghari simpers prettily, the other men around join in the laughter, and Veer Bahadur is soon forgotten. On the drive back to Bhabua later that afternoon, Asghari fills me in on the finer points of her family history that were missing from the public memory of Daya Singh and his family. Teema had found no mention in the chronicles related to me by the good men of Chand. No one seemed to be aware of Asghari's close connection with Daya Singh. This was hardly surprising. Tawaifs, though indispensable to the social and sexual lives of their Rajput lovers, would rarely merit more than a passing reference in the recorded history of their patrons' families.

Targeted daily by Veer Bahadur's moral brigade, Teema's household had neither powerful patrons to act on its behalf nor the resources to hire strongmen. It would either need to relocate or find a backer who could protect them from Veer Bahadur's messianic wrath.

It was around this time that Daya Singh proposed that Teema become his mistress. Bullah and Sa'dullah realised that this was a god-sent opportunity to be rid of Veer Bahadur. If Teema was installed as Daya Singh's mistress, her safety and that of her family would become his responsibility. After taking just enough time to sharpen Daya Singh's desire for Teema, the brothers laid down their condition. Daya Singh would have to prevail upon Veer Bahadur to drop his campaign against the tawaifs of Bhabua. In return, Teema would stop entertaining other men and become his mistress.

Daya Singh had been hearing with distaste about his youngest brother's noisy protests in the tawaifs' quarters. He had little sympathy for the cause. He believed that both tawaifs and their performance were an intrinsic part of Rajput tradition, and was at a loss to understand Veer Bahadur's antipathy to them. Moreover, the crusade was fast becoming a cause of some mirth and much hostility among the Rajputs and other upper-caste landholders of the area. Daya Singh didn't wish the family's prestige to be dented because of his brother's quixotic obsession. He was embarrassed too by Veer Bahadur's harassment and intimidation of women. In Daya Singh's moral framework, this was the lowest a man could stoop.

Veer Bahadur, meanwhile, was incensed when he heard of Daya Singh's interest in Teema. One of the tawaifs he had attempted to harangue had sarcastically told him to lecture his brother instead. Unsure about the veracity of the jibe, he had tried to find out more about Teema and her family. What he heard left him livid.

Keeping mistresses was the norm in his caste and several of his uncles, brothers and cousins had tawaif lovers. That his brother would choose to take on a tawaif mistress at the height of his anti-vice campaign struck Veer Bahadur as selfish and insensitive. Worse, that the girl his brother had picked was, in fact, a common prostitute made Veer Bahadur recoil with disgust. He wanted to confront Daya Singh and yet, as always, was hard-pressed to muster the courage.

It was Daya Singh who sent word that he would like to speak with Veer Bahadur. Wrestling with his fear of his brother, yet gripped by outrage, Veer Bahadur rehearsed the stinging denunciation he would heap upon him about his moral frailty.

Face to face with the family patriarch, however, words failed Veer Bahadur. He heard out in meek silence Daya Singh dismiss his anti-tawaif campaign as 'petty and unmanly, unbecoming of a Rajput'. Briefly but without mincing words, the older man made known his displeasure. Exactly five minutes after he entered Daya Singh's room, Veer Bahadur stepped out, his ears burning with his brother's terse ultimatum: 'Either live in the family home and abide by its rules or move out and do as you please.'

It did not take long thereafter for Veer Bahadur's anti-tawaif movement to peter out in Shahabad. The tawaifs and prostitutes of Arrah, Sasaram and Bhabua were back in business. Daya Singh rented a house some distance from Teema's family home but in the tawaif neighbourhood. And Teema shifted here as his mistress.

CHAPTER 14

Teema and Bindo

PYAARI KHALA'S DEPARTURE FROM THE mortal world has been postponed. She cackles about it and describes herself as a mazboot haddi, a hardy bone. You marvel at your aunt's tenacious hold on life. Everyone knows the clasp is loosening, but no one can tell when she will let go. The relatives assembled in Bhabua to bid her a final farewell have begun to get restive. If Pyaari khala is going to take her time dying, they might as well go back to their homes and lives, and return when the end is confirmed.

We too have packed and are ready to leave for Banaras. Salma has been calling daily to check on your plans. Unaccustomed to the freedom of running the house without your supervision, she wants you back. You too, unwilling to relax your hold on your daughter-in-law and the house, want desperately to return. You are also worried about your long absence as music teacher to foreign students in Banaras. Every class missed cuts into the small but significant income that teaching brings to the family. There is also the anxiety that your students might find another teacher if you are away too long.

Bidding goodbye has taken all morning. After repeated promises to Pyaari khala that you will be back soon, we are finally in the car. Asghari and Rani are coming with us. A free car ride to Banaras seems to be good enough reason for them to take a break from the monotony of Bhabua. In her absence, one of the girls who use the place will keep a key to Asghari's house. For her share of their earnings, Asghari will have to rely upon the girls' honesty in accounting for the number of times they utilise her room while she is away.

She looks remarkably nonchalant about the possibility of being short-changed. You, on the other hand, stiffly holding in your lap a tiffin-carrier packed with food enough for a garrison, sit in the back seat of the car with your lips set thin and your eyes grim at the prospect of hosting your sister in your Banaras home. But, as always in matters concerning Asghari, you keep your misgivings to yourself. Asghari does as Asghari wants, and you know only too well the unpleasant repercussions of obstructing her plans.

Your cousin and best friend, Rajjo, who had accompanied us from Banaras to Bhabua, has decided to stay back to look after Pyaari. This has further soured your mood. It shows up poorly, you fear, your eagerness to leave your aunt and head home. While your love and sense of duty towards Pyaari are undeniable, I am beginning to realise, so is your need to be recognised as the most loving and dutiful of your relatives.

Just as we are about to leave, Ramdaras arrives, his motorcycle piled with three huge sacks of rice and two of arhar dal, your quarterly share from the land that he tills as your tenant. You are proud of your foresight in investing much of your savings, while the going was good, in agricultural lands. Maheshwar Singh added substantially to your holdings. Located in the nearby village of Palakh to which Ramdaras belongs, the landholdings have been the mainstay of your retired life. While some portions have been sold over the years to finance your elder daughter's wedding, the lands that remain provide your household with its annual rations of foodgrains and lentils, besides a small income that comes in as rent.

Ramdaras is about your age, or a bit younger. Before him, his father, Rambharose, looked after your lands. Belonging to the Kurmi peasant caste, Ramdaras's family has done well for itself over the generations. You have told me that he doesn't need to continue as your tenant as he is, in fact, many times better off than you are. His sons have government jobs and Ramdaras, besides looking after his own and your lands, also runs a fertiliser and pesticide depot located on the main road, on the outskirts of Palakh. And yet he carries on with the old tenancy out of respect for the ties that bind his family to you.

Your mood has considerably brightened with Ramdaras's arrival. Reyaz helps him load the sacks on to the top of the taxi, which now groans under their weight. Ramdaras has also brought for you gifts sent by his family—two large earthen bowls set with sajav dahi, clotted cream yoghurt, a speciality of the area, and a cake of fresh, sweet-smelling jaggery. Since your lap already holds the huge tiffin-box, each of the earthen bowls is now deposited in Asghari and Rani's embrace. Sitting in front, next to Reyaz, I carry the cake of jaggery in my lap. Like a quartet of food-bearing mother goddesses enthroned in their modern-day vahan, the Maruti van, we finally set off.

Bhabua is not far from Banaras. It takes only three and a half hours by car; the bus takes a bit longer. The women of your family have made this journey innumerable times. Rani mumbles that Sadabahar had been the first of the family to travel this route. You add that she must have made the journey by bullock cart.

Asghari snorts bossily, 'Bullock cart indeed! Sadabahar was not a rustic slowcoach like you! She travelled everywhere in a horse-drawn carriage.'

Rani quickly turns the conversation towards her mother, Bindo, and aunt Teema. Bindo was the next in line to follow in Sadabahar's wake and travel to Banaras. Sent to the big city at Teema's behest for an education in music and dance, Bindo owed her musical genius to her cousin, says Rani. Pushed into prostitution herself, Teema made sure that Bindo became a tawaif.

Bindo spent her childhood under Teema's care in the house that Daya Singh had rented for her in Bhabua. During his frequent absences on account of work and family responsibilities, Bindo's childish prattle and antics would fill Teema's long days and nights with laughter and warmth. Neither missed the family home that held memories only of fear, want and violence. Older than Bindo by several years, Teema felt a deep maternal love for her little cousin. Bindo too loved and trusted Teema as she would her mother. Daya Singh would visit whenever he could and spend the nights with Teema. He was fond of little Bindo and often brought her toys or sweets, much to Teema's delight.

Asghari tells me that those were happy times for Teema. She lived in great comfort, by her standards, even luxury. Daya Singh provided her with a generous allowance for running the house. Her store-room overflowed with mounds of ghee, sugar, fine rice, wheat and lentils brought in monthly by Daya Singh's retainers from his ancestral home. Teema's kitchen gleamed with heavy brass utensils used to cook and serve the freshest vegetables and the choicest cuts of meat. There was a full-time servant to take care of the housework. She had trunks full of expensive shimmering saris and glittering gold jewellery. Daya Singh had promised to keep Teema like a queen, and he had kept his word.

Not a man known for extravagance, his generosity towards Teema surprised everyone, even himself. Daya Singh wasn't sure why he was so drawn to this girl, but he felt a deep desire to protect and look after her. He expected so little in return that, in the initial months, Teema was hard-pressed to understand how she should make him happy.

In her young life, Teema had only known people to want something from her. She was unused to taking. Daya Singh's simple but sincere assurance that he was happy just being with her and seeing her happy made Teema cry. Filled with gratitude and love, she was resolved to put his comfort, interests and happiness above all else.

She made careful note of his likes and dislikes in food, dress, conversation and lovemaking. Never taught how to cook, Teema painstakingly learnt from her mother and aunt the mysteries of chopping, grinding, frying, stewing and simmering. She loved meal times when, arranging the food in gleaming brass bowls set atop a large, heavy thali, she would serve it to Daya Singh herself.

While eating, Daya Singh would share with Teema news, thoughts and worries related to business, landholdings and even about his family in Chand. He found himself telling this quiet girl things he would never dream of sharing with anyone else. Was it the intelligence in her eyes or the serene composure of her face that elicited confidence, he wondered. Or was it the fact that she always heard him with full attention, without interruption? She neither cast judgement nor made any immediate comment.

If Teema had any response to make, she would do so after careful thought, late at night, when after lovemaking she lay enclosed in Daya Singh's embrace. He would listen quietly while Teema spoke, simply, honestly, objectively and wisely. Usually, her opinions and advice proved useful. In the early years of their relationship, it always amazed Daya Singh that a girl so young and with no experience of either the vagaries of agriculture or the complexities of forest contracts should give such sage counsel. Over time, he began conferring with her before taking any major decision.

Teema built with Daya Singh a home both had long yearned for. If Teema was fleeing the poverty, violence and greed of grasping relatives, Daya Singh was escaping the claustrophobic cacophony of a joint family, the cheerless silences of an incompatible marriage, the demanding duties of an elder son, brother, husband and father. Together, they found friendship, love, sex and joy in their new house.

The rise and fall of Asghari and Rani's voices overlay the bumpy, dusty ride. I notice that Rani invariably leaves her sentences incomplete to be expanded and rounded off by Asghari. Her low-pitched, slow mumbles merge into Asghari's sharp and excitable treble, creating a strangely pleasing aural pattern. They are an unlikely pair of cousins—stocky, plain-faced Rani and petite, pretty Asghari; devout, spiritual, modest Rani and the decidedly unspiritual, transgressive, flamboyant Asghari.

One of the many reasons you grudge having Asghari in your home in Banaras is her habit of standing on the balcony in the evening all made-up—like a 'common prostitute', you hiss embarrassedly. She is old, she has retired, she should behave with propriety, you assert. What will the neighbourhood think, what will people say, how will it affect the girls in the family, you complain. Rani, on the other hand, is always welcome. Head covered, rosary in hand and praying five times a day, Rani adds sheen to the genteel respectability you prize so much.

Yet, these two daughters of Teema and Bindo occupy adjoining houses in Bhabua and lead shared lives. From childhood, Rani cast her lot with Asghari. As a loyal lieutenant, she has followed Asghari through peaceful and turbulent times. Asghari constantly bosses over and berates Rani, who rarely seems to take offence. But on the rare occasion when Rani does speak, Asghari listens. Secure in her cousin's loving acceptance of her routine transgressions, Asghari heeds Rani when she draws the line.

Some nights ago, Asghari threw a tantrum over the quality of meat served at a dinner to commemorate Saleeman's death anniversary. The entire family was sharing the food, consecrated with prayer, in Pyaari's house. Holding up a bone rudely between two fingers, Asghari declared it unfit even to be fed to dogs.

Pyaari had just fallen off to sleep after a long day of pain. You and Rajjo tried unsuccessfully to cajole Asghari into silence. Phoolmani, angered by this disrespect to her mother's memory, threatened to throw Asghari out. Just when things were getting ugly, Rani told Asghari in low but firm tones to calm down and eat her food respectfully. Asghari's belligerence vanished; she subsided into her seat and spent the next half hour devouring the food she had rejected.

Periodically, Rani takes off to seek her spiritual destiny in the many Sufi shrines dotting the countryside. Asghari rarely, if ever, agrees to accompany her on these journeys. If Rani is lucky, she finds a group of pilgrims that she can join. On other occasions, she travels alone, unfettered by fear or the need for material comforts. She moves from one dargah to the next, setting up base and sometimes meditating for days at a shrine. When her absence becomes prolonged, Asghari begins fretting and making enquiries about her cousin's possible whereabouts. Then, cursing Rani for her irresponsible ways, sets off to find her. They return to Bhabua—an extremely cross Asghari, followed by a sheepish Rani.

I am reminded of Bullan and Kallan searching for the spiritually engaged Sadabahar, or the maternal attention that Teema showered on her cousin Bindo; the close bonds shared by women in your family are replicated and transferred over the generations. Rani often says that Teema had wanted for Bindo all that could not be hers: name, fame, respect and independent income as a famous tawaif.

Bindo looked very much like Teema had as a child—short, thickset and unprepossessing. Teema would sometimes be overcome by fear that Bindo too might be pushed into prostitution by Bullah and Sa'dullah. But Bindo was not Teema. Not only did the child already show signs of a remarkable talent for music, she also exhibited a flaming temper and ferocious obstinacy. Bindo could not be pushed around as Teema had been. The realisation would leave Teema happy and relieved.

She recognised quite early on that Bindo's talent demanded a better teacher than Bullah Miyan. Accordingly, with Daya Singh's permission, Teema hired the services of Jhandey Khan, a sarangi player and teacher, to come to her home daily and teach Bindo.

Elderly, cheerful and mild-mannered, Jhandey Khan Sahib had none of the severity that Teema associated with music teachers. Bindo clearly seemed to enjoy her lessons, punctuated by Jhandey Khan's jokes and banter. He belonged to a well-known Banaras-based Dhari family of musicians. For the past few years, he had been living and working in Bhabua, while his wife and children stayed in the family house in Banaras. He brought with him the music of his family, tappa rendition, as also bandish thumri, dadra and hori, chaiti and kajari. He was also an expert in the intricacies of the newly emerging leisurely and expansive bol banao thumri, a style of singing also referred to as the purab ang, or 'eastern style', and linked intimately with tawaif singers from Banaras.

As a novice, Bindo was initiated by her ustad into the formal world of raga-bound music through simple khayal-based songs, learning first their sargam or musical notes instead of the words and then graduating to the composition itself. Over time, he introduced Bindo to his family's speciality, tappa, with its rapid and intricate taans that required prodigious vocal technique. Encouraged by her enthusiasm and rapid progress, Jhandey Khan Sahib also began giving his student basic lessons in bol banao thumri.

While performing bol banao thumri, it should be a singer's aim, Jhandey Khan stressed, to evoke as many different shades of meaning as can be read into the text through melodic elaborations and judicious use of ornamentations. He would demonstrate to her how the simple phrases in a thumri—for instance, *baju band khul khul jaye*; my arm-band keeps coming undone—could be repeated many times over, each time emphasising different moods, such as amorousness, love, anger and even devotion.

Too young to have personal experience of these moods, Bindo would try and faithfully reproduce her ustad's notes. Teema, on the other hand, would find herself profoundly affected by these songs of love and longing that spoke to her in a woman's voice about a woman's life experiences. Free from the pressure of meeting her father's expectations, Teema heard Bindo's strong and confident voice repeat the notes Jhandey Khan Sahib played on his sarangi and took joy in their music, as a listener if not a performer.

This happy state of affairs came to an unexpected end one morning when Jhandey Khan arrived at Teema's house, his face ashen and eyes streaming tears. He had just received news that his wife was seriously ill. Leaving hurriedly for Banaras, he promised to return as soon as her health improved. Teema and Bindo consoled him as best as they could and prayed for his wife's speedy recovery. Then bidding him goodbye, they began counting days to his return.

Jhandey Khan Sahib was gone several months before the news reached Teema that his wife had died a few weeks after his return. Heartbroken, the old teacher was left with no spirit to travel. His family prevailed on him to spend the rest of his days with loved ones in Banaras. This came as a blow to Teema. She sympathised with Jhandey Khan Sahib, but who would now teach Bindo music and prepare her to become the great tawaif that Teema dreamt about? There was no one in Bhabua who came close.

Trying to make the best of a disappointing situation, Teema requested Munnu Maharaj, a young but well-regarded tabla player, to take over Bindo's musical education. Their lessons proceeded adequately and included instructions in kathak, since Munnu Maharaj came from a family of dance teachers. But Teema was far from satisfied. Munnu Maharaj's music, though infused with robust energy and erotic vitality, lacked the exquisite refinement and thorough knowledge of raga-based singing that Jhandey Khan had brought with him from the tawaif salons of Banaras. Still, Teema had little choice but to continue with his services.

Never taught the alphabet herself, Teema was keen that Bindo's education include a thorough knowledge of the letters. On the advice of senior tawaifs in the neighbourhood, she requested a local maulana to guide Bindo through the intricacies of Urdu; a Brahmin widow whom Teema had befriended agreed to teach Bindo to read and write Hindi.

The major test of her commitment to Bindo's future came a few years into her relationship with Daya Singh. Through shrewd investments, manipulation, support of colonial officials and hard labour, his business as forest contractor had expanded phenomenally. Work now demanded that he shift to Ranchi to personally supervise an important contract in the area. While his family would stay on in their ancestral village, Daya Singh wanted Teema to accompany him to Ranchi.

Bullah and Sa'dullah were overcome with panic. A shift to distant lands would slacken their hold over Teema. And put in possible jeopardy the security of the assured monthly allowance from Daya Singh. They tried to cajole Teema into staying back and finding a new patron for herself. But she had tied her happiness to Daya Singh and was adamant about accompanying him wherever he went.

Her major fear was for her cousin. With Teema in far-off Ranchi, who would ensure a brilliant future for Bindo, and protect her from Bullah and Sa'dullah's short-sighted greed? Torn between her love for Daya Singh and sense of duty towards Bindo, a troubled Teema began losing sleep and appetite. Her restlessness and anxiety permeated the house.

Daya Singh empathised with Teema's predicament and understood her reluctance to leave Bindo in the dubious care of Bullah and Sa'dullah. His suggestion that Bindo accompany them to Ranchi, although welcomed enthusiastically by Teema, met with stiff resistance from both brothers. With Teema gone, Bindo was the family's only asset, an insurance against poverty and hunger.

Daya Singh now had to think of a plan that would address Teema's concerns without removing Bindo from her father and uncle's guardianship. He realised too that, as long as Bindo stayed in Bhabua, her still nascent musical talent might go to waste in the absence of the right teacher. Over the decades, the large majority of Rajput landholders, who were traditional patrons of tawaifs in Shahabad, had lost much of the surplus resources needed to support the high-end practice of music and dance. As a result, fewer first-class male musicians now wished to move to towns like Bhabua to teach and accompany the relatively low-paid tawaifs there.

Ambitious and well-placed tawaif families in the district increasingly preferred to send their girls to cities like Banaras and even Calcutta in search of learned teachers and rich patrons. While Rajput landholders in Shahabad continued to patronise tawaifs, the women who remained in the area had usually been forced to stay on due to poverty or a lack of musical talent. The more affluent and powerful landholders in Shahabad considered it a matter of prestige to have liaisons with tawaifs from bigger musical centres like Banaras and to invite them to perform in their celebrations. If Bindo was to make a mark as a tawaif musician, she would have to move out of Bhabua. After much thought, Daya Singh came up with an idea.

Sultana Bai was an old and trusted tawaif who had for long been in the patronage of Daya Singh's uncle, Khazan Singh. She had known Daya Singh since he was a child and they shared a relationship of mutual respect. Whenever Daya Singh visited Banaras, he would try and look up Sultana Bai who lived there with her daughter Mumtaz and granddaughter Roshanara. Sultana Bai too was Baisi, as Teema and Bindo were. She was, therefore, acquainted with Teema's family.

Known for her integrity of character and loyalty to old relationships, Sultana Bai was a true deraydar tawaif who could be trusted to honour her promise. After discussing the matter with Teema, Daya Singh paid the old tawaif a visit.

After careful consideration, Sultana Bai agreed to his request to house Bindo and supervise her education in music and the letters with good teachers. On no account would she allow Bullah and Sa'dullah to initiate Bindo into the profession without first informing Teema and checking out the credentials and offer of the man chosen by the brothers. In exchange, Daya Singh promised a generous monthly remuneration that, at first, true to her deraydar upbringing, Sultana Bai graciously refused but then demurely accepted. In addition, he would send her money for Bindo's education.

Expectedly, Bullah and Sa'dullah protested vociferously at the prospect of sending Bindo away to the care of another tawaif. They feared the possible influence and control that Sultana might in due course wield over Bindo. Daya Singh tried to allay their apprehensions. Sa'dullah could accompany Bindo to Banaras and stay with her there. As soon as she was ready to join the line, Daya Singh would help set her up as a tawaif, independent of Sultana, in her own kotha in Banaras. Sultana would have no share in Bindo's earnings once she entered the profession. The advantages of shifting to Banaras, a musical centre teeming with great teachers and wealthy patrons, Daya Singh reasoned with the brothers, were far greater than the discomfort of living a few years in the house of another tawaif.

Grudgingly, Bullah and Sa'dullah began to see the merit in these arguments. Without needing to spend a paisa, they were getting an opportunity to have another possible Sadabahar in the family. By a strange coincidence, the factor that ultimately decided Bindo's future came in the shape of Veer Bahadur Singh.

After the failure of his campaign against tawaifs, Veer Bahadur Singh lay low for some time, tending his bruised ego and weighing his political prospects. Meanwhile, the Sanatan Dharma Sabha and Arya Samaj agitators were busy once again inflaming sectarian passions in Bhojpuri-speaking districts over the cow-protection issue. As before, they received enthusiastic support from the upper as well as intermediate castes of the region.

Veer Bahadur decided that, while cleansing Shahabad of sin would be a long haul, he should focus his energies on saving the cow from beef-eating Muslims. The cause was dear to his heart, and it might salvage his image after the humiliating retreat from the anti-tawaif agitation.

Like several Rajput and other upper-caste leaders of the movement in Shahabad, he became active in mobilising and leading Hindu mobs in attacking Muslims accused of slaughtering cows.

He got support from all quarters, with the exception of Daya Singh, one of the few Rajput landholders, who was vocal in his opposition to the campaign. Apprehensive of the spiralling violence, Daya Singh had tried to convince Veer Bahadur against getting involved. This time, however, buoyed by the overwhelming success of the cow-protection movement, Veer Bahadur was in no mood to bow to his elder brother. As a precaution, Daya Singh sent a posse of armed retainers to guard the tawaif neighbourhood in Bhabua, with its large Muslim population, where Teema lived.

His fears were not misplaced. Mobilised and led by self-styled leaders like his younger brother, crowds of up to 50,000 Hindus attacked Muslims in 124 villages of the district in 1917. While Bhabua and its surrounds remained relatively peaceful, the rest of Shahabad was plunged into a bloodbath.

Once the violence subsided, Veer Bahadur fled Shahabad to evade the police who were making large-scale arrests of leaders and participants in the violence. Reaching Banaras, he found sanctuary with like-minded young Hindu nationalists in the city. They helped him get an administrative job in Banaras Hindu University, newly established in 1916 by Madan Mohan Malaviya, a prominent leader of the Indian National Congress and sympathiser to the cause of Hindu nationalism.

Upon receiving news that Veer Bahadur had a job in distant Banaras, Daya Singh heaved a sigh of relief. His once-favourite brother had become for him a source of constant tension, embarrassment and personal disappointment. It was best, Daya Singh felt, that he lived far from the family.

This, however, was not to be. After spending a few years in Banaras, Veer Bahadur decided to return to his roots. The country was in turmoil against colonial rule. In 1919, Gandhi's call for satyagraha—non-violent political resistance—against the draconian Rowlatt Act had caught the imagination of large sections of the population. Undeterred by unprecedented British repression, people joined strikes, demonstrations and protests in towns and cities across India, including Delhi, Bombay, Calcutta and Madras.

The protests reached Bihar as well, where Congress support had long been limited to Western-educated, urban professionals, mainly lawyers from upper-caste landholder families. This changed with Gandhi's visit to Champaran in north Bihar, and his institution of an enquiry in 1917 into the condition of impoverished peasants forced by British planters to grow indigo on unfavourable terms. Gandhi now elicited momentous support in the Bihar countryside. He was seen as a Mahatma, a great soul, who the local colonial officers feared was 'daily transfiguring the imagination of masses of ignorant men with visions of an early millennium'.

His call for satyagraha in 1919, therefore, received an enthusiastic response in Bihar. Demonstrations and near-total shut down of work, shops and business establishments in Patna, Muzaffarpur, Chhapra, Champaran, Monghyr, Bhagalpur, Gaya, Jharia and Arrah had marked 6 April, the day of the all-India hartal, or strike, that Gandhi called.

The subsequent firing ordered by Brigadier General Dyer upon an unarmed and peaceful assembly of men, women and children in Jallianwala Bagh, Amritsar, on 13 April 1919, generated outrage among people throughout the country. Veer Bahadur decided that this was the time for him to return home and claim a leadership role in mobilising people against British rule.

On his return to Shahabad, however, his attention was immediately drawn to an unforeseen family emergency that put on hold his political plans. He was appalled to learn that Daya Singh was taking Teema with him to Ranchi. That his brother should have kept a lowly Muslim prostitute as a mistress was bad enough; to sanctify that relationship by taking her along to keep house as a wife was reprehensible.

Veer Bahadur had thus far shared a somewhat thorny relationship with his sister-in-law, Moolan. She had crossed swords with him often about his callous disregard for his young bride, Rukmini. These conflicts were now overshadowed by the outrage he felt about his brother bestowing upon a prostitute the privileges reserved for a wife. His moral indignation was sharpened by his intense hatred for Teema, whom he held personally responsible for the humiliating collapse of his anti-tawaif protests.

For once, Veer Bahadur's rage found some support within the family, for they too were beginning to be alarmed by Daya Singh's emotional attachment to his mistress. If allowed to grow unchallenged, there was no saying what impact this intimacy might have on the patriarch's duties and responsibilities towards his own flesh and blood. Long conditioned to accept the presence of tawaifs, prostitutes and mistresses in her husband's life, Moolan Devi now spent sleepless nights worrying about her future in the wake of his decision to take Teema with him to Ranchi. The influence that the girl could exercise over Daya Singh in a new place, without the counter-balance of family presence, Moolan feared, might erode the security and status assured to her as his wife. Finding an unexpected ally in Veer Bahadur, Moolan began to turn to him for sympathy and advice.

The time had arrived finally for Veer Bahadur to not only right a deeply felt moral wrong but also to avenge his own defeat at Daya Singh and Teema's hands. Fanning his sister-in-law's fears, he instigated her to confront Teema. Getting Moolan to agree wasn't easy since, in all her years as Daya Singh's wife, she had considered it below her dignity to even appear before her husband's mistresses, let alone speak to them directly. Fearful of Daya Singh's wrath, she had even avoided making any critical remarks about his extra-marital relationships. But the crisis now brooked neither considerations of pride nor fear.

Daya Singh was in Banaras for a few days. Seizing upon his absence, Veer Bahadur encouraged Moolan to send word to Teema that she should come and meet her urgently. Taken aback by this unexpected summons, Teema presented herself forthwith at Daya Singh's ancestral home in Chand. With hands folded respectfully and eyes downcast, she stood nervously before her lover's wife, who sat on a bed, staring at her with cold hate.

Tall and slender, with sharply etched features, Moolan was beautiful even well into middle age. That her rival should be this squat, ordinary-looking girl seemed to Moolan so ludicrous that, for an instant, she was overwhelmed with an insane desire to laugh at her fate.

In a voice trembling with rage, she asked the girl, 'Are you the Natin for whom babu sahib has rented a house in Bhabua?' Moolan could not bear to speak Teema's name, derogatorily referring to her as 'Natin'. Teema's nod pierced her heart. Taking a deep breath, she launched into the attack Veer Bahadur had made her memorise before the girl's arrival. The Natin would have her nose cut and ears chopped if she did not immediately stop her prostitute ways. If she ignored the warning and went off with babu sahib to Ranchi, the girl's family would be quartered into little pieces. The choice was hers.

By nature, gentle and soft-spoken, Moolan was shocked by her own venomous words. Unable to continue, she got up and left the room. Teema, who had been silent all this while, stood uncertainly, waiting for Moolan to return. She was bathed in sweat. The memories of a bedroom in an outhouse, in which a child had been raped by an old man, came flooding back. Her limbs felt numb with terror, her thoughts went blank. And quietly, she made her way out of the house and back to Bhabua.

A loud exclamation from you punctuates Asghari and Rani's collective remembrance of their mothers. You have spotted the son of a former Rajput patron family coming from the opposite direction on his motorcycle. And though he drives past without noticing your hands folded in greeting, you keep looking back at his fast receding figure with a wistful half-smile.

'Turn around and sit properly! Flinging yourself out of the car window is not going to make him come back,' Asghari snaps at you. Turning your substantial back on Asghari and Rani, you continue to gaze out in peeved silence at the landscape racing by, burnished the colour of ripened grain in the late afternoon light.

You have often referred to this land of southwestern Bihar and adjoining eastern UP as not only your watan but also your karmabhumi, place of work and recognition of your worth as a tawaif singer and dancer. Even though you began your career in Banaras and have chosen to live there permanently, Maheshwar Singh belonged to a village close to Sasaram in this area. Other Rajput patron families lived in villages and small towns dotting the region. You were invited to perform at their sons' weddings, at festivals and even at official functions.

I have heard from other tawaifs and male musicians in Banaras that, in your prime, you enjoyed a celebrity status that few other singers and dancers of your generation, and even older, including Asghari, had come close to achieving. You were the highest-paid tawaif not only in Banaras but in all of eastern UP and Bihar.

I look at your sullen profile gazing out of the window and comment on your fame in these parts. You turn and blush, pride and shyness in your eyes. While you have no hesitation in talking about your past as a tawaif, you do so always with humility. And so it is now. 'Many tawaifs made a name for themselves here. Those who came before our times were even more famous and respected. No upper-caste family celebrations were considered complete without our presence. The name, fame, fortune and destinies of tawaifs were tied to the Rajput and Bhumihar men of this region.'

I have often been struck by the detailed knowledge of genealogies, clan rivalries, financial fortunes and marital alliances that the tawaifs I have met, including you, have of the sundry Rajput and Bhumihar families in the area. Although never granted formal recognition, tawaifs were often an adjunct of these households. As performers, not only was the tawaif's professional existence inextricably tied to the rise and fall in fortunes of upper-caste patron families, but as lovers and mistresses, they also had children by their Rajput and Bhumihar benefactors.

As long as he lived, Maheshwar Singh, you remember fondly, shared a close bond with his children from you. He paid for their school education and upbringing. While you were busy with your hectic travelling schedule, he would spend time with the children, take them out to the cinema and circus.

Ever mindful of the twenty-five-year age difference that separated him from you, Maheshwar Singh gifted you a share of his landholdings in Palakh as insurance against his death. This land was to be used, according to his wishes, for his daughters' weddings and for setting up his son professionally. He had delegated the responsibility of looking after your lands and interests to his old loyalist Rambharose, father of Ramdaras.

As long as he lived, Rambharose was a pillar of support in your times of need. After his passing, Ramdaras stepped into his father's shoes; his loyalty to you tied inextricably to his family's faithfulness to Maheshwar Singh's memory.

A few days ago, when we visited Palakh to inspect your lands, we had first gone to Ramdaras's house. Our arrival was signalled by excited shouts from the village children, who followed our car through the lanes of Palakh. This rag-tag noisy procession dissolved only after we had been ushered in by Ramdaras and his sons from their outer courtyard shaded by a huge jamun tree into the visitor's room. Large and comfortable, the house reflects its owners' peasant base and prosperity. While the older, inner rooms are still mud-and-thatch, the newer additions to the house, including the visitor's room where we sat, are cemented and painted. The room also boasted of a television, CD player and desert cooler.

I noticed the warmth with which you were welcomed. All the daughters-in-law and children trooped into the room one by one to touch your feet. Heedful of your responsibilities as patron, you had taken a bundle of ten-rupee notes with you; each child was given a note as part of your blessings.

Ramdaras's brand new grandson, swaddled in colourful finery, was brought to you with much fanfare. For the new baby, you had taken a pair of tiny silver bracelets that you slipped affectionately onto his little wrists. Smearing a tiny spot of kohl on his baby cheek, accompanied with much blowing of the air around to ward off buri nazar, the 'evil eye', you mumbled benedictions into the little one's ears.

Ramdaras's wife, who had so far been shyly standing at the door leading to the inner courtyard, then stepped forward to embrace you affectionately. She led us inside to the main house to feed us lunch. You address her as bhoji, or sister-in-law, since you treat Ramdaras as a brother. He and his wife, like everyone else in the family, simply address you as 'bai'.

You are 'bai' for everyone we met in Palakh while walking from Ramdaras's home to the fields. Several people recognised you and offered respectful greetings. This is a largely Kurmi, and predominantly Hindu, village. And yet you, a Muslim tawaif, had walked through its lanes with the confidence of being home.

The complex interweave of power, caste alliances, gender and sexuality that informs the relationship of tawaif families with the wider population of the area has often come to me as a revelation. While the hot winds of a more puritanical sexual morality have no doubt long reached these parts, they have not been able to completely erode the ties of loyalty, duties and responsibilities that bind old tawaif families with that of former powerful patrons and their followers. Therefore, while 'accepted' sexual morality looks down upon tawaifs, relationships with individual women and their family members seem to enjoy relative immunity from moral censure.

You understand the subtle nuances of this paradoxical morality far better than I do. These same men in Palakh, you have said, who speak to you with such respect would not hesitate a moment in describing an unknown tawaif as a paturiya, a prostitute and treating her like scum.

You refuse to take personal credit for the respect you receive in Palakh, attributing it instead to your status as long-term and faithful mistress to Maheshwar Singh, who was a well-known and influential Rajput landholder-turned-businessman of the region. In dry tones you observe, 'Had babu sahib left me early on in our relationship, and had I been unable to find a patron as powerful and influential as him, these same people would have derided me for being a whore.'

Teema perhaps understood this truth as well. Daya Singh brought with him not only love, caring and material comfort; his name and status provided protection and social acceptability, even a modicum of respectability to Teema. Long after she made her way home from Chand, her teeth still chattered and her body shivered at the memory of Moolan's malicious words. Seeking warmth, she curled up under a heavy quilt on the bed she shared with Daya Singh. Moolan's contempt, her threats and her hate had raked up old memories of abject powerlessness that Teema never wished to revisit. She would not allow Moolan to take babu sahib from her, Teema resolved. She would accompany him wherever he went.

And yet she worried about Moolan's warning. Her family would be made to bear the consequences of Teema's actions. With Veer Bahadur Singh as her ally, Moolan could, Teema feared, harm her family in her absence. Bindo would have to be sent off with Sa'dullah to Banaras as soon as possible. The other members of her family—her blind father Bullah, her mother Shakuran, her aunt Saleeman and the many children in the house, including her brothers Yahiya and Yaqub—would have to be relocated to another place until it was safe for them to return to Bhabua.

CHAPTER 15

Husna Bai Calls a Meeting

As the flight lands at Babatpur airport, the air hostess announces with glum satisfaction that the temperature outside is 40 degrees Celsius. It is almost the end of August, but the blazing sun portends an extended summer in Banaras.

The nearly hour-long drive to the old city takes me through the middle-class colonies of the lesser-known 'modern' Banaras. The exceptional ugliness of its layout and architecture flits past my window. This twentieth-century urban sprawl, though inextricably tied to the old city, is not usually on the itinerary of the thousands of pilgrims, tourists, musicians and even researchers like me. We flock instead to the stretch that lies between Raj Ghat and Assi Ghat, seeking, as the case might be, salvation, peace, music, exotica, history and sociology on this span of the eighty waterfronts that constitute, for us, the 'real' Banaras—the old city that claims to offer something to each of its seekers.

After a long, humid drive, we finally reach the chaos of old Banaras. At first glance, nothing seems to have changed. The traffic jams, the narrow, winding roads and even the potholes seem to be much as I had left them a month ago. And yet the city, like all cities, changes all the time.

The driver proudly directs the attention of the European man and woman who share the taxi with me to the glass facade of a spanking new multiplex cinema-cum-shopping mall complex. It stands cheek-by-jowl with old crumbling buildings and their beautiful latticed balconies. The Europeans wear a distinctly disappointed expression and ask if this is where they will have to stay. The driver quickly dispels their fears in a soothing tone, 'No, madam, sir, you live on the ghat next to temple and

Ganga-ji.' 'Eternal' Banaras invents itself again and yet again, even while maintaining an illusion of timeless continuity with an ancient past.

I arrive at your home in Nariyal Bazaar to find you in a state of panic. Your landlord has served you notice to vacate the house you have lived in all your adult life. Before you, Asghari had lived and worked from these premises that Teema had taken on lease on her behalf nearly fifty-five or sixty years ago.

The history of your family, its music practice, is inseparable from this house, you say, sobbing. You began your journey as a tawaif in this house. It is here that you attained celebrity as the most popular and respected performer of your time in Banaras. This house provided sanctuary when you withdrew from the world outside, and witnessed your loneliness, tears and hardship. This house, you declare, in a rare display of the dramatic, is you.

Your present landlord, Babu Radhey Shyam, is a sari retailer with showrooms in several big bazaars of Banaras. He has inherited this property from his father, along with the other buildings surrounding it on three sides, which form a cul de sac in which your house is located. At one time all these buildings housed tawaifs' kothas. Nariyal Bazaar took pride in being the favoured address of elite courtesans, mostly Gandharvas but also some Muslims. The majority of them, like the other tawaifs in Banaras, were tenants of merchant families like Radhey Shyam's.

Through the twentieth century, landlords in Dal Mandi, Nariyal Bazaar, Raja Darwaza and Chatte Tale were under pressure from nationalist reformers to sacrifice profit for the sake of public morality by evicting their courtesan tenants. While some had complied, others had sought refuge in camouflaging their ownership.

Meanwhile, faced with relentless stigmatisation, tawaifs themselves had begun moving out of Banaras. Among the few who stayed back, some were successful in adapting to the changed circumstances and finding new sources of employment. Many others, like your family, made the descent into constant want and deprivation. Clinging precariously to the legal protection old tenants enjoy from either arbitrary rent hikes or forcible eviction, they became increasingly unwanted lodgers for their landlords.

The walls of your house are peeling, the beautiful hand-painted tiles in the visitors' room are broken and chipped with age. Many have fallen out, never to be replaced. The roof of the storeroom on the third floor next to the kitchen caved in a few monsoons ago. You cannot afford renovations, and Radhey Shyam is in no mood to invest in the maintenance of houses occupied by tenants he wants out.

Over the past several years that I have been visiting Nariyal Bazaar, I have noticed the familiar being displaced by the new. The old paanwala, Shambhu, who had directed me to your house on my first visit here, is long gone. The space of his little shop is now occupied by a mobile phone repair kiosk. The milk shop in your katra—as famous for its curdling, rancid smells as for its thick, creamy lassi—has made way for yet another sari store. I see new faces in the old residential properties. With the exception of your immediate neighbours, the Gandharva sisters Chandra and Prabha, yours is the only tawaif family left in Radhey Shyam's cul de sac of buildings.

You have watched in nervous apprehension as he has, one by one, successfully evicted almost all his original tawaif tenants. The process has been long-drawn and at times acrimonious. Many old tenants have been bought off, others vanquished in property cases and the recalcitrant few intimidated by Radhey Shyam's battery of strongmen into leaving. Their apartments have either been rented out to tenants willing to sign short-term leases and pay higher rents, or dismantled and converted into more lucrative commercial establishments like shops and godowns. It is your turn now. Radhey Shyam wants to bring down the old building in which you live and construct in its place a cold store.

'Can you imagine a cold storage replacing the home of living, breathing women musicians?' Tara Bai's outrage is palpable as she gathers you in a comforting embrace. She is on one of her periodic visits to Chanda's home, and I have come to meet her as scheduled. I insisted that you accompany me here in the hope of distracting you from your immediate worries. I hope too that Chanda as a local leader might suggest some way out.

My optimism on that front proves to be unfounded. Other than observing drily that, in a culture where the worth of music and musicians is weighed on the scale of sexual morality, it is hardly surprising that Radhey Shyam should plan to convert your home into a cold storage, Chanda has nothing to offer.

Tara's stories do seem to divert your attention from the spectre of homelessness that haunts you. In particular, she holds us in thrall with her account of a highly unusual meeting held in August 1921 at the behest of the then choudharayin of the tawaif community in Banaras, Husna Bai. It was there that she first met your aunt Bindo, recently arrived in Banaras.

'My mother, Gulab Jan, had taken me along to the meeting,' Tara explains. 'Accompanying us were my aunts Badr-e Munir, or Mannan Jan, and her heartbreakingly lovely younger sister Bittan. They were my mother's cousins, daughters of Shehzadi nani, who, as you know, was Sadabahar khala's closest friend in Banaras.

'In complete contrast to my soberly attired mother, Mannan khala cut a flamboyant figure—middle-aged and fat with flaming red, hennaed hair, wearing a shimmering, sequined red sari. Generous of heart and with an abundance of good humour, she was respected by all for her forceful personality, sharp intellect and wisdom. In fact, after Husna Bai's demise, she was nominated the next choudharayin in Banaras.'

At the entrance to Husna Bai's imposing haveli in Raja Darwaza, Tara's family ran into Sultana Bai, her reclusive and sickly daughter Mumtaz and her granddaughter, the haughty Roshanara. Much older than Tara, Roshanara had begun to gather acclaim for her singing. Fashionably attired in a finely spun chanderi sari with jewellery to match, she was accompanied by a shabbily dressed girl, not more than eleven or twelve, who looked forlorn and lost.

While Gulab Jan and Mannan Jan were exchanging greetings with Sultana's family, the girl let out a frightened squeal at the sight of the grim-faced guards with their swirling black moustaches and menacing staffs posted outside the haveli. Gripping her arm so hard that the girl winced, Sultana snapped at her to stop behaving like a yokel. 'You are entering the house of Husna Bai, choudharayin of the tawaifs of Banaras! If armed guards are not posted here, where else will they be stationed? Outside your little hovel in Bhabua? Now stop embarrassing me in front of everyone!'

Ushered in by maidservants to a vast mehfil ghar, Tara noticed the girl gape in silent wonder at the room that sparkled with chandeliers reflected in full-length mirrors, walls hung with paintings and tall windows draped in rich satin. A rough tug from Sultana brought an abrupt end to her enchantment.

At the entrance to the music hall sat an old woman on an elevated chauki, courteously receiving all the guests. Joining the others in offering a deep salaam to their hostess, Tara saw the girl staring at the many glittering rings that weighed heavy on the old woman's skeletal fingers, and the pipe she gripped of a tall hookah, its base made of pure silver. To Tara's young eyes, the choudharayin looked ancient, a bundle of old bones affixed with the face of a wizened monkey. It was hard to believe that this was the glorious Husna Bai, one of the most accomplished tawaifs Banaras had ever known.

Husna pulled Sultana into a warm embrace. Sultana whispered something in the ear of their hostess, who smiled and nodded before patting the cheeks of Mumtaz and Roshanara. Tara watched the young girl being introduced to Husna Bai as Bindo, grandniece of the famous Sadabahar, and receiving in response the choudharayin's blessings to become as gifted a tawaif as her grandaunt.

As one of the oldest and most respected Gandharva tawaifs of Banaras and as choudharayin, Husna Bai's word was law for the city's courtesans. Little wonder then that the three major tawaif groups in the city—Gandharva, Ramjani and Muslim—trooped in full strength on that humid August afternoon of 1921 to attend a meeting significantly different from the usual panchayats that Husna Bai called periodically to resolve internal disputes or to enforce rules and discipline.

Seemingly impervious to the sticky heat, they sat elegantly on the spotless chandani, white sheets, that covered the gleaming marble floor, with their legs gracefully folded sideways, hands delicately pressed into their laps, shoulders thrown back and heads held high. Tara, trying unsuccessfully to sit without shifting about, marvelled at their ease.

Bindo, seated next to her, seemed to share her thoughts. One of the first things she mumbled to Tara was that her left foot had gone numb. She knew better than to give in to the temptation to stretch her legs and flex her feet, and was trying to wiggle her toes without fidgeting. The old hawk Sultana, she whispered to Tara, would be watching her every move, and for every lapse, there would be hell to pay once they returned home.

'Bindo and I giggled—part admiringly, part derisively—at all the other women, young and old, present there,' Tara recalls with a smile. 'Since we were around the same age, we became friends almost immediately and entertained ourselves through much of what seemed to us then a boring meeting whispering to each other.'

Bindo confided how nervous she was about this formidable venue and occasion where Sultana had chosen to introduce her to the lofty personages and the etiquette that defined the tawaif community of Banaras. And Tara pointed out to her the tawaifs she was familiar with, mostly friends and acquaintances of her mother, Gulab Jan.

Right in front of them sat the volatile Rajeshwari Bai who often visited her mother. Next to her sat her pretty and timid daughter Kamleshwari, lost in thought. Proud of her illustrious lineage, Rajeshwari was grooming Kamleshwari to become as great a tawaif as she herself was and her mother, Myna Bai, had been. But everyone knew that Kamleshwari was more inclined to spending time either sleeping or reading popular romances, and had little interest in music and dance. Few had the courage to tell Rajeshwari that she was wasting money and effort on a pipedream.

Lowering her voice further, Tara directed Bindo's gaze to Siddheshwari, daughter of Rajeshwari's deceased sister Shyama Bai. Holding her aunt's huge paandaan in her lap, Siddheshwari looked just a bit older than Bindo. Though unremarkable to look at, Siddheshwari was, Tara had heard her mother say, blessed with extraordinary talent and interest in music. Sadly, Rajeshwari, in whose house Siddheshwari lived after her mother's death, had chosen to favour her daughter over her niece. Denying Siddheshwari an education in music, Rajeshwari had the girl tend to domestic chores. Over time, Siyaji Maharaj, music guru to Kamleshwari, had prevailed upon Rajeshwari to allow him to teach Siddheshwari too. Although she had been forced to reluctantly agree, Rajeshwari Bai had ensured that Siddheshwari's education in music was made as difficult as possible by burdening her with household responsibilities.

Next to Rajeshwari's family were seated the sombre-looking women of Adaalat Bai's household—old Adaalat herself, along with her daughter Bashiran and granddaughters Batoolan and Rasoolan. Disciples of the highly respected Shammu Khan Sahib from Shori Miyan's family, both the girls were modest in dress and demeanour, even though they were among the most popular young tawaifs in Banaras. The younger Rasoolan, especially, was acknowledged by all as the rising star of the city. Endowed with a rich, resonant voice, she was commended in musical circles as much for the emotional depth and expressiveness of her thumri renditions as for the vigour and agility of her tappas.

Since the family too was from the Baisi Nat clan, Sultana had gone up to greet the much-older Adaalat, and exchanged pleasantries with

Bashiran and her daughters. The interaction had been cordial but brief since Adaalat's household was known for its reticence and reserve.

Up front in the middle of the hall, surrounded by her retinue of young nieces, sat Badi Moti Bai, one of the most esteemed singers of the city. Badi Moti's remarkable musical talent had been recognised early by the great thumri singer from Banaras, Ustad Moujuddin Khan, who in a departure from his usual reluctance to take on tawaif students, had readily agreed to teach the solemn little girl. She had learnt khayal, tappa and tarana from yet another great teacher, Guru Mithailall Mishra.

Fabulously wealthy, Badi Moti Bai was a favourite in princely states like Kashmir, Banswara and Nahan, where she was invited frequently to perform along with other celebrity singers like Malka Jan from Agra and Janaki Bai 'Chhappan Chhuri' from Allahabad. In her own kotha in Banaras, she performed only for select patrons who had to first seek an appointment.

Tara next pointed out the elderly and exquisitely beautiful Chandrakala Bai. Loved by all in the community for her gentle kindness and generosity, Chandrakala's fame was exemplified by the fact that her patron, a wealthy merchant banker from a prominent aristocratic family, was known by her name—as Babu Yadunath Prasad Chandrakala Wale, rather than the more usual other way around of tawaifs being identified through their rich and powerful lovers.

Just a row behind Badi Moti and Chandrakala sat the middle-aged gramophone divas of Banaras, the best friends Wazir Jan and Shiv Kunwar Bai. Maintaining a supercilious distance from the others present, they wore identical bored expressions. Responding to Sultana's greetings with stiff adaabs, they continued to whisper to each other and laugh at private jokes, uncaring of the hostile looks the other tawaifs shot their way. Behind them sat their two maidservants, one carrying a huge silver paandaan and the other a silver spittoon.

'Bindo was especially excited to see Wazir Jan and Shiv Kunwar in person. Their popularity as gramophone stars had impressed her greatly,' Tara remembers. 'Their recordings of thumri, dadra, hori, chaiti and ghazal echoed in those days in the streets of the city. Shiv Kunwar's naat—*Mein toh apney Khwaja ki jogin bani*; I have renounced the world for my Khwaja—was Bindo's favourite. She confided in me that she would hear it often on the gramophone in Sultana's house and spent hours trying to copy it exactly.'

Several other tawaifs present at this meeting had also recorded extensively, including Badi Moti Bai, Rajeshwari Bai, Vidyadhari Bai and their hostess, Husna Bai. Wazir Jan and Shiv Kunwar Bai's recordings, however, by far outnumbered those made by the other tawaif singers of Banaras.

Gazing at them intently, Bindo, with the innocent confidence of the very young, resolved aloud that one day she would be as well known as Wazir Jan and Shiv Kunwar, nay, even better known. One day, Bindo declared to Tara, she would become as famous as Gauhar Jan and Janaki Bai, the brightest stars of the recording world.

Husna Bai's music hall was by then teeming with tawaifs. While high-born, illustrious and wealthy members of the community monopolised the front and middle rows, the larger majority of lower-placed singers, dancers and entertainers crowded the rear portion. Among them sat Munni Jan and her younger sister Anwari, who despite their humble origins were being heard and noticed in the bazaar as singers of unusual talent.

Anwari had shot to fame recently for being among the first tawaifs from Banaras to appear on the theatre stage. Tara informed Bindo that Anwari's songs and dances in the musical interludes of the play *Raja Harishchandra*, being staged nowadays in Banaras by the Kirloskar Sangeet Natak Company from Poona, were playing to full houses. Her dadra, *Maar daala, maar daala*; Slayed me, slayed me, had become so popular that she had been approached to record it for the gramophone.

Anwari's inclusion in Kirloskar's otherwise all-male cast had proved to be short-lived, Tara tells us. The city's culturati attacked the theatre company for promoting public immorality by hiring a tawaif. Under threats of boycott, it issued a public undertaking that it would never compromise again with its policy of hiring only male actors even for female parts. The company tried to make amends by staging in quick succession two plays on nationalist themes, *Bhagwan Tilak* and *Bharat Varsha urf Hindostan*.

Scanning the meeting for more known faces, Tara and Bindo recognised Jawahar Bai dressed in a pitambar, or saffron-coloured, sari. Earlier that year, Jawahar Bai had made it to the columns of the local nationalist Hindi newspaper, *Aaj*, which, under the headline 'Prostitute builds temple', reported at length on the impressive Ram Janaki temple in Kabir Chaura that she constructed at her own expense.

Sultana was among the many tawaifs Jawahar Bai invited to the consecration of idols at the temple. Bindo had tagged along too and watched awestruck. The idols of the presiding deities Ram and Sita (Janaki) were carried through Kabir Chaura on a grand throne in an extravagant procession resembling a wedding party before being consecrated and installed.

While a minor galaxy of ritual specialist pandits recited shlokas in Sanskrit, a group of fifty to sixty elegantly dressed tawaifs had surrounded the throne and, amidst much blowing of conches and ringing of bells, sung songs in praises of the divine couple. Jawahar Bai, dressed in saffron, had stood behind the idols, fanning Ram and Sita with peacock feathers.

Aaj was censorious in its description of the event, using a tongue-in-cheek, sarcastic tone to underline the incongruity of 'prostitutes' advancing the cause of religion. Amidst the tawaif community in the city, however, Jawahar Bai's status had scaled extraordinary heights. Until then a wealthy but relatively unremarkable Ramjani tawaif, Jawahar Bai was now hailed as a prominent member of the community.

Looking after this august gathering of tawaifs was the most celebrated thumri singer of Banaras at that time, Vidyadhari Bai. Accolades and fame seemed to sit light on her slender, middle-aged frame as she discharged her duties as mistress of ceremonies. Keeping an eye on who sat where, who had arrived and who was still expected, she discreetly directed a steady flow of refreshments—silver glasses cool with fragrant khus sherbet and silver platters lined with neatly folded, freshly made paan—to the assembled guests. Dressed in stark contrast to the others in a white khaddar, hand-spun sari with a maroon border, and wearing no jewellery other than a rudraksha rosary around her neck, Vidyadhari Bai looked more like a sadhvi, a female renunciate, than a tawaif who, Sultana had told Bindo, had studied the *Kamasutra* from no less a personage than Goswami Damodarlal.

Tara had heard her mother say that Husna Bai loved Vidyadhari like a daughter. Kotha gossip had it that the choudharayin had called this meeting at Vidyadhari and Sultana's behest. Most of the tawaifs present, however, had little idea about the agenda.

'Mahatma Gandhi ki jai! Bharat Mata ki jai!' Hail Mahatma Gandhi! Hail Mother India! Vidyadhari raised the slogans that were being chanted those days in the mohallas and streets of Banaras.

Tara recalls, 'Bindo and I enthusiastically repeated the chant along with everyone else.' Both girls directed their gaze towards the hall entrance where, on a high table, was placed a heavily garlanded photograph of the man in whose honour this meeting had been organised. They were vaguely disappointed that the hero who inspired these slogans should be so frail and old. Was this the Mahatma-ji or Gandhi Baba that everyone spoke about with such reverence? The girls had somehow imagined him as younger and more muscular. How would he rid India of the goras? Perhaps he would use the mystical powers it was rumoured he possessed? The will of pir (holy men) and paighambar (prophets), after all, worked in mysterious ways.

As the slogans died down, an elderly man dressed in a crumpled and slightly dirty khadi dhoti–kurta made a dramatic entry. With a frayed cloth bag hanging from his shoulder and a sheaf of papers in his hands, Husna Bai's guest appeared completely out of place in this glittering gathering of tawaifs. Bindo recognised the unfaltering severity of his bulging eyes, the irritable twitch of his bulbous nose and the grim, straight line of his thin lips. This was the man she had often seen visiting Sultana.

Arya Samaji reformer, Hindu nationalist and now Congress worker, Prem Kumar Khanna belonged to a Khatri family of traders that had migrated from Punjab to Banaras several generations ago. Whether retailing shawls and saris in the past or selling funereal items like shrouds in the present, business had never really taken off in their family shop in Nepali Khapra. Just about maintaining a precarious foothold in the otherwise affluent Khatri community of the city, the family had waged a constant, losing battle to keep at bay the harshness of genteel poverty.

Prem Kumar Khanna, unable to finish formal schooling, had been forced by his father to start working in the family's bleak shop at a very young age. But a chance encounter with Ramakant Khatri, prominent Arya Samaj pracharak and educationist, opened a new world for him. And much to the dismay of his avowedly Sanatan Dharma practising family, at the age of fifteen, Prem Kumar embraced the creed of Swami Dayanand Sarawati. The prospect of the revival of Hinduism to its Vedic glory imbued the young man with a sense of purpose more elevating than his father's seemingly petty, everyday preoccupations to make ends meet. Guided by Ramakant, he pledged to sacrifice marriage, material security and worldly ambition, and devote his life to the betterment of Hindu society.

Prem Kumar Khanna began his political journey by aligning himself to the cause of Hindi, dedicating several years of voluntary work to the Nagari Pracharini Sabha, active since 1893 in promoting the Devanagari script. He had also been a committed soldier of the 'shuddhi' movement spearheaded by the Arya Samaj, which identified and put pressure on Dalits, from communities like the Doms, who had adopted Christianity in search of a better life, to reconvert to Hinduism. Somewhere along the way, like many other Hindu nationalists in the city, he had aligned himself with the amorphous ideology that defined Congress politics in Banaras, simultaneously accommodating in its ambit various dissonant voices and aspirations.

Prem Kumar nursed no political ambitions, harboured no desire for personal advancement. He had never married. He had no vices. He did not smoke or drink. He had no interest in sex or wealth. He was suspicious of music and dance, and found theatre morally reprehensible. With no interests, hobbies, dreams or desires whatsoever to act as distraction, Prem Kumar Khanna could be counted on to be at the forefront of organising rescue, relief and rehabilitation operations in the event of an emergency or calamity—flood, drought or epidemic. He was a familiar figure in Banaras, going from door to door collecting donations in cash or kind for the benefit of orphans, widows and other such unfortunate members of Hindu society. The cause closest to his heart, however, was the removal of tawaifs and prostitutes from Banaras.

Making good use of his reputation among the merchant elite of Banaras as a selfless social worker, Prem Kumar Khanna had added his loud, rasping voice to the chorus of anti-nautch campaigners in the city. Unencumbered by the constraints of class and caste affiliations that inhibited many elite merchant reformers from putting pressure on members of their own community, as an Arya Samaji social worker from a disadvantaged family, he pursued with ferocious tenacity every tawaif patron, no matter how high-born, wealthy or powerful. Prem Kumar could legitimately derive satisfaction from the fact that several elite patrons had, under pressure from reformers like him, discontinued the practice of hosting tawaifs' performances at public celebrations in their homes. It was reasoned that others would follow if the city's elite showed the way by setting an example.

He was appreciative too of the efforts made by moral reformers from the Sanatan Dharma orthodoxy of Banaras to cleanse temple celebrations of tawaifs' presence, though given his Arya Samaji status, he had played a relatively peripheral role in the campaign. The participation of privileged sections of the city in fairs had also been on a steady decline. Those who continued to patronise these spaces did so with a sense of mounting social embarrassment.

Through the first two decades of the twentieth century, criticism of the Burhwa Mangal had become increasingly strident. The profligacy of organising such extravagance in times of economic distress, its frivolity in the era of nationalism and the central role played in it by tawaifs became standard arguments against the fair. As a result, the maharaja of Banaras had stopped participating in the Burhwa Mangal, as had large sections of the city's elite, especially the English-educated classes. The administration had already denied permission for holding it a few years earlier on grounds that, because of 'rowdy' elements, it posed a law-and-order problem. The merchant aristocracy, which had traditionally played an active role in organising the fair, supported the administration's decision.

Despite all these developments, much to Prem Kumar's disappointment, these early morality drives remained unfinished business through the first two decades of the twentieth century. Though shrill, they did not result in any dramatic decline in participation in fairs by lower castes and classes. Moreover, there were some fairs still where tawaifs' mujra continued to be a major attraction. The demands for purging sringar celebrations and other temple festivities of nach too had thus far been accepted mainly by organisers in the major temples of the city; many smaller places of worship continued to invite tawaif performers. There also remained sizeable numbers of the merchant elite who, while conforming to anti-nautch diktats in their public celebrations, continued to invite tawaifs to perform in the more private setting of mehfils, baithaks and gulab baris at home or in outdoor garden parties. Some of them even maintained courtesan mistresses.

The participation of tawaifs in the literary and cultural public life of the city, though shrinking, had not been completely eroded. The newspaper *Bharat Jiwan* in 1912, for instance, indignantly reported a meeting of aristocratic music lovers, intellectuals and Brahmin pandits at the Baans Fatak home of Babu Suresh Chandra Mukherjee, a wealthy art patron from Calcutta. They had gathered to honour and felicitate a highly respected music scholar and intellectual of Banaras, Aghor Babu.

Much to the consternation of Hindu nationalists, like the editor of *Bharat Jiwan*, this meeting of the high-born, wealthy, religious and cultural lights of Banaras was presided over by none other than the tawaif Husna Bai. It was she, the newspaper reported, who conferred the title of 'Sangeet Ratnakar' upon Aghor Babu. The report concluded with the lament, 'it is tragic indeed that a meeting attended by illustrious scholars such as Pandit Shiv Kumar-ji should be presided over by a prostitute. Has the learning of the pandits of Banaras plummeted to such depths that they should participate in such a function?'

A prolific writer of letters to newspapers, Prem Kumar Khanna had penned long and angry missives about the moral hypocrisy of the respectable classes. Disgusted and frustrated with his lack of success, he decided to combat the menace at its source. From 1918, he began making repeated petitions to the local municipal board to evict tawaifs from their existing quarters in Chowk, Dal Mandi, Nariyal Bazaar and Raja Darwaza—the city centre. Equating tawaifs with thieves, dacoits and murderers, he argued that not only was their presence hazardous for the moral health of the city, it also contributed directly to the rise in crime in Banaras, especially in the areas where they lived and worked. His latter argument was substantively shored up by an 1898 ruling of the Banaras Municipal Board that a prostitute or any other woman of disrepute who allowed criminals and other 'bad' characters to assemble in her house to the annoyance of her respectable neighbours would be asked to vacate her home.

Prem Kumar found sustenance in similar efforts elsewhere. A year earlier, in 1917, the Agra Municipal Board had debated upon passing bylaws to regulate the areas where tawaifs and prostitutes would be allowed to reside. Though the initial proposal to relocate tawaifs out of the city to the other side of the river Yamuna had not carried through, the Board had succeeded in cordoning them off to a small geographical area where they had lived and worked out of for generations. Tawaifs were prohibited from buying or taking on rent any new property even in this area and also from residing elsewhere in Agra. The news that Municipal Boards in other towns like Khurja and Roorkee had followed up by passing similar bylaws emboldened Prem Kumar Khanna to push the municipality in Banaras to do better and evict tawaifs en masse from the heart of Banaras.

❁

Seeking the support of local shopkeepers and non-tawaif residents in areas where courtesans and prostitutes traditionally lived, Prem Kumar made his way one day in the summer of 1919 to Dal Mandi.

The bazaar and its lanes lay deserted in the stupor of afternoon heat. Trying in vain to find shopkeepers or residents to convert to his cause, the only response to his persistent knocks were irritable voices telling him to return at a cooler hour. Exhausted and perspiring, he stood alone on the deserted street with only stray dogs and young urchins for company, his misery compounded by the children's giggles every time he attempted to rouse people from their siesta. The sun was beating down mercilessly. Desperately thirsty, he looked around for water but could find none. And all of a sudden he felt the ground sway under his feet, and everything went black.

After what felt like a long time, Prem Kumar Khanna opened his eyes to a cool darkened room. Someone had just sprinkled water on his face and several people seemed to be fanning him vigorously back to consciousness. Although Prem Kumar did not know this yet, he had woken up in the kotha of Sultana Bai, who lived in the Muslim-dominated Dal Mandi.

Her granddaughter Roshanara, on her way back from a friend's place, had noticed a man lying unconscious not far from her own home. Recognising him as the social reformer who had rudely barged into her mujra at a wedding in the city, demanding that it be stopped, she momentarily hesitated. Then, she alighted from her doli, palanquin, and unsure about what to do next, had the social reformer placed in it and carried home. Once there, she hurriedly woke up her grandmother and informed her of the unforeseen turn of events.

Sultana had initially baulked at the idea of having the community's most vocal opponent on her premises. His vociferous promotion of the anti-nautch movement had made Prem Kumar Khanna a much-hated figure among the tawaifs of Banaras. They would curse him every time an invitation to perform at a wedding or birth was revoked at his behest. And they would mock him when the same patrons quietly invited them to perform at private mehfils.

Like the other tawaifs, Sultana too had been following closely Prem Kumar Khanna's petition to the Municipal Board. It served the obnoxious man right, she thought, that he should faint in the area he wanted emptied of its original residents. Then, as quickly, her natural graciousness had led her to Prem Kumar's bedside, where she took charge of the efforts to revive him.

The horrified, comically helpless look on Prem Kumar's face when he realised the identity of his saviours made Sultana laugh inwardly. Not exactly known for his good manners, the best that the social reformer could muster was a flustered thank you that came out in a strangulated gasp. Sultana and her granddaughter, on the other hand, were courteous hospitality personified, and kept gently pressing upon him the wisdom of resting in their home till it became cooler outside.

Waving aside their suggestion, he insisted upon leaving but, as he took a step towards the door, a nauseous faint enveloped him again. Physically weak and emotionally distraught, Prem Kumar Khanna had little option but to submit to the tender ministrations of Sultana and her family. His head wrapped in a wet towel, he spent the rest of the afternoon miserably eating and sipping various antidotes to heat-stroke, like cooling bel sherbet and raw mango preserve tempered with rock salt and spices.

All this while, Sultana kept up a steady flow of seemingly casual, one-sided conversation that focused largely upon her admiration of the indefatigable efforts made by the indisposed crusader for reform and moral reclamation of Banarasi society—even though, she added with a show of abashed humility, his anti-nautch campaign had caused her family and community immeasurable hardship. With immense satisfaction, she noted the silent but avid attention with which Prem Kumar Khanna heard all that she said.

It was not for nothing that Sultana was counted among the most astute tawaifs in Banaras. Her initial concern for the reformer's plight had been prompted primarily by kindness. But her insistence on prolonging his stay in her kotha sprang from more worldly considerations. Fate had presented her a chance, however slim, of winning over an opponent. It was up to Sultana now to play her cards well.

Trained to read and understand different kinds of men, their strengths and their vulnerabilities, Sultana had vast experience in taming even the most obdurate member of the opposite sex. Her keen-eyed appraisal of her sun-struck, shabbily dressed and ill-at-ease guest had revealed not only an upright and honest man, dogged in his beliefs and uncompromising in his principles; it had exposed too his unarticulated, almost unconscious need for social recognition and affirmation of his selfless striving.

The accidental meeting confirmed what Sultana had gathered from his frequent letters to newspapers. From complaining about the negligence of the Municipal Board towards civic upkeep to protesting against the discourtesy shown to him by a police officer, and bemoaning the moral duplicity of the city's elite with reference to tawaifs, Prem Kumar Khanna wrote often and wrote badly. Sultana had noticed the inelegant language, the poor framing of the letters. She discerned too his recurrent assertions of his own modest background while taking on defaulters among the wealthy and powerful. Indignant, self-righteous and outspoken, the letters had spoken to her about a man who had little love for material gain. A self-made man who had not yet grown out of his humble beginnings. And a man like all men, who could be broken with respect, sympathy and judicious praise.

Sultana and her granddaughter's humility, their admiration of him and their respectful kindness acted like balm on Prem Kumar's prickly soul. The rich and powerful men in the city he was more used to meeting, even while professing support for his cause, had rarely if ever treated him like a social equal. He had tried to convince himself that the causes that repeatedly brought him to their doorstep were more important than the slights and indignities he must suffer in the process. Yet, deep inside, the consciousness of his social inferiority, and their patronising behaviour had hurt.

That these tawaifs should welcome him so warmly into their home, praise his work rather than throw him out for his sustained public campaign against them, and address him with respectful humility as bhai-ji, respected brother, came as a complete shock. And though he could muster only an occasional grimacing smile in acknowledgement, his preconceptions about tawaifs were decidedly shaken by his real-life experience of them as kindly, cultured women.

Equally, he was taken aback at the immaculate cleanliness of Sultana's home; the spotless floors, pristine whitewashed walls, neatly arranged furniture belied all his expectations of filth and disorder that surely would be the natural environs of moral decay and deviancy. The modest sobriety that marked Sultana and her granddaughter's clothes and mannerisms too came as a surprise. They looked and behaved no different, it seemed to his innocent eyes, than women from respectable homes.

Prem Kumar Khanna tried repeatedly to remind himself of all that he had heard of tawaifs' duplicity, their false smiles, their insincere words.

Surely Sultana and her granddaughter's kind solicitousness towards him was just an act that tawaifs were known to be adept at playing? The gentle warmth in their eyes, the sincerity in their voice, however, felt as real to him as the dull, throbbing pain in his head. A man of limited imagination, Prem Kumar had no patience with doubts or multiple possibilities. He cursed his luck for bringing him to the home of women he had thus far single-mindedly hated for their immorality and obscenity.

Finally, he recovered enough to leave Sultana's kotha. Refusing her offer that he be carried back in the doli she and others in the family used, he yielded to her insistence, as she graciously bid him farewell, that her young nephew Fakhru escort him on his walk back home to Nepali Khapra.

Through the afternoon, Sultana had noted with satisfaction the mounting perplexity in Prem Kumar's eyes. This promised to be an exciting game. A game that would spin the world of the pig-headed and priggish social reformer completely out of orbit.

You have invited Babu Radhey Shyam for lunch. I am surprised that he has accepted, but you are not. The relationship goes back two generations—you have known your present landlord since he, as a little boy, accompanied his father, Babu Ghanshyam Das, on his rounds to the tenants.

Since early morning, Salma has been busy preparing the all-vegetarian culinary spread you have ordered. You flit from one room to another in tense anticipation. I am ordered to go to the old sweet shop of Ram Krishna Mishthan Bhandar in Thatheri Bazaar to buy a box of malai ki galouri. These are apparently Radhey Shyam's favourite.

On my return, I run into the landlord on the steep flight of steps going up to your home. I have met him a few times over the years, in your house and at his sari shop in Nariyal Bazaar. In his mid-thirties, Radhey Shyam wears a safari suit and white shiny sandals. He carries a briefcase in one hand, in the other he clutches a cell phone. His name is the only traditional aspect of his outward persona.

Radhey Shyam is fond of describing himself to English-speaking non-Banarasis like me as a 'modern man with traditional sensibilities'. Often, he mixes it up and describes himself as 'a traditional man with modern sensibilities'. And then laughs, shrugs and reasons that it's the same thing. In many ways, that is an apt description. He is modern enough to eat food in a Muslim home, unlike his father. And yet his reasons for accepting a lunch invitation from a Muslim tawaif stem from respect for old relationships forged much before his time. That his visit to your house this time springs from less than benign reasons is not something, I feel, he would want to dwell upon. Perhaps he rationalises it as necessary to fulfil his preordained dharma of making profit as the scion of an old merchant family of Banaras.

Meenu opens the door for us and, after an exchange of polite greetings, leads the guest into the visitors' room. Then calling out to you, she discreetly takes the box of sweets from me and leaves the room. Your entry is dramatic. Slow and laborious, accompanied by much wincing. A wet cloth is tied tightly across your forehead. I am taken aback. You were well enough, even if emotionally charged, until just an hour ago. Now, heroically waving off Radhey Shyam's solicitous inquiries about your health, you insist in a low, quivering voice that you are fine, even while making it manifestly obvious that you are not. Murmured references to diabetes, hypertension and cholesterol float vaguely in the room, adding to the atmosphere of faint decrepitude and depression.

Over the next hour, you acquit yourself perfectly as a gracious, ailing, ageing and vulnerable hostess. Babu Radhey Shyam doesn't do too badly either. Addressing you respectfully as didi in his usual manner, he is concerned and well-mannered. Both of you seem to be playing from a well-rehearsed script. As you ply your 'younger brother' with fluffy, golden puris, you reminiscence about his dear departed father (may Allah grant him heaven) and his principled, considerate and straightforward ways.

Trading memory for memory, Radhey Shyam, munching appreciatively on Salma's potato chops, showers accolades on the integrity and musical talent of Asghari 'didi' and Pyaari 'mausi'. Your aunt's cancer is discussed, her tenacity in holding on to life duly commended, with Babu Radhey Shyam showing touching optimism by declaring that, if she has defied the time that the doctors gave her by almost five months, she will yet live for long. Moving back further in time as kheer and mangoes are served for dessert, homage is paid to Radhey Shyam's grandfather, Babu Shyam Sundar and your aunt, Bindo.

No reference is made through lunch to the termination of lease notice. That is broached, seemingly by accident, when your landlord, burping politely in appreciation of the exquisite repast, is preparing to take his leave. With a great show of absent-mindedness, he first requests a minor increase in rent and then quickly corrects himself, apologising for his memory lapse. You will be moving out next month, of course. You are quick to pounce on the opening he provides.

You are ill. You are unemployed. Meenu has to be married off. There is no way you can shift out of this house just yet. His counter flies sharp. Property prices have gone up everywhere. Rents are rocketing everywhere, except for his old tenants who still insist upon paying the rent they paid thirty years ago. He has made concessions. He has prioritised old relationships over profit. But he has a business to run. And so it goes for the next half hour.

Brisk business takes over the meandering and polite Banarasi rhapsodies to the past. Finally, it is decided that you will stay on for another nine months till Meenu is married off from the house. You assure your landlord of your disinclination to drag him into a lawsuit. He says he always knew you to be reasonable. Nor does he wish to be unfair. He is willing to make a generous settlement that will make you financially more secure and get him back the possession of his property. Figures, beginning in thousands and then going up argument by counter-argument into lakhs, now fly thick and fast between the two of you.

You both prove to be tough negotiators. I am mesmerised by your legal and financial expertise. Clearly, you did all the homework before organising this lunch. You know the fine print of the legal rights you enjoy as an old tenant, your landlord's margin of profit in converting your home into a commercial establishment and property prices prevailing in areas you wish to relocate to in Banaras. And he knows your vulnerabilities. You are neither financially secure enough to fight a long-drawn-out legal case nor equipped to counter the intimidation and threats that could come your way from his strongmen.

Together, you reach the figure he will pay you to vacate his property. It falls far below your stated expectations but soars much above his original offer. You accept. And the deal is sealed with the box of malai ki galouri that is now presented to Babu Radhey Shyam. No compromise is perfect, you tell me later. But life has taught you to wrest from it the most that you can get.

✿

I am reminded of the story that Tara narrated to us the previous evening about Prem Kumar Khanna's chance meeting with Sultana Bai and her granddaughter. The first encounter was followed by seemingly accidental run-ins with Sultana's nephew Fakhru during the reformer's subsequent visits to the area. Prem Kumar would never know that Fakhru, at Sultana's orders, kept close but unobtrusive track of his visits through a network of street urchins and obliging shopkeepers. Son of Sultana's dead cousin, Fakhru had grown up unwanted and unloved on his aunt's charity. Smooth-talking, sharp-eyed and quick-witted, he grabbed at the chance to improve his position in her household. Following the reformer quietly through the by-lanes of the tawaifs' quarters, he would allow himself to be found by Prem Kumar Khanna at an opportune moment with much show of delighted surprise.

A friendship of sorts developed between the two over time. The young man knew everyone there was to know in Dal Mandi, Nariyal Bazaar and Raja Darwaza, and seemed happy to introduce Prem Kumar to all the shopkeepers and non-tawaif residents the reformer wished to convert to his cause. That these were people handpicked by Sultana for their close ties with tawaifs never crossed his simple mind. Satisfied by their earnest promises to support the petition to evict tawaifs from the area, he marvelled at the rapid progress he seemed to be making.

He found Fakhru simple, helpful and generous, and saw in him an admirable young candidate for conversion to the cause of reform, nationalism and, perhaps, if things went well, even of the Arya Samaj. Not wishing to spoil things through hurry, Prem Kumar decided that subtle, sympathetic persuasion might just be the best route to Fakhru's innocent heart. He would encourage the young man to talk in the belief that these conversations would help build confidence and trust for the plans he nursed for Fakhru's redemption.

Fakhru talked about the harsh poverty of their ancestral village, of his family's migration to Banaras in search of a better life, and the bitter choice that the women were forced to make of becoming tawaifs to ensure survival. Fakhru talked well, deftly intertwining fact with fiction. He confided to bhai-ji about his aunt Sultana's struggles to provide for a large, dependent family made up primarily of women, her abhorrence of the tawaif tradition and her unhappiness that her young granddaughter was being forced by circumstances to follow in her footsteps. He spoke repeatedly of the high regard his aunt had for the social reformer, and of her great desire for a direct audience with respected bhai-ji.

Prem Kumar Khanna listened to Fakhru in silence and with increasing bewilderment. His resolute hatred of tawaifs as bearers of sin and immorality wavered under the onslaught of Fakhru's descriptions of the bleak circumstances of their lives. Moreover, in the face of Sultana and Fakhru's kindness, it seemed churlish to refuse a meeting that the old tawaif requested so often and so humbly.

Reluctantly at first, but over time with increasing willingness, Prem Kumar Khanna began dropping in to meet Sultana. Careful never to allude to the petition that had brought him to this part of the city, the ageing matriarch would instead appeal for help on an entirely unexpected front. With tears brimming in her eyes she would exhort him to action. 'We have been shaken out of our slumber by your ceaseless efforts, bhai-ji! Now help us to make honest women of our daughters. Please help us find respectable, reform-minded young men brave enough to marry the young tawaifs in the bazaar.'

Soon other established tawaifs he met through Sultana began chorusing her plea. Husna Bai, Badi Moti Bai and Vidyadhari Bai, taking a cue from Sultana, promised bhai-ji their support to the cause. Bhai-ji also began to be increasingly entrusted with the duties of a local leader. He found himself penning urgent letters to the Municipal Board and local newspapers on the courtesans' behalf, complaining about the bad roads and clogged drains of Dal Mandi, Nariyal Bazaar and Raja Darwaza, oblivious to the irony of demanding better civic amenities for women he wished to remove from the area.

While, very occasionally, his persistent complaints would rouse the Municipal Board out of its legendary lethargy to clean up an odd drain, his efforts to play matchmaker for the young women of the tawaif community proved futile from the start. Just as Sultana and other elders of the courtesan community had hoped, Prem Kumar could not find even a single young reformer willing to marry a tawaif. On the contrary, his efforts drew moral outrage and social isolation. Sultana watched with quiet satisfaction as her community's once-rabid opponent was rebuffed by the morality keepers of the city. Shocked by his attempts to convince their sons to marry the daughters of tawaifs, they were vocal in their admonition. How dare Prem Kumar Khanna try and push into their respectable homes the filth of tawaif quarters? Had he taken complete leave of his senses?

Prem Kumar Khanna's attempts to pressure the Municipal Board of Banaras to evict tawaifs from the city centre too fizzled out. The shopkeepers and non-tawaif residents of the areas went back on their promises, as expected, and found excuses to avoid adding their names to his petition. Among the Board members, many belonged to the same set of people that Prem Kumar had been hounding for years to ban tawaifs from private soirees organised in their homes. They took particular delight in the erosion of popular support for his cause. To his face, they would nod sympathetic agreement but settled instead for restricting tawaif kothas to the areas in which these had traditionally been located.

Outwardly, Prem Kumar Khanna attributed the failure of his proposal to petty politicking rife in the Municipal Board. Deep within, however, a treacherous relief greeted the news of the Board's reprieve to tawaifs. This was a feeling so unexpected that it was some time before Prem Kumar could come to terms with it. Truth be told, the social reformer had lost his passion for evicting tawaifs from Banaras. Instead of blaming them for spreading sin, his failure to find even one man willing to marry a courtesan had made Prem Kumar a bitter critic of respectable society, holding it responsible for forcing poor women into a life of immorality and degradation.

The tawaifs welcomed the Municipal Board's decision with relief. They celebrated their victory over the respectable in the city with a huge jalsa in Sultana Bai's house, where the entire community assembled for night-long festivities of music and dance and merry-making.

Meanwhile, the entire country had begun resounding anew to the cry for freedom. The Congress-led, anti-colonial non-cooperation movement, with its goal of complete Swaraj, was spreading in Banaras with the same fervour as in the rest of India. Closely following these momentous events, the older tawaifs realised that the present spate of nationalism could well wash away with it the tradition they held so dear. Rather than stand in its way, wisdom lay in joining in and swimming with the current. And so, after much thought, Husna Bai, on Sultana and Vidyadhari's advice, called upon all the tawaifs of Banaras to assemble in her house on that sultry afternoon of 8 August 1921. The time had come to convince the community to cast its lot with the very forces that posed the greatest challenge to its survival.

CHAPTER 16

The Call for Freedom

Just as you exhale in relief at the nine-month respite your landlord has offered, you are confronted with another heartbreak. I enter your room to find a crumpled piece of paper on the floor: the response to your application for the post of music teacher in a privately run school for girls in Banaras. Thanking you for your interest in joining their faculty, the school authorities have politely made it clear that you are not a suitable candidate for the job.

This is not the first rejection letter you have received since retiring as a tawaif and seeking other avenues of work. Employment as a music teacher in one of Banaras's many schools had seemed then the perfect choice. After years of futile filling of forms and interviews, you have come to realise that the job you covet so much places respectability well above the ability to teach music. Moreover, notwithstanding your knowledge and practise of thumri, dadra and associative genres, you have no academic degree to back your claims of being a musician—a prerequisite for any formal teaching post in postcolonial, degree-worshipping India.

You complain angrily about how people with a degree in hand, but barely able to string two notes together, secure jobs that genuine musicians are denied. This is especially true of all government-run and government-aided institutions. You have, therefore, concentrated your efforts on private schools, which though miserly in the salaries they offer, and averse to assuring job security, are not as rule-bound as state institutions tend to be. Bitter experience has taught you that the prejudice against employing faculty deemed to be of dubious moral standing is common to all educational institutions, whether state or privately run.

'This is such a small-hearted, mean-minded city!' you say to me by way of greeting. 'A man can be a profiteer, a hoarder, a thief, even a murderer. But if he is rich and powerful, these schools will beg him to join their board of trustees, while they treat a poor woman who sang for a living decades ago like dirt!'

Just then, Meenu comes up and announces Gabriela's arrival. Smoothing your sari, you hurry to the visitors' room on the first floor.

Gabriela is a young business management student from Spain. Taking a temporary break from learning to be an efficient, profit-making manager for big business, she has come to Banaras in search of spiritual enlightenment and that ubiquitous but slippery creature: Indian culture. Accordingly, for the past two months, her days have been spent smoking marijuana on the ghats, attending religious discourses, yoga classes, Hindi lessons and learning from you the basics of Hindustani music.

The hour that Gabriela spends with you three times a week is a potpourri of lessons in spoken Hindi, instructions on etiquette and even on the right posture for sitting on the floor. You also teach her how to eat using her fingers and to drape a sari, and the significance of festivals like Holi, Eid and Diwali. In the little time left, you give Gabriela some rudimentary music instruction, with your old tabla accompanist Sajjan Kumar joining in to provide the necessary percussion rhythm.

You accomplish all this with little knowledge of English beyond the basic 'yes', 'no', 'thank you'. With his elementary English, Sajjan plays translator to Gabriela's fascination for, and your endorsement of, tourist brochure 'Indian culture'. With self-deprecating irony, you say this is your brief as music teacher, cultural guide and spiritual mentor to young European tourists in search of quick-fix nirvana. After paying off the mandatory kickbacks to the chain of hotel managers, tourist guides, taxi drivers and rickshaw pullers linking you to your students, the work brings in much-needed, if meagre, income to your household.

Sajjan Kumar is your primary contact in this network. As an accompanist tabla player in kothas, he had seen bad days after the retirement of the last tawaifs. Rescue came in the form of either teaching tabla to foreign tourists or by sourcing tuitions in vocal music to the singers he formerly played with. As commission, he is assured of regular work as a percussion accompanist in their classes.

Earnest and polite, Gabriela jumps up as soon as you enter the room and self-consciously touches your feet, a lesson in respect presumably learnt from her yoga teacher. You play out your expected response and mumble the appropriate blessings.

'Kaisi hain aap?' How are you? Gabriela carefully, slowly enunciates the question that she no doubt has been taught in her Hindi lessons.

You reply as slowly, *'Mein achhi hoon. Shukriya. Tum kaisi ho?'* I am fine. Thank you. How are you?

Gabriela, giggling embarrassedly, answers in English, 'I am okay, but have forgotten how to say it in Hindi.'

You patiently take over the role of Hindi teacher, *'Bolo, mein bhi achhi hoon.'* Say, I too am fine.

As you begin your lesson, I decide to spend the next hour making notes of my last meeting with Tara and her memories of the community's response to the non-cooperation movement in the city.

Chun chun ke phool ley lo, arman reh na jaye
Yeh Hind ka bageecha, gulzar reh na jaye
Kar do zuban bandi, jailon mein chahey bhar do
Mata pey koi hota qurban reh na jaye
Bharat na reh sakega hargiz ghulamkhana
Azad hoga, hoga, aaya hai woh zamana
Parvah ab kisey hai iss jail voh daman ki
Eik khel ho raha hai phansi pey jhool jana
Bharat watan hamara, Bharat key hum hain bachche
Mata key vaste hai manzoor sar katana.

(You can pluck all the flowers you want
You can destroy this garden that is India
You can try and silence us, throw us into jails
You can kill all those willing to die for the Motherland
But India will no longer remain a prison house
This age brings with it the call for freedom
No one fears your jail, your oppression
Martyrdom has become for us child's play
India is our country, we are the children of India
For our mother's freedom, we will sacrifice our lives.)

On 8 August 1921, in Husna Bai's house, Vidyadhari sang the nationalist song that she had composed, and which she insisted upon performing at every mehfil she was invited to. All the assembled tawaifs joined in. Even

Prem Kumar Khanna, the only outsider at the meeting, made a valiant, if hugely unsuccessful, attempt to sing along.

The song, calling on people to sacrifice all for the country's freedom, had a deep impact on Tara and Bindo. Their eyes filled with tears, their plump arms covered with goose-bumps, and their young, otherwise strong voices choked with emotion, they sang fervently.

In one voice, led by Vidyadhari, the tawaifs laid claim upon the nationalist agenda of the Congress-led non-cooperation movement. Conceived and guided by Gandhi, the movement called for the surrender of titles and honours given by the British government, boycott of foreign goods and institutions run by the colonial state and of the setting up of national schools and colleges, establishment of panchayats or local councils to settle disputes, the promotion of hand-spinning on the charkha and the wearing of khadi. The movement was firmly based on the compulsory observance of non-violence, Hindu–Muslim unity and the abolition of untouchability.

In Banaras, support for the non-cooperation movement was lukewarm through much of the previous year, 1920. The city had for long been a bastion of Hindu nationalists, many of whom were also Congress leaders. Several among them were reluctant to sacrifice the titles and privileges they received from the British government. Most notably, the prominent Congress leader Madan Mohan Malaviya from Allahabad, highly respected in Banaras as a Hindu nationalist and the founder of Banaras Hindu University, refused to give up government aid for BHU. This led to some confusion within the city's Hindu nationalist ranks about supporting the non-cooperation movement.

Gandhi's emphasis on Hindu–Muslim unity too seems to have generated considerable anxiety and suspicion among the Hindu nationalist Congress leaders in Banaras, who had for years rallied around divisive issues of Hindi promotion and cow protection. This problem was not unique to Banaras or to this period. Even at the all-India level, throughout the freedom struggle, the fact that important leadership roles in the Congress were occupied by votaries of Hindu nationalism proved to be the biggest stumbling block to the party's espousal and practice of Hindu–Muslim unity. In a revealing example, Madan Mohan Malaviya, who had vociferously opposed the non-cooperation resolution at the specially convened session of the Congress at Calcutta in September 1920, presided over a cow-protection meeting held in the same city just a few days after the conclusion of the session. This meeting, besides being attended in large numbers by the local Marwari business community, also saw the participation of many Congress leaders.

News from other parts of the country about the use of religious festivals and symbols for the nationalist cause was reported widely by nationalist newspapers in Banaras, like *Aaj*. There were, for instance, reports about Navratra and Dussehra celebrations in cities and towns like Patna, Mirzapur and Agra, where pictures and idols of Bharat Mata, and leaders like Bal Gangadhar Tilak and Mahatma Gandhi, were taken out in festival processions, and religious slogans were replaced by chants of *Bharat Mata ki Jai* and *Mahatma Gandhi ki Jai*. These reports seem to have stirred enthusiasm in Banaras. Increasing demands were made about imbuing the local Ramlila enactments and Dussehra festivities with similar nationalist zeal.

Non-cooperation fervour in Banaras spiked with Gandhi's visit to the city on 25 November 1920. In the two days he spent here, Gandhi addressed several meetings. He spoke at the Banaras Hindu University, where he was cheered by a huge gathering of students, even as Madan Mohan Malaviya remained in the background. He addressed a meeting at the Town Hall too, where a mammoth crowd of 20,000 people gathered on the afternoon of 26 November to hear Gandhi speak of colonial exploitation, of the imperative to protest, and to boycott British-made goods and institutions of the state in order to gain complete freedom based on the principle of satyagraha, or truth-force. The pursuit of truth, he said, shuns violence against the opponent, who must instead be weaned away from error by patience and compassion.

Unknown to Gandhi, a group of tawaifs, led by Vidyadhari Bai, had been part of the vast gathering at the Town Hall. They had been informed about the meeting by Prem Kumar Khanna. Disenchanted by the moral hypocrisy of his erstwhile Hindu nationalist allies, he was now a regular visitor in the tawaif localities.

Prem Kumar had lost none of his earlier fervour against the tawaif tradition. His critique of their lifestyle and art practices as immoral and obscene had, however, undergone a subtle transformation. Instead of his earlier feeling of revulsion and hatred, he now nursed a growing sympathy for tawaifs and prostitutes, whom he saw as victims in need of rescue, reform and rehabilitation.

His growing interactions with the many Muslims among them also made him question his previous communal prejudices and biases. Before his contact with the tawaifs, Prem Kumar had little or no acquaintance with Muslims in his city. His visits to Sultana's home and those of other Muslim tawaifs made him increasingly aware of the ties of common language, culture and history that bound Hindus and Muslims together.

Not surprisingly, Prem Kumar found himself drawn by Gandhi's inclusive call for Hindus and Muslims to come together and liberate India from the yoke of colonial rule. Unmindful of ridicule from the so-called respectable classes of the city, he began to focus his energies upon converting tawaifs to the cause of non-cooperation and nationalism, in the hope that it would lead them to renounce what was, in his view, their demeaning means of livelihood.

The tawaifs, while amused by his clumsy attempts to make respectable women of them, saw in Prem Kumar Khanna a useful counter to the hostility that came their way not only from nationalist quarters but society at large. Moreover, with time, many among them had begun to nurse a grudging respect, even affection, for their morally didactic, thick-headed but scrupulously honest and well-meaning foe-turned-ally. Agreeing to bhai-ji's suggestion that they attend the Mahatma's meeting at the Town Hall, Vidyadhari—who had been following with interest news about non-cooperation-inspired defiance of colonial rule in other parts of the country—had organised a group of tawaifs to accompany her to the gathering.

Gandhi's speech made a great impression upon many of them, especially Vidyadhari. She began performing nationalist songs in every mehfil she was invited to, renounced foreign-made cloth and began wearing only Indian hand-spun fabric.

Over the coming months, Vidyadhari organised a series of smaller meetings at her home to enthuse other tawaifs to the cause of the non-cooperation movement. She was joined in these efforts by Sultana, who too had been closely tracking the unfolding political scenario. Prevailing upon Husna Bai to call a meeting of the entire community, they had worked out the details of the agenda in consultation with the choudharayin and Prem Kumar Khanna.

Once Vidyadhari's song came to an end, Husna Bai addressed the assembly as planned. After thanking Prem Kumar for taking out time to join the meeting, the old choudharayin spoke with characteristic eloquence of the great challenge facing the tawaif community. Times were changing. And tawaifs too would have to keep pace with a fast-transforming world. Mahatma-ji had unleashed a great and powerful storm that would no doubt blow away the British regime. Tawaifs, always on the forefront in earlier wars against foreign rule, would once again have to step forward and contribute their bit to the nationalist cause. This, Husna Bai said, pausing meaningfully, was not just their duty as daughters of this great land but also the need of the hour if they did not wish to be consigned to the dustbin of history.

Except for Tara and Bindo, too young to appreciate the subtext of Husna Bai's nationalist exhortations, everyone present in the hall well understood the real significance of her speech. While many among them had growing sympathy with the nationalist movement, they had also been following with rising apprehension news of renewed morality drives in its present phase.

Following Gandhi's visit to Banaras, local newspapers had been flooded with reports of city-wide meetings at the mohalla level, attended by all sections of the local population—Hindu or Muslim, rich or poor, upper- or lower-placed castes—to pledge support to the non-cooperation movement. Similar meetings were organised too by specific community- and caste-based associations. Taking a cue from reports of developments elsewhere in India, participants at these meetings subsumed the nationalist agenda within an overarching umbrella of social and moral cleansing. These injunctions were then adopted unanimously by all present with the threat of social boycott of those breaking the rules.

High-caste Aggarwal and Marwari merchants and traders and Muslim ashraf, or high-born landowners and religious leaders were among the first to pledge unanimous support to nationalism and social and moral reforms. Then, other castes and communities—from the Hindu Gowala or cow herders, Kurmi or tillers, Kalwar or wine-sellers, Nau or barbers, Mallah or boatmen, to Muslim weavers and tailors, as also Dalits, like the Chamar leather-workers and Dom disposers of the dead—began adopting resolutions against the consumption of alcohol and other intoxicants, like marijuana and bhang, against the use of abusive language and obscenity, against organising and attending performances by tawaifs and gonaharins, and (among the Hindus) against meat-eating and animal sacrifice; using the opportunity as much for upward social mobility as for promising their support to the nationalist movement.

Inspired by Gandhi's strong views against alcohol consumption, which he identified as a major evil causing physical, moral, intellectual and economic ruination, mass picketing of liquor shops became a significant mode of protest in many parts of the country, including Banaras. Special meetings were organised in various localities with speakers holding forth on the evil of addiction to alcohol and other intoxicants.

In an unprecedented show of support for the movement in Banaras, in January 1921, the Kalwar community, traditionally sellers of alcohol, mass-boycotted the auction of liquor shops by the colonial government. There were reports too from rural areas of eastern United Provinces and adjoining Bihar of the Pasi community, whose traditional occupations had included extracting arrack from palm trees, pledging to give up this work and move into other more socially acceptable professions.

The axe of Gandhian morality fell also on the festival of spring and colour, Holi, marked always by an inversion of social mores and a relaxation of sexual boundaries. Through the late nineteenth and early decades of the twentieth century, Banaras newspapers had expended much newsprint lamenting the drunken and drugged revelries integral to the festival—with holis (songs relating to the festival) that included obscene galis, or abuses, being composed and sung (or recited) by the predominantly lower-class Holi merrymakers in the city streets. Respectable classes of the city, complained the newspaper, were forced to stay indoors because of the vulgarity on the roads.

The highlight of these carnivalesque celebrations were public processions with highly sexualised tableaus of comic figures, usually dressed as bride and bridegroom with oversized genitalia. Those passing through Dal Mandi would make their longest stop here to trade abuses and colour with the prostitutes and lower-class tawaifs, both Hindu and Muslim, standing on the balconies of their kothas.

No one in Banaras had seriously thought it possible that the spirit of Holi could ever be subdued. It is doubtful that even those who had supported the resolution for a more sober Holi at a non-cooperation meeting in Banaras a few days prior to the festival had any premonition of how effective their resolve would be in that momentous year.

In a detailed report titled 'Nationalist Holi in Kashi', the Hindi daily *Aaj* exulted:

> In these times of the non-cooperation movement, some youth reformers of the city decided to take out a nationalist procession and sing pure holis that would have a positive impact on people. Accordingly, on 25 March, this procession began from the Town Hall at 4 in the evening.

> It was led by rustic bhajan singers who carried on their shoulders swadeshi crafts for all to see. Behind them was a carriage bearing our national flag and the icons of Bharat Mata and Mahatma Gandhi. Following it was a carriage carrying the charkha, spinning wheel.
>
> All around, young men were enthusiastically raising slogans of *Bharat Mata ki Jai! Vande Mataram!* and *Hindu–Musalman ki Jai*. Many were singing nationalist bhajans and holis about the present state of our country: *Kiya jo zulm Dyer nay, voh honi thee so Holi hai*; The atrocities perpetrated by Dyer, this Holi we shall not forget.

It was indeed a Holi that no Banarasi would soon forget. Fakhru and other young men from the tawaif quarters returned home brimming with excitement about the nationalist passions engulfing the city that day. Sultana and the rest of her household heard from Fakhru about the grand welcome that the procession received in every locality it passed through. Thronging their balconies and terraces, people threw flowers at the procession below as it moved through the city's main thoroughfares to its centre, Chowk. People kept joining, across caste and class boundaries, all walking shoulder to shoulder. Muslims in various parts of the city welcomed the procession with paan and elaichi, green cardamom. And mosques were decorated with lights.

Moving past Dashashwamedh and Kundi Chowki, the procession reached Dal Mandi. Prem Kumar Khanna, as one of the main organisers, had prevailed against bitter opposition in getting the procession to make a special stop here. Eager to be part of these nationalist celebrations, the tawaifs, high and low, came out of their kothas and welcomed the procession with flowers and arti.

Banarsis also began to modify the much-favoured creative hobby of composing and singing holis, songs traditionally imbued with erotic sentiments and imagery. Under Gandhian influence, suitably nationalist and morally pure holis such as this one gained widespread currency in Banaras.

> *Holi hai bhai Holi hai*
> *Hindu, Musalman, Isai*
> *Desh key natey bhai bhai*
>
> Here comes Holi!
> Hindus, Muslims, Christians
> For the cause of the country join hands as brothers.

Appeals were also made for censoring the obscene from enactments of the Ramlila and tableaus taken out in procession during Nakataiyya, a popular Banaras fair linked to Dussehra festivities. Popular entertainments such as the theatre and nautanki too came under the nationalist scanner for obscenity and lewd content, and for employing women actors, singers and dancers from tawaif and other performing backgrounds.

Under the onslaught of Gandhian nationalism, fairs became unwelcoming to tawaifs and gonaharins and took on a more religious purpose and character. The fast-fading Burhwa Mangal was finally abandoned—the fair was not held in 1921. Its demise elicited few tears. On the contrary, angry letters to newspapers castigated the very idea of fairs, entertainments, wastefulness and flippancy at a time when Indians were suffering under colonial rule. Banarsis, it was argued, had an excessive love for frivolous pastimes and would do better to focus their energies instead on national interest.

Not surprisingly, tawaifs and sex workers were the worst hit. Gandhi deplored prostitution as a 'detestable crime', which 'the beast in man has made a lucrative profession'. About the devadasi tradition, he said, 'The Devadasi system is a blot upon those who countenance it. It would have died long ago but for the supineness of the public. Public conscience in this country lies dormant ... it often feels the awfulness of many a wrong, but is too often indifferent or too lazy to move.'

His bitter condemnation found an echo in earlier protests, such as the anti-nautch movement led by Hindu nationalists. Unlike them, however, Gandhi neither held the tawaifs and prostitutes guilty for the 'detestable crime' nor portrayed their prevalence as a legacy of Muslim rule designed to bring about the downfall of Hindu society. Representing tawaifs and prostitutes as hapless victims, he held men accountable for the perpetuation of prostitution. Deploring the practice on grounds of human degradation, and not as a marker of identity politics as projected by Hindu nationalists, Gandhi believed that prostitution damaged men no less than it did women: 'it is a matter of bitter shame and sorrow, of deep humiliation, that a number of women have to sell their chastity for man's lust. Man, the lawgiver will have to pay a dreadful penalty for the degradation he has imposed upon the so-called weaker sex.'

Gandhi's scathing attack on prostitution was closely linked to his ideas about the dangers posed to men and women by sexuality. Sexual intimacy, in Gandhi's worldview, threatened loyalties to higher causes:

to rule over the self and (as a logical extension) to achieving Swaraj. He emphasised restraint, if not complete chastity, for both men and women within marriage, and rejected the possibility of any sexual relationship outside it.

His views on prostitution also need to be understood in the context of his often contradictory views on the status of women. He vehemently opposed the subordination of women but, even while advocating equality, foresaw different roles for the genders. While man was the master of the world outside, the primary function of the woman was to look after the family, and as a wife be 'the queen, not the slave, of the household over which she presides'.

A man of bewildering contradictions and complexities, Gandhi, even while upholding women's primary role as caregivers in the family, not only encouraged their participation in the nationalist movement but also stressed that young women need not aspire solely to marriage and motherhood. To remain unmarried for the nobler purpose of serving society was, in his view, the ideal of self-realisation. Complete chastity, or brahmacharya, was a prerequisite not only for women but also for men choosing this path of service.

He urged Congress women volunteers to work for the rehabilitation of 'our fallen sisters'. Beyond asking prostitutes and tawaifs to give up their 'unworthy profession' and become 'sanyasins of India', Gandhi put forth few ideas about how to combat the practice. Khadi and charkha, his panacea for all ills, were the best that he could offer as alternative employment to women willing to abjure these professions.

As with many other aspects of the movement, Gandhi's followers interpreted his condemnation of prostitution in accordance with their own agendas of moral cleansing. Thus, in Amritsar, Gandhians began picketing the tawaif quarters in an attempt to forcibly prevent male patrons from visiting kothas. Panic-struck tawaifs began to flee Amritsar, and kothas started shutting down. Rumours of similar picketing in other towns and cities across northern India heightened the sense of anxiety among the tawaif community in Banaras, earlier under pressure from Hindu nationalists and now from Gandhi's followers—in many instances, the same set of people.

Prem Kumar did not approve of the picketing. In his view, true change of heart could never be achieved forcibly. The only way it could happen was through non-violent dialogue and reasoning with tawaifs and their patrons. Courtesans in Banaras heaved a sigh of relief when, led by Prem Kumar, one section of Congress volunteers in the city convinced another against picketing areas like Dal Mandi, Raja Darwaza and Nariyal Bazaar.

Profoundly influenced by Gandhi's views on prostitution, Prem Kumar's speech to the tawaifs assembled in Husna Bai's house was precise, forthright and brutal. 'My dear sisters, we have arrived at a historic moment. I appeal to each and every one assembled here to utilise this opportunity to do some collective soul-searching and realise the degrading, immoral and dishonourable lives you are being forced to lead by society, by men and sometimes even by your own greedy and selfish families. By performing obscene songs, vulgar dances and by forging illicit alliances with men, you are bringing shame to yourselves as women. There is no honour in wearing expensive clothes, glittering gold or in having wealthy admirers. True honour for a woman comes in modesty and chastity. These are a woman's true jewels.'

Prem Kumar Khanna had neither the talent nor the desire to embellish his views with pretty phrases and literary figures of speech. Coming straight to the point, he appealed to his sisters to cast off the shameful life they were being forced to lead. Girls who had so far not been dragged into this mire should be married off respectably. Women already in the profession should stop entertaining men in their kothas, renounce meat-eating and alcohol, cast off their practise of obscene songs and dances, and take an oath to lead chaste lives in the service of Mother India and Mahatma-ji.

The assembled tawaifs heard Prem Kumar Khanna's moral exhortations in stony silence. Sultana would grumble later to Gulab Jan that times were indeed bad for the tawaifs. What did this self-righteous idiot know of the long hours of riyaz and diligent art practice that they had put in to become tawaifs?

At the meeting, however, like the rest, she held her peace. Prem Kumar might be a fool, but in the storm that now threatened to destroy the tawaifs' lives and livelihood, he was their only beacon of hope.

In the age of Gandhian non-cooperation, tawaifs were increasingly finding themselves at the receiving end of their urban patrons' growing moral rectitude. As values of thrift, sobriety and abstinence became inextricably linked with national interest, aristocratic patrons of tawaifs in Banaras, who had earlier resisted moralists' attempts to police private musical soirees, now began to discontinue the practice of their own accord.

In addition, one major temple after another shut its doors to courtesan singers and dancers in 1921. The shrinking minority of important temples that continued to provide space for tawaifs' performance faced harsh criticism. 'A correspondent reports that prostitutes sang and danced on the nauvmi (ninth night) celebration of Navratras at Siddh Mata temple. In present times, when people are reforming themselves, why can't the organisers at this particular temple put an end to this vile tradition? Such performances distract the attention of devotees away from the goddess to the dancing prostitutes. Children too are adversely affected. We hope that in the future the organisers will heed this appeal and reform the celebration of festivals in their temple.' (*Aaj*, 20 April 1921)

While all sections of the courtesan community suffered adversely under these morality drives, elite tawaifs were decidedly the worst hit. Their art practice of thumri, dadra, tappa and kathak had defined the 'high' culture of Banaras, associated closely with the aristocracy. With merchant princes and religious establishments taking the lead in shunning them, elite tawaifs were now forced to become more dependent on their other traditional source of patronage, rulers of princely states and zamindars and taluqdars controlling the rural countryside.

Relatively less influenced by the prevailing moral rhetoric, various rajas and nawabs continued to invite tawaifs to perform at public celebrations and in private mehfils. Patronage from the landholding rural elite, however, became less assured. This was especially so in areas of the United Provinces and Bihar, where large sections of the peasantry were getting politicised under the influence of Kisan Sabhas—anti-feudal peasants' groups advocating farmers' rights.

News coming in from Pratapgarh, Raebareli, Sultanpur and Faizabad districts in the Awadh region spoke of a massive, grassroots agrarian movement led by Kisan Sabhas against arbitrary cesses, begar (forced, unpaid labour) and forcible evictions of tenants by oppressive taluqdars who had long enjoyed the support of the colonial government. Along with other symbols of feudal oppression, tawaifs too began to be targeted by the peasantry as markers of exploitative, repressive and debauched taluqdari excesses. The leaders of this peasants' movement in Awadh were little-known sanyasis, or mendicants, like Baba Janki Das and Baba Ram Chandra, a former indentured labourer in Fiji who, on his return home, began propagating the scriptures. Their discourse was marked with appeals for kisan solidarity, combined with the use of symbolism from the Ramayana and other religious texts. Moral righteousness was upheld in the same measure as demands for economic and social justice.

The movement reached a flashpoint in January 1921 when the taluqdars hit back at the protesting peasants with large-scale violence. The immediate catalyst for this action was a farmers' demonstration led by Baba Janki Das against Thakur Tribhuvan Bahadur Singh, the taluqdar of Nanhiyan estate in Raebareli. Interestingly, the peasants were protesting on behalf of the taluqdar's wife, who had approached the Kisan Sabha for help in pressuring her husband to abandon his tawaif mistress.

Protesting outside the haveli of Thakur Tribhuvan Bahadur Singh, the peasants demanded that he not only throw out his mistress immediately but also return to his wife all the jewellery that he had gifted to the tawaif. As punishment for this moral transgression, Baba Janki Das had also levied a token fine against the taluqdar. Furious, Tribhuvan Bahadur called in the deputy commissioner of police, who arrested Baba Janki Das and some of his supporters. This led to widespread peasant protests, which were met with violent and brutal reprisals from taluqdars who rallied together.

The peasantry was in no mood to cow down though. Agrarian riots swept across Awadh from January to March that year. Angry peasants attacked not only houses and standing crops of taluqdars but also properties belonging to merchants and moneylenders—ironically, in Gandhi's name. In certain instances, homes of tawaifs known to be mistresses of especially hated taluqdars were also attacked. On other occasions, angry crowds forcibly stopped mujra performances.

In a bid to buy peace, certain taluqdars, notably their wives, and in some cases widows, began making concessions. A news item in *Aaj* dated 7 May 1921 reported that the senior widow of the taluqdar of Amargarh in district Pratapgarh had lowered the rates of cesses extracted from tenants, and put an end to the practice of forcibly evicting tenants from their land. Moreover, she had refused to organise a tawaifs' mujra to celebrate her adoption of a baby boy. The report concluded by saying, 'this decision by her has made the subject population of Amargarh very happy'.

Terrorised by this turn of events, many tawaifs from Awadh towns of Barabanki, Pratapgarh and Raebareli began fleeing to the safety of friends' and relatives' kothas in Lucknow and Banaras. Beset with anxieties about the erosion of patronage from the urban elite, Sultana and other tawaifs now heard with mounting panic their guests' accounts of rural fury in Awadh.

News of the Awadh peasants' protests had also reached Kisan Sabhas active in other regions of the United Provinces, including the rural countryside surrounding Banaras. Protests began to gain momentum in these areas against not only the exploitative demands of landholders but also against cultural and social practices that an oppressed peasantry now decried as reflective of feudal immorality and vice.

The fair in Sultanpur, near Banaras, traditionally took place a day after Holi. Organised by local zamindars, the fair was famous for the large numbers of tawaif deras, or groups, that were invited to perform here from various cities and towns, but especially from Banaras. Although rural fairs—with their preponderance of peasant buyers and sellers—were usually the domain of lower-placed tawaifs, with elite courtesans considering it below their dignity to sing and dance for an audience of 'rustic bumpkins', the mela of Sultanpur was a performance space sought after by all ranks of women singers and dancers. Even Sultana's picky granddaughter Roshanara made an appearance every year in Sultanpur because of the rich and powerful Rajput and Bhumihar zamindars who showed up in considerable strength. While the more humbly placed tawaifs sang and danced and held sway out in the open, or under the shade of a ragged marquee for the general masses, elite courtesans like Roshanara performed exclusively for the landed aristocracy inside the latter's luxuriously furnished and carpeted tents.

The spring of 1921 in Sultanpur, however, brought with it not the languorous delights of balmy weather and Holi celebrations but the blistering winds of political change. Many among the long-oppressed peasantry, which had earlier looked forward to the fair for months, now began protesting the zamindars' practice of inviting 'prostitutes' to perform there. Sensing trouble, some zamindars agreed to cancel the tawaifs' performances they had organised, but many others, perceiving this as a slight to their position and privileges, refused to withdraw the invitations they had sent to courtesans. In retaliation, several groups of peasants declared that they would, if need be, forcibly stop 'prostitutes' from performing at the fair. Tensions began mounting as rumours spread about the possibility of the Sultanpur fair being engulfed by agrarian riots similar to those in Awadh.

Roshanara was among the tawaifs caught in the standoff between a defiant peasantry and aggressive zamindars. Although deeply anxious about performing at the fair, she could not risk the wrath of her zamindar patrons who would take any attempt by her to back out at this stage as a personal insult. Sultana spent hours in long meetings with several other tawaifs caught in the same predicament. Help, when it arrived, came from unexpected quarters.

Gandhi and other Congress leaders had noted the violent confrontation between peasants and taluqdars in Awadh. Apprehensive about alienating the landed elite, and eager for the sake of national unity to contain the internal schisms in Indian society, the Congress leadership, and especially Gandhi, took a very stern view of the protests against taluqdari excesses. He categorically denounced the use of violence by the Kisan Sabhas and their pitting of peasants against landholders, which he said went against the creed of satyagraha with its stress on non-violent persuasion. In a speech in Faizabad in February 1921, Gandhi 'deprecated all attempts to create discord between landlords and tenants and advised the tenants to suffer rather than fight, for they had to join all forces for fighting against the most powerful zamindar, namely the Government'. (*Leader*, 13 February 1921)

Over the coming months, the Kisan Sabhas in the United Provinces were brought firmly within the ambit of the Congress and non-cooperation activities, with specific peasant demands being relegated to the background. The process was not one of a smooth takeover, of course, but one rife with conflicting impulses—and, as always, with Congress leaders at the local level interpreting Gandhi in the context of their own circumstances.

In the countryside surrounding Banaras, therefore, while some Kisan Sabha leaders continued to mobilise peasants around the issue of land rights, most others utilised the platform to promote the non-cooperation agenda of Hindu–Muslim unity, spinning on the charkha and boycotting of foreign cloth and colonial law courts. Seeking to diffuse the immediate cause of tension brewing between the landholding zamindars and peasantry, Congress leaders based in Banaras, like Prem Kumar Khanna, who used every means to convince urban patrons to shun tawaifs, now searched desperately for a solution that would calm the peasants without jeopardising the zamindars' enjoyment of the courtesans' nach. In the end, they fell back on their Hindu nationalist legacy of using religious symbols in political protest.

Accordingly, Satyadev Shahi, president of the Banaras tehsil Congress committee and a prominent local Kisan Sabha leader, reached Sultanpur a day before the official start of the fair and appealed to all to maintain peace. Without disturbing the nach performances sponsored by the zamindars, Shahi and other local Kisan Sabha leaders organised a yagya, or religious sacrifice, as a parallel event at the fair.

For the moment, peace was brokered and everyone seemed satisfied. Zamindars, thankful for the face-saving settlement, extended all help to the Congress leaders in organising a grand yagya, even as they welcomed their own guests to the tawaifs' nach taking place in their tents. The protesting peasants joined in the yagya and raised rousing slogans of *Bharat Mata ki Jai* and *Mahatma Gandhi ki Jai*. Successful in dousing, in this instance, the fires of agrarian discontent, the Congress leaders returned to Banaras after the fair, happy with the generous contributions made by zamindars and peasants alike to the Tilak Swaraj Fund set up by Gandhi as a means to support the Congress's nationalist and social activities.

Bisraiho na balam hamar sudhiya; O my love, never forget your memories of me ...

Asghari is in a good mood. You are not. This is not unusual when Asghari, lips and nails glittering, visits. The Bhairavi dadra that she trills now, swaying dreamily on your balcony, is a family favourite. I have heard snatches of it from you and Pyaari khala, whose condition, Asghari informs me, is deteriorating fast—'any time now', she announces with a beatific smile and carries on with the dadra.

'And instead of preparing to leave for Bhabua, we sit here and hear you sing,' you retort, attempting to shift on to Asghari's shoulders the guilt you feel. Unusually for her, Asghari refuses to take offence. You whisper primly to me that it's the marijuana that Gabriela must have given Asghari. But you have no proof. Gabriela never smokes it in front of you. And you are too proud to ask whether she shares it on the sly with your sister. You disapprove, as you do all her other excesses, of your sister's love for the weed.

'Come, let's sing together!' Twirling around to face us, Asghari orders you with the enthusiasm of a little girl. You refuse at first but, under her barrage of pleading and demanding, you give in with ill grace. Asghari sings a line and you follow. Both of you reach the third stanza of the dadra. Asghari leads:

Ek mahal do raniya ho balam
Kavan raniya tu soiba ho balam, kavan raniya?
Bisraiho na balam hamar sudhiya

There is one palace with two queens
Which queen will you sleep with, my love? Which queen?
O' my love, never forget your memories of me

You follow:

Ek mahal do raniya ho balam
Kavan raniya tu jaiba ho balam, kavan raniya?
Bisraiho na balam hamar sudhiya

There is one palace with two queens
Which queen will you go to my love? Which queen?
O' my love, never forget your memories of me

Asghari, her benign humour evaporating, looks up sharply and corrects you in a hissed undertone, *Kavan raniya tu soiba ho balam*.

Choosing to ignore her, you repeat your version of the lyrics. Intrigued, I ask about the difference. Asghari elegantly shrugs. 'I sang the song as was taught to me by my ustad, Habib Khan Sahib,' she says, touching her earlobe gently with the right hand as she mentions her teacher's name. 'As far as I am aware, all the other tawaifs of my generation and even earlier ones, like Rasoolan, whose performance of this dadra I have heard on the gramophone, sang the same version. I don't know what this girl was singing now!'

You smile at being called a girl by the original claimant to eternal youth. But Asghari's sharp reprimand has hit home. Embarrassed, you clear your throat and explain, 'Aapa is right. She did sing the original version of this dadra ... but the words of the earlier version are too "open" ...'

'Open' is your euphemism for sexually explicit. I have heard you use it earlier. 'People don't like to hear such "open" songs now,' you explain earnestly. 'They form a wrong impression of artistes who sing such songs.'

My past conversations with you have made me aware that 'form a wrong impression' is your euphemism for saying that the audience labels the singer as sexually 'deviant' and 'available'. You are fond of using euphemisms. As an erstwhile tawaif desperately seeking a foothold in the musical life of contemporary Banaras, you find euphemisms useful.

This city, you say, has a dogala, a hypocritical attitude, towards tawaifs. While Banarsis never tire of extolling their cultural heritage of bol banao thumri and its associative subgenres like hori and chaiti, they have left no stone unturned to shame and victimise the original practitioners of the music they claim to love so much.

As the meeting in Husna Bai's house drew to a close, Sultana presented the real reason behind the call for this gathering. On behalf of all present, she proposed a resolution that had been drafted after careful thought by her, Husna Bai, Vidyadhari Bai and Prem Kumar Khanna.

The motion reiterated the allegiance of all present to the nationalist cause. Furthermore, it proposed the formation of the Gayika Sangh, a registered association of 'singing and dancing girls' that would protect the interests of its members and promote social and moral reform. Members of the Gayika Sangh would weed out obscenity in their performance of music and dance, abstain from the consumption of alcohol and other intoxicants, use only swadeshi hand-spun clothing and promote nationalism by singing patriotic songs on all occasions where they were invited to perform.

The shift from 'tawaif' to 'gayika' is significant. Trying to keep pace with the changing times, tawaifs were attempting a makeover of their traditional identity—an identity that, under sustained attack earlier from colonial quarters and then by the nationalists, had become overlaid with connotations of immorality and sexual vice. More importantly, with the erosion in traditional structures of patronage and customary norms that had earlier protected their lifestyle and art practice, the tawaif community was now reinventing itself as a trade association operating within the legal framework of colonial political economy.

The meeting concluded late in the evening with a vote of thanks moved by Vidyadhari Bai. Thanking Prem Kumar Khanna for gracing the assembly, she brought the proceedings to a close by announcing that a formal public meeting to pass the resolutions moved this evening would take place on the following evening, 9 August 1921, at the Adi Vishweshwara, the only major temple left in Banaras that still kept its doors open to 'gayikas'.

A report that appeared in *Aaj* on 10 August had this to say, 'Yesterday a meeting of prostitutes was held in Adi Vishweshwara temple. It was presided by a framed photograph of Mahatma Gandhi. The meeting began with the prostitute Husna praying for the well-being of the Emperor. She also stressed that the prostitutes needed to reform themselves. Vidyadhari said that we ought to stand by the country in its hour of need ... The prostitute Moti Bai spoke of the need to forsake singing of obscene songs. She also stressed upon the need for prostitutes to reform themselves. An organisation to work for the uplift of prostitutes, the "Gayika Sangh" was also formed.'

The tawaifs of Banaras, when they cast their lot with Gandhian nationalists, were not to foresee his outburst a few years later against what he termed the 'obscene manifesto' of a group of tawaifs in Barisal. Their crime? They had organised efforts to help the poor, nurse the sick and support the cause of Gandhi's satyagraha. Gandhi, when he encountered the group in 1925, declined to recognise them as Congress workers, or even accept their donations unless they gave up their unworthy profession, which made them 'more dangerous than thieves; while thieves merely stole material possessions these women stole virtue'.

In the fading light of an August dusk, I think I see two familiar figures sitting on the steps of Meer Ghat right below Alka Hotel, my home in Banaras. I peer out of my window and recognise Gabriela in her flowered, flowing linen pants and saffron singlet, sitting beside Asghari, dressed in one of her more violently pink saris. I wonder what these two unlikely companions are doing at this time of the evening in this deserted corner, and remember your suspicions regarding the source of Asghari's good humour. But from what I can make out, neither she nor Gabriela seem to be smoking.

My curiosity getting the better of me, I venture down to the ghats. Trying to look casual, I make my way with elaborate aimlessness towards the two women who have their backs to me. Fragments of laughter and snatches of a song that I had heard in your house earlier in the afternoon speak of good times gracing their corner of the now almost empty ghat. Asghari has donned for the evening her earlier avatar of the most successful tawaif in Banaras, and is recreating for a delighted Gabriela the performance of a seated mujra, complete with delicate hand movements and lightning-quick facial expressions, to bring out the many meanings embedded in *Bisraiho na balam hamar sudhiya*. She sings, as she did earlier today, the original 'open' version of the dadra.

The music and mime seem to dissolve the wide chasm of language, culture and age that divides the performer from her audience. Young Gabriela, overcoming the barrier of language that keeps her innocent perhaps of the actual meaning of the lyrics but not the sentiments imbued in the performance, keeps showering Asghari with a volley of '*Waah! Waah!*' that no doubt you taught her.

In the growing dark, hundreds of tiny lights bob on the Ganga, lamps offered by believers to the river at dusk. Behind me lingers the echo of temple bells ringing to signal evening arti. And in front of me, oblivious of my presence, sit an ageing, retired tawaif-turned-brothel keeper and a young European woman sharing a marijuana joint in post-performance silence. I quietly retrace my steps to the solitary confines of my hotel room and take out my notes.

CHAPTER 17

Bindo and Sultana

'Waah, bitiya! You are a mind-reader! Just this morning I was thinking that it would be so nice to have besan ki roti, chaulayi ka saag and lehsun ki lal chutney for lunch and, look, you have fulfilled my wish,' Shanney Khan Sahib beams at the repast laid out in front of him and then at you.

Placing a crisply baked and generously ghee-smeared gram-flour roti on your ustad's plate, you order him with the bossiness of a favourite daughter, 'Abba, now begin eating before it turns cold. And go easy on the chutney. It causes acidity, and I don't want you complaining of a stomach ache.' Spooning a tiny dab of chutney on his roti, you compensate with a generous helping of the chaulayi greens that your old teacher is so fond of.

As long as you have been his student, you have had this simple meal cooked as an offering to your ustad, at least once if not more times, during the monsoon season. Earlier, you would serve him this lunch at your house where he came to impart daily lessons in music. Now, in deference to his indifferent health and old age, we have brought the food, cooked by Salma this morning, to Shanney Khan's home in Chahmama.

Flanked by Dal Mandi on one side and Nai Sarak, the bustling artery of Banaras, on the other, Chahmama used to be closely identified with the Khan sahibs, the term of address in the world of Hindustani music for Muslim male accompanist musicians. In Chahmama, all the Khan sahibs belonged to the Shia Muslim Dhari community. Another branch lived in the outlying area of Shivala ghat, where descendants of the Mughal prince Jahandar Shah had been provided permanent refuge by the British.

The Dhari musicians of Banaras mostly played the sarangi, some the tabla and a few the sitar and harmonium. They were all related to each other by multiple ties of blood and marriage, and traced their lineage to Shori Miyan, the eighteenth-century musician who is credited with the evolution of tappa. His descendants in Banaras, as teachers and accompanists to the tawaifs, became an intrinsic part of the city's musical landscape.

Over the past decades, as tawaifs and their songs fell silent, so did the sarangis, tablas and harmoniums of their accompanists. While a lucky few found new avenues of employment as musicians in All India Radio, or as teachers in music schools or middle-class homes, most others were forced to either retire or reinvent themselves as shopkeepers, entrepreneurs, craftsmen and petty clerks. A large majority moved out of the area to new lands in search of a better future. Chahmama now has new inhabitants, mostly Muslims but also a few Hindu families, with little knowledge or interest in the musical history of their new home.

Shanney Khan's family is among the handful of Dhari musician households that continue to live in Chahmama. Of his seven sons, only two learnt music and, of them, only one, the eldest, carries on the family tradition as a harmonium player. The others earn their living as wholesale dealers in hosiery, small-time construction contractors and small-scale manufacturers of iron lathes.

There is no question of women in the family being taught music. Notwithstanding the historical references to women musicians from the community, in the Dhari households that I visited in Banaras and elsewhere, they play little or no role in the formal transmission of music teaching and learning. According to Shanney Khan Sahib, music learning has always been the domain of the men in his family for as far back as he can remember, with women being confined to running the house and rearing children.

From her inner room, Shanney Khan's wife, whom everyone addresses simply as 'amma', always listens intently to the music being played and sung in her husband's baithak. She might not have been formally taught music by her father, the well-known Shamim Khan Sahib, but her knowledge of the intricacies of raga-based singing and instrument playing is considerable. She discusses music animatedly with you and even points out the occasional flaw in your rendition of a particular piece. Still, amma is as categorical as her husband that no daughter or granddaughter of hers will be allowed to learn and practice music. That prerogative belongs only to the sons and grandsons, she says, sighing at their increasing alienation from the family's tradition.

Shanney Khan accepts the flight of music from his home with resigned equanimity. Music simply has no future in his community, he says. When I ask why, Shanney Khan answers with silence. Articulate only while speaking through his sarangi, he is happiest when playing, bow in one hand, instrument in the other, brows knitted in concentration, eyes half shut, lips parted in an unconscious, thoughtful smile and face lowered in calm repose.

In over six decades of his career as a sarangi player, Shanney Khan has accompanied, on the radio and in music conferences and concerts, some of the biggest names in thumri, dadra and ghazal singing: Rasoolan Bai, Siddheshwari Devi and Begum Akhtar. He has also taught music to a host of tawaif singers who, unable to break the glass ceiling of respectability imposed first by colonialism and then by nationalism, faded into oblivion, unrecognised, unsung.

In the past few decades, as long as his health allowed, he had, much as you do now, taken on as students several European and American tourists out on an India experience. He knew that, for many, their interest in Hindustani music would not outlast their holiday. But the earnings spared him from being financially dependent on his sons, and for this he was grateful. And so he would teach them with the same earnestness as he taught his other students.

Occasionally, Shanney Khan Sahib would also find at his doorstep professional musicians and musicologists genuinely interested in studying the sarangi. Impressed by the depth of his musical knowledge, they have brought him to the notice of academia, and it is not unusual, even now when his failing health does not permit him to take on new students, to find researchers from India and overseas visiting him in his Chahmama home. Bemused at the attention from these rather unexpected quarters, he usually lets his sarangi do all the talking. On the rare occasion that he does speak, he utilises the opportunity to promote you, once his most successful student, and now a musician struggling to earn a living and name in contemporary India's sanitised radio studios and concert auditoriums. It is what he did when I first met him too.

Quietly and without fuss, he tries hard to get you an audience, even if it is a motley one of researchers and tourists, much in the same manner that he promoted you with influential and wealthy patrons in your career as a tawaif. His motives then had not been entirely altruistic, as his name as a music teacher and earnings as an accompanist were linked directly to your fame and popularity as a tawaif. Now, in his winter years, Shanney Khan has no further need for material gain. He promotes your cause entirely in the service of love and loyalty.

Shanney Khan's association with you and your family goes back a generation to his uncle, music teacher and subsequently father-in-law, Shamim Khan Sahib, who had taught your aunt, Bindo. As a young student, he often accompanied his uncle to the double-storeyed house located on the main street of Dal Mandi, where Sultana Bai, her daughter Mumtaz and granddaughter Roshanara lived. Besides them, the house teemed with a host of sundry servants, poor relatives and long-term guests, including the quiet, disconsolate-looking young girl who spent her mornings learning music from his uncle. In your turn, you inherited Shanney Khan as your teacher and accompanist. After you, the musical link between the two families will rupture forever, as will the long association that Shanney Khan's clan has shared with tawaif performers.

Soon, we are joined by Ramzan Khan, old-time resident of Chahmama, and Shanney Khan's friend and neighbour. His father, Shammu Khan Sahib, is best remembered today as the long-time teacher and accompanist musician of one of the most illustrious tawaif musicians from Banaras, Rasoolan Bai

At eighty-plus, about the same age as Shanney Khan, Ramzan Khan is loquacious and eager to talk about the past. His love for music transcends his surprising lack of formal learning. When I ask why, his reply is simple, 'My father never asked me to follow his footsteps. Perhaps he felt that, if I was sufficiently interested, I would approach him of my own accord, because music played all day long in our home. I, on the other hand, kept waiting for him to indicate that he wished me to join the family tradition. When he didn't, I drifted on after schooling to odd jobs till I finally found employment in a shoe store in Dal Mandi. And that is where I worked for over forty years until I finally retired.'

This former shoe-shop clerk, however, knows everything there is to know, not just about the singing style and careers of scores of musicians, women and men, from Banaras but also those from outside. He remembers the details—the highlights and the embarrassing low points—of all the concerts held in the city ever since he was old enough to attend them. Which he did without fail, every single public music gathering organised here. Ramzan Khan's prodigious memory is aided by his labour of love—a pair of voluminous scrapbooks compiled over several decades, full of photographs of musicians, musical gatherings and concerts and Hindi and Urdu newspaper articles about them.

He has brought these at my request to Shanney Khan Sahib's home today. Thick A4-sized notebooks, covered neatly in brown paper like children's schoolbooks. This is Hindustani music history compiled by a music lover for his own enjoyment. I notice that the largest number of photographs and newspaper cuttings are of Rasoolan Bai. As her teacher's son, Ramzan Khan had enjoyed easy access to Rasoolan's home since boyhood. She treated him like a younger brother and, as he grew older, reposed great trust in him as her loyal companion and lieutenant in travels across the country to perform in concerts, music conferences and on the radio. Ramzan Khan travelled with Rasoolan everywhere, from Kashmir to Madras, from Calcutta to Jaipur. He was among the very few who knew Rasoolan Bai beyond her public image as one of Banaras's greatest singers of bol banao thumri.

Leafing through his scrapbooks, Ramzan Khan remembers the little details that give texture to what we know of Rasoolan: her deferential obedience to her ustad, Shammu Khan Sahib; her shyness; her introverted silences; her fretful nervousness before any performance; her blind indulgence of her only child, a son; her great fondness for cashew nuts, almonds and pistachios, which she would munch in fistfuls to relieve the boredom of long train journeys; her love for fine clothes and expensive jewellery in her youth, and her complete disinterest in both as she grew older.

Ramzan Khan's cheerful chatter is contagious. Not given to sharing stories about the many tawaifs he and his family have taught and accompanied, Shanney Khan Sahib, perhaps encouraged by the presence of his friend, begins telling us now, in his usual incoherent manner, the story of Bindo's journey to become a musician. You, with your inheritance of family memories, join your ustad in piecing together your aunt's life.

'Are you deaf, girl? Can't you get a single note right?' Shamim Khan's bushy eyebrows crossed in annoyance, his long, hooked nose quivered in fine frenzy, and his sarangi winced in pain as he gnashed into it with the bow. It was obvious that this morning too ustani had sent ustad off to work hungry after a quarrelling bout.

Ustad's wife, ustani to his students, was endowed with a flaming temper, the price of which was paid by the young apprentice-tawaifs whom Shamim Khan taught music to. He would shower upon them the angry words he dared not squeak in front of his beautiful, tempestuous wife. That day, ever since he settled down cross-legged with the sarangi in his lap, the ustad had raged and ranted at Bindo for the slightest lapse. Even her clumsy attempts at serving him tea and nashta had been brusquely rebuffed. Ustad was too angry and too hungry to eat. For the rest of the day, he would just feed off his students' abject suffering.

Bindo could hear muffled giggles from the adjoining room. Roshanara was, as usual, enjoying herself at Bindo's expense. Anger rose from the pit of her stomach and up her throat, but before it could come hurtling out, Bindo bit her tongue, pressed her lips tight together and swallowed hard. To make any retort would be foolish. Ustad's fury when provoked was many times more punishing than his ill-humour. Besides, he could complain to Sultana. And the consequences of that were too unpleasant to even contemplate.

Keeping her eyes downcast and her voice low, Bindo tried hard to play meek as Sultana had been trying to teach her for two years now. It was easier acting the part with ustad, who was, she had long guessed, behind his stern exterior, a kindly soul wishing his more deserving students well, and among them, he rated Bindo high. More importantly, Shamim Khan Sahib was among the very best teachers that Banaras had to offer tawaifs seeking mastery over purab ang gayaki.

By the second decade of the twentieth century, when Bindo shifted to Banaras, the bol banao thumri of the purab ang was in full bloom in the city, and its cultural hinterland of eastern United Provinces and Bihar, including Gaya, the other major centre of the genre. Its older sibling, the dance-based bandish thumri was in decline, forsaken for the charms of bol banao thumri, which combined the intensely personal expression of local folk songs with the intellectual abstraction of raga-based melodic improvisation. It resounded in mehfils in Banaras and outside, and on the gramophone, performed primarily by tawaif musicians who sang of ecstatic passion, pangs of separation, sexual longing, jealousy, anger, flirtation and even devotion that imbue the poetry of bol banao thumri.

Thumri has often been called by researchers the 'feminine voice' of Hindustani music. The poetic text of thumri is written from a feminine perspective, and is usually centred on the emotions experienced by the woman in love and on the celebration of the romantic play between Radha and Krishna. In bandish thumri, the main motif is usually the dalliance between Krishna and the milkmaids of Braj, but bol banao thumri most often depicts the longing of the heroine as she pines for her absent lover or a celebration of the moment of love. Steeped primarily, but not exclusively, in the rasa or moods of shringar (the erotic) and viraha (separation), much of the poetry of bol banao thumri, so beloved of the courtesans of Banaras, is written in Braj, Bhojpuri, Awadhi and Khari Boli.

Bindo had been introduced to bol banao thumri in Bhabua by Jhandey Khan Sahib. He had talked to her about the premium it placed on emotional expression. Too young to fully understand the meaning of his words, Bindo had sat through the lessons dreaming of the sweet parathas lined with gur that her cousin Teema made for her on special occasions. Then Jhandey Khan Sahib had left for Banaras, and Bindo's initiation into the music of his city had come to an abrupt halt. Now, at the threshold of puberty, Bindo had returned to those lessons under the guidance of Shamim Khan Sahib.

One morning in the early days, her new ustad had taken her for a walk to the river front. Gazing at the calm flow of the Ganga, its surface shimmering in the translucent light of a young sun, Shamim Khan Sahib compared bol banao thumri to the river. Like the Ganga in Banaras, the pace of bol banao thumri too is tranquil and reflective, he said to Bindo. Just like the slow-moving river that flows deep, so too the reposeful tempo of thumri hides within it depths of emotional experience. Like a skilled diver, a performer has to plunge deep inside to explore the many moods enclosed in a given phrase. With all the musical phrases and devices at her disposal, she must then give form to these nebulous feelings, give voice to the abstract expressions.

Bindo also learnt tappa, which was the speciality of the Dhari musician families. She enjoyed its rolling pace, its swift taans, which her ustad would say depict the emotional outbursts of lovers. Her education in this genre would deeply influence her rendition of bol banao thumri and its associative subgenres, hori, chaiti and kajari. Under Shamim Khan's guidance, she learnt how to incorporate varied ornaments of the tappa, like its taans, with grace and clarity into the reflective repose of her thumris. This style, known as tappe ki thumri, or thumri in the tappa style, was in fact a speciality of the Dhari musicians of Banaras, their contribution to the purab ang bol banao thumri.

The best-known exponent of this style was undoubtedly Rasoolan Bai, who could, with seeming effortlessness, incorporate elements from the tappa into her thoughtful and poignantly expressive thumris. Shamim Khan Sahib's favourite student Roshanara too, much to his pride, was being noticed for her rendition of tappe ki thumri.

Shamim Khan Sahib was miserly with his praise. Even Bindo's best efforts elicited only a brusque nod. When speaking about Roshanara, however, Shamim Khan would become uncharacteristically eloquent. Brimming with the impatience of the young, Bindo would be forced to listen, more often than she wanted, her ustad extol Roshanara's musical talent, her uncompromising riyaz and punctilious music practise.

The praise hurt. Everyone made much not just of Roshanara's virtuosity as a musician, but also her humility and polite manners, remarkable in a young tawaif clearly destined for fame. But Bindo knew from personal experience that the modesty masked an imperious arrogance. Roshanara was used to having her way, whether in the choice of men she would entertain, or in how she behaved with the battalion of poor relatives and clan members that camped permanently in Sultana's home. Never outright rude, she treated with calm condescension everyone outside the charmed circle of her immediate family, her grandmother Sultana and her mother Mumtaz.

Bindo did, however reluctantly, see the truth in Shamim Khan's praise for Roshanara's music. From the sidelines, as an apprentice-tawaif allowed occasionally by Sultana to sit behind accompanist musicians in mehfils held in their kotha in Dal Mandi, or at the homes of wealthy patrons, Bindo had secretly been in thrall of the older girl's flawless performance of music, abhinaya and subtle seduction.

'Each man in the mehfil has to be made to feel that he is Krishna himself and I the love-struck gopi. An electric current passes between me and each man in the mehfil.' As a young child, Bindo had heard Mushtari, a popular tawaif in their neighbourhood in Bhabua, boast about her abilities as a tawaif performer. Watching Roshanara in performance, Bindo had finally understood the meaning of Mushtari's words.

Seated on the floor at eye level with her audience in the intimacy of a small gathering, Roshanara would through voice modulation and abhinaya, which included dance gestures and facial expressions, convey the multiple meanings embedded in any given phrase of a thumri. She would make lingering, caressing eye contact with each member of her audience, as if singing for him and him alone. One moment coquettish, the next despondent and then passionate, her face would mirror myriad expressions, her limpid eyes would speak as eloquently as her singing and her hands, with their long tapering fingers, would conjure the illusion of dance.

Although trained in kathak, Roshanara and her class of elite courtesan performers in 1920s Banaras, unlike tawaifs of the previous generations, very rarely incorporated actual dancing in their performance of thumri, dadra, hori, chaiti or kajari. An obvious reason for this lay in the decelerated tempo of bol banao thumri, which did not lend itself to dance, unlike the lively and rhythm-based bandish thumri. A more fundamental cause was the changing social and aesthetic mores of music patrons under the influence of nationalism.

The anti-nautch movement, with its genesis in southern India, had targeted the devadasis and their art practice, comprising vocal music, of course, but more particularly their performance, in religious and secular settings, of dance, sadir. Termed obscene and vulgar by social reformers, sadir came to epitomise, for anti-nautch proponents, much more than her songs, the physicality of the devadasi and her sexuality.

In the context of northern India, the amalgamation of singing, dancing, flirtation and witty repartee that combined to form the tawaif's performance had traditionally been called mujra. When it reached the northern plains, the anti-nautch movement once again heaped the greater scorn upon the aspect of dance. The erotic physicality of the tawaif's dance was viewed by reformers as more threatening to the morals of respectable audiences than the singing, which could, with some modifications in its aesthetics, style and performance practice, be distanced from the corporeal sexuality of the singer.

It is not surprising, therefore, that elite tawaifs like Roshanara, already faced with social hostility and dwindling patronage, especially in urban centres, began weaning dance out of their public performances. When they did perform dance, it was only on special request from long-standing and important patrons in the intimacy of exclusive mehfils, or in the seclusion of their kotha at the opening of a performance devoted primarily to singing accompanied by abhinaya and hand movements.

In performance, the otherwise ordinary-looking Roshanara would transform magically into a ravishing beauty. Her round face and sallow complexion would glow in the light of a hundred candles. Her small eyes would sparkle with a thousand promises, and the playful, coquettish half-smile would somehow make her thin lips look alluringly fuller. As resplendent in a glittering peshvaz if performing in a formal celebration as in a shimmering sari when singing in the intimacy of a private mehfil, the stocky Roshanara would magically change into a lissom sylph, riding the winds with her soaring notes and graceful, quicksilver abhinaya.

Bindo was transfixed by this metamorphosis. She had often heard Sultana say that only tawaifs who could not sing needed a pretty face and lithe figure. Painfully aware as she grew older of her own plain looks, her short and stout frame, Bindo took heart from Sultana's words. Some of the most celebrated tawaif singers in Banaras, including Rasoolan, were in their daily lives as ordinary looking as her, perhaps more. If their singing could so stunningly redeem their physical appearance, then her own prodigious musical talent, once honed to perfection, would decidedly transform her into the most beautiful tawaif of Banaras.

At the threshold of puberty, Bindo was flooded by strange, new desires. She would spend long, solitary hours in front of the mirror flirting with her own reflection. Of the two star-spangled saris that Teema had given on her departure from Bhabua, Bindo would wear one and then the other. Partially covering her face with the sari end, Bindo would practise the half-smile, raising of one eyebrow and then the other, the feigned frown and puckering of the mouth that she had seen Roshanara do in performance. With the same single-minded concentration that she brought to her music practise, Bindo would cast lingering, caressing glances at an imaginary lover, a besotted patron smiling shyly back at her in her make-believe mehfil.

Her fantasies were Bindo's only true companions in the two years she had thus far spent in Sultana's home. Crowded with relatives and servants, the house had no one Bindo could call her own. She missed her family more acutely than she would even admit to herself. In the entire period Bindo had spent in Banaras, she had not even once seen the people she truly loved, her mother, her younger sisters and, most of all, Teema.

After sending Bindo off with Sa'dullah to Banaras, her cousin had left for Ranchi. Missing her desperately, Bindo would request Daya Singh, when he looked her up during his trips to Banaras, to either bring

Teema with him to the city or take her to Ranchi for a visit. Despite his assurances, however, Bindo's wait continued endlessly.

One day, engrossed in her own thoughts, Bindo slowly became aware of raised voices through her bolted door. It was almost noon. So, high and mighty Roshanara had finally deigned to wake up, she thought resentfully. Sultana never allowed Bindo to sleep beyond dawn. Listening closely, she detected a decidedly peevish note in Roshanara's voice, and the soothing sounds Sultana made in response.

Roshanara had not been served the cup of tea that she wanted as soon as she woke up. Bindo heard the older girl blame her for the catastrophe. The brat, Roshanara complained, was always busy either daydreaming or preening like a monkey in front of her mirror. Worse, Bindo was lazy and stubborn, refusing to serve tea as soon as Roshanara called out for it. She hated making a fuss, Roshanara added for good measure, but everyone in the house knew that she got a headache if she didn't get bed-tea on time.

Her eyes blazing, Bindo staggered out of the room to confront Roshanara and Sultana. 'I haven't come to Banaras to make tea for you! You forget that my father and I do not live on your charity. My cousin Teema pays your grandmother good money to keep us in your house. You can throw your weight around with your wretched relatives eating at your expense. But don't you dare expect me to slave over you as you make others do.'

Bindo raged hard, only to be met with the impassive, silent look Roshanara used so effectively to counter dissent. Shrugging dismissively, Roshanara ignored Bindo and addressed her grandmother instead, could ammai please ask the servants to speak softly as she had a headache? Then throwing a supercilious smile in Bindo's direction, she left the room.

In the ensuing silence, Bindo wished that she had kept her cool. Her impulsive fury had once again served her only sour humiliation at Roshanara's hands. She was uncomfortably aware too of Sultana's silence. What storm lurked behind it, she wondered uneasily.

Without a word to Bindo, Sultana stepped out on the balcony and called out to Sa'dullah, who was as usual loitering in the street below, 'Babu, can you come up immediately, please?' Sultana sounded uncharacteristically polite, and Bindo felt a cold shiver run down her spine.

Bindo shared a complicated relationship with her local guardian. Sultana was responsible for her growing ward. And she dispensed her duties well, not only arranging highly qualified teachers for her education in music, dance and the letters but also guiding her, in her typically rough manner, through the maze of cultural and social skills required of an elite tawaif. Sultana also protected Bindo from her father. True to the promise that she had made to Daya Singh, the old tawaif stood like a solid wall between Sa'dullah's greed and Bindo's future, winning her young ward's gratitude in return. As Teema and Daya Singh had wanted, Sultana had stripped Sa'dullah of any intervention in his daughter's life. He had no say in the choice of teachers for Bindo, nor was he asked or allowed to give his opinion about the course and duration of her education.

Yet, there was no denying that Sultana's words were hurtful, her discipline harsh and her favouritism towards Roshanara unbridled. Being treated as a poor relative in Sultana's house tore into Bindo's being like a thorn. She grudged Sultana's rules but also craved to win even the smallest measure of her approval. In the restricted world she had known thus far, there was no one Bindo resented and respected more than the protective and authoritative Sultana who could be as harsh in her reprimands as she was clever in devising ways to render them most punishing.

Bindo was not alone in her nervous foreboding. Shifty-eyed Sa'dullah got a start at hearing Sultana call him upstairs. It was not often that she spoke with him directly and, when she did, it did not augur well. Reluctantly tolerated as an unwanted but unavoidable presence, Sa'dullah had to make do with the pocket money sent for him by Daya Singh, which was just about enough to buy paan, an occasional kulhad of milk and other minor indulgences. An attempt in the early days to generate extra income on the sly one night by trying to pimp the pre-pubescent Bindo to a man he had picked up from the streets had ended in abject humiliation. Sultana had administered him a painful and long-drawn thrashing with her slipper, and had lost no time in suspending his small allowance as further punishment.

Sa'dullah had considered returning to Bhabua, but, while Sultana would be happy to see him leave, she would not allow him to take Bindo without Daya Singh's consent. And Daya Singh and Teema, he knew, would not consent. He could not remove Bindo forcibly from Sultana's custody either, and risk Daya Singh's wrath.

So it was best that Bindo stayed on in Sultana's house. And without her to put to lucrative use, there was little for Sa'dullah in Bhabua. He was better off in Banaras, living under Sultana's roof, eating out of her kitchen. Besides, leaving Bindo alone under Sultana's influence might mean permanently losing a potential breadwinner. Swallowing pride and anger, he had thus stayed on. After some time, Sultana allowed him back his pocket money but under the stern warning that he keep away from Bindo. Thereafter, he spent almost all his time out on the street. Exchanging gossip with shopkeepers, sundry workmen and accompanist musicians, he went up only at mealtimes.

Given his dread of work, this arrangement suited Sa'dullah just fine. He could now avoid most of the duties that other members in Sultana's vast household were obliged to perform. Even when he was given some errand to run, he would either mess it up badly or come up with some excuse or the other not to comply. And so cemented the impatient hostility directed at him by his hostess and her immediate family.

Assuming that he was called up to the house on account of some failed task, Sa'dullah was, therefore, taken aback when Sultana told him in a very calm voice to pack his bags. He and Bindo would have to vacate her house within the hour. Uncomprehending, Sa'dullah just gawked at Sultana.

Bindo too heard her local guardian's command to her father. She could hardly believe that Sultana meant what she had just said, but one look at the impassive face, the cold eyes and Bindo felt her world falling apart. Beset by terrible panic, she fell at Sultana's feet. 'Ammai, forgive me, don't send me away! Ammai, forgive me, don't send me away!' she kept repeating, as if in a trance, tears streaming down her pudgy cheeks, her body convulsed with sobs.

Sa'dullah, meanwhile, grabbed at this unexpected opportunity of removing Bindo from Sultana's control. 'Bai sahib, I don't know what this wretched girl has done to make you so angry. I will immediately take her away, but first please accept my most humble apologies on her behalf.'

Sa'dullah's thinly masked delight snapped Bindo out of her panicked daze. She turned on her father, 'You dirty beggar, don't you dare come anywhere near me. I spit on your face. You are a snake that eats its own children. I will die but not leave ammai's sanctuary. I will die, do you hear, die, but not go anywhere with you, you filthy, greedy bastard!' Bindo finally said aloud the terrible words she had hurled at him in her mind ever since Sa'dullah had smuggled a stranger into her room. She remembered how Sultana had charged in like a tigress and chased out the man and Sa'dullah. Who would protect Bindo if Sultana decided to forsake her? What would become of the shimmering future that Sultana had thus far been painstakingly crafting for her?

Turning back to Sultana, who sat still and seemingly indifferent, Bindo fell once again at her feet, 'Ammai, forgive me! Don't give me for slaughter to this butcher. He and his blind brother ruined my sister's life and now want to destroy mine too. Save me, ammai, from these snakes. Keep me in your sanctuary as you would a slave. I will serve you lifelong. I will drink the water with which you wash your feet. Just forgive me this once, ammai! I will never again give you reason to be angry with me.'

While Sultana remained impassive, Sa'dullah felt as if he had been punched hard in the stomach. He staggered out of the room, his head throbbing and his legs wobbly. Stumbling down in blind panic, he somehow reached his little corner under the staircase where he stored his bedding and took shelter in the bitter cold of winter nights. Curling up in its shadows like an injured dog, Sa'dullah fell into deep wakeful sleep.

He heard harsh voices and saw a pair of young tawaifs, sisters perhaps, clutching slippers in their hands and chasing their father down the street. Their voices merged with that of other tawaifs he had heard abuse their fathers and brothers in the lanes of Dal Mandi. And then he saw Bindo, or was it the docile Teema, her eyes glittering, hair streaming, plunge a knife into him.

Back-stabbing bitch! Ungrateful wretch! Who would have thought that he, Sa'dullah, would be humiliated by his own daughter?

He saw Bindo now in the pandemonium of that night he had brought the man into her room. While the old hag Sultana made a big, unnecessary scene, the girl was silent. She had neither cried out, nor wept, nor complained, but quietly slipped under the razai, quilt, and kept still. Why all this fuss now?

Sa'dullah woke up with a start. His throat felt parched. Sipping water from a broken kulhad, he now saw Bindo as she was a while ago, mouthing obscenities. The girl had poison not blood coursing through her veins. It was all Sultana's fault. She had turned his daughter against him. Girls in his family were obedient and docile. Look at Teema. Had she ever raised her voice until Daya Singh fucked her in body and mind, and turned her against her own father and uncle?

Feeling intensely sorry for himself, Sa'dullah burst into tears. For a long time, he just sat, sobbing. He would teach these snotty bitches a lesson they would never forget. He would get even with them. The thought made him feel much better immediately. It also made him feel hungry. Wiping his face, he crept up the stairs to Sultana's kitchen. There was always something there that he could safely pilfer without it being noticed; a leftover roti or two, a bit of curry, some sweets, a spoonful of homemade ghee.

In the calm that descended after Sa'dullah hurtled out of the room and Bindo fell into exhausted silence, Sultana planned her next move. So far so good, she sighed contentedly. The girl had been shown her rightful place. She deserved to be shaken out of the fancy airs she had begun giving herself. Now, she would think a thousand times before throwing another tantrum.

It didn't hurt either that, in the process, her scoundrel father had received a well-earned kick, that too from his own daughter. He would now know that if he ever dared to sell Bindo again, the girl would not need Sultana to protect her. Better still, the bitterness that had been building up over the years between father and daughter was now congealed into implacable hatred. The old matriarch was a firm believer in the imperial dictum of divide and rule, preferring to have those under her control in a state of mutual war, rather than uniting against her authority. But now what? What was the most appropriate closure to this most satisfactory bout of bloodletting?

As Sultana sat deep in thought, she did not notice the discreet cough at her doorway. Shamim Khan Sahib had arrived a while ago for his daily class with Bindo. Not finding her ready and waiting, the ustad had first fumed at his student's laxity. Soon, however, he became aware of the hurricane raging in Sultana's room. Sultana's nephew, Fakhru, who made it his business to know all there was to know about the goings on in the house, gave him the details of the drama.

As a rule, Shamim Khan maintained his distance from the parasites that thrived in Sultana's kotha. Minding his own business, he shunned the gossip they churned out daily. But today his concern for the fate of one of his favourite students compelled him to listen to Fakhru. What he heard left the ustad deeply anxious for Bindo's well-being.

His worry was underlaid by compassion. He knew of the small indignities, the petty humiliations that were the lot of dependents in Sultana's large household. Treated just a bit better than servants, they were expected to earn their stay by uncomplainingly obeying every command given by her, her daughter and granddaughter. And though Roshanara was undoubtedly his favourite student, he knew only too well the dismissive arrogance that she had inherited from her grandmother and the passive servility that she expected from young girls in the house.

The ustad was alert too to a development that few others in Sultana's household had yet noticed: Roshanara's intense jealousy of Bindo's musical potential. Since Sultana was bound by her promise to Daya Singh that she would arrange for Bindo the very best teachers available in Banaras, Roshanara could not hope to sever the girl's music lessons with Shamim Khan Sahib. Besides, to admit to feeling insecure about a chit of a girl would be too galling for Roshanara's pride. She, therefore, contented herself with making Bindo's stay as difficult as possible, ordering the girl around as if she were her personal maid-in-waiting. Bindo, no walkover herself, was quick to protest. Blind to her granddaughter's petty shenanigans, Sultana would hold Bindo solely responsible for the fierce strife that too often engulfed her household.

The ustad knew too of Sultana's capacity for ruthless manipulation, and understood quickly that she had whipped up the present storm to break his fiery, young student. He had witnessed this rite of passage countless times in tawaif households—the taming and conditioning by veterans of rebellious, impetuous, novice tawaifs into loyal, obedient and malleable contributors to the economy of the kotha. This battle of wills could be relatively brief, or prolonged and with unpredictable consequences, but it invariably left bruised egos, wounded relationships and beaten spirits in its wake.

Shamim Khan feared for Bindo. It was possible that she might be forced either by Roshanara and Sultana or by the good-for-nothing Sa'dullah to return to Bhabua. The ustad did not wish to lose his talented student. But even if Bindo stayed on in Banaras, she was too young and inexperienced, he felt, to survive the elaborate mind-games that Sultana and Roshanara played.

He worried about the effect this would have on her music. Bindo's singing had a fearless quality that very few musicians possessed. His challenge as her ustad had so far been to teach her voice control without obstructing the boldness of her singing. He realised that he was now confronted with a greater challenge yet—of protecting the free spirit that engendered the fearless voice. To meet this challenge, however, he would need to overcome his inhibitions about stepping out of line, beyond his station as a 'low-born' Dhari sarangi player.

In the complex hierarchies that govern the world of Hindustani music-makers, accompanist musicians—tabla, sarangi, harmonium and majira players—have traditionally ranked socially, economically and musically lower than the soloists: vocalists and instrumentalists playing the sarod, sitar and veena. Soloists are valorised for their theoretical understanding as well as practice of music. The vast array of accompanist musicians, on the other hand, are assumed to possess only a practice-based musical knowledge. While it might not be a fair assessment, this assumption governs the traditional hierarchies among Hindustani musicians.

Accompanist musicians are, moreover, dependent upon soloists for the opportunity to perform publicly; it is the soloist who chooses the accompanists. In deference to their status as teachers, the Dhari accompanist musicians were generally addressed in the kotha community as 'Khan sahib' and 'ustad' just as the Kathaks were called 'guru'. The deferential mode of address notwithstanding, there was no denying that they were dependent upon tawaifs for their livelihood. This was reflected in the break-up or baata of an evening's mujra earnings. Tawaifs, as vocalists as well as kotha owners, enjoyed the largest share in the proportion of nine annas of a rupee. The remaining seven annas were shared in varying proportions between the male accompanists—tabla players, sarangiyas and majira players.

Tawaifs also provided leadership to the larger community of musicians attached to the kotha. In Banaras, courtesans from among the Gandharva and elite Muslim clans were traditionally nominated the choudharayins of the musicians' panchayat called the saat taat—or the seven mats which included, besides Gandharva, Ramjani and Muslim tawaifs, accompanist male musicians from the Kathak, Kinnar, Dhari and Bhaat castes.

Acutely aware of his subservient status, Shamim Khan Sahib firmly believed in the saying *'Apni izzat, apney hath'*. One's respect lay in one's own hands. Always dressed in immaculate white, his beard neatly trimmed, hair oiled and combed back, he cut literally and figuratively a tall and imposing figure. His abstemiousness and rectitude complemented the stateliness of his bearing. Particular about offering namaz five times a day, Khan sahib would abjure music during the entire month of Ramzan and through the forty days of Moharram-related ritual mourning.

Unlike many other Khan sahibs and Kathak gurus, Shamim Khan was strict in his shunning of all intoxicants, be it the omnipresent marijuana and bhang or the more expensive alcohol. He rarely, if ever, joined the other accompanists in their paan-stained gossip sessions on street corners, preferring instead to head home at the end of an evening's work. If he was needed at an off-hour to play for an unexpected guest, he would have to be summoned especially from his house, not picked up, as other accompanist musicians were, from off the street.

There were accompanist musicians he knew who thought little of acting as glorified pimps, running messages and arranging meetings between besotted patrons and their favourite tawaifs in return for a few rupees. Such wretches, Shamim Khan Sahib would say, brought shame to the noble profession of music-making. Tawaifs' relationships with patrons, their choice of who to take on as lovers and who to unceremoniously drop, was no business of his. And woe to any patron who even hinted that he, Shamim Khan, compromise his dignity by acting as courier.

His other golden rule was never to spend more time than strictly necessary in a kotha. He disdained those pathetic, musically mediocre tabaliyas and sarangiyas who hung around in kothas, indulged in gossip and even helped with domestic chores in the hope of free meals, extra tips or to ingratiate themselves through flattery and obsequious kowtowing to wealthy and powerful tawaifs.

Hard-working and self-respecting, Shamim Khan was confident of his worth as a musician and as a teacher, and committed to safeguarding the integrity of his music. He expected no more than his fee and respectful obedience from his tawaif pupils, and his fair share in the evening's earnings from the mistress of the kotha. Maintaining a discreet, dignified distance from the household affairs of his students, the ustad refused to get drawn into the quarrels and the power games rife in many salons. He never took sides, never tried to play negotiator, trouble-maker or peace-broker for warring factions.

Little wonder then that he was one of the most venerable figures in the musicians' community in Banaras. Eminent tawaifs like Sultana Bai, Rasoolan's grandmother Adaalat Bai, Rajeshwari Bai, Vidyadhari and even Husna Bai treated him as they would an equal, extending him the honour of seating him on the same carpet, at equal level with them—a rare privilege indeed for a Dhari sarangi player.

Now, his duty as a teacher demanded that Shamim Khan Sahib stake the respect earned over decades for the well-being of his student. One rebuff from the acerbic Sultana, and his years of discipline and effort could come to naught. But it was a risk the ustad decided he must take.

Reaching Sultana's doorway, he coughed politely to indicate his presence. When no response was forthcoming, he coughed again, a little louder, and hesitantly stepped into the room. Sultana seemed to notice him then and, with an imperious gesture, signalled to him to come inside.

One leg placed gracefully over the other, Sultana sat comfortably on a high chair, while Bindo lay in a crumpled heap at her feet. Oblivious to the ustad's entry in the room, Bindo felt a hand pat her gently on the head and was overcome with relief. All would be well now. Sultana had forgiven her.

Bindo looked up and realised with a start that it was not Sultana but her ustad who was patting her on the head. His usually stern face was suffused with solicitous concern. Feeling overwhelmed, Bindo began whimpering softly.

More than a little surprised at Shamim Khan's uncharacteristic entry into kotha drama, Sultana watched his brief silent exchange with Bindo with a speculative look in her eyes. His words, when he finally spoke, took her even more by surprise.

'Bai sahib, I come to you with a humble request that I hope you will grant, with your goodness of heart. I know not what this child has said or done. I can guess that her behaviour must indeed have been reprehensible. As her teacher, I request your forgiveness on her behalf. Please overlook her mistakes this one last time, and allow her shelter in your gracious sanctuary. Her future will be ruined without your wise guidance and kind care. She must have by now realised her folly and will, no doubt, repent long and hard. I can assure you that not only will she mend her ways but will very soon, God willing, make us all proud in the world of music. Everyone will credit you for introducing to Banaras yet another great singer worthy of the name of your great house.'

This was the longest ever that Shamim Khan had spoken to Sultana. His body quivered and his hands trembled in nervous agitation.

Sultana was better trained to hide her emotions under a veneer of cool composure, but she was truly taken aback. In the course of his long association with her kotha, Shamim Khan had never asked for a favour, never made an undue request. He must see some exceptional talent in this girl to cast aside his legendary pride and plead so humbly on her behalf.

This drama was turning more interesting by the minute, Sultana chuckled inwardly. In return for granting forgiveness, she would not only get complete obedience from Bindo but also the ego of a snooty ustad served to her on a platter. She could well afford to be gracious.

'Khan sahib, it is noble of you to feel such concern for your student but please do not make me a sinner by asking me for forgiveness on this girl's behalf. What face will I show to the Maker with the burden of an ustad's apologies weighing so heavy on my shoulders?' With practised false humility, Sultana flashed a sincere smile at the abashed-looking Shamim Khan.

Then, turning towards Bindo, the old tawaif announced with charming grace, 'When your ustad wants you to be forgiven, who am I to stand in the way? Run along now and wash your face quickly, and get some sherbet prepared for Khan sahib. Then settle down for your lesson. I will apologise on your behalf to your ustad for the delay.' Flashing her dimples at both teacher and student, Sultana played the genial matriarch to perfection.

In her tiny cell, Bindo propped up the small, old mirror that had been discarded by Roshanara as too stained by age. Peering into its foggy depths, she saw a pale, stricken face, swollen eyes and a red nose. Weeping was no good for her plain looks.

Combing her dishevelled hair into a plait, Bindo took a deep breath and made three promises to herself. First, she would measure up to the faith that her ustad had reposed in her: one day, soon, she would make him proud of her as a singer—not just as a mehfil singer but as a gramophone artist of renown. Second, as soon as she began life as a tawaif, she would move out of Sultana's home. And third, she would become a musician far more glorious than Sultana's granddaughter. What Roshanara could do, she would do better, Bindo promised herself.

CHAPTER 18

Bindo Makes Her Debut

'LET'S SEARCH IN "B". THE record I was telling you about should be there.'

Peering through thick spectacles, forehead creased in concentration, Krishna Kumar Rastogi browses patiently through his methodically catalogued and neatly arranged collection of early twentieth-century gramophone recordings, a great majority of which are by tawaif singers, including those from Banaras.

The ground-floor baithak, or visitor's room, in Rastogi-ji's family haveli, where his archive is housed, is crowded with music-related memorabilia. Enveloped in a hushed silence, rows of solid steel almirahs line its thick walls on all four sides, their shelves packed with early twentieth-century music records, books about music and dance in Hindi and English, and copies of old Sanskrit, Persian and Bhasha manuscripts pertaining to Hindustani music.

In the centre stands Rastogi-ji's large worktable, strewn with newspapers, adhesive tape, screws, bits of wire, cassettes and CDs, and a two-in-one music system. Next to the table, on a long, low settee, are arranged neatly his collection of musical instruments from Banarasi history: a beautifully carved old tanpura, a sarangi glistening with age, a sitar, a pair of tablas, a mridang and majiras.

It is easy to imagine that time stands still in this room. And yet, much like the mythology of 'eternal' Banaras, the timelessness of this baithak too is illusionary. In the far corner sits a French ethnomusicologist, armed with sophisticated digital camera and scanner, laboriously digitising a big brittle bundle of nineteenth-century music manuscripts. This is his gift of gratitude to the archive, which provided him with a welcoming space for his research. Many of the archival documents in Rastogi-ji's collection have been preserved thus for posterity by grateful users. And many more wait their turn.

Rastogi-ji's collection is among the few music archives I know of that are free of red tape or other rules and regulations. It is open to everyone—music lovers, musicians, scholars and ordinary denizens of the city—interested in exploring the musical heritage of northern India, particularly that of Banaras. His love for music transcends the barricades of possessiveness, secretiveness and insecurity typical of collectors who, while boasting of the cultural gems in their possession, are usually very cagey about sharing them with anyone outside a charmed circle of family, close friends or potential buyers.

Rastogi-ji, while blessed with the collector's obsession to retrieve and acquire, is free of the covetous personal greed that often marks such endeavours. Aptly named Dharohar, or heritage, his music archive—in his own words— 'belongs to all interested in music'.

'Aah! Found it!' With a triumphant look, Rastogi-ji flourishes a record of Mohammad Bandi, which he thinks could be your aunt Bindo's sobriquet as a gramophone singer. Thrilled at the prospect of actually hearing the voice of the woman whose life fragments have come to me from different sources, I eagerly reach for the record.

A closer inspection, however, dampens my excitement. Quite uncharacteristically, Rastogi-ji has failed to notice the serial index imprinted on the record label. This record was made in 1908, a few years before Bindo was born. I discover later that it is of a much-acclaimed tawaif from Patna, Mohammad Bandi, who sang extensively for the gramophone in the early years of the twentieth century. The first two decades of the recording industry in India, since its beginnings in 1902, are inextricably linked with courtesan performers like her.

'Talking machines', the phonograph and gramophone, imported from Europe and America, made an appearance in the Indian market by the end of the nineteenth century. They caught the imagination of the Indian urban elite, who recorded and played back over and over again their own voices and that of loved ones and of well-known personalities and literary, political and cultural icons. There was also at the same time a growing demand for recorded indigenous music that promised a further boost in the sale of talking machines.

By early twentieth century, sensing a huge business opportunity, European and American recording companies entered a frenzied race to capture Indian markets, not only for the sale of phonographs and gramophones but equally for the commercial distribution of recorded music, specifically of recordings made by local singers. The first to arrive on Indian shores in 1902 was the London-based Gramophone and Typewriter Ltd (GTL) that, after 1908, would be known simply as the Gramophone Company Ltd.

The company's first Indian 'recording expedition' was led by thirty-year-old American sound engineer Fred Gaisberg. In his six-week stay in Calcutta, Gaisberg made over 550 recordings of local music talent, the best remembered being the records cut by *'The First Dancing Girl of Calcutta'*, Gauhar Jan.

Although she is widely credited as the first musician in India to be recorded on the gramophone in 1902, that was not, in fact, the case—though it is certainly true that Gauhar Jan was the first vocalist of renown in India to perform for the GTL. The credit for being the first ever to record goes to two young performers associated with Classic Theatre in Calcutta, fourteen-year-old Miss Shoshi Mukhi and sixteen-year-old Miss Fani Bala, described dismissively in his diary by Gaisberg (who had neither any previous experience of India nor any taste or knowledge of Indian music) as 'two little nautch girls ... with miserable voices'.

Condemned to anonymity, Shoshi Mukhi and Fani Bala remain forgotten in the annals of Indian music, as do, with notable exceptions like Gauhar Jan and Janaki Bai 'Chhappan Chhurri', over 300 professional female performers, belonging mostly to either the temple-based devadasi and jogan communities or to tawaif groups. These women comprise the overwhelming majority of vocalists who recorded prolifically in the first two decades of the twentieth century for European, American and Indian record companies: GTL and its subsequent business rivals like Nicole Records from England, Beka Records and Odeon Records from Germany, Parthephone and Cinema Company Records from France, and Kamla Records and Binapani Records from India, including several others.

Among the early recordists were several leading tawaifs from Banaras, including Badi Moti Bai, Chandrakala Bai, Husna Bai, Shiv Kunwar Bai, Vidyadhari Bai and Wazir Jan. Under attack for their customary lifestyle and music practice, they, along with tawaifs from elsewhere, had been quick to embark upon the avenues opened by the newly emerging industries of mass entertainment, such as the theatre and talking machines, to reinvent themselves as stage actresses and gramophone singers.

Male practitioners of Hindustani music, on the other hand, with a few notable exceptions, like Ustad Abdul Karim Khan, had initially shied away from the gramophone because of its time limit of a little over three minutes. The rendition of art music compositions are traditionally based upon abstract melodic improvisation and leisurely elaboration of the subtle nuances of a single raga, sometimes over several hours. Male musicians, therefore, refused to engage with what they saw as a crass instrument that violated the sanctity of music. They were also reluctant to share with an unknown mass audience their exclusive musical repertoires customarily performed in private soirees for a select audience of princely patrons and local elite. Many even feared 'losing' their voices literally to the technology of sound recording and reproduction that was rumoured to 'suck out' the very soul of the performer.

Unfettered by such inhibitions and fears, the tawaif singers quickly adapted to the time constraint of the format. The gramophone made possible the dissociation of their romantic and erotic songs from the sexual physicality of their traditional performance in intimate soirees for male patrons. These songs were recorded now in a functional studio for an anonymous mass audience. Many tawaif gramophone singers used their new identity to distance themselves from their increasingly stigmatised past. Since professional performance of music and dance was associated with tawaif and devadasi communities, several courtesan singers began to insist that recording companies list them as 'amateurs'.

These early gramophone artists enjoyed immense popularity. Black-and-white and hand-painted photographs of them were mass printed in Europe as picture postcards and matchbox covers, and widely circulated as pin-ups in the Indian market for predominantly male buyers. The popularity of their music is corroborated by early twentieth-century cheaply produced, mass-circulated 'chapbooks' containing lyrics and other details of the bestselling songs recorded by tawaif singers.

In these early decades, while many tawaif singers adopted new identities as gramophone artistes, the greater majority continued to straddle the twin worlds of the kotha and the recording studio. The spread of their fame across the country as gramophone singers added mystique to their persona as tawaifs that, though now increasingly reviled, continued simultaneously to evoke fascination.

Despite growing public censoriousness, almost until the non-cooperation movement, tawaifs continued to be feted in private mehfils by merchant patrons like Krishna Kumar Rastogi's grandfather Babu Purshottam Lall in Banaras. His genuine love for the tawaifs' music, combined with an individualistic streak that baulked at meek submission to collective diktats, ensured that Babu Purshottam Lall would maintain the fine balance between conforming and rebelling.

'My grandfather continued to organise private mehfils in the music room upstairs where the best-known ganey walis from Banaras and outside were invited.' Rastogi-ji too prefers the euphemism 'ganey wali' to 'tawaif'.

Purshottam Lall reserved the baithak downstairs, where we sit now, for more nationalist pursuits. With a somewhat embarrassed laugh, Rastogi-ji chooses his words carefully, 'My grandfather would in this very baithak organise Kashi Sangeet Samaj concerts, open to all, where, naturally, no ganey wali was ever invited.'

Credited with being the earliest music society in Banaras, Kashi Sangeet Samaj was founded in 1905 by a group of wealthy merchants from the city, including Babu Purshottam Lall, with the blessings of cultural nationalists Vishnu Narayan Bhatkhande and Vishnu Digambar Paluskar. As part of its mandate to retrieve, safeguard and promote a national tradition of 'classical' music located in ancient Sanskrit texts and modes of learning, the Kashi Sangeet Samaj funded music classes for the teaching of dhrupad and khayal to boys from middle-class families, and organised regular music concerts by overwhelmingly Hindu male musicians, mostly from outside Banaras.

Nationalism had brought with it the need for music that was spiritual, classical, morally uplifting and reflective of India's ancient Hindu heritage. The problem confronting the cultural nationalists was that Hindustani music practice at the turn of the century did not quite conform to these notions. The antiquity of its major genres, like khayal and thumri in their present form, could not be traced back beyond a few centuries. Its close links with court-based patronage imbued Hindustani music practice, in the eyes of middle-class nationalists, with bawdy associations and an unacceptable morality based on pleasure seeking.

Reasons had to be found and blame apportioned to explain the disjunction between an idealised past and, from the nationalists' point of view, a far from perfect present. Accordingly, early twentieth-century cultural nationalists, among them Bhatkhande and Paluskar, focused their attack on the corrupting influence of its past patrons, i.e. Muslim rulers, and its practitioners—tawaif singers and Muslim ustads—seen as interlopers in a sacred tradition.

'The advent in India of the Musalman conquerors marked the date of the decline of all the arts and sciences purely Hindu,' said Vishnu Narayan Bhatkhande in his speech in Baroda in 1916. (Later published as *A Short Historical Survey of the Music of Upper India* by the Indian Musicological Society, Baroda.) He and others of his ilk constantly bemoaned the displacement of Hindustani music in the hands of 'ignorant and narrow-minded' Muslim ustads and 'dancing girls', and argued that Indian music needed to be 'rescued' by morally upright, dedicated and educated men.

Bhatkhande stressed upon the need for music theory to be revamped to make it 'scientific' and in line with Hindu shastra-based 'classical' pedagogy. Music learning, practice and performance had to be simultaneously relocated to suitably sanitised new venues, like music schools and colleges, music societies, music conferences and public concerts largely patronised by the middle classes. To make music acceptable in the homes of the middle classes, Bhatkhande also composed several suitably spiritual and morally uplifting khayal bandishes in an attempt to offset a body of earlier khayal lyrics that were perceived to be obscene and offensive to respectable sensibilities.

Needless to say, tawaifs and Muslim ustads were excluded from this nationalist project. Groping for words to soften hurtful histories, Rastogi-ji says, 'Committed to the promotion of shashtriya sangeet, shastra-based music, Kashi Sangeet Samaj organised music sessions of classical genres like dhrupad and khayal. Patronage of semi-classical and light classical music, like thumri, dadra, ghazal etc., sung more usually by women, fell outside its mandate.'

Catholic in his love for music and non-sectarian in his respect for musicians, Rastogi-ji is an unlikely inheritor of this baithak's cultural nationalist legacy. As the present organiser of the activities of Kashi Sangeet Samaj, he is guided primarily by his commitment to sangeet seva that recognises no barriers in music and between musicians. It is fitting that, under his aegis, an organisation that in the past so zealously excluded tawaifs and Muslim male musicians from its activities should now share space with his music archive and its vast collection of recordings by courtesan musicians, both Hindu and Muslim.

I consider the matter, then ask bluntly, 'Did nationalist hostility towards tawaifs too play some role in Kashi Sangeet Samaj's decision not to invite them to perform at its concerts?'

Flanked by life-size portraits of the presiding deities of Kashi Sangeet Samaj—Vishnu Narayan Bhatkhande and Vishnu Digambar Paluskar—Rastogi-ji's response is straightforward: 'Yes. That, of course, played a major part. But Kashi Sangeet Samaj was not the only music society to shun ganey walis. Most music societies in other cities too kept them out. They were not invited to perform in conferences organised during that period either.' He refers to the twentieth-century cultural phenomenon of music conferences that brought art music out of aristocratic music halls and princely soirees and into the public space.

Organised by cultural nationalists of diverse hues but with a shared vision of promoting Indian music as part of the nation-building activity, music conferences brought together scholars and practitioners before a mainly middle-class audience in different parts of the country. The earliest music conference was organised in 1912 in Thanjavur by a Christian practitioner of ayurveda, Dr Abraham Pandithar, as a 'Sangam' of Carnatic music, with the aim 'to promote an academic interest in and to diffuse a knowledge of all that was best in the science and practice of Indian Music'.

In the north, the best known and most influential initiatives came a bit later from Bhatkhande and Paluskar. Though bitter rivals, the two were united in common cause: that of forging a Hindu-oriented, middle-class-based, classical, national music culture.

Vishnu Narayan Bhatkhande organised the first All India Music Conference in Baroda in 1916, sponsored by the ruler of that princely state. In his opening speech, Bhatkhande reiterated the Hindu cultural nationalists' discourse of holding Muslim rulers and musicians guilty of corrupting shastra-based musical traditions in north India: 'The Mohammedan rulers naturally patronised at their courts their own co-religionists as musicians and who, by pandering to the tastes of their masters, commenced to take all sorts of liberties with the orthodox Sanskrit melodies.' Complaining that 'today the only music we hear is that sung by the dancing girls and their sarangi players', Bhatkhande proposed his agenda for the conference: 'The time has now arrived when the educated classes should take up the subject in hand earnestly.'

Enlisting the support of princely and wealthy sponsors, colonial authorities and influential local music societies, like the Kashi Sangeet Samaj, Bhatkhande organised four more conferences in Delhi (1918), Banaras (1919) and Lucknow (1925 and 1926). The conferences focused on music theory, and the need to develop a classificatory system for Hindustani music, based on ten parent scales, or thaat. Also on the agenda was the devising of a system of notation and the creation of a suitable pedagogy for music-teaching institutions. Speaker after speaker at these conferences waxed eloquent about the existence of a superior understanding of classical music in ancient Sanskrit texts.

Not surprisingly, the events were dominated by the Hindu middle-class intelligentsia. While scholars debated the finer points of music theory and the accuracy of one shastric text over the other, the participating musicians were expected to provide only practical demonstrations. Ironically enough, a great majority of the latter were Muslim khandani musicians upon whose lineage Bhatkhande heaped blame for the downfall of Indian music. Their presence at these events was at the behest of princely patrons who considered it a matter of personal prestige to 'lend' musicians attached to their courts to Bhatkhande's conferences. This, along with generous financial help, were the contributions that the princely classes were happy to make towards the eminently respectable national project of rescuing Hindustani music.

Vishnu Digambar Paluskar too organised several such events during the same period. He convened his first music conference in 1918 in Bombay. In keeping with Paluskar's identity as a practising musician, the agenda of his events was to popularise appropriately Hindu, spiritual and classical music. Although participants in these events too spent considerable time discussing music theory, the focus was on performances, and the events themselves were steeped in Hindu religiosity.

Though smaller in scale and less well-publicised than Bhatkhande's events, and shorn of the participation of princes and wealthy sponsors, Paluskar's efforts helped to popularise the format of music conferences across India. Over the decades, these transformed into marathon performance festivals rather than venues for scholarly debate. Making good use of the rapport he shared with some Congress leaders, Paluskar, besides organising his own events, was also able to make music conferences an adjunct feature of several Indian National Congress sessions.

Differing though they were in emphases and activities, the music conferences convened by both Bhatkhande and Paluskar were informed by a shared contempt for the traditional practitioners of Hindustani music. While Muslim male musicians who actually held the knowledge of music performance desired by the conferences organised by Bhatkhande could not be dispensed with altogether, they, and their Hindu counterparts, were not only seated separately from the middle-class intelligentsia but treated like artisans and craftsmen devoid of theoretical knowledge. In Paluskar's conferences, Muslim male musicians had a minimal presence, with most of the participants being former or current students of his music school, Gandharva Mahavidyalaya, and predominantly Hindu.

Tawaif musicians were not welcome at all, at either set of conferences. With the solitary exception of Veena Dhanammal—a famous veena performer of devadasi origin, who participated in the first All India Music Conference in Baroda in 1916 at the insistence of Sir Tanjore Madhava Rao, the powerful dewan of Baroda—no courtesan musician was invited to perform at these events. An official resolution was passed during the third All India Music Conference organised in Banaras in 1919, formally banning the participation of tawaifs from its proceedings.

'Kashi Sangeet Samaj was closely involved in organising the All India Music Conference in Banaras in 1919. It was a ticketed event and took place at the Vishweshwara Theatre at Bansphatak. Bhatkhande-ji and Paluskar-ji both were present. It was attended by princes of various principalities, big zamindars and their musicians. Eighty-eight male musicians in all, vocalists and instrumentalists, attended the conference,' Rastogi-ji intones sleepily, his penchant for minutiae none the thinner for it.

Then, sensing perhaps my next question, he adds quickly, 'There were no women musicians present.'

I ask him if it was true that a delegation of tawaif singers in the city, led by Husna Bai, had met his grandfather when they heard about the conference, and requested him that they too be invited to perform. It is said that he was sympathetic to their cause but knew that neither Bhatkhande nor the other members of Kashi Sangeet Samaj would agree to the proposal, and so had little option but to turn down their appeal.

Rastogi-ji politely refuses to corroborate the veracity of the story that I heard from Tara. He reiterates, however, that his grandfather did not share the prejudice against ganey walis.

Unwelcome in the emerging new performance spaces of music conferences and music societies, and increasingly pushed out even from their customary venues, such as elite homes of patrons like Babu Purshottam Lall, tawaifs began veering in larger numbers towards the newly emerging technology of motion pictures, and the more established media of the theatre and the gramophone. The gramophone industry had, in the meanwhile, been going through several changes. By the 1920s, attracted by its success, there had been an influx of established male musicians into the arena of recorded music. They were followed a bit later by the first generation of female singers from the middle-classes. The entry of these new voices contributed to a waning in numbers of tawaif vocalists in the industry.

Their marginalisation was accelerated by the increasing stranglehold of nationalist morality over all areas of aesthetic expression, including gramophone recordings. Middle-class consumers of recorded music had reservations about the disreputable origins of tawaif singers in the industry. Even more, they frowned upon the explicitly erotic lyrics of many tawaif songs and the uninhibited style of their singing.

By the 1920s, therefore, the total number of tawaif singers recording for the gramophone was substantially lesser than in the previous two decades. Only those who displayed exceptional musical talent, or already enjoyed high acclaim for their musical skills, were approached by gramophone companies, which were now not only better placed to choose the best among a host of musicians eager to record but had also developed a network of recruiting agents and distributors rooted in the local milieu.

'It is not that ganey walis disappeared from the recording industry after the 1920s,' Rastogi-ji explains. 'Some of the biggest stars of the gramophone of this period, in fact, were ganey walis and singers from related performing backgrounds. Musicians like Janaki Bai "Chhappan Chhurri", Mushtari Bai, Inayat Bai, Imam Bandi, Badi Moti Bai, Vidyadhari Bai, Bai Sundarabai and Mehboobjan made great names in the industry through the 1920s. Bai Sundarabai was even awarded a medal by HMV in 1926–27 for being their highest recorded singer.'

The reigning superstar of the gramophone industry in the 1920s undoubtedly was the pre-eminent tawaif singer, Janaki Bai 'Chhappan Chhurri' of Allahabad. Born in Banaras around 1880, Janaki Bai had been brought to Allahabad at the age of seven by her mother Manki Bai for musical training from Ustad Hassu Khan of Lucknow. Later, she also received training, it is believed, from Ustad Mojuddin Khan, the thumri maestro from Banaras.

Deriving part of her name from the fifty-six (chhappan) knife (chhurri) slashes made across her face by a jealous lover, Janaki Bai was a well-known poet in Urdu and Persian with a published divan, or compilation, of poems, *Divan-i-Janaki*, to her credit. She sang many of her own compositions, setting them to music. Affectionately called Bulbul, or Nightingale, by her admirers, she had been specially invited, along with Gauhar Jan, to perform at the Delhi Durbar of 1911, where together they sang *Mubarak ho, mubarak ho yeh jalsa tajposhi ka* (Blessed is this day of the coronation) to commemorate the coronation of George V as emperor of British India.

Princes and powerful zamindars vied with each other to invite Janaki Bai to perform in their mehfils. Every Dussehra, she sang at the mehfil of the maharaja of Bettiah. She was also a regular performer for the maharaja of Patiala. She was equally popular with music lovers of more modest means who knew her primarily through her gramophone recordings. Beginning her gramophone career in 1907, by 1920, she was the highest-paid gramophone artist, charging Rs 2,000 per recording session.

'You are back!' Tara Bai cackles delightedly when I announce my entry. You and I have dropped in to spend time with her in the evening. I tell her about my unsuccessful attempts to trace Bindo's gramophone recordings.

'I think Bindo probably did record for the gramophone, but I am not absolutely certain because, for a long period in between, I was away from Banaras in the employment of the raja sahib of Fatehpur.' The raja sahib was her long-standing patron and Chanda's father, a two-decade-long relationship that ended only with his death.

'I lost touch with a lot of my friends, including Bindo, during the period I lived in Fatehpur. She and I were close when she was very young and I on the threshold of entering the line. I clearly remember how much she wanted to become a gramophone singer. She idolised Janaki Bai and would often tell me that one day she would become as famous a gramophone artist as her. Whenever she got an opportunity, Bindo would cajole Fakhru into playing for her Janaki Bai's records on the beautiful gramophone gifted to Sultana by an old patron.'

Janaki Bai had a vast and varied repertoire of recordings, ranging from thumri, hori, kajari, dadra to ghazal, bhajan, qawwali and naat, which Bindo would listen to with rapt attention and try to memorise. Occasionally, Bindo's teacher, Shamim Khan Sahib would chance upon

Bindo lost in Janaki Bai's music. An admirer of the great singer himself, he would point out to his young student Janaki Bai's ability to sing even the most difficult songs in an easy flow, without any strain. Marked with rich vocal modulation, her singing, the ustad would explain, reflected both verve and creativity.

It was again through the gramophone that Bindo discovered the music of Ustad Abdul Karim Khan, doyen of the Kirana gharana of khayal singing. He recorded several thumris as well. His reflective renditions were in marked contrast to Janaki Bai's ebullient singing. Deeply inspired, Bindo's singing of bol banao thumri in the years to come would subtly incorporate many elements of the meditative expanse of his khayal renditions and the spiritual pensiveness of his thumris. At the same time, in keeping with her highly individualistic personality, depending upon the composition, her singing would also reflect the effervescence that characterised Janaki Bai's music.

'I remember Bindo's excitement when she heard that she would be making her debut at a mehfil in Patna where Janaki Bai would also be present,' Tara recalls. 'This musical gathering was to be the high point of the celebrations organised by the famous lawyer, Sir Sultan Ahmad, for his son's wedding with the daughter of Nawab Syed Akbar Ali Khan of Patna in 1925.'

A highly successful barrister, Sir Sultan belonged to one of the most influential landowning Muslim families in Bihar. His cousin, Syed Hasan Imam, had served as president of the Indian National Congress. Sir Sultan, on the other hand, played a prominent role in the Bengal Muslim League. He was also a distinguished educationist and instrumental in the establishment of Patna University in 1917, of which he was appointed vice chancellor from 1923 to 1930.

'I tagged along with my mother Gulab Jan and aunt Mannan Jan, both of whom had been invited to perform at the marriage celebrations. The wedding was one of the grandest that I have ever seen and, believe me, I have attended many princely weddings.' Tara has vivid memories of the occasion. 'As the baraat, bridegroom's party, made its way towards the bride's home, almost all of Patna came out on to the streets that evening to witness the magnificent procession of richly caparisoned elephants, camels and horses accompanied by shehnai and drum players playing music non-stop. Illuminated by hundreds upon hundreds of chandeliers carried by porters, the baraat dazzled everyone, particularly its brilliant display of fireworks that Sir Sultan had specially imported from China.'

After the nikah was completed and wedding feast held at the bride's house, the baraat returned next morning to Sultan Palace, where, in the adjoining open fields, a fairy-tale township of beautiful tents had been erected for guests to stay in, and for the festivities that were to last another two days. Music was the highlight of the celebrations. Beginning from early morning Bhairavi mehfils and continuing into the wee hours of the night, several highly respected male ustads, as well as the best-known tawaifs of those times, regaled an over 1,000-strong audience. In the gathering were princes, big landowners, political figures from the Muslim League and Congress, educationists, lawyers, officials in the colonial administration and vast numbers of ordinary people from Patna and outside.

Sir Sultan was a man of many parts. Educated in England and a proponent of English education, he was also a great connoisseur of Hindustani music and patron to a host of musicians, men and women. While his style of living and dressing was Westernised and his politics Muslim nationalist, Sir Sultan, unlike many contemporaries, felt unconstrained about organising family celebrations with customary pomp and splendour, including performance of music and dance by tawaifs.

The star of the show was undoubtedly the famous Janaki Bai from Allahabad. Besides her, there were other luminaries too, like Gauhar Bai from Jaipur, Mushtari Bai from Delhi, Noorjehan Bai from Calcutta, Mohammad Bandi from Patna, and Badr-e Munir from Lucknow, accompanied by her mother Nanuha Jan and aunt Bichhua Jan, the powerful twin choudharayins of the tawaifs in Lucknow.

Also in attendance were the prima donnas from Banaras, including Vidyadhari Bai, Badi Moti Bai, Mannan Jan, Gulab Jan and Rasoolan Bai. Roshanara too had been invited to perform at the celebrations, but had come down with a high fever at the last minute and, much to Bindo's delight, was forced to cancel her participation.

That Bindo was going to make her debut in this galaxy of stars had less to do with her as yet-untested musical talent and more with the resourcefulness of her guardian, Sultana, who had used her old acquaintance with Sir Sultan to contrive for her young ward an invitation to perform. As the youngest, most inexperienced performer present, Bindo would normally have been expected to sing at the beginning of the mehfil while the guests were still assembling. Sultana exercised her formidable charm and considerable influence over the host to circumvent this norm. Regardless of grumblings of discontent from the other tawaifs, Bindo was scheduled to make her professional debut halfway into the pre-dinner evening mehfil, well after lesser known and regarded courtesans had performed but when celebrity musicians were yet to sing. Once her formal debut appearance was over, Bindo was expected to fill in during the lean hours of that evening and the next day, as and when the better-known singers wished to take a break.

Old Sultana had her reasons for planning a debut for Bindo in a mehfil where several well-known musicians were performing, instead of organising a huge gathering in her own kotha, with the girl as the sole performer, as had been the norm. The times were moving against the tawaifs. Most people perceived kothas, even those belonging to elite tawaifs like Sultana, as cesspools of vice and immorality. Tawaifs' customs and norms, such as remaining unmarried but entering into sexual relationships with select patrons, were held up as proof of their inherently deviant lifestyle and sexuality.

High-ranking tawaifs had begun responding to this moral condemnation by modifying some of the more public aspects of their customary norms. The sar dhakna ceremony, for instance, was increasingly delinked from a young tawaif's entry into the profession as a musician. The formal debut of a novice tawaif was now usually marked with her public performance as a musician, foregrounding the cultural aspect of the tradition. The sar dhakna ceremony, which epitomised the sexual role played by tawaifs in the romantic and erotic life of their male patrons, was progressively becoming a quiet and private ceremony.

Once Bindo attained puberty, Sultana decided to mark her debut with a vocal performance even as she waited for the most suitable proposal for the girl's sar dhakna ceremony to come her way. Sir Sultan's celebrations presented the perfect opportunity for Sultana to present Bindo to a gathering of the most influential patrons possible.

There was a risk, of course, in introducing Bindo on a platform crowded with the brightest singing stars, not just from Banaras but across the country. It was a gamble that many well-wishers advised Sultana against taking. The girl could well be completely overshadowed by more experienced performers and washed off the musical landscape before she even had a chance to register her presence. But Sultana knew her music enough to realise that Bindo's was a rare voice. If she was able to prove her mettle in a gathering of the very best musicians of the day, she could, Sultana was confident, conquer the world.

'Bindo and I spent most of our time together at that wedding. She was always on the lookout for Janaki Bai. I got the feeling sometimes that Bindo was more excited about Janaki Bai's presence there than her own debut,' Tara recalls fondly. 'During the Bhairavi mehfil of the first day, Bindo, not scheduled to perform till later in the evening, kept trying to spot Janaki Bai in the crowd of musicians assembled. She looked so distracted, in fact, Sultana had to snap at her to stop behaving like a chhamiya, a lowly dancing girl, and behave instead like the elite tawaif she was trained to be.'

Barely able to contain her impatience with the performances that she was forced to endure before Janaki Bai began singing, Bindo was beside herself with excitement when her idol, known so far to her only through her gramophone recordings, was finally invited on the stage, as befitting her exalted status, at the end of the Bhairavi mehfil. In her late middle age, Janaki Bai was so stout that she could barely walk down the aisle jam-packed with listeners on either side, and on to the slightly raised performance platform in the centre of the marquee.

'Bindo later told me of her initial disappointment at seeing Janaki Bai in person. She didn't look like a Bulbul at all,' Tara recalls with a smile. 'But once the diva began singing, Allah! What magic!'

Everyone assembled was mesmerised by the sweetness of Janaki Bai's voice, the seeming effortlessness of her singing. In those days, there were no microphones. Singers were trained to throw their voices so that even the farthest member of the audience could hear them clearly. The strain would sometimes show in the singing of less talented performers. But not Janaki Bai. She sang easily and naturally, without any strain audible in her voice, even the complex pattern of taans and ornamentations with which she embellished her thumri, dadra and ghazal.

Bindo, Tara remembers, was in a trance for the next couple of hours. But as the evening drew closer, and with it her debut performance, she gradually became a bundle of nerves. Refusing to eat or drink anything, she nervously got ready for the evening's mehfil. Wearing for the first time a peshvaz that Sultana had got specially stitched for this occasion, Bindo, despite her unprepossessing features, looked very fetching in its snug-fitting, shimmering green folds, the colour of rice saplings in the monsoon. In her hair, ears, nose, neck and wrists, she wore the matching jewellery that Sultana had lent her from her own collection.

When the evening mehfil commenced, Bindo's nervousness escalated to a stomach-churning anxiety. Although she had accompanied Roshanara to several mehfils in the capacity of a novice, none of these matched in her memory the terrifying splendour of this gathering that would mark her debut. The marquee dazzled in the light of cut-glass chandeliers the likes of which she had never seen before. There were running fountains, sumptuous Persian carpets, sparkling white satin sheets, and ornate chairs and sofas on which were seated, according to status, princes and nobles, each more richly jewelled than the other. The sophisticated glamour of the other tawaifs and the male musicians present, all immaculately dressed for the occasion, left Bindo feeling extremely intimidated.

What if she couldn't hit a single note right? What if she forgot the bandish while rendering it? What if her throat suddenly ran dry? What if the assembled audience did not enjoy her singing? The doubts kept mounting.

She looked towards Sultana, seated a little ahead of her in the space designated for the performers. Ever since that awful showdown two-odd years ago, Bindo had tried her best not to give her guardian any reason to be angry. She learnt to be as docile and obedient as Sultana expected her to be, running every errand without protest, swallowing every rebuke without a murmur. She had also cut herself away completely, and without much effort, from Sa'dullah, who now lived as a forgotten shadow under the steps of Sultana's house.

Over time, Bindo had been able to win Sultana's approval, if not her affection, which everyone knew was reserved for Mumtaz and Roshanara. Victory made Sultana generous; pleased that she had been able to break Bindo's impudence, she became more tolerant and less critical of the girl. Then, about a year later, an unexpected tragedy had contributed further to a cessation of hostilities. Mumtaz had fallen prey to a mysterious fever and died suddenly, leaving the family shattered. Roshanara, always very close to her mother, had lost her voice due to incessant weeping. Even the best doctors from far-off Calcutta had been unable to help.

Finally, a young hakim, for long a silent admirer of Roshanara's singing, managed to restore her voice. And a grateful Roshanara reciprocated by taking him on as a lover. Surprisingly, Sultana, so hard-headed in matters of the heart and money, had raised no objection. Roshanara resumed singing but the tragedy had imprinted in her a melancholia that even her young hakim could not cure. Troubled by her own demons, Roshanara became less severe in her behaviour. Her interactions with household members, including Bindo, were now, if not exactly warm or kind, devoid of her earlier arrogance and spite.

Sultana too had mellowed. The loss of her daughter and the suffering of her granddaughter made her feel protective of the young girl in her care whom she had once mercilessly crushed into submission. Mindful of her responsibility towards Bindo, Sultana plotted her success with the same single-minded diligence that she had brought to manoeuvring Roshanara's rise in the world of Hindustani music.

Unknown to Sultana or others in the house, however, Bindo had neither forgotten nor forgiven the humiliation inflicted upon her by Sultana and Roshanara. The memory burnt deep in a fierce fire that showed up occasionally in Bindo's eyes before she hurriedly cast them down decorously as her guardian had taught her to. In her lonely, adolescent fury, Bindo had silently rejoiced at the untimely death of Sultana's beloved daughter. She had seen it as divine retribution for the pain that Sultana and Roshanara had inflicted upon her. Neither had she forgotten the three promises that she had made to herself that fateful day. To fulfil those, Bindo needed Sultana's sanctuary. She had, therefore, not allowed her rage to jeopardise her single-minded ambition to become the greatest ever tawaif gramophone singer from Banaras.

The only person who had an inkling of Bindo's inner turmoil was her teacher Shamim Khan Sahib. Much to his relief, the passion that continued to imbue the girl's music indicated that Bindo's spirit had not been broken as he had feared. Such intensity could only arise from either deeply felt love or hate or anger or ambition, the ustad, with his vast experience of music and musicians, knew. He wondered what it was that ignited Bindo's singing.

He noticed her troubled eyes, tremulous lips and clenched fists as she sat now, looking lost, in that opulent assembly, and Shamim Khan Sahib guessed how anxious she must be. It mirrored the apprehension he always felt when his students made their formal entry in the world of professional music practice. Their debut was as much a test of his worth as a teacher as it was of theirs as trained musicians. Bindo's introduction to the world was even more special. After Roshanara, it was in her that their ustad reposed hopes of ensuring immortality for the music associated with his family.

Shamim Khan Sahib patted Bindo gently on the head, his silent touch reassuring the girl that everything would go well. She would perform as brilliantly as her teacher knew she could. Bindo felt considerably calmed. With her ustad playing on the sarangi by her side, guiding her through the musical vistas of each song, she knew she would never get lost.

When her turn came, Bindo felt the nervous tension miraculously ebb out of her being. She had been allotted only twenty minutes, but she suddenly knew that she would make every minute worthwhile for the listeners. The mediocre performances by previous performers had contributed manifold to restoring her confidence. She could sing better than them even on a bad day, she thought, forgetting as she often did the lessons in humility pressed upon her by the old man walking a little behind her now as they made their way to the stage. Each performance was a manifestation of Allah's grace, the ustad had always stressed. Musicians who failed to realise this were eventually vanquished at the hands of their own hubris.

Once she and her accompanists were standing, facing the vast assembly, Bindo spontaneously made a break from customary norm. Instead of greeting the audience first, she turned instead towards her ustad, standing for the first time ever behind her as an accompanist. She offered him a deep salaam of thanksgiving and asked his permission formally to begin the performance. Only after he had extended his hand to her head in blessing did Bindo turn towards the assembled audience and, bowing her head and raising her right hand in salutation, seek their consent to start singing.

Bindo began her performance with a thumri in raga Tilak Kamod as her ustad had decided: *Jaag pari main toh piya ke jagaaye*; I woke up when roused by the beloved. She followed it up with a tappa in Bhairavi, *Lal wala joban*, with which the time formally allotted to her came to an end. The absolute silence that followed pierced her heart. In that suspended moment, she heard a sigh escape Shamim Khan Sahib's lips. 'Was I so bad that he is moaning in disappointment?' Bindo felt sick with despair. And then the silence exploded in a tidal wave of '*Waah, waah! Kya baat! Bahut khoob!*' Bravo! Well done!

That evening, a star was born. In recent times, rarely had a debut performance elicited such effusive praise. Money showered on Bindo that evening like heavy rain, with princes, zamindars and other notables competing to announce generous rewards for her, as they often did on such occasions. Affectionately nicknamed 'Chhoti Bai Sahib' by one and all present, Bindo was allowed to leave the stage only an hour later, after regaling the assembly with one song after another, each met with cries for more.

Her body was quivering and her legs shaking when, finally, she made her way to the space where Sultana was seated along with the other tawaifs, to offer the customary salaam to her guardian in formal acknowledgement of her contribution towards her debut as a tawaif. Just as Bindo was straightening up after bowing low, Sultana suddenly enveloped her in warm embrace. The unexpected affection made Bindo stiffen in shock but Sultana was too elated at her protégé's success to notice: 'Praise be to Allah! You have made me and your ustad so proud! Shabash!' Then, taking off the thick gold chain she always wore, Sultana put it around Bindo's neck as blessing, 'May you always sing like this. May you bring greater glory yet to the name of Sadabahar and your ustad, Shamim Khan Sahib.'

Bindo's eyes smarted with tears. Since childhood, with the exception of her cousin Teema and her teacher Shamim Khan Sahib, everyone else around, and most notably Sultana herself, had only barraged her with rebukes and insults. Sultana's affection and praise overwhelmed her now.

Someone came and whispered to Sultana that Janaki Bai wished to meet Bindo. Apparently, instead of resting in her tent till her performance was due, the celebrated singer had been present for Bindo's recital. She was so impressed that not only did she take off her diamond ring and slip it on to Bindo's finger but she also bestowed her with blessings and added, 'If you continue singing like this, my girl, you will be remembered as another Janaki Bai. But remember never to let praise get to your head. And never forget the debt you owe to those who moulded you into a musician.'

The next few hours of the mehfil were the sweetest in Bindo's life thus far. So many senior tawaifs and male musicians blessed and congratulated her that she lost count. Originally scheduled to perform as a standby, she became over the period of one night one of the most sought-after singers in the mehfil. In no time at all, she was flooded with invitations to perform at other mehfils across princely states and zamindaris of the region.

Tara recounts, 'Sultana was overjoyed. Returns on the expense and effort that had been invested on Bindo's education were coming in faster than anticipated. As her guardian, responsible for all financial dealings on her behalf, Sultana stood to benefit tremendously with this great start to Bindo's career. That mehfil was a bonanza for many other tawaifs as well. Rasoolan, as expected, was showered with accolades, presents and invitations. It was here too that I caught the eye of the raja sahib of Fatehpur. My mother accepted his proposal for me to accompany him to Fatehpur. Many proposals came Bindo's way for her sar dhakna ceremony but Sultana, greedy for the best offer yet to come, politely sidestepped each one of them.'

You have been quiet thus far. Now you suddenly ask, 'Wasn't this the mehfil in which Bindo khala was approached by a gramophone company with an offer to record? I remember my mother mentioning it to me once.'

'Yes, Vallabhdas Runchordas, a Gujarati businessman who was in charge of Odeon Records in India, was also present at that mehfil,' Tara confirms. 'He had launched many musicians' careers in the gramophone industry. Though he was based in Bombay, he had contacts with music patrons and performers across India, and was invited to many mehfils where he would be on the lookout for suitable singers. He was so taken with Bindo's performance that, putting aside her young age and inexperience, he offered Sultana a contract for Bindo with Odeon Records.'

'Bindo must have been overjoyed,' I interject.

'She would have been had she known about it,' quips Tara drily. 'As was the practice in those times, Vallabhdas chose to speak with Bindo's guardian and not directly to the girl. Sultana did not let out a word about this meeting to Bindo, and politely refused the offer that many other tawaifs were only too happy to accept.'

Sultana was disdainful of the gramophone. Its time constraint was to her proof of the superficiality of the medium. Dismissing the gramophone as mere 'showy fashion', she often rued the fall in tastes of music patrons who were so easily dazzled by three-minute songs. Convinced that recording for the gramophone would, in the long run, compromise the integrity and quality of her granddaughter's music, despite repeated offers, Sultana had never allowed Roshanara to sing for it. And she was not willing to allow Bindo, at the threshold of a brilliant career as a musician, to be lured into the distractions posed by music recordings. Besides, Sultana was less than tempted by the relatively low remuneration offered by gramophone companies as compared to the amounts that musicians earned by performing in mehfils.

'Not everyone is a Janaki Bai that gramophone companies will pay them the rates they demand. What's the sense of singing for half the rate you can earn in a mehfil, and in the process erode your charisma as an elite tawaif?' Sultana would rebuke Roshanara if she ever showed interest in the recording offers that came her way. A firm believer in the worth of exclusivity, Sultana feared that the value of Roshanara and Bindo's repertoire would be lowered if it was made available to people outside the select circle of aristocratic patrons: 'Just about any two-bit singer will then learn the songs and style of singing of my girls and be able to stand up in competition.'

Several other tawaifs at that celebration were less dismissive of Vallabhdas Runchhordas's offer. Under pressure from the ongoing morality drives, they had heard with trepidation the news brought by the choudharayins from Lucknow, Nanuha and Bichhua Jan, about the impending likelihood of new anti-prostitution laws, which could adversely affect tawaifs too.

Spearheaded by nationalists, social reformers and early women activists, the abolitionist lobby that advocated the eradication of prostitution as against the policy followed thus far by the colonial government—of surveillance, regulation and segregation of prostitutes—had by the 1920s grown more vocal and robust. Classifying 'dancing girls' alongside prostitutes as the obverse of the idealised chaste Indian woman, they demanded the abolition of them all.

Male nationalists and social reformers had long posited national honour in the figure of the desexualised and chaste Indian mother. Decrying 'dancing girls' and prostitutes as a 'blot' on the face of 'Mother India', they had been quick to raise an outcry in 1923 when the government proposed to send a group of dancing girls from India to the Empire Exhibition in England. Nationalist newspapers like *The Sindhi* in Bombay had carried an angry response, 'It is a pity that India, land of women of high types, should take pride in exhibiting her dancing girls.' Another paper, *Al Wahid*, had bemoaned, 'We are a subject people and must put up with such humiliation until we break our shackles.'

Middle-class women activists were equally vocal in their demand for the abolition of prostitution. Their participation in the freedom movement had been predicated on their endorsement of the ideals of women's sexual purity and chastity. Internalising this discourse, middle-class women nationalists and feminists placed prostitutes and dancing girls outside the pale of Indian womanhood on whose behalf they claimed to speak.

Much like Gandhi, they viewed prostitutes and dancing girls as pitiable creatures in need of rehabilitation and reform. They questioned too the patriarchal double standards that allowed men sexual activity outside marriage, an institution upheld by most early middle-class feminists as sacrosanct. Therefore, while several women's organisations were involved in charitable works for the rehabilitation of prostitutes, they took the lead in demanding a ban not only on brothels but also on the devadasi system—a ban that they hoped would undercut the patriarchal entitlements enjoyed by upper-caste men.

The demands of the abolitionists for more stringent laws against prostitution had received a boost with the introduction of the Government of India Act of 1919, which was based upon the principle of greater self-governance by Indians. Indian lawmakers, both at the level of the Central Legislative Assembly and the provincial assemblies, reflected nationalist aspirations and were more sympathetic to the abolitionist cause. In another development, India, though a dominion state, was made a signatory to the International Convention for the Suppression of the Traffic in Women and Children set up by the League of Nations in 1921.

The spectre of the white prostitute, sexually available to all in the port towns of the Orient, had generated considerable anxiety in Europe and America since the turn of the twentieth century. Her pervasive presence in the brothels of Bombay, Rangoon and Shanghai threatened the racial hierarchy and strict sexual boundaries between the coloniser and the colonised, maintained and enforced by colonial regimes.

Meanwhile, international women's activists, like Josephine Butler, had directed their concern towards the slave-like status of the white prostitutes, whom they saw as trafficked, violated victims of the international sex trade. Termed in Europe and America as 'white slavery', anxiety around the issue had by the 1920s translated into a number of anti-trafficking international laws that, in turn, informed the 1921 International Convention for the Suppression of the Traffic in Women and Children. Broadening the scope beyond 'white slavery', the League of Nations convention aimed to ensure the protection of all women and children from trafficking and sexual exploitation at an international level.

In an attempt to harmonise Indian laws with the international convention on trafficking, the Indian Penal Code was amended in 1923, and the age of consent in cases of kidnapping, abduction, sale and purchase of girls for prostitution was raised to eighteen, as against the earlier limit of sixteen. The colonial government's need to show its commitment to the mandate of the convention combined with the abolitionist enthusiasm of Indian lawmakers, and resulted in the enactment of laws that dealt not only with international trafficking but also the issue of prostitution in the country.

Accordingly, Bombay Presidency, under national and international scrutiny for the large presence of prostitutes—Indian, Asian as well as European—in the port city of Bombay, passed the Bombay Prevention of Prostitution Act of 1923, which made criminal offences of pimping, soliciting, procuring and detaining of women against their will in a brothel. In the same year, the Calcutta Suppression of Immoral Traffic Act (1923) was also passed, and would become a forerunner to similar legislation enacted in different parts of the country through the 1930s.

This flurry of law-making activity in the 1920s had not gone unnoticed by the tawaifs. Alerted to the possibility by their well-wishers and long-standing patrons that members of the legislative council in the United Provinces were in the process of consultation about drafting abolitionist legislation, Nanuha and Bichhua Jan convened a meeting of tawaifs at their palatial haveli in the courtesan-dominated locality of Chowk in Lucknow.

Mirza Jafar Hussain in *Qadeem Lucknow ki Aakhri Bahaar* makes mention of that meeting: 'In either 1924 or '25, when demands were being made for effective legislation to put an end to the profession of public women, a meeting of tawaifs against the proposals was called by the choudharayins, Nanuha Jan and Bichhua Jan, at their house. A number of tawaifs delivered exceptionally fine speeches on this occasion against the proposed bill. The high quality of their reasoning would have held its own in a meeting of highly educated and politically aware gentlemen. Chaudhary Mohammad Ali, the taluqdar of Radauli, and I were also present and were given the responsibility of drafting a legal appeal against the proposed bill.'

Mirza Jafar Hussain writes little about the outcome of the meeting. Perhaps there was nothing more to add. The dice had long been cast against tawaifs and the lifestyle and arts associated with them.

CHAPTER 19

Bindo's Triumph

CHANDA SAILS INTO TARA'S ROOM looking like a battered old ship, her petticoat and nightie billowing in a sudden gust of wind. Wild-haired, ruddy-faced and whisky-breathed, she keels over on to her mother's bed and takes a swig from her hip flask. Blind Tara reaches out and strokes her daughter's hand, while you scramble across the room to shut the now-rattling windows.

Never known for amiability, these days Chanda is almost always on a short fuse. Her son Jaipal has moved out of the family home along with his wife and children after another bitter quarrel over his daughters' Hindu identity. The other two sons, fed up with their mother's refusal to accept their decision to become Muslim, nearly left too, but Chanda has managed to stall their plans. Shocked by Jaipal's unexpected departure, she is prepared to be more accepting of their decision to break with the family's customs. But Jaipal, free at last to pursue his ambitions for anonymous respectability, refuses to return despite Chanda's repeated pleas.

Her surprise intrusion today has nothing to do with family woes, though. She has a message for you from Bitiya, a local social welfare organisation based in Shivdaspur, on the outskirts of Banaras.

Neither quite a village nor really an urban neighbourhood, the ragged suburb of Shivdaspur, with its open drains, unpaved streets, contaminated drinking water, truant electric supply and absent schools and health facilities, has been a hub of prostitution for the past half-century. Located close to the Manduadih railway station, which is a stop for trains running from Kolkata, Darbhanga and Patna in the east to Lucknow, Kanpur and Delhi in the north and Ahmedabad, Pune and Mumbai in the west, the brothels of Shivdaspur are thronged by sex workers, pimps, procurers and the police, and, more recently, by human rights activists and social welfare organisations like Bitiya.

Living either on a permanent basis or in temporary transit, under varying degrees of autonomy and coercion, the sex workers here hail from different backgrounds. Some belong to local families descended from poor prostitutes and gonaharins, mentioned in colonial records as being either based in Dal Mandi brothels or congregating in the outlying area of Manduadih. Another relatively smaller group traces its origins to erstwhile Bedia and Nat entertainers from across northern India, including Banaras, who had once occupied the lowest rung of the tawaif hierarchy. In the transformed moral and cultural landscape, these communities of singers and dancers were forced to reinvent themselves as stage performers and bar dancers or veer towards prostitution, a handful of them emerging as the elite among sex workers and brothel owners in Shivdaspur.

Their establishments teem with daughters from the family, but also with a rapid turnover of other inmates en route to brothels in bigger cities like Mumbai and Kolkata. Among them are girls and young women escorted by their relatives or village elders from poor and marginal communities customarily engaged in sex work. Then there are the first-generation entrants to prostitution. Most of them belong to lower-caste and asset-less families from the impoverished and debt-ridden countryside of Nepal, West Bengal, Assam, Odisha, Bihar and eastern UP. They have come here either to escape poverty or abuse in their natal or marital homes, or have been sent here by parents and relatives lured by promises of a better future.

Living off the earnings of women in Shivdaspur is a parasite population of procurers, middlemen and pimps. Typecast in the popular imagination as smooth-talking and manipulative outsiders—which many in fact are—some are also former female sex workers, and others may well be lovers, influential community or village elders and family members of the girls and women they bring to the doorsteps of brothel owners. Their relationship with the sex workers under their control is complex: manipulative and exploitative undoubtedly, but also often marked with emotional engagement and even intimacy.

For the law enforcers posted in the nearby Manduadih police station, the brothels are a lucrative source of payoffs—financial and sexual. Police raids are a common occurrence, followed by arrests of women on charges of soliciting, unruly behaviour, indecent exposure and obscene performance. As common are the quick bailouts in return for hefty bribes paid by brothel owners, middlemen and pimps, which are deducted from the already squeezed earnings of the women they control.

The advent of HIV/AIDS-related interventions targeting sex workers in the past two decades, followed more recently by the rise in international outrage against trafficking and 'sex slavery', have placed Shivdaspur and other red-light areas in India on the map of activists and organisations working in the areas of health, human rights and trafficking, especially of minors. Bitiya was among the first of such groups to make its appearance in Shivdaspur in the mid-1990s.

Focusing in its initial years on HIV prevention and children's education, Bitiya's activists arrived here carrying condoms, which they distributed among brothel owners and inmates. Although accepted good-naturedly and without demur by the women, the prophylactics were used more often by their children to blow into balloons rather than by clients unconvinced of the need for a safeguard against infections. Despite this, the sex workers welcomed Bitiya on account of the non-formal school it ran in the locality for their children. Although lacking any infrastructure or even a trained teacher, the school was a welcome intervention in the absence of any state-run educational facilities in the area.

Buoyed by this support, the middle-class activists of Bitiya next turned their attention to the realm of culture. In an attempt to encourage a positive self-image among sex workers, from 2000 on, it began organising cultural events in Banaras and other cities to showcase on a formal stage the 'music and dance heritage of tawaifs' for a primarily middle-class audience. While the categorisation of the songs and dance performed by sex workers and entertainers as the cultural heritage of courtesans was somewhat misplaced, Bitiya's initiative nonetheless inspired considerable initial enthusiasm among the women of Shivdaspur. They saw in it an opportunity to claim for themselves a redemptive association with the tawaif. Despised and ostracised in real life, ironically enough, the tawaif as memory has been transformed in contemporary popular culture, notably cinema, as a romantic, troubled, non-threatening figure—evoking pity for her 'fallen' womanhood and a nostalgia for the cultural refinement associated with her in an unhistoricised past.

Tawaif families living in stigmatised anonymity in Banaras were less inspired by Bitiya's cultural initiative. Always careful to maintain a distance from the women of Shivdaspur brothels, former tawaifs like you expressed apprehension that Bitiya's endeavour would further coalesce in public perception the identity of the tawaif with that of the sex worker, a classification used since colonial times to penalise your community. Sharing as they do the larger social contempt for women in prostitution, former tawaifs expressed anger at Bitiya's attempts at appropriation of their legacy—a legacy that they themselves have been forced to disown.

Responding to the criticism they faced, not only from your community but also from their target middle-class audience, of setting up filmy song-and-dance routines performed by sex workers as the art practice of courtesans, Bitiya activists began making attempts to convince retired tawaifs to participate in their events. Their efforts accelerated over the years due to international developments thousands of kilometres away.

From 2000 onwards, there was a resurgence in moral panics internationally about the trafficking of women and children for sexual exploitation. This translated into a shift in international funding and donor focus from HIV-related projects to supporting local initiatives aimed at eradicating 'sex slavery' and child prostitution. Paying lip service to the need to address the core issues of structural inequities, absence of social justice, and growing rural indebtedness and poverty, which fuels the desperate migration of men, women and children from the countryside to often exploitative and hazardous employment opportunities outside, international anti-trafficking discourse has been content to focus instead upon the 'rescue and rehabilitation' of children and women from prostitution and sex entertainment industries like dance bars and pornography.

Dependent on international donor organisations for their survival, local social welfare organisations have often, with good reason, been accused of tailoring their agenda to match the interests of their patrons. Bitiya was no exception, adapting its objectives and activities to fit into the anti-trafficking agenda of international donors. Taking their cue from similar initiatives across the country, Bitiya's activists, escorted by the local police, began conducting raids on Shivdaspur brothels, and forcibly 'rescuing' the often frightened and unwilling inmates they claimed were minors.

Informed by a morality discourse reminiscent of the early twentieth-century anti-trafficking campaigners, these raid-and-rescue efforts lack perspective on how exactly these 'rescued victims' are to be rehabilitated in any meaningful and long-lasting manner in an inequitable political economy. In most instances, they have proved to be counterproductive. Not only have such initiatives compounded the existing stigma and criminalisation of sex work and sex workers, they have had little impact on the continuing migration of women and children into hazardous occupations, and certainly worsened the conditions under which they work. Pushed underground to escape raids and rescue operations, women and children find themselves even more vulnerable to the exploitative terms and conditions imposed by brothel owners, procurers and pimps.

Not surprisingly, a vast majority of sex workers in Shivdaspur began opting out of Bitiya's cultural events. This posed a huge problem for the group that was now marketing its cultural activities as a 'rehabilitation' project aimed at encouraging 'alternative' modes of livelihood among sex workers. Funders, eager to showcase 'grassroots-level solutions' for agendas that they had set sitting in their plush offices in North America and Europe, had thus far been more than generous in their support for Bitiya's cultural interventions. For this funding to continue, the organisation needed the participation of the women whose cause they claimed to champion. Since sex workers in Shivdaspur and other towns of eastern UP and Bihar were loath to extend support, Bitiya had little option but to renew its efforts to woo the thus far recalcitrant tawaifs.

Most former tawaifs in Banaras, including you, remained apathetic to Bitiya's overtures, forcing it to reach out to the community in towns like Muzzafarpur in Bihar and Ujjain in Madhya Pradesh. Simultaneously, in Banaras, it tried to enlist the help of community elders and leaders, which is how they established contact with Chanda, who is always eager to enhance her political leverage by obliging well-connected outsiders. Flush with funds and patronised by the police and local politicians, Bitiya, in Chanda's estimation, was eminently deserving of her support.

As always, Chanda comes straight to the point. Pinning her bloodshot eyes on you, she announces, 'You will be singing at Bitiya's programme next month in Banaras. I have promised them your cooperation. They pay very well, and you are desperate for a new lease of life as a singer. I think the arrangement will work to everyone's benefit.'

You are silent. I have a fair idea of the dilemma you face. Refusing Chanda is not an easy option. She is not only a powerful community leader but also shares old ties with your family. Most importantly, as a single woman heading a large household, you require her help often. She arranges loans for you in times of need, facilitates school and college admissions for children in your extended family, helps find jobs for your many relatives and intervenes on everyday civic issues on your behalf with otherwise unhelpful government officials. You are banking on her largesse for Meenu's forthcoming marriage. And you will most certainly need her help to find suitable accommodation once you vacate your old home. You cannot risk alienating Chanda.

It is true too that you are desperate to reinvent yourself as a singer. You need the earnings as much as you need the return of music in your life. You have left no effort undone to secure entry into the concert circuit. And yet, are you willing to risk the respectability you so crave for a professional break in an event organised by Bitiya?

Tara's room is enveloped in an uneasy stillness. The wind swirling through the house has died down. Chanda drums her fingers impatiently on her mother's bedpost and takes copious swigs from her hip-flask. Tara yawns and stretches back on to her pillow, shutting her eyes. You remain deep in thought.

'Well then, what are you thinking so much about?' Chanda's patience snaps. 'I haven't asked you to murder anyone. I am giving you a wonderful opportunity to not only earn some good money but also to introduce yourself to a highly respectable audience. I would have thought you would be delighted. But if you think it's not good enough, there are many others who will be grateful to grab at the chance.'

You must speak now. 'Aapa, I am always grateful for all that you do for me. Thank you for speaking to the Bitiya people on my behalf.' Your eyes radiate humble gratitude. 'I am so sorry for taking time to reply but, you see, I am in a terrible quandary. I know the Bitiya event is a chance I shouldn't miss but, unfortunately, I am scheduled to perform around the same date next month at two programmes in Delhi that she has arranged especially for me.' To my utter shock, you draw me to your rescue.

You have often said that artful deception always served a tawaif well. To be able to lie convincingly was a skill that a tawaif had to master for self-preservation. Chanda must know that too but does not look suspicious. You sound so sincere, even I almost believe you.

'If I hadn't already accepted advance payment for the programmes, I would have happily cancelled and performed for Bitiya instead. I am wondering now what to do,' you add for good measure.

'Postpone the Delhi programmes. I have already confirmed your participation in the Bitiya event,' Chanda orders, curt and imperious. What Chanda wants, Chanda gets.

While I rack my brain for something to say, you are prepared with a suitably acquiescent reply: 'Aapa, you have taken the words out of my mouth! That's exactly what I was thinking we should do. It's too late in the evening to call now, but tomorrow morning we will request the organisers to shift the programme dates. Since she knows them well,' pointing at me, you say, 'I am hopeful that shouldn't pose a problem.'

I make non-committal, soothing sounds. And Chanda snorts in satisfaction. Having bought some time, you look more relaxed. The room hums again with cordiality. Tara, awakening from her nap, demands tea. The daughter-in-law is summoned to do the needful. You fuss around opening the windows that you had earlier shut. Chanda cruises out of the room, while Tara, refreshed by her catnap, tells me the story of Bindo's triumph in the mehfil circuit.

Following the success of her debut in Patna, invitations poured in for Bindo. Her subsequent equally impressive performances in mehfils organised by the scions of various principalities of western and central Bihar, like Tekari, Dumrao and Hathwa, and in the taluqdari estates of the Awadh region in the United Provinces, kept Bindo busy through the year.

She had also shifted into a kotha of her own. In keeping with the customary practice among Banaras's tawaifs, Sultana had taken this place on rent, adjacent to her own in Dal Mandi. You explain to me that tawaifs in Banaras, even if they were blood sisters, did not perform out of a shared kotha, since these were usually too small to accommodate two or more sets of performers, accompanists and patrons. Thus, in families with more than one tawaif, space was rented in the bazaar for each of the performing women. Senior members of the household were delegated the responsibility of supervising and taking care of money transactions in each kotha.

With Bindo finally graduating to become an independent, earning tawaif, some of her family, including her mother, two brothers and younger sister Phoolmani, had shifted to Banaras to live with her. Sa'dullah too had drifted from under the stairs of Sultana's kotha to an inconspicuous corner of his daughter's new establishment, remaining a shadowy, ignored figure. Since the family had limited knowledge of running an elite tawaif's kotha, with its specific demands of etiquette and upkeep, Daya Singh had requested Sultana to continue to play the role of Bindo's guardian till the girl gained more experience.

Under the new arrangement, in return for a cut from Bindo's earnings, Sultana divided her time between running Roshanara's and her ward's salons. This was a welcome deal for Sultana, although she took care not to show her eagerness to either Daya Singh or Bindo and her family. Truth be told, Sultana was facing difficult times. Roshanara continued to suffer from long bouts of melancholia. She was now a ghost of the talented and spirited tawaif she had been not so long ago. In the face of her constant cancellations due to ill health, invitations to perform were drying up. Also, fewer patrons visited her kotha, which was often shut because of Roshanara's indisposition.

Bindo was now Sultana's hope for a comfortable old age. She not only accompanied her to mehfils outside Banaras but also keenly supervised her evening performances in the kotha, and managed the money transactions.

Chafing under Sultana's continuing control over her life, Bindo resented many of her guardian's decisions. Of these, Bindo felt most bitter about Sultana's interference in her choice of lovers.

Bindo yearned for romance, for a besotted lover who would shower her with attention and gifts. Her sexual initiation had been perfunctory and cold, and had left her deeply disappointed. Sultana had picked the raja of a central Bihar principality for this purpose. Too old and absorbed in astrological charts to be interested in sex, the raja had accepted Sultana's request to become Bindo's first lover for the sake of tradition. Deflowering young tawaifs was simply what rulers like him were expected to do.

In keeping with the times, there had been no public celebrations or feasting to mark the occasion. After an evening's musical performance, Bindo, dressed in bridal red, had been led into raja sahib's bedchamber. A long wait for him to appear ensued. Exhausted, Bindo had just dozed off when she felt someone fumbling with her clothing. With a somewhat preoccupied expression on his face, raja sahib, without bothering to either put out the lights or get undressed, had just pulled down his breeches and pulled up her sari and without much ado entered Bindo. Within minutes, he had rolled over, buttoned himself up and walked away.

Is this what all that fuss is about? Bindo had hazily wondered, getting up and straightening her sari. It seemed to her like a terrible waste of the poetry and music written and composed in celebration of sexual intimacy.

Next morning, Sultana had shown Bindo the gold jewellery set and fifty-one silk and brocade saris that the raja sahib had bestowed upon the girl, besides a sum of Rs 5,501 as payment for the privilege of being her first lover. Noting the delighted greed in her guardian's eyes, Bindo had felt a fresh stab of resentment. All that the old croak was interested in was money. Her happiness meant nothing to Sultana, Bindo thought to herself, rancour welling in her heart.

Following her sexual initiation, Bindo had entertained a modest number of suitably rich and, therefore, predictably elderly lovers that Sultana selected. None of them had come close to satisfying the adolescent desires coursing through Bindo's veins. The only sense of gratification in her early days as a tawaif came from her scintillating success in the musical soirees that usually preceded the dull nights of lovemaking.

One of Bindo's fondest memories was of her triumph in the mehfil organised by the raja of Tekari for a select group of his courtiers and friends. Exclusive, intimate gatherings of royal patrons and learned music lovers like this one, called divan-e-khas, were considered the real test of a tawaif's mastery, not only over music and dance but also etiquette, conversation, banter and flirtation.

As was the norm in princely mehfils, a mix of entertainers, dancers and singers from different strata of the tawaif community had been invited. Lower grades of entertainers known for their physical charms were present, as were tawaifs of a higher grade than them, recognised for their competence in dance and light music. Both these categories kept a respectful distance from elite tawaifs famous for their mastery of raga-based singing. Bindo and several other, more senior, courtesan musicians from Patna, Gaya and Banaras represented the ranks of high-category musician tawaifs at this mehfil. Among them was Wazir Jan, the gramophone celebrity of the first decade of the twentieth century.

During her initial period of exposure to recorded music, Bindo had idolised Wazir Jan. And while her subsequent introduction to recordings of singers like Ustad Abdul Karim Khan and Janaki Bai had somewhat eroded that deity status, she still held Wazir Jan's music in high esteem.

Originally from Karnal in colonial Punjab, Wazir Jan had studied music extensively from Ustad Imdad Khan, grandfather of the sitar maestro, Ustad Vilayat Khan. A versatile singer, she was as famous for her mastery over khayal as of the thumri. Quite early in her career, Wazir Jan had shifted to Banaras and, in 1906, commenced her career as a gramophone singer by recording an impressive twenty-five songs for the London-based Gramophone and Typewriter Ltd, by far the highest number of songs recorded by any singer in India for the company that year. In the years to come, besides recording regularly for Gramophone and Typewriter Ltd, Wazir Jan also performed for its French rival, the Parthephone and Cinema Company.

By the mid-1920s, however, her charisma was on the wane. Long excluded from the select circle of tawaif singers who now recorded for the gramophone, Wazir Jan's advancing years had also diminished her popularity among those patrons for whom a courtesan's youthful beauty was as great, if not greater, an attraction as her musical abilities.

However, the raja of Tekari, renowned for his knowledge of music, was an old admirer of Wazir Jan's and continued to accord her celebrity status at his musical gatherings. Trailed by a maidservant carrying a silver spittoon, Wazir Jan, impeccably dressed in a turquoise-blue Banarasi silk sari, with glittering diamonds adorning her ears, neck and wrists, breezed into the mehfil well after all the other invited performers and accompanists had settled down.

Her appearance set off a flurry of excited whispers. With much tongue-clicking and solicitous head-shaking, the assembled tawaifs gossiped in fierce undertones about the cruel imprint of age on Wazir Jan's fabled Iranian beauty. Her milky clear complexion, they observed with barely concealed delight, had long become sallow. Her petal-smooth skin now resembled weather-beaten leather. Wrinkles had dug deep trenches across her oval face, and the rounded curves of her statuesque figure had turned gaunt.

Trained by Sultana to shun mehfil gossip, Bindo steered clear of the malicious mumblings. She knew besides that the poisonous pity was misplaced. Bindo had noticed Wazir Jan's eyes and seen the steel in them. Wazir Jan had lost neither her legendary hauteur nor confidence in her worth as a musician of a formidably varied repertoire. Selectively acknowledging the greetings of only the best-known and wealthiest tawaifs present, she ignored the deep salaam presented to her by young Bindo, whom she had met briefly at Sultana's house in the mourning period for Mumtaz.

Scheduled to sing towards the end of raja sahib's soiree, in deference to her seniority, Wazir Jan looked characteristically bored through the performances in the earlier part of the evening. The dancing by young and beautiful entertainers made way for tawaif singers, who presented lighter genres likes dadra and ghazal in the main, punctuated by dance. And though there was no hard and fast rule, these performances were usually followed by the appearance of elite tawaifs who sang khayal, thumri, dadra, tappa and raga-based seasonal songs, enacting these through facial expressions and hand gestures and standing up and dancing only occasionally.

Bindo, as the youngest of this elite group, was scheduled to perform before her senior peers. As she began singing, Wazir Jan's boredom fell away. Here was a voice that she instantly recognised as special. Of all the tawaifs assembled in the mehfil, most of whom she had heard on previous occasions, only this short, ordinary-looking girl posed a real challenge to her thus-far uncontested position of being raja sahib's favourite.

Leaning towards her patron and host, seated close by, Wazir Jan began regaling him with a joke in a loud, theatrical whisper. His amused laughter and her own pretty giggling quite effectively destroying the intense romantic mood that Bindo, midway into her first thumri, was trying to create.

Such attempts at disrupting a potential rival's performance were the stock-in-trade of many tawaifs. If lesser, unknown performers disrupted the performance in this manner, they would undoubtedly be rebuked for breach of mehfil etiquette. But a seasoned old hand like Wazir Jan, with the indulgence of the host, could use these tactics not only to successfully decimate a rival's chances of success in that particular mehfil but also cause substantial damage to her self-confidence.

Bindo, still smarting from having her greeting ignored, was now beside herself with rage. Wazir Jan had to be taught a lesson she would not forget. And the time to settle scores was now. Not once stumbling over her ruined first song, Bindo brought it to a swift close. With a suitably bashful smile, she then announced that, since the mehfil was graced by the great Wazir Jan, as a token of respect, she wanted to beg her permission to sing a thumri that the diva had made famous on the gramophone.

Taken by surprise, Wazir Jan had little option but to smile back her permission. Convinced that, despite her undeniable talent, Bindo had bitten off more than she could chew, she waited in happy anticipation for the girl to become a laughing stock for daring to perform a thumri associated with a much greater singer.

A hush fell over the mehfil as Bindo hurriedly consulted with Shamim Khan Sahib. As surprised as everyone else by the risk that his student was taking so early in her career, the ustad knew it was too late to dissuade her. Sensing Sultana's alarm, he quietly gestured to the old tawaif to keep calm. The best that he and Sultana could do now was to give Bindo the support and confidence to succeed in the challenge she had taken on.

Bansuriya re, kaisi bajayi Shyam; Your flute-playing, O Shyam, is incomparable—this was one of Wazir Jan's most famous Bhairavi thumri recordings made for Gramophone and Typewriter Ltd in 1906. Bindo had heard it many times on Sultana's gramophone and committed it to memory. She sang it now with fearless ease as if singing for her own pleasure.

While retaining the broad outline of the celebratory mood that had characterised Wazir Jan's rendition, Bindo imbued it with an expansive imagination of multiple meanings that had been missing in the senior singer's more singular and literal interpretation of the thumri lyrics. Bindo eschewed the profusion of flighty taans and other dramatic attention-drawing ornamentations that had characterised Wazir Jan's rendition in favour of calm repose and emotional expression. Through a leisurely and systematic exploration of the thumri text, she explored its many meanings and moods, from the plaintive cry of a seeking lover to the flirtatious preening of an infatuated admirer, to the yearning for spiritual union of the soul with the divine, in the process making the song immutably her own.

As she sang her final notes, Bindo looked up at Wazir Jan and rejoiced. Revenge tasted so sweet. Her face ashen and crumpled, her eyes dulled by shock, in the course of one song, Wazir Jan had transformed into a defeated, old woman.

Not that anyone else was paying attention. All eyes in the mehfil were transfixed upon the star of the evening, Bindo. Raja sahib and his friends, mesmerised by her performance, had no will left to hear anyone else. Those senior tawaifs who did get a chance to perform were forced to leave after just a song or two because the assembled audience would call for Bindo to return.

Wazir Jan watched her former patron and long-standing loyalist, the raja of Tekari, lavish appreciation and money on Bindo. As she was to confide to Sultana later in the night, in a rare moment of candid vulnerability, watching Bindo that evening, it felt like she was observing herself as a young tawaif being feted by the raja. This sense of déjà vu left her cleansed of her sense of shock, rage and mortification. She felt only a calm bemusement. Fame and adulation, her mother had warned her early on, were transient. Wazir Jan thought she had them firmly in her grip until only a few hours ago. With the passage of only one song, she had lost them both to Bindo, who had not even been born when Wazir Jan recorded the thumri that this young woman had so craftily and spectacularly usurped today.

With her long experience of the world, she knew exactly what Bindo had done and why. And strangely, her earlier hostility had given way to a grudging respect. The musician in Wazir Jan admired the magic that the girl had wrought with her thumri. And the tawaif in her acknowledged that, had she been in Bindo's place, she too might have been as wilfully cruel to an overbearing senior colleague. This evening simply did not belong to Wazir Jan. Perhaps after today no evening would belong to her.

It was just as well that she had recently received an invitation from a long-time admirer, the maharaja of Indore, to shift to his principality and enter employment as a state musician. Unsure until then about leaving Banaras, she now knew that, as soon as she returned home, she would be writing a gracious letter of acceptance to Indore.

Exultant in her triumph, Bindo was oblivious of the sobering reality that Wazir Jan had been forced to confront. Worldly success, her ustad had often warned Bindo, was ephemeral; a crafty illusion, notoriously fickle, that played nasty tricks with those who embraced it as the truth. Too young to understand the import of this wisdom, Bindo gloated in the adoration that came her way that evening.

As was his practice, raja sahib conferred upon Bindo, as the undisputed star of the soiree, the privilege of being driven in his personal car to the palace outhouse where invited musicians were usually lodged once the mehfil came to an end. All the other musicians were expected to either walk back or be transported by horse-driven carriages.

Wazir Jan, used to being driven in her patron's car ever since she began performing in raja sahib's mehfils, opted to walk back in the inky darkness to the outhouse alone, her accompanists trailing behind. Midway into her solitary journey, raja sahib's car came to a screeching halt beside her.

'Bai sahib, at your age you shouldn't be walking alone in such darkness. I am going to the outhouse too and will be happy to take you along in the car,' Bindo's voice, sharp as a butcher's knife and sweet as melon, sliced through the darkness. Ignoring Sultana's commands to let Wazir Jan be, Bindo had been on the lookout for her through the drive. Her pleasure in her victory would not be complete without this final blow to Wazir Jan's self-esteem.

'Thank you, my child! At my age, walking will do me good. I have driven very often in that car, and it is time someone else got a chance. You have richly earned your ride. Enjoy it while it lasts.' Wazir Jan's gentle irony, delivered in a pleasant, even tone, robbed Bindo of the vengeful satisfaction she had sought. She searched hard for a fitting repartee but couldn't think of any.

An acutely embarrassed Sultana had, meanwhile, scrambled out of the car. Wazir Jan was neither likeable nor was she anyone's friend. But she was still a highly respected member of the tawaif community in Banaras, and a wealthy and influential courtesan. Sultana would not allow her upstart ward's foolish arrogance to jeopardise their relationship. Insisting that she had a headache that would do well with fresh air and exercise, with the greatest courtesy, Sultana too joined Wazir Jan, leaving Bindo alone in the car.

'My grandfather stopped organising tawaifs' mehfils during the non-cooperation movement.' Rastogi-ji and I are back in his haveli's music hall. It has been raining heavily for the past couple of days, and a puddle of dirty water has gathered in one corner of the mehfil ghar, thanks to a leaky roof.

Seemingly indifferent to the travails of the present, Rastogi-ji is happily sifting through memories of the past. 'Once the upsurge ebbed, by the mid-1920s, he would occasionally invite the Gayika Sangh to arrange a concert of tawaif musicians in this mehfil ghar.'

A canny businessman, Babu Purshottam Lall must have felt confident that his cautious return to the entertainments associated with tawaif performers, even while raising nationalist eyebrows, would be secretly welcomed by many other merchants yearning for the delights of the cultural pursuits that they were obliged to shun under duress. The task was made easier by the formation of the Gayika Sangh that, as part of its mandate to safeguard the art practice of tawaifs in the age of nationalism, had begun arranging mehfils and music programmes at the invitation of supportive patrons. Retaining a small percentage of the total earnings in the mehfil for its administrative expenses, the Gayika Sangh allowed the rest to be distributed among the participating tawaifs and accompanist musicians.

The arrangement had worked to the satisfaction of everyone involved. Elite tawaifs, who formed the core of the Gayika Sangh, in return for sharing a small cut with the association, managed to retain some degree of access to the music rooms of their erstwhile patrons. Cloaked in its stated ideals of weeding out obscenity in songs and immorality in tawaif lifestyle, the Gayika Sangh became an acceptable alternative for wealthy merchant patrons like Babu Purshottam Lall who now felt a certain inhibition in engaging tawaifs on an individual basis.

His private mehfils were expectedly well attended, even if they could not match the extravagance of his earlier musical soirees. 'Times were not the same. And besides, my grandfather was getting on in years and keeping indifferent health. The few mehfils he organised in later years were low-key and very private gatherings, strictly lasting only the course of one evening,' Rastogi-ji says.

My thoughts go back to Tara and her memories of Bindo's early years as a tawaif. It was at one such musical gathering organised by a rich merchant of the city that she made her debut as a performer in Banaras. A celebration of the rainy season, the kajari mehfil, arranged under the aegis of the Gayika Sangh, saw the participation of three young and upcoming tawaifs—Kashi Bai, Siddheshwari Bai and Bindo. All of them were scheduled to perform kajari, sawan, jhoola and hindol—songs of the beauty of the rainy season, the longing for an absent lover, and of monsoon-drenched romance and sexual intimacy.

It promised to be an exciting evening, with the city's most promising young female performers in attendance. Belying her short, frail figure, Kashi Bai's resonant, powerful voice was being heard and appreciated by music lovers in Banaras and elsewhere. Belonging to an illustrious family of Gandharva tawaifs, she was hailed by her many admirers as a likely successor to the great thumri singer of the previous generation, Vidyadhari Bai. Siddheshwari, on the other hand, had begun performing only recently, after being thrown out by her aunt Rajeshwari Bai for helping her cousin Kamleshwari elope with a lover. Free of her aunt's tyranny, and under the tutelage of her guru, Siyaji Maharaj, Siddheshwari had begun garnering attention as a mehfil singer in small princely and zamindari states like Ranka and Manda, and subsequently in Banaras. Her rise was so meteoric that, even though she began singing professionally much later than many other tawaifs her age, she was being compared to Kashi and Rasoolan as a potential rival.

The mehfil was an important milestone in Bindo's fledgeling career: her first introduction to the merchant aristocracy of Banaras. With the onset of the morality campaigns, tawaifs' kothas had long become out of bounds for the city's merchant elite. Instead, patronage for the salons now came increasingly from rich landowners and contractors from the surrounding countryside, relatively unmoved by the prevailing rhetoric of nationalist morality. Though welcomed warmly by tawaifs, they were not as intimately associated with the music culture of elite kothas as the merchant upper-crust were.

Sultana was, therefore, keen that Bindo be introduced on a suitably respectable platform to the city's merchant aristocracy, which defined the contours of purab ang music. Her logic was simple. Once Bindo was able to win over the knowledgeable and sophisticated music patrons of the city gathered here, her reputation as a musician to reckon with would be assured.

Courtesans of an earlier generation, like Vidyadhari, Rajeshwari and Badi Moti Bai, who began their careers in Banaras, had built impressive musical reputations much earlier in their careers than had younger tawaifs like Rasoolan, Kashi and Siddheshwari. Debuting in the times of nationalist fervour, these tawaifs had been forced to seek wealthy and powerful princely patrons outside before being accorded recognition by the music lovers of their own city.

The mehfil was, as expected, a great success. In the intimacy of a small gathering of musically knowledgeable listeners, all three tawaifs had felt enthused to give their best. Among the audience, unknown to Bindo, was the man who had been so impressed by her debut performance in Patna that he had approached Sultana with an offer to launch the girl as a gramophone singer.

Vallabhdas Runchordas, one of the most influential people in the recording industry at that time, owned The Talking Machine & Indian Record Co. and Viel-O-Phone. These music companies, besides being involved in the sale of all kinds of talking machines, also made and distributed gramophone recordings. He also controlled distribution and marketing for the German-owned Odeon Records in India. Thanks to Vallabhdas Runchordas's vast knowledge of music and musicians, Odeon Records produced the most eclectic and exceptional recordings in India. The success of his ventures had been such that, at one time, he had posed a real challenge to the undisputed leader of the market, the Gramophone Co. Ltd, which was known as His Master's Voice (HMV) after 1916. Many well-known musicians, like Malka Jan of Calcutta, Bal Gandharva and the shehnai exponent Ali Baksh 'Vilayatu' Khan (who was Ustad Bismillah Khan's uncle and teacher) had recorded for him.

Bindo's impeccable performance that evening convinced him that his excitement in Patna had not been misplaced. She had the potential to be a brilliant gramophone star. And it was he, Vallabhdas Runchordas, who would go down in the annals of musical history for introducing Bindo to the wider world.

This time, he decided to talk to Bindo directly. Since her professional debut several months ago, he had gathered enough background information to know that Bindo's relationship with her guardian, even at the best of times, was fragile.

An opportunity presented itself most unexpectedly that evening. Midway through the mehfil, Fakhru came running to call Sultana home because Roshanara, pregnant with hakim sahib's child, had gone into labour. Not wishing to disrupt the flow of the gathering, Sultana decided to quietly rush back, leaving Bindo in the care of Shamim Khan Sahib.

Swooping upon his chance, Vallabhdas Runchordas sought the host's help to arrange a meeting that very evening with Bindo. Happy to oblige, the merchant had a message sent to Bindo through her tabla accompanist, Munney Khan, to step out from the mehfil and meet a guest in the privacy of the smaller end room on the first floor, down the corridor from the mehfil ghar.

Mystified at this unexpected summons, young Bindo felt a shiver of excitement run down her spine. Perhaps a besotted admirer wished to meet her alone? Would he be young and handsome, rich and influential? The gathering of fat, middle-aged and old men in the music hall did not inspire much hope but Bindo remained optimistic.

I imagine Bindo walking down a corridor of the merchant's haveli, brightly lit by electric bulbs newly installed in cut-glass lamps imported from Belgium. At the end of the passage was the door of a room, which she knocked at and pushed open with a mounting sense of anticipation.

As she entered, to her amazement, she saw a person with the body of a child and the face of an old man ensconced in a huge armchair. Vallabhdas Runchordas was tiny. Under five feet tall, he was of such slender build that Bindo felt a strong gust of wind would fly him off his feet. His treble voice with its pronounced lisp only added to the first impression of him being a little boy.

The offer he made left her even more astonished. She blinked several times to assure herself that this was not one of the dreams that she so often had. Bindo was finally going to sing for the gramophone! And the ridiculous-looking man seated opposite was promising to help her become the biggest and brightest star the industry had ever known.

Making no mention of his abortive meeting with Sultana, the gramophone tycoon listed out the prosaic particulars of the dream he was offering Bindo. In exchange for being launched as a gramophone artist, Bindo would have to sign a five-year contract with Odeon. She would not record for any other company in that period. She would be expected to make herself available for all recording sessions on the terms and conditions specified, including the remuneration fee decided by Odeon. In the next few months, Bindo would have to be ready to record ten songs, a mix of popular and rare compositions that he would select from her repertoire.

Caught in a whirr of excitement, Bindo paid little attention to the finer details of the contract that Vallabhdas Runchordas said he would get drafted in the next couple of days for her signature. Nodding mutely, Bindo touched his feet in thanksgiving and took her leave. Through the brief exchange, she did not once wonder why Vallabhdas Runchordas had sought her out instead of approaching her guardian, as was the norm. Nor did it occur to Bindo to suggest that he speak first to Sultana about the offer.

Locking the mehfil ghar door behind him, Rastogi-ji is escorting me down the corridor that runs across the haveli's rectangular first floor, overlooking the inner courtyard. Lined by rooms on one side, the corridor is flanked on four ends by large latticed windows that let in light and breeze. Today, the heavy rain clouds gathered outside cast a gloom on the late afternoon light that usually filters in at this time of the day from the west-facing windows.

Rastogi-ji attempts in vain to switch on sundry light bulbs along the way. Plunged in deep shadows, the corridor is pervaded by the lonely stench of mustiness and bat droppings. As we slowly make our way through the growing darkness, Rastogi-ji speaks of a memory very different from his usual stories: about a grandaunt who had been widowed in childhood.

Shunned by her dead husband's family as 'inauspicious', she had grown up and grown old unloved and unwanted in this very haveli. She kept to herself in a small corner room at the end of this corridor, and is in Rastogi-ji's memories a spectre in white with a tonsured head, whom he occasionally caught sight of as she silently flitted down the passage.

I am momentarily blinded. Rastogi-ji has finally managed to switch on a bulb that actually works. Hanging naked from the corridor ceiling, it engulfs us in a sharp, unforgiving light. Cluttered with discarded furniture, broken electrical fixtures and other odds and ends of past lives, this portion of the haveli houses its unwanted memories. And recalls another haveli not very different from the one I am visiting today.

Behind the genteel facade of havelis, my father would say, festered claustrophobia, loneliness and terrible secrets. Discovering communism while still in school, he had chosen to live far from the shadows of his paternal family's ancestral haveli in Kapurthala, eastern Punjab. Over the years, the growing infighting within the Communist Party and its subsequent fragmentation had exhausted my father's fierce loyalty to a communist utopia but not his disdain for the privileges embodied in the haveli. As children, we were rarely taken on visits to the ancestral house. As we grew up and the house was sold bit by bit to repay mounting debts incurred by my father's younger brother, who had opted to live the haveli life well past its expiry date, my father shed few tears for an inheritance he had long disowned.

I must have been around seven or eight when, on one of our rare visits to Kapurthala, I accompanied my mother to visit my grandmother who lived in the haveli with my uncle. We arrived on a winter's evening, and I remember sleeping in a cold, draughty room that looked large enough to host a cricket match. Early next morning, I wandered around alone, exploring the many terraces, hidden staircases and tucked-away rooms, all abandoned to their state of disrepair. On the second floor, I looked up at the large terrace that occupied the entire third storey of the building. Feeling adventurous, I decided that it would be fun to look down at the street below from the top of the house.

I had almost reached the last high step of a steep, narrow staircase leading to the terrace when I saw HIM. Drooling, clothes torn, one hand and one foot manacled, he was half-sitting, half-lying on the terrace in front of me. Upon noticing me, he let out a terrible howl of despair. I turned and fled down the steps, tripping, falling, getting up and running until I reached the safety of my mother's embrace. Hysterical with fear, I couldn't speak for a long time. And when I did, it was only to say that I wanted to get out of this frightening place and go home.

Much later, I learnt the sad truth of the phantom I had encountered. A distant, poor cousin with scant education and zero prospects had been brought to the haveli to make himself useful to my grandmother and uncle. At some point, when he was about eighteen or nineteen, he was struck by 'madness'. My uncle said that he was probably distressed at the cannibalisation of his beloved haveli into shops and offices and apartments. My grandmother attributed his withdrawal from the real world to the spirits of our forefathers with whom he had begun talking loudly and endlessly.

Doctors, medicines and long incarceration in mental asylums followed. When nothing worked, my uncle brought him back to the haveli and put him in the care of a faith healer. Manic and manacled, he died one night, howling at the skies.

CHAPTER 20

Bindo Takes Flight

'BINDO SNATCHED THE WHIP OUT of the Kunwar's hand, "You bastard! I am a tawaif, not some dumb beast of burden for you to flay," she hissed. Securing a firm grip on the whip, she began flogging the prince furiously!'

Phoolmani, Bindo's younger sister and your least favourite aunt, is uncharacteristically eloquent. 'To make sure that his screams wouldn't alert the sentries guarding the thick bolted doors of the outhouse, Bindo began shrieking loudly and piteously as if in excruciating pain.

'Used to hearing the cries of tawaifs and prostitutes whom the prince brought here every other night, the sentries were momentarily alarmed upon hearing the Kunwar's screams but relaxed when the shrieks of the woman drowned his voice. Perhaps this was some new game he had devised to amuse himself, they thought and went back to rubbing tobacco with lime, which they chewed to keep awake through the long night. If the woman survived in the morning, they would send her packing; if she were dead or dying, she would be thrown into the nearby pond as breakfast for the alligators that the prince loved like his own children.

'The sentries were not to know that Bindo was no ordinary woman. Wild with fury, she continued to whip the prince till he collapsed in a senseless heap on the floor. Stripping him nude, she tied his hands and feet and gagged his mouth. Then taking off her clothes and wearing his, she tiptoed into the adjacent washroom. Jumping out of the window, she ran towards the thickly wooded forest that spread behind the outhouse.'

Stretched out luxuriously on your bed, Phoolmani is clearly enjoying her role as storyteller. Meenu is reluctantly massaging oil into her scalp, while Salma is hovering around with another cup of tea, of which your aunt has had several since morning.

You look glum. To drive home your suffering, you sit on the most uncomfortable stool in the room. Your moroseness is in large measure a result of the nasty earful you got from Chanda this morning when you gathered the courage to lie to her on the phone that the Delhi concerts could not be postponed. Chanda had let her displeasure be known in the loudest terms, underlined with a not-so-subtle threat of abandonment.

You have tried to put on a brave face. Chanda will come around eventually, you have said to me several times, but there is panic in your eyes. You cannot afford to antagonise your powerful benefactor. I wish that there were indeed concerts scheduled in Delhi that could have somewhat compensated for the risk you have taken in refusing Chanda. But no such promise of a new lease of life as musician awaits you. Ironically, the only opportunity available is one you cannot accept for fear of compounding the social stigma and prejudice you endure.

The stressful presence of your difficult and demanding aunt does not help matters. A small-built woman, Phoolmani might have been pleasant-looking if it were not the pinched severity of her paan-stained lips, the suspicious twitching of her hooked nose and the cold glint in her beady eyes. Phoolmani rarely, if ever, smiles, is stingy with kind words and is forever finding fault in others. An intensely unwelcome guest, she has been camped in your house for the past two days to escort her granddaughter Sheem (who arrived here from Bombay yesterday) to Bhabua to visit Pyaari khala.

Phoolmani's excitement at showing off her Bombay-based granddaughter to the yokels of Banaras and Bhabua has, I suspect, contributed to making her relatively amiable. Ever since she arrived in Banaras, she has needed only the most perfunctory prompting to share with me eyewitness accounts of Bindo's life as a young tawaif in Banaras, and other stories gleaned from family lore, like this one of sex, violence and adventure.

'Making her way deep into the forest, Bindo became aware of the fear that gripped at her heart,' Phoolmani narrates. 'What if she was attacked by wild animals prowling in the jungle? Reminding herself that no beast could be more brutal than the prince she had left unconscious, naked, gagged and bound in the outhouse, Bindo steeled herself and doggedly moved on through the moonlit mass of trees, shrubs and undergrowth.'

Bindo knew that as soon as the Kunwar freed himself enough to raise an alarm, his guards would begin hunting for her. She had to find her way out of this jungle as soon as possible. But where would she go? Even if by a miracle she were able to reach Banaras, there was little doubt that the law would catch up with her for assaulting a member of the royalty. Though still young, Bindo knew enough of the world to realise that, in a court of law, the word of a tawaif, no matter how celebrated a musician, would cut no ice against the testimony of a prince, no matter how depraved.

In the silvery shadows of the forest, clutching at a tree like a frightened child clutches at her mother, Bindo yearned for the days when the doors of the world of music were still wide open for her. She remembered the happiness she had felt after the meeting with the gramophone magnate, Vallabhdas Runchordas. How distant that evening seemed now! Too excited to sleep a wink that night, Bindo decided she would tell no one about the meeting.

She knew of Sultana's disdain for the gramophone and had no intention of allowing her guardian to scuttle this opportunity. Sooner or later, Sultana would get to know about the offer that Vallabhdas Runchordas had made to her. Bindo hoped that this eventuality would come to pass only after she had signed the contract with Odeon Records.

It is for this reason that Bindo decided not to confide in Shamim Khan Sahib either. But she had underestimated her teacher's alertness and sense of responsibility. Noticing Bindo's brief, mysterious disappearance during the mehfil, and learning of the meeting through subsequent gossip among accompanists, Shamim Khan Sahib felt obliged to inform Sultana about the matter.

Although he did not have the details of the conversation, Sultana had a fair inkling of the offer that must have come Bindo's way. She had recognised Vallabhdas Runchordas in the gathering that evening. Cursing her naiveté in assuming that he would not approach Bindo after facing rejection from her guardian, Sultana was furious with her ward. Used to controlling the destinies of everyone who lived in her shadow, it was intolerable to Sultana that this girl, moulded by her, should now hatch ambitions behind her back.

'Dulahin, can you warm up water for Sheem's bath? She catches a cold if she bathes in cold water,' Phoolmani breaks off Bindo's story to issue this command. While you purse your lips in barely disguised irritation and Salma looks exhausted, Phoolmani announces to me with obvious pride, 'My Sheem is not used to rough living.'

My response is cut short by Sheem's entry. Even in her night clothes and without any make-up, her sleek loveliness is undeniable. Tall and slender but not thin, true to her name, Sheem shimmers a burnished copper. The oversized T-shirt she wears over a worn-out shalwar does nothing to conceal her feminine curves. The oval perfection of her face is highlighted by the careless knot into which she has pulled up her thick, glossy, long hair. With almond-shaped eyes, high cheekbones and full lips, Sheem's black-and-white era film-star beauty has had me mesmerised ever since I met her at Babatpur airport yesterday.

Dressed in white linen trousers paired with a summery, floral blouse and open-toed sandals, Sheem's only jewellery was a pair of discreet pearl earrings and a delicate gold-chained wristwatch. Her expensive pedicure and designer black sunglasses had made her look, to my inexperienced eyes, more like a glossy fashion model out on a five-star vacation than a bar dancer on her way to Bhabua to meet an ailing grandaunt.

Sheem had walked out of security, past onlookers' stunned stares and straight into Phoolmani's embrace. Her grandmother had boasted non-stop on our drive back to your house about Sheem's popularity, her fabulous earnings and sense of duty to her immediate family. She is her grandmother and mother's ticket to a comfortable present, and hopefully, a secure future. For the extended family, she and the brothel-plying Asghari are an embarrassing come-down from an illustrious past. Sheem is one of the few family secrets you had held back from me till Phoolmani arrived. Only then, shamefacedly, you told me about Seema's only child. As with Asghari, you cannot forgive Sheem the stain that her identity as a bar dancer casts upon your painstakingly woven mantle of respectability.

You justify your contempt for Sheem by casting her as a silly, shallow and selfish brat who thinks of no one besides herself. I have spent too little time with her to form any opinion but do think your criticism of Sheem on the last count might be unfounded. The huge suitcase that she has brought with her on a short trip to Banaras and Bhabua is full of gifts for every member of your immediate and extended family—saris for you and Salma, shalwar-kameez sets and make-up for Meenu's trousseau, a shirt for Nanhe, a teddy bear for Haaris, and goodies galore for relatives in Bhabua.

Neither has she forgotten to bring gifts for Shama, your elder married daughter who, in honour of Sheem's visit, has made a rare trip to Banaras along with her four children—three daughters and a son—to meet her childhood friend. It's difficult to believe that Sheem and Shama are the same age. Weighed under by heavy sequined saris and kilos of gold jewellery, and by the layers of fat she has accumulated in the quest for a prized son, Shama looks a good ten years older than Sheem.

Surprisingly, Shama seems to get along very well with Sheem. Surprising, because, as far as I can tell, Shama does not get along with Meenu, whom she constantly berates for paying too much attention to books and too little to learning household tasks, nor with Salma, with whom she is icily polite and patronising, reminding her forever of the duties expected from an efficient home-maker. Married to a wealthy contractor in the nearby town of Saidpur, your elder daughter is proud of her own model conduct as a wife, daughter-in-law and mother.

I have often heard her brag to the resentfully silent Salma about her admirable management of the servants that she has at her beck and call, and the perfect order in which she keeps her house. Her mother-in-law, Shama never fails to inform Salma, loves her so much that she refuses to be parted from her even for a few days—hence Shama's infrequent and short visits to her natal home. This declaration is usually accompanied by a self-congratulatory sigh. Besides, her children are too used to the plenitude in their father's house to be happy for long in the frugality of their grandmother's home. If you are upset by your daughter's thoughtless dismissal of your financial difficulties, you don't show it.

I have met your son-in-law Amjad a few times. Quiet and reserved, he never stays beyond a night at your place. He is a hard-working, busy man, you say with obvious pride. You often talk about his meteoric climb from being merely comfortably off to becoming enviably well-to-do, his high status in Saidpur's business community, his generosity towards his wife and children. What more could your daughter have asked from life?

Your pride in her good fortune notwithstanding, I have noticed that you look guiltily relieved when it's time for Shama to leave. The demands of her four growing children, and especially her thoroughly spoilt son, play havoc with your carefully budgeted household expenses. The constant tension between her and Meenu disturbs the tranquillity of your home, and Shama's constant complaints about her many ailments fray your nerves.

No one is quite sure what exactly is wrong with Shama's health. She moans incessantly about mysterious fevers that come and go, and various pains and aches, the reasons for which have never showed up in the battery of expensive tests advised by doctors and paid for by her husband.

However, the bruises she almost always carries on her face and body could have a tangible explanation, if only you probed more insistently than you do. You prefer to attribute the black eye, the angry gashes and the injured limbs that Shama invariably shows up with to your daughter's obesity and clumsiness. Parroting your explanations, Shama too makes vague mention of walking into doors and falling off chairs. When I try to talk to you, your disapproval of my questions is obvious. Quick to reiterate that you know your daughter better than I do, you stress that if there was any other reason for her injuries, you would know immediately. And I don't know your son-in-law; he loves your daughter dearly and wouldn't dream of causing her hurt. Shama is a lucky girl, you insist. She couldn't have asked for a better husband and family than the one you wisely chose for her.

Popping yet another painkiller, of which she consumes four or five a day, Shama follows Sheem into the room. 'Amma, I have a splitting headache and can't find my jar of pain balm. Things get lost so easily in this house. Send someone to the chemist to buy me a new jar,' Shama demands in a querulous tone.

'No need to buy a new one, Shama. I am carrying an extra jar of a wonderful pain balm made in Thailand that I bought during my last visit to Dubai. It will make your headache disappear in a flash. I will get it for you,' Sheem says in her eager-to-please, shrill voice, before hurrying off upstairs for the wonder balm.

Sheem's voice is not pretty, nor is her Hindi and Urdu language and diction as polished and educated as that of her mother, grandmother and aunts. Born and brought up in Bombay in the post-tawaif era, her destiny since childhood was tied to the dance bars where the niceties of voice modulation and language skills count for little in comparison to a beautiful face and lithe body.

'The gramophone is for pretty-faced tawaifs and their silly and superficial warbling. I have worked too hard on your education to allow you now to fritter away your talent in singing three-minute songs!' Sultana delivered her judgement to a scowling Bindo.

They had argued all morning about Bindo's decision to record for Vallabhdas Runchordas. At some point, Shamim Khan Sahib walked into the confrontation and, in a rare departure, joined cause with Sultana.

Unlike Sultana, he was not against the gramophone, nor did he think that all music recorded on it was silly and superficial. His objection to the offer stemmed from misgivings about Bindo's youth and inexperience. 'Child, you have just begun performing. Your talent will get stunted if you start recording so early. The gramophone has its own constraints of time and style. You must find your own voice before you sing to the diktats of the gramophone,' the old teacher reasoned with his favourite student who kept staring at the floor in stony silence.

'Musicians like Ustad Abdul Karim Khan Sahib and Janaki Bai, whom you admire so much, had long years of music-making behind them before they agreed to record for the gramophone. They were deeply rooted in their music and could move in and out of the world of recordings and mehfils with ease. Take a lesson from them,' Shamim Khan Sahib pleaded. But no amount of arguing, logic or reasoning seemed to have any effect on the young woman. Her mind was made up. She would sign the contract drawn up by Vallabhdas Runchordas.

'Well then, since you are so sure that you can make your own decisions, you obviously have no further need for a guardian. I suggest you ask your mother to come into the room so that I can inform her of my decision to be out of your kotha and your life.' A furious Sultana issued an ultimatum similar to the one that she had used to merciless advantage years ago.

Bindo, however, was no longer a lonely child from the backwaters of Bhabua, desperate for an education that only Sultana could make possible. Her success in consecutive mehfils, her rising fame and the shift to her own kotha and, with it, the arrival of her family, especially her mother, had done wonders to boost Bindo's not inconsiderable self-belief. Besides, she was sick of being controlled by Sultana. She had argued with Daya Singh during his visits to Banaras against Sultana continuing as her guardian. He had paid no heed. If Sultana of her own accord relinquished that responsibility, neither he nor Teema would have any option, Bindo gloated inwardly, but to allow her to guide her own destiny.

The success of the next part of Bindo's stratagem rested on her mother. A housewife, Saleeman had spent her life confined within the four walls of her home in Bhabua. Innocent to the politics of the kotha and the complexities of the world of music-making, she had no previous acquaintance with Sultana. Naturally, she unquestioningly believed all the stories that Bindo told her about the hardships and deprivations she had suffered at the hands of her tyrannical and mean-minded guardian. Made pregnant again by Sa'dullah as soon as she arrived in Banaras, and preoccupied with managing the house, Saleeman was too exhausted to have the time or the energy to probe the veracity of her daughter's allegations.

Bindo had told her about the meeting with Vallabhdas Runchordas only this morning, but Saleeman had not thought to question her daughter's previous silence on the issue. Bindo had attributed Sultana's unwillingness to allow her to record to jealousy. And Saleeman's heart had gone out to her weeping daughter, who said that Sultana did not wish her to become more popular and famous than her granddaughter Roshanara.

So, when ushered into Sultana's presence, Saleeman made only a token, half-hearted request for her to continue as her daughter's guardian. The slight was not lost on either Sultana or Shamim Khan. Feeling grievously humiliated, Sultana sailed out of Bindo's kotha. Shocked at his student's ingratitude and obstinacy, Shamim Khan had tried in vain to convince Bindo and her mother about their need for the old tawaif's guidance, experience and contacts.

'Yes, I told you, naa ... now stop worrying! Sudhakar just called. He says he can wait for another week. He will not finalise the group till we are back in Mumbai.' Sheem is on the phone as usual, and from the sound of it, talking to Seema, whom she describes as her 'mother, best friend, mentor and malik'.

'Malik?' I ask, flummoxed, the term conjuring up for me visions of nineteenth-century slave girls and their courtesan owners.

'Arrey, malik just means manager,' Phoolmani interjects impatiently.

'It's an old term,' you say, breaking out of your gloomy silence. 'In our community, a young tawaif's mother, aunt or elder sister who managed her career, handled her earnings and took responsibility for her well-being was called her malik. My mother was my malik. Phoolmani khala was Seema's malik. Likewise, Seema is now Sheem's malik.'

An experienced malik, you and Phoolmani impress upon me, tapped into her network of old patrons to give a head-start to a young tawaif's career. As a veteran, she would try and get the best possible musicians to accompany her ward, and hire skilled tailors and jewellers to ensure that she always looked her best in mehfils. She taught the youthful novice in her care the value of professional ethics, to never renege on a mehfil commitment and to make certain that she reached the right place at the right time.

She guided her ward in her selection of appropriate songs for a particular mehfil and kept a sharp eye on her presentation, deportment, etiquette and choice of lovers. Consummate in the art of making even the most miserly patron generous, she passed on these talents to the young tawaif. She handled all the financial dealings and was responsible for investing her ward's earnings to ensure a secure future for her. In short, a responsible and skilled malik was indispensable to the success of a young tawaif.

'Bombay is packed with dancers from all over. They come from all kinds of backgrounds. The Agrewali Bedia, Nat from Rajasthan, Kolahati from Maharashtra, Jogin and Basavi from Andhra and Karnataka, all bring their girls to dance in the bars as do we, the deraydars. Though we all are from different communities and come from different areas, we have music and dance in our blood. We have no need to go through middlemen since our own people are already settled in Bombay and help us establish our girls as dancers. Our girls never travel alone but are accompanied by their mothers, sisters and aunts who look after them. We call them malik, the Bedia call them patelan, and so on, but their duties and responsibilities are the same,' Phoolmani, with her superior knowledge of Bombay bars, explains to me.

'Besides khandani people like us, the line is also full of agents who bring girls with no family background of music and dance from all over the country, even from Nepal and Bangladesh. These girls, travelling on their own without family support, have a much more difficult time than our wards. They are entirely dependent on their agents for work, housing and all other needs, and are exploited by them at every step. The girls know nothing about the profession; they do not know how to protect themselves, have no idea about how to deal firmly with ashiqs and no thought about the future. Not our girls. Guided by us, they do well for themselves, make a fortune while it lasts and invest it wisely for the times when they will no longer be young and pretty, with ashiqs at their beck and call.'

Fed up of the rules and restrictions imposed upon her for years on end by her unwanted malik, Bindo revelled in the freedom that followed Sultana's departure from her life. In the coming days, she signed the agreement with Vallabhdas Runchordas to record for Odeon and spent much time imagining her former guardian's soreness when she became famous as a gramophone star.

Unknown to Bindo, however, the contract that had become the immediate cause of her rift with Sultana was doomed from the beginning. Around the same time as her debut in Patna, the ownership of Odeon records changed hands in Europe. Its holding company, Carl Lindstrom A.G. had sold out to Columbia Gramophone Ltd in October 1925, an inconvenient fact that Vallabhdas Runchordas—sanguine in the hope that the changeover would not affect his stakes in Odeon—had withheld from Bindo when she signed his contract in 1926.

Promising Bindo that he would be back soon for her recording session, he returned to Bombay to discover that there had been a change of agents delegated with the responsibility of managing Odeon records in India. Divested of the lucrative returns from Odeon that he had invested in the running of his own companies, The Talking Machine & Indian Record Co. and Viel-O-Phone, it would take several years for Vallabhdas Runchordas to recover from the financial crisis.

Unaware of this turn of events, Bindo continued to wait for his return to Banaras and the launch of her fortunes as a gramophone singer. Meanwhile, she had to contend with Teema, who upon receiving the news of Bindo's separation from Sultana, arrived unannounced at her cousin's doorstep. This was Teema's first visit to the city in all the years that Bindo had been here.

'Teema looked wonderful!' Phoolmani recalls. 'Although not blessed with beautiful features, the glow of health and well-being on her face, the lustre of her thick, black hair, always coiled in a big bun and the sparkle in her eyes made her look radiant. She had put on weight, and that was most becoming. She was dressed in a simple silk sari. And in her ears, neck, wrists and ankles wore heavy gold jewellery. My mother later remarked that Teema looked every bit a thakurain, Rajput wife.

'My family celebrated their reunion with Teema like Eid. I remember Amma cooked mutton pulao. And she also made dal-puri and kheer, which is always cooked in our parts to welcome back a daughter or a daughter-in-law after an extended absence. You should have seen Bindo's happiness. She rarely smiled, but that day she was beaming from ear to ear. She wouldn't leave Teema's side for a moment. Like a little child reunited with her mother after a long separation, she would keep flinging her arms around Teema in a joyous embrace.'

Bindo's delight was short-lived, though. Teema had come to Banaras with a purpose. Once the tears of reunion had been shed and embraces exchanged, she got down to the business of finding out the exact reasons behind Bindo's split with Sultana. Teema talked with Shamim Khan, Munney Khan the tabla player, Saleeman and to Bindo herself, and came to the conclusion that, if left to her own resources, her cousin's inexperience, mercurial temper, obstinacy and arrogance would, sooner rather than later, destroy her career for good.

Accordingly, she paid a visit to Sultana's home. Apologising profusely for Bindo's behaviour, Teema humbly requested the old tawaif to reconsider taking over once again the responsibility of guiding her career.

'My mother loved Bindo khala very much. She couldn't stand by and allow her to foolishly waste all the effort and money that, at her behest, Babu Daya Singh had invested in khala's success,' you explain.

'Yes of course Teema loved Bindo, but she had no faith in my sister's ability to take care of herself. Teema had no faith in our family and so never tired of running our lives for us,' Phoolmani raises the bitterness of acid over family memories. 'How Bindo wept and raged and pleaded with Teema when she heard of her visit to Sultana! But Teema was unmoved. Refusing to understand the agonies that she had suffered in Sultana's house, Teema even raised her hand at Bindo. Not many tawaifs as successful as Bindo would have tolerated such a beating. But my sister, otherwise so fiery, never once retaliated. It was just as well that Sultana eventually refused to entertain Teema's request. Even she realised that the relationship between Bindo and her had soured beyond redemption, a truth that Teema was refusing to acknowledge.'

'My mother always did her best for her relatives. It's very sad really that all that she ever got in return was blame and ingratitude. Bindo khala and her family had lived off my mother's earnings for years. And yet, the moment Bindo khala began making money, they all conveniently forgot my mother's support.' You are now in battle mode.

'All the efforts that my mother made were for Bindo khala's benefit. It was because of her apologies and pleadings that Sultana softened enough to allow Shamim Khan Sahib to continue his association with Bindo khala. How could she have survived in the line without someone as accomplished and respected as Khan sahib by her side? Postponing her return to Ranchi, my mother stayed on for the next five to six months in Banaras only so that Bindo khala would not be left on her own at the threshold of her career.'

Her prolonged stay in Banaras, you tell me, generated considerable tension between Teema and Daya Singh. He had generously supported Teema's family for years on end. But his patience ran thin when Bindo decided to part ways with Sultana. He was in no mood to put on hold his life with Teema for the sake of a headstrong and foolish young tawaif. Fed up with Teema's absence, Daya Singh personally visited Banaras. Either Teema should immediately accompany him back to Ranchi, he announced, or she could stay back permanently with Bindo. Notwithstanding her concern for her cousin's future, Teema had little choice but to return with Daya Singh.

Sheem, busy so far talking to her many ashiqs on a smartphone and filing her already manicured pink painted nails, suddenly decides to take part in our conversation. 'My mummy is the best mummy in the world!' she declares with filmy child sincerity. 'She never refuses me anything,' stating this emphatically, Sheem goes back to working on her nails.

'It's true! My Seema has devoted her life to Sheem. "You just focus on looking pretty and your dance. I will manage the rest," she tells Sheem,' Phoolmani adds. 'If today Sheem is amongst the highest-earning, top-grade dancers in Mumbai, then the credit goes to Seema. She accepts only the best contracts for her girl, no riff-raff hole-in-the-corner bars for her. And she makes sure that Sheem spends half her year abroad. Tell her, Sheem, where all have you gone?'

'Dubai, Sharjah, Muscat, Singapore, England, America,' Sheem rolls out dutifully.

Bar dancers, it appears, are great travellers, much like tawaifs of an earlier age. Bindo, in her first year as a tawaif under Sultana's guardianship, had already toured several towns and princely states across Bihar and the

United Provinces and built a reputation as a singer of great promise. This came in handy when she set off on her own course, as Bindo continued to be invited not only by patrons familiar with her music but also by guests impressed with her performance in these mehfils. Over the coming years, with Shamim Khan Sahib by her side, Bindo regaled new audiences in the principalities of central India, like Chhatarpur, Datia, Orchha and Panna, besides returning to old patrons in Tekari, Dumrao, Hathwa, Pratapgarh and Manda.

However, there was no denying the fact that, slowly and almost imperceptibly, Bindo lost more opportunities than she gained. Other tawaifs nearer her age, like Rasoolan and Siddheshwari, and even Roshanara who resumed singing after a long hiatus, had graduated to performing in major princely states like Kashmir, Hyderabad and Rampur. Most courtesans in Banaras, including Bindo, had sizzled with envy when Siddheshwari was presented a brand-new car as a token of his appreciation by the maharaja of Kashmir. Since her own house in Banaras had no space outside it for parking, the car was kept in the compound of the Chowk police station with the permission of the officer-in-charge.

Rasoolan and Siddheshwari were also finding appreciation in cities like Calcutta and Bombay, where the English-educated Indian industrialist and business circles now formed the new and powerful patronage establishment for Hindustani music. Bindo, though as musically talented as her peers, continued to be contained in the mehfil circuit of zamindari estates and smaller principalities.

The reasons for this were many. While luck and a chance encounter with a princely patron at a musical gathering no doubt played a role, for newcomers like Bindo, invitations to perform in royal durbars and mehfils were dependent mainly upon recommendations by insiders. After her fallout with Sultana became public, there were few tawaifs and senior accompanist musicians willing to jeopardise their relationship with Roshanara's grandmother by extending support to young Bindo.

Moreover, invitations to perform in princely states were critically dependent on the benevolence of the large and hierarchical bureaucracies surrounding the rulers in these principalities. Old and established tawaifs like Sultana, therefore, paid the greatest attention to cultivating mutually beneficial relationships with the court officials, ranging from courtiers to clerks, who were responsible for organising royal functions and entertainments and the selection of appropriate musicians, dancers and entertainers. This closely guarded network operated on a highly refined system of bribes, commissions, sexual favours and sycophancy. Bindo, who had garnered for herself an unenviable reputation of being ungrateful and disloyal, further compounded the bias against her by often being abrasive and arrogant in her dealings with court officials.

Then there was the increasingly pressing issue of sexual propriety that played a decisive role in the acceptance of tawaif singers into the modern patronage circles of the Indian bourgeoisie. The prevailing prejudice against courtesans had contributed manifold to the anxiety felt by elite tawaifs to fashion for themselves a socially acceptable image.

A further edge was added to this desperation by a flurry of legislation through the 1920s and 1930s of anti-trafficking and anti-prostitution laws, such as the United Provinces Naik Girls Protection Act (1929), United Provinces Minor Girls Protection Act (1929), Bengal Suppression of Immoral Traffic Act (1933) and United Provinces Suppression of Immoral Traffic Act (1933). The criminalisation of prostitution by the state made it vital for elite tawaifs eager to break into the music circuits of the Indian bourgeoisie to distance themselves from a lifestyle associated with immorality and vice.

Siddheshwari, under the mentorship of the venerable teacher Siyaji Maharaj, and Rasoolan, guided adroitly by her grandmother Adaalat Bai, were in the process of refashioning not only their singing styles and repertoires but also their personas to fit into the mould of serious-minded practitioners of raga-bound art music. Ably advised by the shrewd Sultana, Roshanara—though never scaling the heights reached by Siddheshwari and Rasoolan, because of the ill health that plagued her singing career—too was in the process of foregrounding her identity as a musician while simultaneously erasing the markers that associated the tawaif in public perception with prostitution.

Mehfils in Roshanara's kotha, much like the gatherings in Rasoolan and Siddheshwari's salons, began and ended strictly within a given time, and were characterised by their high standard of music, decorum and restraint. Consumption of alcohol and intoxicants by guests was frowned upon, and boisterous behaviour deemed unacceptable. Sultana, renowned for the etiquette that she enforced in Roshanara's kotha, had become more particular still about maintaining discipline and allowing entry only to the 'right' kind of patrons. Premium was placed on family background and old connections, while aspiring guests who flaunted bad manners and new money were politely refused admission. Sacrificing short-term financial gain for long-term social acceptability, Sultana was known to have occasionally cancelled an evening's mehfil in the kotha for want of suitable patrons, instead of allowing Roshanara to perform for anyone and everyone willing to pay as had been the norm.

As she gained maturity, Roshanara was known more for her music than her physical charms and erotic liaisons. Her sexual relationship was discreet and long-term. Notwithstanding the attention she received from rich and powerful patrons, she remained faithful to hakim sahib with whom she had two sons. She was not alone in drawing this line. Rasoolan and Siddheshwari, more successful than Roshanara, had set this rule by personal example.

I remember being told by Ramzan Khan, the son of Rasoolan's teacher Shammu Khan, 'Rasoolan's deportment and observance of etiquette in princely mehfils was impeccable but underlined by a polite reserve. Even the most philandering of princes thought twice before making sexual advances at her. Rasoolan would sing without complaint for as long as her hosts and their guests wished her to perform. And then she would quietly retire to her rooms. Not for Rasoolan the night-long drinking bouts, the sexual encounters that often took place in princely mehfils after the singing. Everyone was aware that she was a serious-minded singer. And for this reason, she was invited only to those mehfils where the focus was on music.'

Bindo, on the other hand, after choosing to part ways with Sultana, had no one to plot her ascent to the highest pinnacle of success. Insecure about money and ignorant about the changing times, her immediate family in Banaras encouraged her to entertain as many wealthy visitors in her kotha as possible. And while she had no trust or respect for her father Sa'dullah who, with Sultana out of the way, tried desperately to reclaim parental authority over her career, Bindo was too inexperienced to gauge the social worth of the men he kept bringing in droves to her kotha. Dazzled, like any young girl her age, by the amorous attention, flattery and expensive presents they showered on her, she would too often ignore the advice of her one sagacious well-wisher in Banaras, Shamim Khan Sahib, to be more selective in her choice of patrons.

Recognising that she was too young to play the role of performer and manager simultaneously, Shamim Khan tried to maintain decorum and etiquette in the mehfils at her kotha. This was easier said than done.

Emboldened by the presence of his wife, who offered him no resistance, and shrugging off his daughter's insults, Sa'dullah was up to his tricks again. Unknown to her, he struck deals with prospective customers who were only interested in a physical encounter with Bindo, and smuggled inside her kotha men too inebriated to be allowed entry into more fastidious salons. His constant meddling often resulted in unsavoury rowdiness and even fisticuffs that disrupted her mehfils.

Police would arrive to quell the fracas. Intractable and inexperienced, Bindo would rage and argue and lay blame upon her next-door neighbour Sultana for lodging false complaints. Sa'dullah would try and use the opportunity to further his importance in her career by seconding her claims. For any elite tawaif, such disturbances, and especially the arrival of police, would have been a matter of grave concern. Not only did these incidents compromise Bindo's reputation among other tawaifs and accompanist musicians, but they also lowered her standing as a musician among more discerning patrons.

The Gayika Sangh, of which she was a member, began to take notice of the goings-on in her kotha. With the passing of anti-prostitution legislation, the scope of the Gayika Sangh's activities had widened considerably. By the 1930s, the association had begun focusing upon securing its members from the stigma of criminalisation unleashed by the new laws.

In an attempt to distinguish tawaifs from sex workers, as a registered trade association, the Gayika Sangh had begun issuing printed 'licences' certifying its tawaif members as singers and dancers. Though these licences enjoyed no legal validity, they were hugely coveted by all tawaifs, because of the considerable goodwill that the Gayika Sangh still enjoyed in the city's law-enforcement circles. The involvement of the most venerable tawaifs of Banaras, like Badi Moti Bai, Rajeshwari, Vidyadhari, Gulab Jan, Mannan Jan and Sultana, ensured for the Gayika Sangh the discreet support of their erstwhile patrons who were among the most powerful men in Banaras, wielding considerable influence with the local administration, police and judiciary. This, combined with Prem Kumar Khanna's continued championing of the Gayika Sangh's interests in official circles, guaranteed its certified members some degree of protection from harassment.

As its activities expanded, the Gayika Sangh soon became indistinguishable from the traditional self-governing council, panchayat or saat taat, of the kotha community in the city, which became subsumed in the association. Besides tawaifs, membership of the Gayika Sangh now included male accompanist musicians from the four communities customarily associated with kotha-based music: Kathak, Dhari, Kinnar and Bhaat. Presided over by Mannan Jan after Husna Bai's death, it was vested with duties and responsibilities of the traditional panchayat that included regulating its members' professional conduct in the community and arbitrating all internal disputes according to customary norms.

Only too aware of the need to protect the increasingly beleaguered tawaifs from the hostile scrutiny of the law, the Gayika Sangh enforced a strict code of conduct upon its members, including the need to maintain decorum at all times in kothas. Any breach of the boundaries of propriety within which tawaifs and accompanist musicians were expected to conduct their professional lives could, and often did, invite censure and even penalty from the association.

The constant disturbances in Bindo's kotha found repeated mention in the crime pages of daily newspapers. Worried that such adverse publicity could stigmatise the wider community and make it more vulnerable to intensified surveillance and persecution by the authorities, Mannan Jan, in her capacity as president of the Gayika Sangh, reprimanded Bindo and her father on several occasions. When Bindo and Sa'dullah failed to comply with Mannan Jan's orders, despite repeated warnings, she decided to bring up their case in a meeting attended by all Gayika Sangh members.

'I, along with my mother, father and brothers, accompanied Bindo to the panchayat held in Mannan Jan's house,' Phoolmani recounts. 'It was a huge gathering with all the tawaifs, gurus and Khan sahibs present. Sultana had instigated everyone against my sister. No one was willing to hear Bindo's side of the story.'

'I have heard about the meeting from Tara khala, who is a very fair-minded person,' you interject. 'She remembers how everyone present tried to instil sense into Bindo khala to become more responsible. But she was beyond reasoning. Instead, she began accusing Sultana of using her contacts in the police to create disturbances in her kotha. No one believed that story. It was becoming obvious to the assembly that Bindo khala was unwilling to take any responsibility for her own actions, and would continue repeating her mistakes, the price of which would have to be borne by the entire community.'

'As if everyone else in the community were saints!' Phoolmani retorts, furious. 'The way you go on sanctimoniously, your friend will think that bhajan–kirtan took place in the other kothas. Come on! Let's not fool either ourselves or others. Let's not pretend that we were nuns living in nunneries. We were tawaifs. Men visited us to have a good time, to hear music, drink, to flirt and, if we were willing, to have sex. There were always guests, however high-born, who would force themselves on a tawaif. They had to be handled. Tempers flared, and even fists would fly between rival claimants for a bai-ji's attention. It happened in all kothas, elite and humble. The only difference was that the police did not barge inside fancy establishments, and the Gayika Sangh too chose to ignore the trouble. They were all part of the same hypocritical pack, each one pretending to be so respectable. You scratch my back, I will scratch yours. Poor Bindo was victimised because she was an outsider, young and on her own.'

Turning your back on your aunt even as she is speaking, you walk out of the room, mumbling about a headache. Leaning over, Phoolmani whispers, 'She is exactly like her mother was. Always pretending to be better than the rest, always quick to point fingers at others.'

Uncomfortable, I try and turn the conversation. 'What was the outcome eventually of the Gayika Sangh meeting?'

'The outcome was predetermined. Mannan Jan and the others threw my sister out of the Gayika Sangh at the end of the meeting. Except for Shamim Khan, she had no one's support. Henceforth, Bindo would have to survive on her own. The Gayika Sangh took back the miserable licence it had issued her. No accompanist could play with her anymore. It was virtually like being excommunicated from the community.'

Bindo's only chance of regaining entry lay in issuing a public apology with an undertaking that henceforth she would abide by the rules of the Gayika Sangh. Anyone who knew Bindo could tell that this would not happen. Fiercely arrogant, Bindo declared that she would rather stop singing than apologise for a wrong that she was convinced she did not commit.

Behind the facade of stubborn belligerence, however, lay deep terror. Too proud to share her fears with anyone, Bindo felt not very different from the lost and vulnerable little girl who had arrived in an unfamiliar city to live among unknown people and face an uncertain future. Her body collapsed under the weight of exhaustion. She felt too drained to carry on the never-ending struggle that had dogged her ever since she embarked on her own as a tawaif. Her expulsion from the Gayika Sangh, though decidedly the worst setback in her career thus far, was not the only disappointment she had faced.

Her early dreams to become a gramophone star had long soured: Bindo had waited for several months after signing the contract with Odeon records before she received news of the collapse of her benefactor's fortunes. Consoling herself that sooner or later she would record for some other company, Bindo had bided time for a good offer to come her way.

As luck or circumstances had it, she missed out on all worthwhile contracts, often by a whisker. Her reputation of being arrogant and headstrong frequently preceded her meeting with company agents, causing her appointments with them to get cancelled at the last minute. Sometimes the negotiations fell through over remuneration. Payments made by recording companies to artists were notoriously low. As the sole provider for her family, ever since Babu Daya Singh cut her off financially, money had become a priority for Bindo. She no longer felt as unconcerned about payments as she had while agreeing to the modest sum offered by Vallabhdas Runchordas. This did not assuage the heartburn she suffered when agents of well-known gramophone companies arrived in Banaras and signed on other tawaif musicians, like Siddheshwari and Rasoolan, who were willing to record for token amounts, based on the reasoning that a wider reach would translate into lucrative invitations to perform at many more musical fora.

While Roshanara, under Sultana's iron hand, continued to refuse all offers to record, Siddheshwari and Kashi Bai had begun recording by the early 1930s, and Rasoolan Bai too had agreed to sing for the Broadcast Company of India in 1935. The popularity of her rivals' recordings had cost Bindo several sleepless nights spent seething in jealousy.

In the midst of this growing darkness, Bindo discovered that she was pregnant. Taken by surprise and not ready to be burdened with yet another responsibility at this critical juncture of her career, she considered abortion. Her father's enthusiastic support of this decision, however, made her waver. She had little respect for Sa'dullah and his manipulative, self-centred greed. Suspicious of his motives, Bindo felt an instinctive defiance flare up.

She began paying more attention to her mother's pleading that she continue with the pregnancy. Within the tawaif community, children were accepted as the will of god, Saleeman said to her. Bindo would not be the first tawaif to carry a pregnancy to term while performing full-time as a singer and dancer, nor would she be the last. Confused and lost, Bindo finally heeded her mother's advice. The first few months were miserable. She felt sick and exhausted all the time. And yet, till her pregnancy began to show, she could not afford to refuse invitations to perform.

Not that she received too many invitations from within Banaras. With the withdrawal of Gayika Sangh membership, she had no access to the music halls of the few tawaif patrons left in the city. Invitations from outside still came her way. Since accompanists from Banaras were forbidden from playing with her, Bindo was forced to make elaborate arrangements to secure musicians from Bhabua and around to accompany her in performance.

She would often find herself desperately missing Shamim Khan Sahib. One of the most accomplished sarangi players of his times, her ustad had been familiar with every nuance of her singing. As her accompanist, he had expertly highlighted her musical strengths during performances and covered up her weaknesses. With him gone, Bindo felt insecure. Forced to sing with accompanists unfamiliar with her music, her performances, she feared, were no longer as dazzling as they were when her ustad had been by her side.

By the time little Rani was born, an exhausted Bindo had slid into debilitating anxiety and depression. Fretting constantly, she blamed the newborn baby and her unknown father, her own family, Sultana and the world at large for conspiring against her destiny as a great musician. She refused to look at her daughter's face when Saleeman brought her to Bindo's bedside. Disinterested in either feeding or looking after the baby, whose care was taken over by her grandmother, Bindo spent the postpartum period staring at the walls and weeping.

'Bindo took no part in the festivities that our mother organised to celebrate Rani's birth. Refusing food or words of kindness, she began shrivelling into a stony silence,' Phoolmani says of her sister's descent into melancholia.

It was around this time that the prince came to Bindo's house. Her kotha hadn't been open in months, but Sa'dullah had not given up on sneaking men into her room. In no shape to entertain anyone, Bindo would furiously throw the visitors out almost immediately. It came as a surprise to everyone, therefore, that she not only refrained from hurling out the kunwar but also allowed him to visit her again the very next day.

Bindo herself wasn't sure why she had thawed with the very first look at the prince. Was it his youth and remarkable good looks that made her heart skip a beat? He was, besides, also attentive and generous, witty and good-humoured. He sympathised with her misfortunes and promised to help with launching her in the gramophone industry, where he claimed to know several people. A broken Bindo found herself being increasingly drawn to him.

The family heaved a sigh of relief. With Bindo shutting herself away, money had been running out. Following their father's example, none of the sons in the household did any work. The daughters, Phoolmani, Pyaari and Sakeena, were too young still to start earning. The family had to eat. Living expenses and fees had to be arranged for the ustad who had been brought in from Bhabua to initiate Phoolmani into music and dance. Bindo had to return to work, and fast, if the family was to survive in Banaras.

No one cared to check on the kunwar's background. Sa'dullah ignored the rumours that he heard in the bazaar about the unsavoury proclivities of his daughter's new lover. For him, all that mattered was that the kunwar was rich and generous. He not only paid Bindo well for her attentions but thoughtfully brought sweets and fruits for the entire family. Most importantly, he never forgot to slip a few extra rupees into Sa'dullah's grasping fingers whenever he visited Bindo, which was almost daily. Sa'dullah wasn't going to spoil this party because of the warnings of some carping mouths.

Soon, the frightening stories reached even Saleeman's ears. No other tawaif in the bazaar was willing to entertain the kunwar. She confronted Sa'dullah.

'Has he done anything to your precious daughter till now?' Sa'dullah had shot back in irritation. 'People are just jealous that, despite their best efforts, our Bindo still manages to attract the attention of wealthy and powerful patrons.'

Saleeman had kept quiet. She needed money to run the house and feed her children. Moreover, Bindo seemed to be returning to her old self under the kunwar's lavish attention. Good times seemed to be returning to the kotha. Saleeman decided to trust Sa'dullah's words and pay no further heed to the gossip of the bazaar.

'What were the stories that your mother heard about the kunwar?' I ask Phoolmani.

'The kunwar, my mother was warned, was a fiend with women. His bedchamber was a slaughterhouse from which no woman came out unhurt. Many even lost their lives in there. Their bodies would then be tossed to the alligators,' Phoolmani replies, evading my eyes.

Rarely stepping out of her house during that period, Bindo remained unaware of the stories that her parents kept from her. Without hesitation, she accepted the prince's invitation to accompany him to his principality in Bihar. Holi was just a few days away, and the kunwar wanted Bindo by his side during the celebrations. Longing to get away from her greedy family, stifling kotha and a hostile city, she paid little heed to Saleeman who, upon hearing of the invitation, woke up at long last to her responsibility as a mother and tried to dissuade Bindo from going. Dismissing her warnings as an excuse to keep her, the golden goose of the family, tied firmly to the household, Bindo fought bitterly with Saleeman.

Bought over by the kunwar's generosity and promises of even greater largesse, Sa'dullah was delighted by his daughter's enthusiasm for the trip. Prudently, he refrained from making his eagerness obvious for fear of Bindo's reaction. She could change her mind just to spite her father, Sa'dullah knew only too well from experience and decided his cause was best served by appearing reluctant to let her leave with the kunwar.

Hiding in the moonlit forest and praying for her life, Bindo recalled the details of the nightmare that had unfolded after her arrival in the kunwar's outhouse. Exulting in the luxurious furnishings of her room, she was taken by complete surprise when the usually gentle prince had appeared flicking a whip in one hand and a strange, jewel-studded, long metallic object in the other. Her surprise had turned to horror when, without warning, he had flicked the whip around her ankles and toppled her to the floor. Then, mounting her quickly, he had opened her legs and tried to thrust the metallic dildo, that at closer quarters revealed saw-like teeth on either side, deep inside her.

Pushing him away with all the strength she could muster, Bindo had protested, 'Kunwar sahib, what is all this? You are hurting me!' Face twisted in a demonic smile, the kunwar slapped her across the face. In a lightning move, Bindo had lunged at him and pulled the whip out of his hand.

Bindo shivered at the memory. She had never imagined that she would end up as a plaything for a degenerate prince. She now realised how far she had drifted from her destiny as a musician. Feeling lost and hopeless, Bindo wept bitter, angry tears of regret for a fruitless life that would now end in a lonely death in an unknown forest.

Suddenly, she heard a voice; a woman's voice singing the most beautiful Sohini, the raga of the hours just before dawn: *Rang na daro, Shyam ji*; Do not throw colour at me, O Dark One (Krishna).

Who could be singing this haunting song in a remote forest? Convinced that she was hallucinating, Bindo peered into the darkness and was shocked to see, in the clearing just ahead, a beautiful girl emanating a radiance that seemed to come from within. Tall and lissom, she had large eyes shaped like lotus petals. She was dressed in a white sari, and her only ornament was the cluster of champa flowers that she wore in each ear. The girl danced to her own singing, seemingly oblivious to the presence of another young woman peering at her through the shrubs.

Dawn was just breaking when the girl finally finished her song. Looking directly at Bindo, who sat bewitched, the girl said, 'It's time we left. The sun will rise shortly and the kunwar's men will reach here by then.'

Nonplussed, Bindo stared at the girl. Finally, finding her voice, she asked, 'Who are you? And how do you know me?'

'I am Sohini,' the girl answered, breaking into a smile as radiant as her being. 'I have been sent by my sisters to bring you into our safekeeping. For long you served us well, until you lost your way. We come now to guide you back on the path destined for you.'

Bindo could not understand anything of what the girl spoke. Yet, she felt her fears ebb. She knew somehow that she could trust this beautiful girl who spoke in riddles. The first rays of the sun had now begun streaking the sky in pale shades of pink.

'Here comes Jogiya,' the beautiful Sohini spoke again, breaking Bindo's trance. Unnoticed by her, they had been joined by an older woman. Dressed in the yellow robes of a yogini, her hair tied into a top-knot and her forehead smeared with sandalwood, she exuded a profound meditative serenity.

Addressing Bindo, Jogiya said softly, 'You might not recognise us, but you do know us as well as we know you. Come with us now. We have not a moment to lose.'

From my limited world of rationality, I try desperately to understand this incredible tale. I ask Phoolmani, 'How do you know all this? Did Bindo return from the forest and tell you her story?'

Phoolmani waves away my questions with an impatient gesture. 'We waited for days on end for Bindo to return. Then the police arrived at our home searching for her. Fearful for Bindo's safety, the family went to Baba Kinnaram's akhada for succour and guidance. We were met there by an old and blind sadhu who, after years of arduous tapasya, could see with his unseeing eyes realities that were out of bounds to ordinary men and women. It was he who told us about Bindo's ordeal and her escape from the prince.

'He explained to my parents: "Among musicians it is known that ragas and raginis come to the aid of the blessed few who serve them faithfully. Bindo was one such rare musician. Betrayed by mere mortals and led astray by her own hubris, she was rescued and provided sanctuary by the melodies she had loved and sung so well. Escorted by them, Bindo disappeared forever deep into the forest, far from the world of human frailties, pettiness, greed and cruelty."' With a sigh, Phoolmani brings to a close the story of Bindo's sad, spectacular life.

CHAPTER 21

Phoolmani

SALMA'S EYES ARE REDDENED AND face drawn when she ushers me into the visitors' room. She neither dimples her usual welcoming smile nor asks if I have had breakfast. She mumbles that you are upstairs and vanishes from the room before I can say anything.

Wondering if Shama, who left last evening, is responsible for Salma's teary demeanour, I consider going upstairs to find you but then decide to wait in the visitors' room. We are scheduled to leave for Bhabua this afternoon with Phoolmani and Sheem. The two of them, I am informed by Salma, who returns looking more composed and with a cup of tea for me, have gone visiting Phoolmani's elder daughter Rajjo and her family.

Salma gets busy clearing away Haaris's scattered toys and tidying up the room. She is now the picture of calm, purposeful efficiency. Stripping the mattresses of the frayed white sheets, she flashes a smile at me before taking them off for washing, her next task for the day.

I have often been struck by Salma's highly confined life, relegated always to the upper storeys of the house, working on never-ending household chores. She rarely comes out in the presence of non-family male visitors who drop in to meet you. Salma's presence is registered, if at all, by a low knock at the door when she brings down food and drink for the guests and at most a glimpse of her hands passing the tray on to you. You say that Salma's seclusion is of her own choice. In all my years of visiting you, I have never once seen Salma step out of your house alone. As a former tawaif disdaining for yourself the claustrophobia of the burqa, you are proud of the fact that Salma, on the rare occasions she does go out, is not only always chaperoned by someone from the family but insists upon wearing the all-covering naqab that leaves only her eyes bare.

Salma is intelligent besides being pretty. Although she has never been to school, she shows a great deal of interest in the outside world she watches on television every night. During the few conversations we have had alone, Salma has told me that she comes from a very poor family. Her parents agreed to marry her off to Nanhe since you made no demands for a dowry.

You confided in me that Salma's family belongs to the Magahiya community, once at the bottom of the tawaif hierarchy. I know that you financed the wedding, including the lunch organised by her family after the nikah was solemnised.

My thoughts are interrupted by the arrival of a very fair, fat and brightly dressed woman. She is trailed by a scrawny, shabbily dressed young boy, weighed down by a basket of fruits, which he balances with one hand on his head, while holding in the other a box of sweets wrapped in cellophane paper as gaudily green as the woman's sari. Gesturing to him to unload the goodies in one corner, the woman tosses a few coins at the child and orders him to leave. Taking no notice of me, the only other person present in the room, she announces her arrival by shouting out your name.

Your reply precedes your hurried footsteps, 'Madhu, you good for nothing! I have been waiting for you to turn up since yesterday and you show up now!' Your obvious pleasure at seeing her is in sharp contrast to your morose mood over the last couple of days on account of the tension with Chanda, compounded by Phoolmani and Sheem's unwanted stay and Shama's stressful presence.

Embracing your guest warmly, you introduce her to me. Madhu, besides Rajjo, is your best friend in Banaras. I have heard a lot about her from you, but this is the first time that I am meeting her in person.

About your age, Madhu belongs to a Ramjani tawaif family from Jaunpur. She shifted to Banaras around the time you moved here from Bhabua. Both of you learnt music and dance from the same teachers and went on to become hugely popular tawaifs. Though professional rivals, you have always been close friends. Today, she is among the wealthier retired tawaifs of Dal Mandi, owning extensive property in the area. The rent she earns has always sent you into raptures of delight and envy.

You envy too Madhu's three kamau, hardworking sons—a rare species in tawaif-headed families. All of them run successful small businesses of their own. They meekly hand over their monthly earnings to Madhu, who apparently is a firm believer in not sparing the rod; the boys still get their share of maternal slaps and punches if they fall out of line.

I have also heard about Madhu's most prized trophy, her husband Dildar Mohammad, who is just about a couple of years older than her eldest son and fifteen years younger than her. A well-off shopkeeper in Dal Mandi, Dildar Mohammad fell so madly in love with Madhu that, unheeding of the despairing warnings of family and friends, insisted on marrying her about seven years ago.

Contrary to dire predictions all around, it has thus far proved to be a happy marriage. Dildar Mohammad, you tell me, not only contributes his husbandly share to Madhu's already substantial earnings but also makes love to her with youthful ardour every night even after the passage of so many years.

At this point, you usually tap your forehead and say, '*Kismet ki baat hai, Saba. Uske paas hamesha jawan hi aye.*' It's destiny, Saba; she always got them young. I know that you say this with a tug in your heart. Masking sexual yearning with wry humour, you have bemoaned to me your luck in attracting the affections of mainly ageing, tired lovers. Madhu's good luck, on the other hand, is still running its course, it would appear.

Madhu has one daughter, Rinku, whom she took to Mumbai several years ago to become a bar dancer. Oddly, you are not only accepting of Madhu's decision but have also expressed genuine sympathy about the fact that, though pretty and vivacious, Rinku's career as a bar dancer was doomed from the start. Suffering from arthritis, her knees hurt every morning after the night-long dancing. You had stated sadly, '*Langdi dancer aur langdi ghodi ek barabar hoti hain ... bilkul bekar.*' A lame dancer and a lame mare are the same ... absolutely useless.

Fortunately for Rinku (and Madhu), a well-off, married jeweller in Mumbai took her on as a mistress and had her installed in a flat that he bought in her name. He not only provides Rinku a generous monthly allowance but also pays Madhu Rs 1,20,000 annually and two pieces of gold jewellery in lieu of removing her daughter from the line. The bounty coming Madhu's way sounds grossly exaggerated to me but I could be wrong. There is no denying that, regardless of the actual sum she receives from Rinku's lover, as the mother of an earning daughter, she is assured for now of a regular additional income every year.

It's her Mumbai connection that has brought Madhu to your house today. She is paying a courtesy call on Phoolmani and Sheem, who is a close friend of Rinku's. Since they are not at home, Madhu directs her attention to me, your new friend about whom, she informs me, she has heard a lot. Settling down on the mattress, Madhu proceeds to give me an intent, unembarrassed, long look. The curiosity is mutual. I have long suspected Madhu to be your alter ego, her bountiful life mirroring the spaces of want in your own. And it is my pop-psychoanalysis that makes me feel unreasonably let down that the fair, fat and plain-looking woman staring at me with shrewd eyes does not approximate the sex goddess-cum-earth mother of your narratives.

The feeling of disappointment seems to be mutual. Without much ado, Madhu comments upon my greying hair. Her advice for me is to use colour. Not unkindly she says, 'What's the need to look like an old woman even before you are one?'

While I don't lose sleep over looking middle-aged, which I am, I must confess that I am not exactly thrilled to hear that I look old. At a loss for words, all I can manage is a weak smile. But you immediately come to my rescue, 'What if her hair is greying? Her face and body are of a young girl!'

Your staunch loyalty makes me feel worse. I am not a young girl and certainly don't look like one. This conversation is not going well, so, turning towards Madhu, I change track, 'I am so glad we could meet. Aapa has talked often about how close you two are.'

As if on cue, you painstakingly enumerate all the many ways in which Madhu has been a supportive and loyal friend through good times and bad. She and Chanda arranged loans for you on relatively reasonable terms when you married off Shama. Madhu also helped finance the extravagance of Meenu's engagement. More recently, following your landlord Radhey Shyam's ultimatum to shift out, it is Madhu, with her vast experience of buying and selling property, who has accompanied you on your rounds to sundry property dealers in search of a house that you can purchase on your limited budget.

Madhu sits impassively through this thanksgiving. I know you are sincere in your gratitude; this is not the first time I am hearing of all this. But in my forays into the world of Hindustani musicians, I have always found this need to enumerate the acts of kindness, even among close friends, a bit difficult to understand. Is it that the hangover of patron–client relationships permeates these more intimate bonds and demands a public reiteration of the giver's generosity and the receiver's appreciation?

You tail off by stating, *'Yeh hamein bahut manti hain.'* A catch-all phrase that can loosely translate, depending upon the context, to: she cares for me a lot, she loves me a lot, she respects me a lot, or I am very important to her.

As expected of me, I turn to Madhu and murmur, 'You have indeed done a lot for aapa.'

With the briefest of nods in acknowledgement, Madhu talks of the difficulties that you have had to face as the mother of a mentally challenged only son. 'She has no one to turn to for support in her advancing age.' Which is why, Madhu had advised you years ago, when Shama was still unmarried, to take her to Mumbai and make her a bar dancer.

I am aware of this. Just a day ago, perhaps triggered by the simultaneous presence of Shama and Sheem in your house, memories of your older daughter's near brush with 'disrepute' had unforeseen made their way into our conversation. You had embarrassedly confessed your bitter turmoil when faced with the choice of putting Shama into the line.

Aware of the family's dire straits, and blessed with a great sense of responsibility, Shama, then only seventeen or eighteen, had begged you to set her up as a bar dancer. After much inner conflict, however, you decided to marry her off instead.

You said with uncharacteristic melodrama, *'Hum uski zindagi barbad nahin karna chahte thhe. Hum chahte thhe ki use woh sab mile jo hamein nahin mila. Ek izzatdar zindagi, shohar aur apna ghar.'* I didn't want to destroy her life. I wanted her to get all that I didn't: a respectable life, a husband and a home of her own.

I remember challenging your assumption that marriage and husband were a great choice for every woman. The argument had led nowhere since you held steadfast that, in Shama's case, as was obvious to all who knew her, marriage and domesticity had brought great happiness.

Today, Madhu reveals something you have not yet told me. 'Since my own daughter had already entered the line, I had taken her and Shama with me to Mumbai. But the girl proved to be selfish and blind to her family's difficulties. All she wanted was marriage. She just refused to dance.'

I notice the swift, small look of alarm you dart at Madhu. I am angry with her for putting out secrets that you don't want revealed. I am also worried that you have been embarrassed. And feel saddened that, in all these years, I have failed to inspire complete trust in you—that you still feel the need to conceal from me parts of your life you fear might be morally repugnant to my middle-class sensibilities. However, once the chaos in my head subsides, I realise that, given the differences of class and sexuality that divide us, it is but natural that you view me as an outsider, hopefully well meaning and well intentioned, but most certainly an outsider.

By now you have regained your composure. 'I have already told you all this, Saba,' you say. You haven't, but I let that pass. I want to say that you owe me no explanation; it is your life and you can choose to represent it any way you want. But you clearly wish to make amends.

You talk about how you had always wanted at least one of your daughters to follow your footsteps and become a performer. Shama was quite pretty then and, more importantly, a good dancer. No, she hadn't learnt 'classical' but could execute better than most film heroines their dance steps that she saw on television. She had won several prizes in dance competitions at school. Shama's friends would gather often at your house and, playing music at full blast, dance. All of them acknowledged that Shama danced best.

You would have liked your daughter to make a name as a dancer in the respectable circuit of dance recitals and shows, but ever pragmatic, you realised these were out of her league, given Shama's lack of training in kathak and the stigma of your background. Then Madhu suggested Mumbai. Initially baulking at the idea, eventually you came around to accepting it as a practical compromise to the uncertain financial future staring at you. The family desperately needed an earning member. On the wrong side of forty and battling difficult circumstances, you were hard put to secure an assured monthly income for your household. And the prospect of having to depend solely on your savings gave you sleepless nights.

Sheem, Seema and Phoolmani were in Mumbai. Sheem, at that point a new entrant to the line, had already begun earning fabulous amounts, you had heard Phoolmani and Seema boast. Other members of your extended family too lived in the city, as did Rinku. Under the protection of family and friends, you felt confident that Shama would come to no harm.

Shama had initially agreed to the plan and willingly accompanied Madhu and you to Mumbai. However, you didn't know that your daughter was in love with Amjad, whose widowed mother had approached you for Shama's hand before the Mumbai plan materialised. You were enthusiastic about the match but the negotiations ran into rough weather when his mother began demanding a huge dowry. You couldn't afford to meet her expectations and backed off, without realising that, in the meanwhile, Shama and Amjad had fallen in love.

Amjad put pressure on his mother to drop her demands but, by the time she buckled under his tears, you had already left for Mumbai with Shama. With his mother in tow, Amjad followed you to the metropolis and demanded that Shama be married to him.

Madhu takes over the story. 'Through my contacts, Shama had immediately got work but then who can undo the will of destiny? Her ashiq and his mother created huge scenes at the bar where she had begun dancing and at my daughter's house where we all were staying. We firmly told them to back off, but then Shama too began behaving like a lovesick fool. Insisting that she wanted to leave the line, she threatened to kill herself if we didn't allow her to marry Amjad. There was little option left eventually but to return to Banaras and get her married.'

I am struck by how familiar this story sounds. The lovelorn heroine-turned-bar dancer, her steadfast lover who braves all odds to get her, and the happy ending heralded by the wail of the shehnai; this is the stuff of Hindi film plots. In keeping with the spirit of the narrative, you bring it to a close by asserting, 'All's well that ends well. I am happy because Shama is so happy in her marriage.'

Recalling the bruises that mark Shama, I say nothing. Madhu gives a dry laugh, 'She might as well be. What option does she have now but to be satisfied with whatever she has? Once married, she has to keep all doors shut.'

Madhu is not talking here literally of the extreme physical seclusion that married women in tawaif families are expected to observe, but is referring at a more metaphorical level to the related rules of fidelity and chastity that must be stringently followed by the grihasthan. Making her point, Madhu presents a further revelation, 'Sometime back, in my presence, when Salma began threatening to run off to Mumbai to join the line, I told her, *grihasthan ho, grihasthan ki maryada mein raho*; you are a married woman, maintain the sanctity of your boundaries.'

I am surprised by Madhu's remark. From what I know of Salma, it sounds unlikely that your meek daughter-in-law would have considered such an option, let alone articulated it to her mother-in-law and her friend. Despite the circumstances of her marriage, she has told me quite clearly that she loves the gentle Nanhe, preferable as a husband in her estimation than most other alcoholic and abusive men around. Seemingly content to be the pivot of the house, although an invisible one, Salma has often expressed admiration, even fondness, for you.

Your feelings towards her are more ambivalent. Salma is the carer and companion that you have ensured for Nanhe in a future when you will not be around. She has given you a much-prized grandson. You oscillate between feeling proud proprietorship of your obedient and respectful daughter-in-law and nursing a gnawing insecurity at the prospect of her weaning Nanhe away from you. While you do acknowledge—albeit not as often or as generously as you ought to—Salma's uncomplaining hard work for the family and her not inconsiderable cooking skills, you are quick to blame her for any friction that arises periodically between Nanhe and you. The other bone of contention is your little grandson Haaris whom you love as your own son and jealously resent Salma's attempts to claim her status as his mother. Most of all, you resent your dependence on her. With her industriously taking care of your house, you are free not only of housework but also to come and go as you please. All of this anxiety and mistrust, unfortunately, brings out the worst in you.

Though you try and conceal your attacks of antipathy, I can't help but notice your belittling of her. Your jibes at Salma for her lack of education, her 'rustic', 'uncouth' ways, her family's poverty and 'low status' are all the more painful since they are made in such a calculatedly casual, seemingly inadvertent manner.

Madhu clearly does not share my unhappiness at your periodic hostility towards your daughter-in-law. She berates you now, in fact, for being too loving and lenient towards Salma. As a result of which, Madhu says, Salma has been thoroughly spoilt. 'If Salma could have the cheek to announce that she will run away to Mumbai and become a dancer, you only have your own good nature to blame,' she says to you sternly.

You grimly assure her that you have brought in line your rebellious daughter-in-law. 'If I can pamper Salma, I know also how to fix her well and proper,' you ominously state.

You stop speaking midway, as Phoolmani and Sheem arrive. Jumping to her feet, Madhu exuberantly embraces first grandmother, then granddaughter. As she showers Sheem with compliments, I notice a subtle shift in her persona. She is more deferential, eager to please and courteous, especially towards Sheem, than she had been thus far with us.

'Money talks,' you grumpily comment in the privacy of your bedroom on the second floor where we sit now, leaving Madhu to spend some time alone with your aunt and niece. Madhu has a heart of gold, you say. Her only weakness is her fascination with the rich and successful.

I am far more interested in discussing Salma. Worried about the storms that have raged in this house, I try (somewhat clumsily) to play peacemaker. 'What is all this about Salma threatening to leave? She is a good girl, aapa. She does so much for the family. You must show your appreciation for her more often.'

'I show her as much appreciation as she deserves,' you retort sharply, 'But what am I supposed to do if she begins throwing tantrums every time I say something she doesn't like? I reprimand her only for her good and that too rarely, unlike other mothers-in-law like Madhu. Anyway, I know how to deal with the likes of her. This morning, she began threatening to run away again. I told her she was free to go wherever she wanted, but she must be prepared to break all ties with Nanhe and Haaris. Neither my son nor my grandson will leave my side and accompany her as she goes about blackening her face. That brought her to her senses. In no time, she was at my feet, begging forgiveness.'

The cold metal in your voice makes a chill run down my spine. Poor Salma! She must have felt really pushed to the wall to turn so desperately defiant.

'I had very nearly decided not to go to Bhabua with you all today,' you break into my thoughts. 'What if the girl scoots off behind my back, with Nanhe and Haaris in tow? Nanhe is as much a child as Haaris and could follow this girl. But then I spoke to Rajjo, who offered to shift in here while I am away. I will ask Madhu too to drop by regularly to make sure that the girl does not do anything foolish. With my friends helping out, I can leave with a lighter heart.'

In the background, the sound of steady beating out of dirt from used bedsheets filters into the room. After washing laundry, Salma will serve lunch and, once you and your relatives have eaten and left for Bhabua, she will do the dishes and clean the kitchen. Then, after ironing everyone's clothes, your daughter-in-law will be back to cooking and serving dinner to Rajjo and Nanhe. Salma's days are long and hard.

✿

'Salma bhabhi always cooks so well!' Sheem lets out a delighted squeal after polishing off four bite-sized samosas stuffed with minced meat that your daughter-in-law has packed for the journey to Bhabua. Sitting beside your aunt and niece on the back seat, you pretend not to hear, while Phoolmani grudgingly concedes, 'Not bad.'

Through the drive so far, you have been wrapped up in silence. You are worried about Salma. But I know too that you are sulking with me for urging you, earlier in the morning, to be more respectful and considerate towards her.

You had accused me of being partisan towards Salma. 'I feel hurt that you who claim to be my friend are always quick to blame me for any tension in the house generated by this girl. You prefer to believe her theatrics and false tears but have no sympathy for my genuine suffering at her hands.' I had protested that this was not true at all. I always took your side when you were in the right.

We have had our share of disagreements earlier but none as acrimonious and heated as this one. Ending on an unpleasant and unsatisfactory note, it had left both of us feeling flushed with anger. After eating lunch in silence and avoiding each other's gaze, we had left with Phoolmani and Sheem for Bhabua.

Hoping that your foul mood will pass, like mine has, I try and tread neutral ground. Turning towards Phoolmani, I ask her what happened after Bindo disappeared forever in the forest.

'When the sadhu at Baba Kinnaram's akhada confirmed our worst fears, my mother was inconsolable and wept for days on end. Blaming herself for believing our father's false reassurances about the kunwar, amma took ill, never to fully recover,' Phoolmani recounts. 'However, we could not afford to grieve for long. With Bindo gone, where would the money come to feed and clothe us all? Besides selling off her jewellery bit by bit, the only security we had was the house that Bindo had had the sense to buy with her earnings.'

'You have forgotten to mention, khala, that following Bindo khala's disappearance, it was the tawaifs of Banaras and, especially Sultana, who helped out the family.' Snapping out of your bad mood, you hasten to score brownie points over your aunt.

'That was the least she could do,' Phoolmani says combatively. 'Sultana had ruined my sister's life. Allah punished her for it, of course. Her precious Roshanara died just a few months after Bindo's disappearance.

That really shook up the old croak good and proper. And so she came to us all sugary sweet and offering help.'

Shaking your head in disapproval, you address a disinterested Sheem, because you are still too annoyed to talk with me directly, 'Sultana had nothing to gain from helping our family. She had lost her only granddaughter, had no other earning member in her household and, yet, out of the goodness of her heart, supported our family through emergencies till khala here began earning. And how did our family behave in return? They took her help and yet continued to speak ill of her.'

'We took what was ours to begin with,' Phoolmani snarls at you. 'Sultana had lived off Bindo when my sister was earning fabulous amounts and her granddaughter was busy being ill. Now, if she began giving us small sums of money, what were we to do if not take it?'

'And what had Mannan Jan taken from Bindo khala that she helped the family?' You refuse to be cowed by Phoolmani's fury.

'As for Mannan Jan, it was her decision to excommunicate Bindo that had led to her disappearance. Had the choudharayin not let herself be influenced by Sultana, my sister would not have been forced to entertain the likes of the kunwar. She must have felt guilty about Bindo's disappearance, and so tried to make amends by throwing charity at us.' Phoolmani will not allow gratitude to tinge her memories.

She does concede that, since her own family could no longer afford to pay for the music teacher they had engaged for her, Mannan Jan offered that Phoolmani, by then approaching puberty, learn alongside her niece Nirmala from Ustad Ata Mohammad Khan of the Patiala gharana who had previously taught Begum Akhtar—at that time famous as Akhtari Bai Faizabadi. In return, Phoolmani would make herself useful at the choudharayin's establishment by helping out with domestic chores.

The family was quick to accept the offer. It was decided that the house would be let out on rent, barring one room in which everyone would live until Phoolmani began earning.

Life as a poor dependent in Mannan Jan's house could have been worse for Phoolmani than the tribulations Bindo suffered under Sultana's guardianship had it not been for Nirmala's protective friendship. The daughter of the choudharayin's younger brother Basudev, Nirmala had been brought up by her father as a Hindu in contravention of the family's tradition wherein girls were Muslims and boys, Hindus. Although this had caused much consternation among relatives, with Mannan Jan initially refusing to accept her brother's decision, Nirmala's gentle and affectionate temperament, her pretty face and the signs of undeniably great musical talent even in early childhood had ensured for her a privileged and pampered upbringing in her aunt's home.

A few years younger than Phoolmani, with no sisters or cousins close to her own age, little Nirmala adopted the older girl as her best friend. As her aunt Mannan's favourite niece, Nirmala's word was law in the family. It was at her insistence that Phoolmani spent all her time with Nirmala, spared from the housework she had been expected to do.

'Nirmala would get furious if anyone ordered me about or said something harsh to me. Sometimes, just to tease her, Mannan Jan would pretend to tick me off and then have a good laugh when Nirmala came charging at her like a little lioness,' Phoolmani recalls with a chuckle.

Phoolmani tells me about Janmashtami in Mannan Jan's house, which celebrated festivals, both Islamic and Hindu, with equal gusto. 'A beautiful wooden palna, cradle, with a bronze icon of infant Krishna would be placed in the main sitting area. Special puja food was cooked and kirtans sung through the day. At midnight, prayers were offered to herald the birth of Krishna Bhagwan. At Nirmala's insistence, an elaborately decorated tableau from Krishna's life would be mounted too in the house. Nirmala, fair and beautiful, was dressed up as Radha in the tableau, while I, much darker in complexion, would be made to wear boys' clothing, with a peacock feather tucked into my hair and a flute in hand, to act out the part of Krishna.'

Nirmala would also try and protect Phoolmani from the wrath of their stern and disciplinarian teacher, Ustad Ata Khan. He had taught the rising star of Hindustani music, Akhtari Bai Faizabadi, for a decade. Disapproving of her involvement with theatre and then films in the 1930s, which he felt took her away from serious practice of music, the ustad had broken away from Akhtari Bai. Subsequently, at Mannan Jan's invitation, he had shifted to Banaras, where he was so impressed by Nirmala's musical potential that he vowed to make her an even greater singer than Akhtari Bai.

Mannan Jan's decision to employ a teacher for Nirmala from the Patiala gharana—pachhaee ang, or western style—of thumri singing had raised eyebrows in Banaras, the undisputed centre of the purab ang. However, there was no denying Ustad Ata Khan's impeccable reputation as a great musician and an exacting teacher. Despite the estrangement, Akhtari Bai always acknowledged his immense contribution to the shaping of her music.

Trained so far in the purab ang by her previous ustad from Bhabua, Phoolmani initially found the lavish ornamentation, the profusion of taans and the ragas derived from the folk music of Punjab and Sindh, so characteristic of the pachhaee ang, difficult to negotiate. Worse, her previous training in voice culture fell far short of Ata Khan's rigorous standards. His own regimen for young Nirmala involved long hours of daily practise that commenced at dawn with exercising the lower voice range and included elaborate vocal exercises to make his student's voice pliant and expressive.

'He would teach us a raga till he was satisfied that Nirmala, if not I, had mastered its intricacies. I remember that during that period, he taught us a lovely bandish in raga Gunkali every single day, for nearly three months. He took away all the pleasure from its learning. The song that had sounded so beautiful in its entirety became a dreadful bore when we had to learn each note, repeating it till the ustad was satisfied.'

Unused to the rigour and too inexperienced to appreciate its value, Phoolmani, unlike the obedient and eager-to-learn Nirmala, found her lessons dull and tedious. Her half-hearted attempts would so enrage Ata Khan that he would fling at Phoolmani whatever came to hand, be it a shoe, a plate or a stick. Nirmala would invariably try and physically shield Phoolmani from the missiles he threw, often hurting herself.

'Ustad would crack mean jokes at my expense all the time. He would call me a tawa, a black iron griddle, on account of my dark complexion, when he got angry. I was nearly twelve by the time he began teaching me. My music lessons from my previous ustads had been a straightforward teaching of different ragas and songs. I found Ata Khan's vocal exercises and his music difficult to catch up with, and the ustad somehow never liked me well enough to make an additional effort. I was just a poor girl, learning music on Mannan Jan's charity. May Allah grant Nirmala heaven! When we were alone, she would try and teach me whatever I had missed out learning from the ustad. She tried hard, but my heart was not in the gurgling the ustad made her do. I craved to sing the songs from theatre and films that I heard on the gramophone.'

Phoolmani's fascination for popular music further irritated her new ustad, who was renowned for his contempt of the gramophone, theatre and cinema. Dismissing Phoolmani as a foolish, flighty girl unworthy of his attention, he focused his energies on Nirmala, whom he had hopes of crafting into a serious-minded and truly committed musician. Nirmala, he felt, wouldn't let him down as Akhtari had.

Ironically, it was precisely Akhtari Bai's success as a celebrity mehfil singer, gramophone artist and singing star in theatre and films that had attracted Mannan Jan to hiring Ustad Ata Khan as a music teacher for her niece. In an era when tawaifs were increasingly being rejected and reviled by all quarters, there was immense pressure on courtesan musicians to reinvent themselves.

The recording medium had long provided a sanctuary for tawaif voices, suitably decontextualised and disembodied. Through the 1930s, vocalists like Rasoolan Bai and Siddheshwari Bai from Banaras, Zohrabai Amabalewali, Amirbai Karnataki, Waheedan Bai from Agra, Jaddan Bai, Shamshad Begum, Akhtari Bai Faizabadi and several others, including Bai Sundarabai, recorded extensively for the gramophone. Bai Sundarabai was also among the earliest musicians to sing on another new medium: the radio.

Tawaif musicians were simultaneously engaged in meeting another challenge. Not only was their art practice being castigated as 'obscene', it was also being trivialised as 'lightweight'. Middle-class music reformers and bourgeois patrons were recasting Hindustani music within a suitably 'classical' mode, with its core vested in raga-based dhrupad and khayal singing associated with male master-musicians. Lyric-driven musical genres, traditionally linked with tawaif musicians—thumri, dadra and ghazal—were, on the other hand, being categorised as 'light' and 'semi-classical' appendages to shastriya sangeet, classical music.

In response, women musicians like Rasoolan Bai and Siddheshwari Bai in Banaras began to focus upon seeking a legitimate, classical musical identity. The two will be remembered for their contribution to the 'classicising' of bol banao thumri from Banaras through adherence to raga rules and controlled formal and systematic musical exploration and expansion of the meanings embedded within a bandish.

Elsewhere, in the new metropolitan centres of bourgeois patronage, like Bombay, now Mumbai, courtesan musicians like Kesarbai Keskar and Mogubai Khurdikar from western India sought public legitimisation through training in the 'classical' tradition of raga-based khayal with immensely respected gharanedar masters like Ustad Alladiya Khan. With hitherto male-dominated musical gharanas formally opening up to women disciples in the early twentieth century, several other courtesan-background women musicians, especially from Goa, Maharashtra and northern Karnataka, like Gangubai Hangal, also adopted the austere personas of khayal singers, eschewing entirely the more 'light' genres of music.

A far greater majority of tawaif performers flocked to Bombay and Calcutta, the colonial centres of political power, commercial activity and cultural patronage, to work in theatre and film. With the establishment of professional Hindustani theatre—referred to in popular parlance as 'Parsi theatre' because of the preponderance of Parsi owners, playwrights and actors in the early years—in the late nineteenth century, a career on stage had attracted many tawaifs across northern India, especially from the lower rungs of the community. Elite tawaifs, however, disdained it for its large numbers of plebeian audiences.

Early cinema of the silent era initially received a similar cold shoulder from high-ranking tawaifs, since it not only divorced its performer's persona from her voice but also—like theatre had done earlier—made its actresses available to all who could pay the price of a ticket. On the other hand, along with women performers from Jewish and Anglo-Indian backgrounds, lower-placed tawaif performers, many of whom had previously worked in theatre, flocked to the new medium. In its initial years, in fact, many Parsi plays were adapted lock, stock and barrel into films.

Early silent films owe much to the contribution of women like Fatma Begum, who was probably the first woman director in India. She also produced and acted in her own films along with her three daughters Zubeida (heroine of the first Indian 'talkie', *Alam Ara*), Sultana and Shehzadi, all highly popular actresses of that era. In 1928, Fatma Begum set up her own studio, Fatma Films, which she later renamed Victoria-Fatma Films. Gauhar—not to be confused with Gauhar Jan, the singer from Calcutta—was another major star of the silent film era. More popularly known as 'Glorious Gauhar', she founded the Ranjit Movietone studio along with director Chandulal Shah.

The introduction of sound in cinema in 1932, with the first talkie *Alam Ara*, saw the influx of many more tawaif performers, cutting across the community hierarchy. Not only did the presence of spoken dialogue generate a greater demand for tawaifs as actresses because of their fluency in Urdu and Hindi, but the emphasis on songs in talkies also created a huge space for musically trained courtesan performers.

The establishment of talkies also coincided with a period of newer anti-prostitution legislation, forcing even elite courtesans, like Jaddan

Bai, to seek a future in cinema. She made her name in Hindi films not only as an actor-singer but also as a director and producer with her own banner, Sangeet Films. Even Siddheshwari Bai briefly tried her luck in cinema during the 1930s, and acted in a few films for the Usha Cinestone Film Company.

Playback singing, a technique unique to Indian cinema, was first introduced in 1935 with *Bhagya Chakra*, a Bengali film directed by Nitin Bose. This opened new avenues for courtesans to recast their identity as musicians. While Amir Bai and Zohra Bai Ambalewali enjoyed huge popularity as playback singers of the 1930s and '40s, Shamshad Begum, already a big name as a radio performer, became the undisputed star of playback singing from the 1940s, until Lata Mangeshkar's ascent in cinema.

In this scenario, glamorous and flamboyant Akhtari Bai Faizabadi, with her exceptional musical talent and a style that was so completely her own that it defied easy classification, crafted a dizzying success as a multifaceted artist, equally celebrated as a ghazal and thumri performer in elite mehfils, as a gramophone singer and as a singing star on stage and the silver screen. Born to Mushtari Bai, a tawaif in Faizabad near Lucknow, Akhtari and her mother had moved from one place to another—Gaya, Patna and Calcutta—in her formative years in search of music learning and then patronage and recognition.

Once in Calcutta, Akhtari began her recording career in 1924 with the Megaphone Company. While her early releases met with lukewarm response, a year later, the stupendous success of Akhtari's 78rpm recording of the ghazal by Behzad Lakhnavi, *Deewana banana hai toh*, made her an overnight singing sensation. Invitations to perform in mehfils in Calcutta and outside—Bardhaman, Darbhanga, Dhaka and Cooch Behar—began pouring in.

Around this time, she also joined Corinthian Theatre of Calcutta as an actor-singer. Here too Akhtari's debut play *Nai Dulahin*, written by Agha Hashra Kashmiri, ran to packed houses. Over the next few years, she established her credentials as a singing star in theatre with plays like *Shirin Farhad*, *Nala Damyanti*, *Laila Majnu* and *Shravan Kumar*.

In 1934, she made a spectacular maiden appearance at a fund-raising concert for the Congress. Sarojini Naidu, who was present, was so impressed by young Akhtari's performance that not only did she go backstage to personally congratulate her but later even sent her a khadi sari as a token of appreciation.

In the same year, Akhtari made her debut on the silver screen as an actress and singer with *Ek Din ka Badshah*, produced by East India Company in Calcutta. The film didn't fare well at the box office but its music proved to be a hit, with all seven songs sung by Akhtari becoming popular. Through the late 1930s, Akhtari acted in several other films, like *Ameena*, *Mumtaz Begum*, *Jawani ka Nasha* and *Naseeb ka Chakkar*. In 1942, she shifted to Bombay and starred in movie mogul Mehboob Khan's *Roti*.

Her acting career added further lustre to her fame as a musician. Akhtari would perform regularly for the maharaja of Kashmir and the nizam of Hyderabad, while the nawab of Rampur, a known connoisseur of Hindustani music, appointed her court musician.

Akhtari Bai's success fuelled Mannan Jan's ambitions for young Nirmala. A career as a full-time tawaif musician in Banaras came with the hazards of social stigma, economic insecurity and cultural marginalisation. Rasoolan and Siddheshwari were the rare exceptions in this dismal scenario, where tawaifs like Bindo, condemned to the wilderness, were the norm. There was also no denying that, regardless of the attention they received outside, even Siddheshwari and Rasoolan found performance opportunities in Banaras fast shrinking. Mannan Jan, therefore, decided that her niece's future lay in becoming a singing star in Hindi films.

'After long years of painstakingly grooming Nirmala to be a top-ranking musician, Ustad Ata Khan was understandably devastated when Mannan Jan announced her plans. All his pleading, reasoning and threats fell on deaf ears. She brooked no interference in her decisions,' Phoolmani recalls her former teacher's defeat with obvious relish.

Young, pretty and musically gifted Nirmala got work within a couple of years of reaching Bombay. She starred in a number of Hindi films through the 1940s: *Sharda* (1942), *Savera* (1942), *Kanoon* (1943), *Gaali* (1944), *Geet* (1944), *Jeevan* (1944), *Chaalis Karod* (1945), *Piya Milan* (1945), *Ghunghat* (1946), *Sehra* (1948), *Anmol Ratan* (1950), *Janmashtami* (1950) and *Jai Mahalakshmi* (1951).

'All seemed to be going according to Mannan Jan's plans when the unforeseen happened,' Phoolmani pauses for dramatic effect. 'Nirmala fell in love with her co-star of several films and, unheeding of her aunt's dire threats that she would be cast out from the family, went ahead and married him.

'Seething with fury, Mannan Jan refused to attend the wedding and returned to Banaras, vowing never again to see Nirmala's face. This was just as well. Nirmala, as a respectably married woman obeying her husband's orders, wanted no connection with her family's courtesan past. Except for the occasional playback singing, she turned her back on music and became a busy housewife and mother of five.'

But then destiny played its hand. Nirmala's husband turned to film production and faced financial ruin. She had no recourse but to go back to earning for the family. And although everyone acknowledged her musical talent, juggling the duties of a wife and mother, seeking concert assignments and cutting a few records, she couldn't really make her mark as a musician. Then her sons grew up and felt embarrassed by the romantic thumris, dadras and chaitis their mother sang. In deference to their wishes, Nirmala had to be content with singing mostly bhajans.

'It was such a waste of a colossal talent.' Overcome with frustrated rage on behalf of a beloved friend, Phoolmani lapses into silence. Sheem, who has been listening intently to her grandmother, solemnly intones, 'Family life, marriage and motherhood are not meant for artists. They take away from the single-minded ambition and effort needed to become a truly great singer or dancer.'

I am taken aback. Ticking myself off for dismissing Sheem as a pretty fluff-head, I try and encourage her to say more, 'Is that why you haven't chosen to get married so far?'

'I am not married because I value my freedom too much, not because I am some great artist,' Sheem says, tossing her glossy hair with nonchalant grace. 'I work hard and am good at what I do, but I have no illusions of being an artist. I am earning well and enjoying life. Why should I leave all this to be at the beck and call of one man? I will think about marriage when I get older and need someone else to foot my bills.' Sheem is unsparingly honest and far more perceptive than I, unable to see beyond her loveliness, have so far credited her to be.

'There is no shame in being a bar dancer! And who says a bar dancer is not an artist? Every night you make countless men forget their dreary lives with your dance, your ada, your smile. What is that if not art?' Phoolmani sounds like an exasperated coach motivating an underconfident student. 'How will others respect you for the artist you are if you do not respect yourself?'

Sheem seems to have lost interest in the conversation. Ignoring Phoolmani, she rummages in her purse for her mirrored compact. Surveying her immaculately made-up face, she powders her nose with close attention. Then looking up, she clarifies, 'The point about family life being a hindrance to women artists was not mine. I was only quoting my grandmother, who feels she lost out on a great career because of family responsibilities.'

Phoolmani rises to the occasion. 'Yes. I do feel family life takes a big toll on women artists. I began working as a tawaif long before Nirmala left for Bombay. I too wanted to try my luck in films. But my parents wouldn't hear of it. Who would feed the family if I went away in search of an unknown, untested future in cinema? My own ambitions had to be shelved for family responsibilities.'

I now begin to understand the perpetual scowl on Phoolmani's face and her bitterness. Her heart was not in being a tawaif. At her family's goading, she would put up a performance every night, but her lack of interest translated into lacklustre singing and dancing. Neither was she pretty enough to compensate for the mediocrity of her mujra. Not surprisingly, as the days and months and years rolled past, fewer and fewer patrons were attracted to her kotha.

Sa'dullah, meanwhile, had cultivated a new passion, gambling. Beginning with petty stakes, he became more desperate and compulsive as his dreams of a comfortable life as the father of a successful tawaif began turning rancid. Undeterred by the stormy quarrels with his daughter and wife over the gambling, he began pilfering all he could lay his hands on—Phoolmani's earnings, odds and ends, including utensils, even picking the pockets of clients coming to the kotha—to finance his addiction.

Finally, without informing anyone in the family, he sold off the house too that, according to community norms, belonged equally to his daughters, his sons and himself after Bindo's death. Phoolmani bitterly recalls, 'We got to know about the fact much after he had taken money on the house sale. According to Islamic law, he, as the father, was the main inheritor of Bindo's house after her death. Accordingly, the sale was deemed valid and, one fine day, we found ourselves on the streets thanks to my good-for-nothing father. That was the first time ever that my mother slapped him across the face. My brothers and I too joined in, and we beat him up outside the house that had been ours. I wish we had thrown him out of our lives before he had the chance to ruin us so completely. Leaving him yelping like a half-dead dog on the streets of Dal Mandi, we made our way back to the family home in Bhabua.'

CHAPTER 22

Return to Bhabua

'THAT WAS RAJJO ON THE phone. She took Salma to the doctor, and guess what? The girl is pregnant!' you announce, hurrying across the terrace where we had been sitting in morose silence. While taking the call from Banaras, you had moved to the farthest corner for privacy. That had hurt. It couldn't have been more obvious that you were still upset with me.

Now, forgetting the arctic freeze you imposed on our friendship, you pull me into a warm embrace. 'Rajjo said that ever since Salma learnt about the baby, she has become her usual quiet, calm self. No more tantrums about running away to Mumbai. I think all that earlier madness was just part of the mood swings that come with pregnancy. Everything will be fine now, you wait and see.'

I offer my congratulations but my thoughts are with Salma. During one of our chats regarding her ambitions for Haaris, she had been definite about not wanting another child. Her logic was simple. Denied schooling herself, she wanted a good education for her son. Nanhe barely earned anything at all and, with the limited resources available to you, it was only possible to bring up one child reasonably well.

In a low voice, Salma confided that she had begun using contraception on the advice of her doctor. You didn't know about this, she said. I asked if she wanted me to tell you. She said no, you wouldn't allow it if you knew. Respecting her right to decide what was best for her, I did not mention it to you. I can only hope that Salma made a conscious choice about getting pregnant this time round and is as happy with the news as you are.

'Allah takes care of everyone He brings to life,' you say, waving away my timid attempt at discussing the financial burden a second grandchild could pose for you. You love children and see them as a gift from the Almighty. In your heyday as a tawaif, unlike some of your contemporaries who chose abortion over burdening their professional lives with unwanted children, you had brought your son and daughters into the world with great joy.

And though you do not say it, I can sense that the news of Salma's pregnancy comes as a reprieve from the agonising anxiety you had about your daughter-in-law. A pregnant Salma is unlikely to run away from her duties as your housekeeper and your son's wife.

You hurry down to share the news with Ghafuran, forgetting your annoyance with her and Naeem ever since we arrived in Bhabua. You hold them responsible for the sorry state of your house. Since we were last here, one of its balconies has caved in, while most of the inner walls are dangerously saturated with seepage. In all the decades that they have lived here, Ghafuran and Naeem have not once whitewashed the house, not to speak of maintenance or repair. You were blunt in voicing your displeasure.

'Sister, where is the money to spend on maintenance of the house?' asked Ghafuran. 'You of all people know of our hand-to-mouth existence. Without you to take care of us, we wouldn't be able to manage two square meals a day.'

Her humble reiteration of the family's dependence on you worked. After making some scathing comments about being taken for granted by Ghafuran and Naeem, you eventually promised them money for repairs. You cannot let your house crumble, after all. Yet, resentful of a burden you can ill afford, you continued to be in a sullen mood, speaking with your sister and brother-in-law only when absolutely necessary.

All that is now put aside in your need to share your joy with your sister. Ghafuran looks delighted. Her eyes welling up with tears, she declares that she will feed ten beggars at the mosque nearby to ensure Salma's safe pregnancy. For this she refuses to take any money from you. 'Is Nanhe not as much my son, sister, as he is yours? I might be poor, but I can afford to feed ten beggars for the well-being of my children,' she says with feeling. You become teary-eyed in response.

You hasten next to Pyaari khala's house, with me in tow. We arrive to find her busy regaling a motley group of relatives with the story she often narrates nowadays to visitors, known and unknown, who throng her house to witness for themselves the miracle wrought by Baba Court Shaheed, the humble saint of Bhabua.

'I was, as all of you know, on my deathbed. The doctors had given up hope and so had the family. My sisters, nieces, grandnieces, nephews, grandnephews would sit around me weeping all the time. Seeing them so hopeless, I too had become convinced that I was going to croak any moment.' Inhaling deeply from the cigarette she holds, Pyaari khala blows out perfect rings of smoke.

'Everyone waited and waited to bid their last goodbyes and give me a decent funeral. But I lingered on. A month passed, then another, then three months passed and then six. One by one, all the relatives began drifting back to their routine. How long could they sit at the bedside of an old woman who refused to die?' The sweetness of Pyaari khala's smile and the gentleness of her tone soften the harshness of her words.

'Left hanging alone with the pain of cancer and the fear of death, I prayed all the time for an early release. "*Ya merey Maula*, O dear Master, I can bear this suffering no more," I would beseech. "Call me to You and grant me reprieve."

'One day, as I lay praying, I must have fallen off to sleep. In my dream, I saw an old man bent with age. He had a long, white beard and exceedingly kind eyes. I knew without being told that he was our own Baba Court Shaheed.

'"Pyaari, why do you fret so?" he asked. "Your time to make that final journey has not yet come. It's a sin to wish for death when the Maker wants you to live. Just open your eyes and see yourself anew." Saying this, he turned back and disappeared in a great mist.

'I woke up with a start. Confused, I looked around but saw no one in the room. But I could smell attar, sweet with the fragrance of roses. Slowly, I became aware that the pain was receding fast. A great sense of peace descended upon me. Baba had been right, I realised. My suffering had been of my own making. For the first time in months, I was able to sit up on my own and reach out for the glass of water that Nawab's wife always keeps on my bedside table. As I sipped the water, I began feeling hungry. My appetite had deserted me for so long that I had forgotten what it felt like to want food. That day, after months, I ate a proper meal of khichdi and curds and fell into a deep restful sleep, free of the pain that always racked my being. And since then, I am back in the bloom of youth,' Pyaari khala declares cheerfully.

It's been two days since her miraculous recovery. Her family does not know what to make of her claims of well-being. While believers like you insist that Pyaari's illness has been vanquished by mystical intervention, sceptics such as Sheem dismiss it as a temporary reprieve due to Pyaari's fighting spirit.

Her doctors are as puzzled. By medical parameters, she ought to have been dead long ago. While Pyaari khala remains bedridden and physically weak, there is no denying that her body has stopped convulsing in pain as it used to. Although she eats very little still, she is able to digest food. She talks a lot. She even smokes occasionally, as she is doing now. Her laughter has returned and her belief in life is unshakeable.

We arrived in Bhabua on the very day that Pyaari had woken up to well-being. None of us had been prepared for the vitality she exuded when she welcomed us. Noting the almost comical transformation of Sheem's face, from deep concern to shocked incomprehension, Pyaari khala chortled with joy, 'Your grandaunt is alive and kicking, my dear, and delighted to have you with her. Come here and give me a big hug like you always do.'

Pyaari khala looks delighted when you inform her about Salma's pregnancy after all the other visitors take their leave. Murmuring blessings upon Nanhe, Salma and their unborn child, she kisses your forehead. Childless herself, Pyaari khala loves children. Cautioning you not to tempt fate by sharing the news of the pregnancy with anyone except your closest well-wishers, she declares that she will shift into your house once the baby is born.

'By the grace of Allah, by then I will be better still and moving around. I will stay with you and look after my great-grandnephew or great-grandniece, just as I have brought up the other children in the family,' she says, stroking your arm.

Pyaari khala has been foster mother to many children, including Sakeena's sons and daughters, Phoolmani's elder daughter Rajjo and various grandnieces and grandnephews. Her first experience of child rearing came early, when she was barely ten or eleven, newly returned to Bhabua, along with Phoolmani and the rest of their family. Teema had arrived soon after, broken in spirit and with two children in tow—four-year-old Asghari and Hanif, who was just one.

From the little that Teema would share, it became clear that, after nearly twenty years of companionship, Daya Singh had got bored of her and taken a new mistress, a young adivasi girl only sixteen years old. One day, without warning, he had brought his new lover to the home he shared with Teema, and had the girl installed in the outhouse. Assuring a bewildered Teema that she would remain in charge of running the household and its finances, he also made it clear that she would have to share him with the younger woman.

Too proud to accept this arrangement, Teema left Ranchi the next morning, along with the two children she had borne Daya Singh, and returned to her family in Bhabua. She brought back with her the jewellery that Daya Singh had gifted her over the years. Besides this, she had nothing, except for a share in the family house that now teemed with people—Teema and her children, her mother Shakuran, brothers Yahiya and Yaqub, Yahiya's wife and son, her aunt Saleeman, cousins Phoolmani, Pyaari and Sakeena, their brothers Saleem, Alamgir and Jahangir, and Bindo's daughter Rani.

Blind and bedridden, Bullah Miyan had died of old age a few years ago. Sa'dullah Miyan, the family learnt, lived on for some time, begging on the streets of Banaras. One morning, he had been found dead, stabbed in the heart by a drunk he had got into a brawl with the previous night.

As the eldest daughter, Teema was now head of the family, responsible for steering it out of the poverty into which it had sunk. The task was daunting. Teema had, by the standards of those times, entered middle age. Never a beauty, with her mounting years, it seemed unlikely that she would find another rich lover like Daya Singh. As for the other girls in the family, with the exception of Phoolmani, whom Teema set up as a tawaif almost immediately, none of the others were old enough. And there was no question of the boys doing any work.

Phoolmani's earnings as a tawaif in Bhabua remained, as in Banaras, paltry. Her mediocre singing and dancing and lack of interest played a part as did the dwindling of wealthy patrons in the area. Many rich Rajput families in Shahabad had migrated to bigger cities like Patna, finding new avenues as lawyers, government officials and contractors. Few of those that remained had the means to splurge on tawaifs outside of the mandatory nach during weddings and other celebrations.

The onset of the Great Depression worldwide too had a debilitating impact, through the 1930s, on the fortunes of many petty zamindars and middle-level Rajput and other upper-caste farmers. A crash in prices of agricultural commodities had translated into a decimation of earnings from the produce they sold in the market, which meant that the burden of revenue and interest payments lay heavy on them. In these circumstances, even wedding-related extravagances, like the nach, had to be cut down.

Tawaifs were hard-hit as a result, and Teema's family was worse off than others. She could have earned something through sex work, a path that some tawaifs past their prime were forced to take. This was not an option that Teema, with painful memories of her childhood and youth, was willing to even consider.

'To supplement Phoolmani appi's less-than-adequate income, Teema began doing work unimaginable for a tawaif. From early morning to sunset, she would toil in the fields as agricultural labour in return for a lowly payment, further reduced because of the Depression. When no work was to be had in the fields, she would trek to the forests to cut grass that she would then sell as fodder,' Pyaari reminiscences, her love and respect for her cousin evident.

'Her self-respect was as great as her sense of responsibility towards us. She never allowed herself to grieve openly about being abandoned by Daya Singh. Not one harsh word against him, not one reproach ever escaped her lips. Her eyes remained stubbornly dry, but her pain was evident in the black clothes she had taken to wearing. Her pretty and colourful saris she distributed among all of us. She stopped wearing any jewellery. No kohl lined her eyes. She looked like a jogan, a female ascetic. People would look at her in awe and agree that Teema was a tawaif unlike any other.

'Though her own life had been so ill-fated, everyone in Bhabua, impressed by the strength of her character, regarded her as mangal, auspicious. If she were passing by in the morning, shopkeepers and vendors would request her to be their first customer so that their business would do well through the day.

'Teema laboured day and night to ensure that we did not go to bed empty-stomached. Asghari and Hanif would be left behind at home. Everyone in the family loved Asghari, who was strikingly beautiful even as a child. My mother, who was bringing up Rani after Bindo aapa's disappearance, took Asghari too under her care. No one was interested in little Hanif, then just about a year old. He would cry with hunger and there was no one around to pay notice. So, I began looking after him, feeding, bathing and playing with him. He would sleep with me at night. He was my first child.' Pyaari khala chokes on her words and memories, and falls silent.

'I remember how Pyaari would carry Hanif around on her waist as if he were a doll. No one else bothered with the boy, not even Teema. On her return home in the evenings, she would shower most of her attention on Asghari, who was even then a spoilt brat,' Phoolmani chips in. She and Sheem are staying with Pyaari, much to the relief of other family members. Ever since we arrived today, we could hear her in the background, peevishly calling out to the wives of Nawab and Wazir to make her some tea. With no answer forthcoming, her voice had become progressively more querulous and edgy. Grumbling about truant daughters-in-law, she has joined us while she waits for her cup of tea to materialise.

Making herself comfortable on Pyaari's bed, Phoolmani recalls that, from childhood, heedless of the difficult times that pressed upon the family, Asghari had always staked her claim to more, confident in the assurance that Teema would meet her every demand, no matter how unreasonable and outlandish. A visit to the local market invariably resulted in Asghari demanding a new dupatta, bangles or some other expensive bauble that caught her fancy. A few tantrums later, Teema would cave in and buy it for her. If Asghari wanted to eat meat then Teema would buy meat, no matter if the family had to eat roti and chutney for the next few days.

'I think, in the early years of her return to Bhabua, Teema wanted to make it up to Asghari for the loss of a wealthy father in whose home every little whim of the child had been met,' Pyaari explains. Phoolmani snorts dismissively.

Pyaari talks about Teema's decision to brave the financial odds and groom the younger girls in the arts of the tawaif. Since her own and Phoolmani's earnings were needed for running the house, Teema sold off almost all the jewellery that she had to pay for this education.

Sakeena, everyone realised, would not make the cut and would be best off learning household chores. But Teema had hopes of both Asghari and Pyaari. Motherless Rani, though not showing any great aptitude for becoming a tawaif, had to be groomed too so that she could be self-sufficient when she grew up. Besides, Teema didn't want her to feel that she had been discriminated against for being an orphan and denied an education.

It was already a late beginning for Pyaari, who was nearly eleven years old by then, and had received only sporadic lessons in music in Banaras. Not wishing to waste any further time, Teema placed all the three girls under the tutelage of Babban Guru, a music teacher in Bhabua. Alongside, a maulavi was engaged to give them lessons in Urdu, polish their diction and teach them some poetry.

Babban Guru tailored his lessons to suit the shifting profile of patrons remaining in and around Bhabua, and their preference for popular, simpler songs over the more esoteric raga-based music performed by elite tawaifs in Banaras. He had trimmed out from his curriculum the long years spent on raga-learning, and focused instead on teaching his students a few basic thumris, a plethora of dadras, seasonal songs like hori, chaiti and kajri that retained their folk flavour, and some popular ghazals.

Pyaari's natural flair for music bloomed under his guidance and, in a few years, she was ready to be launched as a tawaif in Bhabua. Teema, who, as the head of the family, had complete control over Phoolmani's earnings, took charge of Pyaari's career too. She conducted all the negotiations related to money and escorted the girls wherever they were invited to perform.

The fortunes of the family began looking up with the double income coming in. The worst of the Great Depression was also past. World War II had broken out, and while this translated into immense suffering for Europe, in India, then relatively far from the theatre of combat, the early years of the war benefited certain sections of the population, including industrialists, businessmen, traders and contractors. The conflict also boosted demand for agricultural produce as war supplies, resulting in a rise in prices to the benefit of landholders and farmers, including the Rajput and Bhumihar patrons of tawaifs. Many among them were also government contractors who made tidy profits from war-related public works construction and supply of raw materials. With their patrons doing well, good times seemed to be coming back for the tawaifs too.

Musically gifted, pretty, charming and quick-witted, Pyaari was soon a very popular tawaif in the area. Easygoing and obedient, she never questioned Teema's authority. Phoolmani, on the other hand, proved to be a difficult, grudging ward, chafing at the controls exerted by her cousin.

'Teema decided where we would go to perform and where not,' Phoolmani says now. 'She controlled who we could talk to, who we would flirt with. She determined how the family spent the money Pyaari and I earned. Pyaari might have been fine with this arrangement, but I found it intolerable to have to request Teema for permission to even buy a sari with my own hard-earned money.'

A sudden hoot of laughter interrupts Phoolmani's fulminations. Leaning elegantly against the doorway leading to the veranda, Sheem looks every bit a 1940s film star, out of place in Bhabua. Her laughter, though not unkind, is disconcertingly long. Phoolmani withdraws into a stiff, prim silence.

'It was funny to hear you complain about being controlled. You, of all people, nani, who has spent her life controlling others!' Sheem finally says.

Phoolmani explodes with anger. 'Are you trying to say that I control you and your money? Is this what I get for taking care of you? Have I or your mother ever denied you your smallest whim? You waste so much money on expensive clothes, shoes, cosmetics and useless trinkets. Have we ever stopped you?'

'Of course, you haven't, nani. But please don't forget that it's my hard-earned money that you so kindly allow me to spend on myself.' Her point made, Sheem saunters out.

You snigger and Pyaari looks amused. Phoolmani rants on for the next few minutes about the ungratefulness of the young before shuffling off to check on the elusive cup of tea.

'The daughters of this family can be quite a handful,' says Pyaari, chuckling. 'Sheem looks like a pretty doll but, make no mistake, she is no pushover. She might allow appi and Seema to run her career, but she has taken after her grandmother in speaking her mind. Except that she is much gentler, more affectionate and far more generous than appi ever was!'

Pyaari then recalls the acrimonious clash between Phoolmani and the rest of the family over arranging the marriage of Teema's brother, Yaqub. In the community, it was the duty of tawaif sisters to not only look after their brothers but also get them married. While she was with Daya Singh, Teema had managed to marry off her eldest brother, Yahiya. Finding a suitable girl for Yaqub had proved to be more difficult. As a result, well into middle age, Yaqub was the butt of jokes in the community. His single status reflected poorly on Teema and her family too. Tawaifs who failed to 'settle' their brothers, sons and nephews in satisfactory marriages were generally seen as irresponsible and poor.

Teema decided that, with two earning tawaifs in the family, it was time that Yaqub was finally married. She began making enquiries about girls in the community. Soon enough, a suitable prospective bride—docile, obedient and skilled in household chores—was selected and a wedding date fixed. No bride price was paid but, as per the norm, it was agreed that the major expense of the wedding would be met by the boy's household, including gifts to the girl and her family as well as a huge wedding feast, walima, for the entire community once the nikah was solemnised and the bride brought home.

Pyaari and Phoolmani's earnings, Teema calculated, would take care of the expenses. The extravagance, she hoped, would begin the process of reclaiming the influence and authority that her family had enjoyed in the past. Besides, a second daughter-in-law in the family would provide Shakuran and Saleeman with some respite. Despite their advancing years, they still helped Yahiya's wife and Sakeena with domestic chores. The other women in the house, Teema, Phoolmani, Pyaari, Rani and Asghari, were too busy earning or studying to contribute towards housework.

Pyaari, expectedly, was an enthusiastic supporter of Teema's plans. Phoolmani, on the other hand, was vocally resentful. As she saw it, Teema did not in any substantial manner contribute to the family's finances. It had been left to Phoolmani and Pyaari to work hard and feed the entire household. Getting Yaqub married was his sister Teema's responsibility. Why should she expect her cousins to finance the wedding?

Phoolmani got no support within the family or from the larger community. She was seen as miserly and selfish for discriminating between her cousins and siblings when they had all been brought up under one roof. Not surprisingly, Teema felt hurt and let down. Long the sole breadwinner for the entire family, she had never differentiated between her siblings and her cousins. Saleeman was ashamed of Phoolmani's pettiness. Pyaari and Sakeena were embarrassed by their sister's ingratitude. The all-round censure quietened Phoolmani. She grudgingly financed and participated in Yaqub's wedding but, in the long run, she was alienated from the family.

'Go ahead, paint me in the blackest tar! I have always been a target for the family.' Phoolmani has entered the room clutching her cup of tea and is furious.

After subjecting her younger sister to a long, hard glare, she turns towards me, the outsider. 'It wasn't at all as Pyaari makes it out to be.

I was angry with Teema not because of pettiness of heart but out of concern for the family. We had all seen terrible times. Even when Pyaari began earning, it's not as if we became rich. Yes, we were no longer living hand-to-mouth, but given the large number of people in the family, our double income didn't go too far. Money always fell short of needs. And without thinking about how we could afford such lavishness, Teema went ahead and decided to organise a really expensive wedding for Yaqub. Naturally, I felt worried at such mindless profligacy.'

'It wasn't mindless, appi,' Pyaari interrupts in silken tones. 'Teema was not a fool. She decided upon a big wedding only when she was sure that we could afford it. She was thinking about family prestige. And she was proven right. Everyone in Bhabua and beyond talked about that marriage for a long time after it was over. Our family was once again looked at with respect.'

'What good was that respect when the family was weighed under by debts?' Phoolmani's counter makes Pyaari fall silent. 'You know as well as I that, for a long time after the wedding, we were back to cutting corners on basic necessities in order to pay the monthly interest. I was pregnant with Rajjo at that time. To make ends meet, I was forced to work till almost the very end so that the interest could be paid on time. Even Teema felt pushed into accepting that down-and-out Shivendra Singh just to get some extra income into the family,' says Phoolmani, taking a swipe at your father.

'My mother respected my father and so accepted his proposal. He might not have been wealthy but he had integrity of character. He stood by my mother through good times and bad as long as he lived,' you say, voice quivering with indignation.

You talk about him often. A Rajput farmer with a fairly small landholding, Shivendra Singh came into Teema's life when she had given up all ambitions of finding a lover. He could not promise Teema much; whatever little he earned from his lands was crucial for the subsistence of his family—wife, children and old parents. He did not have the surplus to spend on a tawaif mistress. Yet, he fell in love with Teema and promised her, besides a modest monthly allowance, lifelong fidelity and companionship. Teema would continue living with her family and Shivendra Singh would visit her regularly.

Teema had accepted the offer. Perhaps she reasoned that this was the best that life could offer her at this stage, or she may have felt the need for an emotional and sexual attachment, an anchor, a long-term companion. Over the coming years, Teema would have twin daughters with Shivendra Singh—you and Ghafuran.

Much before your birth, though, Phoolmani's relationship with Teema and the rest of the family reached breaking point over her affair with a local boy, Raja, whose mother Naseeran was a tawaif in Bhabua. The two had been meeting clandestinely for a long time, but the family found out only after Phoolmani became pregnant.

Although not binding, the community's norms forbade tawaifs from getting emotionally and sexually involved with men from within the community. This was seen as incest. For tawaif families, the taboo worked as a safeguard against losing women breadwinners to financially non-profitable relationships. As expected, there was a showdown between the family and Phoolmani over Raja.

'Teema ordered the boys—Yahiya, Yaqub, Saleem, Alamgir and Jahangir—to lock me inside the store-room and keep guard day and night to make sure that I didn't escape. It was only when badki amma, Shakuran, and my mother begged her to think of my unborn child that she relented and let me out,' Phoolmani recalls bitterly. 'I was put under continuous guard. I could neither meet nor talk with anyone without either Teema or one of the boys present. Raja too was warned to maintain a safe distance from me. They forgot that I too have the blood of Dharmman Bibi and Sadabahar Bibi in my veins. The more they tried to quell my spirit, the more firmly I resolved to break the walls of their prison.

'Then fate intervened on my behalf. It was the night that Rajjo was born. The women were all gathered in my room, cleaning her up and taking care of me, when we heard the sound of running feet in the lane outside. This was followed by a furore. Soon, we heard the police banging at our door. Yahiya let them in. They said they were searching for some inqilabis, revolutionaries, who had managed to hoist the tricolour flag at the local police station earlier in the evening and were now on the run.'

Turning to you, Phoolmani lets out a dry laugh. 'You might not know this, my dear, since you were born later, but it was courtesy Shivendra Singh that the police ransacked our house that night. He was one among the group of inqilabis they were searching for. Someone had tipped the police off about his relationship with Teema. They turned every room upside down, including mine, even as I lay there helpless with my newborn.'

The year was 1942. To rousing cries of *Karo ya Maro*, Do or Die, and *Angrezon, Bharat Chhodo*, British, Quit India, it was a time of return to the memories of 1857. The Quit India movement, conceived by Gandhi and endorsed by the Congress, spread across the country and became especially strong in eastern United Provinces and western Bihar, areas that had been witness to a long and desperate resistance to foreign rule in 1857. As then, in 1942 too, the western Bihar district of Shahabad was one of the major epicentres of the revolt.

Reeling under war-related inflation and scarcity of essential commodities, exacerbated by the colonial government's failure to control black marketing and profiteering, people joined the movement in massive numbers. They had been following news about the sweeping conquests by Japan of Britain's colonies like Singapore, Malaya and Burma, and were convinced that the end of colonial rule in India was near.

Gandhi envisioned Quit India as a non-violent resistance to the British government. However, with him and most of the Congress leadership under arrest on the eve of the movement, 9 August 1942, the rebellion was largely guided by the circumstances and instincts of local participation as it unfolded over the coming months. In several areas, including Shahabad, it even adopted violent means. Government property, like police stations, railway tracks and telegraph lines, were vandalised, trains were stopped and, in a few places, Europeans were attacked and even killed.

Shivendra Singh had lost his younger brother and uncle in the Japanese conquest of Malaya. Both had worked there as plantation labour. His grief had turned into rage upon learning that the European owners of the plantation had, without informing the workers, or paying their dues, disappeared overnight to escape the Japanese, leaving their hapless migrant employees stranded penniless and defenceless in a foreign, war-torn land. Always sympathetic to the nationalist cause, Shivendra Singh joined the Quit India movement and emerged as a local leader in district Shahabad, rallying villagers cutting across caste and religious lines to stand against colonial might.

In a particularly daring incident, he led a huge crowd of villagers to take over the police station in Bhabua. Easily subduing the few frightened policemen stationed inside, the crowd rescued a group of student leaders who had been arrested the previous day for leading an anti-colonial demonstration in the town. Shivendra Singh and his followers gave the policemen a severe thrashing and put them behind bars in place of the students. Then, scaling the building, they raised the Indian tricolour on the roof.

Later that night, a large police contingent arrived in Bhabua. Guided by the local policemen, it hunted down all those identified as part of the crowd that had stormed the police station. Pyaari tell us, 'We learnt a bit later that, unknown to us all, bhai-ji—all of us called Shivendra Singh 'bhai-ji'—had come to meet Teema after raising the flag, and was in her room when the police knocked at our door. Teema had let him out through the back entrance, which opened into a thicket of trees. He took cover there for some time before making his escape from Bhabua.

'When the police did not find him in the house, they took Teema, Yahiya and Yaqub away for questioning. We were terror struck. All the women were crying. But Teema's courage was amazing. Despite being detained at the police station for almost a week and subjected to regular beatings, she remained steadfast in her account that Shivendra Singh couldn't have been involved in the flag-hoisting since he had left for Calcutta several days ago to look after an ailing relative. This is the story that he had instructed Teema and his family to give the police if questioned by them.'

'Teema did not once think of the danger in which she was putting all of us in by protecting Shivendra Singh,' Phoolmani chips in. 'The police had been merciless in punishing rebels and those sympathising with them. They treated our house like a public thoroughfare in those days. They would barge in whenever they wanted, search every nook and corner, abuse and humiliate the entire family, and beat up the boys. But uncaring, Teema continued to meet Shivendra Singh on the sly to give him money and food. She never once considered what would become of us if the police got to know.'

'Teema did what was right, appi,' Pyaari snaps back. 'Have you forgotten about Dharmman Bibi who joined Babu Kunwar Singh in the battle against the firangis? Teema proved that she had the same blood coursing through her veins. But why don't you talk about what you did?'

Turning towards me, Pyaari says, uncharacteristically angry: 'None of us had informed Phoolmani appi about the brave manner in which

Teema was trying to protect bhai-ji. Appi was weak and bedridden after Rajjo's birth and we didn't want her to worry unnecessarily. But one day she heard of it. And do you know what she did? She threatened Teema that she would inform the police about her continuing contact with bhai-ji unless she was allowed to go off with Raja. We were all shocked by her blackmail. Even though the police harassed us almost on a daily basis, none of us had grudged Teema's actions. We were proud of her contribution to the freedom struggle. But appi was made differently.'

The room is engulfed in an all-out war. Her face suffused an angry red, Phoolmani thunders at Pyaari, 'Why was I expected to feel anything about the freedom of the country when my own freedom had been curbed by my family? All I wanted was to be with the man I loved. I was punished for it and placed under guard at all times. It was only natural that I wanted my liberty before jeopardising my life for the liberty of others.'

Furious at being blackmailed, Teema told Phoolmani that she was free to go wherever she wanted. Shocked at what they saw as Phoolmani's treachery, even her mother, sisters and brothers felt that, regardless of the loss of her earnings, the family would be better off without her malcontent presence. Everyone in the household heaved a sigh of relief when she decided not to take Rajjo along. Phoolmani, they felt, was incapable of taking care of anyone but herself. The baby would be better off in the care of her grandmother and aunts.

'Yes, I left without Rajjo. I did so as a sacrifice for the family. Once she grew older, she would bring earnings to the house. I forfeited my claim upon my daughter so that you all could be assured of an extra earning member. But why would you care to recognise my sacrifice? No elder in the family gave me her blessings. None of my sisters wished me good luck. Shutting the door on me forever, you erased me from your hearts,' Phoolmani sounds at once combative, bitter, self-righteous and sad, a prodigal daughter who never found her way back home.

Pyaari is about to say something but then wryly shakes her head and looks away. You pick up a newspaper and begin leafing through it silently. And Phoolmani leaves the room, looking intensely sorry for herself.

Later that evening, you fill me in on Phoolmani's life after her departure from Bhabua. The following day, I gather more details from Pyaari and even Phoolmani herself. A story of soured hopes, unfulfilled desires and failure, her life makes for depressing hearing.

Leaving Bhabua behind, Phoolmani and Raja reached Calcutta, where his aunt worked in the well-known Moonlight Theatre Company. Though slowly losing its audience to cinema, Hindustani and Bangla theatre still remained a relatively popular means of mass entertainment through the 1940s in Calcutta.

Raja's aunt helped Phoolmani find a job as an actress. Free at last to pursue her dreams of working on stage, Phoolmani was brimming with hopes of stardom. A successful career in theatre had catapulted Akhtari Bai to cinema, celebrity status and more. Why not her?

Not everyone working in theatre was destined to be another Akhtari, though. Phoolmani certainly was not. Not particularly pretty and only an average singer and actor, she was relegated to supporting roles and never became a lead heroine. Raja, meanwhile, drifted into affairs with women who were financially better placed to take care of his needs, abandoning Phoolmani to her own resources.

Heartbroken by his betrayal but obstinate even in defeat, Phoolmani stayed on in Calcutta. With what face could she have returned to Bhabua anyway? In search of a big break, she changed jobs, worked in different companies, including the well-known Saraswati Theatre Company that toured from place to place, putting up performances every evening. Here, she briefly rose to doing more substantial roles as a comedienne and vamp, which brought her to the notice of audiences.

Just when life seemed to be looking up for Phoolmani, communal violence broke out in Calcutta. Pregnant with Seema, she somehow escaped the conflagration and made her way across India to the port city in the west, Bombay.

There, she tried her luck in films but was relegated again to being part of a crowd as a low-paid extra. Her luck only changed with Seema. Pyaari said to me once, 'Seema is appi's only real achievement in life.'

Exceptionally gifted, Seema learnt music from the ustads of Bhendi Bazaar and rose to become the toast of tawaifs' kothas on Grant Road in Bombay. Had her mother allowed it, she might have done better for herself and become a playback singer in films. However, fearful of Seema suffering the same fate as herself, and insecure about money, Phoolmani was not willing to let go of the handsome earnings that she made as a tawaif. The best that she could hope for was that Seema would find a wealthy lover in good time. Her dreams came true when a rich businessman installed Seema as his mistress, buying her the flat that she continues to share with Phoolmani. And then Sheem was born.

I am in Pyaari's room, listening to Phoolmani talk about her life when Sheem hurriedly comes in and announces her decision to head back to Bombay the next morning. Taken by surprise, Pyaari voices her disappointment. Only last evening, Sheem had promised that she would extend her stay in Bhabua by a few days, so why the sudden change in plan?

Sheem is poker-faced. Seema, she says, is insistent that she return immediately or a big contract will slip out of their hands. Sheem's many ashiqs too have been plaguing her with calls. Dashing Phoolmani's hopes of flying out with her, she imperiously tells her grandmother to take the train back to Bombay.

You mutter about the caprice of bar dancers. Pyaari reasons that, as a successful dancer, Sheem's time is not her own. Phoolmani sulks about the long train journey ahead. And Sheem gets busy saying goodbyes to your large, extended family in Bhabua.

Next morning, before her departure, the real reason for Sheem's sudden change of plans presents himself at Pyaari's doorsteps. Reyaz, my cheerful, charming taxi driver and guide, staggers in with dishevelled hair, two-day-old stubble and eyes red with crying. He will die without Sheem, he passionately announces to a flabbergasted Pyaari. Flinging himself at her feet, he begs her to stop Sheem from returning to Bombay.

'Please get her married to me,' he keeps pleading.

Minutes later, his elder brother Aijaz arrives, stick in hand, which he puts to good use on Reyaz's back. No brother of his will marry a two-penny nachaniya, he thunders. When Pyaari tries to stop him, Aijaz lets loose a volley of accusations against Sheem. Ensnaring a gullible, well-to-do boy from a well-connected family is a common trick played by bar dancers. His stupid brother may not be aware of this but he can see through it only too well, he roars. Intimidating at the best of times, a wrathful, raging Aijaz is positively frightening.

Entering the scene with a perfect sense of timing, Phoolmani adds her not inconsiderable histrionics to the drama. Shrieking the house down, she accuses Reyaz of luring her hard-working, successful granddaughter with tall promises of love into abandoning her mother and grandmother and earning for him instead.

Under this volley of charges and counter-charges, Reyaz ducks under Pyaari's bed. It's time now for Sheem to glide in, looking serene and heartbreakingly lovely. With enviable poise, she takes charge, and orders Reyaz to crawl out from his makeshift shelter and speak directly with her. While he is still mustering courage, she tackles Phoolmani, who has flung herself upon Sheem, demanding promises that she will not forsake her and Seema.

Disentangling herself from her grandmother's clasp, Sheem is curt and brutal. 'Nani, stop blabbering and calm down. Your golden goose is not flying off anywhere.' Next, she directs her fearless gaze upon Aijaz and orders the local bully to stop shouting. 'This is my grandaunt's home, not a public meeting. Please get one thing straight. I am not interested in ensnaring your precious brother. It is he who has been chasing this two-penny nachaniya. I am leaving for Bombay today, and have no plans to ever meet your brother again. So take him home and get him married to a nice, respectable girl.'

Aijaz opens his mouth as if to speak but shuts it again, realising perhaps that the 'two-penny nachaniya' he thought he could bully into meek submission is, behind the fluff, a quintessential tawaif, more than capable of giving back as good as she gets.

Sheem now directs her attention to Reyaz who has timidly crawled out from under Pyaari's bed. Giving him a long, pitying look, she douses his passion. 'Grow a spine, Reyaz, before you fall in love again. I told you yesterday and am repeating it again, I don't love you. It is not my fault that you mistook my friendliness and banter for something more. I am happy with my life and have no interest in falling in love or getting married. Now stop acting like a fool and go home.'

While Pyaari props herself up comfortably to enjoy the show, you gently console a sobbing Reyaz. 'Son, she doesn't love you. You are a good boy. Any girl would be happy to have you. But forget about Sheem. Her destiny is not tied to yours.'

Aijaz, fuming and muttering under his breath, drags his brother away. Sheem gets busy on her phone, reassuring her pining ashiqs of her return to Bombay by the evening. Visibly relieved that her worst nightmare has not come to pass, Phoolmani goes off in search of a cup of tea. And you and Pyaari settle down to have a good laugh.

CHAPTER 23

Pyaari Bai, Radio Singer

We are spending the morning at Pyaari khala's home. Sheem and Phoolmani have left for Mumbai. While Sheem is missed by many, and no doubt by the lovelorn Reyaz, Phoolmani's departure is welcome. You are engrossed in reading the newspaper to your aunt. I am trying to make sense of a phone conversation I have just had with an up-and-coming young vocalist in Delhi.

I was surprised to hear from her. I don't know her personally, although I have attended one of her performances. Trained in khayal, she has taken to performing thumri, dadra, hori, chaiti and ghazals, and has garnered attention on account of her attempts to sing in the full-throated style of courtesan vocalists of the past and interweave the histories of tawaif singers into her performance.

Her attempts to locate her newly adopted musical repertoire within its stigmatised and largely invisiblised tawaif past is a departure from the more usual music practice associated with middle-class female practitioners of Hindustani music. Their entry into the realm of raga and tala from early to mid-twentieth century was a direct outcome of nationalist reforms that stressed the need for 'respectable' women to step out of purdah, access formal education and take part in the nation-building process. The importance given by cultural nationalists to music learning and music appreciation by both men and women of the 'respectable classes' also played a key role. The establishment of music schools, colleges and music societies, as part of the efforts to create a 'national music', unlocked hitherto shut doors of music education for middle-class women, as did the fact that hereditary male ustads of gharana-based music learning began formally accepting female students.

Middle-class women, nonetheless, had to wage intense personal struggles through the twentieth century to publicly perform Hindustani music. Patriarchal emphasis on marriage and motherhood posed a major hurdle, as did the association of public music performance with tawaif musicians. There are countless stories of women allowed by their families to learn music as a social accomplishment being ultimately forced to sacrifice their dreams of performing it publicly. Among the few who did manage to sing in those early decades, either for the gramophone or the radio, many took refuge in assumed names for fear of causing social embarrassment to their families. It is not surprising, then, that the few who did brave social infamy and began performing in public without the subterfuge of a false identity, should have been anxious to present a public persona that was the obverse of the stereotype associated with tawaif performers. Preferring the concert space to the stigmatised intimacy of mehfil singing, most of these women performers opted to learn and publicly perform the more austere and raga-based khayal rather than the tawaifs' repertoire of thumri and dadra. Even vocalists from courtesan families, like Gangubai Hangal, made a similar choice in an attempt to distance themselves from their background.

The handful of middle-class women musicians who did opt to perform thumri and its associative genres were more anxious still to distance themselves from the earlier practitioners of these art forms. This translated into an assiduous de-linking of the music practice from the sexuality of the performer. I remember a well-known thumri singer, whom I met as part of my research, snapping at my interest in tawaifs. 'Why have you come to me if you are only interested in "those" kinds of women?' she asked. 'My music is an act of service to the Almighty, while for them it was a means to earn a livelihood.'

An obvious outcome has been to recast thumri as devotional and spiritual, thereby making it a suitable genre for middle-class women musicians to perform. The explicit or implied presence of Krishna in a large number of thumri texts is offered as proof of the 'inherently' devotional nature of the thumri. In several instances, seemingly minor changes have been made to thumri texts. For instance, words that address the patron lover are replaced with a suitable address for Krishna, or words that have sexual overtones, like 'sajariya', or flower-decked bed, are changed to the more decorous 'nagariya', or city. This has resulted too often in road-rolling the delightful ambiguity that exists in thumri texts, where the erotic and the spiritual coexist, overlapping and providing meaning to each other.

There has also been a continuing effort to 'classicise' thumri in a more self-consciously raga mode. Eye contact with the audience and the use of abhinaya through facial expressions and dance movements, are a strict no-no in the decorous presentations of the thumri by a great majority of contemporary women vocalists. This task is made easier by the impersonal and distant space of the auditorium where most contemporary music concerts take place.

In the past few years, however, a small but significant number of prominent middle-class women musicians have questioned the invisibilising of tawaif performers. They have consciously tried to break the wall of respectability that separates courtesan musicians of the past from contemporary women singers. While the majority have focused their efforts on including in their repertoire old thumri and dadra bandishes rendered in a 'voice' associated with earlier courtesan singers, some others, like Vidya Rao, have also been researching and writing about thumri and dadra as shaped and sung by tawaifs. Another prominent vocalist, Shubha Mudgal, has been associated with performance art-based projects aimed at unearthing, retrieving and foregrounding the contributions made by tawaifs to the evolution of Hindustani music.

Their interventions as musicians have immensely enriched the ongoing feminist interrogations in academia, law and the visual arts of different aspects of the tawaif and devadasi traditions. I was, therefore, naturally interested in attending a concert by the woman vocalist whose adoption of the tawaif performance mode was creating such a buzz in the cultural and feminist circles of Delhi.

Jam-packed with audience and media, the concert was held in a small open-air amphitheatre and designed along the lines of a mehfil, with the singer and her accompanist musicians seated at floor level in the centre. Her evening's repertoire consisted of a string of cover versions of well-known thumris, dadras, seasonal songs and ghazals recorded by celebrity courtesan singers of the past, interspersed with a one-way interaction with the audience that combined snatches of musical history and a few jokes laced with some antiseptic flirtation. A nice enough idea, except that the singer's tendency to twist her mouth and twitch her eyebrows in a rather alarming manner, combined with frenetic arm-flailing, seemed less a tribute and more a caricature of the subtle abhinaya that accompanied the singing of erstwhile mehfil performers. Worse, I found myself wishing that her lacklustre and often off-key singing was more in tune with her dazzling attire and jewellery.

The audience, however, comprising known faces from the progressive, feminist and art circles of Delhi, clearly did not share my disappointment. The attempt, even if ham-handed, by an English-speaking, non-tawaif woman musician to conjure the tawaif's phantom on the sanitised respectability of the concert stage was being celebrated by them as so subversive that it overshadowed the mediocre music-making of the event. Torn between sympathy for the politics behind the performance and dismay over the dismal quality of singing and the clumsiness of the act, I decided to reserve my opinion and attend a few more concerts by her before arriving at any conclusive judgement.

Before I had an opportunity to see her in performance again, however, I received this call. Having heard about my research on tawaifs, she wanted to meet me as soon as possible to discuss an urgent matter that might be of mutual interest. I told her that I was not in Delhi and would be out for quite some time. We could discuss the matter over the telephone, I suggested, and after some hesitation, she agreed.

She wanted my help in introducing her to retired tawaifs who would be receptive to sharing with her rare bandishes in their repertoire. This project, she said, would go a long way towards documenting and archiving tawaifs' forgotten compositions, which we could lose forever with the demise of their last remaining practitioners.

I had instantly warmed up to the request. 'What exactly do you plan to do with the bandishes that you collect from retired tawaifs?' I asked, glancing at you and Pyaari khala, deep in conversation about a newspaper report on local civic disrepairs.

'Well, since I am a musician, I plan to perform the bandishes in different fora to ensure the widest possible audience for these forgotten songs,' she replied, sounding somewhat impatient.

I am not sure whether it was her reply or the tone of her voice that made me uncomfortable. But, as I looked at you, head bent, reading aloud a joke to Pyaari khala, I brushed aside my unease and asked, 'Will the tawaifs get paid for sharing their songs with you? Many are in dire financial straits and payment, even if small, would come most handy.'

'Hmm. Well actually that might not be possible,' the vocalist sounded guarded. Then, picking her words carefully, she added, 'You must understand that projects like this one are not commercially viable. We are working on a shoestring budget. There is no money to pay the women. But as partners in a project that aims to highlight tawaif music, they will benefit in other ways.'

'I am sure they will,' I said encouragingly. 'Have you considered inviting former tawaifs to perform their own songs? It would be a wonderful opportunity for them to reclaim their musical identity.'

'But aren't they too old to perform?' came the reply, sharp and fast.

'Many are, but there are quite a large number around who can still sing,' I assured her in my most persuasive tones. In the background, I could hear you reading aloud a ghazal from the newspaper's poetry section.

'Oh! I have no doubt that they can sing.' The voice at the other end sounded patronising. 'But they must be now out of practice for so long. I don't want them to cut a sorry picture in front of a musically informed audience.'

I was astounded by her arrogance. That someone whose performance I had found so musically wanting should be dismissive about musicians she had not even heard was galling.

But worse was to follow: 'What we can plan for, though, is to invite some of these women to the performance. They could sit on the stage with me, perhaps even join in the singing occasionally. What do you think?'

I thought I should tell her to shut up but then remembered your desperation to sing again. Against all hope, I made a last-ditch effort, 'I suppose you will be able to generate funds for their travel and stay? And perhaps once you have heard them perform, you might consider giving them space in your programme to sing some of their own songs?'

'Some money to cover basic travel expenses might be possible. But much as I would love for them to sing, you must understand that people come to hear and see me in performance. I am not sure if the audience or the sponsors will be enthusiastic if we push solo singing by others in an event billed in my name. You know how it is.'

I didn't know how it was, but our conversation had clearly come to an end. I told her I would share her proposal with the former tawaifs I knew, and let her know their reaction. Once again, she pressed upon me the immense political significance of her proposed project and expressed hope that I would be able to convince former tawaifs to 'come on board'.

❁

'What are you so deep in thought about? Missing Delhi?' Pyaari khala's affectionate teasing breaks into my reverie.

'No. Not missing Delhi at all,' I reply, the arrogance of the singer from my city fresh in my mind. I narrate verbatim the conversation I had with her to Pyaari khala and you.

Pyaari khala bursts out laughing. 'I thought I had met all the possible scoundrels and confidence tricksters that throng this world, but this Miss, I must say, is smarter than most. What a novel scheme she has hatched! She wants us to give her our only assets, our songs, for free. She will sing the songs while we will sit around like mute statues decorating her stage. Waah! She will get the accolades for singing our old and rare bandishes. We will get a big fat zero, and yet she wants us to believe that she is doing all this for our benefit. *Shabash! Ismart to Miss Sahib bahut hain lekin shayad yeh nahin jantin ki boodhbi tawaifon ko choona lagana itna aasan nahin.* Bravo! Miss Sahib is smart alright but perhaps she isn't aware that it's not that easy to make fools of old tawaifs.'

I turn to you. You take your time replying. 'Let's give her credit for being honest at least.' I'm surprised to hear this. 'No, really, I mean it. She was blunt about the fact that she wanted our songs but had no interest in us. Someone more unscrupulous would have made false promises, taken our songs and then left us high and dry. At least she has been open about the deal. Please thank her for me, Saba. And tell her that I am simply not interested.'

'Would you like to speak directly with her? Perhaps you might be able to negotiate a better deal for yourself than I was able to get for you?' I ask.

'Saba, life as a tawaif has taught me to sniff out an opportunity if it exists,' you say tersely. 'This offer is dead wood. It carries no promise whatsoever for women like us. The ambitious Miss in Delhi simply wants to use us to promote herself as a singer. I am not interested.'

'Times are indeed changing. I remember when I and many other tawaifs used to sing on the radio, and the absolute horror that izzatdar women and their families had about being confused with us. Today they want to sing our songs! Either way, it is we who will always lose to them,' Pyaari khala, usually so gentle and good natured, sounds unusually bitter.

'I had no idea, khala, that you sang for the radio?' I ask.

Pyaari khala responds with the briefest of nods. 'Yes, I sang on the radio for several years. It all began with an invitation to perform at a zamindar wedding in Patna. One of the guests there—he was addressed as "Sharma-ji" by everyone—worked at the Lucknow radio station. He liked my performance so much that he pressed me to come to Lucknow and sing for the radio. I was very tempted but did not go then. Lucknow seemed too far from Bhabua, and besides there was no guarantee that I would be given a chance to sing. So that was that, although I would often think about his offer.'

Meanwhile, Teema decided that Pyaari ought to shift to Banaras. The war was dragging on, prices were spiralling, food and other necessities were scarce, and suffering stalked Bhabua and its surrounds. In Banaras, on the other hand, Teema had heard that the tawaifs were flourishing. Their kothas, long abandoned by aristocratic patrons, had found new customers in army contractors profiteering from the war and once-petty traders and shopkeepers who had struck gold as hoarders and black-marketeers of basic necessities.

Teema couldn't stay with Pyaari on a permanent basis in Banaras, though, since by then she had taken Asghari to Azamgarh to put her under the tutelage of a well-known dance teacher, Basudev Guru. Accordingly, she arranged for Saleeman, Jahangir, Alamgir, Rani and Rajjo, then just a baby and in her grandmother's care, to shift with Pyaari to Banaras, so that she wouldn't be on her own. Realising that little Hanif would be disconsolate if parted from Pyaari, Teema let him go with her too.

She rented a kotha for Pyaari that was coincidentally located next door to Rasoolan Bai's establishment in Dal Mandi. Her sister, mother and grandmother being long dead, Rasoolan lived here with her only son, Wazir, and a distant cousin and his family. Always rather reserved, the loss of her closest family had left Rasoolan lonely. Perhaps it was this that made her extend a warm welcome to Pyaari, who responded with her usual affection. Missing Teema and unaccustomed to handling her career on her own, she began turning to the older woman for advice, spending much time in Rasoolan's house.

Pyaari says that she would often find Rasoolan in the kitchen, making chapattis for Wazir or cooking his favourite dish. She loved him intensely and was spoiling him silly. He had dropped out of high school and spent almost all his time lolling about the house, doing nothing.

Simple in her habits, Rasoolan, by then middle-aged, had begun dressing in the plainest possible saris. She rarely wore jewellery and never any make-up. She would look genuinely surprised when Pyaari commented on the drab sari she was wearing to go out. 'What's wrong with it? I thought it was rather nice,' she would say and refuse to change into something more colourful.

Rasoolan had also become highly selective about mehfil assignments, accepting only invitations that came from known and respected old patrons. The evening's mehfil in her own kotha, which had earlier been open to all and held daily, was now organised only occasionally for specially invited guests. It was under Rasoolan's influence that, even at the cost of annoying her mother and brothers, Pyaari became choosy about where she would perform, for whom and what she would sing.

'Aapa also made me aware of the shortcomings in my singing and the need to improve my limited knowledge of raga-based music. "Pyaari, we must perfect our music if we wish to survive these terrible times. Only our songs will come to our rescue from all these accusing fingers," she would always say,' Pyaari recalls fondly.

Pyaari realised soon enough that music-making is as dependent on the patronage available as on the singer. In the changing times, most tawaifs couldn't afford to be choosy about patrons. Perforce, they had to perform the film and theatre songs and folk songs littered with sexual innuendo that most of their new patrons preferred. 'Even I would often find myself forced to sing such songs,' Pyaari states matter-of-factly. 'And yet I wanted to earn the respect that Rasoolan aapa had as a musician. So I hired Habib Khan Sahib, one of the best available teachers at that point in Banaras, and continued to learn thumri, tappa and even khayal from him. He also taught music to Rani alongside.'

Following Wazir's marriage, Rasoolan stopped performing altogether at her kotha and in mehfils within Banaras. She did not want her reputation as a tawaif to cause any embarrassment to Wazir and his wife Amiran, and so began cutting down on similar assignments outside too. On several occasions, she would recommend Pyaari instead. Rasoolan preferred now to sing outside the city, mainly at marathon public concerts, referred to as music conferences, where one well-known musician after another performed for huge audiences.

With their genesis in the early twentieth-century initiatives of cultural nationalists like Bhatkhande and Paluskar, by the 1940s, music conferences had come to be firmly established as one of the principal sites of Hindustani music performance. Traditional musicians—male and female—learnt to negotiate and satisfy the diverse tastes of the large heterogeneous audiences thronging music conferences, just as a few decades ago they had learnt to adapt to the challenges of time constraints and market compulsions posed by the technology of sound reproduction. Though the early cultural nationalists had banned tawaif performers, by the 1940s, a handful of courtesan vocalists, including Siddheshwari and Rasoolan, were able to carve out a space for themselves as regular and much sought-after performers at such events.

'One of Rasoolan aapa's most memorable performances had been at a Calcutta music conference where she performed on the closing night along with Siddheshwari and Badi Moti Bai.' Pyaari, who has been deep in thought for some time, now suddenly remembers, her face creasing into a smile. 'I had accompanied her there. The pandal was packed with audience that couldn't have enough of the very best of Banarasi gayaki that these three singers represented. Seated in a semicircle, and accompanied by their respective sarangi and tabla players, each singer picked up from where the other had left. You can't imagine the magic of that night—it stretched on till early morning without a break!

'Aapa also began performing on the radio during this period. The payment wasn't much—if I remember correctly, it was around Rs 50 or 55, a pittance really compared to the earnings she made in private mehfils. But she prioritised her radio assignments, and would decline an invitation from even an old and valued patron if it clashed with her radio dates.'

Radio had emerged as a major performance site by the mid-1930s. It came to India in the 1920s through the efforts of private enterprise and amateur radio clubs. The privately owned Indian Broadcasting Company was the first to start broadcasting in 1927, with a radio station each in Bombay and Calcutta. Apart from issuing a licence to the company, the colonial authorities initially kept their distance, dismissing radio, on the one hand, as mere entertainment but also fearing its subversive potential in India's charged nationalist atmosphere.

In just three years, the Indian Broadcasting Company went bankrupt in 1930 and the government, apprehensive that radio broadcasting could fall either into the hands of the nationalists or of American entrepreneurs, felt obliged to take over the enterprise. Renamed the Indian State

Broadcasting Service, radio was put under centralised government control from the very beginning. Reluctantly at first and then with greater enthusiasm when, despite threadbare investment, profits began showing up from 1935, the colonial government began expanding the base of radio broadcasting in India. In the same year, it appointed Lionel Fielden, a senior and experienced broadcaster from the BBC, to head the enterprise as Controller of Broadcasting.

Under Fielden's stewardship, the Delhi radio station went on air in 1936. Indian State Broadcasting Service too was renamed All India Radio (AIR) in the same year. Expanding its coverage rapidly, AIR established radio stations in Peshawar and Lahore in 1937, and in Lucknow, Madras and Trichinopoly (now Tiruchirappalli) in 1938.

Music occupied pride of place in radio programming from the very beginning, even though the British administrators of AIR had little interest in Indian music. They viewed it at best as a bait to attract listeners to news broadcasts and talk programmes. In the 1939 *Report on the Progress of Broadcasting in India,* Fielden described music as mere 'padding because it does not instruct or inform'. And yet, given the great demand for it by the great majority of listeners, administrators were obliged to allocate the bulk of broadcast time to various genres of Indian music.

The programming of Indian music ranged from Carnatic to dhrupad, khayal to thumri, dadra and ghazals to bhajans, qawwali to folk songs, in an attempt to meet the perceived tastes of different categories of the radio's 'target' audiences, slotted as urban, rural, educated, uneducated, men and women. Getting the mix just right was a headache for radio administrators who slotted the many forms of musical genres into two broad categories: 'classical' and 'light'. The only difference between 'classical' and 'light' in Fielden's opinion lay in the content of the lyrics—in the compositions being either religious or erotic—and in the social status of the performer.

No great votary of Indian music, he was especially critical of 'classical' music, which he dismissed as being too 'limited' and 'rigid'. He had little choice, however, but to give it adequate space in programming for fear of outraging the 'nationalistic outlook' of a section of his listeners and their demands for 'traditional music and the conventionalised vocal acrobatics which it sometimes involves'.

Then there was the issue of negotiating the quagmire of sexuality and morality. Fielden recognised that some sections of AIR listeners 'would demand that all prostitutes and mirasis should be excluded from the microphone and, in fact, that the employment of singers should be regulated by their morals'. He drew the strength to resist this pressure from his belief that an 'equally important and probably increasing number of listeners would not tolerate amateurs at their present stage of development'.

Hindustani and Carnatic musicians, male and female, including some of the most renowned figures of the time, thus performed regularly on AIR, either in the capacity of salaried permanent staff or more usually on a per-programme contractual basis. Within a fortnight of going on air in 1936, for example, the Delhi station of AIR was able to bring to its listeners performances by luminaries such as Ustad Fayyaz Khan, Pandit Vinayak Rao Patwardhan, Ustad Hafiz Ali Khan, Majidan Bai, Ustad Abdul Aziz Khan and Ustad Bundu Khan.

The onset of World War II in 1939 saw AIR increase its daily broadcast time to accommodate the need for more news and talk programmes as counter propaganda against Nazi Germany and the Axis powers. Music programming continued to be a major feature of radio broadcasting. This period coincided with the ascent of A.S. Bokhari to the helm of affairs at AIR as acting controller of broadcasting in the absence of Lionel Fielden, who went on a long leave in 1939. Responding to the colonial government's pressure upon AIR to go all out with war-related news and war propaganda programmes, Bokhari, a well-known Urdu writer, who had been a professor of English literature at Government College, Lahore before joining the radio, wrote, 'In times of war it is all the more important that it (broadcasting) should ... attract and appeal. Entertainment must be developed—not curtailed.' Music and other entertainment programmes were now broadcast to ensure that the greatest number of listeners tuned in to AIR for war-related news and talks, and not turn to German and Italian broadcasts for entertainment.

Over the years, All India Radio emerged as one of the largest avenues of employment for musicians. With the ongoing erosion of the aristocratic patronage earlier available to them, musicians thronged its studios. This state-sponsored patronage relieved many soloists and accompanists of the insecurity that came with the fickleness of individual sponsors. Others were tempted by the vast audience that radio promised. And tawaif musicians like Rasoolan found in AIR suitably respectable patronage to counter the social stigma of their background.

✿

'Rasoolan aapa performed very often at Lucknow radio station,' Pyaari says. 'She would pay Shammu Khan Sahib, who accompanied her on these trips, out of her own pocket, since AIR expected visiting singers to perform with its own permanently employed staff of accompanists. She did not grudge the cost as long as her teacher and long-time accompanist was by her side.

'AIR also did not make any arrangement for the stay or food of musicians coming from outside. Many performers had lodged complaints about this inconsiderate policy. But aapa never raised a fuss and would stay with her cousin Minto, who was a tawaif in Lucknow and lived in the Chowk locality. She would always praise AIR's policy of paying the artist on the spot as soon as the performance was over.'

Pyaari mentioned to Rasoolan her meeting in Patna with Sharma-ji of Lucknow radio. Rasoolan did not know him, but suggested that Pyaari should accompany her to Lucknow and explore the possibility of singing on the radio. Pyaari recalls her initial hesitation and fear of rejection. Moreover, she knew no one in Lucknow with whom she could stay. There was also the question of money and travelling alone by train from Banaras to Lucknow.

'Aapa put many of my fears to rest,' she says now. 'She assured me that I would be treated respectfully by the officers at the radio station. Most of the women singers on radio were, in fact, tawaifs. She offered to arrange for my stay in Lucknow at her cousin's home, and advised me not to let monetary considerations come in the way. The respect I would earn as a radio singer, the audiences that I would reach, would be many times greater compensation than the money I earned in mehfils. I would get a chance to sing on a platform that hosted the likes of Ustad Bade Ghulam Ali Khan Sahib, Ustad Fayyaz Khan Sahib and Baba Allauddin Khan. Most importantly, I would get a chance to sing the music that I wanted to perform but found no listeners for in my kotha. She promised to put in a word on my behalf. That really boosted my confidence, because aapa's standards in music were so exacting that she rarely praised or promoted any other singer.'

Pyaari finally mustered the courage to accompany Rasoolan on one of her trips to Lucknow. Sharma-ji was no longer at the radio station by then but, on Rasoolan's recommendation, she was given a trial programme to sing chaiti and other songs of the summer season. Pyaari performed well enough for her to be empanelled as a singer of 'light' music—thumri, dadra, hori, chaiti, kajri, ghazals and bhajans. She began to be regularly invited to perform for radio programmes, and was accompanied on these overnight trips by Habib Khan Sahib, with whom she shared a part of her payment besides buying his train ticket. They would stay the night in Minto's house.

In the beginning, Pyaari khala says, she found it difficult to sing in a sound-proof room without an audience. Also, almost six weeks in advance, musicians had to provide the radio station with a complete list of the songs they planned to perform, along with their raga and bol, so that these could be printed in AIR's programme journal. In the early days, she felt very nervous about committing herself, so precisely, weeks in advance to a set programme. Like most mehfil singers, Pyaari was used to choosing her songs on the spur of the moment, depending on her mood and that of the audience.

Soon enough, she got used to these constraints. AIR Lucknow invited her to perform every couple of months, and over the next two years, Pyaari began to get noticed as a radio singer. The thrill of her live performance reaching a vast unseen audience was great, she recalls. Many more people now knew about her and her music. She began attracting more patrons to her kotha and getting many more mehfil offers as a tawaif on account of her radio singing.

'But one irritant that continued to gnaw at me was the unspoken rule about different entrances at the radio station for tawaifs and respectable women.' Pyaari khala's eyes, so far lit with happy memories, suddenly turn hard.

'Not that there were too many of them. There was Saiyeda Bano, who was the first woman announcer on Lucknow radio. She also compered the children's programme. Besides her, there were a few others who sang. Most of them observed purdah and performed under assumed names.

'I never got to meet any of them because they were always accompanied by male relatives who whisked them into the studio via the front entrance of the radio station. Tawaifs like me, who formed the overwhelming majority of singers on the radio in those days, would use the rear entrance. Everything was arranged in such a manner that the two sets of women never crossed paths, let alone met or exchanged two words. We all pretended that the rule did not exist but it was very humiliating.'

Pyaari khala's memories about the separate entrances at Lucknow radio station corroborate writer and music aficionado Pran Neville's account of a similar practice that he witnessed first-hand at Lahore and Delhi stations in the 1940s. The reasons behind this segregation are not hard to guess.

At radio stations in the north, like Lahore, Delhi and Lucknow, the persistence of purdah culture made it difficult to get non-tawaif women performers. Social outrage against tawaifs performing on the radio too was the most vociferous here. On account of the very large numbers of tawaifs invited to perform there, the Delhi radio station, for example, was disparagingly nicknamed Sarkari Chawri Bazaar, or the Official Chawri Bazaar—Chawri Bazaar being the tawaifs' quarters of Delhi. During the session of the legislative assembly in 1936, Sant Singh, an Indian member, had drawn the government's attention to the large numbers of 'nautch girls' being invited by the Delhi radio station, and asked if it was aware of 'the strong feelings of the people in this matter'. Govind Ballabh Pant, another member of the legislative assembly, had posed a similar question. Echoes of this criticism were found in the press and in letters sent by some listeners to the radio.

All India Radio responded by pointing out that, as a professional broadcasting body, it had to make use of suitable musical talent wherever it could be located. Was the radio expected to set up a 'Committee of Morals' to examine all artists before inviting them to perform, AIR's programme journal *The Indian Listener* had asked in its issue of 7 May 1936. 'Is there sufficient amateur talent in India to replace the professional to the entire satisfaction of all or even most of the listeners?'

'Amateurs' posed their own problems. Radio programmers complained of the many demands placed upon them by the few non-tawaif women singers available. While some 'amateurs' were willing to perform provided they did so under assumed names, others stipulated that no tawaif step into the studio while they were singing, or that no man was allowed in the vicinity. Still, under pressure from nationalist leaders and sections of its own listeners, AIR did try to attract to its studios as many qualified 'amateurs' as possible. To address their concerns about being 'exposed' to the 'corrupting' influence of tawaifs, AIR appears to have devised an unwritten norm for its stations in the north, mandating the use of separate entrances for 'amateurs' and 'professionals', a euphemism for courtesans. Officially, the radio stations never acknowledged the existence of this practice, nor is there any record of tawaif musicians ever raising a public issue about the segregation. Those associated with

Lahore, Delhi and Lucknow radio stations in this period, however, testify to the existence of this moral apartheid.

'Even a musician as esteemed as Rasoolan aapa was not spared this ignominy,' Pyaari khala recalls. 'The rule did not, of course, apply to male musicians who were free to use any entrance they wished. The staff at the radio station was always so polite and respectful though, that many of us could pretend such a rule didn't exist. I especially remember the courtesy extended to singers like me by Susheela Mishra, the producer for music in Lucknow radio. She was a musician herself and very knowledgeable about music theory. And she would always spend some time chatting with each of the invited performers and putting them at ease before they went on air. People like her made the radio station an attractive space for musicians.

'There were times when Rasoolan aapa would run into Susheela-ji or some other official at the radio station while on her way inside. They would then usher her in through the main entrance which they used, of course. But when aapa arrived on her own, she would always quietly head for the rear gate. She had become, over the years, not only more reserved than she had been earlier, but also very timid. Although she was so highly respected by everyone as a musician, she had become very fearful of being judged for her tawaif past.

'Akhtari, on the other hand, revelled in behaving like the star she was. I met her during one of my earliest trips to the Lucknow station, where she was a regular performer. She was so beautiful. I remember she was wearing an exquisitely embellished typical Lucknow light pink gharara. In her nose, she wore a diamond pin that glittered every time she moved her head. Her plait reached almost to her knees. On her way to the studio, she saw Habib Khan Sahib and came over to greet him. She was surrounded by a bevy of male admirers, including the famous poet Majaz, who at that point worked at the Lucknow radio station. I noticed that she had ignored the unspoken rule about using the rear entrance and breezed in through the front gate. As the most popular singer on Lucknow radio, she could choose to ignore rules. There was no one to stop her. But most others learnt to fall in line.'

This uneasy arrangement came to an end in 1946 with the formation of the interim government vested with the task of assisting the transition of

India from British rule to independence. While Jawaharlal Nehru headed the government, Sardar Vallabhbhai Patel was second-in-command as minister in charge of Home Affairs and of Information and Broadcasting.

Among the very first decisions that Patel took was to ban those musicians 'whose private life was a public scandal' from performing on the radio. Tawaif musicians would find it almost impossible in independent India to gain access to state-sponsored cultural institutions unless they were able to distance themselves from the sexuality associated with them.

This step was part of the larger makeover of All India Radio that Sardar Patel had in mind to make it a suitable official voice for the soon-to-be-independent Hindu-majority India. A.S. Bokhari, who had, in the course of the war years, succeeded Fielden as director general of AIR, was diplomatically removed from his post and sent back to Government College, Lahore. Hindi was proposed as the official language of the radio in place of Hindustani—a mix of Urdu and Hindi—that had been in use thus far. On the eve of India's freedom, the legacy of Hindu nationalists like Madan Mohan Malaviya, Vishnu Digambar Paluskar and Vishnu Narayan Bhatkhande had come to define the direction of the newborn state's policy towards language, culture and music.

In a note dated 13 March 1947, V. Shankar (Private Secretary to Sardar Patel) wrote to P.C. Choudhary, who had succeeded A.S. Bokhari, 'Sir B.L. Mitter has suggested to H.M [home minister, Sardar Patel] that national songs composed by eminent poets ... should be recorded and broadcast from All India Radio stations, instead of the sentimental rubbish and ridiculous drolleries to which one has to listen to daily ... H.M would like the suggestion to be examined.' P.C. Choudhary responded to the missive by directing the stations to weed out 'unsuitable' songs and to suggest suitably high-minded music that could be broadcast instead.

'We in Banaras were stunned when the news about the ban on tawaifs reached the city,' Pyaari khala recalls. 'Most difficult to accept was that this blow to us had come on the eve of Independence from a Congress leader many of us had till then greatly respected.'

Some tawaifs in Banaras went into mourning upon hearing the news, and immersed their musical instruments in the Ganga. Other, more pragmatic courtesans entered into marriages of convenience, mostly with their accompanist sarangi and tabla players and occasionally with long-term patrons, so as to become respectable enough to perform before the radio microphone. Armed with marriage certificates, they changed their names from 'So and so' Bai or Jan to 'So and so' Begum or Devi, the forms of address for married Muslim and Hindu women respectively.

Siddheshwari Bai got married formally to her long-time companion Pandit Iqbal Narain, and changed her name to Siddheshwari Devi. She also moved from her rented accommodation in Chowk to her own recently constructed house in Kabir Chaura, a locality where traditionally male musicians from the Kathak community lived. Here, she continued with her music practice but stopped entertaining patrons in her house.

Rasoolan Bai married Seth Suleiman with whom she had been in a relationship for several years. He was a married man with children and grandchildren. As his second wife, Rasoolan made no demands on him; she had little desire to shift into his house and take on the duties and responsibilities of a co-wife. Instead, she chose to shift out of her rented kotha in Dal Mandi into her own spacious three-storey house in the adjoining Dhari male musicians' mohalla of Chahmama. Inhabited only by Rasoolan and her family, the house was shut to mehfils and outside visitors. The only people welcome were relatives and friends, acquaintances from the tawaif and musicians' community, or people who came to invite her for music conferences and programmes outside Banaras. Seth Suleiman would, of course, visit Rasoolan every other evening.

Rasoolan, says Pyaari, lived a reclusive life but on her own terms. Unlike Siddheshwari and the other tawaifs, she never changed her name. Even after marriage, she remained, proudly and obstinately, Rasoolan Bai.

Many other elite tawaif singers in Banaras made different choices. Shahjehan and Anwari, two of the most popular tawaifs in the city, got married and chose to stop singing altogether, preferring instead to become full-time wives and mothers. Teema Bai did not marry but completely renounced her life as a tawaif. Her love for music was so great that, every evening, she would go to the Radhakrishna temple located in Agastakund and sing bhajans in service of the Almighty.

Then there was Badi Moti Bai, too old to contemplate marriage. Her days of glory as one of the richest and most esteemed tawaifs in Banaras were behind her. A large-scale robbery in her house had left her penniless, while bitter family disputes had decimated her property. Desperately dependent on radio assignments and music conferences, she never recovered from the humiliation meted out by AIR.

Vidyadhari too was by then well into old age and long retired from her life as a tawaif, although she did occasionally sing for the radio. But her heart was no longer in music. She had been emotionally shattered a few years earlier by the death of her long-term patron lover, a wealthy jeweller of Banaras. He was so attached to her that he spent almost all his time in her home, and even breathed his last there.

During his lifetime, he had trusted Vidyadhari so implicitly that he left his most precious jewels in her safekeeping. His wife and sons were not even aware of this, and had Vidyadhari wanted, she could have easily appropriated all these riches. Instead, she called his eldest son to her house, and gave him all the jewels that his father had left with her. He was overwhelmed by Vidyadhari's honesty. But a younger son remained unconvinced, and not only publicly accused her of keeping back some of the jewellery but even filed a court case against her. To make matters worse, the local newspapers made much of her being a 'prostitute' as proof of the claim that she had stolen part of the jeweller's goods.

Though the eldest son was soon able to prevail upon his brother to withdraw the case, the entire episode left Vidyadhari traumatised. She took the news about Sardar Patel's ban on tawaifs as a final signal to stop performing music altogether. Vidyadhari left Banaras, which had long been her home, and returned to her village Jasuri to spend her last days with her younger brother, Sarju Rai, and his family.

'Those years were a terrible time in my life,' Pyaari khala tells me. 'Just before the news of the ban reached Banaras, I had lost my little Hanif to an attack of smallpox. Devastated by his death, I couldn't react to the ban at first. Once I recovered a bit, I began thinking about my future. Performing for the radio had enriched my life in so many ways that it pained me to give it up. But I was reluctant to get married as a way out.

'Marriage held absolutely no appeal for me. I had seen my mother and aunt suffer, and then my sister Sakeena. Moreover, even if I could convince myself to have a paper marriage, there was no one I could ask for the favour. Habib Khan was like a father. I felt sick at the thought of even broaching the subject with him. I didn't trust any of my other accompanists or regular clients enough to ask them to enter into a marriage of convenience with me.'

Patel's bizarre rule had left AIR with almost no women Hindustani musicians, since most of them hailed from tawaif backgrounds. In a quandary about how to carry on with music programming, radio officials in different stations became willing accomplices to the tawaifs' return to the microphone. They accepted without fuss the marriage certificates many had managed to procure and, in some instances, even turned a blind eye to the absence of any proof of marriage. Soon, many of the old tawaif singers, with a respectable 'Devi' or 'Begum' appended to their name, were back to singing on the radio.

'I did not return to the radio for a long time. I had seen the fate of some tawaifs who, within six months of their paper marriages, were forced to deal with demands for money and property from their new husbands and their families.' Looking visibly tired now, Pyaari khala lies down but continues speaking. 'There was this really talented and popular singer in Lucknow, Zahira, whom I got to know during my days of radio singing. She got married to her tabla player in order to beat the ban. But eventually the marriage beat her. Her husband, his first wife who was ailing and bedridden, his battery of children, all became Zahira's responsibility. Whenever she tried to protest, he would threaten her with talaq. He also made it clear that he would claim a substantial portion of her property and earnings as his. So she was trapped in that marriage. I didn't want to suffer a similar fate.'

Meanwhile, the countdown to independence began. Unlike many other places in northern India that were engulfed by communal violence, Banaras remained relatively calm during that period, even though feelings against Muslims ran high. They were being looked upon with suspicion, being told that they were not Indians and should go to Pakistan. The atmosphere was getting more tense by the day. News of riots taking place all around and the arrival of angry refugees from West Punjab to Banaras forced many Muslim families, rich and poor, to migrate to Pakistan.

However, hardly any Muslim tawaifs and musicians in Banaras or Bhabua and surrounding areas left. Free from communal prejudice as a community, Hindu and Muslim tawaifs were united in their suffering at the hands of 'respectable' society. Besides, the livelihood of tawaifs in Banaras was tied to their predominantly Hindu patrons, even if their numbers were dwindling. There was no guarantee that tawaifs would find patrons for their kind of music in Pakistan.

Many Muslim tawaifs in Amritsar, Delhi, Lucknow and other cities and towns were, however, forced to migrate. Their houses were attacked, their families killed. Those who opted to stay on despite the violence, did so at high cost. In Delhi, many Muslim tawaif families living in Chawri Bazaar were forced to take sanctuary for almost a year, along with thousands of other Muslim residents of the city, in the shrine of

Sufi saint Bakhtiyar Kaki in Mehrauli. They were branded as Pakistani spies and, in their absence, their homes were occupied by Hindu refugees. Once the violence abated and normalcy was restored, several tawaif families had to go to court and enter long years of litigation to claim back their properties.

'I remember that, despite our heartbreak over the radio ban, all the tawaifs in Banaras, including I, wore saris of green, white and saffron in celebration on 15 August 1947,' Pyaari khala recalls. 'I also remember the day Gandhi-ji was shot dead next year in January. Dal Mandi, along with the rest of the city, went into deep mourning. Tawaifs shut their kothas in grief. Shopkeepers downed their shutters. I remember everything vividly, as if it happened only yesterday.

'Then, in 1949, the Allahabad radio station came into being. From the beginning, they wanted Rasoolan aapa to perform regularly for them. Finding it far more convenient to travel to Allahabad than Lucknow, she would go there often. At her suggestion, I too tried my luck, and was accepted without too much fuss about my marital status.'

Someone politely clears his throat at the entrance of Pyaari's room. Shambhu Lala has taken to dropping by every couple of hours on some pretext or the other, perhaps to reassure himself that the miracle of her recovery is still holding. In his hand he carries a kulhad full of the sweet, thickened milk that she is very fond of. Wordlessly, he hands it to his lady love.

Pretending to be annoyed, Pyaari pulls a face, 'Lala, why do you pester me through the day? Don't worry, I am not running away with someone else!'

Lala blushes, but says nothing. Pyaari takes a few sips of the milk and holds the kulhad out to him, 'Now you drink.' Smiling shyly, he takes the milk from her and drinks a bit before handing it back.

Feeling like an intruder, I mumble about making a call and step out. You follow.

'This is true love,' you say, stating the obvious when we are safely out of earshot. 'If lala had had his way, he would have married khala long back. He was keen to. But she refused. Their love did not need any official seal, she said. And though he wished otherwise, he accepted her decision and has never left her side.'

CHAPTER 24

Asghari Comes of Age

LEAVING ME FAR BEHIND, ASGHARI scrambles past mounds of mud and dried-up ditches and up the steps of a nineteenth-century Shiva temple, known popularly as Brahmachari Baba ka mandir, on the outskirts of Bhabua. Dressed in a flaming red sari and matching red sandals, with black sunglasses perched on her nose and a flowered ladies' umbrella in hand, Asghari's overstated glamour stands out in the caked brown landscape.

When I finally haul myself up the steps and catch up with her, she purses her red lips disapprovingly. 'You need to lose weight,' she says. At a loss for words, I quietly follow Asghari to the large temple building, which (as she had warned me) we find locked. There is no one else around as far as I can see. A general air of disrepair and neglect clings to its peeling, moss-smudged walls. Peering through the iron-grilled door of the inner sanctum of the temple, I notice a flame burning steadily in the deep darkness. Morning and evening, Asghari informs me, a priest comes and lights a diya and offers prayers to the gods inside. Other than that, the temple remains locked and out of bounds to the general public.

We walk across the temple's sprawling courtyard. There are several tiny alcoves here, some installed with Shivlings, others with just a vermilion-daubed slab of stone bearing offerings of incense and flowers. Asghari says that these are from people living in the neighbourhood who still come here to offer prayers and, on festive days, to bathe in the large sarovar, or water reservoir, on the southern end of the courtyard.

'Summer or winter, dry weather or rain, this sarovar never goes dry,' Asghari informs me with some pride. I bend over the boundary wall and notice the thick green algae that covers the surface of the dark, deep waters.

'Earlier, when the temple was open to all, this courtyard would resound with music and dance performed by tawaifs during Rangbhari Ekadashi, celebrated four days before Holi. In our area and in Banaras too, Rangbhari Ekadashi signals the arrival of gaiety and colour,' Asghari says as she quickly steps under the temple awning to shield her pale loveliness from the sun.

'When I was growing up, Bhabua was filled with tawaifs. The choudharayin here was a very old Gandharva tawaif named Kumari Bai. At her initiative, all the tawaifs, Hindu and Muslim, began gathering at Brahmachari Baba's temple on Rangbhari Ekadashi for an all-night jalsa of music and dance. Kumari Bai had said, "*Hum apne ganey se bahut paisa kamate hain, lekin ek din hum Bhagwan ke durbar mein apni shraddha se gana chahte hain.*" We earn a lot with our singing but we wish to spend one day singing to god in devotion.

'I was very young and still learning music when I performed here for the first time. That was my first ever public performance. Brahmachari Baba, who presided over the celebrations of Rangbhari Ekadashi, was so pleased with my singing that he gave me a rupee as inam, prize. Usually, no singer was given an inam on this occasion because the tawaifs performed here in collective devotion and not in competition with each other. But since I was very young and had still not entered the profession, Baba blessed me with inam.

'My mother told me not to treat it as money but to offer it instead at the feet of god. I was initially reluctant to do so. It was the first public recognition that I had received, and one rupee was a lot of money at that time. But I heeded my mother's orders. When Baba heard of this, he patted me on the head and fed me prasad.

'"You will make a mark as a singer one day, little Asghari," he said in blessing.'

Brahmachari Baba was venerated by everyone in Bhabua, she informs me. He was the oldest person in town. No one quite knew when he had begun living in the temple, but he was in charge of all its activities. Well-versed in Sanskrit, he was also extremely knowledgeable about music and dance and would invite musicians, men and women, to perform at the temple.

'Then Brahmachari Baba went into samadhi and the glorious days of this temple came to an end. A bitter battle over control of it erupted between the Tiwaris, who are Brahmins, and the Choudharis, who are Kurmis. The Tiwaris, as upper castes, expected everyone to accept without demur their claim to the temple and its lucrative earnings from chaddhava, offerings. But the Choudharis would not hear of it. There were pitched battles here between the two warring factions. Police would have to be called in to restore peace. All the celebrations and musical jalsas that took place in the temple during Baba's time came to an end. A long time passed. Ultimately, the dispute reached the courts and the temple was locked. Even the gods are not safe from bitter caste strife in Bihar.'

From the temple, we make our way back to Asghari's house. I am having lunch with her today. Rani, her best friend, cousin and next-door neighbour, will be joining us.

You were mildly amused to hear of Asghari's lunch invitation. 'You should feel flattered that Asghari aapa likes you enough to want to cook for you. Just make sure you tell her that the food is the best you have ever had,' you quipped sarcastically.

But when I compliment Asghari, I do so with deep sincerity. The fish curry, rice and spinach-and-potato saag that she has cooked are superlative. She is, I realise with surprise, a great cook.

I feel guilty, though, that Asghari has spent money she can ill afford on expensive fish and basmati rice to feed me. Her home looks as ravaged by want as it was a few months ago. The kitchen, with its crumbling mud chulha and bare assortment of soot-covered aluminium pots, mocks the gastronomic repast that Asghari has conjured out of its frugality. The sari that screens the bathing area with its hand-pump is the same torn, faded maroon one I had seen before. The corner opposite is still littered with broken, discarded chairs.

The electricity has returned though. I assume that Asghari's brothel-plying has helped clear the pending dues. Later, I learn that, much to Phoolmani's consternation, Sheem took care of the electricity bill while she was here.

I notice too Asghari's cough, recurrent and rasping. She waves away my concern, although Rani, who joins us midway through lunch, says that the cough has been troubling Asghari for some months. Imperiously shutting her down, Asghari insists that it is nothing serious and, ignoring my protests, puts a big piece of fish on my plate.

Fanning me with a newspaper while I eat, she observes, 'My mother cooked fish very well. This is her recipe. She learnt to cook for my father.

He was very fond of fish. He would make me sit with him at meal times and feed me from his thali, carefully taking out all the bones before putting the fish in my mouth.

'You should have seen my father. He was so tall, well built and handsome! He treated me like a little princess. Anything I wanted was mine for the asking. Even as a little child, I had a big wooden box full of the bangles that baba would buy for me wherever he went. I had more dolls than I could play with. Amma would stitch such sweet clothes made of silk and satin for them. I was so happy in Ranchi.

'Then baba brought home another woman, and amma returned with my brother and me to Bhabua. I hated it here. Everyone was so poor and raggedy and miserly, counting every paisa for the smallest purchase. I used to cry all the time and demand to be taken back to my father. Amma would try and cheer me up. No matter how tired she was, she would take me in her arms and kiss and tickle me till I began laughing. Amma loved me a lot, perhaps more than she loved anyone else. She always tried to give me the very best.'

Teema's love for Asghari included hiring the best teachers available in Bhabua to prepare her for a luminous future as a tawaif. Asghari was about five years old when she, along with Rani and a much older Pyaari, began learning music from Babban Guru. One of the oldest male musicians in Bhabua, he was famous for his accomplished playing of a variety of musical instruments, most notably the sarangi and jal tarang.

'I studied under Babban Guru for about five years or more. After his death, my mother took me to Azamgarh to learn dance and music from Basudev Guru. He played the tabla and had taught dance to many tawaifs from Bhabua. Like Babban Guru, Basudev Guru too was a Kathak and belonged to the village of Hariharpur, close to Azamgarh. The entire village was inhabited exclusively by Kathaks who are called Misra in our parts.'

During their first six months in Azamgarh, Teema and Asghari lived as tenants in the house of Allahrakhi, a tawaif and distant relative. Allahrakhi had ruined her career through drinking and scraped out a living by renting rooms to visiting tawaifs. Basudev Guru would come here daily to teach Asghari. He took over from where Babban Guru had left off, and also taught her kathak, which she hadn't learnt thus far. Basudev Guru was a wonderful teacher, Asghari remembers with great affection, and under his guidance she 'took to dance like a fish to water'.

Their stay in Allahrakhi's house, however, proved to be short-lived. Pyaari moved to Banaras during this period, and Teema felt duty-bound to divide time between her and Asghari. Much as Teema wanted Asghari to continue learning from Basudev Guru, she didn't like the thought of leaving her alone in Allahrakhi's home. Hopelessly alcoholic, Allahrakhi would sometimes pass out for days on end, and was hardly the guardian Teema could entrust with her daughter's safekeeping. Besides, the rent and living expenses were proving to be beyond her means. Teema decided to terminate Asghari's education with Basudev Guru and move to Banaras.

'Basudev Guru was reluctant to let me go,' Asghari says. 'He had gauged my potential to be a great dancer and didn't want my future to be jeopardised by a patchy education. Moreover, he had great regard for amma, whom he treated like a sister. He offered to keep me in his family house in Hariharpur at no extra cost, so that I could continue learning from him. I was truly blessed to have a guru like him.

'But my mother remained unconvinced about the wisdom of leaving me in his family's care. To allay her fears, he took us to his home in Hariharpur. His family—his wife and three daughters—were so warm and welcoming that my mother felt immediately less apprehensive. When she pointed out to him and his wife the problems that they, as Brahmins, would face in keeping a Muslim girl in their home, given their rules of purity and pollution, Basudev Guru reassured her, "Asghari is not Muslim or Hindu for us. She is simply my student and will live in our home like a daughter."

'And true to his word, he and his wife kept me for the next three years just like their daughter. Basudev Guru's wife never discriminated between me and her own children, all of whom were around my age. I called her mai. She would sit me alongside her own children at mealtimes. If I fell ill, mai would keep awake through the nights and take care of me, just like a mother would. She would wake me up at dawn for my lessons with guru-ji, and come to my rescue if he got angry and began thrashing me for not paying attention.'

Through this period, Asghari says that she learnt more kathak than she would from all her subsequent teachers over the years. Guru-ji would teach her from dawn to about 8 o'clock in the morning. Then he would leave for Azamgarh to teach in various tawaif households. Back home by late afternoon, he would rest a bit and then again give Asghari lessons till past dinner.

'At the end of three years, Basudev Guru felt confident about introducing me to the other Kathak gurus at the annual puja that the community organised in Hariharpur,' my hostess says, serving me a generous helping of the spinach-and-potato saag. 'All the gurus belonging to the village would be present on this occasion. Katha would be read out and Brahmins fed as part of the puja. The most promising students of all the gurus would be then invited to perform one by one. This was an occasion for the gurus to show off all that they had taught their students.

'When my turn came, as per the norm, the gurus asked someone other than Basudev Guru to accompany me on tabla. The reason for this was simple. *Jo sadhe rehtein hain unke sath toh hum kaise bhi nach kar, gaa kar nikal jayenge.* With those who have taught us as accompanists, we can safely dance and sing our way through somehow. We are confident in the knowledge that our guru will camouflage our weaknesses with his playing. So Phunnu Maharaj was asked to play tabla for me. I performed dance first and then I sang.

'All the assembled gurus were spellbound by my performance and heartily congratulated Basudev Guru for teaching me so well. Even though twenty others students of various gurus performed that day, I was adjudged the best. *Allah ki aisi meharbani rahi hai ki jahan hum jate thhe hum hi rehte thhe.* Allah has been so merciful to me that, wherever I performed, I have dominated the mehfil.

'Basudev Guru looked so happy that day. Basking in his appreciation, I began taking my lessons with him even more seriously. Everything was going well till Yaqub mamu came from Bhabua one day and announced that amma was pregnant and urgently wanted me back.'

The pregnancy had come as a shock for everyone, including Teema herself. She was in her late forties, too old, everyone said, to become pregnant. Asghari reached Bhabua to find her bedridden and looking like death. Her ageing and hard-worked body wasn't strong enough to take the weight of pregnancy, the dai, midwife, had said. Certain that she was past the age of bearing children, Teema had discovered her pregnancy too late for an abortion to be possible.

'Asghari was furious with Teema for putting her life at such risk,' Pyaari khala tells me later in the evening when you and I drop in to spend time with her. 'We were all very frightened. But there was nothing to be done, except take good care of Teema and pray to Allah to be merciful. He heard our prayers because, when Teema went into labour, everything went well and, without much trouble, she delivered not one but two healthy daughters—your friend here and Ghafuran.'

You and Ghafuran, I learn from Pyaari khala, are freedom's children, born the year India gained independence. A delighted Shivendra Singh nicknamed his daughters, Swaraj and Swantantra—Self-rule and Freedom—to attain which he had, during the Quit India movement, put his own liberty and life at stake.

'The twins, being the youngest in the family, were loved by everyone—everyone except Asghari,' Pyaari khala recalls. 'She blamed her half-sisters for putting her mother's life at risk and for being the cause of the abrupt end of her training with Basudev Guru. Through her difficult pregnancy, Teema had wanted Asghari by her side. After the twins were born, Teema decided that it would be best if she shifted with her three girls to my house in Banaras. I was well settled by then. Rani had just entered the line and shifted out to a nearby kotha under my mother's care. Rajjo was with them and learning music from Habib Khan Sahib. He would be asked to teach Asghari too, and Teema would be able to look after the twins peacefully.'

Asghari was not at all happy with Teema's decision. For long used to being her mother's favourite child, she bitterly resented sharing her with the twins. She would pinch their cheeks or push them off the bed when no one was around. And though she was almost thirteen by then, Asghari would throw childish tantrums if she saw Teema cuddling the twins for too long. She would calm down only when Teema put them down and embraced Asghari instead.

Asghari was Teema's only weakness, Pyaari khala points out. As the first-born daughter, Asghari had been loved and pampered by Teema in ways that the other children would never be. The security of her mother's love translated into immense self-belief and confidence for Asghari, Pyaari explains. It also made her completely self-absorbed and self-obsessed.

Used to getting her own way from childhood, she carried her sense of entitlement into adulthood. Teema's decision to groom her to be a tawaif only served to sharpen this feeling. As the future breadwinner for the family, she felt, she had a right to the very best. Perhaps Teema too shared the feeling. She never tired of saying that her fair and pretty, wilful and charming Asghari was sure to make a great success of her career as a tawaif.

'Amma loved Ghafuran and me a lot too,' quiet thus far, you assert your claim on Teema. You acknowledge, though, that her advancing age and the burden of looking after the entire family left Teema with little energy or time to delight in your twin and you individually or indulge your whims. You remember making whimpering sounds persistently as a child to get your mother's attention. Unable to respond in adequate measure, Teema had taken to feeding you whenever you whimpered too long. You have vivid memories of almost always carrying a bowl of food, constantly replenished with leftovers by your mother in an attempt to quieten you down.

'Ghafuran and I are thirteen years younger than Asghari aapa. We were just babies when our mother shifted with all of us to Pyaari khala's house in Banaras. While aapa was busy through the day with her music and dance teachers, Ghafuran and I, barely toddlers, learnt to make ourselves as inconspicuous as possible for fear of inviting her wrath. We dared not make too much noise or come in her way. There was no knowing when she would begin shouting, or when she would throw her slipper at us. Rajjo, who is about five years older than us, would come by daily from Rani aapa's place to play with Ghafuran and me. She would try to shield us from aapa's fury, but even she was scared of her. Amma would reason with aapa but to little avail. At night, she would insist that Ghafuran and I sleep in a separate cot and she alone share amma's bed. Confining ourselves to the topmost floor of the house, we trained ourselves to play quietly, squabble softly and cry noiselessly. We grew up terrified of our older sister,' you say.

'We were happiest when amma took us with her to visit the rest of the family and our father in Bhabua, or when he came periodically to meet all of us in Banaras. Baba called me Swaraj and Ghafuran, Swantantra. He loved us very much. He would seat us on either shoulder and carry us around everywhere.'

Asghari never tired of telling her half-sisters the difference between the privileged status of her own father and that of theirs, the humble Shivendra Singh. She would also fly into a violent rage if the children even touched anything that belonged to her.

'Pyaari khala would often intervene, sternly ticking aapa off, and for a while we would be safe from her wrath, only for it to erupt again at the slightest provocation.' You lean over and lightly kiss your aunt's skeletal hand. Pyaari khala gently pats your cheek.

'Asghari was past puberty and around fifteen years old by then,' Pyaari tells me. 'Her figure had begun showing, her breasts and hips were filling out, and her waist was tapering in. She was beautiful. And she knew it, spending hours in front of the mirror, admiring her looks. We decided that, instead of launching Asghari immediately into the line, her future would be better served if she continued for the next year completing her music and dance education. Habib Khan Sahib, my sarangi accompanist, taught Asghari Banarasi thumri, dadra. And Husn Baksh Khan Sahib used to come in daily for Asghari's taleem in dance.'

'I have faint memories of Husn Baksh Sahib,' you put in. 'He was a very old man and played the tabla. He came daily to teach aapa. I learnt later that he was from Jaipur. He was apparently very religious and particular about his namaz. Besides, he was greatly respected as a musician. In his younger days, he was attached to the court of the maharaja of Jaipur. Everyone said that aapa was lucky to have had him for her teacher.'

'Asghari didn't think so. After learning from him for about six months or so, she threw the most spectacular fit when Husn Baksh ustad reprimanded her over something. Now, there is no denying that the ustad was a strict teacher,' Pyaari adds. 'But then, most teachers those days were strict. We had all grown up being ticked off and even being beaten physically by our ustads. It was accepted that they chastised us for our good. I don't remember anyone ever protesting against it. But then no one was as thoroughly pampered as Asghari was. She just refused to learn any further from him. Teema had no option but to terminate his services.'

'Pyaari khala, don't pass judgement without knowing the full truth,' Asghari's rasping voice breaks in with unmistakable fury. None of us noticed her enter the room. You colour up with embarrassment and make a show of finding a chair for your sister. Ignoring you, Asghari keeps standing.

'Khala, you were away for a radio programme in Allahabad when Husn Baksh was thrown out.' Turning towards you in contempt, Asghari adds, 'And you were just a baby. You had better keep your mouth shut about things you know nothing about. Neither you nor khala know the real reason amma got rid of Husn Baksh.'

'What other reason? Teema told me herself that you refused to learn from him because he had spoken harshly with you,' Pyaari replies in a bantering tone.

Voice quivering with rage, Asghari snaps back, 'He spoke harshly with me not because I was not learning dance well enough but because I stopped him from doing what he wanted. Don't look so shocked, khala. You know as well as I that not all ustads were the saintly father figures we try and make them out to be. The same Husn Baksh who was the picture of piety and decorum when teaching the daughter of a rich and powerful bai-ji would transform into a sleazy lecher with me. He presumed, no doubt, that, since he had agreed to teach me for a lower fee, I would gratefully and meekly submit to his roving fingers. And even if I resisted, my mother, being poor, would keep quiet.

'Initially, when he brushed his hands across my breasts on a couple of occasions, I thought it was an accident. He looked so old and venerable, with his long white beard and his show of offering namaz five times a day, that it didn't even enter my head that ustad-ji was feeling me up. Then one day, finding me alone at home, he untied his pyjama and forced himself upon me. I screamed and screamed in horror. To cover up, he tried to shout me down, pretending that he was angry with me for not paying attention to his lessons. Amma, who had just returned home, came into the room upon hearing the commotion. At first, she believed Husn Baksh's version of events but, after he left, she realised the truth when I told her exactly what had happened.

'Cradling me in her arms, she wept silently for a long time. Then she wiped both our faces clean of tears. She made me bathe and change into fresh clothes. Kissing my hands over and over, she made me promise that I wouldn't tell a soul about the incident. A pubescent tawaif's virginity was a highly prized commodity. She didn't want rumours to circulate and my market value to fall even before I had been launched in the profession. Next day, she terminated Husn Baksh's services.'

There is silence in the room. Pyaari looks shaken. Her voice sounds both hurt and contrite when she finally speaks, 'I didn't know this. Why did neither Teema nor you tell me? Didn't either of you trust me?'

Asghari impatiently clucks her tongue, 'It was not about trust, khala. Of course amma and I trusted you. We just wanted to put the ugly episode behind us. Amma said that the more we talked about it, even to you and other family members, the more it would linger on in our thoughts. She wanted me to forget that it had ever happened. And to tell you the truth, I did forget all about it. I never thought about it till today when you began blaming me for nothing.'

You look at your sister with infinite tenderness. 'I wish amma had skinned the old coot alive instead of worrying about your market price. I wish she had exposed his dirty deeds to everyone so that other little girls could be protected from the ordeal you went through.' This is the very first time that I have heard you being critical of your mother.

'We always speak very respectfully about our teachers. But it is true,' you add, 'that some ustads could be real bastards when it came to young girls, especially those from poor families. Tawaifs, young or old, were assumed to be sexually promiscuous from childhood. And daughters of poor tawaifs, it was understood, had no right to say no even if they were just children. And it's sad that our own families most often hushed up the matter for fear of suffering financially if it became public that a young daughter had been sexually violated before the sar dhakna ceremony.'

While you are speaking, I notice Asghari fidgeting with the pallu of her magenta sari and looking edgy. I wonder if, in spontaneously sharing a long-concealed secret, she is anxious now, face-to-face with memories of fear and vulnerability. It might be too that, long used to being the bossy elder sister, Asghari is unprepared to be the recipient of your sympathy.

Whatever the reason, she clearly has no desire to dwell any longer in the dark room of her adolescence. With an impatient toss of her head, she lights a cigarette from Pyaari's packet and inhales deeply. Asghari is an occasional smoker. Too poor to afford cigarettes, she sometimes smokes beedis, and once in a while helps herself to the packet that Shambhu Lala regularly buys for Pyaari.

'My mother put me in the line soon after. She rented out the kotha in Nariyal Bazaar that she'—Asghari points to you— 'and her family live in now. I took Banaras by storm. I used to dance four or five hours at a stretch, kathak, bhangra, Arabian dance with tambourine in my hand, and the kaherwa from Banaras. My dancing was always hugely appreciated, although people loved my singing too.

'Crowds would gather outside my kotha to hear me sing. People would have to be stopped on the steps so that I could finish performing without any disturbance for the audience already inside. They would wait in a queue to hear me.

'Our music was "chaturmukhi", four-directional. Instead of singing only one kind of song, we sang whatever the audience requested—ghazals, dadra, folk songs, bhajans, film songs or nationalist songs.'

'What about thumri? Didn't you and other tawaifs perform that?' I ask, though I already guess the answer.

'By the time I began performing, few among those who came to tawaifs' kothas were interested in listening to classical songs. The men who visited us were mainly contractors, businessman and shopkeepers who had no taste for classical music. Even if we sometimes sang a thumri of our own accord, as soon as it was over, the audience would immediately demand a change: *"Bai-ji, ab koi thirkati cheez ho jaye."* Bai-ji, let's have a racy number now.'

By the mid-twentieth century, while most elite tawaifs had either renounced music altogether or made a considered decision to only sing at 'respectable' venues like music conferences or on the radio, those belonging to the middle and lower ranks of the community had little choice but to continue with their hereditary calling. Viewed mainly as entertainers, few amongst them enjoyed the status of serious musicians. A century of sustained campaigns by social reformers and nationalists, the flurry of anti-prostitution laws and their boycott by the urban elite had led to the stripping away of the cultural role that tawaifs once performed.

'To be honest with you, most tawaifs were not equipped to sing beyond the mandatory two or three thumris that our ustads had taught us,' Asghari says. 'Unlike the previous generation of singers, who had a long and rigorous education in raga-ragini, the learning of my generation was more jhatpat, rough and ready. A couple of years with one teacher, a few months with another and then another. The best teachers were, in any case, not available. They were either too expensive, or preferred to teach students with a future in classical music performance. The teachers most tawaifs got understood the requirements of our times—a few thumris and many more dadras, simple ghazals, folk songs, etc.

'But I was not like most other tawaifs. Even if the audience I got was not interested in classical music, I wanted to be as skilled in thumri-singing as I was in dadras, ghazals and folk songs. Besides, my popularity was such that I would get invited by the biggest Rajput and Bhumihar zamindars in Bihar. They knew their music, and I wanted to be good enough as a thumri singer to meet their standards.

'Once I began earning, I hired some of the finest ustads available to teach me classical thumri, dadra. I had a sharp mind and learnt fast. Everyone, including my ustads and accompanists, said that I was a truly exceptional singer.'

Pyaari's eyes twinkle at the self-loving Asghari's return to form. These are stories that no doubt your family has heard Asghari narrate very often. You look grumpy, your upsurge of sibling love wilting under the deluge of Asghari's self-admiration.

Later you would scoff at Asghari's assertions of being a great thumri singer. 'Aapa and her tall claims! Yes, she continued to learn from various teachers even after she joined the line, but there was nothing exceptional about that. Tawaifs, including truly great ones, like our own Sadabahar nani, never stopped learning even when they were well established singers. Even our Pyaari khala continued to learn music well after she entered the line.

'And Asghari aapa was too flighty to really give music learning the concentration it requires. She could sing thumri just about adequately, but there was no way she could hold her own in front of even Pyaari khala, let alone the likes of Rasoolan or Siddheshwari. There is no doubt though that she was among the most popular tawaifs in Banaras and got invited to mehfils hosted by landowners in Bihar, more on account of her beautiful face, her silly nakhras and her dancing. Undoubtedly, she was a very good dancer. But she was not expected to sing beyond her usual repertoire of popular ghazals, dadras and folk songs.'

This afternoon, however, while Asghari crows and preens, you maintain a morose silence. Occasionally, you roll your eyes in exasperation.

'I was not only the fairest and most beautiful in the family, I also had the most slender wrists and ankles and the most delicate hands and feet,' Asghari launches into a favourite reminiscence. 'Men would swoon over my feet. "Your feet are so dainty," they would say, "despite having danced so much!"'

I notice Pyaari khala's shoulders shake with silent laughter. The effect is contagious. While I battle hard to suppress my giggles, you break into a smile that reaches your eyes. Oblivious to our mirth, Asghari, now ensconced in the one comfortable chair in Pyaari's room, continues to wax eloquent about her dazzling days and brilliant nights as the brightest star in Dal Mandi's firmament.

'I was a favourite with all the Marwari seths in Calcutta when they visited Banaras. I would also get invited regularly by the wealthy shopkeepers of Thatheri Bazaar; they owned the biggest utensil shops in all of Banaras. Many lawyers and doctors swore undying love for me.

'I was invited often to perform at Rajput and Bhumihar weddings in rural areas. In my days, wedding celebrations would last two days, unlike the old times when they would go on for three or four days. We would be hired by the bridegroom's family. On the wedding day, we would reach the janwasa, community hall, where the baraat was put up in the bride's village. The mehfil would take place there under a shamiana. The nausha, bridegroom, would sit facing east, which is considered the auspicious direction, described as Ganga mukhi. The others in the baraat were seated on mattresses covered with chandani. The audience comprised only men—relatives of the bridegroom, other invited guests and members of the bride's family. No women were present. We would perform in the centre of the mehfil on a dari, also covered with chandani.

'As soon as the nausha was seated, the mehfil would begin, around seven or eight in the evening, and would not end before five in the morning. All tawaifs began the mehfil with dancing. This could last for one or two hours. I would do kathak, followed by other popular and folk dances. I would follow this with sehra, songs in praise of the flower-veil worn by the bridegroom—that was the norm. There were all kinds of sehras. A personal favourite that I made extremely popular went like this:

Layi malin mere naushe ke barabar sehra
Pariyon ney hathhon sey sajaya sehra

The flower girl has brought for my bridegroom a fine sehra
Fairies have with their own hands decorated the sehra.

'This would then be followed by other songs—ghazals, bhajans, Bhojpuri, filmy, depending upon the taste and atmosphere of the wedding party. Once the wedding was solemnised, we would sing the mangal geet, which went like this:

Jai mala ho Siya Ram gale dalo
Dulha toh Sri Ram bane hain
Lachchman devar sehbala ho
Siya Ram gale dalo jai mala ho

O' Sita put the victory garland on Ram
Sri Ram is your bridegroom
Laxman is his best man
O' Sita put the victory garland on Ram.

'Next morning, there would be the Bhairavi ki mehfil. It would begin around nine in the morning. This was the centrepiece mehfil of the wedding celebrations, and was a challenge for tawaifs to perform their best. In the old days, tawaifs from Banaras would begin this mehfil by singing a khayal. I too would do the same. Even if the assembled rustic folk did not understand it, they did appreciate that this was a mehfil for a higher calibre of music. After that there would be a Bhairavi thumri or two, followed by the usual mix of dadras, ghazals, bhajans and Bhojpuri songs.

'Besides these Rajput wedding mehfils in the countryside, where I performed for rough and ready rural folk, I have performed, by the grace of Allah, in mehfils of judges, barristers, zamindars and rajas. I was invited to perform at the marriage celebrations of the daughter of Raja Gopal Narayan of Maanpur, a zamindari near Gaya so large that its landlord was called raja by the people. His men especially came to Banaras to sign me up for the wedding mehfil. Initially, amma refused their invitation since Muharram was due to begin, and all the Muslim tawaifs in the city, including those like us who were Sunni, not only shut our kothas for the forty days of mourning but also avoided performing at mehfils outside during that period.

'Determined to sign me on, they returned the next day to plead their case. My mother refused their invitation again but, while they were there, a mastan who visited our house regularly also arrived. Mastans are naked men of god. In his own way, he too pressed amma to accept the invitation. Not comfortable with refusing him, she finally signed on the satta, legal contract, and accepted the advance payment.'

You have explained that tawaifs entered into a formal agreement to perform in mehfils outside their kothas, countersigned by their hosts. Drawn up on stamp paper with particulars related to date, time and payment, the satta was legally binding on both parties. Any side that defaulted could be sued for going back on a commitment.

'You should have seen the Maanpur palace where the celebrations were being held!' Asghari says excitedly. 'Glittering with lights, it was bigger than any mansion in which I had performed thus far. The sky was ablaze with fireworks and the entire length of the road was lined with fancy cars, in which rajas and maharajas arrived and were received with splendid ceremonial courtesies.

'On our way inside, I got a peek of the palace rooms. They were full of stuffed tigers and cheetahs and deer. I suppose the raja must have hunted them. Expensive Persian carpets covered the marble floors, while huge chandeliers blazed from the ceilings.

'The mehfil was packed with princes, zamindars, colonels, generals and judges. A vast array of musicians and dancers, scheduled to perform that evening, were also present—including Sitara Devi's niece, Annapurna Devi, and the two best-known singers from Patna, Mala Devi and Hira Bai. Kishan Maharaj and the dancer duo, nachwaiyya Ram and Shyam, were also there. But once the singing and dancing began, as Allah is my witness, all the assembled guests wanted just me to perform.

'There were two princes there who were identical twins and very good-looking. They each demanded that I sit in their lap! I said, "I haven't come to sit on your laps. I have come here to sing. Please call someone else if you want a woman to sit on your lap." Everyone laughed at my smart reply. By Allah's grace, wherever I have sung and danced, I have been appreciated the most. I have never come back defeated. That evening, the audience showered me with so much inam every time I performed that my mother got exhausted collecting the piles of currency notes and jewellery.

'Around the same time, my performance in Patna at the mehfil organised by a judge to celebrate his granddaughter's wedding was talked about for days to come. *Baap re baap, aisi mehfil ki mehfil mein jate hue tharthari bolti ththi*. And what a mehfil it was! We were all nervous performing in it! Gudai Maharaj, Lachchu Maharaj, Siyaram Tiwari, Lokai Maharaj and the sarangiya Gopal Maharaj were all present.'

'Wasn't this the mehfil, khala, where you performed and beat all the competition hollow with your thumris?' You jump at the opportunity to score points over Asghari.

'Yes, I was there,' Pyaari khala confirms, but modestly laughs away claims of being the best. 'Besides all the gurus from Banaras that Asghari has mentioned, there were so many other wonderful performers present that I was just a speck of dust compared to them.'

Touching her earlobes lightly, Pyaari adds, 'Ustad Nisar Husain and Ustad Ghulam Mustafa were there. Our own Bismillah Khan Sahib from Banaras was also present. Rasoolan aapa had been invited, but by then she had stopped performing in mehfils altogether. She declined the invitation and suggested my name instead. That's how I was there. Among the women, there was Badi Moti Bai, who was very old by then. But what an electrifying performance she gave—made all the more special since she hardly ever made mehfil appearances anymore. Asghari Bai was also there. She belonged to the court of the maharaja of Orchha and was one of the only known women musicians around who performed dhrupad.'

As Pyaari khala conjures up the magic of music-making by stalwarts of the past, you quietly nudge me from behind. Your eyes direct my gaze towards Asghari. She is yawning ostentatiously, and distractedly flipping through the newspaper. This mehfil, as far as she is concerned, is over.

CHAPTER 25

Pyaari and Zehra

'KHALA, ANY NEWS OF AUSAF SAHIB?' Asghari asks Pyaari. The coquettish arching of her ruthlessly tweezed eyebrows and the cleverness of her smile belie her innocent tone.

'He died years ago. You know that,' Pyaari khala snaps back.

'Oh! Yes of course. Odd how it slipped my mind. And Zehra died a couple of months after he did. I remember now.' This time Asghari's tone is as insincere as her smile.

I wonder where all this is leading. Ausaf might have been an old lover of Pyaari khala, I imagine, and perhaps Zehra was a rival claimant for his attention? I look towards you for clarification. Busying yourself making paan, you avoid my eye.

'Ausaf Sahib was a poet and an admirer of khala's singing,' Asghari informs me with breathless eagerness. 'His wife Zehra was a very generous lady. She was very good to khala. May Allah grant both husband and wife sanctuary in heaven.'

Pyaari khala props herself up on the bed and, flashing a warning look at Asghari, slowly sips water from the tumbler that you extend to her lips. In the intervening silence, I hear Nawab's wife in the kitchen, cooking lunch for Pyaari. The sharp treble of children's voices playing outside filters in.

'Ausaf Sahib and Zehra were good people,' Pyaari says to me in a soft but steady voice. 'Not everyone understood my relationship with them. You might not either. But since I have promised to share with you the story of my life, it's time that you hear this chapter and make what you will of it.'

❁

Ausaf Ali Khan belonged to a wealthy, nationalist family of erstwhile landholders from Jaunpur who had moved to Allahabad in the late nineteenth century. Then the capital city of the United Provinces, Allahabad, with its high court, university and government departments, offered new prospects for the English-educated sons of Ausaf's family, prospects that a life as landowners in the backwaters of Jaunpur did not.

Ausaf's uncle had been among the earliest Indian civil servants in the colonial bureaucracy to resign his job and join the non-cooperation movement in the early 1920s. His father was a well-known lawyer and Congress supporter who shared a close friendship with Jawaharlal Nehru from his days in England as a law student. Ausaf's two elder brothers had also studied in England and returned to set up highly successful practices in Allahabad. His mother was the first girl in her extended family to finish high school. His sister was the first Muslim woman doctor in Allahabad. Ausaf's family had many firsts to its credit.

The youngest in the household, Ausaf proved to be something of a prodigal. If his school years had been a source of some satisfaction to his achiever family, his time at the university generated much anxiety. The boy had little interest in academics and even less in preparing for a career. He spent all his time either fraternising with communists who seemed to be everywhere in the university, or day-dreaming and writing effusive poetry about love and revolution.

Hoping that a wife would steer the young man to the luminous path of purposefulness and success, his parents married him off to Zehra as soon as he completed his graduation. Hailed by all as the perfect match for Ausaf, Zehra belonged to a family of educationists, lawyers and doctors from Aligarh.

Originally from Delhi, her paternal grandfather had been a well-known hakim and religious scholar associated with Delhi College, the first educational institution in Delhi to introduce English learning in 1827. Zehra's father had studied there before becoming professor of history at the Muslim Anglo-Oriental College in Aligarh, later to develop into the Aligarh Muslim University.

A staunch votary of social reform, Zehra's father countered stiff opposition from his own family, not only to ensure that his daughter received the best education available but also that she did not observe purdah on reaching puberty. Zehra, the only sister to four older brothers, completed her schooling from the Aligarh Women's College, which had been founded in 1906 by the social reformer couple Sheikh Abdullah and Waheed Jahan Begum to provide English education to Muslim girls. Outstanding in studies, she loved sports like basketball and hockey too, and represented her school team in inter-school competitions held in Lucknow and Allahabad. Zehra completed her graduation and post-graduation in English from the Isabella Thoburn College for Women in Lucknow, then one of the country's leading educational institutions for women.

She had begun writing short stories in Urdu while still in high school. By the time Zehra was in college, she had become a minor literary celebrity. Many of her short stories had been published in various well-respected Urdu journals for women, like *Khatun*, published by Sheikh Abdullah and Waheed Jahan Begum in Aligarh, and *Tahzib un-Niswan*, a weekly Urdu newspaper for women edited by another social-reformer couple, Mumtaz Ali and Muhammadi Begum from Lahore.

Known for her forthright espousal of gender rights, Zehra broke literary convention with her use of the conversational, everyday language of women. Freedom from patriarchal restrictions was a recurring theme in her writings. Inspired by both the nationalist movement in India and the Russian revolution, she wrote against social injustice and inequality. She loved listening to music and enjoyed poetry.

Zehra had admired Ausaf's poems long before her marriage to him. As predicted by well-wishers, they got along fabulously from the very beginning. So well in fact that, much to her in-laws' dismay, Zehra became an enthusiastic supporter of his decision to pursue poetry as a full-time occupation. Worse, she seemed unperturbed by Ausaf's lifestyle.

From chain-smoking communists to hard-drinking struggling poets, to male and female artists of questionable morals, Ausaf had a wide array of friends and acquaintances. Unkempt and unconventional, they were a source of unremitting tension for his parents. Much to their consternation, Zehra seemed happy to play hostess to all these social misfits that Ausaf brought home to be fed and looked after at their expense. More often, he was away for days and nights on end, with reports reaching his parents of drinking binges and poetry soirees that turned riotous and occasional run-ins with the police. Instead of issuing an ultimatum to Ausaf, as expected by his parents, Zehra would invariably plead with them to bail him out.

There were regular showdowns between Ausaf and his father over not only his apparent lack of purpose in life but, worse, of the trouble he was bringing to his family, already beleaguered for being Muslim in newly independent India. Braving pressures from votaries of Hindu India and Muslim Pakistan that they migrate, Ausaf's family, like the majority of the country's Muslims, had opted to live in India. This choice had come at a heart-breaking price. Unjustly blamed for the creation of Pakistan, Muslims in India often found themselves, in those early years of independence, being treated like strangers and worse in their own land.

Despite his close friendship with the Nehru family, Ausaf's father had been called a Pakistani spy by anonymous rumour-mongers. His brothers faced abandonment by several old-time Hindu clients, who did not wish to take the 'risk' of being represented by Muslim lawyers. A government-run bank had denied his doctor sister a loan to open a hospital, saying that it could turn out to be a bad debt if she and her husband absconded to Pakistan.

Didn't Ausaf realise that, in troubled times such as these, he simply could not afford to compromise the family's reputation, his father asked. His mother begged him to wake up to the challenges that lay ahead. Shrugging off his parents' anxieties as bourgeois self-preservation, Ausaf mumbled about the need for a revolution that would annihilate class and communal divides and usher in true freedom for India.

Desperate with worry, the family heaved a sigh of relief when, following the Indian government's crackdown on communists across the country in the wake of the Telangana rebellion, many of his revolutionary friends were either arrested or went into hiding. Ausaf escaped that fate by a whisker since he was not formally a member of Communist Party of India, which had spearheaded the peasant rebellion. His parents hoped that this brush with the law would cure their son of his revolutionary enthusiasm.

They soon realised the futility of their expectations when they discovered Ausaf and Zehra trying to hide some of his communist comrades in the family house. Fed up with their renegade son and his accomplice wife, his parents decided that the only way the two of them could be made to see sense was to cast them out on their own. This disowning, it was hoped, would not only spare the family further social embarrassment but also force Ausaf to mend his profligate ways. Perhaps Zehra too would now show greater enthusiasm in taming her husband.

Abandoned by the family, some sobriety did indeed seem to dawn upon the couple. They shifted into a rented two-room house in one of the shabbier localities of the town, and had to face the reality of earning a living. Ausaf gravitated towards the newly opened Allahabad radio station and, thanks to his father's large social circle, was able to get a job in the programme department. Zehra got a job as teacher in St Mary's Convent, a missionary school for girls, through a reference from Ausaf's sister. She supplemented this income with her writing.

Pyaari met Zehra and Ausaf for the first time in the early 1950s at the Allahabad radio station, where she had gone with Rasoolan. Zehra, who often dropped in at AIR on her way back from school, immediately recognised Rasoolan, whom she greatly admired. She got talking to both women, and insisted that Ausaf order tea and snacks for them.

Seizing the opportunity, Rasoolan mentioned Pyaari's past record as singer for Lucknow radio and her keenness to perform for the Allahabad station. Zehra immediately pressed Ausaf to put in a word on Pyaari's behalf with the powers that be, paving the way for her entry as a singer without the need for furnishing proof of her marital status.

Hereafter, Pyaari would perform on AIR as 'Pyaari Begum', her background suitably blurred. Her friendship with Zehra blossomed in the coming months over cups of tea at the radio station whenever she went to perform there.

'Zehra seemed just like me—friendly, fun-loving and always smiling,' Pyaari says. 'I would often run into her at the radio station. She had a great sense of humour and both of us would be in splits, cracking jokes. Her face would light up and her eyes would sparkle with laughter. She looked beautiful.

'She was also very sensitive to people's moods. If I was troubled by something, she would immediately sense it and try to help. She was like this with everyone. All the drivers, peons and other junior staffers in AIR Allahabad doted on Zehra. Even though she did not work there, she knew all of them by name and spent time chatting with them, getting involved in their problems and lending a helping hand in whatever way she could.

'She was extremely practical in some ways and a dreamer in many other respects. Zehra always carried knitting needles and balls of wool in her big handbag. These were for the baby garments that she was forever knitting for children from poor families. She was very good at roping in other volunteers too. Once she knew that I could knit, she handed me a pair of knitting needles and wool. Initially I was amused, but soon began to enjoy knitting baby sweaters, caps and mufflers for Zehra.

'She would also hold free tuition classes for children from poor families in her neighbourhood. I thought at first that social work was her way of coping with the one great sorrow in her own life—of being childless. Like me, she too loved children and pined to have one of her own. I realised later that her concern for people and their children came out of her communist ideals.' Pyaari khala slowly and carefully enunciates the word 'communist', as if mispronouncing it would be disrespectful—whether to communists or to Zehra's memory, I am not sure.

'Zehra genuinely believed in the equality and dignity of all human beings,' Pyaari says thoughtfully. 'My background never seemed to matter to her. From the start, she insisted that, since we were around the same age, we call each other by our first names. Just a few months into our friendship, she invited me home. I was shocked, and tried to explain to her that her family might not approve of having a woman like me entertained as a guest by their daughter-in-law. But she explained that she and Ausaf Sahib lived on their own. He too was as insistent in his invitation. After that first visit, I would often go over to spend time with her at their home.'

The house had one large bedroom and a smaller one that served as Ausaf's study, a tiny basic kitchen and a long, covered veranda that had been converted into a sitting-cum-dining room. It was littered with books, music records and photographs. The furniture was old and shabby, curtains threadbare and the bedcovers and cushions flung over rickety settees, colourful but mismatched. To Pyaari's eyes, it was the most beautiful home she had seen. As a tawaif, she had visited a few truly imposing and luxurious mansions presided over by imperious landowners. None of them held for her the warmth and charm of Zehra's untidy home.

'Zehra genuinely had no love for luxury or material things,' Pyaari says. 'She had lived in great comfort in her parents' and in-laws' homes, and yet adjusted remarkably well to her changed circumstances. She never hankered for clothes and jewellery, like so many women do. Except for the pearl earrings that her mother had given her, Zehra wore no jewellery. Always dressed in saris, she wore a few matching glass bangles that clinked in her left wrist, offset by a sombre black ladies' watch on the right one.'

Stoic about her isolation from her family, Zehra was also uncomplaining about the burden of work that now rested on her shoulders. Juggling domestic chores with a full-time job, she was diligent about making her lessons interesting and was popular with her students. Despite her heavy schedule, she found time not only to write but also help others. Her only concern seemed to be about Ausaf and the heartbreak he was encountering in his new life.

One of a small minority of Muslims employed in the programming department in AIR Allahabad, while Ausaf faced no obvious discrimination, he often encountered seemingly innocuous slights and not-so-innocent jokes from his colleagues on account of his identity. The official policy against the language that he had been educated in and wrote in, Urdu, was another form of prejudice. Attacked as a 'foreign' language since the late nineteenth century, in newly independent India, Urdu was being held responsible by many, including several Congress leaders, for being instrumental in the creation of Pakistan. At the heart of this controversy was the perceived 'Muslimness' of Urdu. In the highly polarised north Indian landscape of the late 1940s and early '50s, this rendered the language ineligible for patronage and protection.

In the government schools of Uttar Pradesh, Urdu would no longer be the medium of instruction alongside Hindi, which now became the main language. The marginalisation of Urdu-inspired Hindustani within the radio set-up took deeper root post 1947, when AIR adopted as its official language a highly Sanskritised Hindi that—the joke went—was neither spoken nor fully understood by the vast majority of ordinary Indians outside the radio studios.

'I would get to meet Ausaf Sahib when I went to the radio station for a recording. Although always very courteous, he was a man of few words and mostly kept to himself. I rarely saw him joining the other producers in their long-drawn-out tea-and-paan sessions. I think he felt like a misfit amongst them. The Allahabad station was a small one; everyone knew each other. Although no one said it openly, there was an unspoken bias against Muslims in those days. I felt it too. I would be asked casually why I hadn't left for Pakistan or if I had any plans of leaving. But since I visited the station for only a day every other month or so, it didn't bother me much. For Ausaf Sahib, it must have been much more unpleasant.

And then there was the question of Hindi. Ausaf Sahib had a difficult time writing Hindi in the Urdu script since he didn't know Devanagari.'

Tied down to this thankless work, Ausaf could no longer spend his days in endless soirees. This was just as well, since many of his good-time acquaintances had little use for him now that he could no longer finance their partying at his wealthy father's expense. Left with only a close coterie of time-tested comrades and friends, Ausaf turned to poetry for solace. This period saw him find his true voice as a poet, albeit a largely unrecognised one. Disregarded and dismissed by the literary world, his poetry found its one loyal and committed admirer in Zehra, who kept encouraging him to write even in the face of rejection.

'At times, frustration about his lack of recognition as a poet would overwhelm him,' Pyaari khala tells me. 'Zehra would try and cheer him up as best as she could, but he would become moody and depressed and want to be left alone. At other times, he would go out drinking in the evening with male friends and sometimes not return all night. Always careless about money, he would spend all he had in his pocket on these outings. Worried about his well-being, Zehra would stay awake until he returned but not stop him if he decided to go out again the next evening. She tried to make ends meet on her salary, which in those days wasn't much, and the money that came in from her writing. Since she and I had become very close friends in a matter of months, she would confide in me.

'I would feel angry with Ausaf Sahib for being so irresponsible and self-centred. I have seen many men like him in my life as a tawaif. Without informing Zehra, I quietly tried to find out from my sources in the community in Allahabad if he visited kothas or spent money on some woman. No one seemed to have heard anything. I wished sometimes that I could tell him to be more sensitive towards Zehra. But I knew better than to interfere between husband and wife. So I would listen to her quietly and try and ease her anxieties by telling her jokes or by singing.'

Zehra loved Pyaari's singing. She did not miss a single broadcast of her radio programmes. Looking visibly proud, Pyaari khala says, 'Since I performed regularly on Allahabad radio, many people in the city became familiar with my name. Zehra would tell me in detail everything that she heard others say about my singing. Most of my radio fans, Zehra told me, were women. As a tawaif, I was so used to being praised only by men that this initially came as a surprise. But it felt very good.

'She also helped me broaden my repertoire. Besides thumri, dadra, I began singing more ghazals that she would choose for me. She knew all the well-known poets—Mir, Ghalib, Daagh, Iqbal and Josh—by heart. Her fondness though was for the new poets—Majaz, Kaifi, Makhdum and her own beloved Ausaf Sahib.'

On her trips to Allahabad, Pyaari stayed at the natal home of Rasoolan's daughter-in-law, Amiran. One time, however, Amiran's parents were going to be out of town when Pyaari was scheduled to visit. When Zehra heard of this, she insisted that Pyaari spend the night at her home. Reluctant to accept for fear of putting Zehra in an awkward social position, Pyaari tried initially to make alternative arrangements. But eventually Zehra convinced her to accept the offer.

That evening, Pyaari insisted on cooking the evening meal. Zehra hovered around cheerfully, trying to help. Ausaf had gone out with his friends with a promise to return in time for dinner. Zehra and Pyaari waited for him till late into the night. As time passed, Pyaari noted Zehra wilting; her eyes looked like stones, her lips became crumpled, her shoulders stooped under a heavy weight. Overcome with concern, Pyaari put her arms around Zehra. A storm of emotions poured forth in her embrace.

Zehra wept and talked and wept some more. She loved Ausaf deeply. She loved his handsome face. She loved his poetry. She loved his moody silences. She rejoiced with him when a ghazal that he was writing turned out perfect. She grieved when the same ghazal faced rejection from some philistine editor. Zehra believed in Ausaf's creative genius. She suffered his pain as an unsuccessful poet. She craved for his success.

Pyaari, who had loved many men with pragmatic, professional detachment, listened to her friend with growing wonder. Zehra's love for Ausaf was painful, punishing, all-consuming, but also a love that had hit the hard rock of sexual incompatibility. After the initial years of marriage, Ausaf had stopped approaching Zehra as a woman. He loved her as his best friend, his companion for life, but his romance, Zehra said, was reserved for his poetry. She claimed he no longer felt sexual desire for any mortal woman.

'Are you sure he does not see other women?' Pyaari had asked, unthinking of the effect her question would have. She felt Zehra's slender frame go rigid in her arms.

'Please do not say such a thing! I cannot bear it,' she had groaned in a hoarse voice, dissolving into a fresh flood of tears. 'I will die if this is true. But I know he cannot, will not, ever betray my love.'

At a loss for words that would console the beautiful, passionate woman sobbing in her arms, Pyaari remained silent. Then, struck by a thought, she gingerly tried to find a way to speak without causing pain, 'Is Ausaf Sahib happier with men?'

'He has a lot of male friends but not in the way you think,' Zehra mumbled through her tears.

Pyaari said nothing further. With vast experience of giving and taking pleasure, she felt overwhelmed by sorrow for her friend but knew better than to ask Zehra why she stayed in a sexless marriage. Gently patting her shoulder, Pyaari let her shed the tears she had held back for so many years.

'Well, frankly, if you ask me, Zehra was responsible for her own misery,' Asghari quips dismissively. 'I wouldn't have lived a moment with a man who had no interest in me physically.'

'It's always easier to pass judgement about others,' Pyaari is ferocious in her response. 'You of all people, dear Asghari, should know the ruination that love can cause. And besides, unlike us, Zehra wasn't free to break away from Ausaf and find pleasure in another relationship. Imagine the shame of a divorce for someone from her social background.'

But the truth was, Pyaari explains to me, Zehra loved Ausaf too much to even consider divorce. Finding succour in the deep friendship that she shared with him, Zehra tried to reconcile to a life of celibacy. The decision had not been without pain. The yearning and emptiness that it brought in its wake had, however, been easier to ignore before Pyaari arrived with her friendship. Till then, Zehra had no one with whom she could share her sorrow. Cast away by Ausaf's family, she had also been emotionally distanced from her own relatives, including her parents, whose progressive ideals fell short of accepting a bohemian son-in-law.

Over the years, as the harshness of daily life corroded the wildness of Ausaf's spirit and transformed it into a disillusioned, restless melancholy, his family and Zehra's had grudgingly accepted the couple back into the fold. But they remained suspect on account of their impoverished circumstances and less-than-conventional lifestyle.

Allahabad was a small city where gossip travelled fast. Stories about Ausaf's all-night drinking outings, his socially undesirable friends were well known. Zehra, everyone agreed, was more morally scrupulous than her husband, yet she was considered too 'modern', not only on account of her status as a working woman but also because of her association with Ausaf's wild social circle. This set her apart from the handful of other women, Hindus and a few Muslim, from her background who worked outside the house.

At St Mary's, Zehra, though the only Muslim teacher in an overwhelmingly Anglo-Indian faculty, was highly popular with her colleagues, many of whom she roped in as 'knitting volunteers'. She had many friends and yet shared with none of them the intimacy of baring her hurt.

Zehra had tried to strike friendships with her predominantly Hindu, lower-middle-class neighbours. They liked her for her generosity in teaching their children English for free. Her Muslim identity, her upper-class background, her job and her status as the wife of a social renegade, however, came in the way of being accepted by them as a friend.

Perhaps it is not surprising that, as a social semi-exile, Zehra should have found friendship in Pyaari. An outsider to Zehra's starchy, upper-class background, Pyaari could be told painful secrets that Zehra would dare not articulate even to herself—her sexual yearning and loneliness, her anxieties about Ausaf's alcoholism, her unfulfilled desire to be a mother, her fast-fading hopes for Ausaf's literary success.

After that first night, Pyaari would stay with Zehra whenever she visited Allahabad. Ausaf was often away drinking through the night, and Zehra would find solace in Pyaari's gentle embrace.

'Ausaf Sahib was always welcoming to me when he was home. I think he felt relieved that, at long last, Zehra had found a close friend other than just him. He would always press me to stay for longer since Zehra enjoyed my visits so much.

'She certainly looked much happier when I was around. I too was happy in her company. Everything felt lighter, easier and brighter. I would tell her anecdotes about mehfils, tawaifs and zamindars. She would listen with great interest and beg me for more. She would sometimes read out to me her short stories, which were mainly about women, from backgrounds like her own and from poor families. She wrote very well. She would also talk about the work of other writers, especially women authors like Rashid Jahan and Ismat Chugtai, both of whom also belonged to Aligarh and were known to Zehra personally. Her world of books and literature was unfamiliar to me. I learnt so much just by listening to her. We would sometimes talk through the night, especially when Ausaf Sahib was not home, which was often. Zehra would forget her anxieties, only to be reminded of them when Ausaf Sahib finally stumbled home reeking of cheap alcohol.

'One night, Zehra was very depressed. In a fit of despair, she drank some of Ausaf Sahib's whisky that she found lying in the kitchen cupboard. I joined in too. We didn't drink much, probably not more than two drinks each. On his return home, Ausaf Sahib was furious when he discovered what Zehra had done. I had never seen him lose his temper before and was struck by the fury he was capable of. He didn't say anything to me, of course, but kept repeating to Zehra, "I can't believe that you have done this."

'Fed up with the way he was going on like a stuck record, I finally asked him how he, an alcoholic, could grudge Zehra a drink or two if she wanted it occasionally. He sobered up a bit, insisting that he didn't mind the fact that she had consumed alcohol. What he minded was that she had done so in his absence. Though I did not say anything more to him, I found his reasoning strange. And stranger still that Zehra actually looked sheepish, and promised him that she would never drink again.'

Pyaari's friendship with Zehra had not gone unnoticed by the extended family. How could Zehra befriend a tawaif, they all wondered, and clicked their tongues in disapproval. She and her husband had never cared for convention, everyone knew. But to bring a tawaif home was carrying the disdain for propriety too far. Hadn't Ausaf done enough already to embarrass them socially, that Zehra now felt obliged to add to the ignominy by making friends with a prostitute? Zehra's protests that Pyaari was a well-respected radio singer fell on deaf ears. She would suffer the consequences of making unsuitable friends, her mother and mother-in-law warned her. She would realise her stupidity when 'that' woman stole Ausaf away from her and she would have no one to turn to for support.

This would make Zehra laugh. Pyaari was not out to rob her of her husband, she would reassure them. She was a friend, the most loyal and loving that Zehra could hope to have.

To assuage her family's fear of social embarrassment, Zehra became more discreet about her friendship with Pyaari, avoiding as much as possible being seen in public in her company. If this caused her hurt, Pyaari does not say. All she murmurs in response to my question is, 'I understood Zehra's compulsions. Had I been in her place, I too might have behaved similarly. Our friendship did not suffer. We continued to spend time together as before in her house during my trips to Allahabad.'

The greatest challenge to Pyaari and Zehra's friendship came not from her social circle but the appointment in 1952 as minister of Information and Broadcasting of a man whose official bio-profile as member of Parliament described his hobbies as 'classical music, travel, hiking in mountains and photography'. Born in Pune into a Maharashtrian Brahmin family, and educated at the Kashi Vidyapeeth and Sorbonne University, Paris, B.V. Keskar was a man with a mission: to use radio broadcasting to save India's cultural heritage.

Steeped in Hindu nationalism, Keskar's mission entailed not only the propagation of Hindi but even more of saving the classical music tradition of India. For too long, he argued, Indian music had suffered not only at the hands of colonial rulers indifferent to its worth but more so at the hands of Muslims. Closely echoing the sentiments of his ideological predecessors, Vishnu Narayan Bhatkhande and Vishnu Digambar Paluskar, Keskar blamed Muslim rulers and musicians of appropriating the ancient music of the Hindus and distorting its 'spiritual' core into its present 'erotic' form practised by 'dancing girls, prostitutes and their circle of pimps' (B.V. Keskar, *Indian Music: Problems and Prospects*, Popular Prakashan, Bombay, 1967).

Convinced that the protection and nurturance of classical music was critical to the evolution of Indian culture and society, Keskar asserted, 'Deep down in the roots of the human unconscious, music holds a key position in regulating orderly expression of the primeval emotional forces.' Keskar was loath to leave classical music at the mercy of its 'illiterate' and 'narrow-minded' and mainly Muslim professional practitioners. As minister, he felt it was his duty to formulate a cultural policy that would restore Indian classical music to its former glory.

To this end, he enlisted the help of music theoretician and scholar Dr S.N. Ratanjankar, former principal of the Marris College of Music in Lucknow (now known as Bhatkhande Music Institute Deemed University), established by Bhatkhande in 1926. Ratanjankar shared Bhatkhande's vision of a 'national music' that would be based upon the unification of Hindustani and Carnatic schools, founded on authentic textual authority and reflective of ancient India's classical Hindu heritage. He helped Keskar enlist radio programming staff across the country, giving primacy to theoretical knowledge of music rather than a background of professional performance. Armed with degrees and diplomas from music schools, these new recruits were, in Keskar and Ratanjankar's estimation, the right people to decide on the kind of musicians that deserved to perform on radio and the kind of music that deserved to be broadcast.

In 1952, Keskar started the prestigious National Programme of Music, a ninety-minute weekly concert broadcast from Delhi, distributed simultaneously to various stations. It featured handpicked master-musicians representing Hindustani and Carnatic styles and was part of state-sponsored efforts towards using the radio to revive India's cultural heritage.

The Radio Sangeet Sammelan, started in 1954, was yet another step in this mission, and involved a series of some twenty concerts performed by eminent musicians across the country before invited audiences. Contending that 'classical music has fallen on bad ways and is on the point of extinction in northern India', Keskar concluded in *Indian Music* that 'the main problem before musicians and AIR is to revive public contact with classical music. We must make them familiar with our traditional music, and make them intimate with it.' It was hoped that exposure to musical styles from across the country would eventually lead to the flowering of an appropriately classical 'national music'.

Keskar also set up a committee to look into the broadcast of film songs. These were, in his view, 'vulgar and cheap' and a major impediment to the forging of a truly high-minded classical 'national music'. Not only did Hindi film music use a language that was more Urdu than the Sanskritised Hindi promoted by All India Radio, its lyrics were erotic and its orchestration and rhythm inspired by Western popular music. Keskar wanted a quota of not more than 10 per cent to be imposed on the broadcast of film songs by All India Radio. Besides, the committee he set up was vested with the task of weeding out the more objectionable songs from the few that were broadcast. In 1954, this led to a breakdown of negotiations with the Film Producers Guild of India for broadcast rights to film songs, and for a while, no film music was heard on All India Radio.

Just as Keskar's ban on film music raised many hackles in the film industry and outside, his introduction in 1952 of an elaborate two-tiered system of radio auditions proved to be equally controversial. Each radio station was to have an audition board that would hear (but not see) brief performances by auditioning musicians before asking them questions to test their knowledge of music theory. The recordings of the shortlisted finalists were then sent to a higher audition board, presided over by Professor Ratanjankar in Delhi, for final selection.

Designed to advantage musicians with theoretical knowledge, the audition process increasingly made certification from recognised music academies an added qualification for radio performance. Those selected were graded A, B or C, and either hired as full-time 'staff artistes' or retained on a regular basis as 'casuals'.

Not surprisingly, the audition system created a furore of resentment among the greater majority of musicians who had learnt music in the traditional gharana system or, as in the case of tawaifs, from their accompanist teachers. Senior musicians felt humiliated at being subjected to such an audition before being allowed to perform on radio. There were reports of musicians picketing radio stations in protest.

'I was very nervous about the audition,' Pyaari tells me. 'Many senior musicians had been rejected by the board, so what chance did I stand? But there was no running away from it if I wanted to continue singing for the radio. Rasoolan aapa who too was scheduled to audition tried to boost my confidence, as did Zehra and my ustad, Habib Khan Sahib.

'I did fairly well in the first round of auditions, and Ausaf Sahib told me that I had been shortlisted and my recording had been sent to Delhi for the final audition. I don't know what went wrong there, but I was not selected for empanelment. Even though I had been prepared for the worst, when it came, the news devastated me. Rasoolan aapa, who had been selected in the highest A category, tried to console me by pointing out that, except for her and a few others, most musicians who had learnt music the traditional way had also been rejected. Instead, pipsqueak voices that had been trained in music schools had made the grade. This was hardly any consolation to me. I had been rejected and that's what mattered.'

'Were more tawaifs and Muslims rejected as compared to Hindu male musicians?' I ask Pyaari khala.

'I can't say that with any certainty. A great many performers who were Hindus did not make it through the auditions either. Keskar Sahib was not an easy person to understand. He was an eccentric with some decidedly strange ideas about music and musicians. While it is true that he looked down upon tawaifs and gharanedar musicians, it is also a fact that he genuinely loved music and did much to raise the status of musicians in society. It is under him that AIR began the practice of addressing even accompanist musicians, the sarangi and tabla players, as 'Khan sahibs'. Before his time, they were considered too low in the hierarchy to merit such deference.

'He also went all out to promote musicians who he thought were gifted, regardless of whether they were Muslim or Hindu. He had great respect for Rasoolan aapa. After the initial audition, she was given the status of 'eminent musician' and exempted from appearing for re-auditions that were made mandatory every few years for all radio artists. She performed on several National Programmes of Music and was invited to radio stations across the country for broadcasts. Aapa was awarded the Sangeet Natak Akademi award for vocal music in 1957 during Keskar Sahib's tenure as minister.'

Noting my surprised expression, Pyaari is quick to clarify, 'I am not defending Keskar Sahib! I suffered at the hands of his pig-headed policies myself. I am just trying to give you the complete picture. No one is black-and-white. Neither was he.'

There was no denying, however, that Keskar's attempts to revive a 'national music' through government diktats and bureaucratic procedures emotionally alienated a large number of traditional musicians, who felt forced to comply with a process they found humiliating in order to retain the much-needed patronage AIR provided. In the mid-1950s, Keskar decided to conduct a full-scale re-auditioning of all musicians performing on AIR. Accordingly, a re-auditioning panel was set up, once again headed by Dr Ratanjankar.

The move elicited strong protests from musicians, including Ustad Amir Khan and the Dagar family. Many musicians even went on strike at different radio stations. The fairness of the process was questioned when several esteemed musicians—like Pandit Maniram, doyen of the Mewati gharana; Ustad Chand Khan, khalifa of the Dilli gharana; Ustad Abdul Latif Khan, sarangi maestro from Gwalior—were graded in the lowest category 'C' by Ratanjankar, who though esteemed as a scholar, was not really recognised as a musician. There were complaints too about the brusque and arrogant manner in which he posed questions about theory to leading musicians of the day.

'I was too far away by then from the radio set-up for this gossip to be of much interest,' Pyaari khala tells me. 'To tell you the truth, after being rejected, I didn't want to have anything to do with the radio. I went back to being a full-time tawaif, where at least there were no expectations of punditry from me. I didn't want to ever go to Allahabad again and have memories of my time in radio come flooding back. But then I had to consider my friendship with Zehra.

'She had been even more heartbroken by my rejection at the audition than I was. After she heard the news, Zehra kept repeating that the entire system was a farce if it couldn't recognise real talent like mine. She was so distraught that I had to console her rather than the other way around.' Pyaari khala chuckles at the bitter-sweet memory. 'Promising her that I would try and come often to meet her, I returned to Banaras.'

One morning not long after that, Pyaari was shocked to find Zehra standing outside her house in Dal Mandi. She looked emotionally drained and said very little, except that she had got very tired of waiting alone the previous night for Ausaf Sahib to return home, and so had decided to come to her friend.

Pyaari khala shakes her head. 'I shared the house with my brother Jahangir, his wife and two children, all of whom mercifully were then away in Bhabua. Rani, who lived in a kotha nearby with my mother, and Rajjo had gone with them. But Teema, who stayed close by with Asghari, was in Banaras. Only to her did I reveal Zehra's real identity. To everyone else, I said that she was a distant relative. I didn't want Zehra's reputation besmirched on account of her stay in my kotha. Concerned about Ausaf Sahib, who was undoubtedly searching for Zehra, I asked her to inform him, but she refused outright. Not quite sure what I should do, in a panic, I sent him a telegram without telling Zehra. She stayed with me for the next five days. Those were the happiest in my life.

'I shut my kotha to all outsiders. Zehra and I would spend hours talking, laughing, singing. We knitted a lot, entering into silly competitions about who could make the most baby frocks in a day. Giggling like young girls, we would go roaming around the ghats wearing burqas borrowed from my neighbours. On the pretext of buying saris for myself, I dragged her off to Chowk one day. She eventually allowed me to buy her a

Banarasi silk, a cream-coloured sari with a simple zari border. I made her wear it upon our return home. She looked so beautiful in that sari.' Pyaari begins crying softly.

I notice the smirk on Asghari's face. Rolling her eyes, she blows imaginary kisses into the air. I look away. My eyes meet yours. The tender sadness in them makes mine smart with tears.

'One evening, at her request, I performed a mujra just for her, without the musicians, of course,' Pyaari tells me, wiping her tears. 'Dressed in a red chiffon sari trimmed with a golden border and with all the jewellery that I wore in a formal performance, I sang, danced and flirted with her so that she could have a real-life experience of a mujra.

'In the beginning, I felt quite awkward doing this. But she did not look in the slightest bit flustered. Instead of laughing as I thought she would, Zehra looked solemn, her eyes never once leaving my face. There was an intensity in her gaze that I had not seen before. It began to affect me too, and soon I forgot that I was performing a make-believe mujra.

'At some point of the night I began singing *Baju band khul khul jaye*, and as part of the accompanying bhava began to play with the jewelled armband tied on my left arm. It was then that Zehra stretched her hand out and slowly untied my armband. One by one, she took off each piece of jewellery that I was wearing, and then undid my hair. She looked intoxicated and I felt myself melt as she took me in her arms and lowered her face on to mine.'

'Khala, have some shame!' A gruff male voice intrudes into Pyaari's story, making all of us jump. Aijaz, self-proclaimed guardian of Muslim morals, stands at the door, quivering with indignant rage. Engrossed in the story, none of us had noticed his appearance.

'When did you come, Aijaz?' Asghari exclaims, getting up from her chair.

'Long enough to hear the blasphemy being uttered in this room,' he says, touching his earlobes piously. 'Khala is too ill to know what she is saying, but what about all of you? None of you thought it fit to stop her? But then why should one expect anything better from old prostitutes who run brothels in their homes to make a living?'

'And just who the hell do you think you are to tell us what we should speak or hear or how we should earn our living?' Shoulders thrown back and hands on her hips, Asghari roars at Aijaz. Her fury, I realise, is not the usual playacting. 'Don't you act pious with me, boy! If I start reminding you of the truly blasphemous acts you have indulged in, you will not find a place to hide your face!'

In her rage, Asghari has clearly forgotten the price she might have to pay for taking on the local political goon. But the usually pompous Aijaz shrinks back at Asghari's words. Muttering that khala ought to get some sleep, he stumbles out of Pyaari's room.

Shutting her eyes, Pyaari turns over to face the wall. You sit by her bedside for a long time, massaging her hunched-up shoulders and rigid back. Asghari collapses in her chair and drums out her remaining fury on the armrest. She thunders about the hypocrisy of men like Aijaz, 'He just wanted to get even after Sheem fixed him well and proper over Reyaz.' We nod in assent.

I beg Pyaari to complete her story, but receive only a stony silence in answer. I talk about the beauty of the human spirit embodied in love, be it between man and woman, woman and woman, or man and man. You agree with me, and talk of the women you knew who loved women. 'It was not made a big deal of. It was understood that while the most common form of sexual pleasure was between a man and a woman, there were also those who found pleasure among their own kind. In kothas, as also in the zenanas of respectable ladies, there were those who found their love, their pleasure, with other women.'

Later, when we are back in your house, you complete the love story that Aijaz's moral tirade had so brutally cut short. Ausaf had arrived at Pyaari's house on the sixth day to 'rescue' Zehra who, he claimed, had been kidnapped and brought to Banaras for prostitution. Wild-eyed and in a frenzy, he looked drunk and consumed by the humiliation of being abandoned by his thus far forbearing wife. In no mood to hear Zehra's protestations that she had come of her own free will, Ausaf threatened to call the police if she refused to return with him. To avoid a scandal, Pyaari prevailed upon Zehra to go back with Ausaf, at least for the time being.

'Then what happened?' I ask.

'Then nothing happened,' you reply with grim irony. 'Promising Pyaari khala that she would return soon, Zehra tearfully left with Ausaf. Khala, deeply in love, kept waiting for news from her. At long last, she received a letter from Zehra. She apologised profusely for Ausaf's misconduct, but made no mention of the intimacy between her and khala. Nor did she write about when and where they would meet.'

Not sure what to make of the letter, Pyaari began to fret. Convinced that Zehra had written it under duress, Pyaari decided to see for herself how she was doing. Teema tried to convince her against going, but Pyaari, adamant in her resolve, left for Allahabad. Instead of going to Zehra's house, she went to St Mary's Convent in the hope of speaking to her without Ausaf being around.

School was just letting out when she reached. Zehra met Pyaari with easy, relaxed warmth, as if her presence at the gates of the school was an everyday occurrence. She insisted that Pyaari come home with her for lunch and, refusing to take no for an answer, shepherded her gently into a rickshaw.

Sitting next to her, feeling the softness of her sari caress her arm, inhaling the musk perfume she always wore, Pyaari tried to understand what was going on in Zehra's mind. She looked composed and calm, and not in the least like the passionate woman with whom Pyaari had spent that time of intimacy and love, nor the emotionally distraught woman who had left her home with the promise to return.

Pyaari wanted to ask Zehra about what happened after she went away with Ausaf. She wanted to tell her all about her own desperate yearning since Zehra left. But a curious blend of shyness and apprehension mixed with an insane ecstasy at finally being with her prevented Pyaari from saying anything at all.

Ignoring Pyaari's silence, Zehra kept up a steady, non-committal flow of chatter till they reached her house. Much to Pyaari's discomfort, Ausaf opened the door for them. Extending Pyaari a warm welcome, he too behaved as if nothing had happened in Banaras just a few months ago.

Pyaari noticed that Ausaf looked ill. Gaunt-framed and pallid, he was a shadow of the man that she had known. Neither Zehra nor Ausaf made any mention of his health, although they did refer in passing to the long leave he had taken from AIR for some months now. Feeling too awkward to enquire, Pyaari did not ask why.

The afternoon went by pleasantly enough. Zehra talked the most—about school, about the new knitting volunteers that she had enlisted among the teachers there, and about the writing that she had been doing of late. On Ausaf's insistence, she read out to Pyaari the short story that she had just completed. Unlike her previous work, which usually dealt with female protagonists as central characters, this one was about a man torn in love between his wife and another woman. After much internal dilemma and soul-searching, he chooses his wife over his other love. Surprisingly conventional in its resolution for a story written by Zehra, it was redeemed by interesting characterisation and language.

When asked what she thought of the story, Pyaari said she liked it very much. Then she took her leave of the husband and wife. It was time, she said, that she left for the railway station to catch the train to Banaras. Pyaari never met them again.

'Several years later, khala learnt from a mutual acquaintance that Ausaf, long suffering from liver cirrhosis, had finally succumbed to the disease,' you tell me quietly. 'Zehra died soon after from undiagnosed causes. I remember khala was deeply upset by the news. It was then that she told Asghari aapa and me all about Zehra and Ausaf. She did not perform in her kotha for several days. But then life has to go on.'

CHAPTER 26

The Law

I AM BACK IN BANARAS after nearly two months. I head straight to your home. You look calm, your loss contained in your eyes. Pyaari khala died a few days ago. The end was peaceful, you say. She slipped into the night in her sleep. Her funeral was held the next morning. You returned to Banaras after the third day of mourning, marked with prayers and feeding the poor, wanting no part in the bitter family feuds over Pyaari's property that erupted soon after her burial.

Pyaari khala had loved life, I say, offering my condolences. A gentle warrior, she fought against disease and death to the last. Your eyes well up with tears. Your aunt lived a full life, you say. She experienced in ample measure her share of joy and suffering, and fearlessly faced whatever life threw at her.

My last memory of Pyaari is of her flirting outrageously with Shambhu Lala, who looked both delighted and embarrassed by the attention. Part play-acting, part genuine outpouring of affection, she had held lala's hand and, coquettishly raising first one eyebrow and then another, hummed for his benefit, *Bisariho na balam hamar sudhiya*; Never forget my love, your memories of me.

I found it difficult to believe that this was the forlorn woman of the previous evening, lying with her face to the wall. In response, you described your aunt as a quintessential tawaif—a survivor in love and in life. Zehra had been the love of Pyaari's life. Her betrayal left a deep mark, but it did not erode Pyaari's faith in living. She lived fully and was open to love whenever it crossed her path, unlike Zehra who gave up on life after the death of her love, Ausaf.

A little after I arrive at your place, Shanney Khan Sahib does too. He has put aside ill health to come and share in your grief. He knew Pyaari well, although he had never accompanied her in performance. 'Pyaari Bai was famous in Banaras for her radio singing,' Shanney Khan mumbles. From the faltering, half-sentences that he manages to valiantly string together, it seems that, long after she stopped singing on the radio, your aunt continued to enjoy popularity with those connoisseurs of music who dared to brave social stigma and invite her to perform. Some even continued to visit her kotha as before.

'Khala allowed in only genuine lovers of music,' you add with obvious pride. 'I was very young then but spent long periods of time in khala's home in Dal Mandi. It was very well maintained and kept spotlessly clean. She had inherited many of her regulars from Rasoolan khala who, once she moved away from mehfil singing, directed several music lovers to Pyaari khala instead.'

You talk about Seth Ismail, a cousin of Rasoolan Bai's patron-turned-husband, Seth Suleiman. Like him, Seth Ismail too was a rich silk merchant from Banaras. In an intimate relationship with Pyaari for a few years, it was he who helped her construct her house in Bhabua.

'Didn't Seth Ismail leave for Pakistan quite late, around the mid- to late 1950s?' Shanney Khan Sahib asks you.

'Yes, he did, along with Seth Suleiman and their extended family,' you confirm. 'Khala once told me that Seth Suleiman had been very keen that Rasoolan khala accompany him to Pakistan as his second wife. He promised to look after all her needs there, and even maintain her in a separate establishment if she wanted. One part of her wanted to agree, since she had married him in the hope of spending her old age in the security of his companionship. But after much thought, Rasoolan khala refused his offer, saying, "My songs and I belong to Banaras. We will be lost among strangers in a new land."'

You add that Pyaari khala too dismissed the idea of leaving Banaras. Upon reaching Pakistan, Seth Ismail wrote several letters, urging her to come to Karachi where he and his family had settled. The city, he said, was full of migrants from Lucknow, Banaras and other parts of UP. She would feel at home and never be short of an audience. But Pyaari khala refused to leave Banaras and her family.

After Seth Ismail migrated to Pakistan, your aunt found patronage with a Bhumihar landholder from the nearby district of Ghazipur in eastern UP. He was very old and rarely ever came to Banaras, but regularly invited Pyaari to his family haveli to perform in mehfils and on festive occasions. Over the years, he became very fond of her and occasionally gifted her expensive jewellery. Towards the end of his life, he bought some agricultural lands around Bhabua in her name to ensure security for her in the future.

Meenu arrives with tea and biscuits. Ordinarily quite cheerful, she looks morose. I assume it is because of Pyaari khala's death. I know how fond your children were of your aunt. Nanhe cried when I hugged him earlier in the morning as he was leaving for work. Even little Haaris looks lost as he circles your visitors' room on the red tricycle Pyaari khala had bought him on his birthday. I haven't yet met Salma, now into her fifth month of pregnancy. I know the deep affection that Salma felt for Pyaari, her only supporter in your family. Realising that I ought to offer my condolences to her, I get up to go upstairs but am stopped by you.

'She is sleeping,' you say through primly pursed lips. To my query about Salma's health you are just as terse, 'She is pregnant, not ill.'

In the coming days, I would come to understand that the gloom shrouding your home is only partly due to your aunt's demise. She had been ill for a long time, her going was expected. The quarrels, tension and low spirits besetting you all have more to do with Salma's pregnancy and Meenu's impending marriage.

As I feared, the pregnancy had come as an unwelcome surprise to Salma. Forced by you to carry a child she doesn't want, she has turned into a ghost of the woman I knew. Unwell physically, emotionally disturbed and periodically bedridden, she has no one to offer her solace. Meenu is too preoccupied with dreams of her forthcoming wedding to spare a thought for her sister-in-law. Resentful of Salma's unhappiness over her pregnancy, you are grudging in giving her the love and care she needs.

Unusually edgy and irritable nowadays because of your heightened hostility towards your daughter-in-law, your anxiety is compounded by the pressure to arrange an appropriately lavish wedding for Meenu. You see her marriage, now only three months away, as a challenge to consolidate your status as an impeccably respectable and affluent former tawaif in the community. Meenu's future in-laws expect extravagant hospitality commensurate with their financial status, and that too no doubt weighs heavy on you. And then there is Meenu's constant nagging for a substantial dowry to bolster her status as daughter-in-law in her new home.

On the morning of my arrival, though, you are outwardly the picture of calm composure, graciously receiving visitors who have been coming by to offer their commiserations on Pyaari khala's death. Time goes by. One by one, everyone leaves except old Shanney Khan, who sits by you as a silent, supportive presence.

The last to arrive is Sharafat Khan. Youngest among the seven sons of Rasoolan Bai's teacher Shammu Khan from his second wife, he is the only one who became an accompanist musician, albeit of the harmonium and not the family favourite, the sarangi. He retired five or six years ago, but maintains a link with music-making by occasionally recording marsiyas and other religious recitations, CDs of which are sold in the Dal Mandi market. I have met him at his older brother Ramzan Khan's house in Chahmama a few times. The siblings are neighbours and seem to be constantly in and out of each other's homes.

Eighty-year-old Sharafat Khan cuts an imposing figure with his nearly six-foot frame, aquiline nose, and a thick mane of hair coloured a dull red with henna. He is, as always, immaculately dressed in a crisply starched white kurta-pyjama. After he offers his condolences, you make solicitous enquiries about his and his wife's health. Blessed with a deep baritone, Sharafat's natural manner is oratorical. Ramzan Khan often jokes, 'Sharafat doesn't speak, he makes a speech.' Clearing his throat, Sharafat now declaims, 'Old age itself is an ailment. Bit by bit, imperceptibly, this machine called the human body starts rusting and slowing down. This is the law of nature. But all praise and thanks be to Allah, apart from suffering the unavoidable vagaries of time, we have so far been spared any major illness.'

From here, the conversation moves on to the glories of youth and Sharafat Khan's indefatigable energy as a young, much-in-demand harmonium player. His music career, he says, started late and on the sly, because his father, sensing the changing times, had not wanted any of the sons from his second wife to become professional musicians. He did not teach them music, preferring instead to apprentice them in other trades.

Accordingly, Shammu Khan placed Sharafat under the tutelage of a unani hakim. He had barely begun learning when hakim sahib met with an accident and died. Sharafat returned home and finished his formal schooling. He then joined a watchmaker and eventually set up a watch repair shop of his own. It is at this point, he says, that he discovered his love for music and began learning the harmonium from a friend, Ibrahim, who earned a living by teaching tawaifs.

'Ibrahim began taking me along with him to his teaching assignments in tawaifs' kothas because, although he could play well, he could not sing. In those times, I sang ghazals and film songs well. I would sing on his behalf whenever he needed to illustrate music through singing. After a few days, I became so addicted to this way of life that I would go and open my shop in the morning but then take off with Ibrahim for the entire day. Not unexpectedly, my business collapsed soon after, and I shifted full-time to the music line around 1953,' Sharafat recalls.

His father learnt about these developments quite late. Although he was furious to begin with, Shammu Khan softened once he heard his son play and even offered to teach him a bit.

'New to the line, I was filled with vanity about my own music,' Sharafat admits. 'But once my father began teaching me, my eyes opened. I realised how little I actually knew. Sadly, I could only learn for a few years before he died in 1958.'

'1958 was a terrible year for us,' Shanney Khan Sahib says quietly. 'Shammu Khan Sahib went first, and then came the law.'

He is referring to the Suppression of Immoral Traffic in Women and Girls Act, 1956 (SITA), which was enacted in pursuance of the United Nations' Convention for the Suppression of Traffic in Persons and of the Exploitation of the Prostitution of Others, 1950, to which India was a signatory. Enacted by the Indian Parliament in 1956, the Act came into force across India on 1 May 1958.

While not making prostitution per se a criminal offence, the law aimed instead to 'inhibit or abolish commercialised vice, namely the traffic in persons for the purpose of prostitution as an organised means of living'. Accordingly, the engagement by a woman in individual, voluntary and independent prostitution was not deemed an offence by the law. Trafficking of minors and women for the purpose of prostitution, indulging in prostitution in or near a public place, including places of worship, soliciting for the purpose of prostitution and living off the earnings of prostitution were criminalised by SITA.

The law also permitted a magistrate to order the removal of a person engaged in prostitution from any place and to punish the person upon refusal. Offences under SITA were bailable, but a woman picked up from the street by the police usually did not have either the money or the influence to keep her out of custody.

'An atmosphere of great fear enveloped Dal Mandi and the mohallas adjoining it within the first week of the law coming into force,' Sharafat says grimly. 'No one was sure about its provisions, but the air was thick with speculation that it would be used to forcibly flush out tawaifs and prostitutes from their homes in the old quarters and throw them outside the city.'

Contemporary newspaper accounts reflect some of the anxiety that prevailed among the kotha-dwelling denizens of the inner-city neighbourhoods of Dal Mandi, Nariyal Bazaar and Chowk in Banaras. The usual gaiety of the evenings had given way in the first week of May 1958 to nervous furtiveness. Business took a hit with even regular clients keeping away for fear of the new law. Several better-known and established tawaifs stopped performing altogether. Others did so discreetly—hastily bought thick curtains now covered the partially shut entrances to kothas that had, until recently, been open to all.

Local newspapers reported that large numbers of poorer tawaifs and sex workers had fled in fear of SITA from other cities and towns like Delhi, Meerut and Allahabad and arrived in Banaras's Dal Mandi, seeking sanctuary among relatives and friends. Their accounts of brutal enforcement of the law by the police added further grist to local rumour mills.

There were reports too of tawaifs and sex workers getting organised in cities like Kanpur, Delhi and Calcutta to resist the new law. As early as 1 May, tawaifs in Kanpur organised a meeting in which they decided to challenge the new law in court, with everyone present promising to contribute Rs 25 towards the expenses.

On 6 May, tawaifs and sex workers in Delhi held an impressive demonstration in front of Parliament House to protest against the implementation of the new law. They demanded alternative housing and employment opportunities before being forced to give up their present work and move out of their kothas. Sex workers and bai-jis in Calcutta too organised a public meeting that same week to oppose the new law.

A small number of sympathetic voices from the outside also spoke in support of the beleaguered women. Socialist leader from Gorakhpur, Keshav Singh, had been vocal in his criticism of the new law and advised tawaifs and sex workers to organise in protest. Rustam Setan, well-known Communist leader from Banaras, had expressed concern about the high-handed manner in which the local police were reportedly threatening to evict women from their kothas.

While the central government had drawn up the law and brought it into force across India, the responsibility of implementing it at the local level was vested with the state governments. Through the month of May and the greater part of June 1958, in Uttar Pradesh, apart from hastily setting up a few shelter homes, including one in Jaitapur in Banaras, for girls and women rescued from brothels, officially, there was to be no further action. The state government was still in the process of formulating rules and regulations for putting the law into force.

Seemingly oblivious to such deliberations, however, the local administration and police in UP towns and cities were using the threat of the new law to intimidate tawaifs and sex workers. In Banaras, the police had begun to prepare lists of women involved in sex work. Forcibly entering houses in Dal Mandi and adjoining areas, they would summarily line up all the women and girls present. Accusing them of being involved in prostitution, the policemen would demand names and family details.

In some instances, raids were conducted on brothels, and the women and girls forcibly removed from there and put in the rehabilitation shelter in Jaitapur. Much to the embarrassment of the local administration, though, as reported on 23 May by *Aaj*, within a few days of being brought to the shelter, all the inmates had run away to the brothels they had been 'rescued' from. Undeterred, the police had issued an ultimatum to the women of Dal Mandi and the neighbourhoods adjoining it: they were to vacate their kothas and move out by 1 June.

'The police had taken to barging into the kothas of even the most esteemed tawaifs of Banaras,' Sharafat recalls. 'Mouthing vile obscenities, they would threaten and terrorise the women and their families. By late May, business had come to a standstill. This was the period during which many tawaif families in Banaras, fed up with the daily humiliation and the growing sense of insecurity, decided to shut down their kothas. While many migrated to places like Gaya and Muzzafarpur in Bihar, where SITA had still not been enforced, the wealthier and more established families withdrew from the line for good. Some of those who owned property here stayed on, but many, fearful of continued police harassment, preferred to shift either to their original hometowns or to new places where no one would know their past.'

'I remember that it was around this time that Pyaari khala stopped performing altogether in her kotha,' you add. 'She stayed on in Banaras, but only took up assignments outside the city. There were many admirers of her singing among the Rajput and Bhumihar landholders in eastern UP and Bihar. Invitations from them became her mainstay from this period on.'

Sharafat declaims, 'It was then that Mohini Bai got a public letter drafted on behalf of the tawaifs to make people aware of police high-handedness. She was the president of the Gayika Sangh at the time.'

'Mohini Bai was one of the last great tawaifs that remained. She had retired from singing by then, but still commanded considerable respect in the community,' Shanney Khan murmurs from his corner.

Visibly annoyed at being interrupted, Sharafat speaks more forcefully: 'My father had accompanied Mohini Bai in the past. She was very fond of me, and so I would occasionally visit her to pay my respects. She was very old by then. The Gayika Sangh had been hardly functional for many years when the law came into force in 1958. Its affairs were managed by Mohini Bai's nephews, Ganesh and Bhim. They had some English education and prided themselves on being more knowledgeable about the workings of the world outside than others in the community.'

Sharafat pauses for dramatic effect, and continues, 'I was present when Ganesh and Bhim were drafting the letter about the harassment of tawaifs by the police. I helped in the writing and prevailed upon them that the letter be sent on behalf of tawaifs and prostitutes in general, instead of the Gayika Sangh, so that the organisation was not needlessly identified with ignominy and disrepute.'

Titled 'An appeal from unfortunate sisters—save us from police brutality', the letter was duly published by *Aaj* on 29 May 1958. Assuming the voice of hapless victims seeking redemption, the letter points to thoughtless implementation of the law and police brutality as the main hurdle to the rehabilitation of tawaifs and sex workers:

> We unfortunate women live with the sorrow of being in this profession. As victims of poverty and social ills, we have been forced to enter this shameful way of life ... We can be saved and society too can be cleansed of this sin if the government acts in a responsible manner.

> We were very happy when the government passed the law to end prostitution. We began dreaming of the day when we too would earn a respectable living, stand on our feet and contribute to nation-building. We too wish for the sanctuary of a home, we want to educate our children and lead a life fit for human beings. But our dreams have been shattered by the recent police announcement that we have to vacate our houses by 1 June. You all can well understand that, given our helpless situation, there is little we can do except perhaps commit suicide. The government would be well advised to arrange to educate us in vocational skills and help us find good work so that we can look after our families.
>
> We appeal especially to our sisters. As women, you can understand our suffering. We want to leave this work but find it very unjust that the government should want to put us on the path of starvation. Please save us from certain death. Kindly put pressure on the government to implement the law in a manner that helps us lead cleansed and redeemed lives. Today, instead of being employed to improve our lot, the law is being misused by the police to barge into our houses and issue threats to make our life worse than it is. We feel that the government should entrust the implementation of the law to sisters engaged in social work. They will understand our problems and apply the law in a humane manner. Till the government makes this arrangement, we should not be either evicted from our houses or harassed by the police. We are sure that our wise brothers and sisters will heed this appeal and come to our rescue.

As hoped for, the appeal did evoke some response in Banaras. In the coming days, *Aaj* published several letters from its readers and a statement from Rustam Setan cautioning the administration and the police to desist from hasty and unplanned eviction of tawaifs and sex workers until a comprehensive rehabilitation programme had been put in place.

Interestingly, this advisory had less to do with concern for the women and more with the fear that rash police action would result in prostitution spreading from a well-defined area into 'respectable' localities of the city. Besides, there was also concern that, in a bid to escape SITA, the women might move to towns that had been relatively free of large-scale prostitution. Examples were given of small towns in eastern UP, which thus far had only a few tawaifs and sex workers, but were now flooded with women fleeing from the state's western districts like Meerut. To counter these dangers, it was stressed that, once evicted from their kothas, the women be safely housed away from 'respectable' society in rehabilitation homes and taught vocational skills or be married off.

The Banaras tawaifs' appeal elicited a response from the community in other cities as well. Munir Bai, president of the tawaifs' group in Lucknow, Anjuman-e-Lucknow Sangeet Kalakar, expressed solidarity with her sisters in Banaras and advised them to find courage, organise and struggle against injustice. In the same breath, Munir Bai expressed support for the new law, and emphasised that the government must differentiate between tawaifs and prostitutes in its implementation. Hereditary tawaifs, she argued, were not prostitutes but custodians of traditional music and dance, which the government was trying so hard to promote. The authorities would do well to draw up a detailed list of the different categories of tawaifs and prostitutes in an area before implementing the law. To persecute tawaifs under SITA, which was meant to suppress trafficking and prostitution, would not only be unjust but in the long run do incalculable harm to the cause of art and culture.

On 13 June, responding to the public appeal made by Banaras tawaifs, a state government spokesman in Lucknow clarified that the government had thus far not sanctioned any action under the new law, nor had it issued any directive for the eviction of tawaifs and sex workers from their homes. Police and local authorities were ordered to suspend all further action until the state government formulated appropriate rules and regulations to implement the law.

'The statement from the government was a major victory for Gayika Sangh and revived its influence in the community. Its membership grew overnight,' Sharafat recounts. 'Ganesh and Bhim, who were nobodies till then, began to be looked upon with respect for drafting a letter that had forced the government to respond. Basking in glory, they never bothered to give credit where credit was due. Had I not advised them to send the letter on behalf of all tawaifs and prostitutes, instead of the Gayika Sangh, it would not have had the impact it did with the general public and the government.'

The reprieve proved to be short-lived. By the end of June, the UP government put in place rules and regulations under which SITA would be implemented in the state, and sent orders to its district officials to begin taking action under the law. In cities and towns, the city magistrate was entrusted with the responsibility of implementing the law, assisted by a deputy superintendent of police. In rural areas, the sub-divisional magistrate was in charge. Government officials were to be assisted in their respective areas by organisations and individuals engaged in social work.

As a follow-up to the government's announcement, the Gayika Sangh convened a formal meeting on 30 June 1958 at Mohini Bai's residence. Almost all the members, tawaifs and accompanist musicians, were present. The meeting began with a discussion about strategies to safeguard against police harassment and possible eviction, now that the government had green-signalled implementation of the law.

'Ganesh told everyone present about his correspondence with Malik Dilbar Husain from Delhi,' Sharafat recalls. 'In May, Dilbar had founded the All India Deraydar Sangh to protect the interests of tawaifs. He was the brain behind the demonstration outside Parliament, which was covered by newspapers everywhere.'

My ears prick up at the mention of my old family friend. Dilbar Husain had spoken to me about the All India Deraydar Sangh and his travels across northern India to enlist members. He had also lobbied with political leaders, social activists and cultural figures to make them aware of tawaifs' identity as art practitioners, their rich contribution to music and dance, and the injustice of penalising them under SITA.

'Dilbar had written to Ganesh about a tawaif conference that the All India Deraydar Sangh was planning to organise in Delhi, if possible in that year or in early 1959,' Sharafat tells us. 'He wanted the Gayika Sangh to send representatives to it. Ganesh and Bhim were dismissive of the proposal. "Who is this Dilbar?" they asked. "What are his real intentions behind organising this conference? He just wishes to build his career as a leader at the expense of others in the community." Ganesh and Bhim were basically loudmouths, always suspicious of and threatened by actual doers.

'I tried to argue that we had nothing to lose by accepting Dilbar's invitation. He had plans to invite political and social luminaries to attend the conference and acquaint them with the problems our community faced due to the introduction of SITA. At this, Ganesh had shot back, "Since when have accompanist musicians begun telling deraydars what to do?" I was very angry. How dare a good-for-nothing like Ganesh, living in the reflected glory of his aunt, insult an accompanist musician? Unlike the indolent fathers, sons and nephews of tawaifs, we musicians worked hard to earn an honest living!' Sharafat's voice quivers at the memory of the slight.

Several other accompanist musicians at the meeting also took grave offence at Ganesh's remark and demanded an apology. Ganesh, in turn, found support in his brother and some young men from tawaif families eager to ingratiate themselves with Mohini's nephews. Sharp words were exchanged between the two sides, but male elders among the deraydars and accompanist musicians ultimately brokered a truce.

I am struck by the absence of tawaif voices at the meeting. All the principal actors—the absent Dilbar over whose invitation the standoff took place, Ganesh, Sharafat and the deraydars and accompanist musicians on either side—were men. Neither Mohini Bai, long regarded as the leader of the community, nor any other tawaif present seems to have played any significant part in the unfolding of events.

The meeting moved on to the nomination by consensus of office-bearers for various posts of the Gayika Sangh, which had been lying vacant for years. Mohini Bai was re-nominated president of the organisation. Other than her, only one other tawaif, Kamla Devi, was chosen for the relatively lowly post of deputy secretary. All other posts were now occupied by men, most of them from tawaif families and a few accompanist musicians, with Ganesh as general secretary. In a striking reversal from the past—when tawaifs in Banaras controlled the affairs of the Gayika Sangh and its predecessor, the saat taat or panchayat—by the mid-twentieth century, decision-making appears to have passed increasingly into the hands of men.

'Times had changed,' Sharafat explains. 'As the main breadwinners, tawaifs still called the shots in their relationship with men in their families and with accompanist musicians who were dependent on them for their livelihood. But the world outside had transformed since Husna Bai had first set up the Gayika Sangh. To run any registered association meant dealing with various rules, regulations and government departments, and required paperwork that was beyond the scope of tawaifs. Then there was the law. Dealing with various municipal and police laws had been complicated enough to begin with, but the introduction of SITA meant visits to the police station, lawyers and law courts, which tawaifs, busy running their kothas, had neither the time nor the wherewithal to handle on their own.

'Most tawaifs were neither as educated as the great bai sahibs of the past nor had powerful patrons at their beck and call, happy to pull strings with the administration and police on their behalf. They needed the help of educated men in the community who could run around and get work done. Dilbar had taken on outside responsibilities on behalf of his mother Mumtaz Choudharayin in Delhi. In Lucknow, Munir Bai was helped by her grandsons in the running of Anjuman-e-Lucknow Sangeet Kalakar. But since these women were in robust health, and mentally agile despite their age, they remained very much in command. There were also several other powerful tawaifs in these cities who played an active role in their community's public affairs.

'In Banaras, however, there were hardly any tawaifs left of the stature of Mumtaz or Munir Bai. The community here had been very hard hit by social ostracism. Most prominent tawaifs had opted to leave the profession. Only Mohini Bai remained from the old school, but her health was poor and her memory was going. Other tawaifs did not have the requisite skills or contacts. It was easy for Ganesh and Bhim to take over the Gayika Sangh and fill its posts with their yes-men.'

In the months to come, the Gayika Sangh had its hands full, dealing with harassment of tawaifs by the police, raids and demands for bribes, all of which had become a routine feature in the life of Dal Mandi and its neighbourhood. Rumours about impending eviction orders flew thick and fast. The situation was complicated by the fact that, in most areas, sex workers lived cheek-by-jowl with tawaifs.

Challenging police action against its members, the Gayika Sangh argued that tawaifs earned their livelihood by music and dance and had no links to prostitution. They should, therefore, not be equated with sex workers. Besides arranging bails and filing legal appeals against the arrest of its members, the Gayika Sangh also lobbied with former influential patrons to exert pressure on the police, administration and judiciary to adopt a more sympathetic attitude towards tawaifs.

On 28 October 1958, the police issued a public notice that prostitutes should vacate Dal Mandi and the neighbourhoods adjoining it in the next three days. Tawaifs and sex workers filed legal petitions challenging the eviction order. In the case of tawaifs, though filed in the name of individuals or groups of affected women, the Gayika Sangh played an active role in initiating and following up on the court cases. Bolstered with as many certificates, photographs of performance and commendations as could be found or arranged as proof, the petitions emphasised the difference between tawaifs and sex workers.

At the behest of the Gayika Sangh, a group of tawaifs from Dal Mandi—Tashmeena and sixty others—filed an appeal with the city magistrate, arguing that since they were art practitioners earning their living by music and dance, they should be kept out of the purview of SITA. Another group of tawaifs—Dhaneshwari and sixty-two others—filed a similar appeal questioning the basis of the proposed police action against them.

This strategy evoked scepticism from the press, which had long equated tawaifs with women in prostitution. On 31 October 1958, *Aaj* observed, 'Efforts are being made to shield Gayika Sangh members from the implementation of SITA. It is being argued that members of the Gayika Sangh earn their living exclusively from music and dance ... the public at large, however, is supportive of police action to cleanse areas like Dal Mandi, Nariyal Bazaar, Raja Darwaza and Kundigar Tola of prostitutes.'

The Gayika Sangh's argument stood on firmer ground with the law, though. Responding to the tawaifs' petitions, the court observed that women who earned their livelihood by music and dance alone and did not indulge in prostitution should be free to carry on with their profession without hindrance from the law. The police was asked to postpone the eviction of prostitutes until 12 November, and in this period, verify the number of women who made a living as professional singers and dancers.

'Dal Mandi and other areas that had looked deserted in the immediate aftermath of the eviction order again began humming with activity,' Sharafat tells us. Pausing for dramatic effect, he says, 'It was a strange time. Genuine tawaifs had already left or were leaving the line in large numbers, and prostitutes who couldn't sing a line of music were busy converting their brothels into music salons.'

You describe this transformation of the tawaif neighbourhoods. Following the court's orders, increasing numbers of sex workers, with little or no previous connection to music and dance, began to set themselves up as singers and dancers to protect themselves from eviction and police harassment. Those who could afford it, shifted out from predominantly sex worker neighbourhoods, like Kundigar Tola and Panch Pandav, and rented kothas in mohallas that traditionally housed tawaifs—Dal Mandi, Nariyal Bazaar and Raja Darwaza. In many instances, they rented the houses of tawaifs who were moving out from Banaras for good. To complete their metamorphosis, they began hiring accompanist musicians and learning a few film and folk songs and popular ghazals, which they then performed to keep up appearances.

This repertoire suited the men who now visited kothas just fine, you say in a resigned tone. Over the previous decades, the client profile of Dal Mandi had undergone a major change. Men with an educated taste in music, dance and stimulating conversation had given way to those whose primary interest in frequenting kothas was sex, with the frill of some dance and music thrown in. After the imposition of SITA, even the few discerning patrons who had continued to visit tawaifs stopped coming.

'The entire culture and way of life associated with tawaif mohallas began to change rapidly,' Sharafat Khan interrupts you. 'Prostitutes pretending to be tawaifs took over Dal Mandi, cheap filmy songs drowned out thumri and dadra, riff-raff of all kinds took over as patrons of the bazaar and the Gayika Sangh got crowded by whores.'

Shanney Khan has dozed off in his corner. Ignoring him, Sharafat describes how the court order, hailed as a major victory for the Gayika Sangh, led to a transformation of the identity of the organisation. Its membership, long restricted to tawaifs and accompanist musicians, now began to be coveted by sex workers, since to be a member meant to be a singer and dancer, outside the reach of SITA. Fearful of being identified with sex workers, there was initially stiff resistance by the original tawaif members to the induction of outsiders to the Gayika Sangh. It was argued that the Gayika Sangh had evolved out of the tawaifs' panchayat and was thus the core of the community. Inducting sex workers would irretrievably compromise the identity of the tawaif community and its way of life.

'But bloated with self-importance after the court order, which they saw as a personal victory, Bhim and Ganesh were unable to resist the temptation of lording over a vastly increased membership,' Sharafat says. 'Overriding all other opinion, they opened the doors of the Gayika Sangh to prostitutes. The only concession they made to the tawaif community was to ensure that the prostitutes who were admitted belonged to kindred groups, like Bedia, Kanjar etc., and that some music and dance was performed in their brothels.'

'Let's face facts, Sharafat, there wasn't that much difference left between certain categories of tawaifs and prostitutes.' Shanney Khan Sahib is now wide awake and offering a cogent counter-opinion. 'Today, we might like to think that all tawaifs were great singers and dancers, but the truth we all know is that, by the time the law was enforced, there were many bai-jis who did more or less the same work as prostitutes. Bhim and Ganesh had pointed out as much in one of the Gayika Sangh meetings.'

As the three of us stare at him in surprise, Shanney Khan Sahib, exhausted by his eloquence, slumps back into his corner.

Sharafat is the first to recover. Glowering at your ustad, he snaps, 'Whatever the logic, the Gayika Sangh got crowded with prostitutes. Many respected tawaifs were extremely offended about this, as were several Khan sahibs and gurus, who found it below their dignity to be part of an organisation in which prostitutes were members. In the public eye, we were all tarnished with the same brush.

'Besides, Bhim and Ganesh had become intolerably high-handed. At almost every meeting, there was tension over some issue or the other. In one of the meetings, they claimed that they were badshahs while we, the accompanists, were mere vazirs. At this, Kishan Maharaj stood up in protest and said, "*Hamare bajane se tum badshah bane ho.*" It is because of us that you have become kings. This escalated into a major fight and the Gayika Sangh split in two. The tawaifs mainly remained with the old body, while the accompanists formed a new organisation, Sangeet Mandal, with Kishan Maharaj as president, and I as secretary. Our meetings used to take place in Kabir Chaura at Kishan Maharaj's house.'

Shanney Khan interjects to set the record straight. According to him, with the dipping fortunes of the tawaifs, the Kathaks who, as their tabla players and teachers had been dependent upon the women for economic survival, began asserting their clout in community hierarchy. They demanded a more favourable share in the evening's baata, earnings, which the tawaifs refused. As a result, a group of mainly Hindu male musicians, comprising Kathaks and Kinnars, broke away to register a rival body, the Sangeet Mandal. With notable exceptions like Sharafat Khan, who chose to cast his lot with the Kathak-led new body, most Muslim musicians from the Dhari and Bhaat castes remained in the Gayika Sangh. Being much poorer sarangi and majira players, they felt their interests were better served by retaining traditional links with the kotha economy.

Later, in an interview with me at his beautiful, sprawling family home in Kabir Chaura, the renowned tabla player Kishan Maharaj corroborated Shanney Khan's assertion. The argument between tawaifs and accompanist musicians over the division of mujra earnings in a kotha, he agreed, had been the immediate catalyst for the rupture in the Gayika Sangh, but it had been long in the making.

Sitting in the walled garden of his home, green with myriad flowering plants and fruit trees, Kishan Maharaj talked about the respect for Kathak tabla players in Banaras. He claimed that while this was largely because of their mastery of music, it was also due to their scrupulous 'moral conduct'. For instance, after the imposition of SITA, many Kathaks like him stopped playing for tawaifs in kothas, opting instead to perform only with 'respectable' soloist musicians in music conferences, concerts and on the radio.

Besides, the tabla, which used to be seen only in an accompanist capacity, had begun gaining increasing visibility and respectability as a solo performance instrument. It was drawing appreciation from concert audiences and making stars of players like Sharada Sahai and him, further consolidating the eminent position that Kathak tabla players occupied in the hierarchy of accompanist musicians in Banaras. This is another reason that bolstered their confidence to break away from the tawaifs' fold.

As I spoke to a cross-section of musicians in the city, accompanists and soloists, Hindus and Muslims, it became apparent that many well-known Kathak families in Banaras had been successful in negotiating space for themselves within the nationalist project of an appropriately 'classical' music culture. Their projection of an upper-caste status no doubt helped in gaining greater social acceptance from the votaries of Hindu nationalism, who were the dominant opinion-makers and patrons of art, music and culture in Banaras. The increasing popularity of the tabla as a solo instrument also bestowed greater respectability upon the Kathak tabla players.

Emboldened by these developments, Kathak musicians had demanded a more favourable share in the earnings in a kotha. When this demand was refused by Gayika Sangh tawaifs, the Kathaks had formed their own organisation. Also, by the late 1950s, several well-known Kathak families in Banaras had stopped playing for tawaifs. They could afford to do so because spaces controlled by the upper-caste nationalist middle classes—like music conferences, radio, music societies and public concerts—provided alternative and socially respectable avenues of employment. This also improved their prospects of social acceptance in 'respectable' music circles in Banaras and outside.

Sarangi players, on the other hand, most of whom belonged to the Muslim Dhari community, faced stigmatisation and exclusion from the 'respectable' music culture of Banaras, because the sarangi was seen as an accompanist instrument, associated primarily with tawaifs and their music. Moreover, they were seen as 'low caste' and Muslim in the predominantly upper-caste Hindu public sphere of the city. Muslim accompanist musicians, therefore, had little choice but to either cast their lot with tawaifs or to give up music-making altogether. A minuscule few, like Sharafat, with the advantage of a modern education, were able to make a place for themselves as accompanists in music conferences or find employment on the radio, but they remained the exception rather than the norm.

One late winter's evening, I visit Sharafat Khan's house in Chahmama to explore in greater detail the shift in power dynamics in the mid-twentieth century between accompanist musicians and tawaifs.

He talks about the massive police raid on tawaifs in December 1958 in the Chowk area of Lucknow, about which Amrit Lal Nagar wrote at some length in his *Yeh Kothewaliyan*. Even the kothas of well-known and respected singers and dancers were searched inside out during this hawkish police operation. Old and infirm former tawaifs too were not spared the humiliation of being taken to the police station for further questioning.

The news spread to other cities, like Banaras and Delhi, as a grim reminder of the vulnerability of the kotha community to state surveillance, control and harassment, notwithstanding legal reprieves like the court order exempting professional singers and dancers from the draconian reach of SITA. If the elite tawaifs of Lucknow were not safe from the law then, it was reasoned, no one in the community was. The women's heightened sense of defencelessness led to further decimation of the tawaifs' clout in the kotha community.

Sharafat tells me that the news of the raid led to further divisions in the already diminished membership of the Gayika Sangh. 'Established tawaifs became very apprehensive about sharing Gayika Sangh membership with sex workers and running the risk of being accused of prostitution by the police, as had happened in Lucknow. Arguments and even bitter fights would break out regularly in Gayika Sangh meetings on the issue.'

The Lucknow raid also sharpened the urgency to forge a united front of tawaifs and their accompanist musicians across India in order to effectively lobby for the protection of their interests. Malik Dilbar Hussain toured cities and towns that had sizeable tawaif populations. Under his leadership, the All India Deraydar Sangh hosted its first conference in Delhi in 1960, which was attended by representatives of kotha communities from across northern India. In keeping with the changed times, most of the representatives at the conference were men—deraydars and accompanist musicians—with tawaif participation being much smaller. Sharafat Khan and Hamid Choudhary, a respected deraydar elder, represented the kotha community of Banaras at the conference. Dilbar had also invited sympathetic outsiders, like the well-known thumri singer Naina Devi, to hear the speakers at the event and interact with them. It was hoped that such a dialogue with civil society representatives would help in lessening the misconceptions and prejudice against tawaifs, and hopefully generate greater acceptance in society of their role as cultural practitioners.

As Sharafat thunders on about his electrifying speech at the conference, I receive a panicked call from your home. It is Meenu, who informs me in frightened tones that Salma is missing and that you have gone looking for her. My blood runs cold. Hastily ending my conversation with Sharafat, I rush out and desperately try to get a rickshaw. Not finding one, I walk as fast as I can manage to Nariyal Bazaar.

My thoughts are with Salma. In the past few weeks, I have been noticing with growing concern that she was slipping into an abyss of anxiety and depression. She has spoken intermittently about 'ending it all' but never about the life taking shape inside her womb. Praying for her safety and well-being, my thoughts turn to you.

We have had several heated arguments about Salma's forced pregnancy. I have tried to impress upon you the need to be more solicitous towards her, only to be met with a volley of self-righteous indignation and protestations about your concern for Salma.

'The girl is a drama queen. Don't take her talk of death and doom so seriously,' you have snapped back. 'Don't I provide her with the best possible medical attention? Have I counted paisa when feeding her? Milk, fruit, fish, chicken and eggs—she eats better than we do. Am I not spending beyond my means by engaging a house help to do the cleaning and washing so that Salma is spared hard work? What more does she expect? If despite all this, she is still feeling miserable here then why doesn't she shift to her parents' house?' You know that your daughter-in-law's family is too poor to take on the care of a pregnant daughter. Salma, no doubt, knows it too.

By the time I reach your house, you are back and so is Salma. You found her, wearing no slippers or woollens, seemingly impervious to the cold or the late hour, on a particularly deserted ghat in faraway Shivala. Following the leads provided by inquisitive shopkeepers in Nariyal Bazaar and Dal Mandi, who noticed a pregnant young woman walking barefoot, with hair and face uncovered, you reached Salma just as she was about to leap into the Ganga. Pulling her back, you half-carried, half-dragged her struggling frail frame into a rickshaw.

Physically and emotionally exhausted by her near brush with death, Salma has taken sanctuary in sleep under a pile of quilts and blankets that you have piled on her for warmth. Sitting by her bedside, gently stroking her hair, you are the picture of calm, maternal efficiency. You direct Meenu to take care of little Haaris. The part-time help is ordered to cook some khichdi for your daughter-in-law. When it is ready, you cajole Salma out of her slumber and feed her as you would an ill and sleepy child, one spoon at a time.

Hushing her occasional whimper, you tuck her back in bed once she finishes eating. You wait till she falls back asleep. Then, directing the help to sit by Salma's bedside, you heave your weary frame down the steps to the visitors' room.

You look tired and you look infinitely aged in the span of one evening. Refusing the food I try to feed you, you weep silently for a long time. In all our years of friendship, I have never seen you so distraught, so broken. When finally you speak, your anger at Salma for attempting suicide is matched in equal measure with anger at yourself for forcing your daughter-in-law to carry a pregnancy she doesn't want.

Over and over again, you go over what could have happened had you reached too late. You blame Salma for bringing you within a hair's breadth of a police case, a possible jail term and the shattering of your family's reputation.

'How could she do that to our family?' you ask over and over again. 'What would have happened to Nanhe and Haaris? And what of Meenu's marriage that is due soon? And what about me? My face would have been blackened forever! What a thoughtless, selfish girl Salma has shown herself to be!'

In the very next instant, you berate yourself for being blind to your daughter-in-law's depression. Had you not been so obsessed with having another grandchild, this terrible ordeal might never have come to pass. This trajectory of self-blame is followed by anger at Salma for not wanting a child. What kind of woman wants to abort her unborn child? The girl is hard-hearted with no maternal feelings.

At this, I quietly point to the very real financial concerns for the future of her children that might have prompted Salma's reluctance to carry a second pregnancy. Could you really afford a second grandchild, I ask you pointedly. You fall silent.

And then you begin to weep hard, bitter tears of anger, guilt and remorse mixed in equal measure with fear of what the future holds for you and your family. I let you cry. You are in battle with yourself. Other than hoping that you will emerge from it wiser and more compassionate towards Salma, there is little for me to say or do but sit quietly by your side through this long, terrible night.

CHAPTER 27

Two Sisters

MEENU'S WEDDING IS A MONTH away, but your home is already a hive of feverish activity. Ghafuran arrived a few days ago, accompanied by her daughter-in-law, and has efficiently taken charge of the many tasks that go into the making of an Indian wedding—from preparing guest lists, to giving last-minute tailoring touches to Meenu's trousseau, to cooking long-lasting snacks to go with breakfast and evening tea for the guests who will arrive soon.

The mood in your home is as mellow as the February sun of these days. Whenever you are home in the afternoon, you insist upon massaging oil into Salma's hair, while the rest of the women sit around the two of you on the terrace, taking a breather from household chores. No one refers to that dreadful night. Yet, it seems to have significantly changed your relationship with your daughter-in-law. In its aftermath, you are gentler, kinder towards Salma. At times, your jealousy and insecurity show up in a sharpness of tone but your antipathy no longer gets the better of you. I feel hopeful that these attempts at being more empathetic and caring might over time transform into genuine love for Salma.

Basking in your attention, Salma looks happier than I have ever seen her. Her health has improved. She takes greater interest in her pregnancy. Her doctor, she says, is satisfied with her progress and hopes to perform a normal delivery. She talks often about her hopes for her second child. Her energy levels have revived to the extent that, braving your maternal reprimands to take it easy, she helps out with the endless cooking and sewing of these days.

Meenu contributes little to the wedding arrangements. Not that she is expected to either. Almost always surrounded by her many friends, who fill your home with their whispered confidences and girlish giggles,

Meenu is busy enjoying her special status as a prospective bride. Fussed over by friends and family, she has begun to look indefinably pretty. Her eyes sparkle in anticipation, her face radiates happiness and her skin glows with youthful vitality. And much to your relief, she has become more muted in her demands for an extravagant dowry.

As the provider of the family, your domain is the world outside. You scour the establishments of the most reasonably priced caterers, decorators, marquee arrangers and sundry other service providers you can find to balance your ambitions for a fat Indian wedding with the compulsions of a slim purse. Doggedly bargaining over every single paisa, you patiently move from shop to shop till you are able to locate one where the price fits your budget.

At home, you supervise the whitewash and cleaning that is on in full flow. Every corner of the house is being spruced up to welcome the bridegroom and his family. In between, you make short trips to Bhabua and from there on to Palakh to source provisions—rice, wheat, lentils, ghee, mustard oil and spices—that will feed the wedding party and the hordes of relatives expected in the coming weeks.

You generally come back from these visits looking tired but satisfied. Today, however, you look distinctly edgy. I see why when Asghari follows you into the room.

I know only too well your nervous tension about hosting your flashy elder sister in the respectability of your Banaras home. But the skeletal and frail woman I meet now is a pale shadow of the colourful former tawaif I knew. In the six months since I last met her, Asghari has lost not only a tremendous amount of weight but also the vivacity of her smile and the liveliness of her gait. She looks old and tired and very ill.

Later in the day, Ghafuran tells me that Asghari's recurrent cough turned out to be tuberculosis. Left untreated for long, it had taken a toll on her health. Worse, she suffered a heart attack a few months ago. Asghari has come with you now to Banaras, not so much on account of Meenu's wedding but because there is no one in Bhabua, save Rani, who can take care of her. And Rani is too old and frail to be burdened with the responsibility.

That Asghari is so critically ill comes as a shock. During the past months, you had mentioned only once in passing that Asghari was not keeping too well. Recalling that conversation, I am struck by your understatement. Even now, though you have brought your ailing elder sister home, you don't seem perturbed by Asghari's state as you were about Pyaari khala in the past.

When we are alone in the evening, you grimace in obvious irritation when I broach the subject of Asghari's illness. 'I am supposed to not only find a doctor for aapa but also pay for her treatment since she is penniless, having long ago blown up all her savings. Her daughter has washed her hands of any responsibility and there is no one among our relatives willing to put her up. So what option do I have but to bring her here to stay with me?'

Even though I know of your thorny relationship with Asghari, your uncharacteristically graceless response surprises me. Sensing my unease, perhaps, you remind me of the abuse that you and Ghafuran suffered through childhood and adolescence at Asghari's hands. Treated as no better than poor relatives, you and your twin were denied even your mother's love and care because of her, you say.

It was at her insistence that Teema had been forced to send the two of you, then just five or six years old, back to the family home in Bhabua, while she stayed on in Banaras to look after Asghari and her career. Feeling lost among a horde of distant relatives, Ghafuran and you had clung to each other. Your father Shivendra Singh was no more, and you felt the absence of your mother sharply.

Teema tried to spend a few days in Bhabua every month. You remember awaiting those visits eagerly. Often, she was late, sometimes unable to make it at all on account of Asghari's mujra assignments. Pining for your mother, you would fall ill.

Trips to Banaras were rare, since Asghari was unwelcoming and hostile. She seized upon every opportunity to humiliate the two of you. Even the most minor lapse would invite not just a torrent of filthy abuses but also heavy thrashing.

'Ghafuran and I were so used to being treated like dirt by aapa that we rarely complained to our mother. Just as we had done as little children, we would try and keep out of her way as much as possible,' you say bitterly.

'Aapa is lucky that Ghafuran and I are not like her. Had we been made in the same mould, we would have abandoned her now the way her own daughter has. Ever since aapa took ill, Ghafuran has looked after her and her house in Bhabua. But she herself is poor, so it is I who have to take care of aapa financially. The doctor in Bhabua has advised that she be shown to a specialist in Banaras. Naturally, everyone takes it for granted that I will take responsibility for her. Putting all those years of ill-treatment behind me, I am doing my duty as a younger sister,' you say, adding pointedly, 'But no one can force me to be any more loving towards her than I am.'

Overcome with painful memories, you talk about how, during the few and far between visits to Banaras in your childhood, you would watch in silent wonder the special attention that your older half-sister received from Teema. Asghari was given eggs and milk for breakfast along with a paste of almonds that your mother made just for her. Food for Asghari was cooked in pure clarified butter, and included generous portions of mutton, chicken or fish. She only ate the finest rice and was particular about drinking at least one large glass of fruit juice daily to keep her skin young and glowing.

You and the rest of the family had to make do with the basic fare of rice and dal that was cooked for all non-earning family members. The most that you could hope for was a share in the leftovers of Asghari's meal, if at all.

You remember always being on the lookout for where Teema could have hidden the jars of dry fruit meant for Asghari. Years of helping yourself on the sly to things meant for your older sister had made you an expert at quietly and quickly opening the containers, scooping out a handful of the goodies, replacing the lid on the jar and disappearing from the room as fast as your legs could carry you. Up on the terrace, away from prying eyes, the dry fruit would be savoured hurriedly. At times, Ghafuran caught you out, and you were forced to share the loot with her in exchange for complicit silence. There would be hell to pay if Asghari got to know of your pilfering.

When you were about eleven or twelve, you struggled to convince the family to train you as a tawaif. Jealous about sharing that status with you, Asghari was dead set against the idea. Dismissing you as too ugly to make the cut, she had tried to prevail upon Teema to instead groom you and Ghafuran for marriage. At Teema's insistence that the family needed a second earning member, Asghari had grudgingly chosen the prettier Ghafuran for training to become a tawaif.

Shedding your meekness, you refused to take no for an answer. You loved music and dance. You craved the freedom that Asghari enjoyed.

Above all, you wanted to live in Banaras. The city throbbed with mehfils that went on through the night. Its bazaars spilled over with colour and lights. You wanted to belong here. This was where your mother lived, and you wanted to be with her all the time.

'Whenever I was in Banaras, on the sly, I would watch aapa perform in the kotha, and my desire to learn music grew even stronger,' you tell me. 'I kept pestering amma to convince aapa to allow me to stay on in Banaras and learn music from her teacher and sarangi accompanist Habib Khan Sahib. She would say, "I will talk to your elder sister," but either she forgot or aapa said no, because soon it was time for Ghafuran and me to return to Bhabua.

'One day, during a visit to Banaras, I decided in my twelve-year-old wisdom to take matters into my own hands. Mustering all the courage I had, I approached Khan sahib and asked him to teach me music. He came daily to the house to practise with aapa. He looked amused at my request but, before he could say anything, aapa entered the room and began raining blows upon me. "You black, fat buffalo, you want to become like me! You want to learn music? I will show you how to sing!" Aapa kept shrieking like a mad woman and thrashing me. She had obviously heard me talk to Khan sahib. No one could claim anything or anyone who was hers, as she saw it, least of all me.'

There was only one way to win Asghari over, and that was obsequious flattery. You remark caustically that your elder sister has always been in love with herself. Singled out by Teema and her aunts since childhood as the prettiest girl in the family, as she grew older, Asghari had savoured the attention she received from neighbours and later from male admirers for her looks, her vivacity and for her singing and dancing. Her popularity as a tawaif further validated her complete belief in her own perfection. Her ascendancy as the main breadwinner of the family had given Asghari a taste for the power over those dependent on her. It was hardly surprising that she expected, even demanded, admiration and deference from everyone around.

'Amma would warn aapa about the dangers of falling for flattery,' you add primly. 'Many a great tawaif had been ruined at the hands of their vanity, frittering their hard-earned fortunes on penniless parasites with nothing to offer besides fawning sweet talk and unctuous compliments. Her words would fall on deaf ears. Ever so often, aapa would take a fancy to a good-for-nothing ashiq, and it would require all of amma's wisdom to quietly wean her away from the attachment without overtly showing any disapproval. She knew aapa's headstrong obstinacy only too well. Forbidding her to do something always resulted in more defiance.'

'So what would your mother do instead to get rid of Asghari's unsuitable ashiqs?' I ask, half-guessing the answer.

'Our community had its time-tested ways for such situations,' you reply, shrugging. 'Planting doubts about the sincerity of a man's intentions, generating rumours about his unfaithful ways, subtly putting him in an awkward position in front of aapa, amma was forced to rely on all this in order to save her daughter and family from ruination. It helped that my sister has always been not only self-centred, vain and headstrong but also *kaan ki kacchi*, gullible. If told that a crow had flown away with her ear, she would run after the crow without thinking, rather than check her ear first. She is like that still.'

More often than not, Asghari's infatuations would fizzle out as soon as a newer object of desire caught her fancy, which was often. The constant travel also came in handy when Teema needed to get rid of unsuitable admirers. Few if any had either the resources or the ardour to follow Asghari and her family as they moved from town to town in search of better opportunities.

'Amma travelled with aapa to Bihar, Bengal and even Assam. Next time you chat with her, ask her about her travels. She will be delighted to regale you with stories of her conquests, real and imagined, in faraway lands,' you say, yawning.

It's time I left. You have had a long day and look exhausted. Bidding you goodnight, I make my way down the steps only to notice Asghari sitting at the foot of the staircase, near the entrance, with the door half open to let in some breeze. I look at my watch. It's past nine in the evening, time that I returned to my room. I too am tired.

Asghari has other plans for me, though. As I try and squeeze past mumbling my goodnights, she pats the space beside her and imperiously orders, 'Come, sit down. I have hardly had the chance to speak with you today.' I wearily settle down beside her. If it gets too late, I could sleep here, in the room that you share with Meenu and little Haaris. Banishing thoughts of the pleasures of solitary quietude, a bath and my own bed, I allow myself to be led into the conversation Asghari clearly wants so much.

We talk about her health. She insists that she is doing well and has come to Banaras at your behest to help with the wedding preparations. I look at the wan face of the old woman seated beside me and see the helpless pride in her eyes. Giving her hand a squeeze, I say nothing. For some time, there is silence. I can hear voices from upstairs. Ghafuran is up and so it seems is Salma, no doubt stitching multitudes of gota kinari—golden lace trimmings—to Meenu's trousseau of saris and those to be gifted to the women in her prospective groom's family.

'Has your friend told you about the time when she was eleven or twelve, and had to be brought to Banaras for surgery?' Asghari asks, breaking the silence. Taken aback, I admit I know nothing of it.

'She developed a lump in her breast,' Asghari says, making it sound somehow as if you were to blame. 'I cancelled all my assignments and went with amma to Bhabua to bring her here for medical treatment. We got her surgery done by the best doctor in Banaras. All went well. The doctors removed the lump and the family heaved a sigh of relief. Who paid for everything? Obviously, I did. The doctor said that she would have to stay on for several months in Banaras for follow-up treatment. I said fine. Since Ghafuran would not stay in Bhabua without her, I brought her to Banaras as well.

'The months rolled into years. Every time a date was fixed for their return to Bhabua, your friend would come down with some illness or the other and stay put in Banaras. Serious or minor or even imaginary, her ailments were always attended to by the best doctors. I was never one to be stingy about medical expenses for the family.

'Your friend often complains about the deprivation that she and Ghafuran faced at my hands when they were young. They, along with an army of relatives, lived in my house and at my expense for years. My mother's brother Yaqub, his wife and children were all staying here at that time. My other uncle Yahiya and his family were in Bhabua. Most of my earnings were spent on running both households and meeting the needs of the extended family in Banaras and Bhabua. Amma wanted it that way and, as my malik, she used my earnings as she thought best. I never knew how much I earned nor questioned her about how that money was spent. Does that sound like selfish behaviour to you?

'Yes, I did dress better than my sisters or the other relatives living in my house. As a successful tawaif, I needed to be well-dressed according to the latest fashion in Banaras. It was part of my professional calling. It is also true that I ate more expensive food than the others in the house. But that was how it was in all tawaif households where, at any given time, there would be just one or two women earning and a large number of non-earning relatives. As the sole breadwinner, I not only deserved to eat better than the rest but also needed a rich and nutritious diet, because the long hours of singing and dancing sapped my strength.

'The army of relatives who lived in the house didn't bother me but, other than with amma, I did not like sharing my room, clothes or personal belongings with others. What was so selfish about that? I was working hard for everyone. Didn't I deserve a right over my things? There was no goldmine that I was sitting on. Times were difficult and, to keep my family well, I had to perform for hours at a stretch to attract the generosity of those who still ventured to our kothas.'

In the difficult decade of the 1960s, following the imposition of SITA, well-off patrons had stopped visiting tawaifs. The ones who did were mostly shopkeepers, small-time businessmen and minor government functionaries, whose pockets were not deep enough to keep kothas running in the style they used to. Worse, the criminalising of the tradition by SITA forced kotha doors open to men on the wrong side of the law—goonda and badmash, hooligans and criminals—who in the past could not have hoped to get entry into the salons of well-placed and respected tawaifs. In police FIRs of that period, the terms goonda and badmash began to make a recurring appearance.

Former tawaifs like Asghari blame the entry of erstwhile sex workers into Dal Mandi for the presence of hooligans and criminals in the area. Asghari says that they brought in their wake hooligans and criminals who, as their 'protectors' from the police and from other goons, had always enjoyed a position of domination and control in the brothels of Banaras. They expected and demanded the same deference from traditional tawaifs, who no longer had either the financial resources to be discriminating about their choice of patrons nor, more importantly, the protection of socially and politically powerful men to stand up to such bullying.

Often hand-in-glove with the police and enjoying the patronage of local politicians, hooligans and criminals were a formidable presence in the Banaras of the 1960s. Newspapers of the time spent considerable newsprint bemoaning the criminalisation of the city and the need for firm action by the police. The large presence of hooligans in Dal Mandi was seen as further proof of the deviancy that flourished in kothas and hardened already-existing prejudice against tawaifs and sex workers, who were blamed for sheltering and encouraging criminals.

'Mukand Babu, Pappu Singh, Babu Ram-ji Singh ... they were all notorious goondas.' Asghari reels off the names with ease. 'There were many goondas at that time. They would force their way into kothas, get drunk and begin firing in the air and getting into brawls with each other. The police would arrive soon after.'

Police raids became a regular feature in tawaif neighbourhoods. Most often, the goons slipped away, or the police allowed them to slip away. Instead, tawaifs were forced to pay bribes for allegedly sheltering criminals in their premises. Caught in a vicious cycle, they became increasingly vulnerable to control by both the police and goondas. When harassed by the police, it was to thugs and hooligans that they were forced to turn to for protection. Even tawaifs like Asghari, who tried to maintain the old standards of keeping criminal elements at a safe distance, could no longer afford to openly antagonise them.

'I never faced trouble thanks to Basantu goonda. He was a close friend of Mahendra Bahadur Singh, a lawyer who was devoted to me. Mahendra Babu would come to my help whenever the police tried to harass me. Basantu would protect me from other goondas. He lived in my mohalla, and saw to it that no goonda-badmash entered my kotha. He would hang around this place with a lathi in hand, smiling at everyone. In the evening, he would sit where the visitors took off their shoes. I would invite him to come inside but he always replied—I am fine here.'

Basantu and his lathi also ensured that the goondas did not force Asghari to perform for free in temple festivities within Banaras. From the great, famous ones like Kashi Vishwanath, Durga temple and Sankatmochan, dedicated to major Hindu deities, to small wayside and mohalla shrines offering worship to the birs and mais of the 'little' tradition, each temple has a day or days special to the presiding deity. Called sringar, the day/days were lavishly celebrated in the past by the major temples with rich patrons. Until about the 1930s, the festivities involved performances by courtesans. Smaller shrines, located in poorer neighbourhoods, marked their sringar with simpler festivities.

Over the decades, sringar at these small shrines too became more ostentatious two- or three-day events, drawing greater public attendance.

Given the formidable presence of goonda-badmash in the public life of Banaras by the 1960s, it was not surprising that many of these celebrations were arranged under their patronage. Organising extravagant sringar in their neighbourhood temples provided an opportunity for the strongmen of the city to increase their area of influence and gain public legitimacy.

The highlight of these sringars were performances of music and dance that lasted all night long. Unlike musical performances at the big temples, from where courtesan singers and dancers had long been banished, the sringar celebrations in the small, neighbourhood shrines were now marked by the participation of tawaifs singing an eclectic repertoire of bhajans, qawwalis and film-based songs.

Reviled and ostracised by the elite and middle classes of Banaras, tawaifs found greater acceptance among the city's poorer inhabitants. Although eliciting muted moral censure from the city's working class population too, tawaifs continued to symbolise for them the grandeur and mystique associated with the lifestyle of the traditional elite. The memory of a time when courtesan performances were the highlight of sringar celebrations in the great temples of Banaras still lingered. Financially and socially out of reach for the poor, performances by tawaifs in neighbourhood temples proved to be exceedingly popular.

'Bai-jis were forced to perform at sringars by goondas,' Asghari says. 'To increase their influence in their areas, they competed with each other as to who could bring the most tawaifs to their celebrations. There were regular brawls among thugs to get the same performer. No fee was offered and there was no question of negotiating money with them. The women would weep and cry, but they had to sing at these festivities through consecutive nights. All they could hope to get was inam from the audience, which didn't amount to very much since most of the people were quite poor. I never went. As soon as some goonda even approached my kotha, Basantu would twirl his lathi menacingly and roar, "Which daughter-fucker has the guts to force Asghari to go with him?" That would be enough to send the thugs scuttling away in mortal fear.'

This was also the time when the balance of power between the beleaguered tawaifs and their male accompanists, especially the Kathaks, shifted further in favour of the men. The rift that had already taken place by the late 1950s with the formation of the Sangeet Mandal widened still. In 1965, male accompanists, under the leadership of Kishan Maharaj, reconfigured the Sangeet Mandal and formed the Kashi Sangeet Kalakar Sangh.

According to Sharafat, who had played an important role in the establishment of the new body as joint secretary, almost all the male accompanists, including those from the Dhari and Bhaat communities, now gravitated towards Kashi Sangeet Kalakar Sangh. With Kishan Maharaj as its president and members including other socially well-connected Kathak musicians, the new body not only held promise of protecting their interests better in the changed cultural scenario but also provided a relatively more 'respectable' platform for male accompanists looked down upon otherwise by society.

One of the first resolutions that Kashi Sangeet Kalakar Sangh adopted was that no male musician would play with tawaifs belonging to the Gayika Sangh. The move was sought to be justified on the basis of the argument that most Gayika Sangh members were sex workers pretending to be tawaifs. The resolution made it really difficult for tawaifs to find accompanists. As hoped, it resulted in the further crumbling of the Gayika Sangh, with many tawaifs opting to defect to the Kashi Sangeet Kalakar Sangh.

'The Gayika Sangh had become a joke,' Asghari says in acerbic tones. 'Ganesh and Bhim had totally ruined its original character by allowing in all kinds of riff-raff. Everyone knew that most women there practised prostitution under the garb of being tawaifs. Genuine tawaifs like me naturally felt that our name would get compromised, so many of us left and joined Kishan Maharaj's organisation.'

The Kashi Sangeet Kalakar Sangh issued to all its members licences with registration numbers. Recognised by the administration and police, these licences in turn attracted more tawaifs to the body. The functionaries of the new body also supplied the district magistrate and the superintendent of police with lists of tawaifs who did not indulge in prostitution. Needless to say, these were all members of the Kashi Sangeet Kalakar Sangh. The others, members of the Gayika Sangh, were, by exclusion, stigmatised and harassed further.

'When I heard about Gayika Sangh members being routinely dragged to the police station on some charge or the other, I was glad that my mother had made me join Kishan Maharaj's organisation in the nick of time,' Asghari recalls. 'But even there, we tawaifs faced problems. Two-penny male musicians, many of them still dependent on us for a living, tried to boss over us. Not that we allowed them to get away with it, of course, but it still was quite humiliating.'

An uneasy balance of power seems to have characterised the functioning of the Kashi Sangeet Kalakar Sangh. Since the running of the body was entirely in the hands of male accompanists, issues dear to them, like renegotiating a higher share in the distribution of mujra earnings, often came up during meetings, leading to acrimonious arguments between the men and tawaifs and ending almost always in a stalemate. While tawaifs, as the main performers in a mujra, could still refuse to allow any change in the established norm of baata—wherein the major proportion of an evening's earnings went to them—they found themselves increasingly dependent on male accompanists when confronted with the law and its enforcement agencies. Treated little better than prostitutes by the police and administration, even better-off tawaifs had to allow male accompanists to speak on their behalf.

They also had to put up with the humiliation of being taken to task in meetings about the presence of thugs and hoodlums in kotha premises and the threat of police raids it entailed. Apart from doling out warnings, though, the Kashi Sangeet Kalakar Sangh did little to protect its women members, preferring instead to distance itself from such cases.

Battling police harassment, lack of patrons, bullying by hooligans and criminals, and apathy from their representatives, tawaifs in Banaras tried reinventing themselves. But, by the 1960s, the choices before them were limited.

Cinema was increasingly out of reach. The domination of tawaif voices in film music had ended with the emergence of Lata Mangeshkar as the pre-eminent playback singer. Along with her talented sibling Asha Bhosle, who joined the industry a bit later, she monopolised film music to such an overwhelming extent that it left little room for other female voices to emerge and make a mark.

On screen too, very few actresses from tawaif backgrounds were able to achieve the success that their predecessors had enjoyed even a decade ago. The social taboo against 'respectable' women joining cinema was fast eroding, and many of the new generation of actresses came from English-educated, middle-class backgrounds. They filled the cultural requirement for roles that were being written in Hindi films for the heroine—young, college-educated, 'modern'. This translated to being alluringly westernised but safely rooted in traditional values, and very much a product of the new middle class of independent India.

There were exceptions, of course. The hugely popular Nargis, for example, came from a courtesan background. An exceptionally gifted actor, she essayed a variety of roles and was the trendsetter for the emergence of the modern middle-class persona of the heroine in Hindi films. Not everyone was able to scale these heights.

Asghari tells me about Kumkum, 'She was the daughter of Mannan Jan's beautiful younger sister Bittan, who lived in Patna. Kumkum had learnt kathak from Pandit Shambhu Maharaj and was a very good dancer. But Mannan Jan did not put her in our line. Instead, after Nirmala got married, she took Kumkum to Bombay to try her luck in Hindi films. But much to her disappointment, Kumkum never really made it as a top-line heroine.'

Although Kumkum did appear as female lead in a few films, like *Mr. X in Bombay* (1964), *Raja aur Runk* (1968) and *Jalte Badan* (1973), she is best remembered for her roles as dancer, supporting cast and as second lead in films like *Mother India* (1957), *Aankhein* (1968), *Geet* (1970), *Aan Baan* (1972) and *Lalkaar* (1972). She was also lead in the first-ever film to be made in Bhojpuri, *Ganga Maiyya Tohe Piyari Chadhaibo* (1962), which not only proved to be a commercial success but also garnered critical appreciation for its theme of widow remarriage.

'Padma Khanna too belonged to Banaras and left a mark in Hindi films,' Asghari tells me. She's an actor many old timers like her take pride in. 'She was a Ramjani and a trained kathak dancer. Her family lived in Chhatte Taley where several tawaifs had their kothas.'

Padma Khanna appeared most often in Hindi films as a dancer or second lead but could never make it as a heroine. Her most notable appearances were in the commercial success *Johny Mera Naam* (1970) in which she played the role of a cabaret dancer, and the critically acclaimed *Saudagar* (1973), starring Nutan and Amitabh Bachchan, with Padma in the second lead.

'I got many offers at that time to act in films,' Asghari says, turning the spotlight back to herself. 'People said, "Kumkum and Padma are dust in comparison to you. Your beauty, talent and vivacity will take Bombay by storm." I did dance for a couple of Bhojpuri films. The shooting was in Banaras itself, which was convenient. But much as I was tempted to try my luck in Bombay, ultimately I decided not to go.'

'And why was that?' I ask, surprised that vain Asghari had let go of a chance to immortalise her beauty on film.

'Who would have looked after the large army of dependents that I fed, clothed and provided shelter to if I had taken off to Bombay? Your friend, who now seems to suffer from complete amnesia about the past, had just begun to learn music. I had never wanted her to become a tawaif. Her looks have improved marginally now but, as a youngster, she was fat, dark and ugly. Amma and I had decided to groom Ghafuran for the line and get your friend married.

'But Allah! The pandemonium and drama! She stopped eating, fell ill and cried non-stop. Even that silly twit Ghafuran fell for the ruse. Becoming all noble and self-sacrificing, she declared that she did not wish to become a tawaif, and the family should groom her sister instead. My mother gave in finally, and since I never went against her decisions, I too had to agree,' Asghari recounts your first victory over life.

'So with bai sahib learning how to sing and dance, how could I have gone off to Bombay? Who would have paid for her lessons?' Bitterness choking her voice, Asghari spits out her words.

'There was no guarantee that I would get work in Bombay as soon as I arrived. I would have had to spend on my stay and upkeep. What would have happened to the huge households in Banaras and Bhabua that were completely dependent on me for survival? I might choose not to talk much about all that I have done for the family. Unlike someone we know. But, believe me, I have sacrificed my fair share of dreams at the altar of family responsibility.'

I am at a loss for words that might comfort this ailing and frail woman sitting on the steps of the very kotha that she had once presided over like a queen. I don't know how to tell her that her story is not unique. Their prospects in cinema restricted mostly to low-paying roles as dancers and supporting cast, most tawaifs were unwilling to risk the security of a known, if increasingly difficult, profession for the unknown hazards of starting afresh at the bottom of a new industry. Many of them prefer to look back at that decision in terms of their responsibility towards their families.

Several tawaifs began to look for other doors to open, other vistas to explore. The phenomenal success of Shakila Bano Bhopali in the late 1950s as a qawwali singer—crafting a new idiom for a genre which till then had been performed mainly by men in primarily devotional contexts—provided many tawaifs from across northern India an opportunity to refashion their persona and music.

Characterised by a flamboyant theatricality, Shakila Bano's qawwali performances combined popular music, glamour and entertainment in equal measure. Mostly romantic in content, her presentations came packaged as lavishly designed stage shows, with Shakila herself as the highlight. Dressed in shimmering costumes complemented by heavy jewellery and stage make-up, Shakila would set up her performance as an interactive dialogue with the audience, interlacing her singing with witty banter, flirtatious jokes and enactment of the verse with facial expressions and hand movements. She is also credited with popularising the staging of shows in the form of a qawwali competition between her and a male qawwal, each singer responding in verse to the couplet sung by the other; the premium being on impromptu poetry composition, quick repartee and play of words.

Shakila borrowed liberally from the performativity of the mujra. Her genius lay in successfully evoking the glamour, drama and erotic charge associated with the tawaif's performance, but displacing it safely to the anonymous vastness of a ticketed proscenium stage show. Her success held hope for others. From Delhi-based Chanchal Bharati, a leading tawaif from Mumtaz Choudharayin's family, to Talat Bano and Saba Parveen of Banaras and Mannan Jan of Jaunpur, several tawaifs across northern India contributed from the 1960s onwards to the fashioning of a popular, commercially successful, new idiom in qawwali performance.

A rickshaw bell rings outside. It is followed by the scramble of feet disembarking and raised voices of a woman and man arguing over the rickshaw fare. 'That sounds like Rajjo, squabbling as usual over 50 paise with a rickshaw-puller. She is such a miser!' remarks Asghari, getting up and opening the door wider. Sure enough, dragging a big bundle that appears to be stuffed with clothes, Rajjo staggers inside.

'The daughters-in-law have finally thrown you out, have they?' asks Asghari by way of greeting.

Never one to miss a repartee, Rajjo is quick to respond, 'I heard you were in Banaras scouting for young beauties to set up shop, so came by to try my luck.'

Smiling at me, she embraces her cousin warmly and enquires about her health. The bundle that she carries is curtain fabric that she has bought on your behalf at wholesale rate from a cloth-dealer and former lover. Naeem is reaching tomorrow morning; he will stitch new curtains for your home well in time for Meenu's wedding.

'You came alone, all the way from Pandeypur, at this time of the night to drop some silly curtains?' I sense grudging admiration in Asghari's voice. She is fearless herself, and has little patience with the feminine terrors of the outside that you have instilled in your daughters as part of respectable upbringing. Clearly, Rajjo is a woman after Asghari's own heart.

Tossing her a charming grin, Rajjo replies, 'Aapa, since when did tawaifs shrink from the night? We have dared to venture into lands that the angels had long forsaken. In my days, when invited to perform, I never thought twice about taking off to the most wretched places no one else had heard about.'

Rajjo began her career as a tawaif in Banaras a few years before you joined the profession. She subsequently made a name for herself in qawwali singing as Raziya Bano Banaraswali during the 1960s and '70s. She lingers with us on the steps, chatting about those days.

'I joined the kotha line when I was very young but left after I had my first child. I didn't want him to grow up with the stigma of being a tawaif's son,' Rajjo says. 'Qawwali singing was very popular then. With fewer people inviting tawaifs to perform at family celebrations, space was created for programmes featuring women qawwallas. So I too decided to try my luck at it. I requested a very famous male qawwal from Banaras, Ishaq Anwar, to teach me. I already knew music and sang ghazals and the like. He taught me how ghazal and other song types, like naat, were rendered in qawwali form.'

Rajjo performed extensively in Madhya Pradesh, Bihar and UP in stage shows, wedding celebrations, temples and Sufi shrines. 'I had my own qawwali party. Other than me, there was one harmonium, banjo, naal and dholak player each. They were all men, including the chorus singers, one of whom would also play the khanjari, tambourine.

'Qawwali singers were in regular contact with poets. They wrote original verses for us to sing, of course, but also adapted and rewrote film songs popular at that time. There was always a great demand from the audience for that sort of thing. Very often, our regular poets accompanied us to programmes to be able to write on-the-spot repartees.'

Qawwali programmes were all-night affairs, Rajjo says, beginning at around 10 p.m. and continuing until dawn. The most popular qawwali format featuring women singers was that of sawal–jawab, literally question and answer, in the form of a musical bout, or dangal, between a female and male qawwal. Mostly featuring romantic content, the focus of these musical contests was on a qawwali singer's repertoire of ready verses to match her rival's as also quick wittedness and felicity with flirtatious repartee. Women qawwals, recognised as the main draw of these shows, were paid more than their male counterparts.

'At temples, we would adapt bhajans to qawwali singing. For instance, if we were at a Devi temple, and the male qawwal sang a bhajan dedicated to the Devi, I would have to reply with another bhajan in praise of the Devi. At Sufi shrines, we would sing hamd, naat and manqabat.

'At both such places, however, around one or two o'clock at night, we would shift to ishqiya, romantic, singing. Otherwise, how would we hold the public's attention? If we sang only bhajans and naats all night long, the public would have walked away. So, when we noticed the audience getting restless, we began singing romantic songs and they paid full attention again. The male qawwal sang first. The audience was most interested in the response of the female singer. My poet would be ready with a fitting verse. I sang and interspersed the verses with tongue-in-cheek banter. I was known for my humorous replies. The entire night passed in this "battle" between the qawwals.'

Rajjo chuckles at what are obviously happy memories. Her laughter is infectious and I find myself smiling back. The only person who looks unhappy and bored is Asghari. Deciding that Rajjo has said enough, she steers the conversation back to herself, 'Many people had suggested that I too take up qawwali, but where was the time?' Taking the hint, Rajjo excuses herself and goes upstairs.

'In those years I travelled a lot—Tinsukhia, Dibrugarh, Asansol, Calcutta, Sitarampur, Koderma, Gaya—you name any place in Assam, Bengal and Bihar, I have been there,' Asghari says. 'Your friend and Ghafuran accompanied us wherever we went. As did my accompanists, who taught your friend as well, so that her musical education was not disrupted. Their presence added to the cost, train tickets, food, everything. But I never grudged the money spent on family.

'My popularity as a tawaif was such that I could not stay anywhere for long. As soon as I disembarked from a train, crowds of admirers gathered at the station itself for a glimpse of me. Knives would come out between rivals for my attention, and many a time the police had to escort us away just to bring order. I have come close to losing my life.

'During my first visit to Assam, I was in Dibrugarh. We stayed at the home of three brothers—Babu Khan, Badshah Khan and Bundu Khan. They were contactors and very well off. But then all three decided to fall in love with me and began fighting among themselves! Fed up, I moved out of their house. This was just after the war with China. We were staying close to the banks of the Brahmaputra. I was invited to perform at some army celebration and caught the fancy of the colonel posted there. He just went mad over me!

'*Ab hum jayein toh kidhar jayein? Murat ek aur chahne wale hazar!* Now, with whom should I have gone? One beauty mobbed by a thousand admirers! And so I ran away from Dibrugarh. When we reached Asansol, the men of Babu Khan and the colonel followed us there too. They each offered my mother Rs 2 lakh for me, but she refused.'

Asghari's reinvention of herself as an itinerant tawaif, travelling in search of patrons to distant places, relatively untouched by the implementation of SITA, mirrored an older history. In the eighteenth and early nineteenth century, after the collapse of the Mughal empire, tawaifs and other entertainers, originally from Delhi, had moved with their deras—consisting of family members, servants and accompanists—from one town to another, seeking livelihood. Asghari's family was not alone in falling upon old traditions to survive hostile times. Several tawaif families in Banaras had begun following this practice.

When a dera reached a new place, Asghari tells me, they would rent a place to stay. Everywhere, there were some known tawaifs to help out. A dera could stay at a place for a few weeks or months, and if business was good, even a year or two. But wherever they were, tawaifs made it a point to return to their city or town for the two months of the lagan, or wedding season. There was good money to be made by performing at weddings in the rural hinterland of eastern UP and Bihar. For the rest of the year they would be on the move again from one town to another.

Asghari talks about towns like Muzzafarpur in north-eastern Bihar and Sitarampur in West Bengal that provided sanctuary and livelihood to itinerant tawaifs. Located close to the industrial centre of Asansol, Sitarampur was one of the earliest coal-mining towns in colonial India to attract migrant workers, businessmen, investors and contractors from across the country. Tawaifs and prostitutes too were an intrinsic part of its population, living in a large area of the town called Baijipara, bai-ji's neighbourhood. It was a favoured destination of tawaifs like Asghari, who visited Sitarampur regularly.

'During my time, there were 400 or more tawaifs in Sitarampur,' Asghari says. 'They were from all over. While many lived there on a permanent basis, others like me visited during festive occasions, like Durga puja, when work peaked. We would also be invited to programmes in Asansol and other neighbouring towns.'

Asghari talks about a jalsa, or music programme, organised by the tawaifs in Sitarampur to gather funds for flood relief work in West Bengal. All the money collected from the audience as inam was to be donated to the relief fund. Donations were also sought from regular visitors to the kothas.

'I was in Sitarampur at that time,' Asghari recalls. 'The jalsa took place out in the open on the main road. A stage was erected for the tawaifs to perform on. I was a bit nervous about performing with 400 tawaifs as competition. Allah is always watching and so I cannot lie, but when I began my performance by singing a rashtriya geet, patriotic song—*Aaj zaroorat aa pahunchi hai Bharat ki santan ki, apne watan ke liye laga do bazi apni jan ki*; India today has given a call to its children, Let's wager our all for our beloved country—the audience burst into thunderous applause! I relaxed then.

'The song was a great hit. A lot of money was collected only on the basis of that song. The audience would just not let me leave the stage. I had to beg them finally to allow the other tawaifs to perform too.' With an exaggerated sigh of modesty, Asghari says, 'I have never claimed to be great. It is Allah alone who bestows success. And He has always been kind to me.'

Buoyed by memories of victory and accolades, Asghari is in a mood to talk. She tells me about Muzaffarpur. For long regarded as a mofussil backwater in comparison to better-known Gaya, which had an old tawaif tradition with its own distinctive style of thumri singing, Muzaffarpur came into its own as a tawaif centre by the late 1950s. It was in this period that tawaifs fleeing SITA, especially those from Banaras and other towns in eastern UP, began making their way to Chaturbhuj Sthan, the courtesan's quarters of Muzaffarpur.

A prosperous town and the cultural capital of Maithil-speaking northeast Bihar, strangely, Muzaffarpur seems to have escaped the stranglehold of nationalist morality for long, despite the presence of a sizeable and influential educated middle class. In the 1960s, the town boasted of society gayaki, a musical genre comprised in the main of simply written, easily accessible but literary geets, songs and ghazals in Hindi and Urdu. Associated closely with tawaif performers, society gayaki mehfils were extremely popular with the wealthy. Women too were often a part of the audience, and it was not unusual for entire families to be present at society gayaki mehfils organised to celebrate marriages, birthday parties, wedding anniversaries and other such functions.

The brightest star of Muzaffarpur's music culture was undoubtedly Panna, an unknown tawaif from Banaras, who had risen to dizzying stardom in her new home in Chaturbhuj Sthan. Said to be the genius behind the forging of society gayaki, Panna was a legend in Muzaffarpur. When the first prime minister of India, Jawaharlal Nehru, visited the town in the 1960s, she was invited to perform before him the very best that Muzzafarpur had to offer musically.

'At the height of her career, Panna left Muzaffarpur and migrated to England, where her two daughters were doctors,' Asghari reminisces. 'When I reached the town, everyone said, "A second Panna has arrived! If anyone can fill the void left by her, it is Asghari." Overnight, I became a sensation. Besides my usual repertoire of songs in Urdu, Hindi and Bhojpuri, I learnt to sing in Maithil too, just like Panna used to, for landholding Rajput and Bhumihar patrons in the villages. I was much in demand with them.

'I also learnt the geets and ghazals that were such a staple of society gayaki. Keeping in mind the fact that families, including respectable women, would be present at such functions, one had to be careful about the choice of songs and also the manner in which one performed. Everything had to be decent and in good taste. No cheap pelvic thrusts, bosom-heaving and double-meaning songs. Sometimes, not just the men in the audience but even women would dance at my cajoling. I was very popular with them. Of course, most men present were in love with me but, at such functions, I was careful to pay greater attention to their womenfolk. Just like Panna had in the past.'

'Wasn't it in Muzaffarpur, aapa, that you first met Siddiq bhai?' Your voice echoes in the dark cavernous staircase. You slowly plod down the stairs.

Asghari rises to the bait. 'Yes, I met Siddiq in Muzaffarpur. He was an accomplished tabla player and joined me because I needed one. What of that?' she hisses.

I have heard about Siddiq from you. In your narrative, he is the nightmare of every tawaif household: a good-for-nothing parasite who entrapped Asghari with his sweet words of flattery and declarations of undying love. You hold him responsible for the unprecedented and alarmingly frequent quarrels that began taking place between your sister and mother. Instigating a besotted Asghari against her own family, Siddiq convinced her that she was being exploited by her mother whose real loyalties lay with her younger daughters. Always jealous about sharing her mother with her half-sisters, Asghari now turned against Teema, questioning her financial control over her earnings, casting suspicion on her every decision. It didn't help matters that Siddiq, an alcoholic himself, also encouraged Asghari to drink daily, sometimes even through the day. Teema would object and there would be more fights.

Desperate to be rid of Siddiq, Teema had cut short Asghari's stay in Muzaffarpur and brought her back to Banaras. Siddiq, much to her consternation, followed them. No amount of insults from Teema seemed to have any effect upon him. On the contrary, her harsh words seemed to egg him on even further in his efforts to distance Asghari from her family.

'He destroyed our home. My sister, who till then had never dared to question any of amma's decisions, leave alone raise her voice against her, now thought nothing of shouting at her in front of even strangers,' you had said. 'Drunk out of her senses and blinded by her infatuation for Siddiq, aapa began grilling amma on a daily basis about household accounts and insulting her, without ever showing remorse. Amma tried to deal with her with utmost patience.'

Worried about the dark hole that Asghari was digging for herself, Teema swallowed her pride for a long time and tried to din sense into her. One day, instigated by Siddiq, who now virtually lived in the kotha, a drunk Asghari accused the family of siphoning away her hard-earned money and ordered everyone except Teema to pack their bags and leave. When an elderly relative tried to intervene and calm her down, Asghari hurled filthy abuses at him.

Shocked, Teema sternly ordered her to apologise. Turning on her in blind fury, Asghari hit her mother. Everyone present was stunned.

'Something snapped inside amma,' you had said, recalling Teema's pain with sadness. 'Without a moment's hesitation, she caught aapa's hand in a vice-like grip and twisting it behind her, she gave her a stinging slap across her face. Amma was a very strong woman even at that age. Aapa was no match for her. Then, catching hold of aapa's long hair, amma dragged her out of the kotha and threw her out on the street in full public view. Next, she threw out a cowering Siddiq and aapa's belongings, including all her jewellery, and shut the door behind her. Aapa raged and ranted outside for a long time, demanding to be let in. But amma was unmoved. She was a true deraydar. When she decided upon a course of action, no matter how painful its execution, she would see it through. A renegade elephant has to be shot dead by its mahout to stop him from causing further destruction. A renegade tawaif similarly has to be given up for dead by her loved ones to prevent further damage to the family.'

You, Ghafuran and Pyaari have all narrated to me this painful family history before. Tonight, I hear Asghari's version of the events. Furious at your ham-handed attempt to resurrect the memory of Siddiq, Asghari launches into a bitter tirade against the family, and even Teema.

'I know what you say about Siddiq behind my back,' she confronts you. 'But had I no right to be happy with the man I loved? I was amma's favourite daughter as long as I dutifully sold myself every night to wealthy men who felt no love for me and whom I did not love. But as soon as I fell genuinely in love with a man who loved me in return, amma began behaving as if I had committed some great crime. It is true that Siddiq was not rich. Yes, I supported him financially. For amma and all of you, those were reasons enough to hate him. Amma never spared a thought for my needs. I was getting older by the day. My earning years were limited. Once the line-up of rich lovers dried up, who would comfort me in my lonely years? Didn't I have a right to have a loving man by my side in my old age?'

'You had all the right, aapa, to find a loving companion for yourself,' you respond in a surprisingly gentle voice. 'No one grudged you your happiness, least of all amma. You know as well as I that she loved you the most among all her children. The problem was with your choice of companion. Amma had seen life. She knew Siddiq bhai was unworthy of your love. Where is he now when you most need someone by your side? Where has he been all these difficult years? Didn't he, as amma had said he would, disappear once you stopped performing and your savings dried up?'

I shudder at the harshness of your words, somehow sharper for the softness of your tone. Asghari looks unmoved. Getting to her feet and tossing her head imperiously, she gives you a scathing look. 'Gloat if you must but at the least tell the whole truth. You know as well as I of Siddiq's accident. It is a miracle he survived after being run down by a speeding car. He has been bedridden for more years than I can remember. He went back to his family because he did not wish to be a burden on me. Without any regular earnings, how could I have borne the expense of his medical treatment? I am happy for his sake that his sons are good, hard-working boys, who not only took their father back with good grace but have spared no effort in taking care of him. And now, if you don't mind, I am going up to bed.'

As you look on silently, Asghari makes her way slowly up the stairs of her former kotha. Once you are sure that she is safely out of earshot, you turn to me and say, 'I don't have the heart to say anything to aapa, given her poor health. But someone should ask her why she had no savings left so early on in her retirement. What happened to all the jewellery and land that amma had been wise enough to buy for her while the going was good? Siddiq ate everything away. He ruined aapa, left her a pauper and she still wishes him well! Love is truly, truly blind!'

CHAPTER 28

Your Story

THE BLOW SLICES THROUGH THE joyous singing—unexpected, sharp and brutal. It breaks Shama's nose, letting loose a thick, dark, bloody trickle. She cries out in pain, and your aunts, cousins, nieces and sundry female relatives assembled in the visitors' room fall into shocked silence. Amjad raises his hand again. This time, you spring up and hold his wrist in a strong grip.

'That's enough, Amjad! What do you think you are doing? Go and join the men on the terrace at once,' you snap at your son-in-law.

Amjad looks shocked. It's obvious that he is unused to being rebuked, especially by you. A mountain of a man, over six feet tall and bulky, his bulldog face with its hanging jowls twists into a thunderous scowl. But he turns around and walks out with heavy, menacing steps.

His mother, however, decides that your challenge to her son's authority cannot be allowed to go uncontested. As big-made as her son, she cuts an intimidating figure of unrelieved piety in her widow's plain, black sari and a rosary in hand.

'Baji, sister, you shouldn't have come between husband and wife,' says she angrily. 'I never do. Your Shama can vouchsafe for the fact that my Amjad is a good husband. But he lives by his rules. He does not like women in his house singing and dancing the way Shama was doing just now. She knows he is strict about these things. So why provoke his anger?'

Drawing yourself up to full height, with your shoulders thrown back, you hear her out with an impassive face. Your answer is icily polite and unrepentant, 'I wish you *had* come between husband and wife much earlier. Shama is your daughter-in-law. You have some responsibilities towards her too. Had you stopped Amjad at the first go, perhaps

I wouldn't have had to protect my daughter from him today. And this is not Amjad's house but mine. As far as I can see, Shama broke no decorum by joining in the singing to celebrate her sister's wedding. If you and your son have objections, she will not sing again. But I will not allow anyone to raise a hand at either of my daughters. Now if you don't mind, let's get on with the celebrations.'

You look beautiful today. Dressed in a yellow sari with a maroon border, you wear matching yellow and maroon glass bangles. Yellow suits you; it makes your dusky skin glow a burnished gold. As does the hauteur with which you quell Shama's mother-in-law. I am finally seeing the part of you that proudly belongs to your tawaif past.

You settle down protectively next to a cowering Shama, and bring back on track the disrupted celebration of Meenu's haldi, turmeric, ceremony. Playing the dholak, you exhort your relatives to resume singing. Whispering and gossiping, they take time to respond, but Sheem gets up and sportingly begins dancing. Slowly, the others join in too. Meenu—looking pretty in the yellow clothes worn for the ceremony, with braided white-and-yellow flowers in her hair, on her forehead, in her earlobes, around her neck and wrists—becomes the centre of everyone's attention once again. Amid much revelry, the women give her a rub down with a paste made of turmeric, sandalwood powder, mustard oil and herbs.

Along with one and a quarter kilograms of uncooked rice, five pieces of jaggery, five cones filled with henna, yellow-and-red auspicious thread, kajal and missi (black powder used to darken the gums in order to make the teeth look white), the haldi used for Meenu's scrub had arrived this morning in a big platter ceremonially covered with a green silk cloth from her prospective in-laws' home in Bahraich, as per custom. In her capacity as a suhagan, married woman, Ghafuran had placed the rice and jaggery in Meenu's lap and made three knots on the yellow-and-red thread before tying it to her wrist. With no role to play in the marriage ritual as a former tawaif, you had looked on fondly from the sidelines.

Ghafuran had fed Meenu some jalebi soaked in milk, after which your daughter had untied the first knot of the auspicious thread. For the next two days, she will be fed the same ritual food, which will be followed by the untying of a knot a day. Ghafuran had then ceremonially applied the kajal and missi on Meenu's eyes and gums before putting haldi on her niece, and the assembled women had begun singing the customary, celebratory songs for the occasion.

She was followed by four other married women who too applied haldi and whispered benedictions in Meenu's ear. After them, all the other assembled women guests—married, tawaif and unmarried—had joined in the ritual.

Accompanied by much singing and dancing by the women—family members and guests—the haldi ceremony has been an intrinsic part of wedding celebrations in many parts of India, common to Hindus and Muslims alike. This is slowly changing, with Muslim families like Amjad's abjuring music and revelry that are increasingly seen as a corruption of Islamic tenets.

But you are a believer in the old ways. Ignoring the moral outrage of your more puritanical relatives, you not only observe all traditional wedding ceremonies, including those now decried as 'Hindu', you also insist upon accompanying these with music and dance appropriate to the ceremonies. You know a bewildering variety of wedding songs, and often take the lead in the group singing that nowadays fills your home and spills out into the streets.

I marvel at your calm composure in the face of an ugly situation. I am also happily surprised by your defence of your daughter and feel amazed that you should have done so in the presence of a roomful of guests. Obsessed with maintaining the status quo and keeping up appearances, you have so far turned a blind eye to the tell-tale signs of physical abuse that Shama almost always carries on her face and body.

Once the house clears out, and only immediate relatives staying at your home remain, your aunts, sisters and cousins take you to task. They all feel that you should not have rebuked your son-in-law and his mother in public. Shama will have to pay for the affront, they predict darkly.

You refuse to show remorse. For too long, you have resisted interfering in your daughter's married life, you say to them. As a mother-in-law, you have been affectionate and solicitous towards Amjad, hoping that he will eventually mend his ways. At least, thus far, he had not raised a hand at Shama in your presence. Today, he crossed even that line. As a mother, you have a duty to protect your daughters from harm, especially when it occurs in front of your eyes.

'It's all very well to talk of your duty, but we all know how fragile male ego can be. If Amjad dumps Shama in retaliation, what will you do?' Phoolmani asks unsympathetically.

As if on cue, Jawed comes up to your room and announces dramatically, 'Dulhe bhai has walked out. You all had better come!'

The news is met with consternation all around. With a triumphant 'I told you so' look, Phoolmani leads the way downstairs to the visitors' room where Amjad's mother is in the throes of a spectacular fit of fury. Alternating between threatening to follow her son back home to Saidpur and cursing Shama for being a bad wife and daughter-in-law, she turns her ire upon you, launching into a tirade about the unforgivable manner in which you have insulted her son and her.

Quivering, Shama weeps and apologises to the enraged older woman she calls 'ammi'. In between, she keeps trying Amjad's phone, but he refuses to take her calls. Now, she flings herself into your arms and demands that you apologise to her mother-in-law and husband: 'Amma you shouldn't have said what you did to him and ammi! You shouldn't have come between husband and wife,' sobbing and loudly blowing her nose, she parrots Amjad's mother. Shama reminds me of a child right now, a frightened and browbeaten little girl, convinced that her suffering is her fault.

Although you take Shama into your embrace, your gaze is set hard on the malevolent figure looming behind her. I see the coldness in your eyes and the stern line of your lips. You are furious. Yet, you prudently keep your cool. There is a wedding at hand in three days, and a houseful of guests. You cannot allow Amjad and his mother's nastiness to jeopardise Meenu's celebrations. And so, you gently shush your daughter and attempt as best as you can to soothe her mother-in-law without apologising.

Your relatives pitch in as well. After a hurried family consultation, Ghafuran, Naeem, your aunt Sakeena and her sons, Nawab and Wazir, are dispatched post-haste to Saidpur as peacemakers. They have been entrusted with the task of somehow convincing Amjad to return and play his part as your older son-in-law in Meenu's wedding. Asghari, who is recovering by the day in your care, and your cousin Rani are in charge of keeping Shama's mother-in-law fruitfully occupied with solicitous concern, flattery and pious invocations designed to appease her bruised ego and frayed temper. Even Phoolmani feels obliged to set aside her grievances for once, and join her nieces in cajoling Amjad's mother into a more conciliatory mood. Your cause is inadvertently helped by Asghari and Phoolmani's natural antipathy towards you, which makes their sympathy for Shama's mother-in-law sound genuinely sincere.

Seema goes up to check on Salma. Now eight months pregnant, on doctor's orders, she spends much of the day resting, away from wedding-related excitement. Sheem takes care of Shama. Shepherding her upstairs to your bedroom, she patiently reassures her friend and cousin that Amjad will not abandon her. Seeing their mother weep, Shama's children too have been bawling in different parts of the house, adding to the prevailing chaos. Sheem gathers them together and hushes them into calm. Rajjo takes charge of the kitchen and supervises the extended family's daughters-in-law as they get dinner ready for the relatives camped in your home.

In the midst of this family enterprise, you are busy with preparations for the mehendi, henna, ceremony scheduled for tomorrow morning. The henna that has been sent today by Meenu's prospective in-laws' family will be applied on her hands and feet as part of the customary beauty rituals. Later in the evening is the highlight of all wedding celebrations in your community: the ratjagga, an all-night session of music and dance, ending only with the call to fajr prayers at dawn.

With Madhu loyally by your side, you discuss with the men of the family the seating arrangements for the many women guests expected at the ratjagga on your terrace. The electrician is also called in to ensure there is adequate lighting for the night-long programme.

Satisfied that all is in order, Madhu and you next turn your attention to the food arrangements. Both of you confer for a long time with the cooks, the Muslim bawarchi and Hindu halwai, who between them will cater the dinner before the ratjagga. They will also prepare the wedding feast on the day of the nikah. While the predominantly non-vegetarian dishes cooked by the Muslim bawarchi are meant for your meat-eating guests, the halwai's vegetarian fare will cater to Hindu visitors who observe dietary prohibitions. This twin arrangement for food, you say, is how it's always been at celebrations in tawaif families.

It is late into the night, long after everyone else has had dinner, that you make your way wearily up the stairs. Madhu too leaves for home. Ghafuran calls to say that Amjad has finally agreed to return to Banaras early tomorrow morning. His mother, basking under Asghari, Rani and Phoolmani's collective attention, looks somewhat mollified and even manages a small smile to indicate her approval of Amjad's change of heart. Upstairs, in your room on the second floor, with her children sleeping around her and Sheem for company, Shama begins weeping hysterically upon learning of her husband's impending return.

'He is coming back to beat me up again, I know,' she wails in visible terror.

Sheem is nonplussed. 'Arrey, till a while back, you were howling buckets about being abandoned by him! Now that he has agreed to return, you are bawling about that! Make up your mind. What do you want, Shama?'

In response, Shama only cries more.

Putting your own exhaustion aside, you say with quiet authority, 'He will not lay a finger on you, I promise. We need him to be here for Meenu's wedding. Otherwise, what will people say? You don't want gossip to mar your sister's nikah, do you? Once all the celebrations are over, and Meenu leaves for her in-laws' house, we will talk about you and Amjad. Remember always that this is your home. You can stay back here if you decide not to go with him. I am with you. Now calm down and go to bed.'

Your words have a magical effect upon Shama. Curling up next to her sleeping children, she obediently shuts her eyes. Exhausted by an evening of playing counsellor and child-sitter, Sheem lies down next to her. You sit for some time, looking at your daughter, niece and grandchildren tenderly.

Your day is not yet over. You go over to Salma's room next door to make sure she is fine. Meenu, surrounded by a group of adoring friends and cousins, including Ghafuran's daughters Naseem and Shamim, is busy regaling her sister-in-law with details of the ongoing family drama amidst much muffled giggling. She falls guiltily silent when you enter the room. Pretending that you haven't heard their gossip, you ask Salma how she is doing. Satisfied by her answer, you advise Meenu and the other girls to go to bed. It's late and Meenu needs to sleep well to look her best for her wedding. The girls begin giggling at this but Meenu's eyes well up.

Putting her arms around you, she begins crying, 'Who will look after you, amma, once I am gone?'

I see tears brimming in your eyes before you quickly blink them away. Gently kissing Meenu on her forehead, you smooth back her hair, 'Don't worry about me, my little one. Salma will take care of me. Won't you, Salma?' Your daughter-in-law vigorously nods affirmation.

'Don't worry about amma,' Salma reassures Meenu. 'I am there. I will take good care of her.'

Wiping your daughter's tears away, you add, 'Stop worrying or you will get dark circles under your eyes. Go to sleep now.' You kiss her again and leave the room.

Turning to me, you ask if I am up to accompanying you to the terrace. Your head is buzzing, you can't go to bed right away. I agree but suggest you eat dinner first. You haven't eaten anything since afternoon. You refuse food but agree to have instead your favourite drink—a hot glass of milk sweetened with sugar.

Up on the terrace, a gentle breeze stirs the dark silence. Faint sounds from the lanes below waft up occasionally. From somewhere in the distance comes the insomniac music of a late-night film on television. You make yourself comfortable on one of the terrace chairs and sip the hot milk.

'I did right, do you think, by standing up to Amjad and his mother?' Your question comes as a surprise. Through the afternoon and evening, you had seemed so much in control that it seems inconceivable you harboured any doubts about the rightness of your actions.

'Yes, you were absolutely in the right,' I say with stout conviction. 'As a mother, it is your duty to protect Shama from her abusive husband and mother-in-law.'

'Yes. I think so too. You know, Saba, amma always said, "No matter what the cost, a mother must always protect her children from harm." I tried not to interfere in Shama's married life. You even faulted me for it. But I always felt that, as a tawaif with no experience of the adjustments that couples make to keep a marriage going, I shouldn't be seen as a bad influence on my daughter. More so because, initially, I had other plans for Shama and agreed to her marriage with Amjad only at her insistence. I didn't want people to point fingers at me for breaking my daughter's marriage. But to hell with people! They don't give a damn if my daughter lives or dies. I do. Today, when I saw that hulk of a man hit my daughter as if she were some beast of burden, I couldn't stop myself. No matter what people say about me, it is my duty to protect my daughter from that bully husband of hers and his insufferable mother.'

I couldn't agree more. My only regret is that Shama has already been considerably damaged, both bodily and emotionally, because of the sustained abuse, but I say nothing of this to you. You will now need all support possible to stick to your resolve of being a more supportive mother to Shama.

A companionable silence descends upon us. I hear the sound of steps coming up and cross my fingers involuntarily to ward off any more unpleasant news. Two boyish-looking shadows momentarily hover at the doorway. Then, perhaps noticing us, hurriedly withdraw.

'That must be Jawed and Rafiq, Rajjo's younger son, coming up on the sly for a smoke,' you chuckle. 'Foolish boys! As if we all don't know that they smoke! Have I told you that my mother too took to smoking at a late age? Since she felt embarrassed lighting up in front of me, she would come up here for a furtive smoke. I knew, of course. I could smell the cigarette a mile off on her breath and clothes. But I always kept up the pretence of not knowing.'

'Was this when you had joined the profession and begun performing?' I ask.

'Yes,' you reply. 'Those were very difficult times for our family. Asghari aapa had moved to Bhabua after being thrown out of this house by amma. I was still learning music and not really ready to be launched into the profession. But how would the family have survived without an earning member? So, with a heavy heart, my mother initiated me into the line. I must have been only about sixteen years at that time.

'I was so young that I didn't know how to tie a sari properly! I remember that my mother took me to Kishan Maharaj's house in Kabir Chaura. He was a well-wisher of the family and respected my mother a lot. Knowing our circumstances, he tried to help out by getting me a mehfil assignment with people he knew. He fixed up a meeting with them at his home. To allay their fears that I was not some novice, he suggested that I dance a bit as demonstration of my knowledge of kathak. As soon as I got up, to my utter horror, my sari got entangled in my feet and came off! It was very embarrassing, but Kishan Maharaj saved the situation by treating it lightly and laughing. And since he showed so much confidence in me, his acquaintances signed me on for the mehfil.'

You are in the mood to talk, perhaps hoping to stave off till tomorrow morning the tension of Amjad's return and the pressures of the wedding. The initial years of your life as a young, inexperienced tawaif were difficult. You had to learn to entertain visitors to your kotha. You found the long hours spent waiting for guests tedious as a teenager. 'Like all tawaifs, I would have to dress up and wait. I would sit through the day in the first-floor room. It felt very strange initially, as if I were some doll on display.

'Most people who visited me were known acquaintances of the family. My mother was very careful not to allow unknown men or goonda-badmash entry into my kotha. She would hover around the entrance, and come up with some excuse to politely ward off undesirable visitors.

'I would get up to greet those she let in. After getting them seated, I would order tea and serve them paan. And through all this, I was supposed to keep a conversation going. But what can a sixteen-year-old girl talk about to a middle-aged stranger that he would find engaging? On Pyaari khala's advice, I began reading the newspaper daily. There was always something there that I could use for chatting with the men who visited me. Painfully aware of my limited education, I also began reading books, especially poetry. These helped immensely in entertaining guests.'

Since kothas in Banaras, with their low-paying, often rough clientele and constant insecurity of police harassment, offered limited opportunities, your mother focused on seeking out sattas, or contracts, for Rajput and Bhumihar celebrations in the countryside. There, performances by tawaifs continued to be the main attraction. Rebuffed on account of your inexperience by more discerning and well-paying patrons, she was forced to accept invitations to far-off, small village celebrations disdained by better-established tawaifs.

'There is a village called Surajgadhha beyond Patna,' you recall. 'It is very remote. Even the Rajputs there were extremely poor and rustic in their ways. I went there to perform at a wedding, but nearly starved to death on that trip. There was nothing for the baraat, wedding party, to eat except puffed rice and huge boondi laddus that were so hard that they had to be broken with stones! I would beg my poor mother to give me something edible instead. But there was nothing!

'Then there was the time when dacoits attacked a wedding party I was performing at. It was a fairly common occurrence in Bihar at that time. The village where the wedding was being held was in the back of the beyond. My mother was with me, as was abba, Shanney Khan Sahib. In the middle of the performance, the dacoits arrived in a jeep. I was so young and silly that I didn't realise who they were even though the audience around me scrambled to cover themselves with blankets!

'The dacoits ordered me to sing *Jab pyar kiya toh darna kya?* Why be afraid when you have found love? It was a very popular song those days from the film *Mughal-e-Azam*. Like a fool, I told them I didn't know that song very well but could sing, *Jab raat hai aisi matwali, toh subah ka alam kya hoga*; If the night is so intoxicating, imagine what delights the morning will bring—another song from the same film. I think of that now and laugh at my unfortunate choice of song! Anyhow, I began singing. One of the dacoits caught hold of my hand and tried to pull me towards him. I angrily pulled back my hand and shouted, "Have you lost your mind?"

'It was then that abba gestured at me to shut up and with folded hands pleaded with the dacoit to let go of me. My mother too fell at his feet, "We are just poor dancing girls," she said. "My daughter is young and doesn't know the ways of the world. Please let us go." It was only then that I realised that they were dacoits and got very frightened.

'Meanwhile, we heard shots being fired. Most of the dacoits had gone straight to the bride's house to do the looting. The remaining few had surrounded my mehfil to ensure that none of the guests went to the family's rescue. I could hear shouting and screaming coming from the house and non-stop gunshots! It was a terrifying experience.

'The dacoits who had been talking to my mother and ustad, however, were very nice to us. "Don't worry your head about all this. It has nothing to do with you. Please continue singing," they said to me. Overcoming my fear somehow, I folded my hands and pleaded with them to leave. "A girl's honour is at stake," I said to them. "The bridegroom's family will now run away without the marriage taking place. The poor girl's life will be destroyed. No one else will marry her."

'Surprisingly, the dacoits heeded my appeal, though in their own way. They took away the loot but, before leaving, forced the bridegroom to marry the bride at gunpoint. Next day, the bridegroom's father, who had hired me to perform at the wedding, refused to pay my fee! He said that since the dowry that was to come to them had been looted, there was nothing to celebrate. I was very angry. I told him to go to hell!

'I have performed in wedding mehfils with thousands of guests in the deep interiors of rural Bihar. Early on, I learnt to gauge my audience and choose my repertoire of songs accordingly. In my experience, it is very difficult to hold the interest of rustic audiences who haven't been exposed to the niceties of thumri, dadra and ghazal. For them, after performing the mandatory sehra during the mehfil on the wedding evening, I would sing a couple of popular, racy ghazals, a few dadras and bhajans, and then focus on the standard popular mix—Bhojpuri folk songs and film songs. I would interweave this with dancing with a tambourine in hand, keeping the beat fast and pacey. The audience would be very happy and say, "Oh, she sings and dances so well!"

'At the Bhairavi ki mehfil the next morning, I would begin by performing two or three Bhairavi thumris. That was mandatory. I followed this up with dadra, folk songs, bhajans and filmy songs. By noon, the sun would be blazing. Tawaifs were expected to keep performing in that heat. It was hard work. The powder, lipstick and kajal on my face would melt and run down in streaks with the perspiration. Then, mercifully, it was time for the mid-day meal and the mehfil came to a close.

'Often, people say that our money was haram, earned through illicit means. But that was simply not true. Tawaifs worked very hard for a living. Our money was more halal, lawful, than of the so-called respectable in society who earn it too often by exploiting and cheating others. After the Bhairavi mehfil in the morning, I would have to be ready to perform again in the evening.

'I have performed without a break for eight days and nights, moving from one wedding celebration to another. I hardly got any sleep during those days and tried and catch up on it during the travel itself. *Bahut mehnat kiya jata thha aur bahut mehnat ka paisa tha*; I worked very hard and the money I earned was literally by the sweat of my brow.

'We were routinely harassed by goonda-badmash. Bihar was such a rough place. It was assumed that women who sang and danced for a living were fair game for any man. Very often, Rajput landholders themselves were goonda-badmash who thought nothing of getting tawaifs picked up and raping them. I am thankful to Allah that, more often than not, I came out of such encounters unscathed.

'Goonda and badmash men are at least honest about what they want from a woman. Not like so many respectable men who treat women like dirt. My mother, as you know, had never wanted me to join this line. I insisted because I had a very different notion about the profession in my head. You might find it difficult to believe but, honestly, I had assumed that being a tawaif entailed singing and dancing, earning my own money and always having my mother by my side. I knew about sex, of course, but had never realised how central it was to being a tawaif. By the time I began performing, it was the most important part of the line.

'Amma would try to protect me by making it clear that I would sing and dance but not be available for sex. We lost many contracts on that account. And even the ones we got, while many people were decent enough to respect our wishes, there were always those who tried to get their way once we were there, as if it was their birth right to have sex with the tawaifs they hired. My mother would fight like a tigress to protect me. She was very clear that she wouldn't make me do anything I didn't want.

'I remember this village near Arrah where, even before the mehfil ended, the host made it clear that he wanted me in his bed later that night. My poor mother resisted valiantly but how much can one woman fight against a group of men armed with rifles and lathis? His men overpowered her soon enough, and began hitting her and heaping filthy abuses upon the two of us. I then decided that I could not put my mother in such mortal danger. Since I had joined this line willingly, I would have to cast aside my squeamishness about sex with strangers. But I always resented being forced against my will and resisted it till there was no option. Amma always supported me, "Don't do anything you don't want," she would say.

'To tell you the truth, once I was reconciled to that aspect of my profession, it wasn't so bad. With the right kind of men, it was even pleasurable. Most times, however, it was just indifferent. Amma had warned me early on, "Child you will experience all kinds of pleasure, but very little of one pleasure." Now I can't explain this to you in detail, but I did feel it. Most of the men who could afford tawaifs were at least in their middle age. At sixteen or seventeen years of age, I had to entertain men who were forty-five or fifty, or even older. That's a huge age difference. They were all married and were usually too weak in their bodies and set in their ways to even want to give a woman pleasure. They just knew how to take. I would then just switch off and let them do what they wanted. But as a young woman, naturally, the yearning to give and receive pleasure was there.

'After spending an entire night writhing on the bed, the next morning, I would have to sing and dance. The frustration of the night would come out in my singing and dancing. People would say admiringly, "She has so much dard, pain or yearning, in her voice! She dances with so much junoon, passion!" So, even the less-than-satisfying sex helped me evolve as a singer and dancer.'

Naturally modest, you rarely talk about yourself, your desires and feelings unprompted. And yet tonight I am enthralled by the candour of your story.

'I worked very hard on my music,' you say. 'Even after joining the profession, I diligently continued my taleem with abba, and even sought out other good teachers. I was painfully aware of my far-from-complete music education at the time I had joined the line, and was set upon learning all that I didn't know. No matter how tired I was after performing day and night at a celebration, I was punctilious about doing riyaz with abba.'

Within a few years, you began to be noticed for your singing, and to be invited by the wealthiest Rajput and Bhumihar families in eastern UP and Bihar. 'In my times, I was the highest paid tawaif in Dal Mandi,' you say with obvious pride. 'I hiked my rate to Rs 10,000 at a time when tawaifs were happy to perform for a Rs 1,000–2,000 fee. Then I raised it further to Rs 15,000 and later to Rs 20,000. I worked very hard, so I wanted to be paid accordingly.

'The speciality of my singing was that every man present at my mehfil would feel that I was singing just for him. "She is looking at me," he would whisper to the man seated next to him, who would say, "I think she is looking at me!"'

Your growing reputation as a singer was matched with respect for being serious-minded about your calling. Beyond the actual mehfil, you avoided socialising and flirting with the gathered men. Making do with your professional fees and the inam you won for your singing and dancing, unlike many other tawaifs, you resisted the temptation of using these opportunities to wheedle expensive gifts and ask for favours, since these always came with strings attached. Intimidated by your reputation, men now thought twice about forcing themselves upon you.

'Once, at the mehfil of a very influential family in Arrah, the wedding party wouldn't let me leave. There were various legislators, politicians and all kinds of other important people in the audience. They demanded that I shake hands with each one of them. Now I could have used that opportunity to promote myself and curry favour, but knowing better, I folded my hands instead and said, "Brother, I am not what you are taking me to be." They were so stunned by my straightforward reply that they backed off.

'At another wedding near Sasaram, the mehfil was held in a huge orchard. The audience was so large that there was no space to accommodate even a grain of rice on the chandani spread across the vast grounds. Many in the audience had been forced to find seating space on top of trucks parked just outside the orchard, and many more had climbed trees and were sitting on the branches like monkeys. As soon as I sang a couplet, they would shake the branches in appreciation and shower money at me from above! Believe me, it was very heady!

'What followed later that evening was not heady at all, though. Most of the men had been drinking. That was not unusual in Rajput weddings. Everyone drank. Periodically, they would fire shots in the air. This too was usual during wedding festivities. Almost all Rajputs carried firearms those days.

'At this wedding, however, two groups began fighting over me. Each wanted me to sing songs of their choice, and began competing by trying to outdo each other in the money they would give me in inam after every song. This was a great point of prestige, especially among Rajputs at mehfils—so and so has given so much and so and so has given that much. At some point, the competition got out of hand, with each side feeling slighted. They then began firing at each other. Two men died as a result. It was horrible. Worried about my safety, the hosts advised me to leave the village as soon as possible.

'I became very careful after that about not encouraging such competition. I didn't wish to compromise my dignity and safety. Even otherwise, with patrons and lovers, it never entered my head that I should make them paupers. If they gave something willingly, then good, otherwise it was okay too. I let it be. Most other tawaifs did not behave like this. All my friends and family would say, "You are an idiot. How did you let the man leave with money still in his pocket?" I would reply, "Should I have cut his pocket then?"

'I had once gone to perform at a mehfil in a village beyond Sasaram. There was this man there who was completely taken with me. And though he was not a Rajput, he was obviously very rich. He was probably a superintendent engineer or something like that. I am not sure. Whenever I sang a new couplet, he extended his hand to the manager standing behind him, who placed a wad of Rs 1,000 in his hand, which he then gave to me. In this manner, he must have given me over Rs 50,000 through the course of that evening. I thought to myself, this man has lost his head completely!

'Then perhaps he ran out of money. So he took off his ring and gave it to me. After that, he gave me his watch. Next, he handed me a gold necklace that was in his pocket and said, "Now I have nothing left to give you except the clothes that I am wearing!"

'I said, "Please keep your clothes on, otherwise there will be a breach of the mehfil's etiquette and decorum."

'When the mehfil had come to an end and everyone was departing, he came up to me and said, "It was wonderful hearing you. I am leaving now."

'I said, "Please don't go just yet."

'At this, the crowd gathered around began excitedly whispering to each other, "She is telling him to wait!" He too looked utterly delighted, probably imagining all kinds of scenarios.

'I took him away from the crowd and made him sit down. I had bundled his ring, watch and necklace in a handkerchief, which I now placed in his hand and said, "Babu sahib, you have been most generous with me and I truly appreciate all your gifts. I must humbly request you, however, to please take back your ring, watch and gold necklace."

'He was completely taken aback and asked, "Why?"

'I said, "You showed your appreciation enough for my singing by your enjoyment and wah-wah! You were very generous in showering me with money. I feel truly honoured and grateful. However, I don't expect people to take off the gold they are wearing to give to me. I don't accept such gifts."

'Haughtily he said, "I don't take back things that I have given away."

'I said, "You will have to take back your ring, watch and necklace. I don't wish to be cursed by your family. They will blame me when you return home empty-handed. They are bound to assume that I extracted all this from you and will no doubt wish me ill."

'My mother wasn't angry when I returned the man's jewellery and watch to him, but the ustads were quite upset, "You grandly gave his gifts back. We too had a share in them." They were right, of course. Tawaifs did have to share a part of their earnings with ustads; mostly it was cash but sometimes, as in this crazy fellow's case, it could also be gold and silver. But how could I have kept a necklace that he had probably taken off his wife's neck? Saba, it is because I did not earn the curses of wives that life, on the whole, has been kind to me. As a woman myself, I did not want to be the cause of another woman's suffering.

'I know that I am not bathed in milk and blameless. You have faulted me about my behaviour with Salma and Shama. Maybe I have failed them at times and added to their distress. But as Allah is my witness, I have wanted to be a good mother-in-law and mother. But circumstances have not always allowed me to do my best. The compulsions of our circumstances, Saba, sometimes make us act in a way that, in better times, we might not have done. I can honestly say that I have never wished any woman ill.

'Even when I became involved with Maheshwar Singh, I was always very careful never to encroach upon the rights of his wife. You might say that I shouldn't have become the mistress of a married man if I was so concerned about his wife. But what choice did I have? As a tawaif, I was expected to provide sexual services to men besides music and dance. Rather than be passed around like a box of sweets from one man to another, I preferred to be the mistress of one person. Maheshwar Singh's name elicited both fear and respect. Being his mistress protected me from the unwelcome advances of other men. Free of the constant tension of warding off unwanted attention, I could single-mindedly focus upon excelling in my singing career.

'I made sure, however, to give the greatest respect to his wife. Her name was Lachchi, although I always called her didi. She must have resented me in the beginning. Which wife would like her husband to be involved with another woman? But once she got to know me, we began to get along very well. We would meet, I would visit their home, eat there, stay there but I took care not to overstep boundaries. Both she and Maheshwar Singh were around the same age and nearly twenty-five years older than me. She had seen many mistresses come and go from her husband's life. But she always said that I was different.

'If I was staying in their house, I would always insist that he spent the nights with her. I never tried to throw my weight around and behave like the mistress of the house, bossing over servants, giving orders. I knew my place and was at peace with it. I was just Maheshwar Singh's lover. She, as his wife, was the mistress of the house, vested with the power to run it as she willed. I had no desire to usurp that. If she had a quarrel with Maheshwar Singh, I would take her side. Likewise, she would stand by me if I had a fight with him over something. Neither of us tried to use the other's quarrel to score points. Maheshwar Singh would often complain that we ganged up against him.

'If he was staying at my place, then after three days, my mother would sternly tell me to send him home. At that age, I obviously wanted him to stay with me not just for three days but for much longer. But my mother would advise me to never separate him from his family. *Woh asra dekhti hogi*; She must be waiting for him, my mother would say. *Uski aah padegi to tum kabhi panap nahi sakogi*; Her sighs will not let you prosper. I would then tell him to leave immediately.'

As I hear you speak about your relationship with Maheshwar Singh's wife, I think of your mother. There are striking similarities between

Teema's relationship with Daya Singh and yours with Maheshwar Singh, but equally strong differences in the relationships the two of you shared with the wives of your respective lovers. Teema guided you to be more empathetic towards your lover's wife, and yet the circumstances of her own life had not allowed her the choice of showing Moolan similar consideration. Perhaps Teema's sympathy for Lachchi arose out of a desire to make up for that lapse. Or perhaps it came from her pain at being abandoned by Daya Singh for a much younger lover.

You continue with the story: 'Maheshwar Singh traded in coal, which he brought in from the collieries in Dhanbad. He also ran trucks and was a forest contractor. His wife and children mostly lived in Banaras, since his business was based here. The rest of his family was in Sasaram. He had seven brothers. They managed the family's lands and properties. They had vast tracts of land. They were a very important and influential family of the area. Their word was law in Sasaram.

'Much before I got to know him, Maheshwar Singh and three of his brothers, Someshwar Singh, Shivaadhar Singh and Bachan Singh, had been sentenced to death on murder charges. Their family apparently had a dispute with some backward caste members in their area, who had therefore murdered one of Maheshwar Singh's brothers, Tilakdhaari Singh. In retaliation, Maheshwar Singh and his brothers murdered thirteen people of the backward community. While all of them together launched the attack, it was Maheshwar Singh's eldest brother, Someshwar Singh, who killed all thirteen. He used neither gun nor bullet but a sword. This was as their mother had wanted. On hearing the news of Tilakdhaari Singh's death, she had ordered Someshwar Singh to repay his debt for mother's milk by putting to the sword all those who had snatched her son from her. "They have spilled my son's blood. I want blood for blood. I will find peace only when I see his murderers' blood on your sword."

'And so the brothers wiped out an entire family, except a woman and her little daughter. It was she who testified against them during the trial. After committing the murders, they first went to their mother and put the blood-stained sword at her feet. Then they marched off to the police station and announced to the darogah, station house officer, that they had committed murder. The darogah said, "That's alright, babu sahib. Please be seated. This is not a major issue for you to worry about. Just how many people have you murdered?" Someshwar Singh said, "Thirteen." The darogah nearly fell off his chair in shock.

'Someshwar Singh, Maheshwar Singh and their two other brothers were then sentenced to death. Their family, however, was very close to the Congress leader Jagjivan Ram. He belonged to Sasaram too. They addressed him as babu-ji and he valued their support. He helped to get them released.'

Better versed than I in the realpolitik of caste dynamics in rural Bihar, you do not find it ironic that a Dalit leader like Jagjivan Ram, espousing the cause of social justice in his public utterances, might have helped the upper-caste Rajput family of Maheshwar Singh go scot free in the murder of thirteen backward caste members. 'Caste wars are a reality of Bihar. But personal loyalties are more important and often override all other considerations,' you say with a shrug.

'Maheshwar Singh was not like his brothers. He was the most educated in his family. Education does make a difference,' you say, reiterating a firmly held belief. 'The other brothers were violent and boorish in their ways. They were involved in all kinds of criminal activities, murder, kidnapping for ransom, etc. People called them mafia dons, but since they enjoyed political patronage, the police were scared to touch them. They were known to have lower-caste women picked up. And they misbehaved with tawaifs too.

'There was this tawaif in Banaras called Babita. She was very popular at that time. Babita was involved with a very good man. He was also a Rajput from Sasaram. They were, however, lower in status to Maheshwar Singh's family. The family would often invite me to perform at their functions and were always very respectful with me. Babita and I were friends. She was a mediocre singer but a very good dancer.

'Once, she was invited to perform at a family function organised by Someshwar Singh. This incident took place a couple of years before I got involved with Maheshwar Singh. Babita initially accepted the invitation but later got cold feet when she heard stories of the way the men in that family misbehaved with tawaifs. She got her Rajput lover to write a letter to Someshwar Singh saying that she would not be able to come and perform at his function. *Bas iss par baat badh gayi*; The situation turned bad from here. How dare she refuse to perform? Their Rajput pride was wounded. That's how fragile their sense of prestige was—it could be hurt by the refusal of a tawaif to perform for them! They threatened to burn down Babita's house in Banaras and kill her lover's entire family if she didn't come as promised.

'To avert a bloodbath, Babita agreed to go, but she went under police protection arranged by her lover. The police darogah was nervous and embarrassed about having to escort Babita to babu sahib's house and asked forgiveness of Someshwar Singh as soon as they reached, saying that he was just following orders. Someshwar Singh and his brothers reassured the darogah that they understood his predicament and were not going to harm him or his men. They were, however, furious with Babita for bringing the police with her. She had to be shown her aukat, status.

'They said nothing to her just then. She began dancing. The mehfil was milling with Rajputs from all over Bihar. Mid-performance, Someshwar Singh and his brothers went up on the stage and stripped Babita of her sari. The entire mehfil fell silent. The police escort just looked on helplessly. Then, at gunpoint, the brothers made her dance naked in front of everyone. Abba was there. He was one of the ustads playing with Babita. He told me the entire story. Babita's mother fell at Someshwar Singh's feet and asked forgiveness for her daughter. The ustads too begged him to spare the girl as did the two other tawaifs who had also been invited to perform.

'Someshwar Singh said to them, "*Yeh kya soch kar police darogah sath le kar ayee thhi*; What did she think she was doing by getting a police escort? What can the police do to us? We are the law here." They would probably have killed Babita had some Rajputs present, who also knew her lover, not interceded. Eventually, they let her off.

'Maheshwar Singh wasn't like his brothers at all. He was respectful to women and always treated me with consideration. During an argument, if I was in the right, he would hear me out quietly and make amends. Not like most other men who are convinced that they are always right and hate being corrected by women. He was also very proud of my success as a singer, and never came in the way of my work. Unlike many smaller men who are insecure about their women, he was too confident to feel threatened by the admiration I received from others. Moreover, he trusted me completely. I never broke his trust and was faithful to him as long as he lived.

'I cared a lot for Maheshwar Singh. Perhaps I loved him for his sharafat, decency, or perhaps because he was the father of my three children. *Kis cheez par marte thhe yeh hamein nahi pata*; Why I loved him so much I myself don't know. He was so much older than me. But he had love, concern and respect for me and my family.

'Mindful of the huge age difference between us, he tried to ensure a comfortable future for me. He helped in constructing the house in Bhabua, although the land for it was bought with money I had earned. He also bought agricultural land for me in Palakh. Over the years, he gifted me gold jewellery, all of which has now gone to my daughters and daughter-in-law.

'Besides, he gave me money every month for running the house. He was very particular about never being late. Once, he had gone to Calcutta and got stuck there for longer than he had anticipated. So, he sent his driver all the way back to Banaras to reach me the money on time. He had such a high sense of responsibility. He paid for my children's education and their other expenses. All the foodgrain came from his lands. Worried about my safety, he gave me a car and a driver for travel. Everyone recognised the white Ambassador car as his, and so I was never troubled even in remote, dacoit-infested places.

'He was one of the few people in my life who gave me love, money, respect and material security, expecting nothing in return, except love and faithfulness. Most others in my life, including my own family, only knew how to take. Like all tawaif families, mine too treated daughters as money-making machines.

'At one time, I was counted as the premier tawaif of Banaras, who earned Rs 6 lakh altogether every wedding season. My major earnings came from performing at weddings and other celebrations outside Banaras. I also earned by performing at my own kotha when I wasn't travelling. My mother handled all my money. Out of these earnings, a part went to the accompanists as their payment. Some of it was spent on buying new clothes and so on for me and the family, household expenses, medical expenses and other contingencies. A substantial part of it was sent to Bhabua for the rest of the family. I had two mamus, maternal uncles. One of them had died when I was quite young; the other one passed away a couple of years before I joined the line. His widow went back to her parents, but their two daughters stayed with us and were our responsibility. My mother got them married.

'Then there was Bafati bhaiyya, who was my elder mamu's son and lived in Bhabua. My mother had got him married. We provided for his family. My sister had looked after them all earlier. After her estrangement from amma, I took her place.

'In later years, I also had to marry off Asghari aapa's daughter, Gindo, because by that time, my sister had frittered all her savings on that good-for-nothing Siddiq. Ghafuran and her family, in any case, I have always taken care of. With all this spending, I was left with very little by way of savings. This is how it always was in our community. Even the highest-earning tawaifs managed to save only a fraction of their earnings.

'I am thankful that amma wisely used the money we saved to buy agricultural lands for me. She also invested a part of the money, on Maheshwar Singh's advice, in fixed deposits made in my name and buying shares for a future income for me. All this is what has sustained me through these long years.

'I was at my peak during my time with Maheshwar Singh. It was then in the early 1970s that I began recording for a Calcutta-based music company, Kohinoor Records. They had a set-up in Banaras to record Bhojpuri songs, qawwalis, etc. by local artists who mostly came from tawaif and qawwali backgrounds.'

In all the years that I have known you, there has been no mention of a recording career. Taken by surprise, I say, 'I didn't know you had recorded! Why didn't you ever mention it to me when I was researching your aunt Bindo's possible recordings as a gramophone singer?'

Your answer is characteristically self-deprecatory, 'You never asked. And to tell you the truth, I had almost forgotten about it till now. In any case, I was never a grand gramophone singer like Bindo khala wanted to be, or like Siddheshwari and Rasoolan were. They recorded for major music companies like HMV and enjoyed all-India fame. I thought you were interested in only big names like them. I recorded only Bhojpuri songs for local Banaras-based music companies. My reach was limited to eastern UP and Bihar.

'I sang for Kohinoor and a bit later, around 1974–75, for Madhur Records, which was Banaras-based. Kohinoor Records had shut down by then, but Madhur did good business. It was located at Bulla Nala in Banaras and was owned by Madan Electronics. I think they paid around Rs 1,000–1,500 for one recording. I wasn't interested in the money; for me, the important thing was that there were records being made in my name.

'These records had a huge market in UP and Bihar. Since the songs were mostly in Bhojpuri, they would sell a lot in rural areas. Most of these records were bought by people who hired out music systems for weddings and other public functions. This kind of music was played mostly at big public celebrations. Many of the songs were quite racy and "open". People didn't listen to them so much in their own homes. One of my most popular songs, for instance, went:

Guiyan kaisan suhag wali raat hui,
jaiha pehle piya se mulaqat hui,
Rama kavan gati hui,
dheel det na hi koi.

Friend, how was the wedding night
And the first meeting with your beloved?
Rama! Don't ask of my state
There was no respite given or taken through the night.

'I would get a thrill at hearing my recordings being played in all the places where I went to perform in programmes. I had become quite famous by then, and so my records sold well. Besides the usual romantic and "open" songs, I also recorded other kinds of music—nationalist, seasonal and the like—which also sold very well. A nationalist song that I originally recorded went on to become hugely popular. It was about an Indian soldier, Abdul Hamid, who was martyred in the 1965 war against Pakistan, and was posthumously awarded the highest gallantry medal, the Paramvir Chakra. Hamid belonged to village Madhopur in district Ghazipur of eastern UP. He was, therefore, a major local hero in this entire area. The song that I recorded in his memory was set to an aalah:

Kaun naam deswa mein Hamid more bhaiyya,
jaika gaon Madhopur, zilva Ghazipur,
watan ke karanwa taj de hun paranwa,
teen teen tankwa ke kar liye choor choor.

What land did Hamid come from, my brother?
He belonged to village Madhopur, district Ghazipur
For the love of his country he sacrificed his life
Three tanks he smashed to smithereens.

'This song was hugely popular in mehfils. *Bahut iski farmaish hoti thhi*; There were many requests for it. People appreciated the thehrav (a restful abiding in each note) and depth with which I sang the lines, and my voice too by Allah's grace was very powerful. Many other tawaifs sang it too, but people especially loved my version. Many of my other songs were equally popular, and so were sung by other singers too. But in public memory they remained closely associated with me.

'I had kept many of my records for a long time. But then they got warped with age and so, unthinkingly, I threw them away. I went to Madan Electronics a few years ago to ask for my records once I began to understand the importance of keeping such things. But Madhur Records had shut down by then. No one at the shop knew who I was and weren't interested in helping me find my old records.

'Dixit Photo Studio used to be located right next to their shop. In my heyday, I had got several portraits done there, because when I was singing for Madhur Records, they needed my photos to print on the record covers. Those were such lovely photographs. Sadly, those too are gone.'

Letting out a deep sigh, you fall silent. Although it's still dark, birds have begun chirping. Milk men are tinkling their cycle bells in the lanes below. From some temple close by, a loudspeaker comes to life with bhajans in preparation for the morning arti. Soon, it will be dawn. In a few hours, the hustle and bustle of the mehendi ceremony will begin. You heave yourself up from the chair, 'In the old days, my mehfils would last through the night and break only around this time. I would often bring my performance to a close with a song that became very popular, *Chalti beriya, Nazar bhar ke dekh lo*; It's time to leave, Give me a full, final look.'

CHAPTER 29

Jo Beet Gayi Soh Baat Gayi

'I HAD MAYBE A DOZEN cases against me in the courts during my time as a tawaif in Bhabua,' Asghari announces with a flourish. We are in your room upstairs with her daughter Gindo, Madhu and you. While Gindo sniggers and Madhu maintains a polite silence, your response is predictable.

Flinching with embarrassment, you let out a mumbled protest, 'Aapa, this is nothing to brag about! And do speak softly. Meenu's friends are in the next room. What will they think?'

Your older sister is unfazed. 'Shut up, you silly prude! No one can hear me outside this room. And your friend is enjoying my story. *Hamesha ki tarah rang mein bhang mat dalo!* Don't be a spoilsport like always!'

Gindo's is now hooting with rude laughter. It is not clear whether she is jeering her mother or you, since her eyes keep darting from one to another. Slender and fair-skinned like her mother, Gindo has inherited neither Asghari's girlish prettiness nor her vivacity. The slyness in her eyes and a near-constant sneer rob her face of the narcissistic charm that is so abundant in Asghari. Ever since she arrived from Patna yesterday, her husband and three children in tow, she has spent most of her time gossiping and scoffing at her relatives, especially Asghari and you.

I can understand her antipathy towards her mother. As a child, she had been brought up by Teema, unloved and unwanted by the self-absorbed Asghari. Much against her wishes, Gindo had then been dragged off to Bhabua by her mother, only to be relegated to the background in Asghari's preoccupation with herself and Siddiq. Married off at a very young age, she has had little to do with Asghari, and has been a shadowy, forgotten presence in the extended family, making an appearance only at weddings and other such occasions.

Gindo's hostility towards you is harder to fathom, given that you have often stepped in to fulfil responsibilities that Asghari was unable or unwilling to shoulder. It was you who arranged her marriage, and you again who took care of Gindo during her pregnancies. You say that she resents everyone. Convinced that life has given her the short shrift, this is how she is. What you leave unsaid is that Gindo, in turn, is an unwelcome presence in your family.

As she continues sniggering, you direct a look of intense suffering in my direction. Ignoring her daughter and you, Asghari is in full flow, 'People jealous of my popularity would lodge complaints against me at the local thana. The police would arrive and arrest me along with those listening to me sing, and register a case. But there were so many lawyers who were in love with me! One or the other of them would bail me out immediately and fight my case for free and win!

'During a raid, the darogah had once threatened me, *Tumhari khal kheench kar usme bhoonsa bhar denge*; We will skin you alive and stuff you with straw! The Rajputs present at that time in my kotha said, "The day you come even close to doing that, we will burn down your police station!" The police never dared to insult me again or use physical force. In any case, I was earning so much that there was plenty of money to bribe off the policemen. That is what they were really after.

'On another occasion, the police came and arrested me and the two girls who used my house for their own work on charges of being minors. I was sleeping when the police came. The ustads began protesting that I was not a minor. The police said that I was accused of prostituting minors. So they took me along with the two girls, one of whom was genuinely a minor. When we were produced in front of the judge, he ordered that we be locked up till our bail was arranged.

'On hearing the judge, both girls put their heads on my shoulder and began weeping, "Oh khala, they are going to lock us up!" I told them to shut up. Then I told the police that we would not go inside the lock-up. If we were forced in, then both the girls and I would die there and then of heart failure!

'The policemen replied, "Do you want us to lose our jobs?"

'I assured them that their jobs would not be in jeopardy. Our lawyers would be coming any moment to arrange our bail. I gave them Rs 20 and said, "Take this and go and have tea. This court belongs to us. You have nothing to worry about."

'Finally the policemen took out a bench from inside the lock-up, and we sat there. In less than an hour, our bail was arranged by some Rajputs who used to come to hear me sing. They were happy to stand surety for us. We were not some thieves or dacoits who would run away!

'Then there was the time when I was sent off to jail for a day for contempt of court. The prison was full of all kinds of murderers and dacoits. They were all standing and staring as I passed by. Some among them, especially the Rajputs, recognised me, "Oh Asghari, how are you here?"

'I replied jokingly, "I was missing you all, so I came to be with you!" We all had a good laugh, including the policemen.'

'So were you lodged in the men's jail?' I ask Asghari. Your eyebrows are arched with disapproving scepticism.

'No, I was put in the women's jail but had to pass through the men's prison to reach there. There was a huge courtyard. The men's jail was on one side of it and the women's on the other. There were two or three other women prisoners in the cell that I was put in. They took me to be a fancy lady, because soon food arrived for me from home, kababs and parathas. My bedding too came from home. I ate dinner and made myself comfortable. The other women in the cell were very nice to me.

'After a while they said, "Please, sister, sing something so that the time passes."

'I said, "Certainly, let's have some music, but where are the musical instruments?"

'So they found a thali. I sat down and, beating at the thali, sang all kinds of rustic songs. The women were delighted. I made them dance vigorously to my songs! Even the woman guards outside our cell began dancing, and all the other women prisoners too. It was such fun!'

You snap in utter exasperation, 'Fun! Have you no sense of shame at all, aapa? Think of the heights from which you began your career and where you reached by the end of it! There is no glory in getting arrested and being put in prison like a criminal!'

You stop abruptly, no doubt regretting your words already. Asghari is dangerous when provoked. And sure enough, Asghari retorts, 'Well, not all of us were lucky to be the mistress of one of the biggest dons in Bihar. Murder, kidnapping, extortion, rape and what not, your precious Maheshwar Singh and his brothers had done it all, so don't give me lessons in respectability!'

With a look of malicious pleasure, Gindo settles down to enjoy what promises to be an intense spat. Duly chastened, you maintain a glum silence. Your house is full of guests sleeping away the revelry of the ratjagga. Meenu's nikah is tomorrow. You are best served avoiding a full-on war with the mercurial Asghari. There is no saying where the confrontation might lead.

Asghari, her eyes narrowed and chin tilted up belligerently, senses victory and smiles.

I try and broker peace by talking about the great time everyone had at the ratjagga. Music had flowed like wine. Dipping into their treasure-trove of songs, the women in your family and your friends had relived their days as tawaifs. They had performed in groups, singly and in good-natured competition with each other. Putting aside her ill health, Asghari had been the sparkling star of the evening with her singing, dancing and stories of conquests and glory. You had matched your sister song for song, joke for joke in perfect jugalbandi.

As dawn broke, signalled by the call of azan, the singing stopped. The women of the family lit earthen lamps filled with desi ghee and arranged these on five trays, alongside flower garlands, gulgulas and raham, sweet rice dumplings. You all then carried the trays to the local mosque. Placing the lamps on the minbar or pulpit, you and your women relatives put the garlands, gulgulas and raham in the five takhs—niches—carved into the mosque walls. After offering prayers, you removed the gulgulas and raham from four takhs, leaving one niche full, and brought these home to be distributed among relatives.

After a long time, you had looked happy, and with good reason. Yesterday went off without a hitch. The mehendi earlier in the day was a joyful ceremony. Even Shama had looked cheerful. Her mother-in-law condescended to sit through the function, and Amjad returned to your house as promised and accepted your brief but gracious apology.

Later, when I expressed my disappointment about the apology, you were frank, '*Museebat mein gadhey ko bhi baap banana padta hai*; In a crisis one has to show respect even to an idiot. I had to buy peace with Amjad and his mother because I can't afford to fight in the midst of a wedding. Just wait and see how I deal with them once Meenu has left for her in-laws' house.'

You are proud of your capacity for patience in the face of provocation; one of the many lessons you say you learnt as a tawaif. Aware of your vulnerability as a stigmatised woman, you could not afford to be hot-headed in your response. You have always preferred to buy time, think coolly through a crisis and respond to it prudently.

Asghari, your polar opposite, is always geared up for war. Visibly itching for a fight in the face of your cold silence, she eggs you on now, 'I am sure you are dying to tell your friend about your own impeccable record with the police! So let's hear you talk, Miss Washed-in-milk!'

You sigh. Before you can respond, however, Madhu speaks on your behalf, 'She has no need to say anything. All of Nariyal Bazaar and Dal Mandi can vouch for her unimpeachable conduct as a tawaif. The shadows of police batons never blackened her home! Even in the days of Ranjit Singh, she was perhaps the only bai-ji he could find no excuse to summon to his thana.'

I have heard of Ranjit Singh from you and many of your tawaif friends, including Madhu and Chanda, and from former accompanists like Shanney Khan and Sharafat Khan, who have talked to me at length about the turbulent period of the 1970s. It was a time of moral panics in Banaras. It was also a time of growing disillusionment with the failed promises that India had made to itself upon gaining independence, a time of widespread protests against rural inequalities, poverty and urban unemployment.

Beginning with the peasant uprising in 1967, spearheaded by the Communist Party of India (Marxist-Leninist) in Naxalbari, West Bengal, the late 1960s and early 1970s saw the advent of radical politics in large parts of India. In Uttar Pradesh, landless peasants led by the Communist Party of India had launched the 'land grab' movement. Especially strong in eastern Uttar Pradesh, in areas like Chakia, the movement saw attempts by landless cultivators to forcibly seize parts of government wastelands and the private land of large landholders. There was also a rise in radical student politics, inspired by the ideas guiding the Naxalbari uprising. University and college students in Banaras too, authorities alleged, were being indoctrinated into the Naxalite ideology.

The state's response to what it saw as a crisis in the established social order was twofold: suppression of the peasant and student protests through swift and harsh punitive action and an increasing preoccupation with public morality. Prohibition was imposed in major pilgrimage centres of UP, like Banaras, Ayodhya, Mathura and Allahabad. Drives against the presence of goondas and prostitutes in public spaces were intensified. The media played its part too through shrill amplification of moral panics and its wholehearted support of state-sponsored morality drives.

Ranjit Singh, a police officer known for his messianic zeal to cleanse his area of immorality and vice, was specifically posted as station house officer (SHO) at the Chowk police station in 1970 as part of the anti-prostitution drive initiated in Banaras by the new kotwal, or chief inspector of police, Nirmal Chandra Joshi. Self-righteous in his beliefs and authoritarian in his functioning, Ranjit Singh began featuring in newspaper headlines almost as soon as he took charge of the Chowk police station in May 1970. His morality drives were primarily directed at sex workers. Tawaifs suffered too, the distinguishing line between them and sex workers becoming thinner by the day. Police raids, mass arrests and public humiliation of sex workers, pimps and tawaifs suspected of indulging in prostitution became the order of the day in the tawaif and sex worker neighbourhoods that were under his jurisdiction.

'Upon taking charge, Ranjit Singh had stated that he would not harass genuine tawaifs if they earned their livelihood by music and dance. He would only act against prostitutes. And he really did go after them. Barging into their brothels at all times of the day and night, beating up the inmates and customers before arresting them, harassing prostitutes and their pimps when they stepped out of their homes, public beatings and forced evictions, all this created an atmosphere of utter terror in Dal Mandi,' says Madhu, an old resident of the area herself. 'Uma Shankar Dube, a pimp, had written to the authorities protesting against Ranjit Singh's tyranny. In retaliation, Ranjit Singh forced the woman Dube lived with in Kunji Tola to beat him publicly with chappals. He then had Dube paraded with his face blackened through Dal Mandi and Chowk.'

'I remember, during that time, there was a massive raid in Nariyal Bazaar on brothels that had come up in the past few years,' you recall. 'Our immediate neighbourhood still housed only tawaifs' kothas but those too were raided that night. In all that confusion, Ranjit Singh landed up here and demanded to search the house. Maheshwar Singh was upstairs with me, so my mother went down to speak with the police. All the neighbours and shopkeepers who were out on the street by that time told Ranjit Singh that he was knocking on the wrong door, but he was so arrogant that he wouldn't listen to anyone. He was rude to my mother too. Hearing the commotion, Maheshwar Singh came down the steps and confronted Ranjit Singh. You should have seen the SHO's face once he recognised who he was speaking with! The same man who strutted around humiliating poor women stood stammering in front of Maheshwar Singh, who told him that I was a well-known singer and his woman. All that Ranjit Singh could say was, "Yes, of course, babu sahib! Sorry for the disturbance!" before fleeing and never coming back.'

'Yes, I heard about that from Pyaari,' Asghari attempts a re-entry into the conversation. 'I told her that, had I been in your place, I would have fixed Ranjit Singh for good without needing any babu sahib to speak up for me.'

You ignore the jibe, but Madhu shoots back, 'Aapa, only a while back you were boasting about all the babu sahibs who bailed you out in Bhabua. So why have different standards for us? And please, don't mind it if I say that it's always easier to pass judgement from a distance! You have no idea about Ranjit Singh's high-handedness. He would barge into tawaifs' kothas on all sorts of pretexts, like if the mujra extended even five minutes beyond the 10 p.m. deadline he had set, or if the mehfil was too noisy. He would beat up the men gathered there listening to music. Even if he made no arrests, the men were frightened enough to never return.'

As part of the clean-up drive against badmash-goondas in the city, raids upon tawaifs' kothas had become frequent under Ranjit Singh's tenure. While having little or no impact on goondas, who usually managed to slip away in connivance with the policemen, these raids frightened away regular visitors to the kotha. Anti-obscenity drives too became a regular feature in Dal Mandi and adjoining neighbourhoods, with tawaifs being booked for performing obscene songs and dances.

The police also attempted to mark out properties across the city that allegedly housed brothels. A public notice was issued in July 1970 to house owners, demanding why action should not be initiated against them for leasing out their properties to sex workers. A great majority of the houses identified were located in areas like Dal Mandi and Kundigar Tola.

As a follow-up to this notice, the kotwal led massive raids across the city, and many sex workers were arrested. Police locked up the vacated houses and threatened to auction them off as a punitive measure against the owners. Emboldened by these actions, Ranjit Singh began getting sex workers forcibly evicted in neighbourhoods under his jurisdiction, and pressurising landlords into leasing these properties to suitably 'respectable' tenants.

Sex workers responded by coming together and forming their own organisation—the Gayika, Nayika, Veshyavritti Sangh—which held a public meeting on 9 August 1970 to condemn Ranjit Singh's high-handedness, describing him as a taanashah, or dictator (*Aaj*, 10 August 1970). Speaker after speaker at the meeting held forth on the unimaginable hardships faced by sex workers, who were generally poor women with no other resources. The extensive shutting down of brothels had resulted in the starvation and destitution of thousands of families dependent on sex workers for their survival. Asserting their willingness to forsake sex work, the speakers demanded that the state first make provisions for alternative sources of livelihood for the women.

Tawaifs were more divided in their response to Ranjit Singh's morality drive. While privately they bitterly resented his high-handed intrusions into their kothas, in public, they preferred to maintain a distance from the sex workers. The Gayika Sangh had been quick to issue a public statement in support of his actions. Asserting that prostitution and prostitutes brought a bad name to tawaifs, who earned their livelihood through singing and dancing, the statement expressed satisfaction at the 'cleansing' of Dal Mandi and the neighbourhoods adjoining it of 'vice' and 'illicit' activities.

Its rival organisation, the Kashi Sangeet Kalakar Sangh, was more nuanced in its approach. While extending support to police actions against sex workers, it decried the SHO's authoritarian style of functioning and his unwarranted actions against tawaifs in the name of purging Dal Mandi of prostitution.

'I was the secretary of the Kashi Sangeet Kalakar Sangh at that time, and had written a complaint against Ranjit Singh to the authorities, stating that he was committing excesses with artists,' Sharafat Khan had told me. 'That letter made the rounds of the minister and officers concerned, and came back to the Chowk Police Station. When Ranjit Singh read it, he was furious. Vindictive as he was, he ordered that I be caught hold of and brought to the thana. When I heard of this, I disappeared from Dal Mandi. I told Ustad Bismillah Khan of this matter. At that time, the governor, B. Gopal Reddy, had come to Banaras on a visit. I met him at Bismillah Khan Sahib's house and shared our plight with him. He promised help but then seemed to forget all about the matter. Ranjit Singh's terror continued for some years. Even after he left, the others who came in his place indulged in much the same tyranny.'

Backed by state might, Ranjit Singh and his successors were successful in forcing sex workers to flee Dal Mandi and its adjoining neighbourhoods. The inner-city area, traditionally associated with tawaifs and sex workers, was, by the mid-1970s, officially and permanently 'cleansed' of prostitution. A large majority of sex workers shifted base to the outlying area of Shivdaspur, transforming it into the hub of prostitution in Banaras.

The state's drive against goondas, however, proved less successful. Many of them enjoyed the patronage of powerful politicians in return for providing muscle power in the hurly-burly of electoral politics. Goondas, therefore, continued to thrive in the city, including in Dal Mandi and the neighbourhoods adjoining it. The tawaifs who remained in the area too continued to be in business, although under increasingly difficult circumstances.

'After I got involved with Maheshwar Singh, I had almost stopped entertaining visitors in my home. He didn't care for it, and I was earning so well performing in mehfils in Bihar and eastern UP that I didn't really need the income that came from the kotha,' you say.

Asghari wanders out of the room. Gindo follows, bored perhaps with the serious turn in the discussion.

Ignoring their exit, you continue, 'At that point, I was the highest-paid tawaif from Banaras performing in Bihar. My relationship with Maheshwar Singh was public knowledge, and ensured protection and respect for me. No one dared to behave amiss in my mehfils. In Banaras, I would occasionally make an exception to entertain known and valued patrons, who might come by especially to my house to hear me sing while on a trip to the city. However, after Ranjit Singh tried that once to barge into my home, I stopped entertaining here altogether. I didn't want to compromise my name and dignity by having the police come to my house again. Once my children were born, I also stopped performing in mehfils within Banaras. I didn't want them to be taunted at school for being a tawaif's children. Consciously, I led a very low-key life in the city, focusing instead upon my career as a mehfil singer outside Banaras.'

Madhu, your contemporary in Banaras, has a very different experience of the time. 'Though I did take on outside assignments, my main income came from performing in my own kotha and mehfils in Banaras. My mother, Prabhati Bai, who was handling my career, felt insecure about allowing me to travel outside. I think the main reason behind her reluctance was the severe arthritis in both knees that had left her homebound. Maybe she was not sure how safe I would be, travelling on my own, accompanied only by the ustads. Anyway, I was doing well in Banaras and many good, wealthy people still came to my kotha regularly. And I was the star of mehfils held in the city. These were not like the mehfils of old that used to be organised in peoples' homes on weddings and other celebrations, but more like private parties of visitors to the city who were keen on seeing a mujra, and were usually held in guest-houses and hotel rooms. The money was good since they were mostly organised by businessmen.

'During Ranjit Singh's time, my mother had become very particular that only the right kind of people be allowed into my kotha, so that there was no trouble. But despite her best efforts, sometimes big-time goondas, like Kamal Singh and Pappu Singh, would bully their way inside, get drunk and create a ruckus. Reputed tawaifs like me tried to avoid such scenes at all costs, because the police would arrive immediately. Instead of arresting the troublemakers, they would harass us, and drag us to the thana for sheltering the goondas, whom they quietly let off. That was so typical of the police. They were a terror to all those they could bully, like prostitutes, pimps, tawaifs and ustads, but they would kowtow to powerful men like Kamal Singh, whose father was an important and influential politician.'

In my research, I have frequently encountered references to Kamal Singh, who has been described to me in singularly unflattering terms by former tawaifs and accompanists as a 'goonda' and 'badmash'. He first came into the limelight as a student leader in 1970, in violent confrontation with a group of students who were on strike to protest against lack of college educational infrastructure. With the backing of college authorities, Kamal had attempted to break the strike by physically assaulting the protesting students whom he accused of being Naxalites.

By the mid-1970s, he had graduated to becoming a full-time political thug. His father was a powerful minister in the UP government at that time. Enjoying political protection, Kamal Singh had a free run of Dal Mandi and other mohallas near it, terrorising tawaifs, leading police raids against them and evicting them from their houses.

Much of this period, from June 1975 to '77, coincided with the nationwide imposition of the Emergency, during which elections were suspended, civil liberties curbed, political critics of the then powerful Congress prime minister, Indira Gandhi, arrested in large numbers, and the press brought under heavy censorship. The history of the Emergency is a chronicle of unbridled state control and excesses committed by constitutional and extra-constitutional authorities in the name of national interest and security. At the local level, it is also a history of the misuse of state machinery by a political thug to victimise the tawaifs in Banaras.

Madhu describes Kamal Singh as, '*Bade baap ka bigda beta*, the spoilt son of a big man. His father was a minister. The Emergency was on and the police did his bidding. No one dared say anything. He did as he pleased.'

You add, 'He would barge into kothas, get drunk and even rape tawaifs. He carried away a tawaif to a hotel and, along with five or six men, took turns raping her. She finally managed to cover herself with a bedsheet and jump out of the hotel room window. Miraculously, she survived. She was pregnant at that time. He also abducted another tawaif, Pushpa. No one could stop him. Even when people tried to lodge a complaint against him, the police would respond only after he had done whatever he wanted. He used to burn women by stubbing cigarettes on them. He had burnt Pushpa in this manner too.'

'There was a tawaif called Leena who was pregnant with his child,' says Chanda walking in, her face flushed with whisky and the exertion of climbing the two flights of stairs to your room. Her steps are, as always, a bit unsteady. Instead of the usual housecoat over a petticoat that she wears at home, Chanda is dressed in her preferred attire for the outside—a masculine-cut shalwar-kurta without a dupatta draping her shoulders and bosom.

As community leader, Chanda rarely deigns to visit peoples' homes, expecting them to seek her out instead. In recognition of your friendship, she makes an exception, and has been dropping by at your house to participate in Meenu's wedding festivities. You have taken to gently boasting to your family about the special place you have in Chanda's heart. Jumping up now to welcome her in, you solicitously get her seated and call out for tea and refreshments. Madhu too makes a show of getting up as a mark of respect to her seniority and status. Accepting the courtesies imperiously as her rightful due, Chanda waves at you the ever-loyal hip-flask that she always carries, and declines the tea but accepts the paan that you press upon her.

Chanda never gossips and rarely ever talks about other people. But today, she says of Kamal Singh, 'He often beat up Leena badly. Desperate to escape, she tried to run away to Calcutta. But he followed her there and forcibly took away her newborn baby. Leena's mother Siromani was a known tawaif in Dal Mandi. To teach Leena a lesson, Kamal Singh had her evicted and her house broken down.

'He got the police to carry out massive raids on Siromani along with many other tawaifs in Dal Mandi. He had them all arrested on trumped-up charges of doing sex work or some other false cases. He justified his actions as "cleansing" Dal Mandi of immorality and maintaining law and order. But everyone knew that the real reasons behind the raids and arrests were to punish Leena and to force tawaifs out of their houses so that he and his supporters could occupy these and make profit.

'Siromani, Bittan, Naurangi Bai, Lakshmi, Shahjahan were all old, respected tawaifs, and were among those whom he got evicted from their rightful properties. He forcibly bought two of the houses at much below market rates. He developed a market in one of them. At his insistence, the other houses were sold off at low prices to his supporters and other people. He also got other tawaifs evicted who were tenants in Dal Mandi and had been living in their houses for years. The house owners were powerless in the face of his bullying.

'He revelled in throwing his weight around. He could summon anyone, barge into anyone's home in the name of curbing immorality. It was a joke that a goonda like Kamal Singh should go about bragging of his heroic deeds at the expense of poor women for whom there was no redress! He would come with the police in tow—who would dare to question him then?'

You add, 'He landed up at my place once, accompanied by four or five men. Maheshwar Singh was present in my room at that time and, on hearing his voice, came down. Kamal Singh promptly got up and respectfully touched his feet. He was a Rajput too, so knew Maheshwar Singh and his family. He then talked Maheshwar Singh into agreeing to host him and his friends for a drinking session in my house.

'I was very annoyed. I didn't want Kamal Singh and his goonda friends drinking in my home but could not say anything since Maheshwar Singh had acquiesced. Anyhow, that evening, for some reason, Maheshwar

Singh got drunk very quickly. Excusing himself, he went upstairs and fell asleep. Kamal Singh kept drinking and insisting that I sing for him and his friends. I kept refusing politely, hinting that he and his gang should go now that Maheshwar Singh had left the party.

'As I was speaking, Kamal Singh lunged at my breast. A thin gold chain that I was wearing around my neck got entangled in his hand. Part of my blouse also got ripped off. He put his face close to mine and said, "Come darling, give me a kiss."

'I was furious, "I would rather die first," I told him. "Shame on you!"

'Stung by my words, he threw a bottle at the wall opposite. Meanwhile, my mother rushed upstairs and woke Maheshwar Singh. It was around 10.30 at night. Someone from my house also went running to the police station, which was located close by. The police reassured him that they would come soon but never turned up.

'Maheshwar Singh, in the meantime, followed my mother downstairs, where Kamal Singh stood facing me with part of my blouse sleeve in his hand. Seeing him enter the room, the men accompanying Kamal Singh entwined themselves like snakes around Maheshwar Singh. Shaking them off, he lunged at Kamal Singh from the back. Dragging him bodily out of the room, Maheshwar Singh threw him down the stairs.

'In the melee, he too got pushed down by Kamal Singh's henchmen. But Maheshwar Singh proved far too strong for the likes of Kamal Singh and his goondas. He pulled up Kamal Singh by the collar and, thrashing him all along the way, dragged him to his father's house, which was located quite close to Nariyal Bazaar.

'This became a very big incident. All the Rajputs requested Maheshwar Singh not to make an issue of it with Kamal Singh's family, but he refused saying, "This woman has devoted her life to me. How dare he misbehave with her?"

'Then there was a meeting in the house of Kamal Singh's father. Maheshwar Singh was invited, as were many other Rajputs. All of them believed in violence and killing, and had come with their guns. I begged Maheshwar Singh not to attend the meeting. I was fearful that there might be bloodshed.

'He shrugged me off saying, "This has nothing to do with you. This is a matter to be settled between Rajputs."

'He saw to it that Kamal Singh apologised to me. He was also made to promise that he would never come to my house again. And he never did.'

Madhu turns to me and says, 'Everyone talked about it for days. She was the only tawaif that Kamal Singh had been forced to apologise to. He kept troubling the other tawaifs, though. Everyone was frightened of him. He ruined the lives of many women. He humiliated so many old tawaifs that we would weep for them. Like Babban mausi from Gaya who had spent a lifetime here. She was very old and a contemporary of my mother. Her singing was wonderful.

'Five or six elderly and influential tawaifs of the area, including Babban mausi, had got a letter drafted and planned to collectively go to Kamal Singh's father and ask, "What wrong have we done? Why have there been police raids against us? Why are we being evicted from our homes?" Many women were quite poor. Where would they go?

'When Kamal Singh got to know of this, he summoned everyone involved, but only Babban mausi was around. He piled really filthy abuses upon her. She was so shattered that she left Banaras for good, and went back to Gaya. She is now dead. So many tawaifs left Banaras because of him and began living in other places. Most left this line altogether.

'Eventually, the Emergency period got over. Some of us who still had our houses resumed singing and dancing. Dal Mandi and the other areas were never the same again. Most of the tawaifs had left. The few who remained carried on for some time but the bazaar was dead.'

Bringing the story of the locality to a close, you say, 'First Ranjit Singh came along and threw out all the prostitutes, and then Kamal Singh tyrannised the tawaifs into leaving. By the 1980s, there were no tawaifs, no music or dance to be heard or seen in Banaras. It was as if the beautiful, shimmering evenings of Dal Mandi, Nariyal Bazaar and Chowk had been just a passing dream.'

Surrounded by your closest friends and confidantes, you finally speak at length about the chapter in your life that you seldom revisit. I have only rarely been given a glimpse of this particular phase, and that too only in fragments and through euphemisms.

'Maheshwar Singh died on 25 March 1984 in a road accident.' The date is forever etched in your memory. 'Some people said that he was murdered by rivals in the guise of an accident. Whatever the cause, my world was destroyed. He was the world to me. With him gone, I was emotionally shattered. Financially too, without him and the regular monthly maintenance he provided, I was in a very difficult situation. My children were very little. Meenu was only three months old. Nanhe, the doctors had said, would need medical support throughout his life to be functional. Besides, I had a family to provide for back home in Bhabua. My mother, who had been my anchor, also passed away within a few months of Maheshwar Singh's death. My life seemed to go black.

'But I had responsibilities. Life had to go on. *Toh karein toh kya karein?* So what way out did I have? *Bihar mein hamari tooti bolti thhi*; I was at my zenith in Bihar. This was due to my talent, of course, but also because Maheshwar Singh's name was attached to mine. No one dared to misbehave with me. They would treat me with respect as an artist, not the way they treated other tawaifs. I didn't wish to go back there now that Maheshwar Singh was gone, and risk being treated differently.

'Neither was I willing to compromise my dignity by reopening my kotha here. In any case, there was hardly anyone left who visited kothas, except low-life goondas. I didn't want to get mired in that muck. But then how would we survive? I was desperate for a way out. There was no income coming in and, at a relatively young age, with three children to look after, I was already eating into my savings.

'Maheshwar Singh's wife tried to help out, but she was now completely dependent on her sons, and they hated me. When I had gone to visit didi after Maheshwar Singh's death, his eldest son told me never to come to their house again. "You are now free to take on any man you want," he had said. It was very humiliating.

'Later, though, when I thought about it, I felt this was the only path open to me. It was then that I met Mishra-ji. He was a businessman from Delhi and extremely clever and canny. Before meeting me, he had done his homework well, and found out all about my desperate situation. Flashy in his ways, he had a lot of experience, since he was much older than me and had been involved with several women. He would brag about his affairs and tell me names of tawaifs that he had known intimately, women whom I addressed as granny or aunty. Even after he entered into a relationship with me, he continued seeing other women.

'He would have me travel to Delhi for long periods, and put me up in a guesthouse. I preferred that because I didn't want to entertain him or anyone else in my home in Banaras. My children were growing and I didn't want strange men around them. I would call someone from my family, like Ghafuran, to come and stay with the children when I had to go to Delhi. My old maid also lived with us, and was a very good woman. At times, I would call Pyaari khala to help out. She would come and stay for ten days, two weeks with the children.

'Mishra-ji put on airs about belonging to a big city. He was also very good at doing things for show. For instance, I would be sitting with the ustads in the guesthouse, and Mishra-ji would arrive. The ustads, as was their habit, would begin fawning over him. He would open his briefcase in front of all of them, and take out saris and a gold chain or bangles, making it out as if these were for me. He would tip the ustads too. When Rs 500 would have sufficed, he would give each one of them Rs 1,000. Everyone naturally sang paeans of praises for him. No one knew that, once we were alone, Mishra-ji would promptly put back the jewellery and the saris in his briefcase, saying that he would give them to me later. But he never did.

'I might have been a tawaif, but I had led a simple life with Maheshwar Singh, who was a man of his words. He gave me so much without ever making a show of it. Essentially a down-to-earth person, he had no attraction for chamak-dhamak, flashiness. He lived modestly, and loved and respected me for who I was. I hardly ever put on any make-up. It made no difference to Maheshwar Singh. I didn't spend hours dressing up. I would wear Hawaii chappals and go to perform! And yet I got respect for my music and my behaviour.

'Mishra-ji, on the other hand, had no respect for my simplicity. He would scoff at my lack of style and my plain looks. Inwardly, he did realise that I was not a run-of-the-mill tawaif. That is why he had singled me out. He wanted to exploit me and my tawaif training for his own purpose.'

'Men like Mishra are the worst, lowest motherfuckers around,' intones Chanda, taking a swig of her whisky. 'The only way they know to control women is by running them down and humiliating them. If you recall, I had warned you about Mishra even then. He had been a regular in Dal Mandi since before your time and enjoyed a lousy reputation. He was just a glorified pimp, who used women for his own gain.'

You nod. 'I realised soon enough that Mishra-ji wasn't interested in me for himself. He had chosen me thinking that, since I had been such a successful tawaif, I would be an asset in furthering his interests. He had contacts at the highest level in Delhi's political and official circles. He wanted to use me to oblige them and so promote his business. I hated it all.

'What I resented most was that Mishra-ji gave me no choice. I was a tawaif, Saba, I had known several men before I got involved with Maheshwar Singh. But my mother hadn't ever forced me to do anything I didn't want. Mishra-ji, on the other hand, wouldn't take no for an answer. I would protest, but to little effect. To make me feel insecure and to put pressure, he would try and make me feel inferior. He made it seem like he was doing me a favour by taking me on as his mistress.

'I hated the situation so much that I began avoiding going to Delhi. And so he stopped sending me money. It was a pressure tactic to force me to do what he wanted. He knew that I would not sing and dance in Banaras. Bihar, he knew, was a closed chapter. What other option did I have but to go back to him? And he was right. I had to return to him and entertain his friends.

'Dazzled by his showy ways, my musicians, even my family, thought that Mishra-ji must be giving me a lot of money. Firstly, he never gave me much, and secondly, they had no idea of the ways in which I had to swallow my pride to get him to pay the little he did. It was a nightmare to entertain his friends night after night, sing trashy songs for them, hear their filthy jokes about women and be passed around like an inanimate doll from one man to another. I, who had enjoyed so much respect and adulation as a tawaif, was now reduced to nothing! I felt so ashamed of what I had become.

'Mishra-ji would devise all kinds of ploys to humiliate me for his sadistic pleasure. Every year, on Karva Chauth, he would insist that I fast the entire day for his long life if I wanted maintenance for that month. And to make sure that I did keep the fast, he would be around through the day gorging silly on food while I starved.

'I will always be grateful to abba for insisting that I go with him for an audition at Gorakhpur radio station. He understood how unhappy I was, and tried to help me find a way out. Mishra-ji was very dismissive when I got selected in the audition. I think he felt threatened that, with radio opening up for me, I might slip out of his control. He said, "What will the radio give you? Peanuts! I had such high hopes of you, but you can't do anything."

'It is true that singing for the radio did not bring me too much money. But it gave me back my confidence, which had really taken a beating through my years with him. Most of the people there were nice to me and treated me with respect. I valued that greatly over money. It was not always smooth sailing, of course. Everywhere, there are good people and bad. My tawaif past would sometimes catch up with me at the radio station. Someone or the other would recognise me and crack a nasty joke. That was deeply hurtful.

'Yet, however difficult the path, I couldn't bear the thought of going to Delhi and entertaining Mishra-ji's friends and associates. My visits to him became more sporadic. But he was not willing to let me escape his grasp so easily. He would come to Banaras and insist on staying in my house, even though he knew that I didn't like it. He worked on my insecurities psychologically, and tried to convince me that, without the steady income he had to offer, my children and I would starve. He added up my earnings from the radio to show that they amounted to nothing. He spoke of me being a single woman in need of male protection.

'Despite all this pressure, when I still resisted going to Delhi, he had me thrown out of Gorakhpur radio. I was a freelancer there, performing whenever they invited me. Mishra-ji was a fixer, whose business it was to cultivate people and get his work done. He somehow found a contact in Gorakhpur radio, who obliged him by getting me removed from the empanelled list of singers. Mishra-ji told me this himself. "Don't think you can fly away. I can clip your wings whenever I want," he said.

'I begged him to get me back on to the radio. He said he would consider it only if I behaved well with him. Swallowing my pride, I did as he wanted. My visits to Delhi resumed. I hated every moment there. The life he had to offer me was so humiliating, so suffocating! More than a couple of times, I even ran back to Banaras without informing him.'

'Yes, I remember that time in your life so well,' Madhu says, not mincing words. 'Which is why I suggested that you take Shama to Bombay. But then Shama let you down. And you had to turn to Mishra-ji for financial help for her wedding expenses. He promised much but ultimately, as always, went back on his word and stingily extended only a fraction of what he had said he would give. Had Shama shown a greater sense of responsibility towards the family, you would not have been in dire straits at that point.'

You are quick to come to your daughter's defence, 'My situation was not of Shama's making. I should never have agreed to become Mishra-ji's mistress in the first place. Abba would always advise me to never stop singing. "Music is your strength, child," he would say. "Music will always be your saviour." I should have heeded him and not stopped performing in mehfils after Maheshwar Singh died. My decision to not go back to Bihar was my worst mistake. It was just false pride that stopped me. What was the worst that could have happened had I continued singing? That I would have been treated as other tawaifs were? Even that might have been preferable to becoming Mishra-ji's goongi gudiya, dumb doll. At least I would have been my own mistress.

'Then one day, after twelve hellish years of being with him, I got my freedom! Mishra-ji, in his seventies by then, died of a heart attack. One shouldn't speak ill of the dead, but to tell you the truth, I felt so relieved, so light in my being, when I heard the news of his passing. That night, I wept and prayed to Allah to never put me at the mercy of a man again. I promised that I would never complain about the hardships I might have to endure being on my own as long as I never had to do the bidding of a man. Never ever.

'Allah has been kind and merciful. He has given me the love and support of friends like Madhu, Rajjo and Chanda aapa. Without them to turn to in times of difficulty, I wouldn't have been able to come so far on my own. He brought you into my life. You have helped me in more ways than you can guess. Your interest in my life has helped me regain pride in myself, in my past.'

You are crying. I have tears in my eyes, as does Madhu. Chanda just looks drunk. Brusquely patting you on your shoulder, she says in her gruff manner, 'Enough of this crying over the past. *Jo beet gayi soh baat gayi*; That which is over, is over. Your daughter is getting married tomorrow. Get going now with the preparations.'

CHAPTER 30

Kab Tak, Merey Maula?

THE MOOD IN THE ROOM is sombre. Sitting opposite your son-in-law, arms crossed purposefully, you are unusually blunt, 'Kindly understand what I am saying. I will not allow Shama and the children to go with you unless you take an oath on the Quran in front of everyone present here that you will never again lift a hand at my daughter.'

There is a murmur in response. Also present in the room are Shama, Amjad's mother, his married elder sister and her husband, Ghafuran and Naeem, Rajjo, Madhu, Chanda and me. Your other relatives, save Asghari, have left after the wedding celebrations ended last night.

Amjad's mother is quick to jump into the fray. 'How dare you speak to my son in this manner, baji! Just till yesterday, you were as sweet as sugar and now you speak to him as if he were some criminal!'

You do not reply, but Shama, sitting close to you, begins shivering in fear and crying. Chanda, in her role as community elder, speaks next. Her tone is conciliatory and surprisingly gentle, 'Amjad is a good boy. I am sure he realises his fault and will have no hesitation in taking a solemn oath that the mistake will never be repeated.'

'I am not at fault!' Amjad thunders back in mutinous fury. 'First teach your daughter some decency. I want a wife, not a dancing girl, in my home. Like mother, like daughter!'

Amjad rages hard and incoherently. The core of his rant seems to be sexual insecurity about Shama. He accuses her of immodest behaviour, sexual impropriety and even cheating. He blames you for encouraging her, since, as a tawaif, that is all that you are capable of teaching your daughters. Shama bawls louder at each accusation. Even Amjad's mother looks shocked, and orders him several times to keep quiet. His sister and brother-in-law embarrassedly try and intervene. You say nothing and hear him out to the end.

Then, standing up to full height, you reply, 'Yes, I am a tawaif, as were your grandmother and aunt. What of that? We are all from the same ilk in this room. So, let's not pretend to be better than the other. I have taught my daughters to be loving, respectful and dutiful wives and daughters-in-law. If my daughter has wronged you in any way, I will be the first to punish her, but I need proof of the misdeeds you say she has committed. Can you find one person who will second the accusations that you have made against her? If you cannot, then keep quiet and listen to me.'

Taking a long pause, you now pull out your surprise revelation like a magician, 'I know all about your affairs with other women. I have proof. You dare accuse my daughter of infidelity when you have been cheating behind her back? I am going to get police cases filed against you for cheating and physically abusing my daughter. I am already in talks with lawyers and will have no hesitation in dragging you to the courts if need be. But I am not going to send Shama and her children back to your home.'

You have prepared well. Whether Shama was aware of her husband's infidelity is not clear, but her piteous weeping heightens the drama of your pronouncement. Amjad looks ashen, as do his mother and sister. Your threat of invoking the Domestic Violence Act has a further sobering effect. His first reaction is to demand that he be allowed to speak alone with Shama. When you refuse to oblige, Amjad tries blackmail. He will abandon Shama, he threatens, by giving her a divorce. Your response is swift. He is welcome to divorce your daughter, you say, but he has to be prepared to lose his children, especially his beloved son.

Ultimately, you win this round. Increasingly isolated, even by his own family, Amjad is left with little option but to take an oath upon the Quran, as you demanded. Peace is restored. Generous in victory, you revert to being the solicitous, respectful mother of a married daughter that you have always been. Plying Shama, Amjad, his children, mother and sister with the customary boxes of sweets and return gifts, you bid them a warm goodbye. Next, you get down to the business of supervising the post-wedding pack-up, taking inventory and settling bills.

Bit by bit, your home is stripped of the finery in which it was decked up till last night. The lights, festoons and buntings are removed. Chairs are carted off. Carpets are rolled up in piles and are now being used by the neighbourhood children as hurdles across which they frenziedly jump back and forth. The marquee that covered the street outside your house is taken down, only its naked bamboo poles still stand. In one corner, stray dogs feast on the remains of the wedding lunch off used plates that will be washed and carted back to the warehouse by the contractor.

It's been over a decade now since that day. You have had to fight many rounds of battle with Amjad in this time. He reneged on his oath within months of returning to Saidpur. Shama spends longer and longer periods in your sanctuary, and yet adamantly clings to her abusive marriage. Caught in a vicious cycle of suffering at Amjad's hands, running back to you when the going becomes unbearable and then returning to him at the slightest hint of remorse, she masks her dependence on him as love and duty towards an errant husband. Prayers have become her substitute for breaking free from an increasingly brutish Amjad. Shama's hopes of redemption now lie in her fifteen-year-old son, Ali, whom she has pampered and indulged over the years. He is the mirror image of his father.

You oscillate between a feeling of deep protectiveness for your daughter and exasperation at her lack of resolve, and try to do the best you can by her under the circumstances. Meenu's marriage, on the other hand, is a source of much satisfaction. Arshad, her husband, has proven to be a loving, responsible life partner and father. He is open-minded and supportive of Meenu's ambition to run her own beauty parlour. Meenu, you say proudly, has fought her own battles for a happier, more fulfilling life. She has not expected you to fight on her behalf. Shama, you say resignedly, must fight for herself too. You cannot forever fight for her. Besides, you have your own daily battles to wage.

Life posed its greatest challenge to you soon after Meenu's wedding. Salma went into convulsions while delivering your second grandchild. The doctors were able to save the baby but failed to revive Salma, who died on the operation table. You returned home with the granddaughter you had wanted so much and with the guilt of Salma's death.

Over and over again, you would ask me if I held you responsible for her demise. Not knowing what to say, I replied, not quite truthfully, that I didn't. The pregnancy had not killed Salma. She had died of complications during childbirth, the cause of which we didn't quite know.

You would look unconvinced and reply, 'It's the same thing. The pregnancy led to childbirth.'

Finally, one day when you posed the same question again I asked, 'Do you hold yourself guilty for pushing Salma to carry her pregnancy?'

You did not reply, but your eyes brimmed over with tears.

Eventually, you stopped asking me that question. Perhaps you had resolved your guilt. More likely, you were too weighed under by new responsibilities to spend time seeking answers to difficult questions.

There was a house to run. Thus far, it was Salma who kept it shipshape. Her children were now your children. Three years old, Haaris looked lost without his mother and cried for her often. Baby Hina had to be nursed. Nanhe, inconsolable in his incoherent grief, required comforting. And in the midst of the terrible loss, shock and mourning that gripped your family, you had to vacate the house that had been your home for over forty years and put down new roots.

Girding up for the challenges ahead, you had been ill prepared for the nasty combat that the highly suggestible Asghari declared, even as she stayed in your home. Under your care, she was making a quick recovery from tuberculosis, yet that did not stop Asghari from being Asghari.

Instigated by Gindo, she demanded that the financial settlement your landlord was prepared to make with you be made with her instead. Citing her tenancy before you had shifted in, Asghari claimed that she was the actual tenant of the house and you an interloper. Eventually, she had to back off in the face of forty years' worth of monthly rent receipts you were able to produce to buttress your claim. But the row resulted in the final rupture of the always thorny relationship that you had shared with your elder sister.

In the first flush of anger, you demanded that she return all the money that you had spent on her medical expenses over the years. To spite Gindo, you staked a claim on Asghari's house in Bhabua as compensation. Once your fury abated, you let go of the claims but refused to allow Asghari to stay in your home any longer.

She returned to Bhabua, since Gindo had no intention of taking her in. Living in the precarious care of an ailing Rani and on the uncertain charity of the extended family, Asghari succumbed to a weak heart and a blocked artery a few months later. Dry-eyed, you went to Bhabua to take charge of her last rites. There was no one else who would.

❁

Meanwhile, you had been busy identifying a new home for yourself, your grandchildren and Nanhe. It had taken time and dogged exertion. After months of searching, with Madhu's help, you had finally chosen a two-storeyed house that miraculously not only fit your budget but was also spacious enough to be let out to tenants and earn for you a monthly income.

The flip side was its location. Far from the familiarity of the old inner-city neighbourhoods of Nariyal Bazaar and Dal Mandi, where you spent the greater part of your life, your new home is situated in one of the unplanned, unkempt, suburban colonies that have been coming up since the twentieth century to accommodate Banaras's growing working-class and lower-middle-class population. The last house on an unpaved lane, which spews dust clouds in the summers and ankle-deep muddy slime through the monsoons, your home is next to a vast gurgling swamp that gorges on the locality's garbage and lets out shiny green bubbles of gaseous malevolence.

Sharing in the tribulations posed by erratic electricity, contaminated water supply and the ever-present mosquitoes are your new neighbours, relatively recent migrants to the city—tailors, artisans, clerks, petty traders, shopkeepers and schoolteachers—who have no association with the music and dance that is your past. While you value the anonymity this new home offers, there is also the isolation and loneliness of living among strangers.

You are now housebound, and have had to acquire new skills of keeping home, cooking and cleaning that, as a tawaif, you had never had to master. In the last ten years, our conversations have entered new realms. We often find ourselves exchanging recipes and household tips—subjects we rarely, if ever, discussed earlier.

Retired and with no earnings, save the paltry monthly rent you get from tenants and interest from your savings, you are reconciled to the lack of familial enthusiasm to help with the running of your house. Though it hurts, you have also stoically accepted abandonment by relatives and friends who thronged your old home on social visits. Your new house is too inconveniently located and too uncomfortable, without Salma's efficient hospitality, for them to make the effort. Television is your faithful companion now. The simulated life offered by its dramas fills the silence of empty rooms. What does rankle, though, is the absence of the always-dependable Ghafuran. You reluctantly earned her resentment by selling the house in Bhabua to meet the increasing needs of two growing grandchildren.

At the threshold of old age, you have had to parent Haaris and Hina on your own. Though well aware of your remarkable ability to rise up to life's challenges, I am amazed by the success you have made of bringing them up. You forego basic necessities for yourself but indulge their childish whims. And yet, maintaining a fine balance, you also enforce discipline to instil in them the virtues of being responsible. Always a believer in education, you have insisted on sending them to a good school, taught yourself anew to be able to help them with their homework, spent long hours keeping vigil while they prepared for their exams, enthused them to do better if they fared poorly and exulted in their success when they did well.

There is also Nanhe to look after. He never recovered from Salma's loss, and has long given up the valiant fight against his disability that he put up when she was alive. He lost his job early on as a result. He refuses to come out of his room and has become a recluse, completely dependent on you. His hearing is impaired and he has been steadily losing his eyesight. You have shown him to doctors, made him undergo umpteen medical tests. The diagnosis is always the same. Nanhe's condition will deteriorate progressively. The best that you can do is keep him comfortable.

Over the years, you have had to confront your mortality in the face of the death of near and dear ones. Your aunts Phoolmani and Sakeena and your gentle cousin Rani are no more. Tara too is gone. Perhaps the most wrenching loss has been Shanney Khan Sahib's death. Gone with him is the reassurance of love and support that he always extended to you like a father. Gone too are the opportunities he created, to introduce and promote you with outstation musicians and researchers who sought him out during visits to Banaras.

Though you rarely dwell upon it, the demands of your new life have been at the cost of music. As a full-time home-maker and a mother, you have had to sacrifice your riyaz and ties with associates from your musical past. You are only sporadically in touch with your old tabla accompanist Sajjan Kumar, since he no longer brings foreign students to your doorstep. Your new home is just too far from the attractions of the ghats and temples of 'eternal' Banaras for most foreign tourists to make the trudge. Besides, you now neither have the time nor the inclination to teach music. No one in your neighbourhood knows of your past as a singer. They think of you as an elderly Muslim widow leading an eminently respectable, if difficult, life looking after her family. And you wish to keep it that way. Foreigners and the sound of music would make neighbours curious. You don't want them to ask questions. You want your grandchildren to grow up untouched by the stigma of your past.

It is for this reason that you haven't taught Haaris and Hina any music. Haaris especially has inherited from you a love for music and a strong singing voice. You have noticed that he is sureela, tuneful, and are proud of it but reluctant to teach him yourself. At my repeated insistence that music not be allowed to die out in your family, you have made vague promises about sending him to learn khayal from a Shashtri-ji living close by, but have thus far found some reason or the other to defer doing so.

You have, however, been firm that both your grandchildren attend daily classes to learn the Quran. Haaris spends an hour before school at the neighbourhood mosque, while little Hina goes to an ustani living close by after school hours. This does not come as a surprise. I am well aware of your deep religious convictions. Your own children too were brought up as Muslim, sent for Quran lessons during childhood, and initiated into the practice of offering prayers and observing Ramzan as they grew older.

The actual observance of these practices, you left to their discretion, never imposing your will upon them. Your own practise of faith has always been private and free of dogma. I have not known you to need external markers of religion to prove your identity as a practising Muslim. The depth of your faith has imbued you with the quiet confidence to sidestep orthodoxy, insularity and sectarianism. Rooted in the observance of South Asian Islam, your faith has been catholic, with room for the syncretic practices that your family has followed through generations as part of community tradition.

Your adoption of more public markers of religion and emphasis on more orthodox practices for yourself and your grandchildren over the past few years, therefore, came as a surprise initially. Whereas in the past, the milestones in your children's religious schooling were marked by simple, low-key family festivities, you celebrated Haaris and Hina's ameen—completion of the first reading of the Quran—a couple of years ago with an elaborate function. Relatives and friends from Banaras and elsewhere and your entire neighbourhood were invited, an extravagance you could ill afford.

Even though Hina is only ten years old, you insist she wear a headscarf whenever she steps out. You have taken to wearing a chador in public, after spending a lifetime eschewing hijab. You have abandoned the more catholic term for goodbye, Khuda hafiz, for the more Islamic Allah hafiz, and made your grandchildren adopt it as well. You have become punctilious about offering namaz five times a day, and are firm that thirteen-year-old Haaris offer Friday prayers even if he has to miss his much-loved cricket practise at school. You are equally insistent that he observe fast through the entire period of Ramzan as you do. Little Hina too is encouraged to keep as many rozas as she can at her young age.

Over time, as your friend, I have come to understand your achingly deep loneliness that seeks solace and a sense of belonging. Isolated from family and friends and living among strangers, you attempt to address these needs within the orthodox parameters of organised religion. Linked to this is your intense desire for acceptability in the small Muslim community of your new neighbourhood. They are mostly educated, and as clerks, shopkeepers and schoolteachers, form the 'gentry' among the majority working-class Hindu population in your area. You crave the respectability of your Muslim neighbours for Haaris and Hina, and often talk with pride about the easy access they enjoy in these 'respectable' homes on account of being well-mannered, 'good' children. You are proud of the compliments that come your way for bringing them up to be such pious Muslims at this young age.

The increasing religious polarisation over the past decade in your neighbourhood and city plays on your mind too. Never a believer in religious divides, you had shared warm and friendly relationships with your primarily Hindu neighbours in Nariyal Bazaar and had hoped to replicate the same in your new home. Your new immediate neighbours, almost all Hindus, responded politely enough to your overtures. But there is no mistaking the distance that they have continued to maintain, despite your best efforts at friendliness.

Part of their reserve is due to cultural differences. Your sophisticated urbanity is at a remove from the rustic lifestyle of your working-class neighbours, many of whom are first-generation migrants to the city. The main reason, though, is your Muslim identity. Even vegetarian food cooked in your home is suspect and rarely, if ever, partaken by your Hindu neighbours. Family celebrations and community festivals distance you from them, instead of bringing you closer as they had in the past. Only a handful among them came for your grandchildren's ameen, although you had invited the entire neighbourhood and made provisions for the separate cooking of vegetarian food by a halwai. Invitations to religious celebrations, like katha recitations and pujas, organised in your neighbours' homes are infrequent. Few, if any, Hindu neighbours make the effort to visit you on festivals, despite your warm invitation. Hina came home crying last Eid because the little children in the neighbourhood taunted her that her family slaughtered cows to celebrate the festival. A cricket enthusiast, Haaris is targeted every time India loses to Pakistan in an international match. He has now stopped playing cricket in the neighbourhood.

Though seemingly minor, the slights, taunts, jeers and derisive comments mirror more ominous developments. Over the past few years, you have noticed bands of boys in khaki shorts gather early in the morning in the nearby maidan in front of a saffron flag. Their aggressive gestures and angry slogans make you fearful. You have never seen such gatherings before, either in Bhabua or in your old mohalla of Nariyal Bazaar.

These boys often take the lead in organising celebratory processions through the neighbourhood on festive occasions. As a long-term Muslim resident in Banaras, you are no stranger to huge Hindu pageants that are so much a part of your city's annual calendar. They have never before inspired fear in you. Rather, their pomp, gaiety, colour, noise and anarchy provided a welcome break from the routine of daily life. Not anymore. The sinister intermixing of aggressive political rhetoric, saffron and tricolour flags, intimidating martial symbols of unsheathed swords and trishuls, and the religious passion of the processions organised by the boys in khaki shorts makes you apprehensive. On several occasions, the participants have been known to verbally abuse and sometimes even physically bully visibly Muslim-looking onlookers. This is again a new and frightening development in variance with your experience of the old city where Hindu and Muslim neighbours stood together and not against each other.

You have been witness in the past to the fires of sectarian passions that have periodically engulfed Banaras. You vividly remember the violent outbreaks in the early 1990s, resulting from the anti-Muslim rhetoric of Hindutva fanatics over the Babri mosque, and in 1992, after they demolished the mosque. There were curfews through this period in Banaras, including in Nariyal Bazaar. But you had lived with the confidence of being in the safekeeping of your Hindu neighbours who shared with you, when there was need, their rations of food and other essentials.

It is an assumption that you can no longer afford to make, not just about your new neighbourhood but about your city. Banaras voted in an avowedly chauvinistic Hindutva leader as its representative to the Lok Sabha. He was also the right-wing Bharatiya Janata Party's prime ministerial candidate. His chilling anti-Muslim utterances, and the subsequent rise in systemic discrimination against minorities, the frequent attacks on Muslims in the name of beef-eating and love jihad, the elevation as chief minister of Uttar Pradesh of a Hindu religious head known more for his anti-minority fanaticism than his spiritual beliefs, have all made you achingly aware of your vulnerability as a Muslim.

With every passing day, the scorching fires of hatred and violence spreading across the country seem to draw in closer. Rajjo's youngest son Rafiq and his wife Preeti have had to leave the family home and go into hiding for daring to fall in love and get married across the lines of religious divide—a union now described as 'love jihad'. After initial objections to the match, Preeti's parents have made their peace with her choice. Self-proclaimed protectors of the faith, however, have been harder to convince. Declaring the marriage part of a 'jihadi conspiracy' to convert Hindu girls to Islam, they have labelled Rafiq a criminal and Preeti a misguided victim in need of rescue from her legally wedded husband.

You remark upon the irony of the situation. Rajjo's children, like your own, are born of Hindu fathers. Today, there are ugly demonstrations outside her house, demanding custody of the Hindu daughter-in-law whom she and her son stand accused of brainwashing to the jihadi cause.

You are fearful about the safety of your family and baffled by the accusations levied at Rajjo and Rafiq. 'What is jihadi about falling in love and getting married?'

You understand the larger politics behind the manufacture of fear, mistrust and hatred. But the senseless violence perpetrated with terrifying regularity by seemingly ordinary people has left you shocked. You called me up upon hearing of the brutal murder of a schoolboy by the passengers of a local train in Delhi. His only fault was that he was a Muslim. 'He was just a boy, Saba,' you wept for the unknown Junaid. 'He was only two or three years older than my Haaris.' Understandably, you have become nervous about allowing your grandchildren, and especially Haaris, to venture out on his own.

Your heightened sense of insecurity is shared by the other Muslim families in your area. Pushed to the margins, they have sought safety in each other and in the markers of organised religion. Though hailing from different castes and regions, they form a close-knit community in which you too have carved out a space for yourself. As khala to everyone, you help out young wives and mothers with sage advice, share in the gossip with elderly matriarchs and take active part in the collective celebrations and sufferings of the community.

The community too stands by you when there is need. Recently, your attempts to get rid of a tenant who continued to default on regular payment of rent got caught in the quagmire of shrill sectarian-political rhetoric. The tenant counter-accused you of cooking and eating beef, and thus hurting his religious sentiments. He sought the help of the neighbourhood boys in khaki knickers to intimidate you and threatened to report you to the police. Terrified and alone, you found yourself in the humiliating position of explaining your dietary habits to your neighbours. The matter was resolved only after some politically influential Muslim elders in the locality used their connections with the local councillor and legislator to prevail upon the boys in khaki to back off and to have the tenant ousted from your house.

Your sense of hurt is palpable. 'I have never made any difference between people on account of their religion, but today I get threatened and insulted just because I am a Muslim! What madness is this?'

In desperate need of solace, like a homing bird, you go back to Chowk in the old city and pray at the tiny mazar of Baba Zahid Shareef, your local guardian in Banaras. You then walk down to the ghats on the Ganga and feed the fish. These rituals have provided you spiritual succour in the past and remain intrinsic to your being.

The visit somewhat calms the restlessness in your heart, the anxiety that gnaws at your being, but not entirely. You then make a special trip to Bhabua. The death of Pyaari khala and Asghari and the sale of your agricultural lands and the house in Bhabua, and especially the resultant coldness in your ties with Ghafuran and her family, have meant that you rarely have reason to visit the town as you did so often in the past. Yet, Bhabua will always be your watan, the place where your story began.

Alighting at the bus stop, you make your way straight to the shrine of the Sufi protector of your family, Baba Court Shaheed. In your hand you clutch a platter of malida, flowers and incense sticks. After making your offerings, you sit down near Baba's grave. Clutching the latticed railing surrounding it, and resting your head upon the rails, you whisper fervently to Baba, as a daughter does upon her return home, about the sorrows that lie heavy in your heart. Seeking his continued benevolence upon you and your family, you share with him your anxieties about being a single woman and a Muslim in the India of today.

Tears streaming down your face, deep in prayer, you sit at the dargah for a long time. Slowly, the shadows lengthen and the shrine empties of other devotees. As the caretakers of the shrine begin to light lamps, your feverish prayers take on the form of music. After many years of being parted from your songs, you find yourself singing a bandish that, breaking free from the deep recesses of your heart, rises as a plaintive cry to your lips:

Kab tak, merey Maula? Kab tak, merey Maula?
Mein harf-e-tamanna hun
Badi der sey chup hun
Kab tak, merey Maula?

Select Bibliography

Aalok Paradkar, *Padma Vibhushan Pandit Kishan Maharaj*, Pandit Kishan Maharaj Abhinandan Samaroh Samiti, Varanasi, 2002.

Abdul Halim Sharar (E.S Harcourt and Fakhir Hussain, Trs and Eds), *Lucknow: The Last Phase of an Oriental Culture*, Oxford University Press, New Delhi, 2004.

Acharya Chatursen, *Vaishali ki Nagarvadhu*, Hind Pocket Books, Delhi, 2001.

Alain Danielou, *The Ragas of Northern Indian Music*, Munshiram Manoharlal Publishers, Delhi, 2010.

Amaresh Misra, *War of Civilisations: India AD 1857*, Vol. 1 and 2, Rupa and Co., New Delhi, 2008.

Amlan Das Gupta (Ed.), *Music and Modernity: North Indian Classical Music in an Age of Mechanical Reproduction*, Thema, Kolkata, 2007.

Amritlal Nagar, *Yeh Kothewaliyan*, Lokbharti, Allahabad, 2001.

Aneesh Pradhan, *Hindustani Music in Colonial Bombay*, Three Essays Collective, New Delhi, 2014.

Anis Azmi (Ed.), *Agha Hashra Kashmiri ke Chuninda Drame*, Vol. 1 and 2, National School of Drama, Delhi, 2004.

Anna Morcom, *Courtesans, Bar Girls & Dancing Boys: The Illicit Worlds of Indian Dance*, Hachette India, Gurgaon, 2014.

Anuja Agarwal, *Chaste Wives & Prostitute Sisters: Patriarchy and Prostitution among the Bedias of India*, Routledge India, New Delhi, 2008.

Arthur Golden, *Memoirs of a Geisha*, Vintage Books, USA, 2005.

Ashok Da. Ranade, *Some Hindustani Musicians: They Lit the Way!*, Promilla & Co. Publishers, New Delhi, 2011.

Ashok Da. Ranade, *Music Contexts: A Concise Dictionary of Hindustani Music*, Promilla & Co. Publishers, New Delhi, 2011.

Ashok Da. Ranade, *Hindustani Music*, National Book Trust, New Delhi, 2002.

Ashraf Aziz, *Light of the Universe: Essays on Hindustani Film Music*, Three Essays Collective, New Delhi, 2003.

Ashwini Tambe, *Codes of Misconduct: Regulating Prostitution in Late Colonial Bombay*, Zubaan, New Delhi, 2009.

C.A. Bayly, *Rulers, Townsmen and Bazaars: North Indian Society in the Age of British Expansion, 1770–1870*, Cambridge University Press, Cambridge, 1990.

C.S. Lakshmi, *The Singer & the Song*, Kali for Women, New Delhi, 2000.

Charu Gupta, *Sexuality, Obscenity, Community, Women, Muslims, and the Hindu Public in Colonial India*, Permanent Black, Delhi, 2000.

Christopher Hibbert, *The Great Mutiny: India 1857*, Allen Lane, London, 1980.

Daniel M. Neuman, *The Life of Music in North India: The Organization of an Artistic Tradition*, University of Chicago Press, Chicago, 1989.

Davesh Soneji, *Unfinished Gestures: Devadasis, Memory and Modernity in South India*, University of Chicago Press, Chicago, 2012.

David Arnold, *Colonizing the Body: State Medicine and Epidemic Disease in Nineteenth Century India*, Oxford University Press, New Delhi, 1993.

Deana Heath, *Purifying Empire: Obscenity and the Politics of Moral Regulation in Britain, India and Australia*, Cambridge University Press, UK, 2010.

Deepa Ganesh, *A Life in Three Octaves: The Musical Journey of Gangubai Hangal*, Three Essays Collective, New Delhi, 2013.

Deepti Priya Mehrotra, *Gulab Bai: The Queen of Nautanki Theatre*, Penguin India, New Delhi, 2006.

Diana L. Eck, *Banaras: City of Light*, Routledge, London, 1983.

Eric Stokes, *The Peasant and the Raj: Studies in Agrarian Society and Peasant Rebellion in Colonial India*, Cambridge University Press, UK, 1980.

Eric Stokes (C.A. Bayly, Ed.), *The Peasant Armed: The Indian Rebellion of 1857*, Clarendon Press, Oxford, 1986.

F.C. Daly, *Manual of Criminal Classes Operating in Bengal*, The Bengal Secretariat Press, Calcutta, 1916.

Fouzia Saeed, *Taboo! The Hidden Culture of a Red Light Area*, Oxford University Press, Karachi, 2001.

Francesca Orsini (Ed.), *Before the Divide: Hindi and Urdu Literary Culture*, Orient Blackswan, New Delhi, 2011.

Francesca Orsini, *The Hindi Public Sphere: 1920–1940—Language and Literature in the Age of Nationalism*, Oxford University Press, New Delhi, 2009.

Francis Buchanan, *An Account of the District of Behar and Patna in 1811–12*, Bihar and Orissa Research Society, Patna, 1939.

Francis Buchanan, *An Account of the District of Shahabad in 1812–13*, Bihar and Orissa Research Society, Patna, 1934.

Gyanendra Pandey, *The Construction of Communalism in Colonial North India*, Oxford University Press, New Delhi, 1992.

H.H. Risley, *The Tribes and Castes of Bengal*, Vol. I, reprinted by Firma Mukhopadhyay, Calcutta, 1981 (First Edition by Bengal Secretariat Press, 1891).

H.R. Luthra, *Indian Broadcasting*, Publications Division, Ministry of Information and Broadcasting, Government of India, New Delhi, 1986.

Hasan Shah (Qurratulain Hyder, Tr.), *The Nautch Girl*, Sterling Publishers, New Delhi, 1992.

Indrani Chatterjee and Richard M. Eaton (Eds), *Slavery & South Asian History*, Indiana University Press, Bloomington, 2006.

Janaki Bakhle, *Two Men and Music: Nationalism in the Making of an Indian Classical Tradition*, Permanent Black, Delhi, 2006.

Janaki Nair, *Women and Law in Colonial India: A Social History*, Kali for Women, New Delhi, 1996.

Jawaid Alam, *Government and Politics in Colonial Bihar, 1921–1937*, Mittal Publications, New Delhi, 2004.

Jean D' Cunha, *The Legalization of Prostitution: A Sociological Inquiry into the Laws Relating to Prostitution in India and the West*, Wordmakers and CISRS, Bangalore, 1991.

Joep Bor, Francoise 'Nalini' Delvoye, Jane Harvey and Emmie Te Nijenhuis (Eds), *Hindustani Music: Thirteenth to Twentieth Centuries*, Manohar, New Delhi, 2010.

Joep Bor, *The Raga Guide: A Survey of 74 Hindustani Ragas*, Nimbus Records, Charlottesville, VA, 1999.

Kamehwarnath Mishra, *Kashi ki Sangeet Parampara*, Bharat Book Centre, Lucknow, 1997.

Kathryn Hansen, *Grounds for Play: The Nautanki Theatre of North India*, University of California Press, Berkeley, 1993.

Kay Jordan, *From Sacred Servant to Profane Prostitute: A History of the Changing Legal Status of the Devadasis in India, 1857–1947*, Manohar Publishers, New Delhi, 2003.

Kenneth Ballhatchet, *Race, Sex and Class Under the Raj: Imperial Attitudes and Policies and their Critics, 1793–1905*, Vikas Publishing House, New Delhi, 1980.

Kumar Prasad Mukherji, *The Lost World of Hindustani Music*, Penguin India, New Delhi, 2006.

Lakshmi Subramanian, *Veena Dhanammal: The Making of a Legend*, Routledge India, New Delhi, 2009.

Lakshmi Vishwanathan, *Women of Pride: The Devadasi Heritage*, Lotus Collection, New Delhi, 2008.

Lalita du Perron, *Hindi Poetry in a Musical Genre: Thumri Lyrics*, Routledge, New York, 2007.

Leela Gulati and Jasodhara Bagchi (Eds), *A Space of Her Own: Personal Narratives of Twelve Women*, SAGE Publications, New Delhi, 2005.

Liza Dalby, *Geisha*, Vintage Books, London, 2000.

Louise Brown, *The Dancing Girls of Lahore*, Fourth Estate, New York, 2005.

M.A. Laird (Ed.), *Bishop Heber in Northern India: Selections from Heber's Journal*, Cambridge University Press, Cambridge, 1971.

M.A. Sherring, *Benares the Sacred City: In Ancient and Modern Times*, Book Faith India, Delhi, 2000.

M.A. Sherring, *Hindu Tribes and Castes as Represented in Benaras*, Thacker, Spink and Co., Calcutta, 1872.

Madhu Kishwar, *Gandhi and Women*, Manushi Prakashan, New Delhi, 1986.

Madhu Trivedi, *The Emergence of the Hindustani Tradition: Music, Dance and Drama in North India, 13th to 19th Centuries*, Three Essays Collective, New Delhi, 2012.

Martin Gaenszle and Jorg Gengmagel (Eds), *Visualizing Space in Banaras: Images, Maps, and the Practice of Representation*, Oxford University Press, New Delhi, 2008.

Michael Kinnear, *The Gramophone Company's First Indian Recordings, 1899–1908*, Popular Prakashan, Bombay, 1994.

Michael Kinnear, *The 78 R.P.M. Record Labels of India*, Apollo Bay, Victoria, 2016.

Michael S. Dodson, *Banaras: Urban Forms and Cultural Histories*, Routledge India, New Delhi, 2012.

Mirza Ghalib (Saiyyed Ainul Hasan, Tr.), *Dastambu: Mirza Ghalib ki Diary*, Sandarbh Prakashan, Delhi, 1989.

Mirza Jafar Hussain, *Qadeem Lucknow ki Akhiri Bahar*, Taraqqi e Urdu Bureau, Vizarat e Taleem, New Delhi, 1981.

Mirza Mohammad Hadi Ruswa (Khushwant Singh & M.A. Husaini, Trs), *Umrao Jan Ada*, Sangam Books, Delhi, 2009.

Montgomery Martin, *The History, Antiquities, Topography and Statistics of Eastern India*, Vol. 1, Behar (Patna City) and Shahabad, Cosmo Publications, Delhi, 1976.

Moti Chandra, *The World of Courtesans*, Vikas Publishing House, Bombay, 1973.

Mrinalini Sinha, *Specters of Mother India: The Global Restructuring of an Empire*, Duke University Press, Durham, 2006.

Namita Devidayal, *The Music Room*, Penguin India, New Delhi, 2008.

Nandi Bhatia, *Performing Women, Performing Womanhood: Theatre, Politics, and Dissent in North India*, Oxford University Press, New Delhi, 2010.

Nazir Ahmad, *The Bride's Mirror: A Tale of Life in Delhi a Hundred Years Ago*, Permanent Black, New Delhi, 2002.

Neepa Majumdar, *Wanted Cultured Ladies Only!: Female Stardom and Cinema in India, 1930s–1950s*, Oxford University Press, New Delhi, 2010.

Nita Kumar, *The Artisans of Banaras: Popular Culture and Identity, 1880–1986*, Princeton University Press, Princeton, 1988.

Unknown, *Sachitra Mashhoor Gawaiyye*, Varanasi.

P.C. Roy Chaudhury, *Bihar District Gazetteers*, Shahabad, Superintendent Secretariat Press, Patna, 1966.

P.J.O. Taylor, *What Really Happened During the Mutiny: A Day-by-Day Account of the Major Events of 1857–1859 in India*, Oxford University Press, New Delhi, 1997.

Peter Manuel, *Cassette Culture, Popular Music and Technology in North India*, Oxford University Press, New Delhi, 2001.

Peter Manuel, *Thumri in Historical and Stylistic Perspectives*, Motilal Banarsidass, New Delhi, 1990.

Prabha Kotiswaran (Ed.), *Sex Work* (part of the series 'Issues in Contemporary Indian Feminism'), Women Unlimited, New Delhi, 2011.

Prabhat Ranjan, *Kothagoi: Chaturbhuj Sthan ke Kisse*, Vani Prakashan, New Delhi, 2015.

Pran Neville, *Nautch Girls of the Raj*, Penguin India, New Delhi, 2009.

Pratibha Agarwal (Ed.), *Master Fida Hussain: Parsi Theatre mein Pachas Varsh*, Natya Shodh Sansthan, Calcutta, 1986.

Premchand, *Sevasadan*, Manoj Pocket Books, Delhi, 2012.

Qurratulain Hyder, *Agle Janam Mohe Bitiya Na Keejo*, Rajkamal, Delhi, 1999.

Radha Kumar, *The History of Doing*, Zubaan, New Delhi, 1993.

Radhika Singha, *A Despotism of Law: Crime and Justice in Early Colonial India*, Oxford University Press, New Delhi, 1998.

Reginald Heber, *Narrative of a Journey: Through Upper Provinces of India*, Vol. 1, Low Price Publications, Delhi, 1993.

Rimli Bhattacharya (Ed. and Tr.), *Binodini Dasi: My Story and My Life as an Actress*, Kali for Women, New Delhi, 1998.

Rita Ganguly and Jyoti Sabharwal, *Ae Mohabbat: Reminiscing Begum Akhtar*, Stellar Publishers, New Delhi, 2008.

Rohini Sahni, V. Kalyan Shankar and Hemant Apte (Eds), *Prostitution and Beyond: An Analysis of Sex Work in India*, SAGE Publications, New Delhi, 2008.

S.K. Ghosh, *Bihar in Flames*, APH Publishing Corporation, Delhi, 2000.

S.G. Bannerjee, *The Princes and the Dancing Girls*, Kamala Press, Varanasi, 1967.

Malka Pukhraj (Saleem Kidwai, Tr.), *Song Sung True: A Memoir*, Kali for Women, New Delhi, 2003.

Sandria Frietag (Ed.), *Culture and Power in Banaras: Community, Performance and Environment, 1800–1980*, Oxford University Press, New Delhi, 1992.

Sashi Bhusan Chaudhuri, *Civil Rebellion in the Indian Mutinies, 1857–1859*, World Press, Calcutta, 1957.

Savita Devi & Vibha S. Chauhan, *Ma Siddheshwari*, The Lotus Collection, Roli Books, New Delhi, 2000.

Shanti Hiranand, *Begum Akhtar: The Story of My Ammi*, Viva Books, New Delhi, 2005.

Sheila Dhar, *Raga'n Josh: Stories from a Musical Life*, Permanent Black, New Delhi, 2005.

Sonia Faleiro, *Beautiful Thing: Inside the Secret World of Bombay's Dance Bars*, Hamish Hamilton, New Delhi, 2010.

Sumanta Bannerjee, *Dangerous Outcast: The Prostitute in Nineteenth Century Bengal*, Seagull Books, Calcutta, 1998.

Sumathi Ramaswamy, *The Goddess and the Nation: Mapping Mother India*, Zubaan, New Delhi, 2010.

Susheela Misra, *Some Immortals of Hindustani Music*, Harman Publishing House, New Delhi, 1990.

Tapan Raychaudhuri and Irfan Habib (Eds), *The Cambridge Economic History of India*, Vol. 1: 1200 to 1750, Cambridge University Press and Orient Longman, Delhi, 1984.

Thomas Babington Macaulay, *Critical Historical and Miscellaneous Essays and Poems*, Vol. 2, American Book Exchange, New York, 1880.

Thomas R. Metcalf, *Land, Landlords and the British Raj: Northern India in the Nineteenth Century*, South Asian Edition, Oxford University Press, New Delhi, 1979.

Thomas R. Metcalf, *The Aftermath of Revolt: India, 1857–1870*, Manohar Publishers, New Delhi, 1990.

T.J.S. George, *MS: A Life in Music*, HarperCollins India, New Delhi, 2007.

T.J.S. George, *The Life and Times of Nargis*, East West Books, Chennai, 2007.

Uttam Kamble (Kishore Divse, Tr.), *Devadasi*, Samvad Prakashan, Mumbai, 2008.

Vamanrao H. Deshpande, *Indian Musical Traditions, An Aesthetic Study of the Gharanas in Hindustani Music*, Popular Prakashan, Mumbai, 2001.

Vasudha Dalmia, *The Nationalization of Hindu Traditions: Bhartendu Harischandra and Nineteenth-century Banaras*, Oxford University Press, New Delhi, 1997.

Vikram Sampath, *My Name is Gauhar Jan!: The Life and Times of a Musician*, Rupa, New Delhi, 2012.

W.W. Hunter, *A Statistical Account of Bengal*, Vol. XII: Districts of Gaya and Shahabad, Concept Publishing Company, Delhi, 1976.

Zoë Yalland, *Traders and Nabobs*, M. Russell, Salisbury, 1987.

Zoya Hasan, *Forging Identities: Gender, Communities and the State*, Kali For Women, New Delhi, 1994.

Articles, Papers and Essays

Badri Narayan, 'Popular Culture and 1857: Memory Against Forgetting', *The 1857 Rebellion* (Biswamoy Pati, Ed.), Oxford University Press, New Delhi, 2011.

Bernard S. Cohn, 'The Census, Social Structure, and Objectification in South Asia', *Caste in History* (Ishita Banerjee-Dube, Ed.), Oxford in India Readings: Themes in Indian History, Oxford University Press, New Delhi, 2008.

David Lelyveld, 'Transmitters and Culture: The Colonial Roots of Indian Broadcasting', *South Asia Research*, SAGE Journals, Vol. 10, No. 1, May 1990.

David Lelyveld, 'Upon the Subdominant: Administering Music on All India Radio', *Social Text*, Duke University Press, No. 39, Summer 1994.

Erica Wald, 'From begums and bibis to abandoned females and idle women: sexual relationships, venereal disease and the redefinition of prostitution in early nineteenth-century India', *The Indian Economic and Social History Review*, SAGE Publications, 5 May 2009.

Gyanendra Pandey, 'Rallying Round the Cow: Sectarian Strife in the Bhojpur Region, 1888–1917', *CSSSC Occasional Paper*, Centre for Studies in Social Sciences, Calcutta, No. 39, 1981.

Jon Barlow, Lakshmi Subramanian, 'Music and Society in North India: From the Mughals to the Mutiny', *Economic and Political Weekly*, Vol. 42, Issue No. 19, 12 May 2007.

Kunal M. Parker, 'A Corporation of Superior Prostitutes: Anglo-Indian Legal Conceptions of Temple Dancing Girls, 1800–1914', *Modern Asian Studies*, Cambridge University Press, Vol. 32, No. 3, July 1998.

Lakshmi Subramanian, 'Faith and the Musician', *Economic and Political Weekly*, Vol. 41, No. 45, 11 November 2006.

Lata Singh, 'Women Performers as Subjects in Popular Theatres: Tamasha and Nautanki', *History and Sociology of South Asia*, SAGE Publications, 1 January 2010.

Max Katz, 'Institutional Communalism in North Indian Classical Music', *Ethnomusicology*, University of Illinois Press on behalf of Society for Ethnomusicology, Vol. 56, No. 2, Spring/Summer 2012.

Melita Waligora, 'What is Your "Caste"? The Classification of Indian Society as Part of the British Civilizing Mission', *Colonialism as Civilizing Mission: Cultural Ideology in British India* (Harald Fischer-Tine, Michael Mann, Eds.), Wimbledon Publishing Company, London, 2004.

Prashant Iyengar, 'Navigating the Public Private Divide through the 19th-century Legal Archive', LASSNET Conference, December 2010.

Rimli Bhattacharya, 'The nautee in "the second city of the Empire"', *The Indian Economic Social History Review*, SAGE Journals, Vol. 40, No. 2, 2003.

Sadanand Menon, 'From National Culture to Cultural Nationalism', *On Nationalism* (Romila Thapar, A.G. Noorani and Sadanand Menon, Eds.), Aleph, New Delhi, 2016.

Sandria Frietag, 'Crime in the Social Order of Colonial North India', *Modern Asian Studies*, Cambridge University Press, Vol. 25, No. 2, May 1991.

Sandria B. Freitag, 'Sacred Symbols as Mobilizing Ideology: The North Indian Search for a "Hindu" Community', *Comparative Studies in Society and History*, Cambridge University Press, Vol. 22, No. 4, October 1980.

Sanjay Nigam, 'Disciplining and Policing the "Criminals by Birth"—Part 1: The Making of a Colonial Stereotype: The Criminal Tribes and Castes of North India', The *Indian Economic Social History Review*, SAGE Publications, Vol. 27, No. 2, 1990.

Sanjay Nigam, 'Disciplining and Policing the "Criminals by Birth"—Part 2: The Development of a Disciplinary System, 1871–1900', *The Indian Economic Social History Review*, SAGE Publications, Vol. 27, No. 3, 1990.

Sanjay Srivastava, 'Thinking About, but Beyond, "Lata Mangeshkar"', *Economic and Political Weekly*, Vol. 40, No. 28, 9 July 2005.

Shadab Bano, 'Women Performers and Prostitutes in Medieval India', *Studies in History*, SAGE Journals, 10 January 2012.

Sharmila Rege, 'The Hegemonic Appropriation of Sexuality: The Case of the Lavani Performers of Maharashtra', *Contributions to Indian Sociology*, SAGE Journals, 1 January 1995.

Sheba Chhachhi, 'The Householder, the Ascetic and the Politician: Women Sadhus at the Kumbh Mela', *India International Centre Quarterly (India: A National Culture?)*, Vol. 29, No. 3/4, Winter 2002–Spring 2003.

Stephen Hennigham, 'Quit India in Bihar and Eastern United Provinces: The Dual Revolt', *Subaltern Studies 2*, (Ranajit Guha, Ed.), Oxford University Press, New Delhi, 1983.

Suresh Chandvankar, 'Odeon Label Discs in India', *The Record News*, The Journal of The Society of Indian Record Collectors, annual issue, TRN 2010.

Veena Talwar Oldenburg, 'Lifestyle as Resistance: The Case of the Courtesans of Lucknow, India', *Feminist Studies (Speaking for Others, Speaking for Self: Women of Color)*, Vol. 16, No. 2, Summer, 1990, pp. 259–287.

Vidya Rao, '"Thumri" as Feminine Voice', *Economic and Political Weekly*, Vol. 25, No. 17, 28 April 1990.

Acknowledgements

I WOULD LIKE TO THANK New India Foundation for the fellowship that made the research for this book possible. I am deeply indebted to Ramachandra Guha for his encouragement at all stages of writing and for his very useful comments after reading through the first draft of the manuscript. Grateful thanks also to Rivka Israel for her painstaking editing of the first draft.

My gratitude to the publishers, Westland, for the faith they reposed in me. I would especially like to thank Ajitha G.S. not only for her valuable inputs as an editor at every stage of the book but also for the warmth and cheer she brought to our collaboration. Heartfelt thanks too to Orijit Sen for his inspired cover illustration and to Vishwajyoti Ghosh for the striking cover design.

The book comes out of the documentary that I made in 2009, *The Other Song*. My gratitude to the India Foundation for the Arts for supporting the making of the film that started me on this exploration of the social history of the tawaifs.

Warmest thanks to my research associates: Shrimoyee Nandini Ghosh for her invaluable help with archival research, especially in the area of law-making and the ways in which it impinged upon the traditional lifestyle and customary practices of the tawaif community, and Rizvan ul Haq for his meticulous research of archival and literary material in Urdu and Hindi. I would also like to acknowledge the invaluable help with research that I received in Bihar from Manoj Kumar.

For their friendship and generosity in sharing with me their memories and experiences, my most grateful thanks to Malik Dilbar Hussain, Rani Begum, Zarina Begum, Qurban Hussain, Banno Begum and Daya Kumari. Without them to show the way, this book might not have been possible.

I am deeply indebted to Krishna Kumar Rastogi, Vaidya Shiv Kumar Shashtri, Rai Anand Krishan, Ramzan Khan, Sharafat Khan, Mehtab

Khan, Dr Anjan Chakravarty, Girdhar Das Parekh, Chitranjan Jyotshi and all the other Banarasis in the book who prefer to remain unnamed for opening to me the doors of their city's music and its history. I feel privileged to have had long conversations with Girija Devi and Pandit Kishan Maharaj, both of whom were very generous in giving me their time. I would also like to thank Rajiv Arora of *Daily Gandiv*, Varanasi, Shashi Dhar of *Aaj*, Varanasi, Dr T.K. Biswas and L.D. Vyas of Bharat Kala Bhavan, BHU, for all the help they extended to the research. Heartfelt thanks to Alka Hotel, my home away from home in Banaras.

Gratitude to Saleem Kidwai, Pran Nevile, Francesca Cassio, Lalita du Perron, Julien Jugand, Amlan Das Gupta, Urmila Bhirdikar, Vidya Rao, Manjari Chaturvedi, Lateef Siddiqui, Aslam Mehmood, Prof. Nayyar Masood and Thakur Ranvir Singh for their enriching conversations and insights. Many thanks to Bharat Shekhar, Dr Deepak Mehta and Dr Saif Mehmood for their valuable comments on the manuscript. I am grateful to Gauhar Raza for taking out the time to translate for me Urdu verses written by courtesan poets. And very thankful for the friendship of Sanjay Kak, who has been always there to give good advice when I have needed it.

My thanks to Nehru Memorial Museum and Library and the National Archive for providing a welcoming space to me and my research associates for archival research. Thanks also to Nagari Pracharani Sabha, Varanasi; Bharat Kala Bhavan, BHU; Dharohar and Kashi Sangeet Samaj, Varanasi and the record room of Kotwali police station, Varanasi for facilitating research. Gratitude too to the School of Cultural Texts and Records, Jadavpur University and Bhatkhande Music Institute University, Lucknow.

It's been a long journey and one that I could finally complete only because of the love and support of family and friends—my husband, comrade and fellow traveller, Rahul Roy, has always been by my side, enthusing me when I flagged, pushing me to do better; my mother Manorama Dewan; my in-laws, Premlata and J.N. Roy; my sister and brother-in-law, Samira and Rakesh Suri; my niece, Sara Suri; my aunt and uncle, Nusrat and Ahmed Rashid Shervani, and my dearest friends Jaya Sharma and Amina Shervani. And Shobhna Sonpar. I am grateful to have you all in my life.

Index